International Investment Law and Development

FRANKFURT INVESTMENT AND ECONOMIC LAW SERIES

The Frankfurt Investment and Economic Law Series addresses a core field of international law whose importance is likely to increase further as globalization progresses: international economic law. Serving as a forum for dialogue and cutting-edge debate, its scope takes in the legal regime governing international economic relations at large with a particular focus on international investment law.

Seeking to look beyond practical concerns raised in this field, the series addresses conceptual and foundational issues relating to the theory of international investment law – including questions of legitimacy and policy, the interaction with other fields of international and domestic law (both public and private), and interdisciplinary approaches to investment law and policy. Its intellectual foundations link to the workshops held in Frankfurt in connection with the annual Frankfurt Investment Arbitration Moot Court.

International Investment Law and Development

Bridging the Gap

Edited by

Stephan W. Schill

Professor of International and Economic Law and Governance, University of Amsterdam, the Netherlands

Christian J. Tams

Professor of International Law, University of Glasgow, UK

Rainer Hofmann

Professor of Public Law, Public International Law and European Law, University of Frankfurt, Germany

FRANKFURT INVESTMENT AND ECONOMIC LAW SERIES

Edward Elgar
PUBLISHING

Cheltenham, UK • Northampton, MA, USA

Published by
Edward Elgar Publishing Limited
The Lypiatts
15 Lansdown Road
Cheltenham
Glos GL50 2JA
UK

Edward Elgar Publishing, Inc.
William Pratt House
9 Dewey Court
Northampton
Massachusetts 01060
USA

A catalogue record for this book
is available from the British Library

Library of Congress Control Number: 2015943237

This book is available electronically in the **Elgar**online
Law subject collection
DOI 10.4337/9781784711351

FSC
www.fsc.org
MIX
Paper from
responsible sources
FSC® C013056

ISBN 978 1 78471 134 4 (cased)
ISBN 978 1 78471 135 1 (eBook)

Typeset by Columns Design XML Ltd, Reading
Printed and bound in Great Britain by TJ International Ltd, Padstow

Contents

Contributors

Walid Ben Hamida, Ph.D., is Professor of Law at the University of Evry and Sciences Po, Paris (France). He has authored more than 50 publications on arbitration, alternative dispute resolution and investment law in Arabic, French and English and taught investment law in more than 30 countries. Dr Ben Hamida served as arbitrator, expert and counsel. His practice focuses on international law, investor-state dispute settlement, Arab laws and arbitration. Since July 2012, he has been a member of the Court of Arbitration of the International Chamber of Commerce.

Christina Binder is Professor of International Law at the Department of European, International and Comparative Law at the University of Vienna and Deputy Director of the Interdisciplinary Research Centre 'Human Rights'. She was Visiting Fellow at the Lauterpacht Centre for International Law in Cambridge (2007–8) and at the Max Planck Institute for Comparative Public Law and International Law in Heidelberg (2008–10). She is a member of the Executive Board of the European Society of International Law and of the ILA Committee on the Implementation of the Rights of Indigenous Peoples. Ms. Binder also served as legal expert for EU and OSCE/ODIHR election observation and assessment missions in several countries and acts as electoral expert for the Congress of Local and Regional Authorities for the Council of Europe.

Jonathan Bonnitcha is a Visiting Fellow in International Investment Law and Policy at the Australian National University, and a Senior Lawyer in the Australian Government's Office of International Law. He holds the degrees of DPhil, MPhil, and BCL from the University of Oxford and LLB and BEc from the University of Sydney. He has advised both developing and developed country governments on investment treaties, and published a monograph and several articles on the subject. He currently lives in Myanmar. His contribution to this volume expresses his personal view only.

Marie-Claire Cordonier Segger, DPhil (Oxon), MEM (Yale), BCL and LL.B. (McGill), BA Hons, is a senior director, jurist and leading scholar of international law on sustainable development. She serves as Senior

Director for the Centre for International Sustainable Development Law, Senior Research Associate for the Centre for International Forestry Research (CIFOR), and Senior Legal Advisor to the Ramsar Convention on Wetlands. She is also Senior Legal Expert, Sustainable Development, for the International Development Law Organization. She holds a fellowship in the Lauterpacht Centre for International Law, University of Cambridge, and an international professorship in the Law Faculty of the University of Chile. Dr Cordonier Segger has published 18 books and over 80 papers, including 'Sustainable Development in World Investment Law' (Wolters Kluwer 2010), she edits a CUP Series on 'Implementing Treaties related to Sustainable Development', and serves on Editorial Boards of several law journals.

Diane A. Desierto, JSD (Yale), is Professor of International Law, International Economic Law, International Investment and Commercial Arbitration, and ASEAN Law at the University of Hawaii William S. Richardson School of Law, USA, Co-Director of the ASEAN Law & Integration Center and Adjunct Fellow of the East-West Center. She is Scientific Advisory Board Member at the *European Journal of International Law*, Contributing Editor of *EJIL:Talk!*, Associate Editor of the *Asian Yearbook of International Law*, Special Projects Team Leader at Oxford Investment Claims, former Law Clerk at the International Court of Justice, and forthcoming Director of Studies for Public International Law at the Hague Academy of International Law.

Melaku Geboye Desta is Professor of International Economic Law at the Leicester De Montfort Law School in England. Prior to joining De Montfort University, Melaku was Reader in International Economic Law at the Centre for Energy, Petroleum and Mineral Law and Policy (CEPMLP), University of Dundee, in Scotland.

Isabel Feichtner, Dr. iur. (Frankfurt), LL.M. (Cardozo Law School) is Associate Professor of Law and Economics at Goethe University, Frankfurt. Before joining the law faculty in Frankfurt in 2011, she worked as a corporate associate at Cravath, Swaine and Moore in New York, was visiting researcher at NYU Law School, Senior Research Fellow at the Max Planck Institute for Comparative Public Law and International Law in Heidelberg and Research Fellow at the German Institute for International and Security Affairs in Berlin.

Markus W. Gehring, LL.M. (Yale), Dr. iur. (University of Hamburg), MA (University of Cambridge), is Deputy Director of the Centre for European Legal Studies (CELS) and University Lecturer at the Faculty of Law, University of Cambridge. He is Director of Studies in Law and

Fellow at Hughes Hall and serves as pro bono Lead Counsel for Trade Law with the Centre of International Sustainable Development Law (CISDL). Dr Gehring has been a Visiting Professor at several universities and is ad personam Jean Monnet Chair in Sustainable Development Law in the Faculty of Law, at the University of Ottawa.

Antonius R. Hippolyte is a Doctoral Candidate at the University of Hull in the United Kingdom, having completed an LL.B. and an LL.M. at the same institution. His area of expertise is in international economic law and governance. Specifically, his work examines the fairness of the rules of the international investment regime from the perspective of third world States, using Third World Approaches to International Law (TWAIL) to evaluate the place of the third world in international economic governance. He is due to complete his doctoral studies in 2015.

Rainer Hofmann is Professor of Public Law, Public International Law, and European Law, and Co-Director of the Wilhelm Merton Centre for European Integration and International Economic Order at the University of Frankfurt/Main. He is Member of the Advisory Board on International Law of the German Ministry for Foreign Affairs and Secretary-General of the German Branch of the International Law Association (ILA). He sits on the Executive and the Management Board of the EU Fundamental Rights Agency, representing the Council of Europe. He was co-Rapporteur of the ILA Committee on Reparation for Victims of Armed Conflict (2003–12) and President (1998–2004 and 2008–12) of the Advisory Committee under the Council of Europe Framework Convention for the Protection of National Minorities.

Kendra Magraw is a doctoral candidate in international law at the Graduate Institute for International and Development Studies (IHEID) in Geneva, Switzerland. She specializes in international investment law and international commercial arbitration. Her doctoral topic is on treaty interpretation in public international law; she has also authored other articles on public international law issues. She has worked in varying capacities in private practice, as well as at the United Nations Conference on Trade and Development, the International Centre for Settlement of Investment Disputes and the International Court of Justice. She has a Masters in International Law from IHEID and a J.D. from the University of Minnesota.

Krista Nadakavukaren Schefer is Swiss National Science Foundation Professor of International Law at the University of Basel's Faculty of Law. Previously at the University of Bern and the World Trade Institute, she continues to cooperate with these faculties. She is a member of the research council of the Swiss Network on International Studies (SNIS), sits on the executive committee of the Society of International Economic Law (SIEL), and is a member of the London School of Economics' Sounding Board of its Investment and Human Rights Project. A native of the United States, she graduated from Georgetown University Law School before writing her dissertation and Habilitation at the University of Bern. She is a member of the New York State Bar.

Vid Prislan is a Research Fellow and Ph.D. Candidate at the Grotius Centre for International Legal Studies, Leiden University. He obtained degrees in International Relations from the University of Ljubljana, Slovenia, and in Dutch Law and Public International Law from Leiden University. His doctoral research focuses on the role of domestic courts' decisions in investor-State arbitration, but he is also interested in the interaction of foreign investment law with other subfields of public international law and Dutch foreign investment policy in general. He is the Book-Review Editor at the *Leiden Journal of International Law*.

Yannick Radi, Ph.D. (EUI), is Assistant Professor in International Law at the Grotius Centre for International Legal Studies of Leiden University. He is specialized in international investment law and arbitration. He is a Senior Editor of the *Leiden Journal of International Law*.

Andrea Saldarriaga is co-Lead of the Investment & Human Rights Project at the London School of Economics and Political Science (LSE). She is an international lawyer whose practice has focused on international arbitration, international investment law and human rights. In addition to her work at LSE, Andrea is a fellow of the Columbia Center on Sustainable Investment and a member of the International Investment Agreements expert network of UNCTAD. She teaches business and human rights at ESSEC Business School Paris and ESCP Business School Europe.

Stephan W. Schill, Dr. iur. (Frankfurt), LL.M. (NYU), LL.M. (Augsburg) is Professor of International and Economic Law and Governance at the University of Amsterdam and Principal Investigator in the ERC-project on 'Transnational Public-Private Arbitration as Global Regulatory Governance'. Formerly he was Senior Research Fellow at the Max Planck Institute for Comparative Public Law and International Law in Heidelberg. He is admitted to the bar in Germany and New York and is a Member of the ICSID List of Conciliators. He is also the Editor-in-Chief of the *Journal of World Investment and Trade* and the author of several books and articles on international investment law.

Muthucumaraswamy Sornarajah, LL.M. (Yale), Ph.D. and LL.D. (London) is CJ Koh Professor of Law at the National University of Singapore. He is the author of 'The International Law on Foreign Investment', the fourth edition of which will be published by Cambridge University Press in early 2016. His most recent book is 'Resistance and Change in the International Law on Foreign Investment' (Cambridge University Press, 2015).

Christian J. Tams is Professor of International Law at the University of Glasgow, where he directs the Law School's LL.M. programme in international law. He is also a visiting professor at Sciences Po Law School in Paris, and a fellow of the Young Academy of Scotland. He is a member of the German Court of Arbitration for Sport and the scientific advisory board of the *European Journal of International Law*. In addition to his academic work, Professor Tams is an associate member of Matrix Chambers London and regularly advises States and investors in proceedings before international courts and tribunals.

Celine Tan, Ph.D., is Associate Professor at the School of Law, University of Warwick, UK. Her research centres on exploring aspects of international economic law and regulation with a focus on the international financial architecture and international development financing law, policy and governance. She is also co-Director and one of the founders of the Centre for Law, Governance and Regulation of the Global Economy (GLOBE) at Warwick. Prior to Warwick, she was a lecturer in law at the School of Law, University of Birmingham, UK and has worked with non-governmental and intergovernmental organisations around the world.

Ruben Zandvliet is a Ph.D. candidate at the Grotius Centre for International Legal Studies, Leiden University. His research focuses on labour standards in international economic law. He holds an LL.M. (cum laude) from Leiden University and an LL.M. (James Kent Scholar) from Columbia University. During his doctoral studies, he worked as a visiting scholar at The Hague Institute for Global Justice (2013–14) and the Lauterpacht Centre for International Law (2015). Previously, he worked as a policy advisor for a Member of Parliament in the Netherlands in the fields of economic policy, corporate law, and constitutional law.

Preface

This book marks the start of a new series, the Frankfurt Investment and Economic Law Series. As editors, we hope the series will establish itself as a forum for dialogue and debate about a core field of international law whose importance is likely to increase further with progressing globalization: international economic law. Open to the legal regime governing international economic relations at large, its particular focus is on international investment law. Rather than focusing principally on practical concerns raised in this field, we intend the series to become a forum for the discussion of conceptual and foundational issues of international investment law: this includes questions of legitimacy and policy, the interaction with other fields of international and domestic law, both public and private, and interdisciplinary approaches to investment law and policy, among others. The focus of the series reflects our belief that, while international investment law and international economic law are firmly established, perhaps too much of the academic discourse today remains in the form of a coda to practice. Books in this series will be diverse in their approaches; but, as series editors, we hope they will contribute to an independent and rigorous analysis that does more than retrace developments in practice.

The series has grown out of a range of workshops held in Frankfurt and organised by our respective institutions – the Wilhelm Merton Centre of European Integration and International Economic Order, the School of Law of the University of Glasgow and the Max Planck Institute for Comparative Public Law and International Law in Heidelberg. Prior inquiries mapped out the relationship between International Investment Law and General International Law, International Investment Law and Its Others, and evaluated the impact of Preferential Trade and Investment Agreements on international investment law. Resulting volumes – inspired by the workshops, but revised and much expanded – were published by Nomos publishers, and remain available. While we encourage the submission of other manuscripts, especially monographs, we expect to continue the tradition of the Frankfurt Investment Law Workshops, which we hope will be the nuclei of future edited volumes.

* * *

The first book of the Frankfurt Investment and Economic Law Series, which grew out of the Frankfurt Investment Law Workshop held in March 2013, addresses one of the great challenges facing contemporary investment law – its relationship with development. As is set out in our thematic introduction, the linkages between investment and development are plain, and yet for a long time there has been relatively little scholarship exploring them. According to much-quoted dicta of tribunals, without some contribution to development (however defined), an economic transaction does not qualify as an investment. More generally, if international law seeks to promote and protect investments, this is due, at least partly, to the fact that investments are considered to be conducive to development. Conversely, the recent legitimacy crisis of international investment law reflects growing uncertainty about the impact of investment on development.

Against this background, the contributions to the present volume assess the relationship between investment law scholarship and development discourses. They are organized around two competing visions of that relationship – investment and development as 'friends' or 'foes'. The contributions reflect both visions, from the highly critical to the very harmonious. Read together, we believe they not only fill a gap in the literature, but are an important attempt to bridge the gap between international investment law and development.

Rainer Hofmann
Stephan W. Schill
Christian J. Tams

October 2015

Acknowledgments

In the preparation of this book we have incurred many debts. Philipp B. Donath and Jakob Kadelbach, both at Goethe University Frankfurt, provided vital support in planning and organizing the 2013 Frankfurt Investment Law Workshop that inspired the publication of this book. At the University of Glasgow, Athene Richford and Dr. Alessandra Asteriti commented on manuscripts. At the Max Planck Institute for Comparative Public Law and International Law in Heidelberg, where the bulk of the preparatory work was undertaken, Nadine Berger, Felix Boos, Vladislav Djanic, Daniel Litwin, Raphael Schäfer and Katrine Tvede helped with editing and complementing references.

In organizing the Workshop, and in relying on editorial support, we have been able to draw on resources made available by our host institutions, which we gratefully acknowledge. Stephan W Schill would particularly like to acknowledge support in editing this book by a European Research Council Starting Grant on 'Transnational Private-Public Arbitration as Global Regulatory Governance: Charting and Codifying the Lex Mercatoria Publica' (LexMercPub, Grant agreement no: 313355) during his tenure both at the Max Planck Institute for Comparative Public Law and International Law in Heidelberg and the University of Amsterdam.

Finally, our thanks are due to Edward Elgar Publishing. Ben Booth and his team have supported the establishment of the Frankfurt Investment and Economic Law Series and overseen a smooth commissioning process. During the finalization of this book, we have benefited from David Fairclough's editorial skills. We are grateful to all of them.

PART I

Introduction and keynote

1. International investment law and development: Friends or foes?

Stephan W. Schill, Christian J. Tams and Rainer Hofmann

I. INTRODUCTION

The relationship between international investment law and international development law has long been a history of ignorance and mistrust. This need perhaps not have been so, as the two fields seem rather closely linked. Investment law is, as the First Recital in the Preamble of the Convention on the Settlement of Investment Disputes between States and Nationals of Other States (ICSID Convention) indicates, premised on a development nexus.[1] Moreover, there is broad consensus that investment, including foreign investment, can have a positive impact on economic development at a macro-economic level and serve as an instrument both for the transfer of technology and for financing specific development projects.[2] The connection between investment and development is also

[1] Convention on the Settlement of Investment Disputes between States and Nationals of Other States (adopted 18 March 1965, entered into force 14 October 1966) 575 UNTS 159, Preamble, First Recital ('Considering the need for international cooperation for economic development, and the role of private international investment therein').

[2] On the economic interrelationships see Giorgio Barba Navaretti and Anthony J Venables, *Multinational Firms in the World Economy* (Princeton UP 2004) 151–85; OECD, *Open Markets Matter – The Benefits of Trade and Market Liberalisation* (OECD 1998) 25–58; Henrik Hansen and John Rand, 'On the Causal Links between FDI and Growth in Developing Countries' (2006) 29 *The World Economy* 21; Abdur Chowdhury and George Mavrotas, 'FDI and Growth: What Causes What?' (2006) 29 *The World Economy* 9.

recognized in a large number of development policy instruments, including the Agenda 21 of the UN Conference on Environment and Development (1992),[3] the Monterrey Consensus and the Johannesburg Plan of Implementation (2002),[4] the Doha Declaration on Financing for Development (2008),[5] and the UN Millennium Development Goals (MDGs).[6]

---

[3] UNCED, 'Agenda 21: Programme of Action for Sustainable Development' (14 June 1992) (UN Doc A/Conf.151/6/Rev.1) para 2.23 ('Investment is critical to the ability of developing countries to achieve needed economic growth to improve the welfare of their populations and to meet their basic needs in a sustainable manner, all without deteriorating or depleting the resource base that underpins development. Sustainable development requires increased investment, for which domestic and external financial resources are needed. Foreign private investment and the return of flight capital, which depend on a healthy investment climate, are an important source of financial resources.').

[4] United Nations, 'Monterrey Consensus of the International Conference on Financing for Development' (22 March 2002) (UN Doc A/AC.257/32) para 21 <http://www.un.org/esa/ffd/monterrey/MonterreyConsensus.pdf> accessed 18 May 2014 ('[a] transparent, stable and predictable investment climate, with proper contract enforcement and respect for property rights, embedded in sound macroeconomic policies and institutions that allow businesses, both domestic and international, to operate efficiently and profitably and with maximum development impact.'). See also United Nations, 'Plan of Implementation of the World Summit on Sustainable Development' (26 August–4 September 2002) (UN Doc A/Conf.199/20) 7 ff.

[5] United Nations, 'Doha Declaration on Financing for Development' (9 December 2008) (UN Doc A/CONF.212/L.1/Rev.1) para 23 ('We recognize that private international capital flows, particularly foreign direct investment, are vital complements to national and international development efforts.'). See also the recent Outcome Document of the 'Third International Conference on Financing for Development: Addis Ababa Action Agenda' (Addis Ababa, 13–16 July 2015) (15 July 2015) (UN Doc A/Conf.227/L.1) para 45 ('We recognize the important contribution that direct investment, including foreign direct investment, can make to sustainable development, particularly when projects are aligned with national and regional sustainable development strategies.'). For further statements, including of the G8, G20, the Organisation for Economic Co-operation and Development (OECD), the World Bank, and UNCTAD, see Markus W Gehring and Andrew Newcombe, 'An Introduction to Sustainable Development in World Investment Law' in Marie-Claire Cordonier Segger, Markus W Gehring and Andrew Newcombe (eds), *Sustainable Development in World Investment Law* (Kluwer 2011) 3, 4–5.

[6] See United Nations Development Program, *Investing in Development: A Practical Plan to Achieve the Millennium Development Goals* (2005) <http://www.unmillenniumproject.org/documents/overviewEngLowRes.pdf> accessed 20 May 2014. Similarly, the Rio+20 Conference more recently led to the adoption of the Outcome Document 'The Future We Want' that called for

In fact, one may ask with some justification whether international investment law would exist as a privileged body of law for the promotion and protection of foreign investment unless it was assumed, rightly or wrongly, that investment contributed to development?

Notwithstanding the nexus between investment and development, the literature and jurisprudence on international investment law until recently have largely treated the law of international development in passing.[7] Similarly, models for international investment agreements (IIAs) have only rarely been conceptualized from a development perspective.[8] Notably, the rich debates surrounding the purported 'right to development' are only rarely explored from an investment law perspective. If

---

increased investment in sustainable agriculture and rural development, water resources and sanitation services, clean energy technology, sustainable tourism, infrastructure, research and development, and education. See Annex to UNGA Res No 66/288 (11 September 2012) (UN Doc A/Res/66/288) paras 110, 123, 127, 131, 149, 154, 188, 201, 232, 271. The promotion of private investment will also remain an important pillar of the post-2015 development agenda. See Annex 'Transforming Our World: The 2030 Agenda for Sustainable Development' to UNGA Draft Res (12 August 2015) (Un Doc A/69/L.85) paras 20, 67 Goal 1.5.b, Goal 2.5.a, Goal 7.3.a, Goal 10.7.b, Goal 17.5.

[7] For the more recent surge in literature on investment and development see infra n 18. Before 2013, by contrast, there has been relatively little reflection on the relationship between investment and development. But see Andrew P Newcombe, 'Sustainable Development and Investment Treaty Law' (2007) 8 JWIT 357–407; Peter Muchlinski, 'Holistic Approaches to Development and International Investment Law: The Role of International Investment Agreements' in Julio Faundez and Celine Tan (eds), *International Economic Law, Globalization and Developing Countries* (Edward Elgar 2010) 180–204; Cordonier Segger, Gehring and Newcombe (n 5); Diane A Desierto, 'Development as an International Right: Investment in the New Trade-Based IIAs' (2011) 3 *Trade, Law and Development* 296; Olivier De Schutter, Johan Swinnen and Jan Wouters (eds), *Foreign Direct Investment and Human Development – The Law and Economics of International Investment Agreements* (Routledge 2012).

[8] An early exception is the 2005 International Institute for Sustainable Development (IISD) Model International Agreement on Investment for Sustainable Development; see Howard Mann et al, 'IISD Model International Agreement on Investment for Sustainable Development' (April 2005) <https://www.iisd.org/pdf/2005/investment_model_int_agreement.pdf> accessed 7 April 2015. For more background and further documentation see <https://www.iisd.org/investment/capacity/model.aspx> accessed 7 April 2015. Another development-inspired model IIA was the 2007 Norway Model BIT, available at <http://www.italaw.com/sites/default/files/archive/ita1031.pdf> accessed 7 April 2015 that was shelved in 2009 following largely critical input received during consultations.

investment lawyers have for a long time tended to ignore development discourses, their lack of interest has been reciprocated by development lawyers. Many works on international development law – including in its 'sustainable' variant – pay no more than lip-service to investment protection.[9] This contrasts starkly with world trade, human rights, global finance, etc. – where much discourse exists about the 'streamlining' of international law in light of developmental principles. Yet, all too often, the debate has bypassed international investment law. This is all the more surprising since at least one source of inspiration for the right to development, namely the long-standing controversies surrounding the establishment of a New International Economic Order, was very much investment-focused, if from a decidedly critical vantage point.[10]

More recent initiatives suggest that change is under way. Rather than in terms of ignorance or mistrust, the United Nations Conference on Trade and Development (UNCTAD) recently launched its Investment Policy Framework for Sustainable Development (IPFSD) which views the relationship between investment law and development in a positive light.[11] As its title indicates, it aims to make investment law development-friendly. For that purpose, the framework introduces a toolbox of principles for investment policy-making, guidelines for national investment policies, and options for the design of IIAs, which seek to ensure that investment meets countries' development needs. In UNCTAD's words:

> *'New generation' investment policies place inclusive growth and sustainable development at the heart of efforts to attract and benefit from investment.* This

[9] See only Marie-Claire Cordonier Segger and Ashfaq Khalfan (eds), *Sustainable Development Law: Principles, Practices, and Prospects* (OUP 2004); Duncan French, *International Law and Policy of Sustainable Development* (Juris Publishing 2005); Marie-Claire Cordonier Segger and Christopher G Weeramantry (eds), *Sustainable Justice – Reconciling Economic, Social and Environmental Law* (Martinus Nijhoff 2005); Nico Schrijver, *The Evolution of Sustainable Development in International Law: Inception, Meaning and Status* (Martinus Nijhoff 2008); Asif Qureshi and Xuan Gao (eds), *International Economic Law: Critical Concepts in Law*, Vol V: 'International Development Law' (Routledge 2011); Isabella D Bunn, *The Right to Development and International Economic Law: Legal and Moral Dimensions* (Hart 2012). An exception is Krista Nadakavukaren Schefer (ed.), *Poverty and the International Economic System – Duties to the World's Poor* (CUP 2013), which contains several chapters on international investment law and investment arbitration.

[10] See the discussion infra Parts II.B and III.A.

[11] See UNCTAD, *World Investment Report 2012 – Towards a New Generation of Investment Policies* (2012) 97 ff.

> leads to specific investment policy challenges at the national and international levels. At the national level, these include integrating investment policy into development strategy, incorporating sustainable development objectives in investment policy and ensuring investment policy relevance and effectiveness. At the international level, there is a need to strengthen the development dimension of international investment agreements (IIAs), balance the rights and obligations of States and investors, and manage the systemic complexity of the IIA regime.[12]

The Framework marks but the start of a more general agenda of UNCTAD to reform international investment law in order to serve better as an instrument for development.[13] How to achieve this goal is addressed in an ongoing policy process at UNCTAD. Independent of the outcome, the process is based on the premise that investment law and development can be reconciled: they can be friends. UNCTAD is not the only forum where development figures prominently in the debates on the future of international investment policy. Development equally plays an important role, for example, within the OECD,[14] the Association of South-East Asian Nations (ASEAN),[15] the Southern African Development Community (SADC),[16] or the Commonwealth Secretariat.[17] In

---

12 Ibid xii (*emphasis in the original*).

13 UNCTAD, *World Investment Report 2013 – Global Value Chains: Investment and Trade for Development* (2013) 110 ff; UNCTAD, *World Investment Report 2014 – Towards a New Generation of Investment Policies* (2014) 126 ff; UNCTAD, *World Investment Report 2015 – Reforming International Investment Governance* (2015) 119 ff.

14 See, e.g., Kathryn Gordon, Joachim Pohl and Marie Bouchard, 'Investment Treaty Law, Sustainable Development and Responsible Business Conduct: A Fact Finding Survey' (2014) OECD Working Papers on International Investment, 2014/01 <http://dx.doi.org/10.1787/5jz0xvgx1zlt-en> accessed 7 April 2015.

15 See the ASEAN Comprehensive Investment Agreement (adopted 26 February 2009, entered into force 29 March 2012) <http://agreement.asean.org/media/download/20140119035519.pdf> accessed 7 April 2015.

16 See South African Development Community (SADC) Model Bilateral Investment Treaty Template with Commentary (2012) <http://www.iisd.org/itn/wp-content/uploads/2012/10/SADC-Model-BIT-Template-Final.pdf> accessed 7 April 2015.

17 See J Anthony VanDuzer, Penelope Simons and Graham Mayeda, 'Integrating Sustainable Development into International Investment Agreements: A Guide for Developing Countries' (Commonwealth Secretariat 2012) <https://www.iisd.org/pdf/2012/6th_annual_forum_commonwealth_guide.pdf> accessed 7 April 2015.

parallel, there has been a surge in the literature in international investment law that addresses the field's relationship to development.[18]

Not everyone shares an optimistic view on investment and development though. While UNCTAD emphasizes sustainability, inclusiveness, and opportunities for reform, for many the relationship between investment and development is beyond repair. The former is an enemy of the latter: investment law impedes development needs. M. Sornarajah's work contains a particularly prominent version of this critique. It presents the relationship as one of irreconcilable conflict: investment law and development are foes.[19]

In his keynote to the Frankfurt Investment Law Workshop, which is reproduced in this volume, Sornarajah presents a scathing critique of the existing investment treaty system.[20] For him, 'investment treaties are based on lies' because there is no proof that their rationale to contribute to economic development by providing legal stability and independent

---

[18] Anne van Aaken and Tobias A Lehmann, 'Sustainable Development and International Investment Law: A Harmonious View from Economics' in Roberto Echandi and Pierre Sauvé (eds), *Prospects of International Investment Law and Policy* (CUP 2013) 317–40; Ilze Dubava, 'The Future of International Investment Protection Law: The Promotion of Sustainable (Economic) Development as a Public Good' in Marise Cremona et al (eds), *Reflections on the Constitutionalisation of International Economic Law: Liber Amicorum for Ernst-Ulrich Petersmann* (Kluwer 2013) 389; see further the contributions by Markus W Gehring and Avidan Kent, Wolfgang Alschner and Elisabeth Tuerk, Pierre-Olivier Savoie, Diane A Desierto, Ursula Kriebaum, and Maria Gritsenko in Freya Baetens (ed.), *Investment Law Within International Law: Integrationalist Perspectives* (CUP 2013); the contributions by Lise Johnson and Rahim Moloo, Rahim Moloo and Jenny J Chao, Caroline Henckels, Stephan W Schill, Vid Prislan and Ruben Zandvliet, Mavluda Sattorova and Alessandra Asteriti as part of the 'Symposium on Sustainable Development and International Investment Law: Bridging the Divide' in Andrea K Bjorklund (ed.), *Yearbook on International Investment Law & Policy 2012–2013* (OUP 2014) 265–473; as well as the contributions by Anne-Juliette Bonzon, Anne van Aaken, Laurence Boisson de Chazournes and Brian McGarry, Faraz Rojid and Maria de Carmen Vasquez, Krista Nadakavukaren Schefer, and Tarcisio Gazzini in the Special Issue on 'Special Issue: Towards Better BITs? – Making International Investment Law Responsive to Sustainable Development Objectives' (edited by Andreas R Ziegler) in 15 JWIT 803–963.

[19] See, e.g., Muthucumaraswamy Sornarajah, 'Mutations of Neo-Liberalism in International Investment Law' (2011) 3 *Trade, Law and Development* 203. See further Muthucumaraswamy Sornarajah, *Resistance and Change in the International Law on Foreign Investment* (CUP 2015).

[20] Muthucumaraswamy Sornarajah, 'Developing Countries in the Investment Treaty System: A Law for Need or a Law for Greed?', in this volume, 43.

dispute settlement mechanisms holds true.[21] Instead, Sornarajah criticizes deeper structural concerns, noting that investment treaties are asymmetric because they *de facto* limit only the sovereignty of developing countries which are recipients of foreign investment from developed countries. Investment treaties limit host governments' policy space for the protection of public interests, such as environmental concerns or public health, and create potential liabilities of, not chances for, development for developing countries. Instead, Sornarajah opines, '[t]he only economic development the treaties bring are to the arbitrators who interpret these treaties and lawyers of large law firms who represent and argue before the arbitral tribunals.'[22] In consequence, investment treaties' 'true purpose is plunder under the cloak of a law made through the instrumentality of power'[23] that prolongs colonial domination of developing countries through new mechanisms of 'global governance'. Sornarajah therefore proposes 'to put an end to this falsehood that the system created benefits for the development of the poor.'[24]

So are international investment law and development friends or foes? Or perhaps a bit of both? The contributions in this book are organized around these questions. They do not yield one clear answer, but perhaps can help overcome the problems of ignorance and mutual mistrust. They do not tackle the underlying economic question of whether investment treaties in fact attract foreign investment,[25] have an impact on the cost of

---

[21] Ibid 44.

[22] Ibid 46.

[23] Ibid 47.

[24] Ibid 46.

[25] There is an increasing amount of studies on this topic, with diverging results. Contrast only Jennifer Tobin and Susan Rose-Ackerman, 'When BITs Have Some Bite' in Catherine A Rogers and Roger P Alford (eds), *The Future of Investment Arbitration* (OUP 2009) 131 (finding a positive correlation between investment agreements and investment flows) with Emma Aisbett, 'Bilateral Investment Treaties and Foreign Direct Investment: Correlation and Causation' in Karl P Sauvant and Lisa E Sachs (eds), *The Effect of Treaties on Foreign Direct Investment: Bilateral Investment Treaties, Double Taxation Treaties, and Investment Flows* (OUP 2009) 395 (negating a correlation between investment agreements and investment flows). In more recent refined studies, however, evidence is becoming more robust that there is a positive correlation between investment agreements and the inflow of foreign direct investment. See, for example, Axel Berger et al, 'Do Trade and Investment Agreements Lead to More FDI? Accounting for Key Provisions Inside the Black Box' (2012) 10 *Int'l Economics and Economic Policy* 247; Tim Büthe and Helen V Milner, 'Foreign Direct Investment and Institutional Diversity in Trade Agreements: Credibility,

capital by reducing political risk,[26] or are able to have positive influence on macro-economic growth of host States;[27] instead, the focus is on the conceptual relations between international investment law and development. A significant problem in this context is not only that there is a gap between investment and development in the practice of international investment law, but also that the notion of development is itself elusive, or at least multi-faceted. This also makes it more difficult to integrate international investment law and development.

Against this background, the present chapter is intended to set the stage. It starts with an analysis of the multi-faceted and multi-layered notion of 'development' (Part II). It then discusses the gap between international investment law and development within international investment policy and the practice of investment arbitration, and, more recently, in the debate about the 'legitimacy crisis' of international investment law (Part III). This gap, the chapter then suggests, can be overcome through a more comprehensive and integrated vision of the relationship between investment and development and by considering and critically analyzing the conceptual linkages between international investment law and development as done in the chapters of this book (Part IV).

II. THE LEGAL REGIME OF (SUSTAINABLE) DEVELOPMENT

Compared to the international investment regime, the international legal regime of (sustainable) development seems fuzzy. There is no equivalent

Commitment, and Economic Flows in the Developing World, 1971–2007' (2014) 66 *World Politics* 88 (with further references).

[26] See Srividya Jandhyala and Robert J Weiner, '*Institutions sans frontières*: International Agreements and Foreign Investment' (2014) 45 J Int'l Bus Studies 649.

[27] There appears to be no research that examines the link between IIAs and economic growth directly. It is arguable, however, that this link can be drawn by understanding IIAs as requiring contracting states to implement economic institutions, such as property and contract protection, government according to the rule of law and effective dispute resolution mechanisms, and linking this to the question to which extent institutions contribute to growth and development. See on this link Stephan W Schill, *The Multilateralization of International Investment Law* (CUP 2009) 3–6; Stephan W Schill, 'Fair and Equitable Treatment, the Rule of Law, and Comparative Public Law' in Stephan W Schill (ed.), *International Investment Law and Comparative Public Law* (OUP 2010) 151, 177–81 (with further references to literature on institutional economics).

to the relatively homogenous governance structure of large numbers of IIAs.[28] Whereas international investment law has been gradually built, treaty by treaty (or 'BIT by BIT', as is often said),[29] the legal regime of development has evolved in different waves and in a less linear fashion. The contemporary regime draws on, and seeks to integrate, a broad range of overlapping, and partly competing, influences. It is multi-layered, and any attempt to assess its relevance for, and linkages with, contemporary investment law must take account of these various layers.[30] They include rules on development that emerged first on the inter-State level after World War II and during the debates in the 1970s about the emergence of a New International Economic Order (A.), the human rights dimension with the right to development (B.), the concept of sustainable development that emerged in the 1980s (C.) and the debates about development and good governance that started in the 1990s (D.). These multiple layers of international development law contribute to the lack of conceptual clarity when assessing the relationship between international investment law and development.

A. 'Development Age' and 'New International Economic Order'

In the discourse on development, President Truman's 1949 inaugural address is widely seen as a starting point. In its famous Point Four, the US President proposed to 'embark on a bold new program for making the benefits of our scientific advances and industrial progress available for the improvement and growth of underdeveloped areas.'[31] In its emphasis on creating conditions conducive to economic and social progress, this was not entirely new: it notably took up ideas that had been articulated in

---

28 Schill, *Multilateralization* (n 27).

29 See Jeswald W Salacuse, 'BIT by BIT: The Growth of Bilateral Investment Treaties and Their Impact on Foreign Investment in Developing Countries' (1990) 24 *The International Lawyer* 655.

30 For a fuller analysis see Gilbert Rist, *The History of Development: From Western Origins to Global Faith* (4th edn, Zed Books 2014); Philipp Dann, *The Law of Development Cooperation* (CUP 2013), especially Part I (35–154); Philipp Dann, Stefan Kadelbach and Markus Kaltenborn (eds), *Entwicklung und Recht. Eine systematische Einführung* (Nomos 2014).

31 Harry S Truman, 'Inaugural Address' (20 January 1949), reproduced in *Department of State Bulletin*, 30 January 1949, 123; also available at <http://www.presidency.ucsb.edu/ws/?pid=13282> accessed 7 April 2015. Rist (n 30) 70–71 provides context.

the 1944 Declaration Concerning the Aims and Purposes of the International Labour Organization (the Declaration of Philadelphia),[32] but added a particular idealist twist.

Point Four not only marked the beginning of a new presidency, but also, as Gilbert Rist notes, 'inaugurated the "development age"'[33] during which specialized institutions and programs devoted to development policy were to be established at the national and international levels. It was a peculiar beginning though: one based on modernization theory that aimed to create, in 'underdeveloped areas', conditions for the 'faithful re-creation of the successful economic and social development of modern Western societies.'[34] In line with the scientific focus of the project, law was primarily seen as an instrument, a tool of and for modernization. This implied the export of Western (domestic) legal concepts as part of a 'law and development' agenda.[35]

While the institutions of the 'development age' were being set up, the modernization theory underlying President Truman's Point Four came under fire during the process of decolonization.[36] The poor economic circumstances besetting many of the newly independent countries were no longer explained as an 'absence of modernity', but as a result of structural inequalities in the international economic system.[37] This added a new, more critical dimension to what was now being referred to as the

---

[32] 15 UNTS 35. For a recent (benevolent) re-evaluation see Alain Supiot, *L'esprit de Philadelphie* (Seuil 2010).

[33] Rist (n 30) 71.

[34] Dann (n 30) 58.

[35] See, e.g., David M Trubek, 'Towards a Social Theory of Law' (1972) 82 Yale LJ 1; and the overview in Elliot M Burg, 'Law and Development. A Review of the Literature and a Critique of "Scholars in Estrangement"' (1977) 25 AJCL 492.

[36] See Brun-Otto Bryde, *The Politics and Sociology of African Legal Development* (Metzner 1976); David M Trubek and Marc Galanter, 'Scholars in Self-Estrangement: Some Reflections on the Crisis in Law and Development Studies' [1974] Wisc LR 1062.

[37] See Francis G Snyder, 'Law and Development in the Light of Dependency Theory' (1980) 14 *Law & Society* 723. As Ahmed Mahiou, 'Development, International Law of' in Rüdiger Wolfrum (ed.), *The Max Planck Encyclopedia of International Law* (OUP 2015) <http://opil.ouplaw.com/home/EPIL> accessed 2 April 2015 succinctly notes, it would be necessary to overcome 'the unbalanced structure of international economic relations and the relationships of domination established to the advantage of certain States. In order to break the vicious cycle of underdevelopment, these relations of dependence and domination preventing the countries of the South from pursuing a coherent strategy of development must first be addressed' (ibid para 3).

'law of development' or 'international development law':[38] 'international development law [would] challeng[e] classic [international] law to work towards the reduction of inequalities and the realization of a new order.'[39] It had become a 'committed branch of law.'[40]

Nowhere was this more clearly felt than in the heated debates about a New International Economic Order (NIEO). Drawing on the relatively scarce UN Charter references to 'economic and social progress and development,'[41] a series of UN resolutions adopted during the 1970s – among them the Declaration on a New International Economic Order[42] and the Charter of Economic Rights and Duties of States[43] – sought to formulate firmer rules requiring industralized States to provide 'active support for the industrialization of developing countries, more equal global trade relations, and the general goal of international social justice and the harmonization of living standards.'[44] This differed markedly from President Truman's idea of industrialized nations benevolently (and of their free will) making 'the benefits of [their] scientific advances and industrial progress available for the improvement and growth of underdeveloped areas.'[45] Yet while the diagnosis was radically different, the cure prescribed remained rather similar: development remained a question of

---

[38] For doctrinal expositions see notably Michel Virally, 'Vers un droit international du développement' (1965) XI AFDI 3; Georges Abi-Saab, 'The Independent States and the Rules of International Law: An Outline' (1962) 8 Howard LJ 95; Oscar Schachter, 'The Evolving International Law of Development' (1976) 15 Colum JTL 1; Mohammed Bedjaoui, *Pour un nouvel ordre économique international* (UNESCO 1979); Michel Virally, 'Où en est le droit international du développement' (1975) 20 *Revue juridique et politique: Indépendance et coopération* 279.

[39] Mahiou (n 37) para 9.

[40] Ibid.

[41] Article 55(a) UN Charter.

[42] Declaration on the Establishment of a New International Economic Order, UNGA Res 3201 (S-VI) (1 May 1974) (UN Doc A/RES/S-6/3201); and further Programme of Action on the Establishment of a New International Economic Order, UNGA Res 3202 (S-VI) (1 May 1974) (UN Doc A/RES/S-6/3202).

[43] Charter of Economic Rights and Duties of States, UNGA Res 3281 (XXIX) (12 December 1974) (UN Doc A/RES/29/3281).

[44] Dann (n 30) 64. For further comment see, e.g., SK Chatterjee, 'The Charter of Economic Rights and Duties of States: An Evaluation after 15 Years' (1991) 40 ICLQ 669; Gillian M White, 'The New International Economic Order: Principles and Trends' in Hazel Fox (ed.), *International Economic Law and the Developing States: An Introduction* (BIICL 1992) 25; DHN Johnson, 'The New International Economic Order' (1983) 37 *The Yearbook of World Affairs* 204.

[45] Cf Truman (n 31).

economic growth.[46] To incentivize economic growth, independence of developing countries from developed countries and self-determination in order to allow countries to set their own development objectives and strategies, rather than an international governance framework for development, was propagated.

During the 1970s, a number of reforms were initiated with a view to implementing the NIEO agenda.[47] GATT contracting parties agreed to a preferential treatment for developing countries; international funds were set up to regulate and stabilize the price of commodities; and various UN agencies engaged in attempts to formulate codes of conduct for transnational corporations. Yet many of the more concrete proposals at the heart of the NIEO agenda – binding provisions on technology transfer; a lessening of expropriation standards;[48] a right to receive development assistance, etc. – met with resistance.[49] And when (as Sacerdoti notes) '[b]y the end of the 1970s, new economic policies and a new assertiveness in international affairs emerged among industrialized nations', such as Great Britain and the United States, hopes for an international consensus faded; and the 'unity of the NIEO project' gave rise to separate regimes governing trade and investment, on the one hand (in which market sector principles prevailed), and a specialized regime of international cooperation for development, on the other.[50]

While the NIEO project lost steam and gave way to a neoliberal agenda limiting the role of the State as an economic actor,[51] three further strands of the multi-layered 'development agenda' came to assume normative relevance: human rights, sustainable development, and good

---

[46] Philipp Dann, 'Ideengeschichte von Recht und Entwicklung' in Dann, Kadelbach and Kaltenborn (n 30) 24.

[47] For a helpful summary see Giorgio Sacerdoti, 'New International Economic Order (NIEO)' in Wolfrum (n 37) paras 21–4.

[48] See notably Article 2(2)(c) of the Charter of Economic Rights and Duties of States, which recognized the right of States to 'nationalize, expropriate or transfer ownership of foreign property, in which case appropriate compensation should be paid by the State adopting such measures, taking into account its relevant laws and regulations and all circumstances that the State considers pertinent.'

[49] For example, the Charter's recognition of a right to nationalize property (see last footnote) was rejected by sixteen capital-exporting States. In the award in the *Texaco case,* Arbitrator Dupuy held the provision *not* to reflect general international law: see *Texaco Overseas Petroleum Co & California Asiatic Oil Co v The Government of the Libyan Arab Republic*, 53 ILR 389, 489 ff.

[50] Sacerdoti (n 47) paras 26–7 (quote at para 25).

[51] The process is summarized by Dann (n 46) 26–8.

governance. They continue to shape the contemporary regime of development and, existing side by side, account for its multiple layers.

B. Adding a Human Rights Dimension: The Right to Development

The move towards a 'right to development' is the first of the contemporary layers.[52] The right can be seen as an attempt to blend demands for a just world economic order and for self-determination with human rights discourses. The link between human rights and economic and social conditions had long been recognized – notably in the ILO's Declaration of Philadelphia, but also in Article 28 of the Universal Declaration of Human Rights, which recognized the need to establish 'a social and international order in which the rights and freedoms set forth in this Declaration can be fully realized.'[53] Two decades later, the concluding document of the Teheran Human Rights Conference of 1968 found '[t]he widening gap between the economically developed and developing countries' to be an impediment to 'the realization of human rights in the international community' and considered 'lasting progress in the implementation of human rights [to be] dependent upon sound and effective national and international policies of economic and social development.'[54]

In retrospect, it seems almost natural that once human rights discourses had trickled down, they would gradually begin to shape debates about development. A 'human rights-based approach' would measure development not only in terms of economic growth, but place emphasis on the growth of individual liberties.[55] This broader understanding of development emphasized the role of the individual as the beneficiary of

---

[52] For recent assessments and many further references see Bunn (n 9); Felix Kirchmeier, 'The Right to Development – Where Do We Stand? State of the Debate on the Right to Development' Occasional Papers No 23 (Friedrich-Ebert-Stiftung 2006); Alhagi Marong, 'Development, Right to, International Protection' in Wolfrum (n 37). See also Diane A Desierto, 'The International Mandate for Development: Building Compliant Investment within the State's Development Decision-Making Processes', in this volume, 333.

[53] Universal Declaration on Human Rights, UNGA Res 217 A (III) (10 December 1948) (UN Doc A/RES/3/217A).

[54] See Articles 12 and 13 of the Proclamation of Teheran, Final Act of the International Conference on Human Rights, Teheran (1968) (UN Doc A/CONF.32/41) 3.

[55] That engagement was a gradual process, as perceptively noted by Philip Alston, 'Revitalising United Nations Work on Human Rights and Development' (1991) 18 MULR 216.

development policies; and it placed development discourses squarely into a framework of individual rights: the 'law of development' was complemented by a 'right to development'.[56] The 1986 General Assembly Declaration on the Right to Development, adopted by an overwhelming majority of 146:1 votes (8 abstaining), completed that process on the universal level.[57] Since 1986, the right to development is regularly counted among the widely-recognized solidarity (or 'third generation') rights.[58]

Yet, notwithstanding its formal recognition, the substance of the right has remained hazy. According to the 1986 Declaration, the right combines individual and collective aspects, entitling 'every human person and all peoples … to participate in, contribute to, and enjoy economic, social, cultural and political development, in which all human rights and fundamental freedoms can be fully realized.'[59] Since 1986, various UN institutions – among them the Office of the High Commissioner for Human Rights, a dedicated Working Group on the right to development and the United Nations Development Program – have sought to operationalize the right.[60] Since 2000, this process has been increasingly integrated into the wider attempt to formulate and implement the MDGs.[61]

---

[56] The argument is typically traced back to Kéba M'Baye, 'Le droit au developpement comme un droit de l'homme' (1972) 5 *Revue des droits de l'homme* 505.

[57] For an earlier recognition at the regional level see African Charter on Human and Peoples' Rights (adopted 27 June 1981, entered into force 21 October 1986) 1520 UNTS 217, art 22. That provision however focuses on the collective dimension of the right to development, which is viewed as a right of peoples.

[58] See, e.g., 'Vienna Declaration and Programme of Action' World Conference on Human Rights in Vienna (25 June 1993) (UN Doc A/Conf.157/24) Part I, section III (Article I.10): right to development an 'integral part of fundamental human rights'. For many further details see Bunn (n 9) 46–52.

[59] Declaration on the Right to Development, UNGA Res 41/128 (4 December 1986) (UN Doc A/RES/41/128) art 1(1).

[60] For a comprehensive account see the High Commissioner's *Realizing the Right to Development: Essays in Commemoration of 25 Years of the United Nations Declaration on the Right to Development* (OHCHR 2010).

[61] See United Nations Millennium Declaration, UNGA Res 55/2 (18 September 2000) (UN Doc A/RES/55/2) and the comprehensive documentation at <http://www.un.org/millenniumgoals> accessed 1 April 2015. Para 11 of the Millennium Declaration reflects the centrality of the right to development; it runs as follows: 'We are committed to making the right to development a reality for everyone and to freeing the entire human race from want.' In line with this, the

In the quest for operationalization, the right to development seems to be gradually transformed into a benchmark against which national and international policies across a range of sectors are being evaluated. For example, in its work towards the implementation of the eighth MDG ('to develop a global partnership for development'), a High-Level Task Force on the Right to Development, established in 2004,[62] identified a large number of criteria and indicators to assess the policies in three core areas: development policy, participatory human rights processes, and social justice in development.[63] Nearly three decades after the adoption of the 1986 Declaration on the Right to Development, this much more fine-grained approach indeed seems promising; yet at the same time, it suggests that the right to development is now seen as a framework of analysis for assessing policies towards development, not as a free-standing enforceable right.

C. Integrating Ecological Concerns: Sustainable Development

In parallel to debates about a 'right to development', global public concern for environmental protection resulted in yet another strand of development discourses, which perhaps today is the most prominent: the demand that development be sustainable. Following the widely quoted definition of the Brundtland Report, sustainable development is understood not only as economic development (and can neither fully be captured by individual rights discourses); instead it needs to be understood as 'development that meets the needs of the present without compromising the ability of future generations to meet their own

---

eighth millennium development goal (MDG 8) is to 'develop a global partnership for development'. For brief comment see Bunn (n 9) 169–71. The 'integration' of development discourses into the MDG process is not uncontroversial. According to Rist (n 30), the 'division of "development" into a set of discrete goals actually paralyses thought and stands in the way of their systemic linkage' (ibid 235); in his poignant words, the MDG process leads to 'development in shreds' (ibid 233).

[62] See UNCHR, Res 2004/7 (13 April 2004) (UN Doc E/CN.4/RES/2004/7). Detailed information about the work of High Level Task Force is available at <http://www.ohchr.org/EN/Issues/Development/Pages/HighLevelTaskForce.aspx> accessed 1 April 2015.

[63] See HRC, 'Consolidation of Findings of the High-level Task Force on the Implementation of the Right to Development' (25 March 2010) (UN Doc A/HRC/15/WG.2/TF/2/Add.1).

needs.'[64] Sustainable development therefore encompasses economic growth, environmental protection, and social development in an intragenerational perspective.[65]

While the 1986 Declaration on the Right to Development had not mentioned the environment, most of the major documents adopted subsequently recognize it as a key public policy goal. The 1992 Rio Declaration on Environment and Development emphasizes the link between environmental protection and economic development: 'In order to achieve sustainable development, environmental protection shall constitute an integral part of the development process and cannot be considered in isolation from it.'[66]

As with the right to development, sustainable development needs to be operationalized; it is 'not an action-oriented rule but rather a principle that guides States in their decision-making.'[67] Yet, compared to the right to development, that operationalization seems rather well under way. As Virginie Barral notes, quite apart from the debate about its customary status, references to sustainable development have been included in approximately 300 international treaties.[68] References to that notion have served to legitimize dynamic readings of treaty provisions in light of environmental concerns.[69] And depending on the wording of a particular clause, these treaties either require States in some general manner to

---

[64] World Commission on Environment and Development, *Our Common Future* (OUP 1987) 43.

[65] On the notion of sustainable development, its emergence and legal nature see, e.g., Virginie Barral, 'Sustainable Development in International Law: Nature and Operation of an Evolutive Legal Norm' (2012) 23 EJIL 377; Klaus Bosselmann, *The Principle of Sustainability: Transforming Law and Governance* (Ashgate, Aldershot 2008); Ulrich Beyerlin, 'Sustainable Development' in Wolfrum (n 37); Nico Schrijver, *The Evolution of Sustainable Development in International Law: Inception, Meaning and Status* (Brill 2008); International Law Association, 'New Delhi Declaration of Principles of International Law Relating to Sustainable Development' (2002) 49(2) NILR 299.

[66] United Nations Conference on Environment and Development, Rio Declaration on Environment and Development (12 August 1992) (UN Doc A/CONF.151/26) Principle 4.

[67] Beyerlin (n 65) para 17.

[68] Barral (n 65) 384.

[69] The *Shrimp Turtle* case is a prominent example; in it, the WTO Appellate Body drew on (amongst other things) the reference to sustainable development in the preamble to the WTO Agreement to justify its evolutive interpretation of Article XX(g) GATT: see WTO, *United States – Import Prohibition of certain Shrimp and Shrimp Products*, Report of the Appellate Body (12 October 1998) WT/DS58/AV/R, para 127.

integrate environmental considerations into economic development projects, or specify the measures that will need to be adopted in fulfilment of their obligations.

D. Back to the State? Development and Good Governance

Finally, alongside human rights-based and ecologically informed approaches, the contemporary understanding of development is informed by concerns for governance structures. According to this approach, successful development depends on functioning political and economic structures in the recipient countries. In line with this, national and international agencies, from the 1990s onwards, began to tie development to rule of law standards and institutional reform.[70]

Compared to the neoliberal agenda of the Washington Consensus, this resulted in a re-evaluation of the State: market forces no doubt remained crucial, but themselves depended on functioning structures, which development policies would need to bolster.[71] As Philipp Dann notes perceptively, while the agendas differed, this in some ways meant a return to the roots: 'Law reform in developing countries, the hallmark of the law and development movement [of the 1950s and 1960s], was rediscovered by development agencies in the 1990s.'[72] This adds a further normative layer

---

[70] For early initiatives see the World Bank's report on *Sub-Saharan Africa: From Crisis to Sustainable Growth* (World Bank 1989) and on *Governance and Development* (World Bank 1992). See further Beate Rudolf, 'Is Good Governance a Norm of International Law?' in Pierre-Marie Dupuy et al (eds), *Völkerrecht als Wertordnung. Festschrift Christian Tomuschat* (Engel 2006) 1007; Jan Kooiman, *Governing as Governance* (Sage 2003); Matthias Koetter, 'Good Governance' in Dann, Kadelbach and Kaltenborn (n 30) 553; and the contributions to Perry Kessaris (ed.), *Law in the Pursuit of Development Principles into Practice?* (Routledge 2009).

[71] See Stefan Oeter, 'Fragile Staatlichkeit und Entwicklung' in Dann, Kadelbach and Kaltenborn (n 30) 471. As Anne-Marie Slaughter and William Burke White, 'The Future of International Law is Domestic (or, The European Way of Law)' (2006) 47 Harvard ILJ 327 have argued convincingly, this new focus on governance and functioning State structures seems a general feature of contemporary international law.

[72] Dann (n 30) 7. Unsurprisingly, the move towards governance discourses has met with resistance: for an influential critique see, e.g., Anthony Anghie, *Imperialism, Sovereignty and the Making of International Law* (CUP 2005) 245–72.

to the notion of development: functioning normative structures in recipient countries were now considered a prerequisite of development. As Stefan Kadelbach notes, 'law has become part of the notion of development.'[73]

E. Interim Conclusion

As this brief summary highlights, the concept of development has itself been in a state of almost permanent development. On its journey from 'western origins to global faith'[74] the notion of development has acquired many meanings. Debates about its human rights, ecological and governance dimensions highlight the openness of the concept, which can be imbued with different layers of normativity. The result is an extremely heterogeneous normative concept that operates in conjunction with other rules and principles of international law. In order to be effective, developmental imperatives or demands need to make themselves felt in other legal regimes. For present purposes, the relevant other legal regime is that of international investment law. To be successful, it is thus crucial that the idea and notion of development is enculturated in that legal regime. This is not always without problems. Indeed, as the subsequent section discusses, there is a considerable gap between international investment law and the notion of development and developmental principles.

III. THE INVESTMENT/DEVELOPMENT GAP IN INTERNATIONAL INVESTMENT LAW

Despite the widespread view among economists and many international organizations that investment is instrumental for development, there has long existed a significant gap between the discourse on international investment law and that on development. This is not only true in respect of the literature on the concept of development, the right to development, and the concept of sustainable development, but also in the practice of international investment law. This gap can be seen when considering the evolution of investment law in the struggle between capital-exporting and capital-importing countries (A.), the way development is viewed within investment arbitration (B.), and the ongoing debate about the 'legitimacy

---

[73] Stefan Kadelbach, 'Entwicklung als normatives Konzept' in Dann, Kadelbach and Kaltenborn (n 30) 57 ('Recht wird ... Teil des Entwicklungsbegriffs').

[74] See the sub-title of Rist's influential account (n 30).

crisis' of international investment law (C.). Yet, there are also some glimpses of a more positive attitude towards development concerns within international investment law and investor-State dispute settlement as investment law contains gateways for development concerns to seep in (D.).

A. The Evolution of International Investment Law

The evolution of international investment law is characterized by a clash of interests between capital-exporting and capital-importing countries, which is often equated with the clash between investment protection and development. In fact, the international law of foreign investment has evolved mainly as a law of investment (or investor) protection against the background of conflicts of interests of investors from capital-exporting States and those of capital-importing host countries.[75]

Following a period of gunboat diplomacy by capital-exporting states during the 19th and early 20th centuries,[76] the roots of modern investment law stretch back to the struggle over the content of customary international law on the protection of aliens in the wake of the Soviet and Mexican revolutions after the end of World War I.[77] While capital-importing countries argued against an independent standard for the protection of foreign investments under international law, supporting instead protection exclusively by national law in national courts, European powers and the United States argued for an independent system of protection under international law. These capital-exporting countries not only advocated for an independent system of protection that would provide for prompt, adequate, and effective compensation for expropriation under the Hull formula but also supported the existence of a minimum standard of treatment in customary international law.[78]

After World War II, capital-exporting countries continued to make efforts to garner support for a multilateral investment treaty. Such efforts

---

[75] For a comprehensive take on the history of investment law see Andrew Newcombe and Lluís Paradell, *Law and Practice of Investment Treaties* (Kluwer 2009) 1–73.

[76] See O Thomas Johnson and Jonathan Gimblett, 'From Gunboats to BITs: The Evolution of Modern International Investment Law' in Karl P Sauvant (ed.), *Yearbook on International Investment Law & Policy 2010–2011* (OUP 2012) 649.

[77] On this see also Rudolf Dolzer, *Eigentum, Enteignung und Entschädigung im geltenden Völkerrecht* (Springer 1985) 13 ff.

[78] Permanent Sovereignty over Natural Resources, UNGA Res 1803 (XVII) (14 December 1962) (UN Doc A/RES/1803(XVII)). The resolution constituted a compromise in this context.

failed, however, due to the conflicting interests of developed and developing countries,[79] preventing the establishment of the International Trade Organization in the late 1940s,[80] as well as the OECD Convention on the Protection of Foreign Property of 1967.[81] In both cases, the lack of a consensus on the appropriate scope of protection of property under international law was decisive. The ICSID Convention was the only example of a successful multilateral instrument on international investment law. Yet, following the maxim 'procedure before substance',[82] it does not contain provisions on substantive investment protection, but only provides for procedural rules for the settlement of disputes through arbitration.

Instead, in the 1970s, as already alluded to above, developing and socialist countries mobilized against an independent customary international law standard of protection of foreign investment, in particular through UN General Assembly Resolution 3201 of 5 May 1974 ('Declaration on the Establishment of a New International Economic Order')[83] and UN General Assembly Resolution 3281 of 12 December 1974 ('Charter of Economic Rights and Duties of States').[84] In parallel, and foreshadowing modern debates about corporate social responsibility,[85] attempts were made within the United Nations Centre on Transnational Corporations (UNCTC) to impose duties on multinational corporations through a code of conduct, including the duty to respect human rights.[86] Through these approaches, developing and socialist countries emphasized

---

[79] On the development after 1945 see Schill, *Multilateralization* (n 27) 31–6.

[80] On this see William Diebold, 'The End of the ITO' (1952) 16 *Essays on International Finance* 81.

[81] Draft Convention on the Protection of Foreign Property and Resolution of the Council of the OECD on the Draft Convention, 7 ILM 117 (1968).

[82] See Rudolf Dolzer and Christoph Schreuer, *Principles of International Investment Law* (2nd edn, OUP 2012) 9.

[83] See *Declaration on the Establishment of a New International Economic Order* (n 42).

[84] See *Charter of Economic Rights and Duties of States* (n 43).

[85] On this see Peter Muchlinski, 'Corporate Social Responsibility' in Peter Muchlinski, Federico Ortino and Christoph Schreuer (eds), *The Oxford Handbook of International Investment Law* (OUP 2008) 637, 638.

[86] See 'Draft United Nations Code of Conduct on Transnational Corporations (1985)' in UNCTAD, *International Investment Instruments: A Compendium*, Vol I – Multilateral Instruments (United Nations 1996) 161 ff; see comprehensively Carsten-Thomas Ebenroth and Joachim Karl, *Code of Conduct – Ansätze zur vertraglichen Gestaltung internationaler Investitionen* (Universitätsverlag Konstanz 1987); Karl P Sauvant, 'The Negotiations of the United

their interest in development and countered the demands of capital-exporting countries for investment liberalization and protection. Although their attempts did not prevail at the time, the position of developing countries caused an intensive debate about the scope of the protection of property under customary international law.[87]

However, despite the rejection of a customary standard of investment protection, developing countries soon felt the need to attract foreign investment in order to meet their own economic development goals (especially given their limited financial resources and the lack of technology for more sophisticated economic activity). This need was further exacerbated by the debt crisis in the 1980s and the limited availability of official development assistance. Such events ultimately led to the rise of bilateral investment treaties (BITs), in particular after the end of the Cold War, when the adoption of a market economy promised more economic growth and development than alternative models.[88] Although BITs are now a truly global phenomenon (being regularly concluded between typical capital-exporting and capital-importing countries as well as between developed and among developing countries), the evolution of this area of law in North-South struggles explains, at least historically, the gap between the investment and development discourses.

B. Development Discourse in Investment Arbitration

The gap can also be seen in the limited number of instances where investment law and development have come into contact in dispute settlement practice under investment treaties. The notion of development, or considerations relating to it, play a role in only three areas: in respect of the definition of what constitutes an investment, regarding the question of whether the host State's level of development influences the substantive standards of protection, and as regards the object and purpose of international investment law. Tellingly, investment protection and development are often understood from the perspective of conflicting interests and objectives. Development, in other words, is regularly used as an argument to limit the protection of foreign investments, and hence as antagonistic to investment.

First, there is significant debate in investment arbitration with regard to the importance of development for the definition of investment in Article

---

Nations Code of Conduct on Transnational Corporations: Experiences and Lessons Learned' (2015) 16 JWIT 11.

87 Dolzer (n 77) 35 ff.

88 On the development of BITs see Schill, *Multilateralization* (n 27) 40–44.

25(1) ICSID Convention.[89] Following the decision in *Salini v. Morocco*,[90] which developed the so-called *Salini* test,[91] arbitral tribunals debate whether the requirement of a contribution to the host country's economic development should be a constitutive element of the definition of investment.[92] The main argument to justify the inclusion of such a requirement is the object and purpose of the ICSID Convention, as set out in its Preamble.[93] However, it is doubtful whether, on these grounds, the existence of an investment can be made dependent on whether an identifiable economic activity contributes to the development of the host country. Legal certainty is endangered if it is unclear at the time the investment is established if it contributes to the development of the host

---

[89] See Devashish Krishan, 'A Notion of ICSID Investment' in Todd J Weiler (ed.), *Investment Treaty Arbitration and International Law* (Huntington 2008) 61; Julian D Mortenson, 'The Meaning of "Investment", ICSID's Travaux and the Domain of International Investment Law' (2010) 51 Harvard ILJ 257; Nitish Monebhurrun, 'The Political Use of the Economic Development Criterion in Defining Investments in International Investment Arbitration' (2012) 29 J Int'l Arb 567; see further Diane A Desierto, 'Deciding International Investment Agreement Appicability: The Development Argument in Investment' in Baetens (n 18) 240, 243–8.

[90] *Salini Costruttori SpA and Italstrade SpA v Kingdom of Morocco*, ICSID Case No ARB/00/4, Decision on Jurisdiction (23 July 2001).

[91] See, e.g., *Biwater Gauff Ltd v. United Republic of Tanzania*, ICSID Case No ARB/05/22, Award (24 July 2008) para 319 (with reference to *Salini* (n 90)); cf also Christoph H Schreuer, Loretta Malintoppi, August Reinisch and Anthony Sinclair, *The ICSID Convention – A Commentary* (CUP 2009) Art. 25 para 153. Under this jurisprudence the characteristics of an investment are: (1) a monetary contribution to a project by the investor; (2) a certain duration of the economic activity at stake; (3) the investor's intention to make profit; (4) the assumption of risk; and (5) a contribution of the investment to the economic development of the host country.

[92] Comprehensively on the relevant arbitral jurisprudence see Mortenson (n 89) 268-80. See in particular the decisions in *Malaysian Historical Salvors, SDN, BHD v Malaysia*, ICSID Case No ARB/05/10, Award on Jurisdiction (17 May 2007) paras 123 ff; *Malaysian Historical Salvors, SDN, BHD v Malaysia*, ICSID Case No ARB/05/10, Decision on the Application for Annulment (16 April 2009) paras 56 ff and ibid, Dissenting Opinion of Judge Mohamed Shahabuddeen paras 14 ff (where the majority of the Annulment Committee supported that contribution to development did not form part of the definition of investment, while the sole arbitrator as well as the dissenting Committee member supported that contribution to host State development was a necessary criterion).

[93] See supra n 1; drawing on the Preamble, e.g., *Patrick Mitchell v Democratic Republic of the Congo*, ICSID Case No ARB/99/7, Decision on the Application for Annulment of the Award (9 February 2004) paras 28–9.

country and whether its activity is consequently an investment in the meaning of the ICSID Convention. This uncertainty would also negatively affect investments that are conducive to economic development and hence desirable from the host country's perspective. Moreover, the host State always remains free to regulate and block the admission of undesired investments[94] and to regulate investor conduct under domestic law, including by establishing obligations not to harm the environment or to respect interests of the local population. All of this makes it doubtful whether introducing the contribution to economic development as a criterion for the very protection of an investment is actually conducive to development interests.[95]

Second, development also plays a role in whether the host country's level of development has an impact on the interpretation of substantive protection standards. This may come up, for example, when considering whether the interpretation of fair and equitable treatment is different depending on whether the host State is a developed or a developing country.[96] While some tribunals explicitly take into account the level of

---

[94] Note however that some treaties do impose pre-establishment obligations and market access requirements, and some also restrict performance requirements that can be used by host States in order to obtain development benefits from an investment. Admittedly, with these treaties, host States do not remain completely free to regulate the admission of foreign investments; yet these obligations are also not absolute and it remains an open question, which is hardly addressed in the literature, whether admission requirements have negative effects on sustainable development. In any event, even market-access obligations do not do away with the ability of States to regulate investor conduct in the public interest as discussed below.

[95] Similarly, but with partly differing argumentation, see Mortenson (n 89) 280 ff. For more recent decisions rejecting that the protection of an investment should depend on its contribution to the host State's development, see, e.g., *SGS Société Générale de Surveillance SA v The Republic of Paraguay*, ICSID Case No ARB/07/29, Award (10 February 2012) paras 106–108; *Quiborax SA, Non Metallic Minerals SA and Allan Fosk Kaplún v Plurinational State of Bolivia*, ICSID Case No ARB/06/2, Decision on Jurisdiction (27 September 2012) paras 218–25 (with further references to arbitral jurisprudence); *Deutsche Bank AG v Democratic Socialist Republic of Sri Lanka*, ICSID Case No ARB/09/2, Award (31 October 2012) para 295; *Electrabel SA v Republic of Hungary*, ICSID Case No ARB/07/19, Decision on Jurisdiction, Applicable Law and Liability (30 November 2012) para 5.43; *KT Asia Investment Group BV v Kazakhstan*, ICSID Case No ARB/09/8, Award (17 October 2013) paras 171–3.

[96] See comprehensively and with reference to further arbitral cases Nick Gallus, 'The Influence of the Host State's Level of Development on International Investment Treaty Standards of Protection' (2005) 6 JWIT 711–29; Ursula

development in order to negate a violation of investors' rights,[97] other tribunals refuse to do so when interpreting substantive standards.[98] Despite a lack of consensus on this issue among arbitral tribunals, the debate illustrates that the development perspective of international investment law is, albeit in a rudimentary manner, reflected in investment arbitration and that the stability of investment protection and the expectations of foreign investors need to be considered relative to the state of development of the host country.

Finally, development-related considerations play a role in arbitral jurisprudence when considering the object and purpose of the ICSID Convention and international investment treaties more generally. Even though arbitral tribunals perceive the protection of foreign investment as the main purpose of these treaties, they also take into account broader overarching concerns of development. Most famously, the tribunal in *Amco v. Indonesia* stated that 'the [ICSID] Convention is aimed to protect, to the same extent and with the same vigour the investor and the host country, not forgetting that to protect investments is to protect the general interest of development and of developing countries.'[99] Furthermore, development as the object and purpose of IIAs also often informs

---

Kriebaum, 'The Relevance of Economic and Political Conditions for Protection under Investment Treaties' (2011) 10 LPICT 383; Maria Gritsenko, 'Relevance of the Host State's Development Status in Investment Treaty Arbitration' in Baetens (n 18) 341; Ursula Kriebaum, 'Are Investment Treaty Standards Flexible Enough to Meet the Needs of Developing Countries?' in Baetens (n 18) 330.

[97] For example, the tribunal in *Alex Genin v Estonia* argued that the irregular cancellation of a banking license in the 1990s did not constitute a violation of the fair and equitable treatment standard because the investor knowingly accepted that Estonia was in transition from socialist planning to a market economy. See *Alex Genin Eastern Credit Limited, Inc and AS Baltoil v Estonia*, ICSID Case No ARB/99/2, Final Award (25 June 2001) paras 348 ff. Similarly, *Pantechniki SA Contractors & Engineers v Republic of Albania*, ICSID Case No ARB/07/21, Award (30 July 2009) paras 76–82 (finding that the host country's level of development, namely the environment of desolation and lawlessness at the time of the establishment of the investment needed to be taken into consideration when applying the substantive investment treaty standards); see also *White Industries Australia Limited v Republic of India,* UNCITRAL, Final Award (30 November 2011) paras 10.3.15, 10.4.18 (arguing in favor of taking the development level into consideration).

[98] In this sense, e.g., *Gami Investments, Inc v United Mexican States*, UNCITRAL, Final Award (15 November 2004) para 94.

[99] *Amco Asia Corporation and others v Republic of Indonesia*, ICSID Case No ARB/81/1, Decision on Jurisdiction (25 September 1983) para 23.

the interpretation of investment treaties more generally. For instance, in the context of the protection of legitimate expectations as part of fair and equitable treatment, the tribunal in *Lemire v. Ukraine*, having recourse to the preamble of the applicable BIT, stated that the purpose of the treaty was not the protection of foreign investment per se; instead, the protection pursued a farther-reaching objective, namely to help the development of the host country.[100]

Even if the references to development mentioned above are not the general rule in arbitral jurisprudence, they nevertheless illustrate an awareness that international investment law is related to, and relevant for, development. Nonetheless, a broader discourse on the relationship between investment protection and development is missing within arbitration practice. This is certainly not least due to the fact that the majority of counsel and arbitrators have a background in international commercial arbitration and practice investment law as a sub-discipline of international arbitration without necessarily having in-depth awareness of its development implications.[101] This contributes to isolating the discourse within investment arbitration from the underlying development objectives of international investment law and the broader discourse and scholarship on the international law of development.

C. The 'Legitimacy Crisis' of International Investment Law

Finally, the gap between investment and development also reflects in the debates about the legitimacy crisis of international investment law.[102] This debate focuses on the democratic accountability of arbitrators, the extent to which their interpretations of investment treaties restrict the right to regulate in the public interest, and the institution of investor-State dispute settlement.[103] Symptoms of this crisis can be seen in the recent

---

[100] *Joseph Charles Lemire v Ukraine*, ICSID Case No ARB/06/18, Decision on Jurisdiction and Liability (14 January 2010) paras 272–3.

[101] On this see Stephan W Schill, 'International Investment Law and Comparative Public Law: An Introduction' in Schill, *Comparative Public Law* (n 27) 3.

[102] See Charles N Brower and Stephan W Schill, 'Is Arbitration a Threat or a Boon to the Legitimacy of International Investment Law?' (2009) 9 Chicago JIL 471, 473 (with further references).

[103] On this and on the following, see Gus Van Harten, *Investment Treaty Arbitration and Public Law* (OUP 2007) 152 ff; see also David Schneiderman, *Constitutionalizing Economic Globalization: Investment Rules and Democracy's Promise* (CUP 2008) (specifically on the threat of investment law to democracy); Kyla Tienhaara, *The Expropriation of Environmental Governance* (CUP 2009).

withdrawal of some States from BITs and the ICSID Convention[104] and in the efforts of many countries to recalibrate their investment treaty obligations and restrict investment treaty arbitration.[105]

This criticism of investment law can also be read as relating to development concerns. In essence, some critics have argued that investment protection is becoming an obstacle to the development objectives of host countries and sustainable development more generally. As such, the many vague legal terms used in BITs raise concerns that arbitral tribunals may interpret the treaties to curtail state measures aimed at the protection of the environment, human rights, labor and social standards, or taken in reaction to financial crises, for the benefit of the protection of investors, without sufficiently considering the public interests involved. This can be seen as affecting (sustainable) development, as this concept is understood as encompassing the right of States to further social development as well as the protection of the environment or human rights. International investment law's 'legitimacy crisis' therefore shows how acute the gap vis-à-vis the notion of development and developmental principles has become.

It is not least for this reason that Sornarajah argues, as was alluded to above, that international investment law and investment treaty arbitration are so flawed that bridging the gap is not only practically difficult, but structurally impossible because the system as such is fundamentally flawed and detrimental to the development of developing countries. For him,

> the episode of investment treaty arbitration, which began with *AAPL v. Sri Lanka* in 1990, brought out the worst tendencies in international law and in international lawyers. The neoliberal age sought to use international law instrumentally in order to advance the precepts of its own market-driven agenda. It sought to construct a law that was conducive to liberal flows of foreign investment. The ethos for it was created by international financial institutions – the International Monetary Fund and the World Bank – which saw in instruments like BITs the means of purveying the tenets of neoliberalism. They encouraged these treaties. … These premises were acted upon by arbitrators who enhanced the scope of the law that was contained in

---

On the criticism of investment law see also José E Alvarez, 'The Public International Law Regime Governing Foreign Investment' (2009) 344 RdC 193, 246 ff.

[104] For example, Bolivia, Ecuador and Venezuela have denounced the ICSID Convention in 2007, 2009 and 2012, respectively.

[105] See José E Alvarez, 'Why Are We "Re-calibrating" Our Investment Treaties?' (2010) 4 *World Arbitration & Mediation Review* 143 (2010).

> the treaties ... This was an age in which international law served the interests of greed. The sooner that situation is ended, the better for the credibility of international law. ... It is time that international law is redirected to serve man's need rather than his greed.[106]

Sornarajah therefore offers a view of international investment law and development as two irreconcilable antagonists. Accordingly, the gap between them cannot be bridged because of the power structures between developed and developing countries in the making of international investment law, because of the one-sided content of the rules that benefit investors to the detriment of competing public concerns, and because of the biases of those who apply them.

D. Existing Gateways for Development Concerns

The investment/development gap notwithstanding, various attempts exist to make international investment law more receptive to development concerns. Changes in treaty-making are one such attempt. They focus, above all, on institutional changes to investor-State arbitration, ranging from a return to State-to-State arbitration,[107] via introducing a common appeals body in order to review investment treaty awards,[108] to establishing a permanent international investment court.[109] However they also involve development-focused reforms, including the inclusion of preambles in investment treaties that make reference to development, the recalibration of substantive investment treaty standards, and the inclusion of exception clauses in order to grant host States sufficient policy space to pursue their development strategies.

Another gateway through which development concerns can enter international investment law is treaty interpretation. In fact, the jurisprudence of investment treaty tribunals illustrates how the protection of foreign investment can be reconciled with the pursuance of development strategies of host States. For example, many arbitral tribunals are

---

106 Sornarajah (n 20) 66 (internal citations omitted).

107 For example, the Australia-United States Free Trade Agreement has chosen this option; see William S Dodge, 'Investor-State Dispute Settlement Between Developed Countries: Reflections on the Australia–United States Free Trade Agreement' (2006) 39 Vanderbilt JTL 1 (2006).

108 In this sense, for example, Susan D Franck, 'The Legitimacy Crisis in Investment Treaty Arbitration: Privatizing Public International Law Through Inconsistent Decisions' (2005) 73 Fordham L Rev 1521, 1617 ff.

109 In this sense see Van Harten (n 103) 180 ff.

increasingly having recourse, even under old-style, lean BITs, to argumentative structures and principles of reasoning that ensure host States considerable policy space to implement their own development strategies and to take measures to comply with international treaties that aim at sustainable development, such as environmental or human rights protection. Proportionality analysis is such an argumentative strategy, which tribunals increasingly use in order to balance the protection of foreign investments and non-investment concerns that are part of the concept of sustainable development.[110] In fact, proportionality balancing itself is often considered as a function of the concept of sustainable development.[111] Exercising (degrees of) deference in the review of government conduct is another strategy tribunals employ.[112] Similar to proportionality balancing, this could ensure that host States are given sufficient policy space to pursue their development strategies. Overall, the practice of international investment law illustrates that even traditional, more restrictive investment treaties, and their interpretation by arbitral tribunals, need not necessarily restrict the development strategies of host countries and instead can be construed to leave policy space for States to pursue them. Much, however, depends on the willingness of arbitral tribunals to make use of these options.

---

[110] See Benedict Kingsbury and Stephan W Schill, 'Public Law Concepts to Balance Investors' Rights with State Regulatory Actions in the Public Interest – The Concept of Proportionality' in Schill, *Comparative Public Law* (n 27) 75; Alec Stone Sweet, 'Investor-State Arbitration: Proportionality's New Frontier' (2010) 4(1) *Law & Ethics of Human Rights* <http://www.bepress.com/lehr/vol4/iss1/art4> accessed 7 April 2015; Erlend Leonhardsen, 'Looking for Legitimacy: Exploring Proportionality Analysis in Investment Treaty Arbitration' (2012) 3 JIDS 95; Caroline Henckels, 'Indirect Expropriation and the Right to Regulate: Revisiting Proportionality Analysis and the Standard of Review in Investor-State Arbitration' (2012) 15 JIEL 223. Examples from arbitral jurisprudence include *Tecnicas Medioambientales Tecmed SA v United Mexican States*, ICSID Case No ARB (AF)/00/2, Award (29 May 2003) para 122; *Saluka Investments BV v Czech Republic*, UNCITRAL, Partial Award (17 March 2006) para 306; *Total SA v Argentine Republic*, ICSID Case No ARB/04/1, Decision on Liability (27 December 2010) paras 123 and 197; *El Paso Energy International Company v Argentine Republic*, ICSID Case No ARB/03/15, Award (31 October 2011) paras 241–3 and 373; *Occidental Petroleum Corporation and Occidental Exploration and Production Company v Republic of Ecuador*, ICSID Case No ARB/06/11, Award (5 October 2012) paras 384 ff; *Deutsche Bank v Sri Lanka* (n 95) para 522.

[111] Barral (n 65) 395–7.

[112] Stephan W Schill, 'Deference in Investment Treaty Arbitration: Re-Conceptualizing the Standard of Review' (2012) 3 JIDS 577.

Finally, investment treaty disciplines themselves can be viewed as good governance instruments that require States to implement decision-making patterns and legal principles that are conducive to economic growth, and hence further an important aspect of sustainable development. This can be illustrated, for example, in respect of the arbitral jurisprudence on the fair and equitable treatment standard.[113] Indeed, arbitral tribunals have concretized the standard to reflect a number of more specific legal principles that run parallel to the concept of the rule of law, as we know it from domestic administrative and constitutional law,[114] but also from how the United Nations understands it.[115] Thus, arbitral tribunals regularly interpret fair and equitable treatment to encompass the following elements that are part of the concept of the rule of law: (1) the requirement of legal security and predictability; (2) the principle of legality; (3) the protection of legitimate expectations; (4) basic due process requirements for administrative and judicial proceedings; (5) the protection against arbitrariness and discrimination; (6) legal certainty and transparency; and (7) the concept of proportionality or reasonableness.

Understanding the fair and equitable treatment standard as an expression of the concept of the rule of law shows how investment treaty disciplines aim at implementing structures of good governance for investor-State relations that are conducive to economic growth, and hence further the economic component of sustainable development. Similar considerations also apply to other investor rights in international investment treaties such as the protection against expropriation without compensation and national and most-favored-nation treatment. Even these principles can be understood as characteristics of a State that acts in accordance with the rule of law, respects the property interests and the freedom of its citizens, and restricts them only for overriding public

---

113 See in more depth Schill, *Fair and Equitable Treatment* (n 27).

114 Cf, e.g., Tom Bingham, *The Rule of Law* (Penguin 2010) 8.

115 United Nations, 'Delivering Justice: Programme of Action to Strengthen the Rule of Law at the National and International Levels, Report of the Secretary General' (16 March 2012) (UN Doc A/66/749) para 2 ('the rule of law [i]s a principle of governance in which all persons, institutions and entities, public and private, including the State itself, are accountable to laws that are publicly promulgated, equally enforced and independently adjudicated, and which are consistent with international human rights norms and standards. It requires, as well, measures to ensure adherence to the principles of supremacy of law, equality before the law, accountability to the law, fairness in the application of the law, separation of powers, participation in decision making, legal certainty, avoidance of arbitrariness and procedural and legal transparency.').

interests. An international investment law understood and applied in a way so as to require compliance with the concept of the rule of law could then be seen as part of a broader international legal framework that promotes (sustainable) development goals.

E. Interim Conclusion

As this section has highlighted, concerns for the notion and principles of development have been made too little explicit in international investment law so far. On the contrary, investment protection and development are often conceived as mutually exclusive objectives. At the same time, we have pointed out how even within the existing discourse on international investment law the interests of developing countries and concerns for sustainable development can find recognition and be integrated. International investment law, in other words, is not necessarily inimical to bridging the investment/development divide; instead, a closer nexus with the notion of development and developmental principles can be sought, and can guide the interpretation and negotiation of investment treaties.

In the end, much depends on the vantage point from which one conceptualizes the relationship between international investment law and development. After having clarified the different facets of the notion of development and having traced both the investment/development gap in international investment law, as well as potential gateways for development concerns to come into international investment law, we now turn to how the contributions in the present book approach the relationship. The attempt we make here is not to provide ready-made solutions to how the relationship between investment and development should be viewed. Rather this book provides different perspectives and attempts at clarification of the relationship of these concepts. The overarching objective is to bring the discourses on investment and development closer together and to explore whether and how the investment/development gap can be bridged.

IV. BRIDGING THE INVESTMENT/DEVELOPMENT GAP

As noted above, the book opens with a keynote by M. Sornarajah that contains a forceful and scathing critique of international investment law. By contrast, most of the subsequent chapters adopt a more nuanced approach. Rather than criticizing international investment law in a lump-sum fashion, these other contributions explore ways in which investment law can be made compatible and reconciled with development interests. They do so from different angles, including both general and more concrete analyses of the relationship between investment law and development, focusing on both the application and interpretation of existing, and the making of new, investment treaties. They are grouped into three clusters. Part II of the book contains chapters that analyze the relationship of international investment law and development from different conceptual angles (A.). Part III contains chapters that take a closer look at how international investment law interacts with self-determination as one core aspect for the implementation of development strategies. It includes the classical topic of investment protection and natural resources as well as the more recent concern of how investment disciplines affect transitions to democracy (B.). Part IV, finally, looks at the interaction of international investment law and the social dimension of development, namely social inclusion and the participation of all members of society in the benefits of economic growth as an indicator of development (C.).

A. Reconceptualizing the Relationship between Investment and Development

Part II starts with an analysis by Yannick Radi of the conceptual history of the relationship between international investment law and development, which differs quite radically from Sornarajah's account. Pointing out the importance of the epistemological context in which the relationship between international investment law and development is analyzed, Radi argues that viewed from within the investment regime 'IIL has always been a "friend" to development.'[116] This is so, above all, because the principal objective of international investment law, he argues, has always been the promotion of development; the protection of foreign investment, by contrast, has been but a subsidiary objective. In Radi's view, the problem with the investment/development gap is therefore one of the epistemic limits of the investment arbitration community. which has simply forgotten or ignored the 'subsidiary' nature of the protection granted under investment treaties when elevating it to the prime objective of the investment regime.[117] In this perspective, the 'reintegration' of investment and development in modern, recalibrated investment treaties

116 Yannick Radi, 'International Investment Law and Development: A History of Two Concepts', in this volume 69, 70.

117 Ibid 71–72.

is a way to make the original *telos* explicit, rather than to lower the level of protection granted to foreign investment.

In investment treaty-making, envisioning a constructive relationship between international investment law and development is becoming the prevailing mindset. This requires us – as Markus W. Gehring and Marie-Claire Cordonier Segger show – to understand investment treaties as tools for 'harnessing FDI [i.e. foreign direct investment] for sustainable development.'[118] This is not only desirable from the perspective of sustainable development, but also possible. It requires, as Gehring and Cordonier Segger show, 'to situate investor rights within a wider normative context, to interpret investment agreements (especially early ones emphasising investor rights only) in a systematically integrated way, and to allow for reform from within.'[119] The integration of investment law into a broader sustainable development framework can be achieved through innovative procedural and substantive advances in how IIAs are negotiated. Participation of civil society and transparency in the negotiation of IIAs, capacity-building of negotiators of developing countries, and ex-ante development impact assessment of IIAs could enhance their sustainability. The contribution to sustainable development could further be enhanced through preambular language alluding to the development aspirations of IIAs, as well as including appropriate exceptions and reservations, provisions on development cooperation, and corporate social responsibility.

The formulation of development-friendly investment treaty policy is also at the heart of the involvement of the United Nations, in particular of UNCTAD. Andrea Saldarriaga and Kendra Magraw focus on UNCTAD's involvement in bringing investment law and development together.[120] They not only stress that various UN statements for a long time have set out a positive relationship of investment and development, but also explain how current challenges for sustainable development stemming from the investment regime are being addressed by UNCTAD. Thus, the sole focus of investment treaties on investment protection, the lack of transparency of and public participation in investment arbitration, vague rules in investment treaties that give arbitral tribunals broad discretion to

---

[118] Markus W Gehring and Marie-Claire Cordonier Segger, 'Overcoming Obstacles with Opportunities: Trade and Investment Agreements for Sustainable Development', in this volume, 93, 99.

[119] Ibid 94.

[120] Andrea Saldarriaga and Kendra Magraw, 'UNCTAD's Effort to Foster the Relationship between International Investment Law and Sustainable Development', in this volume, 125.

restrict governments' policy space, and the lack of investor obligations inform UNCTAD's agenda for IIA reform. This has not only resulted in the IPFSD already mentioned, which aims at rethinking investment law and the content of IIAs in a development perspective, but continues as part of UNCTAD's ongoing work on IIA reform, which aims at encouraging investment for development.

An important guiding concept for IIA reform and the implementation of existing IIAs is that of good governance and the rule of law, to which the contribution of Celine Tan turns.[121] Indeed, investment treaty disciplines are often justified as providing the good governance structures that are necessary for increasing foreign investment and economic growth more generally but do not exist in many host States. Yet, Tan doubts whether a loosely institutionalized system, such as investor-State arbitration, is able to use the concept of good governance to justify its own existence, when it may not live up to the normative demands of the good governance concept itself. This is so because she questions whether arbitration is appropriate for settling private-public disputes from the perspective of the rule of law in the first place; furthermore, she wonders to which extent investment treaty disputes do not stifle domestic law reforms because the interpretations by arbitral tribunals may cause regulatory chill. Tan is therefore critical of whether good governance discourse should be used as guidance for reforming the international investment regime. Rather than leading to a more legitimate and balanced system, the use of good governance language to justify and reform international investment law may do nothing more than 'masking and further legitimising its systemic deficiencies.'[122]

The epistemic and ideological context of all analyses of the relationship of international investment law and development is also emphasized in Antonius R. Hippolyte's chapter on Third-World Approaches to International Law (TWAIL).[123] The TWAIL movement, which shares much of Sornarajah's ideological background, understands international law generally, and international investment law in particular, as a product of hegemonic dominance of Western capital-exporting States that is biased towards the developing world. While Hippolyte appreciates the

---

[121] Celine Tan, 'Reviving the Emperor's Old Clothes: The Good Governance Agenda, Development and International Investment Law', in this volume, 147.

[122] Ibid 179.

[123] Antonius R Hippolyte, 'Aspiring for a Constructive TWAIL Approach Towards the International Investment Regime', in this volume, 180.

theoretical depth TWAIL approaches display, he criticizes them for sticking to an outdated economic and political framework which is unable to make constructive contributions to reforming international investment law for the benefit of developing countries. According to Hippolyte, TWAIL should embrace investment law as an instrument that can potentially further developing countries' interests, rather than continue opposing it due to its North-South pedigree. Such a new openness is needed, in his view, not least because economic reality has undergone fundamental changes during the last decades. After all, we do not see autonomous national economies interstitially interacting anymore, but rather observe their integration into one global economic system. Switching from destructive analysis to constructive criticism would therefore, Hippolyte argues, be a true contribution of TWAIL to the interests of developing countries.

B. Development and Self-Determination

Part III of this book turns to the relationship between international investment law and development understood as self-determination. As Melaku Desta shows in his chapter,[124] self-determination has played a particularly prominent role in the natural resources sector during NIEO times in order to make developing countries politically and economically independent from their former colonial masters. In this context, claims for self-determination and sovereignty went hand in hand. Yet, once political independence had been achieved, reliance on unbounded sovereignty could become inimical to achieving development goals in cases where cooperation with foreign investors was necessary to exploit cost- and technology-intensive natural resources. This justifies restrictions on sovereignty, such as those contained in investment treaties. Yet again, absolute stability of investor-State relations would not be appropriate either as the social, political, and environmental circumstances may change during the life of a multi-decade natural resources project. The solution would therefore be to balance sovereignty and self-determination, on the one hand, and the protection of foreign investments in the natural resources sector, on the other. To achieve this aim, Desta argues, developing countries should actively contribute to making and reforming investment law and avoid fundamental opposition à la NIEO.

---

[124] Melaku Desta, 'Sovereignty over Natural Resources and International Investment Law: The Elusive Search for Equilibrium', in this volume, 223.

Isabel Feichtner's chapter focuses on the method of resolving disputes over natural resources. She points out that during NIEO times there was a preference for the political resolution of such conflicts at the inter-State level, while legal norms and judicial as well as arbitral procedures played a lesser role.[125] This has changed fundamentally. Disputes about natural resources today are resolved through the application of legal principles in binding, allegedly de-politicized, procedures, including investor-State arbitration. Using the example of Zambia, Feichtner illustrates the problems of such a move to law and legal dispute resolution: in her view, the host State now is solely responsible for handling the complex private-public relations, which previously had been resolved in a political process involving host and home States. Moreover, Feichtner points out, the interests of the host State's population are not internationalized, but remain mediated through the host State and are thus not necessarily reflected in conflicts over natural resources. As a remedy, she emphasizes that the political element in resolving investor-State disputes, in particular in the natural resources sector, should not be forgotten: this would enable dispute settlement processes to be more socially inclusive and might lead to results that reflect the self-determination of an entire country.

Jonathan Bonnitcha then turns to another aspect relating to the interaction of international investment law and self-determination, namely the role investment treaties play in the transition from authoritarian rule to democracy.[126] This is a core concern for development because only participation of people in government will enable them to set their own development priorities and strategies. According to Bonnitcha, investment treaties can hinder this transition by protecting investments made during the preceding authoritarian rule, thereby complicating, or even preventing, the incoming government's own development strategies. At the same time, protecting investments against a new government's interference may also help break investor support for the old regime and thereby facilitate transition to democracy. To find the right balance between empowering incoming governments to implement new laws and policies, but also to break ties between the old regime and its economic supporters, is, as Bonnitcha argues, the task of those interpreting investment treaties. Such interpretations are, as he insists, possible.

---

[125] Isabel Feichtner, 'International (Investment) Law and Distribution Conflicts over Natural Resources', in this volume, 256.

[126] Jonathan Bonnitcha, 'Democracy, Development and Compensation under Investment Treaties: The Case of Transition from Authoritarian Rule', in this volume, 285.

Walid Ben Hamida complements Bonnitcha's analysis by focusing specifically on the revocation of contracts and concessions agreed to by a former authoritarian regime.[127] Ben Hamida argues that international investment law, in principle, is agnostic towards the reasons leading to a transition of power. Whether change takes place from democratic to autocratic rule, or vice versa, is immaterial for the protection of investments under investment treaties. Accordingly, contracts and treaties concluded by a non-democratic government must be honored by the successor government. Developments during the Arab Spring may however have led to a gradual qualification of this time-honored rule, Ben Hamida suggests. Notably, he points to a number of multilateral Arab investment treaties, which require foreign investors to observe public order and morality. Such provisions, according to Ben Hamida, may give rise to arguments that contracts with undemocratic governments are themselves immoral and cannot be enforced. Another source for such an argument are references to the need for democratic forms of government, inter alia in agreements concluded by the European Union. The application of investment treaties to governmental transitions may therefore itself be in transition.

C. Development and Social Inclusion

The final Part of the book brings together contributions that address the relationship between investment law and development from the perspective of social inclusion. It opens with a chapter by Diane A. Desierto on the right to development, as articulated in the 1986 UN Declaration on the Right to Development.[128] As she points out, understanding development – in line with the Declaration – as an inclusive process, rather than as achieving a specific end result would do away with the need to provide an objective and uniformly applicable definition. Instead, what development means could differ from country to country, similar to the idea of development as self-determination, provided that the process for concretizing self-determination into specific policies involves all stakeholders and represents all social interests. In this context, the right to development, as Desierto argues, corresponds with the 'specific responsibility of States to build in an enabling environment for international human rights

[127] Walid Ben Hamida, 'Investment Treaties and Democratic Transition: Does Investment Law Authorize Not to Honor Contracts Concluded with Undemocratic Regimes?', in this volume, 309.

[128] Desierto (n 52) (in this volume).

protection as part of the State's economic decision-making processes.'[129] This responsibility must also be met in the negotiation of IIAs and investor-State contracts and in the management of investment disputes. This would require States to move away from an inter-State approach to investment relations and towards a more inclusive system that allows people to participate in decision-making processes and put their interests center stage.

Social inclusion also plays a core role in Krista Nadakavukaren Schefer's assessment of international investment law's relationship to the fight against poverty.[130] In her view, international investment law is problematic from the perspective of poverty reduction because it does not empower the poor, neither substantially, nor procedurally; instead it fosters inequalities by granting special protections for foreigners against the redistribution of existing resources. Nadakavukaren Schefer is right when arguing that investment law does not actively combat and reduce poverty. At the same time, it is important to note that investment law does not prohibit wealth redistribution as such. While uncompensated expropriations are prohibited, other redistribution instruments, such as taxation, remain available.

Social inclusion is also the theme of the contribution by Vid Prislan and Ruben Zandvliet.[131] Focusing on the interaction between investment protection and labor standards, they note that a comprehensive notion of development cannot be limited to enhancing benefits for investors. Instead, a development-friendly investment law needs to ensure that investor benefits do not come at the expense of labor standards. As Prislan and Zandvliet observe, for this reason, references to labor rights can increasingly be found in international investment treaties. Some of them prohibit contracting States to use the deregulation of labor standards as an investment incentive; others aim at ensuring that enhancing labor rights at the domestic level will not constitute breach of investment treaty disciplines. Other clauses go further: they actively encourage, or even require, governments to adopt internationally recognized labor standards. Finally, investment treaties now increasingly also consider ways of enhancing compliance of foreign investors with labor standards through better enforcement mechanisms, mostly in the form of soft

---

129 Ibid 338.

130 Krista Nadakavukaren Schefer, 'The Law of Investment Protection and Poverty Reduction', in this volume, 369.

131 Vid Prislan and Ruben Zandvliet, 'Mainstreaming Sustainable Development into International Investment Agreements: What Role for Labor Provisions?', in this volume, 390.

obligations as part of corporate social responsibility. Some of these obligations may well mature into hard law obligations in the future. As Prislan and Zandvliet show, investment treaties today, in particular in the context of broader economic governance agreements, 'no longer allow the goal of economic development to be achieved at the expense of social concerns, but instead promote a more holistic concept of sustainable development.'[132]

Finally, Christina Binder addresses a specific and often overlooked aspect of the inclusive function of development, namely the rights of indigenous peoples.[133] According to her, a truly development-friendly regime has to do more than recognize the host State's right to national self-determination. Focusing on the effects of investment projects and investment disputes on indigenous peoples and their (land) rights, Binder emphasizes that the host State's population is not necessarily a homogenous group with a uniform majoritarian public interest. Instead, (sustainable) development must mean 'inclusive development',[134] so that 'the protection of indigenous peoples as culturally distinct peoples is a necessary part of sustainable development.'[135] Similar considerations may also apply to other vulnerable groups within a host State if development is to benefit all parts of a society. International investment law has to meet that challenge through procedural and substantive accommodation of the interests of indigenous people, such as making use of principles for their protection in the interpretation of investment treaties and through the promotion of amicus curiae submissions by indigenous people. None of this requires any treaty reform; the options are available under the existing legal framework – but of course they need to be used.

V. CONCLUSION: MAINSTREAMING DEVELOPMENT IN INTERNATIONAL INVESTMENT LAW

This broad survey of the relationship between international investment law and development yields a mixed picture. On the one hand, investment and development appear to be closely inter-connected from an economic perspective. Achieving the aims of sustainable development in

---

[132] Ibid 422.

[133] Christina Binder, 'Investment, Development and Indigenous Peoples', in this volume, 423.

[134] Ibid 424.

[135] Ibid.

particular seems barely possible without investment, including foreign investment. After all, only by means of additional investment will it be possible to transition to more environmentally-friendly technologies without cutting back economic, cultural, and social development. On the other hand, the discourse on investment and development, especially in international legal scholarship, has rarely sought to integrate investment and development. Although those who practice and analyze international investment law and investment dispute settlement are aware of the development implications of the field, they seldom understand their practice as part of an international law of development.

Things may change, however, with the conclusion of a new generation of investment treaties that draw more explicit links between investment protection and development, with the interpretation of investment treaty disciplines in light of the concept of sustainable development, and with the emerging analysis of the impact of the right to development on international investment policies. Nevertheless, a significant part of the scholarship on international investment protection law remains stuck in a conceptual framework that is structured by the contrasts between interests of capital-exporting and capital-importing States, investors and States, claimants and respondents, pro-State and pro-investor arbitrators, neo-liberalism and neo-communitarianism, and that views international investment law and development as antagonists rather than as mutually supportive disciplines.

As the preceding discussion indicates, there are numerous possibilities to strengthen the link between investment and development in international investment law, both methodologically and thematically, and to overcome the existing isolation and polarization without fundamentally changing the functioning of the current investment regime. This could involve changes in treaty practice that stress the development-dimension of investment treaties, such as ensuring policy space, including environmental and human rights safeguards, and inclusiveness in the procedures for negotiating investment treaties and settling investor-State disputes. It could also see a more active involvement of developing countries in debates about the making and reforming of international investment law and empowering host States to effectively regulate foreign investment in a balanced manner. All this requires, first and foremost, a willingness to think about international investment protection and development not as antagonists, but as two aspects of a common project. Overcoming the existing 'silo-thinking' that separates investment protection from development concerns would allow scholars and practitioners to mainstream development concerns in international investment law and investment dispute settlement and to reconceptualize international investment law as a regime that forms part of international development law.

This having been said, perhaps the dispute is less one about an abstract relationship between two notions than about the proper means of ensuring that investment benefits (sustainable) development. Even the most ardent supporters of investment protection are likely to accept that not all investments are always beneficial, and that some in fact adversely affect sustainable development goals. In particular, investments that are not well regulated by the host country may adversely affect the environment, the local population and its living conditions. There are numerous examples, especially in the area of natural resources, in particular in oil and gas exploitation and mining (but also in other high-risk ventures), where actions of foreign companies have resulted in damage to the environment, living conditions, or the health of local populations. As a consequence, it is necessary to distinguish between beneficial and detrimental investments and to ensure that potential harm is prevented. This not only requires effective regulation by the host country, but is also dependent on the companies, their home countries, and the international community as a whole.

Joint and concerted efforts at all levels in linking the admission of foreign investment to host countries development strategies, in regulating foreign investment projects effectively, and in ensuring sufficient policy space for legitimate government (re-)regulation will enable investment law to serve as an important component of international development law. Under these conditions, international investment law and development would be friends, not foes.

2. Developing countries in the investment treaty system: A law for need or a law for greed?

Muthucumaraswamy Sornarajah

I. INTRODUCTION

We have always been led to believe that investment treaties contribute to the economic development of the poorer states of the world. The theory is that they promote the stability that is lacking in the developing countries due to their absence of proper laws and functioning courts which could grant effective protection to foreign investment. By creating definite rules which result in remedies provided through arbitration, investment treaties provide stability for foreign investors. In that context, their fears having been effectively removed, foreign investors will move into developing states that sign investment treaties, providing secure treatment standards enforced through arbitration tribunals.

Economists have challenged this rationale for investment treaties in recent times. Many argue that there is no evidence to show that investors choose to invest in developing countries because these countries have investment treaties.[1] Instead, any cursory look at the picture will show that foreign investors invest not because there are investment treaties, the

[1] There is an increasing debate amongst economists as to whether there is any link between investment treaties and flows of foreign investments. The studies are inconclusive. See Emma Aisbett, 'Bilateral Investment Treaties and Foreign Direct Investment: Correlation Versus Causation' in Karl P Sauvant and Lisa E Sachs (eds), *The Effect of Treaties on Foreign Direct Investments* (OUP 2009) 395; Mary Hallward-Driemeier, 'Do Bilateral Investment Treaties Attract Foreign Investment? Only a Bit and They Could Bite' World Bank Pol'y Res Working Paper No 3121 (2003); Jason Yackee, 'Do Bilateral Investment Treaties Promote Foreign Direct Investments?' (2010) 51 Va JIL 397. This is not an exhaustive list. There is a summary of these articles in Christian Bellak, 'How Bilateral Investment Treaties Impact on Foreign Direct Investment' (2013)

existence of which some investors do not even know of, but for other reasons such as the ready availability of mineral resources, cheaper labour, large markets for manufactured goods and the need to meet competition of other investors who would move into these states if they did not. If these reasons are the dominant ones, and if it is true that there is no correlation between investment flows and the signing of treaties, host states lose sovereignty unnecessarily by entering into investment treaties. The only rationale for investment treaties is that, for the loss of control over foreign investment that results from conformity with the standards in the investment treaty, the quid pro quo is the greater flow of foreign investment. If this equation, however, does not hold, no rationale for investment treaties exists. In fact, economic studies throw great doubts with the validity of this rationale.

Investment treaties are asymmetric treaties which benefit only multinational corporations from developed states.[2] Though stated as creating reciprocal obligations, this is a fallacy as developing states are hardly capable of sending substantial investments into the major developed economies of the world. Investment treaties are based on lies. Developing states derive no benefit from the system of protection devised through arbitration. What is more, they stand in peril of multi-million dollar arbitral awards resulting from the violation of the treaties at times when they are least able to meet such awards. This is illustrated by the experience of Argentina, which had to face 52 arbitrations involving claims of several billion dollars while recovering from an economic crisis.[3] The damages are so exorbitant that they undermine economic plans of the state. The costs of litigation are equally high. As estimated in the Philippine parliament, the legal costs of meeting the arbitration in *Fraport v. Philippines*[4] cost over fifty million dollars, money which could have been used to build schools, hospitals and roads.[5] Neither has the

---

<http://www2.gre.ac.uk/__data/assets/pdf_file/0006/822705/Christian-Bellak-How-Bilateral-Investment-Treaties-Impact-on-Foreign-Direct-Investment-A-Meta-analysis-of-Public-Policy.pdf> accessed 30 October 2014.

[2] They are technically invalid as unequal treaties. For the notion of unequal treaties, see Mathew Craven, 'What Happened to Unequal Treaties? The Continuities of Informal Empire' (2005) 74 *Nordic Journal of International Law* 335.

[3] Paolo Di Rosa, 'The Recent Wave of Arbitrations against Argentina under Bilateral Investment Treaties: Background and Principal Legal Issues' (2004) 36(1) *University of Miami Inter-American Law Review* 41.

[4] *Fraport AG Frankfurt Airport Services Worldwide v The Republic of the Philippines*, ICSID Case No ARB/03/25, Award (16 August 2007).

[5] Gil C Cabacungan Jr, 'House to Probe Huge Lawyers' Fees in NAIA 3 Case' *Philippine Daily Inquirer* (Makati City, 28 March 2011) <http://newsinfo.

investor in the dispute received a single cent of his USD 400 million investment. The benefits of the system to states and investors therefore need to be examined afresh.

II. RE-EXAMINING THE ECONOMIC BENEFITS OF INVESTMENT TREATIES

From the point of view of states, investment treaties have been disastrous. The regulatory powers of states to deal with abusive investments are considerably curtailed as a result of these treaties. The ability of the state to deal with environmental crisis, to protect the health of its people or to promote the public interest has been curtailed by investment treaties as well. They bring about a regulatory chill in that the threat of investment arbitration they contain results in states drawing back from measures that are necessary to deal with issues of public interest. States also have other competing interests that are imposed through multilateral treaties. These involve matters of global interest, such as measures necessary to deal with climate change or to protect human rights, cultural property and global health. The need for investment treaties, therefore, has to be re-examined.

To reiterate a point already made, investment treaties are not the reasons for the flow of foreign investments. Multinational companies have many reasons for going into developing countries. It makes sense to invest in large markets of developing countries. In imperialist days, the imperial outposts served as markets for manufactured goods of the imperial power. The same situation prevails now as it is obvious that multinational corporations need the large markets found in China, India and parts of Africa and Asia. If they do not enter these states, their competitors will. The profits the competitors make will affect the home markets as the profits will be used for innovation and expansion. If a multinational corporation operates in the resources sectors, it will enter states that have the resources, whether or not they have treaties. For example, energy companies enter Ecuador not because it has investment

inquirer.net/breakingnews/metro/view/20110328-328066/House-to-probe-huge-lawyers-fees-in-NAIA-3-case> accessed 23 January 2015. On costs involved in arbitrations generally, see Diana Rosert, 'The Stakes Are High: A Review of Financial Costs of Investment Treaty Arbitration' (International Institute for Sustainable Development 2014) <http://www.iisd.org/sites/default/files/publications/stakes-are-high-review-financial-costs-investment-treaty-arbitration.pdf> accessed 23 January 2015.

treaties but because it has plenty of energy resources. If they do not enter, their competitors will. In the modern world, China, India and other states are hungry for resources and provide effective competition. Their national oil companies are as effective as any Western oil company. They do not necessarily depend on investment treaties. The largest investors in Ecuador are from Brazil and Mexico, two states with which Ecuador has no investment treaties. The largest investors in South-East Asia are the multinational companies of the United States. The United States has no investment treaties with the states of the region (except with Singapore). It is pretty obvious that resource-based multinational corporations will enter states which have an abundance of resources. With heavy competition for resources, such entry simply has to be made for these corporations to survive in business. Equally, large manufacturing companies will enter lucrative markets whether they are protected by treaties or not. It is a canard to say that investment treaties promote investment flows or aid in economic development. This is only how investment treaties have been sold to developing countries.

The premise of investment treaties rests on a lie. The only economic development the treaties bring are to the arbitrators who interpret these treaties and lawyers of large law firms who represent parties and argue before the arbitral tribunals.[6] They have created a system of investment treaty arbitration through which they profit tremendously. So much so, that vulture funds have emerged to fund arbitrations.[7] It is best to put an end to this falsehood that the system created benefits for the development of the poor. Nothing of the sort takes place. As in the historical past of the 'white man's burden',[8] an altruistic justification used to plunder the wealth of Africa and Asia, the present altruistic mantra that investment

---

[6] The point is made in a scathing manner in Corporate Europe Observatory, 'Profiting from Injustice: How Law Firms and Arbitrators Are Fuelling an Investment Arbitration Boom' (2012) <http://corporateeurope.org/trade/2012/11/profiting-injustice> accessed 30 October 2014. For a more academic analysis of the same issue, see Sergio Puig, 'Social Capital in the Arbitration Market' (2014) 25 EJIL 387.

[7] Jonathan Lippert, 'Vulture Funds: The Reason Why the Congolese Debt May Force a Revision of the Foreign Sovereign Immunities Act' (2008) 21 New York ILR 1.

[8] The 'white man's burden', a term used by Rudyard Kipling who wrote a poem under the title, was to bring the colonized people of Asia and Africa to the standards of civilization of the imperial powers. This 'duty' was the justification for imperial rule and the plunder of the wealth of the people of Africa and Asia. The maintenance of a standard of civilization was seen as a purpose of international law. Gerrit Gong, *The Standard of Civilization* (OUP 1964).

treaties benefit economic development is a myth. Their true purpose is plunder under the cloak of a law made through the instrumentality of power. History always repeats itself. The idea of colonialism never went away. It was quickly replaced by a system of 'global governance' or a 'rule of law' very reminiscent of the standard of civilization that justified imperialism and formed a cornerstone of imperialist international law. The picture may well change as developed states are now increasingly at the receiving end of the system they had devised to pillory developing states.

It has been suggested that the system of investor-state arbitration is based on the awards made by just 16 arbitrators and that a handful of law firms practise in the area.[9] Hence, the area is based on a restrictive practice that purports to make law for the whole world. Had there been a global competition law, this operation would have merited its attention. Yet, it is a system in which the World Bank participates, as the major arbitration centre that churns out these awards is the International Centre for Settlement of Investment Disputes (ICSID). ICSID was created under the auspices of the World Bank. The World Bank created this Centre on the basis of its ideological preference for the view that secure investment tribunals will promote foreign investment flows. This neo-liberal vision was further stabilized through investment treaties which created jurisdiction in ICSID when treaty standards were violated.[10]

The law that has resulted is one that is geared to the advantage of private interests of large multinational corporations, arbitrators and law firms. Recent studies in this field indicate that the law had been made by a handful of aging men with a few token women in attendance. Very few of them come from the developing world. Those who have come from the developing world have drunk deeply not only of the exquisite wine that is offered at the parties of arbitrators, but equally deeply of the notions of neoliberalism and the prevailing culture of investment arbitration. You cannot join the club without servilely subscribing to the holy tenets of the absolute standards of investment protection. The members of the select club are touted as 'highly qualified publicists' though there is little evidence of their deep learning, but greater evidence of their deep prejudice. They make law for the world without any legitimate power to do so. The poor of the world, in whose name this chicanery takes place, have their resources robbed and the ignominy of being recalcitrant

---

9 Puig (n 6).

10 The creation of such jurisdiction dates from the award of *Asian Agricultural Products Ltd (AAPL) v Republic of Sri Lanka*, ICSID Case No ARB/87/3, Award (27 June 1990).

offenders of the treaty standards heaped on them through the expansive interpretation of treaty standards by arbitral awards. Their states stand in peril of being prey to vulture funds. Their states were induced into signing investment treaties in the belief that good would come out of such action. Instead, what has resulted is a heaping of misery in times of crises.

It is untrue that development takes place on the basis of investment treaties. States without investment treaties like Brazil have made spectacular economic progress. Many states have now withheld their treaty programmes. South Africa and several Latin American states are among them. Many have also withdrawn from participation in the ICSID system. There will be nothing to show that they have suffered any ill effects in investment flows as a result of withdrawing from investment treaties. It would appear that investment treaties only bring trouble. They impose a regulatory chill through the threat of arbitration by an investor, and make states forgo action in the public interest.

III. A LAW IN THE HANDS OF ARBITRATORS

What is worse for developing countries is that the law, which was agreed to under the investment treaties, has been expanded by arbitrators beyond its original basis. In some instances, obvious frauds and malpractices have been overlooked in order to uphold jurisdiction of foreign investors. I take as one instance, the use of corporate nationality, widely relied on to define the investor who is protected. Here we see cases, like *Tokios Tokelés v. Ukraine*,[11] holding that assets, which originally belonged to the host state, could be taken into another treaty state and brought back as protected investment. Obviously, such a view subverts the purpose of the investment treaty, which is to promote economic development through the injection of fresh funds.

Another fraudulent manipulation of the investment treaty system is the so called 'Dutch sandwich' whereby the mere insertion of a subsidiary in the corporate structure enables a large multinational corporation to exploit the better protection under an investment treaty, usually the Dutch treaty with the disputing state. This is again a fraud on the system as the subsidiary so incorporated to achieve jurisdiction is not the one which sends out the investment.

---

[11] *Tokios Tokelés v Ukraine*, ICSID Case No ARB/02/18, Decision on Jurisdiction (29 April 2004).

Relief has been provided on the most spurious basis after the assumption of such jurisdiction, *ConocoPhillips v. Venezuela*[12] being the classic example of such an award. In that dispute, jurisdiction was assumed under a Dutch treaty on the basis of the insertion of a Dutch subsidiary in the corporate structure with no proof that any investment was channelled through that subsidiary. The majority of the tribunal found liability on a point hardly argued in the case, namely that there were no good faith negotiations in fixing compensation. The case demonstrates a situation in which some arbitrators will find rather atrocious ways of ensuring that resource-rich developing countries toe the line that is drawn in order to ensure that foreign investors are given secure protection. The legitimacy of investment arbitration becomes suspect as a result. It is as if once gunboat diplomacy had failed,[13] investment arbitrators are the insidious troops that are the hidden guardians of foreign investment dressed up in expensive civilian suits instead of military uniform.

Likewise, the whole saga relating to the use of the most-favoured-nation (MFN) clause to widen jurisdiction in a manner favourable to the claimant has yet to run its course. It is evident that a tribunal should first have jurisdiction to pronounce on the effect of the MFN clause and the clause itself cannot be the basis of its jurisdiction to pronounce on the issue. It defies logic to say that a tribunal can extend its jurisdiction through the MFN clause when it does not have jurisdiction to so rule unless it can use that very clause. But logic has never mattered. In investment arbitration, it is possible to pull oneself up by one's own bootstraps. The only consideration has been to ensure that the goal of foreign investment protection is advanced.

In an area of low visibility, sixteen men, are said to make the law for the world, or rather for the developing countries. But, as a spate of recent cases against European states, including the *Vattenfall* arbitration against

---

12 *ConocoPhillips Petrozuata BV, ConocoPhillips Hamaca BV and ConocoPhillips Gulf of Paria BV v Bolivarian Republic of Venezuela*, ICSID Case No ARB/07/30, Decision on Jurisdiction and Merits (3 September 2013).

13 Apologists admit that the area of investment protection was once the area for gunboat diplomacy but that it has been replaced by arbitration. The admission is instructive only for the reason that the rules that are applied are insidious and further the purpose of investment protection more effectively than gunboat diplomacy, which was direct, whereas the system of investment arbitration comes cloaked as 'neutral rules' applied by 'neutral' tribunals.

Germany,[14] demonstrates, the boot that was intended to kick the poorer countries is on the other foot and is starting to kick the wrong states, which thought they were immune from the system that they had created. The law was originally intended to apply to 'economic development agreements', and developed states do not make such agreements. So, there are rumblings within Germany, which started the treaty system, about the need for such treaties as there are rumblings within other developed countries, which are slowly losing their power in the emerging multipolar world. The investment treaty arbitration system is coming home to the developed states to roost. It will prove uncomfortable for these states as this happens. The developed states themselves are doing a lot of rethinking on investment treaties. The making of a European investment treaty and the debates surrounding it indicate considerable anxieties concerning treaties that are devoted to the protection of investment.

The hegemonic world legal order is founded on many lies. Grotius lied when he spoke of the natural law basis of the international law on freedom of the seas when his objective was seeking to justify the right of the nascent Dutch naval power to traverse the world and found colonies in Asia. Hegemonic English international lawyers lied when they argued that Australia was *terra nullius* and so could be occupied by white settlers, ignoring the nomadic aborigines who could not hold land. Hegemonic power has used the instrumentality of international law to provide justifications in altruistic terms so that it could justify its domination. Colonialism was justified through the lie that it was the white man's civilizational burden when in fact there was a massive plunder of the wealth of the colonies. International law's founding in lies is an unfortunate history that it has been unable to shake off.

Investment treaty law lied when it stated that it is fashioned to promote economic development in the poorer world. The financial institutions insisted that investment treaties were made. The Washington Consensus cultivated the belief that investment protection was necessary to ensure investment flows. Investment treaties were made based on this cultivated lie, propagated by various institutions and governments of the West. Over three thousand treaties resulted from the pressures to conform to the lies or otherwise access to loans and other facilities would be denied. Coercion was the basis of many of the laws that were made through treaties. These treaties are potentially void because of such coercion. The

---

14 *Vattenfall AB and others v Federal Republic of Germany*, ICSID Case No ARB/12/12 (registered 31 May 2012).

hegemonic power, which drove this system espoused a neoliberal vision, which was translated into international law through coercive power.

The law that is purveyed is said to be a neutral and depoliticized law, when in fact it is a purveyor of the economic philosophy of the hegemonic power and its allies. When Charles N Brower plaintively pleads that the law is being politicized by writers from the developing world,[15] my answer is to ask in return the question as to what the arbitrators and writers of the West have been doing, employing and expanding the instrumental law of investment protection, having no regard at all to the fact that their position as well involves a politicization no less evident only because it is done with a pretence to neutrality. Institutions have also cultivated this pretence. It is in realization of that fact that we now have a plenitude of cases involving the United States and Canada – like *Methanex v. United States*[16] and *Chemtura v. Canada*[17] for instance – which show the need to have a law based on other considerations besides inflexible investment protection. The new trends initiated by countries with the resources to mount such arguments indicate exceptions to standards of investment protection that considerably undermine the old law on investment protection.

IV. EXPANSIONARY TRENDS IN INVESTMENT TREATY ARBITRATION

Let me give you some examples of the expansionary law that I suggest has been made to further the aim of investment protection. Expansion of the law with an evident purpose of furthering a political aim of enabling the domination of multinational capital is also politicization of the law. It is a fallacy to argue that in this field the law remains unpoliticized as its rules always have had their roots in the preferences of the powerful states. It is futile to argue that standards such as the international investment standard of full protection and security, which are still the staples of investment treaties, did not come from US relations with Latin America and are not politicized rules resulting from American power. With the exception of the fair and equitable standard, which has been the

[15] Charles N Brower and Sadie Blanchard, 'What's in a Meme? The Truth About Investor-State Arbitration' (2014) 52(3) Columbia JTL 689, 690.

[16] *Methanex Corporation v United States of America*, UNCITRAL (NAFTA), Final Award of the Tribunal on Jurisdiction and Merits (3 August 2005).

[17] *Chemtura Corporation (formerly Crompton Corporation) v Government of Canada*, UNCITRAL (NAFTA), Award (2 August 2010).

focus of modern politicized expansion, the other treaty standards are the result of an American dominance. They reflect American international law which was resisted by Latin American states.

It would be invidious to say that these are neutral rules and equally invidious to say that the sixteen arbitrators who interpret them do so in a depoliticized manner. Arbitrators themselves are not 'depoliticized'.[18] Arbitral neutrality is another myth that supports the system. Arbitrators have expanded the standards of protection in investment treaties. The law is then theorized and entrenched by eager, usually young, sycophantic aspirants to recognition by the club or its potential members. We hear that the law has become customary international law, when you cannot demonstrate that the practice of even a single state like the United States is constant as regards provisions in the investment treaties though they are negotiated on the basis of a model[19] or that it is multilateralized when it is not possible to show that the techniques used in multilateralization, such as the MFN clause, have uniform acceptance.

Let me illustrate my views by having regard to incidents within the two principle areas of investment arbitration: jurisdictional bases and the substantive rules for liability. First, we have the jurisdictional areas. The MFN treatment provision in treaties has been used to a significant extent in order to ensure that the better provisions of third-party treaties are used by claimants in this field. Likewise, theories of corporate nationality make it possible for treaty-shopping to take place. Thus, it is possible to incorporate in places like the Netherlands in order to take advantage of the better provisions of treaties that one would find in there. This enables round-tripping of investments. As decided in *Tokios Tokelés v. Ukraine*,[20] it is possible for citizens of one state to accede to the protection of an investment treaty with another state by incorporating their business in that other state and to channel their money back to their home state, now benefiting from the protection of an investment treaty. So what one finds here in this jurisdictional sphere is the situation where the law is expanded so that the techniques of litigation are more

---

[18] Michael Waibel and Yanhui Wu, 'Are Arbitrators Political?' (2012) <http://www.wipol.uni-bonn.de/lehrveranstaltungen-1/lawecon-workshop/archive/dateien/waibelwinter11-12> accessed 30 October 2014.

[19] The United States has had three models since 1987. The latest are from 2004, available at <http://www.state.gov/documents/organization/117601.pdf> accessed 30 October 2014, and 2012, available at <http://www.state.gov/documents/organization/188371.pdf> accessed 30 October 2014.

[20] *Tokios Tokelés v Ukraine,* ICSID Case No ARB/02/18, Award (26 July 2007).

favourable to multinational claimants who resort to actions under investment treaties. A shameful example in this context is the adoption of the same technique by an American tobacco company, which would not have investment-treaty arbitration under the treaty between its own state and Australia, to register a subsidiary in Hong Kong and sue Australia on the basis of the Hong Kong treaty on the ground that the plain packaging requirements introduced by Australian laws to protect its public from the effects of smoking amounted to expropriation.[21]

The definition of a protected investment has also brought about its share of disagreements. We know that there is no definition of investments under the ICSID Convention but that bilateral investment treaties (BITs) contain a rather long list of investments that are identified for protection. The issue essentially is which treaty is to dominate. The neoliberal view would be that the definition in the investment treaty should be accepted, but the contrary view is that the ICSID Convention should be more relevant as it is the one from which a tribunal draws its jurisdiction. The neoliberal vision is that as broad a definition of investment protection should be used as this enables liberal movement of investments around the world.[22] The other view is that the ICSID Convention is aimed to promote economic development and that investments that do not promote such development should not give rise to ICSID jurisdiction.

Arbitrators are divided. The division cannot be based on treaty interpretation alone, but is really based on purely ideological grounds. Obviously, teleological interpretation of the ICSID Convention favours the narrow view that only investments that lead to economic development should be protected. This is the very basis of the ICSID Convention, created by the World Bank. The World Bank has no power to provide general arbitration facilities. Its only rationale for the creation of ICSID is that it has a developmental function. So, it would be correct to hold that only investments that can lead to economic development are protected.

---

21 *Philip Morris Asia Limited v The Commonwealth of Australia*, PCA Case No 2012-12 (registered 22 June 2011).

22 The current controversy is triggered off by the line of awards which regard financial and derivative instruments as investments, including *Ambiente Ufficio SpA and others v Argentine Republic*, ICSID Case No ARB/08/9, Decision on Jurisdiction and Admissibility (8 February 2013); *Deutsche Bank AG v Democratic Socialist Republic of Sri Lanka*, ICSID Case No ARB/09/2, Award (31 October 2012).

Yet, such a conclusion does not tie-in with the neoliberal vision. So, the traditional refuge of teleological interpretation that is the basis of expansionist views has to be cast aside in this situation. Arbitrators, who have the unique capacity to commune with the spirit of the ICSID Convention, cast aside their uniqueness, put the ICSID Convention aside, and rely on the investment treaty definition instead. Of course, the investment treaty does not create jurisdiction in ICSID tribunals. They merely refer disputes to ICSID. It is for the ICSID tribunal to decide on its jurisdiction and in this, the sole factor that has to be satisfied is the criterion for jurisdiction under the ICSID Convention. The capacity of the neoliberal arbitrator and his academic acolytes to change with the winds is infinite. I could go on to demonstrate other instances of jurisdictional expansion but this should suffice. I turn now to the second expansionary activity.

The second area relates to the expansionary changes that have been made to the substantive law relating to the causes of action under the treaties. These include expropriation as well as other standards of treatment. There has also been expansion of the substantive law. Such expansion means that there is encroachment on the sovereignty of developing states. The most glamorous change through expansionist interpretation concerns the fair and equitable treatment standard. When I wrote the first edition of my book, *The International Law on Foreign Investment* in 1994, I researched the standard and found that it was without any substantive content.[23] The international minimum standard had been around for over one hundred years, and beyond the notion of denial of justice and the standards for a lawful expropriation, the standard had no definite content. I asked around from my colleagues and students as to what was meant by fair and equitable treatment. They told me that they were just lawyers' terms for standards that were subjective and did not exist in any concrete sense.

Yet, this dormant standard sprouts into life. Suddenly, we are told that it is the ceiling with the old international minimum standard being the floor. This is new wisdom that did not exist previously. Suddenly, the fair and equitable treatment standard sprouts new meaning. Created by the magic wands of a selected group of arbitrators, this amorphous standard assumed strange meanings that very competent lawyers could not have dreamed it had. In 1999, there was an exhaustive study of the fair and

---

[23] M Sornarajah, *The International Law on Foreign Investment* (1st edn, CUP 1994) 250–52.

equitable standard in the *British Year Book of International Law*.[24] In it, Stephen Vasciannie concluded by saying that the standard had no precise content.[25] Yet, in five short years from that study, Christoph Schreuer wrote saying that the standard had now become an autonomous standard with definite content.[26] Clearly, there was law-creation that had taken place by persons who were vested with no power to create law. The legitimacy of their power to do so is greatly suspect. Yet, there was no way that this arrogation of power could be challenged within the system.

The most important rule that constitutes the content of fair and equitable treatment, we are told in a series of contemporary awards in which certain arbitrators belonging to the exclusive club recurrently feature, is the rule that where a state creates legitimate expectations in a foreign investor, a failure to ensure that the expectations are met results in liability for the breach of fair and equitable treatment.[27] The quick effort to conserve this rule, developed by a group of identifiable arbitrators, as customary international law demonstrates the febricity and the imagination of the neoliberal vision. It is interesting to know that when major international lawyers argue about the difficulties of creating norms of international law through the practice of sovereign states, it is possible for a pack of individuals to create customary international law through just a few arbitral awards. The world is being conned. The pitifulness of it is that the poor of the world are being deceived of their natural resources by the 'college' of international lawyers who are supposed to stand as a bulwark against injustice. It is a matter for sadness. But, leaving this aside, it is necessary to explore the soundness of the development of the view that violation of assurances given at the time of investments are actionable as violations of fair and equitable treatment and the protection it is said to grant to 'legitimate expectations'.

The rule is to a large extent the work of identifiable arbitrators. Francisco Orrego Vicuña had written several articles suggesting the rule

---

24 Stephen Vasciannie, 'The Fair and Equitable Treatment Standard in International Investment Law and Practice' (1999) 70(1) BYIL 99.

25 Ibid 130–47.

26 Christoph Schreuer, 'Fair and Equitable Treatment in Arbitral Practice' (2005) 6 JWIT 357, 385.

27 See Marc Jacob and Stephan W Schill, 'Fair and Equitable Treatment: Content, Practice, Method' in Marc Bungenberg and others (eds), *International Investment Law: Handbook* (CH Beck/Hart/Nomos 2015) 700, 723–728 (with further references to arbitral awards on this point).

in international investment law largely by drawing parallels between it and the English administrative law principles on legitimate expectations.[28] He later sat on several arbitrations, the facts of which lent themselves to the application of such a principle. The Argentinian arbitrations, arising from the economic crisis in that country, provided an ideal setting for the articulation of the rule that violations of assurances made at the point of entry by the state will be actionable as violations of the fair and equitable treatment standard.[29] The Argentinians, in a change of policy advised and supported by the neoliberal institutions of the Washington Consensus, had announced full protection for all incoming investments. In the energy sectors in particular, they had announced that there would be parity between the US Dollar and the Argentine Peso and that the prices of commodities would be in accordance with an American price index. After holding out for some time, the Argentine government responded to a severe public emergency arising from widespread riots by devaluing the peso and refusing to keep the prices fixed to the American index. This resulted in loss to several US investors who had entered Argentina through share purchases in the privatized industries. 52 different arbitrations resulted on the basis of the violation of treaty provisions.

The claims of expropriation were dismissed as the facts did not show dispossession or that the investors could not have continued to remain shareholders despite the devaluation. As expropriation became difficult to establish under the circumstances, some other avenue had to be found. The dormant fair and equitable treatment standard was given the kiss of life by the arbitrators. The easy way was to identify the rule they were formulating that the violation of assurances given at the commencement of the investment would amount to a violation of the fair and equitable treatment standard in the idea of legitimate expectations in domestic English law and farm it off as a general principle of law. So, there was investment of effort in this by a small group of arbitrators formulating the rule in exorbitant terms, which, as one writer was to point out, even the

---

[28] Francisco Orrego Vicuña, 'Regulatory Authority and Legitimate Expectations: Balancing the Rights of the State and the Individual under International Law in a Global Society' (2003) 5 *International Law Forum* 180.

[29] *CMS Gas Transmission Company v The Republic of Argentina*, ICSID Case No ARB/01/8, Award (12 May 2005) paras 273–84; *Enron Corporation and Ponderosa Assets, LP v Argentine Republic*, ICSID Case No ARB/01/3, Award (22 May 2007) paras 256–8; *Sempra Energy International v The Argentine Republic*, ICSID Case No ARB/02/16, Award (28 September 2007) paras 296–304.

most sophisticated state could not meet.[30] That did not matter. All that mattered was that developing countries could hardly aspire to the standards as formulated. After all, this was law that was aimed at the vassalage of the developing countries, not at the liability of developed countries.

To justify this line of jurisprudence, the idea was that it reflected a formulation of a public law standard of governance. There was sycophantic scurrying for the discovery of the principle in the public law of some European systems, but no one has done sufficient work to show that there was indeed a notion in European public law that hampered change of public policy because legitimate expectations had been created by the state in a person. It would indeed be difficult to find such a notion in the public law of any state. Changes of policy are necessary in any constitutional system so as to meet public emergencies and changes in public circumstances. It is for that reason that in the English law-based administrative systems, there is ready interference on the basis of procedural unfairness in violating expectations but not in the ready offering of relief for the violation of any substantive rights. In fact, it is in the remotest of situations, as where a special right is granted to an individual in very special circumstances as in the *Coughlan* case,[31] that the English courts think of providing a substantive remedy.

The extraction of the rule of legitimate expectations does not depend on a general principle of law as there are no general principles relating to this that could be exacted from European systems. Rather, it is a concocted rule that owes its existence to the whim of a small group of arbitrators who price investment protection above other values. They have made law on the basis of an error but, since only a handful of them have made the error, it is a reversible error. No arbitrator has sought to reverse the error. Armies of young Ph.D. students will write theses, some of them already published, without questioning the legitimacy of how this principle had come to be such a major part of modern investment protection

---

[30] Zachary Douglas, *International Law of Investment Claims* (CUP 2009) 28 referred to the *Tecmed* standard as 'the description of perfect public regulation in a perfect world, to which all states should aspire but very few (if any) will ever attain'. The Tribunal in *El Paso Energy International Company v The Argentine Republic*, ICSID Case No ARB/03/15, Award (31 October 2011) para 342 said that 'the description of the FET standard looks *like a programme of good governance that no State in the world is capable of guaranteeing at all times*' (emphasis in the original).

[31] *R v North and East Devon Health Authority Ex Parte Coughlan* [1999] EWCA Civ 1871 (16 July 1999).

law. It is symbolic of the malaise in legal academia that no young scholar has dared to question the basis of the doctrine.

Yet, one tribunal has sought to question the legitimate expectations doctrine somewhat by pointing out that the legitimate expectations rule exists in domestic systems to question the discretionary decisions of subsidiary officers or organs like ministers or provincial councils but not the legislature of a state as to where such a legislature changes policy to meet an economic crisis.[32] Most tribunals that have hesitated to apply the doctrine of legitimate expectations, by contrast, have sought to restrict its scope by pointing out that the circumstances may not give rise to expectations or that such expectations in the given situation could not be considered legitimate.[33] So, those arbitrators who want to keep away from the rule do not confront it simply because it is not politic to do so, but merely avoid its use by finding that the facts show that it would be difficult to show that there could be legitimate expectations in the given situation.

Thus, there are cases where it has been held that countries emerging from socialist rule were not ones in which expectations of stability could be considered legitimate.[34] Some have held that the rule is not there to provide an insurance policy against obvious risks that should have been anticipated by a prudent businessman.[35] So, there is a group of arbitrators, who are not adventurous enough to be expansionist, yet not bold enough to question the basis of a rule which cannot be maintained as it has no basis for recognition as a rule under the investment treaty. One has to explain this absence of boldness in the second group of arbitrators who do not say the obvious that the first group has erred in identifying the legitimate expectations rule as a part of fair and equitable treatment without showing a sufficient basis for such identification. Instead, they compound the error, by finding ways around applying the rule on legitimate expectations.

---

[32] *Total SA v The Argentine Republic*, ICSID Case No ARB/04/01, Decision on Liability (27 December 2010) para 313.

[33] *Saluka Investments BV v Czech Republic*, UNCITRAL, Partial Award (17 March 2006) para 304; *Continental Casualty Company v Argentine Republic*, ICSID Case No ARB/03/9, Award (5 September 2008) para 261; *Total v Argentina* (n 32) paras 120, 121, 164.4.

[34] *Alex Genin, Eastern Credit Limited, Inc and AS Baltoil v The Republic of Estonia*, ICSID Case No ARB/99/2, Award (25 June 2001).

[35] *Emilio Agustín Maffezini v The Kingdom of Spain*, ICSID Case No ARB/97/7, Award (13 November 2000) para 29; *Waste Management Inc v United Mexican States*, ICSID Case No ARB(AF)/00/3, Award (30 April 2004) paras 160, 177.

In contract arbitration, the stabilization clause, which was based on the notion of freezing the expectations of the foreign investor at the time of his entry, has lost its significance. In *Aminoil v. Kuwait*, the tribunal held that the stabilization clause has limited validity in a long term contract protecting the investment for the period necessary for the recovery of the initial investment and reasonable profits.[36] The tribunal also held that changing circumstances will always affect the contractual balance so that a new balance will have to be drawn, notwithstanding the stabilization clause. There was also discussion in the award as to whether the stabilization clause can fetter the regulatory power of the state exercised in the public interest. As later commentators have pointed out, as far as natural resources contracts are concerned, *Aminoil* announced a change in trends.[37] In a sense, the use of the production sharing agreement, with power heavily tilted towards the state entity, has confirmed the trends initiated in *Aminoil.*

What has happened in investment treaty arbitration has been to offset these trends in contract-based arbitration and to put the clock back to the days when assurances made by the state, particularly in the form of a stabilization promise, made at the time of the entry of the investment are given watertight protection. A concerted effort has been made in investment treaty arbitration to offset the developments in contract-based arbitration. We see frenetic activity in this regard, particularly in the early Argentine cases and the cases that follow them. There is an effort to bolster up the legitimate expectations doctrine so that assurances, such as the statements made by the Argentine government regarding the Peso-Dollar parity or the fixing of commodity prices to an American price index, are given sanctity. We see that stated in absolute and absurd fashion in the *Tecmed* award.[38] *Tecmed* is followed in the other awards until a realization dawned that the standards it advocated could not be met by even the most advanced state in the world. When regulatory measures as exceptions to police powers are rediscovered in the *Methanex* award,[39] it comes with the exception of assurances given to the

[36] *Government of the State of Kuwait v American Independent Oil Co (AMINOIL)*, Ad-Hoc-Award (24 March 1982) (1982) 21 ILM 976, 1021–4, 1037.

[37] M Sornarajah, *The International Law on Foreign Investment* (3rd edn, CUP 2010) 283–4.

[38] *Técnicas Medioambientales Tecmed, SA v The United Mexican States*, ICSID Case No ARB(AF)/00/2, Award (29 May 2003) paras 152 ff.

[39] *Methanex v USA* (n 16) pt III ch A paras 20 ff (giving a chronology of Californian regulatory measures); see pt IV ch D paras 7–10 and 15 for the Tribunal's findings on the merits.

foreign investor, though no authority was cited for the exception and no authority in fact exists for such a limitation.

But, we see that the second group of arbitrators, though not directly challenging the validity of importing legitimate expectations doctrine into investment law through the fair and equitable treatment standard, have nevertheless whittled its scope considerably by having regard to the specific circumstances of each case. The situation-specific manner in which they have approached the rule ensures that the awards they make are not capable of creating single specific rules. Firstly, there are the statements that the concept of legitimate expectations does not provide an insurance policy against risk and that the foreign investor should anticipate the risks that arise from his business in the particular circumstances in which the investment is made. Secondly, the context in which the investment is made must be taken into account in judging the legitimacy of the investment. So, for example, when entry is made into a former socialist state of Eastern Europe which is nearly emerging into the capitalist system, it would not be legitimate to expect perfect conditions of business. Leeway has to be made for imperfections. Legitimate expectations have to be modulated to fit the particular circumstances.

There are many other instances of such expansionary interpretations building up a neoliberal system of investment protection. So that I will not be accused of making too much of the single instance of legitimate expectations, let me quickly note some other instances of such expansionary adventurism. Another instance concerns the full protection and security clause in the provision on treatment standards. It has always been accepted that the clause referred to the customary international law which required that the state would incur state responsibility if it did not give protection to aliens threatened with violence. The clause, instead, came to be read as requiring stability of investment.[40] In the area of expropriation too, the view that any depreciation in the value of property could be expropriation had been articulated.[41] The law that had been

---

[40] *Československá Obchodní Banka AS v The Slovak Republic*, ICSID Case No ARB/97/4, Award (29 December 2004) para 70; *Azurix v Argentine Republic*, ICSID Case No ARB/01/12, Award (14 July 2006) paras 406, 408; *Compañiá de Aguas del Aconquija SA and Vivendi Universal v Argentine Republic*, ICSID Case No ARB/97/3, Award (20 August 2007) paras 7.4.13–7.4.17.

[41] *Metalclad Corporation v United Mexican States*, ICSID Case No ARB(AF)/97/1, Award (30 August 2000) para 103; *Middle East Cement Shipping and Handling Co SA v Arab Republic of Egypt*, ICSID Case No ARB/99/6, Award (12 April 2002) para 107; *Alpha Projektholding GmbH v Ukraine*, ICSID Case No ARB/07/16, Award (8 November 2010) paras 408–410.

created through interpretation was far in excess of the law contained in the treaties. It has gone well beyond the law intended by the parties. The glaring instance of this was in the *Ethyl* case where the statement of the Minister for Environment of Canada, that she was contemplating the abolition of a carcinogenic substance manufactured in Canada only by the foreign investor, was alleged to be an expropriation.[42] Canada settled by paying compensation. It is well-known now that on similar facts, the tribunal in *Methanex* decided that the measure was a regulatory expropriation effected to protect the health and welfare of the society.[43]

The contention that I make is that there is simply an inordinate expansion of the law well beyond the original intention of the parties through an interpretation of the provisions of the treaty by using methods of interpretation that seem unsound. The interpretation makes economic development more illusory than when the treaties were made. At the time of the making of these asymmetrical treaties, the only justification could have been that they contributed to the economic development of the host developing countries. It was an unprovable assumption but at least this mere hope provided a ground for the loss of sovereignty the treaties entailed. But, with the unwarranted expansion of the law through interpretation, the original intention of the parties has been clearly bypassed beyond the range of the surrender of sovereignty the treaties entailed. Clearly, the time has come to ditch these treaties. The treaties cannot contribute to the economic development of the states. Instead, the type of investments that get shelter under the treaties through enormous sums awarded in their favour are ones that were clearly deleterious to the interests of the states. If one were to look at some of the cases against Ecuador, the statement would become clear. In the *Texaco-Chevron* case,[44] for example, massive desecration of tribal lands of the Amazonian people were involved, but the tribunal may be bent on awarding large sums to the foreign investor almost as a prize for his environmental pollution of a pristine area of the world.

---

[42] *Ethyl Corporation v The Government of Canada*, UNCITRAL (NAFTA), Award on Jurisdiction (24 June 1998).

[43] *Methanex v USA* (n 16) pt IV ch D para 15.

[44] *Chevron Corporation and Texaco Petroleum Corporation v The Republic of Ecuador*, UNCITRAL, PCA Case No 2009-23 (initiated 23 September 2009).

V. REBALANCING BY DEVELOPED COUNTRIES AS HEGEMONY

There is an obvious cause for concern that is reflected even in the attitudes of rich countries. The rich states feel that their regulatory space has been constrained by investment treaties. They believe that they need to act in order to protect public interests against foreign investors and cannot be deterred by reasons of investment protection from doing so. When poor countries engaged in regulatory expropriations, no one raised an eyebrow in concern. One wonders whether the archetypal Mexican expropriations in pursuance of land-reform following the Zapatist Revolution in Mexico from 1910 to 1940, in the context of which much expropriation law is discussed, were not regulatory expropriations as the state was seeking to free land from the exploitative domination of monopoly capital and redistribute it to the landless who cultivated it.

Many post-colonial expropriations were similarly regulatory in that they sought to redirect the economy into the hands of the local people and divest it from the hands of nationals of the imperial powers. The premises on which investment protection law was based were purposefully tilted against the developing state, which simply did not have the power to object. Now that the targets of arbitration suits are developed countries, we see the emergence of the regulatory expropriation exception to provide for the situation, despite the fact that no meaningful distinction can be made between regulatory expropriation and non-regulatory expropriation in the case of measures taken by the modern state.

The picture is now changing dramatically. Developed states like the United States and Canada are fast becoming the largest recipients of foreign investment. They are becoming restrictive of flows of foreign investment, using national security exceptions to keep foreign investment out. They have been subjected to several arbitrations and can anticipate very many more. This picture is repeated as far as European states are concerned. German views have been considerably altered as a result of the *Vattenfall* arbitration. The boots which kicked the developing countries with fervour are now on other feet. The attitudes are consequently changing. The US Model BIT[45] and the Canadian Model BIT,[46] both

---

[45] US Model BIT of 2004 (n 19) art 12 (environment protection), art 13 (labour standards), art 18 (essential security interests), art 19 (disclosure of information), art 20 (prudential measures for financial services), art 21 (taxation measures), Annex B (letter on expropriation: exemption of regulatory measures).

released in 2004, are replete with defences against liability. They provide for environmental safeguards, labour standards and, most of all, contain provisions stating that measures taken to protect the health, welfare and safety of the public should not be considered as violations of the investment treaty. They contain subjective statements of the national security defence. The new Model treaties shift the focus of investment treaties from investment protection and seek to balance them against other interests, such as the environment, labour standards and other public interests.

So are born the balanced treaties. The balanced treaties have now become established practice with the new American and Canadian treaties being based on their respective model treaties. The call for balance also has resulted in other so-called balanced treaties, instances being the ASEAN Comprehensive Investment Agreement (2009),[47] the SADC Model Treaty[48] and the Commonwealth Guide for Developing Country Negotiators.[49] These treaties strike the balances within them differently. Stephan Schill optimistically suggested that investment treaties multilateralize investment law.[50] It is like talking of the BITs Revolution on the basis that the investment treaties create customary international law. Both are figments of imagination. The internal structures of investment treaties are carefully negotiated striking different compromises and they can neither create custom nor multilateralize the law.

---

46 Canadian Model Foreign Investment Promotion and Protection Agreement (FIPA) (2004) art 10 (general exceptions), art 11 (health, safety and environmental measures), art 16 (taxation measures), art 17 (prudential measures), Annex B 13(1) (elaboration of expropriation, not to include regulatory measures) <http://investmentpolicyhub.unctad.org/Download/TreatyFile/2820> accessed 30 October 2014.

47 ASEAN Comprehensive Investment Agreement (adopted 26 February 2009, entered into force 29 March 2012) <http://agreement.asean.org/media/download/20140119035519.pdf> accessed 30 October 2014.

48 South African Development Community (SADC) Model Bilateral Investment Treaty Template with Commentary (2012) <http://www.iisd.org/itn/wp-content/uploads/2012/10/SADC-Model-BIT-Template-Final.pdf> accessed 30 October 2014.

49 J Anthony VanDuzer, Penelope Simons and Graham Mayeda, *Integrating Sustainable Development into International Investment Agreements: A Guide for Developing Countries* (Commonwealth Secretariat 2012) <https://www.iisd.org/pdf/2012/6th_annual_forum_commonwealth_guide.pdf> accessed 23 January 2015.

50 Stephan W Schill, *The Multilateralization of International Investment Law* (CUP 2009).

Of course, much is going to depend on how the neoliberal arbitrators are going to read these developments. Their usual approach has been to read whatever inroads states make on investment protection as narrowly as possible. It could well be that such an approach would be attempted with the so-called balanced treaties. But, this would provoke states into rasher reactions. It could also be that the newer, balanced treaties would become a larger playing field for lawyers. The balanced treaties, with a plethora of defences and with the rule on regulatory expropriations are essentially unworkable because they contain considerable subjectivity, the need to provide a margin of appreciation to the state exercising its discretionary power and the uncertainty involved in the wide formulation of regulatory space.

The reaction of arbitrators has been the discovery of the proportionality rule, picked out of the air without any basis in treaty language.[51] There is no demonstration as to how this is made applicable to the situation of investment disputes. As in other instances, a rule of domestic law, of uncertain origin and not demonstrably a general principle, is plucked out of thin air as if through a magical process and made relevant to control the new threat to investment protection and to investment arbitration. The proportionality test reserves some power in the arbitrator to determine whether the measure taken was proportionate to the end achieved by the state. The domestic courts give a large margin of appreciation to the state in these matters. Arbitrators, hardly qualified to perform such an exercise as they are by no means acquainted with the internal situation of the state within its political and social context, have arrogated unto themselves the power of performing such a function. They will only alienate states further from investment arbitration and bring more contempt for investment arbitrators as self-serving mercenaries who do not want to give up on the system that produces good earnings for them.

---

[51] See, for example, *Occidental Petroleum Corporation and Occidental Exploration and Production Company v The Republic of Ecuador*, ICSID Case No ARB/06/11, Award (5 October 2012) paras 402–404; see further also *LG&E Energy Corp, LG&E Capital Corp, LG&E International Inc v Argentine Republic*, ICSID Case No ARB/02/1, Decision on Liability (3 October 2006) para 194; *Total v Argentina* (n 32) paras 123 and 197; *El Paso Energy v Argentina* (n 30) paras 241–3 and 373.

VI. CONCLUSION

What then are the answers? We see that many states of Latin America have terminated treaties and have withdrawn from the ICSID Convention. The trend will continue with a return of Latin American states to the Calvo doctrine. The Australians attempted to give up investor-state arbitration in their treaties as well. Their experience with the Philip Morris arbitration may well see them have an entrenched view on this. It could possibly be that other states will also dispense with investor-state arbitration and there is growing evidence as to this taking place. Many treaties are approaching termination. The chances are that the treaties will not be extended beyond their period of validity. In this way, the treaties will lapse, though of course, the rights of existing investors would continue for the period specified. Eventually, one can see the system of investment treaty arbitration going into desuetude. But, in its last years, it will like all wild beasts, thrash about for life, giving rise to unimaginable crudities.

To me, the episode of investment treaty arbitration, which began with *AAPL v. Sri Lanka* in 1990,[52] brought out the worst tendencies in international law and in international lawyers. The neoliberal age sought to use international law instrumentally in order to advance the precepts of its own market-driven agenda. It sought to construct a law that was conducive to liberal flows of foreign investment. The ethos for it was created by international financial institutions – the International Monetary Fund and the World Bank – which saw in instruments like BITs the means of purveying the tenets of neoliberalism. They encouraged these treaties. Often, through conditionalities imposed on loans and other financial assistance, they required developing states to make these investment treaties holding out the economic advice that the treaties would promote flows of foreign investment and result in economic development. These premises were acted upon by arbitrators who enhanced the scope of the law that was contained in the treaties. All this has been explained above.

But, what is unconscionable was the active participation of international lawyers in maintaining this system built on the unprovable and aimed at only the poorer states of the world despite the fact that the system had turned against the interests of the humanity that inhabited these states. It is a system built on a falsehood. If the international law profession did so because its members profited personally from the

52 *AAPL v Sri Lanka* (n 10).

maintenance of this system, it is indeed an indictment of the international lawyers of this particular age that they subverted the system of international law in order to serve their selfish interests. One may say that this was not a phenomenon of this age alone but previous ages as well, but one can speak with the authority of observation only of the age in which one has lived and worked.

This was an age in which international law served the interests of greed. The sooner that situation is ended, the better for the credibility of international law. As Mahatma Gandhi once put it, the world has sufficient to meet man's need but never enough to meet man's greed.[53] It is time that international law is redirected to serve man's need rather than his greed. I talk of man's greed for it is man who lusts for power, sex and wealth. A woman is guided, it is said, by considerations of motherly love, care for the hungry child and the easing of suffering. At a time when few women have now emerged into arbitration, let us hope that they may show a change towards a need-based law that is yet not visible despite their entry. Let not history show that their kind also acted with the same chicanery and pursued greed rather than the need of mankind.

---

[53] This citation was reported by Pyarelal, *Mahatma Gandhi: The Last Phase*, vol 2 (Navajivan Publishing House 1956) 522.

PART II

Conceptual linkages between international investment law and development

3. International investment law and development: A history of two concepts

Yannick Radi*

I. INTRODUCTION

As suggested by the title of this edited volume, a historiography of the relationship between international investment law (IIL) and development reveals that the question of the nature of their relationship has generated passionate debates in particular within the investment law community. Indeed, some regard IIL as a threat to development and as the source of 'regulatory chill',[1] while others conceive of IIL as a tool to foster development.[2] Beyond the empirical evidence used to support these respective viewpoints, these different perspectives are often the result of diverging approaches to IIL. Underlying these approaches are different legal backgrounds, methodologies and research objectives. In that epistemological context, *the* history of the concepts of IIL and development can hardly be told. No scholar can pretend to tell the objective

* The author is grateful to the editors and the participants to the workshop for their comments on the first draft of this chapter.

[1] See, e.g., Muthucumaraswamy Sornarajah, 'A Coming Crisis: Expansionary Trends in Investment Treaty Arbitration' in Karl P Sauvant (ed.), *Appeals Mechanism in International Investment Disputes* (OUP 2008) 39; Jeff Waincymer, 'Balancing Property Rights and Human Rights in Expropriation' in Pierre-Marie Dupuy, Ernst-Ulrich Petersmann and Francesco Francioni (eds), *Human Rights in International Investment Law and Arbitration* (OUP 2009) 275.

[2] See, e.g., Peter Muchlinski, 'Holistic Approaches to Development and International Investment Law: The Role of International Investment Agreements' in Julio Faundez and Celine Tan (eds), *International Economic Law, Globalization and Developing Countries* (Elgar 2010) 180; Stephan W Schill, 'International Investment Law as International Development Law' [2012–2013] *Yearbook of International Investment Law & Policy* 327.

history of this relationship, nor can they pretend to have an all-encompassing approach to this history.

In light of the above, this chapter proposes *a* history of international investment law and development that aims at retracing the *legal* relationship between these two concepts from within the 'box' of IIL, i.e. by analyzing the way states and arbitration tribunals have conceived of the relationship between IIL and development. More precisely, one endeavors to demonstrate that from this perspective, IIL has always been a 'friend' to development. To do so, this chapter unravels and examines the policy objectives and challenges, the legal uncertainties and innovations that have characterized the relationship between IIL and development in the practice of states and arbitrators.

To reach the above-mentioned objective, it is first necessary to briefly depict and 'pierce the veil' of these two concepts. The concept of development has evolved and its scope has been enlarged over the second half of the 20th century. From this conceptual transformation, three 'sub-concepts' of development have emerged.[3] At the outset, in the context of the claim of decolonized states to the economic sovereignty over their natural resources, the concept of development referred to a *droit du développement* understood in terms of economic prosperity.[4] Progressively, and as illustrated by the semantic shift from *droit du développement* to *droit au développement*,[5] development has been linked to human rights in its various components and been considered as a human right on its own. This is well illustrated by the Declaration on the Right to Development whose Article 1.1 states:

> [T]he right to development is an inalienable human right by virtue of which every human person and all peoples are entitled to participate in, contribute to, and enjoy economic, social, cultural and political development, in which all human rights and fundamental freedoms can be fully realized.[6]

---

[3] The exact content of these 'sub-concepts' is not clearly defined in the practice and is discussed in the literature. In this context, the present introduction does not intend to enter into the discussion of their precise content, but instead to depict their mainstream understanding.

[4] See Resolution on the Permanent Sovereignty over Natural Resources, UNGA Res 1803 (XVII) (14 December 1962) UN Doc A/5217.

[5] See Keba M'Baye, 'Le droit au développement comme un droit de l'homme' (1972) 5 *Revue des Droits de l'Homme* 503.

[6] UNGA Res 41/128 (4 December 1986) UN Doc A/RES/41/128 <http://www.un.org/documents/ga/res/41/a41r128.htm> accessed 14 April 2014.

Finally, development has been conceived of in terms of sustainable development, encompassing – in an intergenerational perspective – the promotion/protection of social rights/human rights, the environment and economic prosperity.[7] In that sense, heads of State and Government as well as high level representatives renewed in 2012 'their commitment to sustainable development, and to ensure the promotion of an economically, socially and environmentally sustainable future for [the] planet and for present and future generations'.[8] All these objectives – the promotion/protection of social rights/human rights, the environment and economic prosperity – are key components of the public interest of states. Consequently, public interest can be regarded as the conceptual cornerstone of sustainable development.

International law, and especially customary law, had protected property abroad since the 19th century. It is at the time of the decolonization that IIL emerged and then exploded in the 1990s.[9] The identity and features of this regime are reflected in its 'components' and the objective it pursues. Regarding its components, one should not reduce IIL to international investment agreements (IIAs), despite the impressive number of bilateral investment treaties (BITs) currently in force. Indeed, IIL is also made of two other components: investment arbitration and investment guarantees. Altogether, they constitute the pillars of the IIL regime. Which objective(s) does this regime pursue? Contrary to mainstream opinion, I argue that IIL aims and has always aimed primarily at promoting development in one or all of the above-mentioned public interest dimensions of states. More precisely, while IIL has, since its genesis, aimed at the promotion of economic development, it is increasingly pursuing the protection and promotion of sustainable development. This teleological focus on development and the transformation of the concept of development has resulted in the changes of the features and nature of IIL as well as of the underlying policy challenges and conflicts of interests stirring it.

In this teleological account of IIL that will be further explained below, the protection of foreign investments is viewed as a subsidiary objective

---

7 See in particular Declaration on Environment and Development, UNGA Res 47/190 (22 December 1992) UN Doc A/RES/47/190 <http://www.un.org/documents/ga/conf151/aconf15126-1annex1.htm> accessed 14 April 2014.

8 See Declaration on 'The Future We Want' UNGA Res 66/288 (27 July 2012) para 1, UN Doc A/RES/66/288 <http://www.un.org/disabilities/documents/rio20_outcome_document_complete.pdf> accessed 14 April 2014.

9 See, e.g., Kenneth J Vandevelde, 'A Brief History of International Investment Agreements' (2005) 12 UC Davis JILP 157.

aimed at attracting foreign investors to foster development. The subsidiary nature of protection is sometimes forgotten or ignored by the investment law community. From the perspective of arbitration, this is highly problematic inasmuch as this leads some arbitrators to 'apply' IIAs in a way that fails to adequately take into account the public interests attached to the concept of the right to development and sustainable development. From the standpoint of scholarship, the above reading by some arbitrators reinforces the understanding of IIL by many academics who regard IIL as ontologically and teleologically hostile to development. But as argued and examined in this chapter, although the relation between IIL and development is complex and its history evolving, development constitutes the teleological focus of IIL.

To tell this complex history, one that puts at the forefront of IIL the public interests attached to the concept of the right to development and sustainable development, this chapter distinguishes between two periods when the focus and attention of foreign investment policy-makers has been respectively on economic development (II.) and sustainable development (III.).[10]

II. INTERNATIONAL INVESTMENT LAW AND ECONOMIC DEVELOPMENT

At the time of the New International Economic Order,[11] newly independent states and developing states more generally endeavored to gain economic independence. This led to a dismantling of the customary international law of the protection of aliens abroad.[12] As a result, foreign investors were faced with the risk of being expropriated without compensation or of suffering discriminatory and arbitrary treatments,[13] and for

---

[10] This distinction pursues didactic motives. It goes without saying that the history of international investment law and development does not reflect such 'clear-cut' divided periods.

[11] See Declaration on the Establishment of a New International Economic Order, UNGA Res 3201 (S-VI) (1 May 1974) UN Doc A/RES/29/3201; Charter of Rights and Economic Duties of States, UNGA Res 3281 (XXIX) (12 December 1974) UN Doc A/RES/29/3281.

[12] As to the relation between the international law of the protection of aliens abroad and international investment law see Patrick Juillard, 'L'évolution du droit des investissements' (1994) 250 *Recueil des Cours* 9, 76.

[13] Customary international law provided indeed the minimum standard of treatment as embodied in the *Neer* decision of the Mexico-USA Claims Commission and the compensation of expropriation as formulated by the US

that reason, they became reluctant to operate in developing states. Such mistrust threatened the economy of those states, which were largely dependent on foreign direct investments.[14]

In light of this context, it is first argued that IIL was conceived and designed, first and foremost, with the view to promote economic development (A.). Second, it is put forth that this focus on economic development and the traditional 'absence' of the public interests attached to the right to development and sustainable development in the 'old' and great majority of IIAs still in force should not lead to the conclusion that IIL has 'sacrificed' development considerations (B.).

A. International Investment Law in the Service of Economic Development

Given its original features and the context of its inception, IIL can be conceived of, at the time of its genesis, as a 'systemic package deal' concluded between developing states and developed states.[15] On this basis, it is claimed that from a teleological point of view the protection of foreign investors has always been used instrumentally for the promotion of economic development (1.). Furthermore, I put forward that the substantive and procedural protection of foreign investors cannot be considered in isolation, but should instead be considered in combination with the investment insurance accorded by developed states to their investors (2.).

1. The objectives of international investment law: Protection-for-economic development

In all likelihood, because of the traditional 'one-sided' dimension of IIAs in terms of the addressees of treaty obligations, investment protection is often perceived as the only objective of IIL.[16] This perception is mistaken inasmuch as, from the outset, IIL has aimed at the promotion of states'

Secretary of States, see *LFH Neer and Pauline Neer (USA) v United Mexican States* (15 October 1926) 4 RIAA 60; Letter of the US Secretary of States to the Mexican embassy (21 July 1938), quoted in Andreas F Lowenfeld, *International Economic Law* (OUP 2002) 398.

[14] See Aron Broches, 'The Convention on the Settlement of Investment Disputes' (1972) 136 *Recueil des Cours* 331, 343.

[15] See Yannick Radi, *La standardisation et le droit international – contours d'une théorie dialectique de la formation du droit* (Bruylant 2013) 256–61.

[16] See, e.g., Howard Mann, 'Reconceptualizing International Investment Law: Its Role in Sustainable Development' (2013) 17 *Lewis & Clark Law Review* 521, 524.

economic development. This is evidenced by the 'founding convention' of BITs practice, i.e. the 1963 OECD Draft Convention on the Protection of Foreign Property that recognizes in its Preamble 'the importance of promoting the flow of capital for economic activity and development.'[17] Likewise, the Preamble of the first BIT ever concluded between Germany and Pakistan provides that 'an understanding reached between the two States is likely to promote investment, encourage private industrial and financial enterprise and to increase the prosperity of both States.'[18]

Not only does the objective of prosperity and development exist, but it should also be regarded as the main objective pursued by IIAs. Indeed, IIAs do not aim at favoring investment operations *per se*, but at promoting the economic prosperity of states more broadly. The protection of foreign investments is both a secondary and an indirect objective of IIAs: indirect, because this protection aims at encouraging and promoting investment operations, secondary, because the protection of investments and their promotion has been conceived of as a tool to stimulate states' economic prosperity. In this sense, the Tribunal in *Joseph Charles Lemire* stated:

> The object and purpose of the BIT – the third interpretive criterion – is defined in its Preamble: the parties 'desir[e] to promote greater economic cooperation between them, with respect to investment by nationals and companies of one Party in the territory of the other Party' and recognize that the BIT 'will stimulate the flow of private capital and the economic development of the Parties.' The main purpose of the BIT is thus the stimulation of foreign investment and of the accompanying flow of capital. But this main purpose is not sought in the abstract; it is inserted in a wider context, the economic development for both signatory countries. Economic development is an objective which must benefit all, primarily national citizens and national companies, and secondarily foreign investors. Thus, the object and purpose of the Treaty is not to protect foreign investments per se, but as an aid to the development of the domestic economy.[19]

---

17 OECD Draft Convention on the Protection of Foreign Property (1963) <http://www.oecd.org/investment/internationalinvestmentagreements/39286571.pdf> accessed 14 April 2014.

18 Treaty for the Promotion and Protection of Investments concluded between Pakistan and the Federal Republic of Germany (adopted 25 November 1959, entered into force 28 April 1962) <http://www.iisd.org/pdf/2006/investment_pakistan_germany.pdf> accessed 14 April 2014.

19 *Joseph Charles Lemire v Ukraine*, ICSID Case No ARB/06/18, Decision on Jurisdiction and Liability (21 January 2010) paras 271–3; see also *AWG Group Ltd v Argentine Republic*, UNCITRAL, Decision on Liability (30 July 2010) para 218; *Suez, Sociedad General de Aguas de Barcelona, SA and Vivendi*

Following the same rationale, the ICSID Convention is also exemplary of the primacy of economic development in the objectives pursued by IIL. Indeed, the Preamble of the Washington Convention starts by mentioning 'the need for international cooperation for economic development, and the role of private international investment therein.'[20] The Report of the Executive Directors on this Convention is even more explicit:

> In submitting the attached Convention to governments, the Executive Directors are prompted by the desire to strengthen the partnership between countries in the cause of economic development. The creation of an institution designed to facilitate the settlement of investment disputes between States and foreign investors can be a major step toward promoting an atmosphere of mutual confidence and thus stimulating a larger flow of private international capital into those countries which wish to attract it.[21]

In light of the above, it is not surprising that the *Amco* tribunal expressed the view that the ICSID Convention is aimed to protect, to the same extent and with the same vigor, the investor and the host State, not forgetting that to protect investment is to protect the general interest of development and of developing countries.[22]

As is evidenced by this teleological overview, IIL has always aimed primarily at the promotion of economic development, with the protection of foreign investors being only instrumental to it.

Universal, SA v Argentine Republic, ICSID Case No ARB/03/19, Decision on Liability (30 July 2010) para 218; *Suez, Sociedad General de Aguas de Barcelona, SA, and InterAguas Servicios Integrales del Agua, SA v Argentine Republic*, ICSID Case No ARB/03/17, Decision on Liability (30 July 2010) para 200.

[20] Convention on the Settlement of Investment Disputes between States and Nationals of Other States (1965) (ICSID Convention) <https://icsid.worldbank.org/ICSID/StaticFiles/basicdoc_en-archive/ICSID_English.pdf> accessed 14 April 2014.

[21] Point 9, Report of the Executive Directors of the International Bank for Reconstruction and Development on the Convention on the Settlement of Investment Disputes between States and Nationals of other States, attached to the ICSID Convention <https://icsid.worldbank.org/ICSID/StaticFiles/basicdoc_en-archive/ICSID_English.pdf> accessed 14 April 2014.

[22] *Amco Asia Corp v Republic of Indonesia*, ICSID Case No ARB/81/01, Award on Jurisdiction (24 September 1985) para 23.

2. The instruments of international investment law: Protection-for-insurance

The primacy of economic development and the instrumental dimension of the protection of foreign investments is further evidenced by the role and status of IIAs in the IIL 'machinery'. Indeed, they should not be viewed in isolation but in the broader context of a 'bargain' concluded between developing and developed states to promote economic prosperity. IIAs were concluded in return for an investment insurance to investors granted by their home states.[23] In other words, developed states accepted to grant insurances to their investors for their investments in developing states subject to the condition that those developing states had concluded an IIA with them. The interconnection of investment insurances and treaty protection is further illustrated by the subrogation clauses of IIAs which confer identical rights upon the parties to the IIA and the indemnified investor.[24] In that sense, investors' protection and

---

[23] For instance, France had two insurance mechanisms in the 1970s controlled by the Compagnie Française d'Assurance du Commerce Extérieur (COFACE) and by the Banque Française du Commerce Extérieur. For an analysis of domestic insurance mechanisms see in particular Dominique Carreau and Patrick Juillard, *Droit international économique* (Dalloz 2007) 515–20.

[24] See, e.g., Agreement between the Government of the United Kingdom of Great Britain and Northern Ireland and the Government of the Republic of Angola for the Promotion and Protection of Investments (adopted 4 July 2000) art 10: '(1) If one Contracting Party or its designated Agency ("the first Contracting Party") makes a payment under an indemnity given in respect of an investment in the territory of the other Contracting Party ("the second Contracting Party"), the second Contracting Party shall recognise: (a) the assignment to the first Contracting Party by law or by legal transaction of all the rights and claims of the party indemnified; and (b) that the first Contracting Party is entitled to exercise such rights and enforce such claims by virtue of subrogation, to the same extent as the party indemnified. (2) The first Contracting Party shall be entitled in all circumstances to the same treatment in respect of: (a) the rights and claims acquired by it by virtue of the assignment; and (b) any payments received in pursuance of those rights and claims, as the party indemnified was entitled to receive by virtue of this Agreement in respect of the investment concerned and its related returns. (3) Any payments received in non-convertible currency by the first Contracting Party in pursuance of the rights and claims acquired shall be freely available to the first Contracting Party for the purpose of meeting any expenditure incurred in the territory of the second Contracting Party.' <http://unctad.org/sections/dite/iia/docs/bits/uk_angola.pdf> accessed 14 April 2014.

investments' insurance were constitutive of a 'systemic package deal', the aim of which being the stimulation of the economic development of states.[25]

The interconnection of investors' protection and investments' insurance is also well illustrated by the 1985 Convention Establishing the Multilateral Investment Guarantee Agency (MIGA).[26] As to the primary objective of the Convention, its Preamble provides:

> Considering the need to strengthen international cooperation for economic development and to foster the contribution to such development of foreign investment in general and private foreign investment in particular; Recognizing that the flow of foreign investment to developing countries would be facilitated and further encouraged by alleviating concerns related to non-commercial risks.

However for an investment to be eligible for insurance and for the MIGA to be willing to contribute to development, the Agency should be satisfied that the host state provides a fair and equitable treatment as well as legal protection for the investment.[27] In this sense, Article 24 of the Seoul Convention provides that the MIGA should promote and facilitate the conclusion of agreements among its members on the promotion and the protection of investments. As it appears with the MIGA as well, the objectives and instruments constituting the IIL regime can be conceived of as a 'systemic package deal' aimed at the promotion of economic development.

---

[25] That being said, this does not mean that developed states were not individually interested in the furtherance of this common interest. Indeed, such a 'systemic package deal' was also beneficial for the growth of their foreign direct investment operations. Going one step further, it is also argued that, beyond the objectives stated, IIAs hurt developing states in practice, see, e.g., Andrew T Guzman, 'Why LDCs Sign Treaties that Hurt Them: Explaining the Popularity of Bilateral Investment Treaties' (1997) 38 Va JIL 639.

[26] Convention establishing the Multilateral Investment Guarantee Agency (MIGA Convention) (adopted 11 October 1985, entered into force 12 April 1988) <http://www.miga.org/documents/miga_convention_november_2010.pdf> accessed 14 April 2014.

[27] Article 12(e)(iv) of the MIGA Convention; following the same rationale, see also para 3 of the Preamble of the MIGA Convention.

B. International Investment Law and the Taking into Account of Public Interests

Having originally focused on economic development, international investment law has conferred substantive and procedural protection to foreign investors. In view of this, does it nevertheless entail that IIL has sacrificed the protection/promotion of the public interests, i.e., human rights, labor conditions, the environment, which are attached to the concepts of the right to development and sustainable development?

A section of the literature on this matter as well as NGOs have answered this question positively.[28] In addition to the argument that IIAs place no obligation upon foreign investors, this claim is based on the traditional general wording of IIAs provisions that are silent on public interests and states' regulatory power to protect/promote these interests.

Obviously, IIAs place obligations only upon states and public interests are rarely 'visible' in the 'old' generation of IIAs. However, the existence of broadly-worded obligations does not equate to the granting of an absolute protection to foreign investors, nor to the deprivation of states' ability to regulate for the benefit of the public. In that sense, I first argue that public interest comes into play to fill in the space of indeterminacy that characterizes IIAs provisions (1.). Secondly, I contend that mainstream arbitration practice uses indeterminacy to take into account and safeguard the various public interests attached to the concepts of the right to development and sustainable development (2.).

1. The 'invisible presence' of public interests in IIA provisions

Among the obligations provided in the 'old' generation of IIAs which are deemed to hurt most developing states, obligations of fair and equitable treatment (FET) and indirect expropriation are often mentioned.[29] These provisions are characterized by their normative vagueness. This means that beyond their normative core, which enshrines a balance of interests struck by states parties, there exists a space of indeterminacy to be substantiated by arbitrators, on a case-by-case basis, by taking into account all the relevant interests at stake in the dispute at hand.[30]

---

[28] See, e.g., supra n 1.

[29] See, e.g., Mann (n 16) 533–4.

[30] As noted in the literature, the customary rules on state responsibility provide that the weighing of the interests of states and investors forms part of the determination as to whether a substantive violation has occurred, see Suzanne A Spears, 'The Quest for Policy Space in a New Generation of International Investment Agreements' (2010) 13(4) JIEL 1037, 1046, who refers especially to

In the context of investment arbitration, these interests consist of the public interest of the host state and the private interest of the foreign investor. As FET and the concept of indirect expropriation are characterized by their normative indeterminacy, the taking into account of these interests and their balancing gives them a normative substance in a given factual situation. In that sense, even though the normative core of the above-mentioned provisions protects investors' interests, they do not exclude public interests. On the contrary, in light of the telos of IIAs,[31] public interests play a key role to 'substantiate' these treaty provisions.[32]

As it appears here, conventional practice does not fix the relationship between the public interest of the host state and the private interest of the foreign investor on its own, nor does it settle the conflict between these interests in a given case. In the normative frame of FET and indirect expropriation, it is up to investment arbitration tribunals to decide on the extent to which the public interests that are attached to the right to development and sustainable development should be taken into account.

---

the Restatement (Third) Foreign Relations Law of the United States, s 712(g) (1986) and the work of Louis B Sohn and Richard R Baxter, 'Responsibility of States for Injuries to the Economic Interests of Aliens' (1961) 55 AJIL 561.

31 This is reinforced by the potential application of international law to the settlement of the dispute and the interpretation of IIA provisions conducted under Article 31(3)(c) of the Vienna Convention on the Law of Treaties. Indeed, both the application of international law and systemic interpretation offer the opportunity to arbitrators to take into account international law rules, for example, human rights and environmental law, which protect and promote various public interests.

32 By the same token, given this normative vagueness, it is argued that the narrative on 'conflicts' should focus on interests instead of on norms. Indeed, it is often said in the context of the debate about the fragmentation of international law that IIL is in conflict with other areas of international law, such as international human rights law. Furthermore, when non-investment provisions are incorporated within the 'box' of investment arbitration to settle the dispute through applicable law or systemic integration, scholars often regard the situation at stake as a conflict of norms. On the contrary, I argue that such a situation should not be regarded as a normative conflict. Due to the vagueness of IIA provisions, a vagueness that is also characteristic of international human rights norms for example, it cannot be said *ex ante* that there is such a conflict. The only conflict that exists at this stage is a conflict between the respective interests of the parties to the dispute; see Yannick Radi, 'The "Human Nature" of International Investment Law' (2013) 1 TDM 4.

2. The balancing of public and private interests in international investment arbitration

From the decision of arbitration tribunals on the extent to which public interests should be taken into account, we can derive the scope of the regulatory space that is left to host states to protect/promote public interests. Have arbitration tribunals deprived states of their regulatory power; have they annihilated this regulatory space? Beyond the few often-cited decisions that are used to stigmatize the investment law regime,[33] I argue that arbitration practice *as a whole* safeguards the regulatory space of host states by striking a balance between the private interest of foreign investors and the public interest of host states. This is evidenced by the arbitration case-law on indirect expropriation and fair and equitable treatment.

The provision on indirect expropriation protects foreign investors against state measures having an effect tantamount/equivalent to (direct) expropriation. The vagueness of this provision results precisely from its silence as to the criteria of this equivalence. In any case, it is through criteria elaborated by investment tribunals themselves that arbitrators balance between public and private interests and thereby 'substantiate' the notion of indirect expropriation.

In the past, arbitration practice was on the surface 'manichean' inasmuch as it appeared to focus either on the effect of state measures ('sole effect doctrine'), favoring thereby foreign investors' interests, or on their purpose ('police power doctrine'), favoring host states' interests. However, beyond the *dogma* of the 'sole effect'[34] and 'police power'[35] doctrines, as asserted in obiter dicta, and beyond the divergences among tribunals as to the exact weight to be given to the various circumstances, it is put forth that, whatever the starting point of tribunals' reasoning, most tribunals have increasingly relied on the following test: a state measure aiming at the protection/promotion of a public interest amounts

---

[33] See the *Metalclad* decision as to indirect expropriation quoted, for example, in Howard Mann, 'Investment Agreements and the Regulatory State: Can Exceptions Clauses Create a Safe Haven for Governments?' Background Paper for the Developing Country Investment Negotiators' Forum (2007) 4–5; see *Metalclad Corp v United Mexican States*, ICSID Case ARB(AF)/97/1, Award (30 August 2000) para 103.

[34] For a radical expression of this doctrine see in particular *Metalclad Corporation v Mexico* (n 33) para 103.

[35] For a radical expression of this doctrine see in particular *Methanex Corporation v United States of America, UNCITRAL (NAFTA)*, Final Award (3 August 2005) para 7.

to an expropriation only in extreme situations, namely when they result in the loss of control or in the complete destruction of the value of the investment.[36] As a matter of principle, investors have to bear the brunt of the satisfaction of the public interests pursued by state measures without being compensated; however, if these measures annihilate their investment, it is up to host states to accept the consequences of such satisfaction and to offer compensation.[37] While being at the core of the case-law, this balancing is made explicit in the test of proportionality that has been used by some arbitration tribunals, in particular the *Tecmed* tribunal, which reasoned:

> After establishing that regulatory actions and measures will not be initially excluded from the definition of expropriatory acts, in addition to the negative financial impact of such actions or measures, the Arbitral Tribunal will consider, in order to determine if they are to be characterized as expropriatory, whether such actions or measures are proportional to the public interest presumably protected thereby and to the protection legally granted to investments, taking into account that the significance of such impact has a key role upon deciding the proportionality. Although the analysis starts at the due deference owing to the State when defining the issues that affect its public policy or the interests of society as a whole, as well as the actions that will be implemented to protect such values, such situation does not prevent the Arbitral Tribunal … from examining the actions of the State … to determine

---

[36] Compare, for instance, on the one hand, the *Feldman* and *Tecmed* cases and, on the other hand, the *EnCana* case; see *Feldman v Mexico*, ICSID Case No ARB(AF)/99/1, Award on Merits (16 December 2002) para 152; *Tecnicas Medioambientales Tecmed, SA v United Mexican States*, ICSID Case No ARB(AF)/00/2, Award (29 May 2003) para 115; *EnCana Corporation v Republic of Ecuador*, LCIA Case No UN3481, Award (3 February 2006) para 169.

[37] In that sense, the distinction between regulation and expropriation can be discussed. As asked by Judge Higgins: 'Is not the State in both cases (that is, either by a taking for a public purpose, or by regulating) purporting to act in the common good? And in each case has the owner of the property not suffered loss?', Rosalyn Higgins, 'The Taking of Property by the State: Recent Developments in International Law' (1982) 259 *Recueil des Cours* 267, 331. In fact, the author shares the view expressed by Judge Higgins, arguing that the difference between expropriation and regulation based on public purpose is hardly viable intellectually. In this regard, the conclusions reached by Judge Higgins in the context of international law are equally pertinent for investment law: 'A regulation that amounted (by virtue of its scope and effect) to a taking, would need to be "for a public purpose" (in the sense of in general, rather than for a private, interest). And just compensation would be due. At the same time interferences with property for economic and financial regulatory purposes are tolerated to a significant extent', ibid.

> whether such measures are with respect to their goals, the deprivation of economic rights and the legitimate expectations of who suffered such deprivation. There must be a reasonable relationship of proportionality between the charge or weight imposed to the foreign investor and the aim sought to be realized by any expropriatory measure. To value such charge or weight, it is very important to measure the size of the ownership deprivation caused by the action of the state and whether such deprivation was compensated or not … it should be also considered that the foreign investor has a reduced or nil participation in the taking of the decisions that affect it.[38]

In light of the case-law of arbitration tribunals, I argue that despite the 'silence' of the indirect expropriation provision, mainstream arbitration practice has protected the regulatory space where states protect/promote the various public interests that form part of the concepts of the right to development and sustainable development.

The same holds true with respect to FET. Indeed, diverging from the *Tecmed obiter*,[39] most arbitration tribunals follow this practice as formulated notably by the *Saluka* tribunal:

> The determination of a breach of Article 3.1 by the Czech Republic therefore requires a weighing of the Claimant's legitimate and reasonable expectations on the one hand and the Respondent's legitimate regulatory interests on the other. A foreign investor protected by the Treaty may in any case properly expect that the Czech Republic implements its policies *bona fide* by conduct that is, as far as it affects the investors' investment, reasonably justifiable by public policies and that such conduct does not manifestly violate the

---

[38] *Tecmed v Mexico* (n 36) para 122; see also *Total SA v République d'Argentine*, ICSID Case No ARB/04/01, Award (27 December 2010) para 232.

[39] 'The foreign investors expects the host State to act in a consistent manner, free from ambiguity and totally transparent in its relations with the foreign investor, so that it may know beforehand any and all rules and regulations that will govern its investments, as well as the goals of the relevant policies and administrative practices or directives, to be able to plan its investment and comply with such regulations. Any and all State actions conforming to such criteria should relate not only to the guidelines, directives and requirements issued, or the resolutions approved thereunder, but also to the goals underlying such regulations. The foreign investor also expects the host State to act consistently, i.e. without arbitrarily revoking any pre-existing decisions or permits issued by the State that were relied upon by the investor to assume its commitments as well as to plan and launch its commercial and business activities. The investor also expects the State to use the legal instruments that govern the actions of the investor or the investment in conformity with the function usually assigned to such instruments, and not to deprive the investor of its investment without the required compensation', *Tecmed v Mexico* (n 36) para 154.

> requirements of consistency, transparency, even-handedness and non-discrimination. In particular, any differential treatment of a foreign investor must not be based on unreasonable distinctions and demands, and must be justified by showing that it bears a reasonable relationship to rational policies not motivated by a preference for other investments over the foreign-owned investment.[40]

Arbitration practice as a whole strikes a balance between private and public interests by relying on the legitimate expectations that one has conceptualized elsewhere as a 'two-step' test assessing first, the existence of expectations, and second, the legitimacy of their breach.[41] Thereby, it pays due respect to the regulatory space of states and the public interests attached to the right to development and sustainable development.

In light of the above, one may wonder why IIL has been regarded as a foe or at least as 'insensitive' to the public interest. A few explanations for this perception may be suggested. A first explanation can be found in the practice of arbitration tribunals themselves. Indeed, beyond the subjective fact that arbitrators may not all have the same sensitivity to public interest considerations and the objective reality that few tribunals have accorded a broad protection to investors' interests to the detriment of the public interest,[42] the reasoning in support of the decisions of tribunals plays an important role here. The wording and the argumentation used – as illustrated by the above-mentioned example of the 'sole effect doctrine' – may give the impression that arbitrators discarded public interest considerations.

In addition to arbitrators, scholarship also contributes to the vision of IIL as a foe to the public interest. As just mentioned, the quality of arbitrators' reasoning can be improved. Contrary to civil society, which may be misled by the deficiencies of legal reasoning or may make a strategic use of them to caricature and stigmatize IIL, the basic task of scholars is precisely to analyze and to make sense of judicial and arbitration decisions. In that sense, investment scholars should more often 'pierce the veil' of the wording of awards and uncover their *ratio decidendi*. Furthermore, beyond the unavoidable plurality of approaches within the investment law epistemic community, they should not use the

---

[40] *Saluka Investments BV (Netherlands) v Czech Republic*, UNCITRAL, Award (17 March 2006) para 306.

[41] See Yannick Radi, 'Realizing Human Rights in Investment Treaty Arbitration: A Perspective from Within the International Investment Law Toolbox' (2012) 37 NC J Int'l L & Com Reg 1108, 1149–51.

[42] See, e.g., *Tecmed v Mexico* (n 36) para 154.

few ill-argued and pro-investor decisions[43] to create an 'academic artefact' which differs from the practice of arbitration tribunals.

In addition to arbitrators and scholars, states also contribute greatly to the perception of IIL as a system at odds with the public interest through IIA practice. The following famous quote helps to understand the key problem generated by this practice: 'Justice must not only be done; it must be seen to be done.'[44] The traditional secrecy opted for by states in the settlement of investment disputes has very likely contributed to the 'invisibility' of the taking into account of public interests, as has done the above-mentioned terseness of the 'old' generation of IIAs. In that regard, the increasing publicization of international investment arbitration through mechanisms such as amicus curiae,[45] is likely to contribute to the mitigation of this perception. In the same vein, the current 'formalization' of this taking into account in new treaty provisions and the increasing mention of sustainable development as an objective of IIAs will contribute to the realization that IIL is doing justice to public interests.

III. INTERNATIONAL INVESTMENT LAW AND SUSTAINABLE DEVELOPMENT

As evidenced by the preambles of the 'new' generation of IIAs and of free trade agreements (FTAs) in particular, sustainable development is an objective increasingly pursued by IIL.[46] This entails that in addition to

---

[43] It has been empirically evidenced in the literature that host states have prevailed more often than they have lost, see Susan D Franck, 'Empirically Evaluating Claims About Investment Treaty Arbitration' (2007) 86 NC L Rev 1.

[44] See *R v Sussex Justices, Ex Parte McCarthy* (1924) 1 KB 256, (1923) All ER 233.

[45] See, e.g., Rule 37 of the ICSID rules of procedure for arbitration proceedings <https://icsid.worldbank.org/ICSID/StaticFiles/basicdoc/CRR_English-final.pdf> accessed 14 April 2014.

[46] See, e.g., the Preamble of the United States-Chile Free Trade Agreement (2003): 'The Government of the United States of America and the Government of the Republic of Chile, resolved to: … PROMOTE sustainable development' <http://www.ustr.gov/trade-agreements/free-trade-agreements/chile-fta/final-text> accessed 14 April 2014; the Preamble of the North American Free Trade Agreement (1992): 'The Government of Canada, the Government of the United Mexican States and the Government of the United States of America, resolved to: … STRENGTHEN the development and enforcement of environmental laws and regulations' <https://www.nafta-sec-alena.org/Default.aspx?tabid=97&language=

economic development, IIL is nowadays conceived as a tool to protect/promote labor rights/human rights and the environment.

Although sustainable development constitutes a unique objective, I argue that it is pursued through two strategies whose objectives are notably different. This section unearths and analyzes these two strategies and reflects on their implications on the evolution of the relations between IIL and development. The first strategy relates to state measures enacted to protect/promote public interests and makes explicit the limits of investors' protection under IIAs *vis-à-vis* such measures (A.). Conversely, the second strategy addresses other situations where labor conditions and the environment are at risk *because of* state conduct. It aims at controlling the use of states' regulatory power for the benefit of these two categories of public interest (B.). In that sense, it constitutes a (r)evolution in the role assigned to IIAs and more generally to IIL.

A. The Promotion of Sustainable Development through the Express Protection of States' Regulatory Power

As explained above, the application of vague provisions that are typical of the 'old' and still mainstream IIA practice has not resulted in the annihilation of the regulatory power of states. It remains that the 'new' generation of IIAs is characterized by an express protection of this power and an explicit taking into account of public interests. To make sense of this evolution, one first needs to unravel the motives of this evolution (1.) and then assess – in a prospective manner – the added-value of the provisions that explicitly protect states' regulatory power and public interests (2.).

1. The motives of the evolution: The de facto bilateralization of BITs and the reinforcement of the public dimension of investment disputes

The evolution of IIAs – from implicitly to explicitly protecting states' regulatory power and taking into account public interests – is the product of two phenomena that met in the last decade of the 20th century. The first one relates to the multilateralization of capital flows and the consequent *de facto* bilateralization of the BITs concluded between

en-US> accessed 14 April 2014; the Preamble of the Netherlands-Namibia BIT (2002): 'Considering that these objectives [of investment protection] can be achieved without compromising health, safety and environmental measures of general application' <http://www.unctadxi.org/templates/DocSearch____779.aspx> accessed 14 April 2014.

developing states and developed states. Indeed, although BITs protected the foreign investments of both parties, the lack of FDIs originating from developing states deprived the *de jure* treaty protection granted to their investors of any effectiveness. The growth of FDIs emanating from those developing states has changed the situation and conferred a proper reciprocity to BITs. In that economic and political context, the notion of developed states and home states, on the one hand, and developing states and host states, on the other hand, cannot be fully assimilated anymore.[47] Developing states are increasingly home states of foreign direct investment operations.[48] On the other hand, developed states are increasingly in the position of host states; as a result, they can be faced with a claim emanating from an investor of a developing state. This explains why developed states are becoming more and more supportive of the protection of public interests and of the protection of states' regulatory power.

The second phenomenon relates to the reinforcement of the public dimension of investment disputes. For a long time, arbitration has been based on state contracts concluded by host states and foreign investors.[49] Investment disputes were at that time of a contractual nature and mainly concerned themselves with the alleged violation of these state contracts by the host state. Since the 1990 *AAPL* decision[50] and its view that a foreign investor can rely on the BIT dispute settlement provision irrespective of the prior conclusion of a state contract – a development known as 'arbitration without privity'[51] – most investment disputes have

---

[47] In that sense see, for example, Andrew Newcombe, 'Sustainable Development and Investment Treaty Law' (2007) 8 JWIT 357; Spears (n 30) 1042–3.

[48] Developing countries' transnational corporations now account for a quarter of global foreign direct investment (FDI) outflows, see United Nations Conference on Trade and Development (UNCTAD), *World Investment Report 2010: Investing in a Low-Carbon Economy* (UN 2010) xix.

[49] For a discussion of the legal status of state contracts see in particular Pierre Mayer, 'Le mythe de l'ordre juridique de base (ou *Grundlegung*)' in Philippe Fouchard, Philippe Kahn and Antoine Lyon-Caen (eds), *Le droit des relations économiques internationales – études offertes à Berthold Goldman* (Litec 1982) 199; Prosper Weil, 'Problèmes relatifs aux contrats passés entre un état et un particulier' (1969) 128 *Recueil des Cours* 94.

[50] *Asian Agricultural Products Ltd v Sri Lanka*, ICSID Case No ARB/87/3, Final Award (27 June 1990).

[51] See Jan Paulsson, 'Arbitration Without Privity' (1995) 10 ICSID Rev 232; see also Walid Ben Hamida, *L'arbitrage transnational unilatéral. Réflexions sur une procédure réservée à l'initiative d'une personne privée contre une personne publique* (Bruylant 2004).

a conventional dimension and concern the alleged violation of BITs.[52] This development has increased the impact of investment arbitration on public interest and public policies. Indeed, it has resulted in an explosion of the number of claims filed by foreign investors and thereby contributed to the multiplication of proceedings where domestic public interests and policy choices are under arbitration scrutiny.[53] Furthermore, one should realize that investment arbitration does not only impact the public interest in the domestic scene of the host state involved in the proceedings, but that it has larger consequences. Indeed, given the similarity of IIA provisions, the decision of a tribunal in one case is of interest for the policy choices of all the states parties to IIAs.[54]

These two phenomena met to shed a brighter light on public interests and states' regulatory power in IIL and have greatly contributed to the emergence of new provisions that protect explicitly those public interests and states' regulatory power.

2. The explicit 'presence' of public interest in international investment agreements

The body of IIA provisions that address public interest issues and states' regulatory power follow two main strategies: the provision of exceptions and the refinement of substantive standards.[55]

Although the provisions on exceptions diverge as to the exact substantive and procedural requirements to which those exceptions are conditional,[56] they have in common to enable states to enforce measures

---

[52] Among the disputes registered by the ICSID in 2010, IIAs amounted to 73% of the instruments constituting the basis of consent to arbitration, while contracts and domestic legislation amounted respectively to 22% and 5%, see ICSID, 'Cases – Statistics' Issue No 2010–2 (2010) 20 <https://icsid.worldbank.org/apps/ICSIDWEB/resources/Documents/2010-2%20English.pdf> accessed 5 February 2015.

[53] See in particular Gus Van Harten and Martin Loughlin, 'Investment Treaty Arbitration as a Species of Global Administrative Law' (2006) 17 EJIL 121, 122; Rudolf Dolzer, 'The Impact of International Investment Treaties on Domestic Administrative Law' (2005) 37 NYU J Int'l L & Pol 953, 956.

[54] See Radi (n 15) 359–70; Stephan W Schill, 'International Investment Law and Comparative Public Law – An Introduction' in Stephan W Schill (ed.), *International Investment Law and Comparative Public Law* (OUP 2010) 3 and 18–20.

[55] See Spears (n 30) 1048.

[56] For a typology of these different types of exception clause see ibid 1060–62.

which are necessary to protect human, animal or plant life or health. The key element in these provisions is the notion of necessity.[57]

The second 'sustainable development' strategy, i.e. the refinement of substantive standards, often consists in the reaffirmation that the exercise of regulatory power by states with respect to health and the environment cannot be considered a violation of IIAs.[58] However, most of the provisions which embody this strategy provide that this could be the case in only rare circumstances. For instance, the Annex B of the 2012 US Model BIT makes this clear as to expropriation: '*Except in rare circumstances*,[59] non-discriminatory regulatory actions by a Party that are designed and applied to protect legitimate public welfare objectives, such as public health, safety, and the environment, do not constitute indirect expropriations.'[60]

These evolutions of treaty practice aimed at the protection of public interest and states' regulatory power have been criticized on various grounds. Some have expressed the concern that the provision of an exhaustive list of policy objectives may result in a restriction of the normative space left by traditional substantive standards.[61] Others have

---

[57] 'Subject to the requirement that such measures are not applied in a manner that would constitute arbitrary or unjustifiable discrimination between investments or between investors, or a disguised restriction on international trade or investment, nothing in this Agreement shall be construed to prevent a Party from adopting or enforcing measures necessary: (a) to protect human, animal or plant life or health; (b) to ensure compliance with laws and regulations that are not inconsistent with the provisions of this Agreement; or (c) for the conservation of living or non-living exhaustible natural resources', Model Agreement for the Promotion and Protection of Investments (2004) <http://italaw.com/documents/Canadian2004-FIPA-model-en.pdf> accessed 14 April 2014.

[58] See, e.g., Common Investment Area Agreement (COMESA CIAA) (adopted 23 May 2007) art 20(8): 'Consistent with the right of states to regulate and the customary international law principles on police powers, bona fide regulatory measures taken by a Member State that are designed and applied to protect or enhance legitimate public welfare objectives, such as public health, safety and the environment, shall not constitute an indirect expropriation under this Article.'

[59] Emphasis added.

[60] 2012 US Model BIT (2012) <http://www.state.gov/documents/organization/188371.pdf> accessed 14 April 2014.

[61] See, e.g., Nicholas DiMascio and Joost Pauwelyn, 'Non-Discrimination in Trade and Investment Treaties: Worlds Apart or Two Sides of the Same Coin?' (2008) 102 AJIL 48, 82–3.

also raised the question as to whether it makes any sense to import general exceptions provisions from trade agreements into IIAs.[62]

In light of the features of the two above-mentioned strategies, i.e. the necessity of state measures as to exceptions clauses and the restrictions to the protection of public interests and of the states' regulatory power in the refined substantive standards, I put forth that the main issue raised by these two strategies relates to their efficiency. Indeed, from a prospective point of view, it seems that their 'substantive' added-value will be virtually insignificant. This is so because, as argued previously, the 'silent' provisions typical of the 'old' generation of IIAs enable the taking into account of public interests in a way similar to the exception provisions and the refined substantive standards. And as evidenced by the analysis of the case-law, arbitration practice as a whole has paid due respect to the regulatory power of states and to their public interests.

The above-mentioned Annex B of the 2012 US Model BIT illustrates that point. Indeed, I believe that the 'rare circumstances' it refers to will likely correspond to situations where mainstream arbitration practice concludes in the violation of the indirect expropriation provision, i.e. a loss of control or a complete destruction of the value of the investment. The future will teach us whether the practice of investment tribunals confirms this opinion. Meanwhile, it remains that the explicit presence of public interests in the new generation of IIAs makes the justice that is done to public interests in IIL more visible and thereby participates to the legitimization of the regime in the eyes of local populations and the civil society.

B. The Promotion of Sustainable Development through the Control of the Use of States' Regulatory Power

Contrary to the above-mentioned provisions, the provisions of the 'new' generation of IIAs controlling the use of states' regulatory power with the view to protect/promote sustainable development objectives constitute a major innovation in IIL. Indeed, they address situations where public interests are harmed by state conducts and they aim at prohibiting/preventing these conducts. This primary focus on state conducts responsible for the harm to public interests constitute in my view an important (r)evolution of the role assigned to IIAs and IIL. In light of the examination of these mechanisms (1.), it is therefore necessary to take

62 Mann (n 16) 11–12.

good note of this innovation and to inquire into its policy motives and implications (2.).

1. The normative features of the (r)evolution

In order to protect and promote sustainable development, the 'new' generation of IIAs contains innovative provisions as to the conduct that is expected and required from states with respect to the environment and labor conditions. Irrespective of the issue of their (non-)bindingness, these provisions *mutatis mutandis* reaffirm the commitments of states with respect to their labor standards and environmental international obligations. This is illustrated by Article 13.1 of the 2012 US Model BIT: 'The Parties reaffirm their respective obligations as members of the International Labor Organization (ILO) and their commitments under the ILO Declaration on Fundamental Principles and Rights at Work and its Follow-Up.'[63]

'Non-lowering provisions' relating to these two fields are also typical provisions of the 'new' generation of IIAs. For instance, Article 13.2 of the above-mentioned model provides:

> The Parties recognize that it is inappropriate to encourage investment by weakening or reducing the protections afforded in domestic labor laws. Accordingly, each Party shall ensure that it does not waive or otherwise derogate from or offer to waive or otherwise derogate from its labor laws where the waiver or derogation would be inconsistent with the labor rights referred to in subparagraphs (a) through (e) of paragraph 3, or fail to effectively enforce its labor laws through a sustained or recurring course of action or inaction, as an encouragement for the establishment, acquisition, expansion, or retention of an investment in its territory.[64]

Most of the provisions mentioned above are coupled with a dispute settlement mechanism that generally consists of inter-state consultation. This is also illustrated by the 2012 US Model BIT whose Article 13.4 provides:

> A Party may make a written request for consultations with the other Party regarding any matter arising under this Article. The other Party shall respond to a request for consultations within thirty days of receipt of such request. Thereafter, the Parties shall consult and endeavor to reach a mutually satisfactory resolution.[65]

---

[63] 2012 US Model BIT (n 60).
[64] Ibid.
[65] Ibid.

These provisions constitute an important step in the promotion of sustainable development, but also in the role assigned to IIL.

2. The policy motives and implications of the (r)evolution

Over the last decades, states and international organizations have placed issues of interest for the international community as a whole at the core of their policy agenda. In addition to democracy, the rule of law, one finds among their priorities the protection and promotion of sustainable development and its various components: labor rights/human rights, the environment and economic development.[66]

This political agenda has led states to make of IIL an international tool in the service of those public interests attached to the concept of sustainable development. This strategy has revolutionary features and implications as to states' regulatory power. Concerning the provisions in which states reaffirm their commitments states are required – in a more or less binding manner – not to violate, for example, their international labor law obligations, irrespective of any objective relating to the attraction of foreign investors. As to 'non-lowering provisions' and the objective of attracting or maintaining the presence of foreign investors, states are under treaty control not only vis-à-vis investors of state parties but also often vis-à-vis investors of third parties. More generally, one should realize that this evolution constitutes a direct interference with the choices that often have to be made – in more or less 'easy' cases – between various public interests, i.e. the protection/promotion of labor conditions and the environment, on the one hand, and other public interest, e.g., national security. These choices to be made are not underlain by the classical public/private conflict of interests the investment community is familiar with, but instead, by a conflict between different public interests. These provisions that aim at controlling the use of states' regulatory power evidence another evolution in the role that is attributed to IIL in the promotion of development.

IV. CONCLUSION

From the aftermath of decolonization to today's globalization, IIL and development have had a long and common history. This chapter endeavors to demonstrate that – from a legal point of view – IIL has always

---

66 See, e.g., United Nations Millennium Declaration (8 September 2000) UN Doc A/55/L.2 <http://www.un.org/millennium/declaration/ares552e.htm> accessed 16 April 2014.

aimed at promoting development: yesterday, economic development, today, sustainable development. At each stage of this history, I put forth that this regime, taken as a whole, has never sacrificed the public interests attached to the concept of the right to development and sustainable development, i.e. the environment, human rights and labor rights. This transformation from economic development to sustainable development has impacted on the design and content of IIL. Beyond the explicit protection of public interests and states' regulatory power *vis-à-vis* foreign investors' interests, I claim that the focus on sustainable development has led, most fundamentally, to the targeting of states' conduct in new situations that were so far unknown to IIL. This nascent (r)evolution marks the start of a new era in the history of IIL and development.

4. Overcoming obstacles with opportunities: Trade and investment agreements for sustainable development

Markus W. Gehring and Marie-Claire Cordonier Segger*

I. INTRODUCTION

'Sustainable development' has been recognised as a key global policy objective by all countries of the world through a progressive series of international policy debates and declarations over the past three decades.[1] The concept draws attention to the potential long-term sustainability of

* This chapter shares thoughts with the previous work of the authors and of the Centre for International Sustainable Development Law, where Dr Cordonier Segger serves as Senior Director.

[1] See, inter alia, 'Rio Declaration on Environment and Development' UN Conference on Environment and Development (Rio de Janeiro, Brazil, 3–14 June 1992) (14 June 1992) UN Doc A/CONF.151/26 <http://www.un.org/documents/ga/conf151/aconf15126-1annex1.htm> accessed 20 September 2015; 'Johannesburg Declaration on Sustainable Development' UN World Summit on Sustainable Development (Johannesburg, South Africa, 26 August–4 September 2002) (4 September 2002) UN Doc A/CONF/199/20; 'Doha Ministerial Declaration' WTO Ministerial Conference, Fourth Session (Doha, 9–14 November 2001) (14 November 2001) WTO Doc WT/MIN(01)/DEC/W/1. For a more detailed review see Marie-Claire Cordonier Segger and Ashfaq Khalfan, *Sustainable Development Law: Principles, Practices & Prospects* (OUP 2004) 3–4 and Marie-Claire Cordonier Segger, Markus W Gehring and Andrew Newcombe (eds), *Sustainable Development in World Investment Law* (Kluwer Law International 2011); see also Marie-Claire Cordonier Segger, 'Sustainable Development in Regional Trade Agreements' in Lorand Bartels and Federico Ortino (eds), *Regional Trade Agreements and the WTO Legal System* (OUP 2006) and Markus W Gehring, Marie-Claire Cordonier Segger, Fabiano de Andrade Correa, Patrick Reynaud,

development, especially whether such development is able to respect social, economic and environmental priorities in a balanced and coherent manner.[2]

Just as other features of the 'development agenda' addressed in this volume, sustainable development does not always go hand in hand with investment protection. The social, economic and environmental priorities sustainable development seeks to promote can clash with investor rights recognised under investment treaties. In many ways, much of the recent discourse on 'investment and …' disciplines can be read in that manner: as a story of conflict, collision and the quest for hegemony.

The present contribution adopts a different approach. Rather than looking at confrontations and collisions, it approaches the relationship between investment protection and sustainable development constructively. It highlights options for international investment law to take account of international and domestic environmental priorities and socio-economic development imperatives. This no doubt requires a willingness to situate investor rights within a wider normative context, to interpret investment agreements (especially early ones emphasising investor rights only) in a systemically integrated way, and to allow for reform from within. However, as the subsequent sections clarify, all this is, not only called for, but also possible. What is more, the purpose of sustainable development – devised, after all, to integrate objectives and imperatives hitherto considered to clash – provides a useful conceptual framework within which social, environmental and economic perspectives on investment protection can be balanced – and hence made sustainable.

Perhaps the most commonly accepted definition of 'sustainable development' was proposed almost 25 years ago by the Brundtland Report, in which it was described as 'development that meets the needs of the present without compromising the ability of future generations to meet their own needs.'[3]

In essence, for economic law, this suggests that the quality of development being stimulated by the trade, investment or financial rules should also respect environmental protection and social inclusion priorities.[4] As Sir Elihu Lauterpacht has recently explained in this respect:

Alexandra Harrington and Rodrigo Mella, *Climate Change and Sustainable Energy Measures in Regional Trade Agreements (RTAs)* (ICTSD/CISDL 2013).

[2] Cordonier Segger and Khalfan (n 1) 3–4.

[3] Gro H Brundtland and World Commission on Environment and Development, *Our Common Future: The Report of the World Commission on Environment and Development* (OUP 1987).

[4] Cordonier Segger and Khalfan (n 1) 103.

> Sustainable development, therefore, represents a commitment to a different kind of economic development, one that focuses on achieving important improvements in the opportunities and quality of life without jeopardizing the interests of future generations.[5]

Foreign Direct Investment (FDI), as defined by the Organisation for Economic Co-operation and Development (OECD), 'reflects the objective of establishing a lasting interest by a resident enterprise in one economy (direct investor) in an enterprise (direct investment enterprise) that is resident in an economy other than that of the direct investor.'[6]

It is usually assumed that such investments include several features, such as the transfer of funds, long-termed activity, at least partial participation of the investor in the management of the project, and business risk.[7] The promotion of FDI is regulated, in international law, by myriad international investment agreements (IIAs), including a growing number of bilateral investment treaties (BITs). These treaties are designed to provide security and certainty for foreign investors, in order to promote foreign direct investment, often with the objective of achieving economic growth or development from the viewpoint of the host State.

The relationship between FDI and sustainable development can be described as 'dual-natured'.[8] On the one hand, the activity of transnational corporations and other foreign investors may, and often does, promote certain aspects of sustainable development. Foreign investments might foster economic growth, leading to the transfer of technology and knowledge, the creation of good quality jobs for educated professionals, and even gains in productivity. Further, FDI may directly promote sustainable investments, for instance generating capital for renewable energy technologies and infrastructure which help to mitigate climate change, investments in watershed restoration which improves water supplies for people, adoption of new agricultural techniques which

---

[5] Elihu Lauterpacht, in his foreword to Cordonier Segger, Gehring and Newcombe (n 1).

[6] Secretary-General of the OECD, *Benchmark Definition of Foreign Direct Investment* (4th edn, OECD 2008) para 117 <http://www.oecd.org/industry/inv/investmentstatisticsandanalysis/40193734.pdf> accessed 20 September 2015.

[7] Rudolf Dolzer and Christoph Schreuer, *Principles of International Investment Law* (OUP 2008) 60.

[8] This term was recently used to describe the more specific relationship between FDI and climate change, see United Nations Conference on Trade and Development (UNCTAD), *World Investment Report 2010: Investing in a Low Carbon Economy* (United Nations 2010) 136.

support and generate domestic markets for organic and fair trade food products, or dissemination of information and communications technologies which improve quality of life and open new educational opportunities in developing countries. On the other hand, the activities of investors may also frustrate sustainable development, promoting large-scale natural resources exploitation projects that externalise important social and environmental costs, generating significant negative impacts on the environment and on communities. For example, the UN Special Representative of the Secretary-General on the issues of Human Rights and Transnational Corporations has revealed serious allegations of a wide range of human rights violations by transnational corporations, particularly in the extractives, construction and textiles sectors.[9] Similarly, FDI can also adversely affect the global environment, particularly ill-considered new investments relying on obsolete technologies in the extractives, energy, agriculture or transport sectors which externalize damage caused by greenhouse gas emissions, hazardous chemical risks, or degradation of biological diversity and ecosystem services, for instance.[10]

The prospect of a 'global green economy' in the context of poverty eradication and sustainable development addresses precisely these issues, supporting the trade, investment and development efforts which spur a more ecologically and socially beneficial outcome.[11] For example, in the context of climate change, the demand for emission credits is predicted to reach USD 100 billion by 2050.[12] An increase in the demand for low-carbon technologies might be anticipated, with potentially significant economic gains to the producers and investors in these technologies. In a

---

[9] Report of the Special Representative of the Secretary-General on the issue of human rights and transnational corporations and other business enterprises, John Ruggie in Human Rights Council (HRC), 'Promotion and Protection of all Human Rights, Civil, Political, Economic, Social and Cultural Rights, including the Right to Development' (7 April 2008) UN Doc A/HRC/8/5/Add.2.

[10] See, for example, the factual background of the Vattenfall case, *Vattenfall AB, Vattenfall Europe AG, Vattenfall Europe Generation AG v Federal Republic of Germany*, ICSID Case No ARB/09/6, Award (11 March 2011).

[11] See, for example, Céline Kauffmann and Cristina Tébar Less, *Transition to a Low-Carbon Economy: Public Goals and Corporate Practices* (OECD 2010) paras 105–109 <http://www.oecd.org/investment/mne/45513642.pdf> accessed 20 September 2015.

[12] UNFCCC Secretariat, *Investment and Financial Flows to Address Climate Change* (2007) para 637 <http://unfccc.int/files/cooperation_and_support/financial_mechanism/application/pdf/background_paper.pdf> accessed 20 September 2015.

converse sense, paying inadequate attention to sustainable development challenges and attendant risks is increasingly perceived as poor economic decision-making and financial management. For example, as identified by Sir Nicholas Stern's Report on the economics of climate change, the negative effects of climate change are expected to disrupt the global economy 'on a scale similar to those associated with the great wars and the economic depression of the first half of the 20th century.'[13] These economic impacts should be prevented, not ignored.

In essence, there is a great deal to gain by the successful integration of sustainable development as an objective for sound and careful investment policy and rule making. Such integration can take place in the context of a series of imperfectly embedded, multi-layered governance systems and regimes. For instance, it has been suggested that the protection offered by IIAs could be integrated within the United Nations Framework Convention on Climate Change (UNFCCC) regime's flexible mechanisms, as means to promote low-carbon or renewable energy investments globally.[14] But as noted by Sussman, given the complex questions that climate change negotiators already struggle to resolve, adding the negotiation of a multilateral agreement on investment into this process seems impractical.[15] Careful research, dialogue and analysis will be needed, over the course of years, to ensure such climate change treaty-led market-based instruments are designed and implemented to both reliably mobilize and harness sustainable investments on all levels.

This chapter focuses on an alternative and eminently practical possibility: the integration of sustainable development priorities, through innovative procedural and substantive advances, in the purpose and provisions of IIAs themselves.[16] Indeed, such innovations, as will be discussed below, are already being tested in the context of international trade and investment agreements on bilateral and regional levels. Looking forward, such integration of sustainable development within the text of IIAs might take place on several levels, facilitated by important procedural changes in treaty negotiation and design.

---

13 Nicholas Stern, *The Stern Review on the Economics of Climate Change* (CUP 2007) ii.

14 Edna Sussman, 'The Energy Charter Treaty's Investor Protection Provisions: Potential to Foster Solutions to Global Warming and Promote Sustainable Development' in Cordonier Segger, Gehring and Newcombe (n 1) 513, 528.

15 Ibid 529.

16 See supra n 1, especially Marie-Claire Cordonier Segger and Andrew Newcombe, 'An Integrated Agenda for Sustainable Development in International Investment Law' in Cordonier Segger, Gehring and Newcombe (n 1) 99.

In terms of procedural innovations, sustainable development objectives can be integrated into the steps of preparing for the IIA negotiations. For example, public participation and inter-agency consultation processes can be adopted to ensure that environmental, social and economic policy priorities are balanced in decision-making. As another example, impact assessment mechanisms can provide more complete and accurate data for decision-makers to understand potential impacts (positive or negative) that the investments encouraged by the treaty are likely to have on sustainable development in the partner countries.

In terms of substantive innovations, sustainable development can be integrated – by the Parties during the negotiations – within the substantive provisions of IIAs themselves. For example, the IIA preamble can expressly recognize the Parties, joint commitment to sustainable development. The substantive rules of IIAs can clarify that the Parties do not intend to restrict States from enacting environmental or social regulations, reserving existing laws and standards, providing general and specific exceptions, or even providing guidance in areas where overlaps with other international commitments are possible. Moreover, IIAs can also be designed to actively promote sustainable investment. This can be achieved, inter alia, by creating a privileged business environment for investments that respond to international commitments to sustainable development, such as the UNFCCC focus on investment in renewable energy or the United Nations Convention on Biological Diversity call for investment into sustainable uses of biological diversity. Such treaty texts can assist tribunals to ensure that sustainable development considerations are taken into account in IIA dispute settlement resolution, particularly if the principle of public participation, as outlined in the International Law Association's New Delhi Declaration of Principles of International Law Relating to Sustainable Development,[17] has been integrated through the inclusion of the public's right to submit amicus curiae briefs in investment disputes, or by allowing free access to documents.

In light of the procedural and substantive innovations adopted by the Parties to recent trade and investment agreements, this chapter explores how carefully crafted treaties might serve to convert investment rules from obstacles to opportunities for sustainable development.

---

[17] International Law Association, 'New Delhi Declaration of Principles of International Law Relating to Sustainable Development' (2002) 49(2) *Netherlands International Law Review* 299.

II. HARNESSING FDI FOR SUSTAINABLE DEVELOPMENT THROUGH TREATY LAW

States agree, on the level of global policy, that FDI is a key component of any sustainable development agenda. Indeed, according to the 2002 Johannesburg Declaration and the Johannesburg Plan of Implementation of the World Summit for Sustainable Development,[18] where states highlighted over 60 existing economic, environmental and social international agreements that play a role in achieving sustainable development while mentioning 200 others,[19] there is a need for balance between risk and opportunity. Essentially, as the Plan explains, it is important to prioritize the role that trade and finance could play to foster sustainable development in developing countries:

> Globalization offers opportunities and challenges for sustainable development … Globalization should be fully inclusive and equitable, and there is a strong need for policies and measures at the national and international levels, formulated and implemented with the full and effective participation of developing countries and countries with economies in transition, to help them to respond effectively to those challenges and opportunities. This will require urgent action at all levels to … [c]ontinue to promote open, equitable, rules-based, predictable and non-discriminatory multilateral trading and financial systems that benefit all countries in the pursuit of sustainable development.[20]

From a sustainable development perspective, when states embark upon new IIA negotiations they should be able to take three dimensions into account: economic development, social development, and environmental protection. However, although sustainable development has been enshrined as an explicit objective in several binding international treaties, is at the core of the mandate of many international organizations, and is also the subject of various soft law declarations and standards, it remains challenging to include in new IIAs.[21]

---

[18] 'Plan of Implementation of the World Summit on Sustainable Development' in Report of the World Summit on Sustainable Development (Johannesburg, South Africa, 26 August–4 September 2002) 6 (4 September 2002) UN Doc A/CONF/199/20 [hereafter Johannesburg Plan of Implementation].

[19] Cordonier Segger and Khalfan (n 1) 1–60.

[20] Johannesburg Plan of Implementation (n 18) 47.

[21] Kathryn Gordon, 'International Investment Agreements: A Survey of Environmental, Labour and Anti-corruption Issues' in OECD, *International Investment Law: Understanding Concepts and Tracking Innovations* (OECD

Traditional Preferential Tariff Agreements (PTAs) which were popular in the 1970s do not often mention broader concerns related to sustainable development. Since the early 1990s, there has been a marked increase in Regional Trade Agreements (RTAs), and the well-trodden grounds examining whether RTAs can be considered 'building blocks' or 'stumbling blocks' to deeper WTO liberalization,[22] fall beyond the scope of this chapter. Of special interest, however, is that these RTAs increasingly incorporate investment, social, environmental and other sustainable development considerations to varying degrees within the unique economic liberalization and cooperation frameworks provided by each treaty.[23] Indeed, many 'regional trade' agreements are neither regional, nor uniquely trade: encapsulating entire IIAs as chapters, such economic accords could be more accurately termed 'international trade and investment agreements' (ITIAs). The Parties to such ITIAs are increasingly less likely to hail from a contiguous 'region' of the world in any geographical, economic or environmental sense of the word (i.e., the US-Oman Agreement, or the Canada-China Agreement). And in such ITIAs, states not only often commit to trade liberalization that is deeper than the World Trade Organization (WTO) Agreements, but also to key investment law commitments which extend beyond the minimal provisions of the WTO plurilateral agreement on Trade-Related Investment Measures (TRIMs). Indeed, many such accords actually enshrine the deep investment liberalization commitments normally found in BITs as does the North American Free Trade Agreement

---

2008) 135 <http://www.oecd.org/daf/inv/investment-policy/40471550.pdf> accessed 20 September 2015.

[22] Jagdish N Bhagwati and Robert Hudec, *Fair Trade and Harmonization: Prerequisites for Free Trade* (MIT Press 1996); Jagdish N Bhagwati, Arvin Panagariya and Paul Krugman, *Trading Blocs: Alternative Approaches to Analyzing Preferential Trade Agreements* (MIT Press 1999); Lorand Bartels and Federico Ortino, *Regional Trade Agreements and the WTO Legal System* (OUP 2006); Kyle W Bagwell and Petros C Mavroidis, *Preferential Trade Agreements: A Law and Economics Analysis* (CUP 2011); Won-Mog Choi and Yong-Shik Lee, 'Facilitating Preferential Trade Agreements between Developed and Developing Countries: A Case for Enabling the Enabling Clause' (2012) 21 Minn JIL 1; Jong Bum Kim, 'Dual WTO Notifications of RTAs with Non-Reciprocal Trade Liberalization' (2012) 15(2) JIEL 647.

[23] IISD, 'The Rush to Regionalism: Sustainable Development and Regional Approaches to Trade and Investment Liberalization' (2004) 2 <http://www.iisd.org/pdf/2005/trade_rush_region.pdf> accessed 10 August 2015; see also the contributions in Section 3 in Cordonier Segger, Gehring and Newcombe (n 1) 403 ff; Cordonier Segger, 'Sustainable Development in Regional Trade Agreements' (n 1).

(NAFTA) and other examples involving the US, Canada, Mexico, Chile and others, or at least provide guarantees on establishment for investment promotion purposes, as do the EU-Chile Agreement and other examples involving the EU, MERCOSUR and others.

Principal incentives for the negotiation of such ITIAs are often described in general terms, such as opening new markets, increasing economic growth, accessing cheaper imports and increasing foreign investment. This recognized, a diversity of regional conditions generates myriad priorities and opportunities for trade and investment cooperation, which in turn shapes a varied RTA and ITIA landscape. Many strategic considerations are relevant to the negotiation of new trade and investment agreements, such as efforts to send a strong signal that a country is considered a priority economic partner (for example the US-Korea Free Trade Agreement and the US-Colombia Free Trade Agreement), the desire to build regional economies of scale as a counterweight to other regional economic powers (such as MERCOSUR), or efforts to avoid being excluded from a powerful economic bloc – such as the Central America Free Trade Agreement (CAFTA). Further, leading countries are now seeking to harness economic integration initiatives under their ITIAs in order to achieve other objectives that are not exclusively economic, addressing regional concerns for sustainable development through cooperation on issues of public policy and law.

Based on the analysis of recent regional accords, research is beginning to reveal that, with respect to sustainable development, several distinct models now exist for RTAs, particularly the ITIAs.[24] These collaborative ITIAs, many negotiated in the recent two decades, tend to include provisions on further issues such as labour standards, environmental protection and sustainable development. Such ITIAs may commit to sustainable development objectives in their Preambles, provide gnomic reassurances in the event of conflicts between the ITIA provisions and other international agreements on the environment and/or human rights and social inclusion, offer general and specific exceptions for domestic policies related to health, the environment, natural resources and other priorities, or even provide for labour and environmental chapters or side agreements, establishing mechanisms or institutions responsible for monitoring respect for human rights or environmental standards, assisting

[24] Anna Joubin-Bret, Marie-Estelle Rey and Jörg Weber, 'International Investment Law and Development' in Cordonier Segger, Gehring and Newcombe (n 1) 15, 23; Cordonier Segger, 'Sustainable Development in Regional Trade Agreements' (n 1); also Gehring, Cordonier Segger, de Andrade Correa, Reynaud, Harrington and Mella (n 1).

with environmental data collection and exchange, and even stimulating legislative reform and dealing with complaints.[25]

Though these ITIAs are negotiated in diverse circumstances, and vary extensively in content, focus and scope, they are all shaped by the policy priorities of the states that are signatories, and certain trends can be noted as a result. The EU adheres to a sustainable development strategy, adopted in 2001 and revised in 2006, which seeks to promote sustainable development, requiring the EU's internal and external policies to integrate environmental, social and economic decision-making.[26] In the US, the Trade Act of 2002 imposes a responsibility on the US to ensure that trade, labour and environmental policies are mutually supportive and to seek to protect and preserve the environment and promote human rights, enhancing international means of doing so. This also includes obligations to ensure that trade agreements do not weaken or reduce protections afforded in domestic environmental laws as an encouragement for trade and to include provisions on environmental protection.[27] In this way, powerful economic actors, such as the EU and the US, give priority in ITIA negotiations towards the inclusion of sustainable development, labour, environment and other provisions, though the exact measures adopted in each treaty varying according to the specific economic, social and environmental circumstances of the relationship.

III. SUSTAINABILITY THROUGH PROCESS: TURNING OBSTACLES TO OPPORTUNITIES THROUGH PARTICIPATION, CAPACITY AND IMPACT ASSESSMENT

The first step to including sustainable development firmly in international trade and investment treaties is crucial, and procedural. In recent years, many states have adopted a practice of including certain innovations in the negotiations process itself for a new ITIA. Several important new procedures have been adopted to ensure that, while the momentum

---

[25] OECD, Joint Working Party on Trade and Environment, 'Regional Trade Agreements and Environment' COM/ENV/TD(2006)47/FINAL (2006) 19 <http://www.oecd.org/env/38599779.pdf> accessed 20 September 2015.

[26] Council of the European Union, 'Renewed EU Sustainable Development Strategy' (26 June 2006) <http://register.consilium.europa.eu/pdf/en/06/st10/st10917.en06.pdf> accessed 20 September 2015.

[27] US Bipartisan Trade Promotion Authority Act of 2002, 19 USC 3801 Sect 2012 (relating to 'Trade Negotiating Objectives').

gained in negotiating the trade agreement is not lost, sustainable development considerations form part of the trade agreements.[28]

Participation is one key point. Successful ITIA negotiations have, for instance, benefited from the involvement of civil society and the promotion of high levels of transparency during the negotiation process. Facilitating public participation and consultation in negotiations has allowed stakeholders and even individual experts to influence the process. Such openness can help environmental or social concerns that may have been overlooked to be considered and addressed in the trade treaty. Participation of other agencies during negotiations, such as environmental ministries or authorities, labour and human rights authorities, agriculture, energy or transport departments, can lead to stronger and more balanced environmental, social and economic development ITIA provisions, and secure greater buy-in for implementation. Participation of the public, including civil society and academic experts as well as the private sector, can be crucial both to complement and facilitate a more in-depth understanding of key considerations and issues, and also to ensure transparency and access to information, leading to greater legitimacy.

Capacity is a further innovation in ITIAs. In recent negotiations, states have established bilateral or multilateral capacity-building mechanisms to support the treaty negotiations and implementation, often facilitated by an intergovernmental organization in which all Parties are members to ensure neutrality and objectivity. For instance, countries may be reluctant to accept new sustainable development and environmental responsibilities in ITIAs, owing to fears that such obligations would impose burdensome financial and institutional requirements that they are incapable of providing. Capacity-building programs can review recent successful experiences in this field and support the establishment of new domestic institutions for continued learning, training officials and providing support for policy reform, also assisting in monitoring and enforcement of social, environmental and sustainable development provisions. Such instruments and programs, if they include a funding mechanism to ensure financial support for such initiatives, can alleviate concerns and contribute to a balanced outcome in the ITIA.[29] Such procedural changes can assist in securing the integration of environmental and social concerns in recent trade and investment treaties, and might be considered for future investment accords as well.

---

28 OECD (n 25) 33.

29 Morocco, for example, benefits from capacity-building arrangements through both its US RTA and a partnership agreement with the EU.

At the heart of the procedural questions is the issue of impartial and relevant data. It is understood that FDI can bring social, economic, and environmental benefits to countries, and can have a positive impact on such issues as income growth, modernization, employment and productivity.[30] However, the exact scenarios and impacts that might result from liberalization and promotion of investment between two particular parties, or two regions, are often unknown or poorly understood. While great quantities of scientific studies might exist, quite simply, no-one has specifically looked at the question of 'what would happen if investment and trade increased tenfold in this particular sector', from a social and environmental perspective. Without this information, and resulting careful treaty crafting to enhance benefits and flank or minimize risks, ITIAs – and by extension other IIAs – may well frustrate sustainable development objectives, creating conflicts between the commercial, social, and environmental goals.[31] Moreover, well-drafted agreements can achieve more than their inherent goals. For example, trade and investment agreements can, at least potentially, also support and promote responses to climate change, or poverty eradication objectives. One way to avoid potential conflicts on the one hand, and promote possible synergies on the other, is the use of impact assessment mechanisms.[32]

To ensure that potential ITIA provisions can be identified which respond the economic, social and environmental circumstances of each accord, many developed and developing countries now undertake ex-ante or ongoing environmental, developmental, human rights or sustainability impact assessments and reviews of trade liberalization policies and draft treaties. Indeed, the use of impact assessment mechanisms has increased in recent years. A brief overview of the approaches to impact assessment mechanisms applied by Canada, United States and the European Union, among others, for free trade agreements and for ITIAs, is helpful in this regard.[33]

---

[30] OECD, Committee on International Investment and Multinational Enterprises, 'Foreign Direct Investment for Development: Maximising Benefits, Minimising Costs' (2002) <http://www.oecd.org/investment/investmentfordevelopment/1959815.pdf> accessed 20 September 2015.

[31] For a review of the potential conflicts see Cordonier Segger, Gehring and Newcombe (n 1).

[32] For a more detailed review of this topic, see Markus W Gehring, 'Impact Assessments of Investment Treaties' in Cordonier Segger, Gehring and Newcombe (n 1) 145.

[33] For a more detailed review see ibid 156–68.

Impact assessment mechanisms can be found both at the domestic and international level: On the national level, domestic environmental planning and often social (health, gender, human rights) laws and standards often require the impact assessment of major economic development projects and policies. On the international level, a growing number of trade and investment negotiations include requirements for assessing the impact negotiated agreements might have on sustainable development.

Indeed, countries increasingly adopt mandates to require such reviews and assessments. In the US, Executive Order 13141, Environmental Review of Trade Agreements (November 1999) – later embodied in the Trade Act 2002 – and the Guidelines for Implementation of Executive Order 13141 (December 2000) establish the process for the assessment of environmental factors in the development of trade agreements by way of an environmental review. Similarly, in Canada, the 1999 Cabinet Directive on the Environmental Assessment of Policy, Plan and Program Proposals and the 2001 Framework for Conducting Environmental Assessment of Trade Negotiations together require federal governments to undertake Strategic Environmental Assessments (SEAs) that analyse the environmental impacts of policy, plan and program proposals and lay out the guidelines for doing so.

The EU goes even further in what it terms its Sustainability Impact Assessments (SIAs). The SIA process is even more comprehensive in its analysis, as it also requires an examination of the social and economic aspects and impacts. All three programs involve an initial scoping exercise, where all possible impacts and mitigation measures are considered, and all include a public consultation element, which allows members of the public to become involved in the process, including the scoping process, so that all possible effects and the opinions of the public are taken into account at an early stage. For example, as part of the EU-Canada negotiations of a Comprehensive Economic and Trade Agreement (CETA), SIAs were prepared so as to assess the impact of both international trade and investment, on economic, social, and environmental issues.[34]

Trade and investment treaty impact assessments are a process of decision-making, based on comprehensive independent studies in which scenarios of the potential impacts of negotiated treaties are carefully assessed. In the past, for trade agreements and ITIAs, the focus of these

---

[34] See report commissioned by the European Commission, 'A Trade SIA Relating to the Negotiation of a Comprehensive Economic and Trade Agreement (CETA) Between the EU and Canada' (Final Report, June 2011) 337 <http://trade.ec.europa.eu/doclib/html/148201.htm> accessed 20 September 2015.

mechanisms was limited to the environmental effects. Such assessments are known as Environmental Impact Assessments, Environmental Reviews, or Environmental Assessments.[35] Currently, however, the scope of impact assessments has expanded. For example, some impact assessments are specifically designed to review the impact of international trade or foreign investments on human rights.[36] More widely, and in accordance with the 'holistic' concept of sustainable development,[37] some impact assessment mechanisms attempt to provide a fuller picture, by assessing the economic, environmental, and social implications of investment and trade agreements.[38] For example, the EU Commission 'Handbook' on this topic proposes the examination of such issues as energy use, poverty, gender equality, external debt, public health, living conditions, access to education, labour standards, unemployment, and more.[39] These wider assessments are known as SIAs.

Impact assessments of trade agreements often follow four steps:[40] First, (1) the 'screening and scoping' phase. In this stage the relevant issues are framed, and the measures that are most likely to impact the environment (or broader issues in the case of SIAs) are identified. This

---

[35] See supra n 1.

[36] For a detailed review see James Harrison and Alessa Goller, 'Trade and Human Rights: What Does "Impact Assessment" Have to Offer?' (2008) 4 *Human Rights Law Review* 587. For an example of impact assessment for foreign investment, see International Centre for Human Rights and Democratic Development, 'Human Right Impact Assessments for Foreign Investment Projects: Learning from Community Experience in the Philippines, Tibet, the Democratic Republic of Congo, Argentina, and Peru' (2006) <http://publications.gc.ca/collections/collection_2007/dd-rd/E84-21-2007E.pdf> accessed 20 September 2015.

[37] The EU Commission's 'Impact Assessment Guidelines' indeed mentions that one of the objectives of impact assessments is to ensure coherence and consistency with the EU's sustainable development strategies; see European Commission, 'Impact Assessment Guidelines' SEC(2009)92 (15 January 2009) 6 <http://ec.europa.eu/smart-regulation/impact/commission_guidelines/docs/iag_2009_en.pdf> accessed 20 September 2015.

[38] See supra n 1.

[39] European Commission, External Trade, 'Handbook for Sustainability Impact Assessment' (2006) 52–6 <http://trade.ec.europa.eu/doclib/docs/2006/march/tradoc_127974.pdf> accessed 20 September 2015.

[40] The exact classification varies between one jurisdiction to another. However, in essence these stages are mostly similar. For example, for the EU classification of these stages, see European Commission (n 39) 12, 17–19, or European Commission (n 37) 7. For a more detailed review of the classification proposed in this chapter, see Gehring (n 32) 154–5.

step often includes expert meetings and public consultations. The next step (2) is the initial review. In this phase the potential impact of the negotiated agreement (or more accurately, of the measures identified in the first step) on the environment (or on issues such as social well-being, in the case of SIAs) are identified. The scope of this examination varies from one mechanism to another. While in certain countries only local effects are examined (Canada, for example), in other jurisdictions trans-boundary and global effects are also assessed (the EU, for example). Following the initial review, a preliminary assessment (3) is often published. The purpose of this review is to inform the negotiators about the projected impacts of trade liberalization in the identified areas. Lastly, an ex post final report (4) is prepared following the conclusion of the negotiations and after the final text of the agreement has been concluded. The final report outlines how certain negotiating positions might have changed due to the content of the preliminary assessment, as well as the trade-offs and balances made between economic liberalization and environmental protection.

Though not as thorough as EU and North American provisions, other countries also have similar measures in place to ensure that the impacts of trade measures are considered up front and inform the negotiation process. For example, New Zealand requires a National Interest Assessment (NIA) for all treaties to which New Zealand may become a party. This assessment must consider environmental, economic, social and cultural impacts of the proposed treaty.[41] Japan's Ministry of the Environment commissioned a study to investigate the environmental impact assessment methods that would be applied during Japan's FTA negotiation process and bases its Guidelines on Environmental Impact Assessment of Economic Partnership Agreements and Free Trade Agreements in Japan on the results of this study.[42] Japan has also collaborated with Korea's Ministry of Environment to conduct case studies on hypothetical

---

[41] New Zealand Parliamentary, Standing Order No 398, 'Standing Orders of the House of Representatives' (2014) 117 <http://www.parliament.nz/resource/en-nz/00HOHPBReferenceStOrders4/eb7c8b9e4a6c7aa88a47d14dc4100513b2557e60> accessed 20 September 2015.

[42] See Government of Japan, Ministry of the Environment, 'Guideline on Environmental Impact Assessment of Economic Partnership Agreements and Free Trade Agreements in Japan' (2004) <http://www.env.go.jp/en/policy/assess/epa_fta/index.html> accessed 20 September 2015.

trade agreements and in 2005 held a Joint Expert Seminar on Methods for the Assessment of Environmental Impacts by Free Trade Agreements in Japan.[43]

Ultimately, the results of these assessments can be useful, as they assist negotiators to identify the areas where preventive, cooperative or enhancement initiatives could be useful to promote climate-change objectives in a trade or investment treaty. Such IAs can promote sustainable development goals in several ways. As has been seen in numerous trade treaty and ITIA negotiations, IAs allow negotiators to identify aspects of agreements that require mitigation or enhancement measures, in order to achieve the fullest benefits of the economic cooperation.[44] By assessing economic, environmental, and social impacts of potential measures, decision-makers have a better idea of the advantages and disadvantages of each proposed negotiating position (and eventual treaty provision). IAs allow decision-makers to fully understand the synergies between the different fields, and how one policy can support another. Alternatively, by addressing more than just environmental or economic aspects, IAs equip decision-makers with better tools to perform any trade-offs which are necessary in places where the promotion of one policy inherently frustrates the goals of another. Lastly, where the public is effectively invited to take part in this process, IAs also increase the democratic legitimacy and the quality of negotiated agreements. These assessments also have the potential to identify areas where domestic law and policy reform is needed and can help to shape the reforms by providing timely guidance. As they have already been for ITIAs, these benefits might all be available to decision-makers negotiating other IIAs, such as BITs, through the adoption of an IIA SIA methodology and mandate.

IV. TURNING OBSTACLES INTO OPPORTUNITIES FOR SUSTAINABLE INTERNATIONAL TRADE AND INVESTMENT AGREEMENTS?

There are multiple forms of turning obstacles into opportunities for sustainable development. This part proposes a careful study of preambular language, reservations and exceptions, enhanced cooperation on sustainable development between the parties and corporate social

43 OECD (n 25) 43, 44.
44 For a detailed review of SIAs see Gehring (n 32) 145.

responsibility as parts of new RTAs which can enhance the opportunities for sustainable development. It studies existing examples and highlights how these can overcome sustainable development obstacles in trade and investment regimes.

A. Preambular Language and Purpose – Reconciling Environment and Development

In the 1987 Report of the World Commission on Environment and Development,[45] the 1992 Rio Declaration and Agenda 21,[46] the 2002 Johannesburg Declaration and Plan of Implementation,[47] and the 2012 United Nations Conference on Sustainable Development Declaration,[48] countries clearly recognized that trade and investment law has the potential to provide important contributions to sustainable development. From a sustainable development perspective, the main challenge faced by treaty negotiators is to balance the conflicting interests present in the essence of foreign investments. Treaty negotiators, for example, can design tools which will promote sustainable investments by providing them with a secure and stable business environment. On the other hand, they may need to secure ample regulatory flexibility so States will be able to reform and adapt their policies.

Although increasing,[49] the explicit recognition of sustainable development objectives in investment treaties remains relatively low.[50] The following section discusses some of the examples offered by RTA and ITIA substantive declarations and rules in order to address sustainable development objectives. It should be mentioned that this is not an

---

45 World Commission on Environment and Development, *Our Common Future* (OUP 1987).

46 Rio Declaration on Environment and Development (n 1); 'Agenda 21', UN Conference on Environment and Development (Rio de Janeiro, Brazil, 3–14 June 1992) <http://sustainabledevelopment.un.org/content/documents/Agenda21.pdf> accessed 20 September 2015.

47 Johannesburg Declaration on Sustainable Development (n 1) and Johannesburg Plan of Implementation (n 18).

48 'The Future We Want', Declaration of the United Nations Conference on Sustainable Development (2012) UNGA Res 66/288 (27 July 2012) Annex, UN Doc A/RES/66/288.

49 Kathryn Gordon and Joachim Pohl, 'Environmental Concerns in International Investment Agreements: A Survey' OECD Working Papers on International Investment (2011) 8 <http://www.oecd.org/daf/inv/investment-policy/WP-2011_1.pdf> accessed 20 September 2015.

50 See Gordon (n 21).

exhaustive list of possible solutions. In fact, the complex nature of sustainable development requires many different approaches for the numerous issues embedded in these goals. Indeed, what is right for climate change will not necessarily work for smoking prevention, or bio-diversity. However, the review below can be used as a point of departure, from which more complex solutions can be developed.

One approach adopted by states is the inclusion of references to sustainable development objectives in preambles to ITIAs. The importance of preambular language that is worded in a 'purposive' manner can be understood from Article 31(2) of the 1969 Vienna Convention on the Law of Treaties (VCLT), according to which the context and the purpose of a treaty is to be derived inter alia from the treaty's preamble.[51] In light of the different interpretations given to legal terms such as 'expropriation', 'legitimate expectations' and 'like-circumstances', and the effects these can have on sustainable development objectives,[52] the role preambular language can fulfil is significant.[53]

A second type of preambular language, while not referring to sustainable development as a treaty objective per se, imposes upon parties to behave consistently with this principle. This type of language can be found in certain US and EU ITIAs. The preamble to the US-Rwanda IIA, for example, defines as treaty objectives inter alia the promotion of economic cooperation, the stimulation of private investment, and the creation of a stable business environment. It continues, however, by stating that the Parties are:

> [d]esiring to achieve these objectives in a manner consistent with the protection of health, safety, and the environment, and the promotion of internationally recognised labor rights.[54]

A third example of preambular language can be defined as 'non-derogation' language. This language can be found in many of the IIAs

---

[51] Vienna Convention on the Law of Treaties (adopted 23 May 1969, entered into force 27 January 1980) 1155 UNTS 331 (VCLT) art 31(2).

[52] For a review of these terms and their relations to sustainable development see Cordonier Segger, Gehring and Newcombe (n 1).

[53] Marie-Claire Cordonier Segger and Andrew Newcombe, 'An Integrated Agenda for Sustainable Development in International Investment Law' in Cordonier Segger, Gehring and Newcombe (n 1) 126.

[54] See similar language in the US Model BIT (2004) and the US-Uruguay BIT (adopted 4 May 2005, entered into force 1 November 2006) <http://investmentpolicyhub.unctad.org/Download/TreatyFile/2380> accessed 24 August 2015.

signed by States such as Finland, the Netherlands, Japan and the US.[55] According to these references, the treaty's objectives (often economic in nature) are to be achieved without relaxing regulatory standards in fields such as the environment, health or safety.

Lastly, on very rare occasions references to sustainable development treaties can be found in the preamble to IIAs. An example can be found in the preamble to the Singapore-EFTA FTA (which includes investment protection), in which the Parties reaffirm 'their commitment to the principles set out in the United Nations Charter and the Universal Declaration of Human Rights,'[56] and in the Energy Charter Treaty, in which the Parties are

> [r]ecalling the United Nations Framework Convention on Climate Change, the Convention on Long-Range Transboundary Air Pollution and its protocols, and other international environmental agreements with energy-related aspects.[57]

A shared commitment to sustainable development is found more broadly in other ITIA preambles, those commonly described as RTAs. The incorporation of sustainable development concerns in preambles generally offers clues as to the object and purpose of the ITIAs themselves, providing guidance to the Parties, and any dispute settlement bodies, on how they might interpret the agreement in the event of a dispute. For example, the Parties to the 1994 NAFTA jointly recognize the need to

---

[55] See, for example, Finland-Ethiopia BIT (adopted 23 February 2006, entered into force 3 May 2007); Finland-Armenia BIT (adopted 5 October 2004, entered into force 20 March 2007); Netherlands-Suriname BIT (adopted 31 March 2005, entered into force 1 September 2006); Netherlands-Burundi BIT (adopted 24 May 2007, entered into force 1 August 2009); US-Mozambique BIT (adopted 1 December 1998, entered into force 3 March 2005); US-Jordan BIT (adopted 2 July 1997, entered into force 12 June 2003); US-Bahrain BIT (adopted 29 September 1999, entered into force 30 May 2001); Japan-Korea BIT (adopted 22 March 2002, entered into force 1 January 2003); Japan-Vietnam BIT (adopted 14 November 2003, entered into force 19 December 2004); for treaty texts see UNCTAD, 'International Investment Agreements Navigator' <http://investmentpolicyhub.unctad.org/IIA> accessed 20 September 2015.

[56] EFTA-Singapore FTA (adopted 26 June 2002, entered into force 1 January 2003) <http://investmentpolicyhub.unctad.org/Download/TreatyFile/2638> accessed 20 September 2015.

[57] Energy Charter Treaty (adopted 17 December 1994, entered into force 16 April 1998) 2080 UNTS 95.

'promote sustainable development' within the preamble of the treaty.[58] Indeed, ITIAs entered into by the US and Canada subsequent to NAFTA all incorporate similar assertions regarding the promotion of sustainable development. The Canada-Chile Free Trade Agreement,[59] the Canada-Costa Rica Free Trade Agreement,[60] the Canada-Peru Free Trade Agreement,[61] the Oman-US Free Trade Agreement,[62] the US-Colombia Free Trade Agreement[63] and the Chile-US Free Trade Agreement[64] all enshrine commitments to pursue and support policies that promote sustainable development in environmental and natural resource management. The US-Australia Free Trade Agreement provides that parties will conduct their activities 'in a manner consistent with their commitment to high labour standards, sustainable development, and environmental protection.'[65]

The 2003 United States-Singapore Free Trade Agreement recognizes that

> economic development, social development, and environmental protection are interdependent and mutually reinforcing components of sustainable

---

[58] North American Free Trade Agreement (NAFTA) (adopted 17 December 1992, entered into force 1 January 1994) (1993) 32 ILM 289, 605.

[59] Canada-Chile FTA (adopted 5 December 1996, entered into force 5 July 1997) <http://www.sice.oas.org/trade/chican_e/chcatoc.asp> accessed 20 September 2015.

[60] Canada-Costa Rica FTA (adopted 23 April 2001, entered into force 1 November 2002) <http://www.sice.oas.org/Trade/cancr/English/cancrin.asp> accessed 20 September 2015.

[61] Canada-Peru FTA (adopted 29 May 2008, entered into force 1 August 2009) <http://www.sice.oas.org/TPD/AND_CAN/Final_Texts_CAN_PER_e/index_e.asp> accessed 20 September 2015.

[62] US-Oman FTA (adopted 19 January 2006, entered into force 1 January 2009) <http://www.sice.oas.org/Trade/USA_OMN_FTA_e/USA_OMN_ind_e.asp> accessed 20 September 2015.

[63] Colombia-US FTA (adopted 22 November 2006, entered into force 15 May 2012) preamble <http://www.sice.oas.org/Trade/COL_USA_TPA_e/Index_e.asp> accessed 20 September 2015.

[64] US-Chile FTA (adopted 6 June 2003, entered into force 1 January 2004) (2003) 42 ILM 1026.

[65] US-Australia FTA (adopted 18 May 2004, entered into force 1 January 2005) preamble <http://www.sice.oas.org/Trade/US-AusFTAFinal/USAusind_e.asp> accessed 20 September 2015.

> development, and that an open and non-discriminatory multilateral trading system can play a major role in achieving sustainable development.[66]

Embracing the promotion of sustainable development as part of broader trade and investment agreements does not end with the NAFTA partners. For example, the EU-Chile Association Agreement goes further than many of the US and Canadian ITIAs by requiring Parties to implement their obligations in accordance with a 'principle of sustainable development.'[67] The 2012 EU Association Agreement with Central America seeks to

> The Parties confirm their commitment to the promotion of sustainable development, which is a guiding principle for the implementation of this Agreement, taking notably into account the Millennium Development Goals. The Parties shall ensure that an appropriate balance is struck between the economic, social and environmental components of sustainable development.[68]

In a more integrated context, the parties to MERCOSUR's treaty establishing the common market note in the preamble that

> the broadening of the current dimensions of national markets through integration is a fundamental condition to accelerate economic development with social justice [and that] this objective must be achieved through more effective use of available resources, preserving the environment … .[69]

Through ITIAs between North and North, North and South and even South and South countries, sustainable development has been recognized as a key objective, not only in the abstract, but in the very arenas that

---

66 US-Singapore FTA (adopted 6 May 2003, entered into force 1 January 2004) preamble <http://www.sice.oas.org/Trade/USA-Singapore/USASingind_e.asp> accessed 20 September 2015.

67 Chile-European Community Association Agreement (adopted 18 November 2002, entered into force 1 February 2003) <http://www.sice.oas.org/Trade/chieu_e/ChEUin_e.asp> accessed 20 September 2015.

68 EU-Central America Association Agreement (adopted 29 June 2012) art 1.2, OJ L 346 (15 December 2012). The States involved are Costa Rica, El Salvador, Guatemala, Honduras, Nicaragua and Panama.

69 Treaty Establishing a Common Market between the Argentine Republic, the Federal Republic of Brazil, the Republic of Paraguay and the Eastern Republic of Uruguay (adopted 26 March 1991, entered into force 29 November 1991) <http://www.sice.oas.org/trade/mrcsr/treatyasun_e.asp> accessed 20 September 2015.

most seek to encourage economic growth – investment and trade policy and law.[70] As discussed, the NAFTA preamble notes a joint resolve to promote sustainable development by the Parties, it was also the first ITIA to be accompanied by an environmental side agreement. The provisions of this side agreement declare the promotion of sustainable development 'based on cooperation and mutually supportive environmental and economic policies' as one of its main objectives.[71] Subsequent ITIAs have followed suit, either with side agreements or with chapters and provisions relating to the environment and sustainability that are integrated into the text of the regional economic accord itself. In the Canada-Peru FTA, at Chapter 17, the Parties pledge to

> … recognize the mutual supportiveness between trade and environment policies and the need to do so in a manner consistent with environmental protection and conservation and the sustainable use of their resources.[72]

In the EU-Colombia-Peru Agreement, parties agree to

> … promote international trade in a way that contributes to the objective of sustainable development, and to work in order to integrate and reflect this objective in the Parties' trade relations.[73]

But, these general statements of intent, no matter their potential interpretive value, are not the 'state of the art' in ITIAs. To operationalize these preambular and related declarations, many states have taken on further and more specific commitments. These include provisions for (1)

---

[70] Marie-Clare Cordonier Segger and Markus W Gehring, 'Introduction' in Markus W Gehring and Marie-Claire Cordonier Segger (eds), *Sustainable Development in World Trade Law* (Kluwer Law International 2005) 1, 3.

[71] North American Agreement on Environmental Cooperation (adopted 17 December 1992, entered into force 1 January 1994) art 1(b) <http://www.cec.org/Page.asp?PageID=1226&SiteNodeID=567> accessed 20 September 2015.

[72] Canada-Peru FTA (adopted 29 May 2008, entered into force 1 August 2009) art 1702(2) <http://www.sice.oas.org/Trade/CAN_PER/CAN_PER_e/CAN_PER_index_e.asp> accessed 20 September 2015; similar provisions are found in the Chile-Colombia FTA (adopted 27 November 2006, entered into force 8 May 2009) art 18.1 <http://investmentpolicyhub.unctad.org/Download/TreatyFile/3089> accessed 20 September 2015.

[73] Trade Agreement between the EU and its Member States, of the one Part, and Colombia and Peru, of the other Part (adopted 26 June 2012, entered into force 1 June 2013) art 4(j), OJ L 354 (21 December 2012).

'waivers or windows' to avoid conflicts with climate change and other sustainable development-related provisions, (2) deeper cooperation arrangements through specific provisions in side agreements and other chapters of ITIAs, (3) actual enhancement of trade and investment in specific sectors of relevance to climate change, such as environmental goods and services, renewable energy, carbon markets, organic agriculture, sustainable transport and sustainably harvested forests. Such texts also serve to inform international dispute settlement procedures of sustainable development dimensions to their cases.

B. Exceptions and Reservations

Another way in which States attempt to promote sustainable development objectives is the use of exceptions and reservations in ITIAs. ITIAs, like almost any international agreement, impose certain restraints on states' regulatory flexibility. Through the use of exceptions, States ensure that their ability to regulate certain fields will not be restricted by investment treaties.

Exceptions in ITIAs appear in several forms. First, some ITIAs include provisions that allow for treaty reservations, which are sector-specific carve-outs from treaty obligations. For example, Annex I of the Canada-Peru FIPA includes a list of sectors that are exempted from the IIAs' substantive rules.[74] Second, many ITIAs adopt general exceptions provisions, modelled on Article XX of the General Agreement on Tariffs and Trade ('GATT'). These general exceptions exclude from the scope of ITIAs measures relating to the protection of inter alia 'human, animal, or plant life or health', or to the conservation of exhaustible natural resources. As in Article XX of the GATT, these exceptions are subject to non-discriminatory treatment and should not be used as disguised restrictions for investment or trade.[75]

Third, several ITIAs include so-called 'non-precluded measures' ('NPMs').[76] NPMs are intended to exempt certain subject areas (e.g. public health, public security, morality) from the scope of the treaty, or

---

[74] See, for example, Canada-Peru FIPA (adopted 14 November 2006, entered into force 20 June 2007) art 9 <http://investmentpolicyhub.unctad.org/Download/TreatyFile/626> accessed 20 September 2015.

[75] For examples and detailed discussion see Andrew Newcombe, 'General Exceptions in International Investment Agreements' in Cordonier Segger, Gehring and Newcombe (n 1) 356, 358.

[76] William W Burke-White and Andreas von Staden, 'Investment Protection in Extraordinary Times: The Interpretation and Application of Non-Precluded

from specific treaty obligation. For example, the protocol following the Germany-Bangladesh BIT states:

> [m]easures that have to be taken for reasons of public security and order, public health or morality shall not be deemed 'treatment less favourable' within the meaning of Article 2.[77]

Exceptions, at least in theory, can promote sustainable development objectives. Their main contribution in this respect is by preventing conflicts between investment rules and sustainable development regulation. The recent Philip Morris claims made against Australia and Uruguay following their anti-smoking regulations (mainly plain-packaging rules) is an excellent example of a case in which general exceptions would have been helpful.[78] However, exceptions can be taken with care. As stated by Newcombe, in several cases, tribunals have already approved that measures aimed at the protection of public policy objectives do not breach investment treaty obligations, and as such, it is important that any list of protected areas is worded simply as an open set of examples, without limiting the scope of what can be considered as bona-fide public policy objectives.[79]

C. Sustainable Development Cooperation

Particularly among the broader RTAs and ITIAs, there are increasing instances in which Parties have actually agreed not just to seek to prevent their economic accord from being an obstacle to sustainable development, but actually to provide for proactive opportunities for sustainable development cooperation alongside. For instance, NAFTA is formulated

---

Measures Provisions in Bilateral Investment Treaties' (2007) 48 Va JIL 307; see also Newcombe (n 75) 358.

[77] Germany-Bangladesh BIT (adopted 6 May 1981, entered into force 14 September 1986) <http://investmentpolicyhub.unctad.org/Download/TreatyFile/264> accessed 20 September 2015; for an example for general exclusion see US-Panama BIT (adopted 27 October 1982, entered into force 30 May 1991) art X <http://investmentpolicyhub.unctad.org/Download/TreatyFile/2146> accessed 20 September 2015.

[78] *Philip Morris Brands Sàrl, Philip Morris Products SA and Abal Hermanos SA v Oriental Republic of Uruguay*, ICSID Case No ARB/10/7, Request for Arbitration (19 February 2010); *Philip Morris Asia Limited v The Commonwealth of Australia,* UNCITRAL, PCA Case No 2012-12, Written Notification of Claim (22 June 2011).

[79] Newcombe (n 75) 357–8.

as a straight free trade and investment agreement, but it also establishes separate side-agreements to provide frameworks for environmental and labour cooperation. The North American Agreement on Environmental Cooperation (NAAEC), a separate side agreement to NAFTA, establishes the Commission for Environmental Cooperation (CEC) as its implementation body, which is responsible for information exchange on environmental issues, assessing environmental impacts of proposed projects and dealing with complaints from private individuals concerning non-implementation of environmental laws by NAFTA Parties.[80] This model of ITIA, with attendant side agreements, is often used by Canada, Mexico and the United States when negotiating with other countries. Most recently, Australia and Japan are also adopting similar approaches. It is notable, however, that even in cases where side agreements exist, there are often further 'core provisions' or chapters within the associated ITIAs that address environmental and social inclusion concerns, reference plans for cooperation and exchange on these issues, and provide general exceptions to ITIA provisions for related public policy priorities (as mentioned above).

Further, broader ITIAs may also be formed in contemplation of regional economic integration objectives. These ITIAs focus on the formation of a common market, or an economic union, and progressively integrate their rules, often shaping collaborative agendas on different policy priorities as part of this process. While agreements forming the European Community provide the quintessential example, less complex arrangements include the MERCOSUR in Latin America and the Economic Community of West African States (ECOWAS). Despite having been formed with a view to encouraging trade and investment liberalization in the regions, these regional integration arrangements address their member States' shared concerns, such as good governance, legislative harmonization, the environment, health, human rights and social inclusion. Such ITIAs and their derivatives among regions (EU-Central America, EU-CARIFORUM) or bilaterally (EU-third party) increasingly provide instruments to promote political dialogue and joint cooperation measures among the signatories, focused on ways to support sustainable development, environmental and social collaboration, with trade as simply part of the broader regional agreement. Such is the case in the EU Partnership Agreement with The Forum of the Caribbean Group of

---

[80] See supra n 1; see also John Kirton, 'The Commission for Environmental Cooperation and Canada-U.S. Environmental Governance in the NAFTA Era' (1997) 27 *The American Review of Canadian Studies* 459.

African, Caribbean and Pacific (ACP) States (CARIFORUM), the Euro-Mediterranean Partnership and the different association agreements signed by the EU, which target various aspects of environmental and social development in the cooperation and trade chapters.[81]

D. Corporate Social Responsibility

Another layer in which IIAs can promote sustainable development objectives, is by activating and supporting the efforts of Parties to promote Social Corporate Responsibility (CSR). The modern concept of CSR can be traced back to the 1950s, when CSR was defined as 'obligations of businessmen to pursue those policies, to make those decisions, or to follow those lines of action which are desirable in terms of the objectives and values of our society.'[82]

Although nowadays some debate still takes place on the exact definition of CSR,[83] for the purposes of this chapter the words of Judge Gonthier will suffice:

> [CSR] generally embodies the notion that a corporation must act in a responsible manner with regard to the environment, community and the society in which it operates. In its most basic form, CSR emphasizes an approach to corporate governance and operations that integrates and balances the self-interests of the corporation, and those of its investors, with the concerns and interests of the public.[84]

Perhaps the most eminent example of a CSR code is the OECD Guidelines for Multinational Enterprises (OECD Guidelines) which have been described by some as an 'emerging consensus on the social obligations of MNEs.'[85] The OECD Guidelines represent a comprehensive code of conduct, including voluntary standards for environment,

---

[81] See supra n 1.

[82] Howard R Bowen, *Social Responsibility and Accountability* (Harper & Row 1953), as cited in Archie B Carroll, 'Corporate Social Responsibility: Evolution of a Definitional Construct' (1999) 38 *Business & Society* 268, 270.

[83] Peter T Muchlinski, *Multinational Enterprises & the Law* (OUP 2007) 101.

[84] Charles D Gonthier, 'Foreword' in Michael Kerr, Richard Janda and Chip Pitts (eds), *Corporate Social Responsibility: A Legal Analysis* (LexisNexis 2009), as cited in Jarrod Hepburn and Vuyelwa Kuuya, 'Corporate Social Responsibility and Investment Treaties' in Cordonier Segger, Gehring and Newcombe (n 1) 585.

[85] Muchlinski (n 83) 103.

employment, combating bribery, science, competition and taxation.[86] A more recent example, albeit one that focuses exclusively on human rights, is the 2011 'principles for responsible contracts', that were formulated by John Ruggie, the Special Representative of the Secretary-General on the issue of human rights and transnational corporations and other business enterprises.[87] These principles include inter alia the planning and management of potential adverse impacts on human rights, project operating standards, community engagement, and grievance mechanisms. The vast majority of CSR norms can be considered as 'soft law', as they are voluntary and rely on self-governance. This, however, does not make them ineffective. Soft law mechanisms often include other 'sticks and carrots' besides the threat of legal action.[88] In some cases CSR 'soft law' norms have indeed proven successful in enforcing higher standards of social responsibility.[89] The activity of foreign investors, as discussed above, can impact social, economic, and environmental issues. But while some governments are equipped with the means to regulate and control these effects, others are not. This situation can be aggravated where States are eager to attract foreign investment and consequently are willing to ignore the adverse effects on issues like human rights or the environment. Furthermore, the existence of governmental corruption, or the mere inability to enforce high standards of regulation, can result in the exploitative behaviour of foreign multinationals. All of these scenarios are the result of inefficient enforcement of high standards of corporate social 'behaviour' on foreign investors. The role CSR can play in this respect is evident. By adhering to external norms, on top of, or in place of, the norms imposed by host States, higher standards of behaviour can be achieved. Furthermore, following CSR principles such as

86 OECD, *Guidelines for Multinational Enterprises* (OECD 2011) <http://mneguidelines.oecd.org/text/> accessed 20 September 2015.

87 UN Human Rights Council, 'Report of the Special Representative of the Secretary-General on the Issue of Human Rights and Transnational Corporations and Other Business Enterprises, John Ruggie' (21 March 2011) UN Doc A/HRC/17/31/Add.3, <http://business-humanrights.org/sites/default/files/media/documents/ruggie/report-principles-for-responsible-contracts-25-may-2011.pdf> accessed 20 September 2015.

88 Roya Ghafele and Angus Mercer, 'A Mountain Biker Cannot Start a Journey in Sixth Gear: An Assessment of the UN Global Compact's Use of Soft Law as a Global Governance Structure for Corporate Social Responsibility' (2010) 17 UC Davis JILP 41.

89 John M Conley and Cynthia A Williams, 'Global Banks as Global Sustainability Regulators?: The Equator Principles' (2011) 33(4) *Law & Policy* 542.

those proposed by John Ruggie,[90] will assist foreign investors to plan and avoid potential conflicts and enhance their acceptance by the local community.

CSR norms can be imported into ITIAs, and even BITs more narrowly, in several ways. First, several of the provisions already discussed in this chapter are designed to enforce (as 'hard law') higher standards of social activity.[91] With respect to self-governed 'soft law' norms, these can be mentioned in the preambles to IIAs and serve as a source for treaty interpretation. The preamble to the Canada-Peru FTA for example, 'encourages' enterprises to respect CSR norms. A more comprehensive example can be found in the preamble to the IISD Model BIT, where one of its aims is described as:

> Affirming the progressive development of international law and policy on the relationships between multinational enterprises and host governments as seen in such international instruments as the ILO Tripartite Declaration on Multinational Enterprises and Social Policy; the OECD Guidelines for Multinational Enterprises; and the United Nations' Norms and Responsibilities of Transnational Corporations and Other Business Enterprises with Regard to Human Rights.[92]

Furthermore, IIAs can also include more specific treaty provisions with respect to CSR. The IISD Model BIT for example, includes a CSR provision (Article 16), according to which foreign investors must adhere to a list of CSR codes and guidelines. Another possibility is an ex ante review of the investors' CSR policies and their suitability for designated projects. The implementation of such a review may be prescribed as a precondition for certain types of investments, especially for those that were identified as sensitive by SIAs. Alternatively, as implied by Article 13.6(2) of the EU-Korea FTA (which specifically refers also to FDI), States can also grant preferential treatment to investors that comply with CSR obligations.[93] If such a strategy is to be adopted, States should adjust other treaty provisions, such as the non-discrimination provisions for example, in order to ensure that CSR-based preferential treatment will not be considered as a treaty violation.

---

[90] For example, Ruggie suggests to maintain community engagement, and to establish 'grievance mechanisms', to which individuals and local communities will be able to approach, UN Human Rights Council (n 87) 19–20.

[91] See a review in Hepburn and Kuuya (n 84) 599.

[92] IISD Model International Agreement on Investment, <http://www.iisd.org/pdf/2005/investment_model_int_agreement.pdf> accessed 20 September 2015.

[93] Hepburn and Kuuya (n 84) 609.

Interesting developments in this respect can be found in the evolving EU policy of international investment law. Pursuant to the entry into force of the Treaty of Lisbon, FDI has been integrated into the EU common commercial policy. While the formulation of the EU's future investment policy is still ongoing, it may be predicted that the inclusion of CSR in this policy is highly likely. First, the EU's latest FTAs with Korea and with Colombia and Peru mention CSR standards as a means to promote sustainable development goals.[94] Secondly, in two recent Resolutions the European Parliament expressed its will to see CSR provisions incorporated into future investment and trade agreements.[95] Most notably, in its Resolution on the future European international investment policy it was stated that the Parliament is calling 'for a corporate social responsibility clause and effective social and environmental clauses to be included in every FTA the EU signs.'[96]

Similar recognition was also made by the European Council, in its 'conclusion on a comprehensive European international investment policy' from 2010.[97]

V. CONCLUSIONS

Sustainable development is no longer optional. In many ways the social licence for investment protection rules depends on its ability to balance

---

[94] In both cases FDI are specifically mentioned; see EU-Korea FTA (adopted 6 October 2010, entered into force 1 July 2011) art 13.6, OJ L 127 (14 May 2011); EU-Colombia-Peru FTA (n 73) art 271.

[95] European Parliament, 'Resolution on Corporate Social Responsibility in International Trade Agreements' (25 November 2010) <http://www.europarl.europa.eu/sides/getDoc.do?pubRef=-//EP//NONSGML+TA+P7-TA-2010-0446+0+DOC+PDF+V0//EN> accessed 20 September 2015; European Parliament, 'Resolution on the Future European International Investment Policy' (6 April 2011) <http://www.europarl.europa.eu/sides/getDoc.do?pubRef=-//EP//NONSGML+TA+P7-TA-2011-0141+0+DOC+PDF+V0//EN> accessed 20 September 2015.

[96] EU Parliament, 'Resolution on the Future European International Investment Policy' (n 95).

[97] Council of the European Union, 'Conclusion on a Comprehensive European International Investment Policy' (3041st Foreign Affairs Council Meeting, Luxembourg 25 October 2010) para 16 <http://www.consilium.europa.eu/uedocs/cms_data/docs/pressdata/EN/foraff/117328.pdf > accessed 20 September 2015.

economic, human rights and environmental priorities. Three consequences are particularly cogent to help turn obstacles into opportunities for international trade and investment law.

First, current uses of existing IIAs can be re-thought. These instruments can provide less of a second chance for a foreign investor to influence difficult governmental negotiations and even less exceedingly preferential treatment of the foreign investor in comparison to domestic companies.[98] Rather, investment law can serve the sustainable development objectives of the host country, and the global community. It is not inconceivable that investors in future will have to demonstrate that they have done precisely this. Standards are becoming increasingly detailed and clear, and the global reputation of a transnational corporation, or an investment bank, increasingly hinges upon their social and environmental performance, not just their economic profits and losses.

Second, as this chapter has demonstrated, there remains ample opportunity to innovate for sustainable development in investment treaty making. Several examples from ITIAs and even narrower RTAs have been discussed but further innovations, for instance making CSR standards binding, can be considered in the future to properly balance environment and development concerns in investment treaty making. With the arrival of the European Union as a new actor,[99] many IIAs will need to be re-written or re-concluded. This window of opportunity should allow for better balancing provisions and procedural innovations to be enshrined.

Finally, a wealth of international sustainable development treaties also provides international standards that can influence how fifty-year-old treaty instruments can be interpreted.[100] The norm users of investment law, particularly arbitrators on tribunals, may need to take special care to engage in the kind of balancing of socio-economic development and environmental priorities discussed above, particularly when engaging a new generation of investment treaties drafted along the lines discussed above. The precautionary principle allows for reversal or lessening of the

---

98 See, for example, Gayle Allard and Candace Agrella Martinez, 'The Influence of Government Policy and NGOs on Capturing Private Investment' (OECD Global Forum on International Investment 27–28 March 2008) <http://www.oecd.org/investment/globalforum/40400836.pdf> accessed 20 September 2015.

99 See Angelos Dimopoulos, *EU Foreign Investment Law* (OUP 2011).

100 UN Treaty Secretariat, *Multilateral Treaty Framework an Invitation to Universal Participation: 2010 Treaty Event: Towards Universal Participation and Implementation* (United Nations 2010).

burden of proof as has long been the case in the world trading system.[101] Certain arbitrators have tried to make amends in the award stage, such as in the *Bywater* decision, but further development for example with regards to the burden of proof is recommended. Dispute settlement is becoming increasingly transparent and the new UNCITRAL rules should influence how the majority of arbitral tribunals will act. Any procedural innovations should be coupled with a contemporary interpretation of investment obligations.

Modern IIAs offer greater possibilities to balance environment and socio-economic development objectives. This is mainly due to the growing concern of the Parties involved in the negotiation of the agreements regarding the widespread impact that these instruments can have, not only on the environment but also on trade, labour conditions, health issues, etc. This chapter reviewed some of the tools States may find useful when attempting to incorporate sustainable development objectives into their IIAs. It was explained that the challenge faced by treaty-drafters is multilayered, as States must strike a balance between the need to secure ample regulatory flexibility on the one hand, and to create a stable, transparent and inviting business environment, on the other. These tools, it was emphasised, should be developed and refined in order to maximise the potential embedded in FDI for supporting sustainable development.

In order to conclude this chapter, three final remarks can be made. First, the essence of the term 'sustainable development' lies in the desired balance between economic, social and environmental concerns. All three pillars are important, and all should be taken into consideration. This is what distinguishes 'sustainable development' from pure environmental or economic approaches. Following this view, it is argued that states may consider the measures discussed above, among others, as illustrative examples of the creativity and careful treaty-crafting that is possible for the next generation of FTAs, IIAs and even ITIAs. For example, it may be that the easiest way to prevent future conflicts actually frustrates potential synergies. The use of blanket rather than specific exceptions, for example, might hinder foreign investments and thus frustrate technology transfer or the creation of new jobs in new industries focused on sustainable development of renewable energy, sustainable use of biodiversity, or sustainable and organic agriculture for food security.

---

101 Marie-Claire Cordonier Segger and Markus W Gehring, 'Precaution, Health and the WTO: Moving Towards Sustainable Development' (2003) 29 *Queen's Law Journal* 133.

Second, the concept of sustainable development deliberately includes numerous interests, with each stakeholder requiring different balances and different treatment. IIAs should therefore avoid using 'one size fits all' solutions for sustainable development. For example, it would be wrong to address the interaction between economic development and climate change mitigation with the same legal tools used for the interaction between human rights and economic development, or to assume that the implications of an agreement between two small countries focused on trade and investment in agriculture are the same as those of an agreement between a large country with unexplored petroleum resources and a region with high energy demand.

Finally, to convert investment law from obstacle to opportunity for sustainable development, the details and nuances of the treaty rules themselves are crucially important. These must be carefully critiqued, as well as considered, by competent legal research, analysis and decision-making on all levels of a complex and multi-layered international system.

5. UNCTAD's effort to foster the relationship between international investment law and sustainable development

Andrea Saldarriaga and Kendra Magraw*

The categories of legal thought are obviously conceived along lines parallel to the categories of economic conduct. The logically formal rationality of legal thought is the counterpart to the purposive rationality of economic conduct.[1]

I. INTRODUCTION

Foreign direct investment (FDI) is one of the main drivers of the global economy. Global FDI flows reached USD 1.45 trillion in 2013 and they are expected to grow to USD 1.7 trillion in 2015.[2] The positive correlation between FDI and development has long been acknowledged in economic and political circles. In contrast, the question about the relationship between international investment law (IIL) and development – more specifically sustainable development – has emerged relatively recently and remains an issue of debate. How has IIL evolved and how does it relate, if at all, to development?

In Part II, this chapter sketches the way the relationship between investment and development has evolved and how this evolution has

* The authors would like to thank Elisabeth Tuerk, Chief of UNCTAD's International Investment Agreement Section, for providing comments. The views expressed in this chapter are those of the authors and do not reflect the views of the UNCTAD Secretariat or its Member States. All omissions and errors remain those of the authors.

1 Max Rheinstein, 'Introduction' in Max Rheinstein (ed.), *Max Weber on Law in Economy and Society* (Harvard UP 1954).

2 UNCTAD, *World Investment Report 2014* (United Nations 2014).

influenced the role of IIL. Part III highlights some of the developments that have prompted calls for a reassessment of the purpose and functioning of IIL. Part IV then introduces the contribution of the United Nations Conference on Trade and Development (UNCTAD) to investment, development and the role of IIL. Part V offers a brief conclusion.

II. THE RELATIONSHIP BETWEEN INVESTMENT, SUSTAINABLE DEVELOPMENT AND INTERNATIONAL INVESTMENT LAW

Already in 2002, the Monterrey Consensus synthesised the positive correlation between FDI and development by affirming that FDI plays a key role in financing sustained economic growth and that it is especially important for

> its potential to transfer knowledge and technology, create jobs, boost overall productivity, enhance competitiveness and entrepreneurship, and ultimately eradicate poverty through economic growth and development.[3]

The Monterrey Consensus reflected the optimism of the 1990s, characterised by the growth of global FDI flows and the belief in its capacity to generate positive impacts for development. International organisations and mainstream economic theory supported that view and amplified the need for developing countries to focus their efforts on attracting high flows of FDI. In this context, the law, and in particular, the regime that governs foreign investment, played a very specific role: that of promoting and protecting foreign investment.

In this regard, the Monterrey Consensus noted the necessity to create domestic and international conditions to facilitate FDI flows and therefore the need for countries to achieve 'a transparent, stable and predictable investment climate, with proper contract enforcement and respect for property rights… .'[4] The Consensus went on to stress the need for special efforts in priority areas such as regulatory frameworks for promoting and

---

[3] 'Report of the International Conference on Financing for Development' (Monterrey, Mexico, 18–22 March 2002) (22 March 2002) UN Doc A/CONF.198/11, ch 1, resolution 1, annex, 9–10, para 20.

[4] Ibid para 21.

protecting investments and noted the importance of investment agreements.[5] This approach was reiterated in 2008 during a follow-up conference in Doha where it was further specified that '[b]ilateral investment treaties may promote private flows by increasing legal stability and predictability to investors.'[6]

The beliefs reflected in the Monterrey Consensus were held by the international community long before its conclusion. Such beliefs have contributed to the rapid development of IIL into a vast network of international investment agreements (IIAs) geared predominantly towards protecting – and indirectly promoting – FDI through broadly drafted standards of treatment and their enforcement through international arbitration.

However, the optimism of the 1990s turned towards criticism as it became evident that FDI did not automatically catalyse positive contributions to host States and their communities, and that instead, it could raise challenges, such as environmental degradation, infringement of human rights, crowding out of domestic industries and exacerbation of social inequalities.[7] In addition, the focus on economic growth also revealed its shortcomings and exposed the risks it creates for other social and environmental goals of governments and societies.

Over approximately the same time period, the notion of sustainable development was conceptualized and grew in importance, becoming the overarching goal of national governments and international organisations

---

[5] The Monterrey Consensus noted: 'To attract and enhance inflows of productive capital, countries need to continue their efforts to achieve a transparent, stable and predictable investment climate, with proper contract enforcement and respect for property rights, embedded in sound macroeconomic policies and institutions that allow businesses, both domestic and international, to operate efficiently and profitably and with maximum development impact. Special efforts are required in such priority areas as economic policy and regulatory frameworks for promoting and protecting investments, including the areas of human resource development, avoidance of double taxation, corporate governance, accounting standards, and the promotion of a competitive environment. Other mechanisms, such as public/private partnerships and investment agreements, can be important' (ibid para 21).

[6] 'Doha Declaration on Financing for Development: Outcome Document of the Follow-up International Conference on Financing for Development to Review Implementation of the Monterrey Consensus' (Doha, Qatar, 29 November–2 December 2008) (9 December 2008) UN Doc A/CONF.212/L.1/Rev.1, 12, para 25 [hereinafter Doha Declaration].

[7] J Anthony VanDuzer, Penelope Simons and Graham Mayeda, *Integrating Sustainable Development into International Investment Agreements – A Guide for Developing Country Negotiators* (Commonwealth Secretariat 2013) 22.

alike.[8] This notion embraced the need to balance economic growth with social and environmental concerns. As the concept was defined and applied, it developed even further: as noted by the International Law Association Committee on the International Law on Sustainable Development 'the international community has now endorsed a broader conception of sustainable development than previously envisaged … .'[9] This broader conception of sustainable development 'must take into account three intersecting factors – economic development and social (human rights) development, as well as environmental protection.'[10]

In this context, it became clear that investment should support the pursuit of sustainable development objectives. The case has also been made with respect to the United Nations' sustainable development goals (SDGs):[11] according to UNCTAD estimates, the attainment of the SDGs requires global investments in the order of USD 5 trillion to USD 7 trillion a year. At current investment levels in SDG-relevant sectors, developing countries alone face an annual gap of USD 2.5 trillion. Clearly, international investment policies have a role to play in this regard. Thus far, however, the importance of sustainable development considerations, and the role investment has to play, have not yet translated into the mainstream of international investment policymaking: while some modern IIAs include references to sustainable development

---

8 The New Delhi Declaration states that 'sustainable development is now widely accepted as a global objective and that the concept has been amply recognized in various international and national legal instruments, including treaty law and jurisprudence at international and national levels.' See also ibid 4. For a discussion of the legal character of SD commitments see ibid 110.

9 Committee on International Law on Sustainable Development, 'First Report' 71st Biennial Conference of the International Law Association (Berlin, Germany, 16–21 August 2004) 9 <http://www.ila-hq.org/download.cfm/docid/917ADCC2-76B0-4D5B-889D9BA9AFD2BB95> accessed 18 August 2014.

10 Marie-Claire Cordonier Segger and Ashfaq Khalfan, *Sustainable Development Law: Principles, Practices and Prospects* (OUP 2004) 1.

11 UNCTAD (n 2). UN Member States have agreed that they need to establish SDGs which will build upon the Millennium Development Goals and converge with the post-2015 development agenda. As a contribution to the development of the SDGs, the 2014 World Investment Report addressed investing in them.

and other considerations,[12] the accumulated stock of older agreements follow a more traditional pattern.[13]

Faced with the potential challenges that FDI may raise and given the prominent place that sustainable development has come to occupy among the goals of the international community, it appears to be imperative that IIL go beyond its overarching goal of protecting FDI only. There is an urgent need for IIL to adapt to the changing circumstances and address the challenges posed by FDI to help ensure that it contributes to sustainable development.

Moreover, the question as to the role IIL plays in relation to sustainable development comes at a time when the evolution of investment arbitration has revealed the extent of the protections afforded to investors in IIAs and the discretion granted to arbitral tribunals, which has led to rising voices of dissatisfaction with IIAs and the functioning of investor-State dispute settlement (ISDS), as discussed below.

III. THE UNFOLDING OF IIL THROUGH ARBITRATION AND THE CHALLENGES FOR SUSTAINABLE DEVELOPMENT

From 1959 up to around the beginning of the 2000s, States signed several hundreds of IIAs, thus setting up the rules of a 'game' that no one really knew how to play. It was only with the increase of investment arbitration

---

[12] For example, a review of a selection of IIAs concluded in 2013 by UNCTAD show that most of them had sustainable development-oriented features (such as those identified in the Annex Table III.3 of the 2012 World Investment Report and Annex Table III.1 of the 2013 World Investment Report, e.g., references to the protection of health and safety, labour rights, the environment or sustainable development in the treaty preamble), see UNCTAD (n 2) 116.

[13] According to a recent survey conducted by the Organisation for Economic Co-operation and Development (OECD), only 12% of the entire stock of IIAs contains language relating to sustainable development and responsible business conduct. The most often addressed issue is environmental protection (10%), followed by labour standards (5.5%), anti-corruption (1.5%) and human rights (0.5%), see OECD Informal Ministerial Meeting on Responsible Business Conduct, 'Investment Treaty Law, Sustainable Development and Responsible Business Conduct: A Fact Finding Survey' (26 June 2014) <http://www.oecd.org/daf/inv/mne/2014RBCMinisterial-TreatyRBC.pdf> accessed 18 August 2014.

cases that followed the Argentine crisis in 2001–02[14] that the game's players and spectators realised the amplitude of the rules and the implications of 'the game'. In this context, a number of concerns with IIAs and the functioning of ISDS were revealed. Although not necessarily expressed in terms of 'sustainable development', most of the current criticism of IIAs and ISDS in fact impacts values and elements that are essential to its realization. Sustainable development embraces goals beyond economic growth, and integrates a social and environmental dimension to the notion of development. By doing so, sustainable development incorporates into the notion of development the need to: promote good governance; safeguard the environment; protect, respect and observe human rights; and promote transparency, participation and accountability.[15]

---

[14] UNCTAD, 'Recent Updates in Investor-State Dispute Settlement (ISDS)' IIA Issues Note No 1 (April 2014) 2 <http://unctad.org/en/PublicationsLibrary/webdiaepcb2014d3_en.pdf> accessed 18 August 2014.

[15] The UN Department of Economic and Social Affairs (UN DESA) has prepared guidelines for supporting states in developing their national sustainable development strategies (NSDSs). In its guidance, it notes that: 'Sustainable development has three principal components: economic growth, social equity and protection of the environment. Underlying the economic component is the principle that society's wellbeing would have to be maximized and poverty eradicated through the optimal and efficient use of natural resources … The social component refers to the relationship between nature and human beings, uplifting the welfare of people, improving access to basic health and education services, fulfilling minimum standards of security and respect for human rights. It also refers to the development of various cultures, diversity, pluralism and effective grass roots participation in decision-making. The issue of equity, i.e., the distribution of benefits and access to resources remains an essential component of both the economic and social dimensions of sustainable development. The environmental component, on the other hand, is concerned with the conservation and enhancement of the physical and biological resource base and eco-systems.' see, UN DESA, 'Guidance in Preparing a National Sustainable Development Strategy: Managing Sustainability in the New Millennium' (2001) 7. In addition, in a recent discussion paper on 'Governance for Sustainable Development,' the United Nations Development Programme (UNDP) discusses the various elements and values integral to the notion of sustainable development. In particular, the document notes: 'Democracy, good governance and the rule of law at the national and international levels, as well as an enabling environment, are essential for sustainable development including sustained and inclusive economic growth, social development, environmental protection and the eradication of poverty and hunger (General Assembly resolution 66/28) … Accountability is a key theme running through and underpinning many aspects of governance – both vertically, from government to people, and horizontally

This section provides a brief overview of how IIAs and ISDS relate to these elements and values, and create potential challenges for their realization.

A. 'Single-Goal Game'

In the early days of IIA negotiations, investment flows were predominantly North to South and, in the wake of decolonisation, it was the capital-exporting countries that sought to conclude IIAs to protect the investments of their nationals.[16] The key objective of these countries was ensuring that investments were protected primarily from expropriation and discriminatory treatment because they considered that domestic laws in developing countries did not adequately protect investments from such actions. It is therefore not surprising that IIAs were drafted with investment protection as the primary goal.

This approach was strengthened by the correlation established between FDI and development as reflected in the Monterrey Consensus. Developing States that wanted to attract FDI in the hope of spurring development were required to offer specific protections to foreign investment – signing

---

between parts of the state, such as the executive and the judiciary. Sustainable development will require that public officials account for actions taken in the public's name and with public resources … Openness and transparency are essential to achieve sustainable development. There is evidence that informed citizens and the private sector are better able to engage in developing policy; they are better collaborators and partners with government on service delivery, and also better able to hold governments to account, leading to improved development outcomes … Participation is both a right, and a means to more sustainable development …', UNDP Discussion Paper 'Governance for Sustainable Development – Integrating Governance in the Post-2015 Development Framework' (March 2014) <http://www.undp.org/content/dam/undp/library/Democratic%20 Governance/Discussion-Paper–Governance-for-Sustainable-Development.pdf> accessed 18 August 2014.

[16] See, e.g., UNCTAD, 'Bilateral Investment Treaties: 1959–1999' (15 December 2000) 1–2 <http://unctad.org/en/docs/poiteiiad2.en.pdf> accessed 18 August 2014; Simon Lester, 'Liberalization or Litigation? Time to Rethink the International Investment Regime' (Cato Institute Policy Analysis No 730, 8 July 2013) 3 <http://object.cato.org/sites/cato.org/files/pubs/pdf/pa730_web.pdf> accessed 18 August 2014; Krista Nadakavukaren Schefer, *International Investment Law: Text, Cases and Materials* (Edward Elgar 2013) 6–10.

IIAs was considered one of the key tools in this regard.[17] The attraction of high levels of FDI emerged as an overriding concern of many of these States.

While the number of IIAs grew significantly over time, other measures necessary to build a transparent, stable and predictable investment climate that encourage FDI did not figure prominently in the agendas of policymakers. In particular, IIAs were largely unable to prompt regulatory and behavioural changes in host States: the signature of IIAs by States was generally not followed by regulatory or institutional changes at the domestic level to enable States to meet their newly acquired commitments. States would sign IIAs and then proceed in their national affairs as before without holistically examining their national investment policies and practices, or improving governance. As a result, access to arbitration became the main feature by which IIAs guaranteed investment protection. The increase of ISDS created a dynamic where such protection was achieved by winning cases against host States. Winning ISDS cases appears to have become the 'single-goal' of IIAs, and litigation turned into the core of the dynamic created by these treaties.[18]

The focus on the ISDS mechanism and on winning cases has failed not only to contribute to improving investment practices and good governance, but also has created financial pressure arising from high defence costs and amounts of damages awarded in investment cases.

B. Lack of Transparency and Public Participation

Investment arbitration initially followed the commercial arbitration model from which it drew the procedural rules that govern the proceedings. Confidentiality was among these rules; thus investment arbitration began functioning behind closed doors, far from public scrutiny. However, as the International Centre for Settlement of Investment Disputes (ICSID) permitted awards to be published in certain circumstances and the number of cases increased, it became clear that matters of public interest

---

[17] See UNCTAD (n 16) 1; Dirk W Te Velde, 'Foreign Direct Investment and Development: A Historical Perspective' (Overseas Development Institute, 30 January 2006) <http://www.odi.org/sites/odi.org.uk/files/odi-assets/publications-opinion-files/850.pdf> accessed 18 August 2014.

[18] It has then been argued that IIAs therefore have failed to improve host States' investment climates and good governance, objectives that development agencies were hoping that IIAs would bring; see, Celine Tan, 'Reviving the Emperor's Old Clothes: The Good Governance Agenda, Development and International Investment Law', in this volume, 147.

were being brought to investment arbitration and that the decisions of arbitral tribunals had an impact beyond the two parties to the arbitration. Yet many of those affected by these decisions were not able to take part in the proceedings and, most of the time, were not even aware of their existence or of their outcome.

Civil society groups and academics therefore began raising concern about the lack of transparency and opportunity for effective participation in ISDS cases with public policy dimensions.[19] Transparency and participation are not only necessary to ensure that social and environmental concerns of affected communities are adequately aired and represented, but are also central features of good governance and sustainable development.[20]

C. Broad Rules, Arbitral Discretion and Potential Constraint on Regulatory Space

The rules set out by States in investment treaties were drafted in broad terms. This breadth began to be a cause of concern when States started to 'play the game' and realised that it was for the arbitrators to define the contours of such rules. The broad formulation of IIA provisions, combined with arbitrator discretion in their interpretation and the lack of precedent in IIL, has resulted in at least two unanticipated consequences.

First, IIAs rules have developed in a non-uniform fashion due to different treaty formulations and arbitral interpretations, resulting in unpredictability and lack of clarity regarding the legal standards contained in the treaties. Unpredictability and lack of clarity, in turn, make it

---

[19] ICSID has limited transparency provisions and the UNCITRAL Rules (pre-2013) contain no disclosure mechanism. In regard to participation, some arbitral tribunals have accepted submissions from amicus curiae, but it is generally not required by IIAs or arbitral rules.

[20] The New Delhi Declaration provides that public participation is central to sustainable development and good governance. International Law Association, 'New Delhi Declaration of Principles of International Law Relating to Sustainable Development' (2002) 2 *International Environmental Agreements: Politics, Law and Economics* 215, principle 5. Further, the Office of the High Commissioner for Human Rights has noted that 'good governance relates to political and institutional processes and outcomes that are deemed necessary to achieve the goals of development' and that it includes as its key attributes: transparency, accountability, responsibility, participation and responsiveness (to the needs of the people), see OHCHR, 'Good Governance and Human Rights: Overview' <http://www.ohchr.org/en/Issues/Development/GoodGovernance/Pages/GoodGovernanceIndex.aspx> accessed 18 August 2014.

more difficult for both States and investors to navigate IIAs, as it is hard to anticipate with a reasonable degree of certainty what conduct might constitute a breach under the treaty.

Second, as tribunals interpreted the typically open-ended provisions contained in IIAs, it emerged that the levels of protection granted to foreign investments and investors in these instruments was expanding beyond that which many States may have anticipated when they entered the IIL system. On the one hand, the underlying State conduct challenged by investors included issues that went far beyond what was expected to be covered by claims on expropriation or minimum standards of treatment, which arguably were the primary concern of States.[21] Over time, investors began to challenge State regulatory actions that touched on the public domain, such as regulations regarding health, human rights or the environment.[22]

On the other hand, the interpretation of IIA provisions by arbitral tribunals seem to have resulted in levels of protection that go beyond what national courts would extend, even in developed countries. A recent analysis by Lise Johnson and Oleksandr Volkov illustrates this point by examining the question of liability for generally applicable government measures that may impact investments in both arbitral case law and the decisions of US courts. The chapter argues that some arbitral interpretations have established a sort of *de facto* rule providing that the stability of a legal framework is an essential element of the fair and equitable treatment (FET) standard. Therefore changes to national legislation that

---

21 Nadakavukaren Schefer (n 16) 8.

22 See, e.g., *Methanex Corporation v United States of America* (UNCITRAL) (challenging regulation seeking to ban a petrol additive for reasons of public safety, health and the environment); *Vattenfall AB, Vattenfall Europe AG, Vattenfall Europe Generation AG v Federal Republic of Germany*, ICSID Case No ARB/09/6 (challenge to environmental restrictions placed on a coal-burning power plant); *Metalclad Corporation v United Mexican States*, ICSID Case No ARB(AF)/97/1 (amongst others, challenge of the designation by ecological decree of the claimant's property as a protected natural area); *Técnicas Medioambientales Tecmed SA v United Mexican States*, ICSID Case No ARB(AF)/00/2 (challenge to denial of a licence to a landfill operator on environmental grounds); *Piero Foresti, Laura De Carli and others v Republic of South Africa*, ICSID Case No ARB(AF)/07/1 (challenge to government measure aimed at ensuring that historically discriminated against persons had adequate opportunities); *Philip Morris Brands Sàrl, Philip Morris Products SA and Abal Hermanos SA v Oriental Republic of Uruguay*, ICSID Case No ARB/10/7 (challenge to regulation on tobacco packaging designed to protect human health).

are inconsistent with a promise previously made to an investor can be a breach of FET, prompting compensation. Some tribunals have qualified this 'stabilization rule', but it is still flexible and inconsistent. Meanwhile, US courts have analysed this same question for over 200 years. Using the doctrines of 'sovereign acts' and 'unmistakability', which contain strict conditions for liability, US courts give much more deference to government actions than IIL arbitral tribunals.[23]

Therefore, rather than having a positive impact on States' institutional and regulatory framework, it could be argued that the ISDS game may also place new limitations on governments' policy space that prevent them from enacting measures that are necessary to meet their development goals. Thus, IIAs are sometimes perceived as unduly inhibiting the ability of States to use their sovereign power to regulate areas key to sustainable development such as human rights, the environment and public health, resulting in what has been called a 'chill' effect on governments' ability to regulate.[24]

---

[23] Lise Johnson and Oleksandr Volkov, 'Investor-State Contracts, Host-State "Commitments" and the Myth of Stability in International Law' (2013) 24(3) *American Review of International Arbitration* 362, 374–5 and 382–401.

[24] A recent case highlights this phenomenon quite well. In 2011, Philip Morris brought an IIA case against Australia for State regulations relating to tobacco packaging that it claims violated an IIA. Australia had passed its national legislation in order to comply with its obligations under the Framework Convention on Tobacco Control (FCTC), a World Health Organization (WHO) treaty that obliges signatory States to enact national legislation of the sort that Australia did – for example, one aspect of Australia's legislation requires packaging that does not indicate that certain cigarettes are 'lighter' or 'milder' than others, see UNCTAD, 'International Investment Law and the WHO Framework Convention on Tobacco Control', IIA Issues Note (forthcoming). While this case is pending, New Zealand, another party to the FCTC Convention, indicated that it was putting on hold its plans to enact similar national legislation in order to see what the outcome of the *Philip Morris v Australia* case becomes. See Statement by Tariana Turia, Associate Minister of Health of New Zealand (19 February 2013) <http://www.beehive.govt.nz/release/government-moves-forward-plain-packaging-tobacco-products> accessed 18 August 2014. A similar reaction was adopted by parliamentarians in Malaysia when presented with proposed legislation to limit advertising for tobacco products. See Bill O'Toole, 'Mandalay Civil Society Calls for EU Treaty Halt' (*The Myanmar Times*, 7 July 2014) <http://www.mmtimes.com/index.php/business/10915-mandalay-civil-society-calls-for-eu-treaty-halt.html> accessed 18 August 2014.

D. Asymmetry in Rights and Obligations between Investors and States

IIAs have been criticised for being a 'one-way street' justice system where investors enjoy broad standards of protection enforced through international arbitration with no counterbalance or safeguards that conditions these protections on a minimum standard of responsible conduct. States have undertaken obligations in IIAs with little or no corresponding obligations on investors, and most IIAs do not explicitly provide that the host State has the ability to assert counterclaims. Further, IIAs do not expressly offer a way to foster responsible business conduct[25] or require positive contributions to the sustainable development of the host State.[26] On the contrary, many IIAs limit the possibility to request those contributions by, for example, prohibiting performance requirements.[27] Finally, IIAs have few safeguards to prevent investors that have allegedly been involved in illegal conduct or have caused negative impacts on

---

[25] Recent IIAs, in particular in the form of free trade agreements (FTAs), have started to include provisions exhorting governments to promote corporate social responsibility. However, according to the OECD, only 12% of the entire stock of IIAs contains language on sustainable development or responsible business conduct, see OECD (n 13).

[26] Some arbitral tribunals, however, have determined that in order for there to be a covered investment, the investment must contribute to the development of the host State, which puts some obligation on the investor. This is called the *Salini* test. However, there is a debate between arbitration professionals as to whether an investment needs to contribute to the host State development in order to qualify as an investment and there is a divide in the approaches taken by tribunals; see, e.g., *Jan de Nul NV and Dredging International NV v The Arab Republic of Egypt*, ICSID Case No ARB/04/13, Decision on Jurisdiction (16 June 2006) para 91; Emmanuel Gaillard, 'Identify or Define? Reflections on the Evolution of the Concept of Investment in ICSID Practice' in Christina Binder and others (eds), *International Investment Law for the 21st Century: Essays in Honour of Christoph Schreuer* (OUP 2009) 403.

[27] The Canada-Colombia FTA offers an interesting example. While it includes a provision urging governments to encourage companies to voluntarily incorporate corporate social responsibility standards (Article 816), this provision prohibits States from imposing or enforcing a series of requirements, including: achieving a given level or percentage of domestic content; purchasing, using or according preference to goods produced in the territory of the host State; or the transfer of technology, a production process or other proprietary knowledge to a person in the host State. Although some of the prohibitions are subject to exceptions, these are limited and difficult to interpret and apply.

people and the environment from being covered by the protection of the treaty and receiving compensation.[28]

E. Roles and Power of Arbitrators

Criticism has been made of the fact that IIAs have vested arbitrators with the power to review sovereign acts involving the exercise of public authority by the host State – including potentially any executive, legislative or judicial acts of the State – without the guarantees of accountability, openness and independence of the judiciary.[29] In fact, an increasing number of challenges to arbitrators may suggest that arbitrators are perceived as biased or predisposed.[30] Concerns have also arisen from the perceived tendency of disputing parties to appoint arbitrators that may be sympathetic to their cases. The interest of arbitrators of being re-appointed in future cases and their frequent 'hat changes' (serving as arbitrators in some cases and counsel in others) has been cited as increasing independence and impartiality concerns.[31]

More broadly, it has been alleged that arbitrators lack contextualisation regarding the issues that they have to address. In addition to originating from a small community, arbitrators are generally geographically uniform, as they tend to come from Europe and the United States, and often have experience with commercial law rather than with public matters and

[28] For example, in *Siemens AG v The Argentine Republic* (ICSID Case No ARB/02/8), the investor was compensated more than USD 200 million for Argentina's breach of its IIA obligations with respect to a contract that had been obtained through corruption. In other instances, the investor's conduct has been contested either by the State or by interested third parties that take part in the arbitrations (e.g. *Chevron Corporation and Texaco Petroleum Corporation v The Republic of Ecuador,* UNCITRAL, PCA Case No 2009-23; *Biwater Gauff (Tanzania) Ltd v The United Republic of Tanzania,* ICSID Case No ARB/05/22; *Suez, Sociedad General de Aguas de Barcelona SA and Vivendi Universal SA v The Argentine Republic*, ICSID Case No ARB/03/19).

[29] Gus Van Harten, *Investment Treaty Arbitration and Public Law* (OUP 2007) 5.

[30] Chiara Giorgetti, 'Challenges to Arbitrators in International Disputes: Two Tribunals Reject the "Appearance of Bias" Standard' (2012) 16(20) ASIL Insights <http://www.asil.org/insights/volume/16/issue/20/challenges-arbitrators-international-disputes-two-tribunals-reject-> accessed 18 August 2014; Karel Daele, *Challenges and Disqualification of Arbitrators in International Arbitration* (Kluwer Law International 2012).

[31] See UNCTAD, 'Reform of Investor-State Dispute Settlement: In Search of a Roadmap' IIA Issues Note No 2 (June 2013) 4 <http://unctad.org/en/PublicationsLibrary/webdiaepcb2013d4_en.pdf> accessed 18 August 2014.

the exercise of normative and regulatory powers. Further, these arbitrators are unlikely to be familiar with the nuanced needs of and realities facing respondent States, thus overriding public interest concerns of the States affected by arbitral awards.[32] This raises serious concerns regarding the protection of interests inherent to sustainable development, such as the protection of human rights and the environment.

* * *

In sum, as applied by arbitral tribunals through ISDS, IIAs have revealed a series of features that not only seem to go beyond what was initially intended by States, but also appear to pose challenges to sustainable development objectives. An increasing number of stakeholders consider that IIAs' focus on protection has resulted in a 'single-goal litigation game' that is ineffective in improving investment climates and good governance, while lacking transparency and effective public participation. Similarly, there are concerns that IIAs contain broad and ambiguous rules, may constrain regulatory space, and have asymmetrical rights and obligations between States and investors. Finally, the role and power of arbitrators has also been called into question. These concerns have led to calls of re-assessing IIAs and IIL, with an increasing focus on sustainable development considerations, and have prompted efforts by UNCTAD to contribute to re-thinking IIL through a development lens.

IV. UNCTAD'S CONTRIBUTION TO RE-THINKING IIL AND ITS RELATION TO SUSTAINABLE DEVELOPMENT

UNCTAD has contributed to shaping not only the notion of sustainable development but also the evolution of IIL. In this way, UNCTAD is in a unique position to gauge the relationship between sustainable development and IIL and to develop practical tools to assist States that are examining this relationship and their investment policies. This Part will first discuss UNCTAD's mandated role regarding IIL and sustainable development, before describing some of its contributions to this area: the

[32] Sundaresh Menon, 'International Arbitration: The Coming of a New Age for Asia (and Elsewhere)' (ICCA Congress, Singapore, 11 June 2012) 12, para 32 <http://www.arbitration-icca.org/media/0/13398435632250/ags_opening_speech_icca_congress_2012.pdf> accessed 18 August 2014.

Investment Policy Framework for Sustainable Development (IPFSD) and paths for reform of ISDS and the IIA regime.

A. UNCTAD's Role Regarding the Development of IIL and Sustainable Development

As the principal UN body for investment and development matters, UNCTAD has an important role to play, as reflected in the mandate it is given by its 194 members.[33] The Accra Accord and Accra Declaration that came out of the 2008 UNCTAD XII Conference provided that UNCTAD should focus on the development dimension and effects of IIAs.[34] The Accra mandates contain a number of important reflections on the role that investment plays in development, which are crucial to understanding the need to re-assess the role of IIL:

- First, the Declaration acknowledged that the benefits that FDI can bring to host economies are not automatic but that in order '[t]o seize opportunities, countries need active and well-sequenced policies to maximize the development benefits of investment flows.'[35]
- Second, the Accord made it clear that FDI could not only bring benefits but that it could also result in negative impacts. The Accord noted that '[a]long with the expected benefits of FDI, potential risks include crowding out local investments, anti-competitive practices, transfer pricing and environmental and social impacts.' The focus on generating high levels on FDI therefore had to switch to one that considers 'both the quality and quantity of FDI.'[36]

With respect to IIAs, the Accra Accord emphasised the need

---

[33] For more on UNCTAD's original mandate and historical evolution see Diana Rosert and Elisabeth Tuerk, 'UNCTAD's Role in Addressing International Investment Trends and Challenges' (2013) 4 *European Yearbook of International Economic Law* 537; UNCTAD, 'UNCTAD at 50: A Short History' (2014) <http://unctad.org/en/PublicationsLibrary/osg2014d1_en.pdf> accessed 18 August 2014. For a list of current UNCTAD Member States see <http://unctad.org/en/Pages/About%20UNCTAD/UNCTADs-Membership.aspx> accessed 18 August 2014.

[34] UNCTAD, 'UNCTAD XII: Accra Accord and the Accra Declaration' (Accra, Ghana, 20–25 April 2008) 58, 60, paras 146, 151 <http://unctad.org/es/Docs/iaos20082_en.pdf> accessed 18 August 2014 [hereinafter Accra Accord and Accra Declaration].

[35] Ibid 3, para 13.

[36] Ibid 50, para 111.

> to balance the interests of home countries, host countries and foreign investors. The settlement of disputes between investors and States deserves special attention, and national capacities to negotiate development-friendly investment agreements need to be enhanced.[37]

Regarding UNCTAD, it further noted that:

> UNCTAD's work on investment should continue to assist all developing countries … [with] the objective of sustainable development and a supportive investment climate in national development strategies … It should focus on the development dimension of IIAs and examine the effects of IIAs … .[38]

The 2012 Doha Ministerial Conference that followed the Accra Conference further called for focusing on the impact of FDI on inclusive growth and sustainable development.[39] The Conference recognized that FDI should be promoted in a manner complementary to the development priorities of host States, particularly through investment policies with a strong focus on sustainable development and inclusive growth.[40]

Against this background, UNCTAD has carried out its work programme on IIAs, which led to the launching of the IPFSD[41] in 2012 and to proposing ways for re-thinking and reforming IIAs and ISDS as described below.

B. UNCTAD's IPFSD

The IPFSD clearly sets out the challenges posed by national and international investment policymaking and offers concrete policy guidance on how to develop investment policies that are geared towards sustainable development. It is a tool created to meet the needs of governments that wish to ensure the promotion of investment in their territory and at the same time ensure that this investment contributes to

---

37 Ibid 51, para 113.

38 Ibid 60, para 151.

39 'The Doha Mandate' (Doha, Qatar, 21–26 April 2012) (31 May 2012) UN Doc TD/500/Add.1, 13–14, paras 58 and 65.

40 Ibid para 58.

41 The IPFSD seeks to, on the one hand, ensure sustainable development goals are incorporated into IIAs, thus balancing the IIA regime, and, on the other hand, promote FDI. UNCTAD, 'Investment Policy Framework for Sustainable Development' (2012) <http://unctad.org/en/PublicationsLibrary/webdiaepcb 2012d6_en.pdf> accessed 18 August 2014 [hereinafter IPFSD].

sustainable development. The IPFSD is not a negotiated text or undertaking between States, but rather the result of numerous consultations with IIL and development experts.[42]

The IPFSD consists of: (i) eleven Core Principles, which aim to inform national and international investment policymaking; (ii) Guidelines for National Investment Policies; and (iii) Options for IIA negotiators.

The eleven Core Principles of the IPFSD are: 1) investment for sustainable development; 2) policy coherence; 3) public governance and institutions; 4) dynamic policymaking; 5) balanced rights and obligations; 6) right to regulate; 7) openness to investment; 8) investment protection and treatment; 9) investment promotion and facilitations; 10) corporate governance and responsibility; and 11) international cooperation.

The Guidelines for National Investment Policies translate the overarching eleven Core Principles into concrete guidelines at the national level. While maintaining an attractive investment climate in States, the Guidelines aim to ensure that a State's investment policy is coherent with its overall development strategy, augment the sustainable development impact of FDI projects, and promote responsible investment.[43]

The Core Principles also translate into Options for IIA negotiators in the form of clause-by-clause suggestions and comments on the various options, where appropriate, with emphasis on their contribution to sustainable development.[44] These policy options can help address some

---

[42] During its conception, its drafters took stock of related instruments, such as the UN Guiding Principles on Business and Human Rights, the World Bank Guidelines on the Treatment of Foreign Investments, the UN Global Compact, and the OECD Guidelines for Multinational Enterprises, amongst others; see IPFSD (n 41) 10, box 3.

[43] For example, the IPFSD proposes that environmental impact assessments (EIAs) be carried out in a non-discriminatory, stable, predictable and transparent manner as part of national investment policies as a way to enable a State seeking to attract FDI to try to ensure that such projects would be environmentally sustainable.

[44] The IPFSD does not provide sample treaty language. UNCTAD has other resources that offer examples of clauses and alternative drafting such as the APEC Handbook and the Pink Series; see APEC Committee on Trade and Investment, Investment Experts Group, 'International Investment Agreement Negotiators Handbook: APEC/UNCTAD Modules (IIA Handbook)' (December 2012) <http://investmentpolicyhub.unctad.org/Upload/Documents/UNCTAD_APEC%20Handbook.pdf> accessed 18 August 2014; see also, e.g., UNCTAD, *Scope and Definition: A Sequel* (United Nations 2011).

of sustainable development and overall challenges discussed in Part II, as illustrated below.

First, the IPFSD can help change the 'single-goal' game into a 'multi-goal' game that is better suited to meeting today's sustainable development imperative, for example, by providing drafting options for provisions that refer to investments' contribution to sustainable development and good governance.[45] Further, the earlier focus on investors obtaining compensation through arbitration is complemented by an emphasis on the development of institutional, regulatory and policy capacity (in particular, through the IPFSD's section on national investment policies).[46]

Another contribution of the IPFSD in this regard is its focus on maximizing development benefits from FDI. This includes States' abilities to be selective in their FDI attraction efforts, focusing them on the type of investments that better fulfil their development needs (e.g. by carving out specific policy areas and/or industries from the scope of the treaty or selectively entering into liberalization commitments), or to use performance requirements and related operational constraints when necessary to achieve legitimate policy purposes.[47]

Second, the IPFSD also contains suggestions for strengthened transparency and stakeholder engagement, such as by fostering the accessibility of documents and public participation.[48] Transparency of ISDS claims can also allow for more adequate representation of stakeholder interests, prevent non-transparent deals and stimulate tribunals to integrate in their analysis relevant sustainable development concerns that ensure a balanced and contextualised assessment of the case.

Third, the IPFSD provides clause-by-clause options for different treaty provisions to reduce their ambiguity and reach, for example, by including an exhaustive list of State obligations under FET.[49] The IPFSD also suggests including interpretive guides to tribunals in the preamble, such

---

[45] IPFSD (n 41) 48, Option 1.

[46] Capacity building for the implementation of IIAs, rather than a focus on enforcement, is also at the core of UNCTAD's work on Dispute Prevention Policies (DPPs). IPFSD Option 2.1.8. of national policies and Options 2.3 and 4.9 of policy options for IIAs. Performance requirements need to be in compliance with international obligations and would typically be imposed principally as conditions for special privileges, including fiscal or financial incentives.

[47] See IPFSD (n 41) 58, Option 7.

[48] Ibid 57, Option 6.3.

[49] Ibid 51, Option 4.3.

as stressing that the objective of investor protection shall not override States' right to regulate.[50] The IPFSD also considers the inclusion of clauses in IIAs that stipulate that if there is a conflict between an IIA and a host State's other international commitments in areas related to public policy, such as health or the environment, the latter shall prevail.[51]

The IPFSD can additionally help address concerns about the limitations that IIAs can pose on governments' policy space and reduce the exposure of the host State to litigation: for example, the IPFSD has options to include carve-outs and exceptions for measures of general applicability that relate to the adoption of domestic regulatory measures that aim to pursue legitimate public policy objectives such as the protection of human rights, public health and the environment, or preserving cultural diversity.[52] The IPFSD notes that:

> To date few IIAs include public policy exceptions. However, more recent treaties increasingly reaffirm States' right to regulate in the public interest by introducing general exceptions. Such provisions make IIAs more conducive to SD [sustainable development] goals, foster coherence between IIAs and other public policy objectives, and reduce States' exposure to claims arising from any conflict that may occur between the interests of a foreign investor and the promotion and protection of legitimate public-interest objectives.[53]

Fourth, the IPFSD can help reduce the asymmetry inherent in IIAs. The UNCTAD framework provides options for IIA clauses that contain investor obligations,[54] incorporate corporate social responsibility (CSR) standards,[55] or permit States to make counterclaims.[56]

Finally, the IPFSD provides policy options to address some of the perceived problems surrounding investment arbitrators and, more generally, the institutional set-up of the ISDS system. For example, the IPFSD suggests considering permanent or quasi-permanent arbitrators or an appellate mechanism, or placing caps on arbitrator fees.[57] Further, IIAs

---

50 Ibid 48, Section 1.

51 Ibid 58, Option 8.

52 Other policy objectives could include ensuring compliance with laws and regulations that are not inconsistent with the treaty, allowing for prudential measures (e.g. to preserve the integrity and stability of the financial system) or ensuring the provision of essential social services (e.g. health, education, water supply).

53 IPFSD (n 41) 55, Option 5.

54 See ibid 58, Option 7.

55 Ibid.

56 Ibid 56, Option 6.2.1.

57 Ibid 57, Option 6.3.

can provide that certain types of disputes concerning sensitive policy areas, such as tax or prudential measures, be submitted to the competent authorities of the parties for a preliminary joint determination of the existence of a breach under the treaty.[58]

As shown by the above examples, the IPFSD offers a framework that helps policymakers make investment supportive of sustainable development. The IPFSD notes that it is crucial for States to examine their national investment policies and their existing or future IIAs as a comprehensive whole in order to ensure that sustainable development and governance needs are catered for.

The clause-by-clause policy options laid out in the IPFSD are not just for prospective treaties, but can also be used in treaties that are already in existence, for example, by inspiring governments to adopt notes of interpretation of and protocols to existing treaties.[59] They can also be used in the process of renegotiating treaties. As documented in the 2013 World Investment Report (WIR), by the end of 2013, more than 1,300 bilateral investment treaties (BITs) were at the stage where they could be terminated or renegotiated at any time, creating a window of opportunity to address inconsistencies and overlaps in the multi-faceted and multi-layered IIA regime, and to strengthen its development dimension.[60]

However, the IPFSD, even if used by an increasing number of countries, cannot resolve all of the perceived or actual shortcomings of the current IIA regime. Instead, there is need for a holistic approach, an issue that was discussed in more depth in the 2013 and 2014 WIRs.

C. Towards Comprehensive Reform of the IIA Regime

Since the launch of the IPFSD, UNCTAD's work on IIL and sustainable development was expanded upon in UNCTAD's 2013 and 2014 WIRs (and is anticipated to continue in the 2015 WIR). The 2013 WIR laid out five paths of reform for ISDS: 1) promoting alternative dispute resolution; 2) tailoring the existing system through individual IIAs; 3) limiting investor access to IIAs; 4) creating an appeals facility; and 5) creating a

---

58 Ibid.

59 See UNCTAD, 'Interpretation of IIAs: What States Can Do' IIA Issues Note No 3 (December 2011) <http://unctad.org/en/docs/webdiaeia2011d10_en.pdf> accessed 18 August 2014.

60 However, in determining whether to renegotiate or terminate IIAs, States should weigh the pros and cons in the context of their investment climate and their overall development strategies, see UNCTAD, *World Investment Report 2013* (United Nations 2013) 109.

standing international investment court. Each suggestion goes toward specific concerns with the current regime as discussed above, and each has its own advantages and disadvantages.[61]

Building on the recognition that almost all countries are parties to one or several IIAs, but that many are dissatisfied with the current regime, UNCTAD's 2014 WIR lays out four ways of responding to the current situation: 1) maintaining the status quo, i.e., continuing to sign traditional IIAs without incorporating sustainable development elements into them; 2) disengaging entirely from the IIA regime, by, for example, terminating IIAs or denouncing multilateral arbitration conventions; 3) making selective adjustments, such as by including considerations discussed in the IPFSD (sustainable development considerations, exceptions, carve-outs, etc.) into IIAs but leaving most of the current system untouched; and 4) undertaking systematic reform that aims to address the IIA challenges holistically.[62] Each of these paths of action has benefits and drawbacks; however, the systematic reform path could most effectively address the complexities of the IIA regime and bring it in line with the sustainable development imperative.[63] As stated in WIR 2014:

> [S]ystematic reform means designing international commitments that promote sustainable development and that are in line with the investment and development paradigm shift (WIR 2012). With policy actions at all levels of governance, this is the most comprehensive approach to reforming the current IIA regime. This path of action would entail the design of a new IIA treaty model that effectively [increases the development dimension, rebalances rights and obligations, manages the systemic complexity of the IIA regime and] focuses on proactively promoting investment for sustainable development. Systemic reform would also entail comprehensively dealing with the reform of the ISDS system … .[64]

V. CONCLUSION

The effort to re-think IIL to ensure it is compatible with sustainable development is on-going and needs the support of all actors concerned, in particular, States.

---

[61] UNCTAD, *In Search of a Roadmap* (n 31).

[62] UNCTAD, 'Reform of the IIA Regime: Four Paths of Action and a Way Forward' IIA Issues Note No 3 (June 2014) <http://investmentpolicyhub.unctad.org/Upload/IIA%20ISSUES%20NOTE%20NO%203.pdf> accessed 18 August 2014.

[63] Ibid.

[64] UNCTAD, *WIR 2014* (n 2) 130.

Some States have determined that exiting multilateral arbitration conventions or ceasing to negotiate IIAs is the best method to protect the ability to regulate and account for sustainable development and good governance. Whether other States in the system will accept this to be the case remains to be seen, and some reports indicate that some States still believe that IIAs provide the best guarantees of protection for the investments of their investors.[65] However, for those deciding to maintain their IIAs, the IPFSD provides useful tools for alleviating the strains caused on the system by those aforementioned features of IIL by enhancing policy space for countries' development strategies.

In addition, re-fashioning IIAs following the IPFSD and other efforts to integrate sustainable development concerns will pose important challenges to arbitrators. They will need to get acquainted with new concepts that will play an increasingly relevant role in the system, such as sustainable development, human rights due diligence, environmental and human rights impact assessments and CSR. A judicious assumption of the decision-making process under the renewed IIAs will require arbitrators capable not only of addressing the conceptual challenges but also of understanding the needs of the communities and governments affected by their adjudicatory function. The work of counsel will also need to adapt to these changes.

In sum, holistic, coordinated and sustainability-oriented reform has many dimensions. IIA negotiators and the arbitration community both have many options at hand to help ensure that IIL and sustainable development build a fruitful friendship. UNCTAD has played, and will likely continue to play, an important role in providing policymakers and States with tools to ensure that they are able to reap the most sustainable benefits of that friendship.

---

[65] See, e.g., Linda Ensor, 'Move to Ease German, EU Doubts over Investor Risk in SA' (*Business Day BDlive*, 20 August 2013) <http://www.bdlive.co.za/economy/2013/08/30/move-to-ease-german-eu-doubts-over-investor-risk-in-sa?utm_source=API&utm_medium=twitter> accessed 18 August 2014; Chantelle Benjamin, 'Swiss Govt Reacts to Termination of Investment Treaty with SA' (*Mail & Guardian*, 1 November 2013) <http://mg.co.za/article/2013-11-01-swiss-govt-reacts-to-termination-of-bilateral-investment-treaty-with-sa> accessed 18 August 2014.

6. Reviving the emperor's old clothes: The good governance agenda, development and international investment law

Celine Tan*

I. INTRODUCTION

The concept of 'good governance' has long occupied a central space in contemporary development policy. Originally conceived and promulgated widely by development agencies, notably the World Bank, in response to concerns over the effectiveness of development assistance, the good governance agenda quickly gained broader currency as a tool of international economic law and policymaking. In the realm of international investment, the notion of good governance has been regularly enrolled by its proponents to advocate for and facilitate institutional reforms in developing countries aimed at creating what is termed 'an enabling climate' for foreign direct investment (FDI). Here, the design of the institutional framework of domestic governance, particularly those which manage and regulate the entry and conduct of foreign investors, are seen as crucial to capacity of developing countries to attract and sustain FDI and thereby engendering economic growth and development.

In terms of international investment law, the language of good governance, its associated rule of law narrative and their relationship to development outcomes have been used to justify the normative and institutional evolution of law and policy in this area. Specifically, notions

* I would like to thank Rumana Islam for her research assistance and Ryan Ferro for his editorial work on this chapter and to the editors of this collection, especially Christian Tams and Stephan Schill, for their constructive suggestions and comments. I am also grateful to Koen de Feyter and Andrea Saldarriaga for their comments on an earlier draft of the chapter. All errors and omissions remain my own.

of stability, predictability and efficacy that feature prominently on the good governance and rule of law agenda have been widely conscripted to legitimise the rapid proliferation of international investment agreements (IIAs) and the attendant ascendency of the investment arbitration regime over the past two decades.

More recently, as global criticism of and dissatisfaction with the current regime of investment law have intensified, the narratives of good governance and development have re-emerged as instruments of both critique and crisis containment of the legal framework for international investment. Reflecting the contested interpretative terrain that underpins these discourses, the concepts of good governance and the rule of law have alternately provided the language for challenging contemporary international investment law while supplying the scripts for a counter-discourse that seeks to rehabilitate the normative and institutional credibility of the existing investment regime. Crucially, the discourse of good governance, framed in the context of development outcomes for host states, has once again been harnessed to justify the regulatory reforms of and limits placed on governmental action by international investment law.

This chapter examines the problematic revival of the good governance agenda and its relationship to international investment law and development. First, the chapter reviews the origins of the good governance concept as a tool of development policy and practice, locating its inception and evolution within a particular policy and operational context. Second, the chapter interrogates the agenda's pivotal role in supplying the conceptual framework on which contemporary international investment law and policy is premised. In particular, the chapter examines how the language of good governance has been instrumental in providing a justificatory link between international investment law and economic and social development in host states. The chapter then proceeds to evaluate how the contemporary investment protection regime measures up to the same indicators of good governance subscribed to and promulgated by international development agencies.

In doing so, the chapter considers how the same discourse has alternately served as a potentially transformative narrative for confronting the negative dislocations of the investment framework at the same time as it is being utilised to diffuse systemic criticism and rehabilitate the credibility of the regime. Here, the chapter cautions against the ahistorical import of the good governance agenda into the international investment law and policy unless accompanied by a broader systemic review and reform of the regime. It argues that while the discourse of good governance and development offers a useful prism for reflecting upon and/or challenging the substantive and procedural limitations of international investment law, the utility of these concepts must be placed within the broader context in which they were conceived and applied in law, policy and practice.

II. GOOD GOVERNANCE AS A DEVELOPMENT CONSTRUCT

A. Crisis Containment

The genesis of the good governance agenda can be traced back to the conceptual shifts in development policymaking in the late 1980s and throughout the 1990s, driven by rapidly changing global economic and geo-political circumstances. Led by the World Bank, its key intellectual actor and financier, the emergence of the good governance project can be situated within a broader movement by the international development sector to recast the conceptual and operational premise of official development assistance in light of growing criticism that the development interventions of the postwar period were failing to deliver the outcomes envisioned by its architects, with developing countries remaining mired in a chronic poverty and debt trap.

Specifically, international development practitioners were confronted with two distinct but interrelated challenges at the close of the 1980s. Firstly, the Washington Consensus model of economic organisation that informed the design of structural adjustment programmes over the past decade was failing to engender the expected economic growth and generating social and economic dislocations, including the exacerbation of income disparities and structural inequalities within and between states.[1] Instead, the withdrawal or reduction of state support in key economic and social sectors, coupled with the removal of government controls over trade and financial flows, had 'weakened the state as an institution'[2] removing not only its productive role in the economy but also much of its regulatory and administrative functions. Secondly and

---

[1] Rita Abrahamsen, *Disciplining Democracy: Development Discourse and Good Governance in Africa* (Zed Books 2000) 37–8; Structural Adjustment Participatory Review International Network (SAPRIN), *Structural Adjustment: The SAPRI Report: The Policy Roots of Economic Crisis, Poverty and Inequality* (Zed Books 2004) 1–4.

[2] SAPRIN (n 1) 76.

relatedly, concerns with weak governance of state agencies and fractured mechanisms for public accountability and democratic decision-making in aid recipient states had led to increasing public awareness in both donor and recipient states over the efficacy of development assistance. This, along with frustration with fragmented aid structures and processes, resulted in corresponding demands for greater transparency of and accountability for aid.[3]

Influenced by the institutional turn in economics, rooted in the work of Robert Coase and popularised by Douglass North and, latterly, Joseph Stiglitz, chief economist at the World Bank at the time of this conceptual shift,[4] good governance provided an expedient conceptual framework for addressing these latent concerns of the development practitioners while maintaining the credibility of past and future aid programmes. Emerging from and refined by a series of reports from the World Bank,[5] the good governance agenda reconceptualises the relationship between the state and the market, viewing the state as central to the promotion of economic

---

[3] Martin Doombos, '"Good Governance": The Rise and Decline of a Policy Metaphor?' (2001) 37(6) *The Journal of Development Studies* 93, 97–102; Stephen Humphreys, *Theatre of the Rule of Law: Transnational Legal Intervention in Theory and Practice* (CUP 2010) 133–5; Carlos Santiso, 'Development Finance, Governance and Conditionality: Politics Matter' (2004) 7(1) *International Public Management Journal* 73, 75–6.

[4] Toby Carroll, *Delusions of Development: The World Bank and the Post-Washington Consensus in Southeast Asia* (Palgrave Macmillan 2010) 70–82; Tor Krever, 'The Legal Turn in Late Development Theory; the Rule of Law and the World Bank's Development Model' (2011) 52(1) Harv ILJ 287, 302–4.

[5] The concept of good governance was first mooted in a World Bank report on sub-Saharan Africa that characterised the crisis in Africa as 'a crisis of governance' and elaborated and expanded in subsequent documents, most notably in its landmark report on *Governance and Development* in 1992 (World Bank 1992), the Bank's governance and anti-corruption strategy, *Reforming Public Institutions and Strengthening Governance* (World Bank 2000) and successive editions of its annual flagship *World Development Reports (WDR)*, including that of 1997 on *The State in a Changing World* (World Bank and OUP 1997), *Building Institutions for Markets* in 2002 (World Bank and OUP 2002) and *A Better Investment Climate for Everyone* in 2005 (World Bank 2005). For a historical review of the Bank's conceptual thinking see Krever (n 4); Carlos Santiso, 'Good Governance and Aid Effectiveness: The World Bank and Conditionality' (2001) 7(1) *The Georgetown Public Policy Review* 1; Santiso (n 3).

development, not as a primary provider of goods and services but rather as 'a partner, catalyst and facilitator' of the market.[6]

The central message of the good governance agenda was and continues to be that structural and macroeconomic reforms are insufficient to generate economic growth and social development outcomes without an enabling institutional environment to underpin them. According to this approach, success of economic reform programmes and efficacy of development interventions are dependent on the effectiveness of institutions – including the civil service, judicial systems, financial regulators and supervisory authorities, legislatures, and civil society groups[7] – to support them. Good governance, it was argued, entailed not only 'effective participation in public policy-making' but also 'the prevalence of the rule of law and an independent judiciary' and 'institutional checks and balances through horizontal and vertical separation of powers, and effective oversight agencies.'[8]

For its proponents, the good governance agenda served as a credible foil to critics of mainstream development policy and practice at the time, supplying both a conceptual framework to explain the substantive failures of development assistance while providing a technocratic arsenal for tackling the more instrumentalist concerns of aid delivery and effectiveness. The failures of earlier development interventions had therefore less to do with the content of the economic prescriptions themselves than with how these reforms are implemented by recipient governments and whether these governments possess the necessary institutional framework to successfully embed them in pursuit of social and economic objectives. At its core, the good governance agenda seeks at once to both problematise and reinvigorate the role of the state in economic development and social welfare. It recognises the importance of public institutions in the economy but at the same time places the burden of institutional development and effectiveness on the state while legitimising the interventions of

---

[6] World Bank, *WDR 1997* (n 5); also Carroll (n 4) 2–3; David Craig and Doug Porter, *Development Beyond Neoliberalism? Governance, Poverty Reduction and Political Economy* (Routledge 2006) 10–15; David Trubek, 'The Political Economy of the Rule of Law: The Challenge of a New Developmental State' (2009) 1(1) *Hague Journal on the Rule of Law* 28, 31.

[7] World Bank, *WDR 2002* (n 5) 2, Table 1; World Bank, *WDR 1997* (n 5) 7–11.

[8] Santiso, 'Good Governance and Aid Effectiveness' (n 5) 5.

the international development community where such institutional failures are perceived of as inadequate.[9]

B. Disciplining the New Developmental State[10]

A central plank in the good governance agenda is the concept of the rule of law, an instrument through which state power can be curtailed, diffused, and channelled towards creating the environment for economic growth and social development. The rule of law provides a mechanism through which the aforementioned invigorated role of the state in the economy can be managed and delimited. With its emphasis on developing functional judicial, legislative, administrative and regulatory regimes within developing countries, the rule of law supplies 'the normative and institutional structure'[11] to support the construction of a market economy. It does so through the promotion of legal systems which are entrusted 'with the task of protecting individual rights', notably property and contractual rights, 'by constraining the inclination of political power to expand, to act arbitrarily and to abuse its prerogatives.'[12] An effective rule of law is therefore seen as a requirement of this new regulatory developmental state, a bulwark against the exercise of arbitrary state power and excessive state intervention in the economy and a guarantor and an enforcer of private contracts and property transactions.[13]

This emphasis on institutions and the rule of law makes good governance an attractive conceptual paradigm for embedding the law and policy of a nascent international investment regime predicated on liberalisation and investor protection. Indeed, an important component of the governance approach to development policy has been the creation of the aforementioned 'enabling climate' for foreign investment in developing countries and transition economies as a means of incentivising foreign

---

[9] Abrahamsen (n 1) 41–5; Carroll (n 4) 76–8; Santiso, 'Good Governance and Aid Effectiveness' (n 5) 5.

[10] This term is adopted from Trubek's conception of the new functions of the state in contemporary international political economy that is qualitatively different from the classical notion of a developmental state; see Trubek (n 6) 31. In the former, the state assumes a productive role in the economy while the latter conception views the state as a driver for and regulator of private sector activity; ibid.

[11] Pietro Costra and Danilo Zolo, *The Rule of Law: History, Theory and Criticism* (Springer 2007) 19.

[12] Ibid.

[13] Humphreys (n 3) 138–40; Krever (n 4); World Bank, *Initiatives in Legal and Judicial Reform* (World Bank 2004) 2.

direct investment in efforts to deliver developmental outcomes. Efforts to foster this investor-friendly environment in developing countries have ranged from embedding legal and regulatory reform of economic sectors in broader developmental policy loans from the international financial institutions to discrete judicial reform and legal training projects funded through multilateral loans and bilateral donor grants.[14] The World Bank Group, in particular, has been at the forefront of advocating this 'investment climate approach' to development, arguing that countries' transition towards market economies cannot be achieved without legal and institutional reform and 'firmly establishing the rule of law to create the necessary climate of *stability* and *predictability*.'[15]

The emergence of an international legal framework of investment protection in the past two decades builds on the reforms promoted through international development interventions. Consisting of a proliferating network of bilateral investment treaties (BITs) and investment chapters of free trade agreements and an increasingly sophisticated international arbitral system, this regime constitutes a major 'paradigm shift' in international investment law.[16] Unlike the previous, *ad-hoc* landscape of investment protection predicated on customary legal principles and espousal of claims through home states, contemporary international investment law is much more codified, juridified and, some would argue, depoliticised.[17] Proponents of this emerging universe of

---

[14] International Finance Corporation, *International Finance Institutions and Development through the Private Sector: A Joint Report of 31 Multilateral and Bilateral Development Finance Institutions* (International Finance Corporation (IFC) 2011) 33–4; World Bank (n 13) 3–4.

[15] World Bank (n 13) 2.

[16] Stephan W Schill, 'Enhancing International Investment Law's Legitimacy: Conceptual and Methodological Foundations of a New Public Law Approach' (2011) 52 Va JIL 57, 74–5.

[17] See José E Alvarez, *The Public International Law Regime Governing International Investment* (Brill 2011) 59; Ibrahim FI Shihata, 'Toward a Greater Depoliticization of Investment Disputes: The Roles of ICSID and MIGA' in Kevin W Lu, Gero Verheyen and Srilal M Perera (eds), *Investing with Confidence: Understanding Political Risk Management in the 21st Century* (Multilateral Investment Guarantee Agency 2009) 2. The depoliticisation aspect refers to the right of foreign investors under investment treaties to bring claims directly against host states in an ostensibly neutral international forum, thereby extricating host states from involvement in such disputes as was the case under the system of state espousal of claims; see Alvarez (n 17) 99; Susan D Franck, 'Foreign Direct Investment, Investment Treaty Arbitration, and the Rule of Law' (2007) 19 *Global Business & Development Law Journal* 337, 343–4; Shihata (n 17) 4–6.

IIAs and arbitral tribunals argue that it provides a stable and predictable regime of investment governance that is crucial because of the evolving nature of 'political risk', especially in emerging markets and developing economies. This language correspondingly finds currency among advocates of the good governance agenda in development policy circles, reinforcing the structural and institutional reforms promoted by the World Bank and other international development agencies. In particular, the emphasis on securing a stable and predictable regulatory framework for the conduct of foreign investment in developing countries was attractive given the changes in the economic fabric of developing countries in the past three decades.

The rapid liberalisation of cross-border capital flows and the mass privatisations of key economic sectors, such as extractive industries and utilities, in developing countries since the mid-1980s significantly shifted the landscape of foreign direct investment. Specifically, the aforementioned changing role of the state from a producer of goods and services to a regulator of a multiplicity of private actors charged with the ownership and operation of economic sectors had led to new concerns over the exercise of state power *vis-à-vis* foreign investors. In a complex domestic landscape which posits the state as an interlocutor between a myriad of local and foreign private actors within an intricate web of transnational and national commercial arrangements, new political risks are argued to arise not from the actions of the government itself but how it balances the relationships between different domestic and foreign constituents.

In other words, risk to investors today is perceived not as stemming primarily from overt interference of states with the proprietary rights of the investor, such as through forced nationalisations of entities or industries, or from the impact of civil insecurity and failure to maintain law and order. Instead, political risk is said to arise from broader use of state regulatory power and the institutional framework – or lack thereof – under which governmental authority is exercised.[18] This is compounded

[18] See Patrick Garver, 'The Changing Face of Political Risk' in Lu, Verheyen and Perera (n 17) 81; Thomas W Wälde, 'The Effectiveness of International Law Disciplines, Rules and Treaties in Reducing the Political and Regulatory Risk for Private Infrastructure Investment in Developing Countries' (Conceptual Study in Preparation for the World Bank Conference on Political and Regulatory Risks in Private Infrastructure Investment, Rome, Italy, 9–10 September 1999) <http://www.dundee.ac.uk/cepmlp/gateway/index.php?news=32119> accessed 18 August 2014.

by the increasing devolution of regulation, including to quasi-governmental and private agencies, and political decentralisation to sub-national entities that further destabilises the domestic framework in which foreign investment takes place. At the same time, the transactional complexities of contemporary investments – that can include multilevel and multinational firm contracting – demand greater institutional and legal stability for enforcement of agreements between private entities to reduce the so-called transactional costs of doing business.[19]

The good governance agenda therefore provides a legitimising discourse for the new structure of international investment law, providing a frame of reference through which the discipline of governmental action *vis-à-vis* the private sector can be justified. The logic of this confluence between development policy and investment rules maintains that good governance is key to attracting foreign investment which in turn translates into economic growth and resources for social development.[20] Here, the problematisation of host state legal and governance regimes as weak and inadequate for the purposes of global economic integration legitimises the interventions of the international community by way of the aforementioned good governance and rule of law projects and latterly by way of legal reform induced by IIAs.

III. INVESTMENT LAW AS GOOD GOVERNANCE

A. Externalisation of Investment Governance

The structure of contemporary international investment law externalises the internal governance of foreign investment by subjecting the exercise of state power in respect to investment policy and practice to an *external* source of law. It requires the exercise of government authority in this area

---

[19] Garver (n 18) 82–3; Thomas W Wälde, 'Changing Directions for International Investment Law in the Global Economy – An Overview of Selected Issues' (1999) 4(2) *CEPMLP Online Journal on Natural Resources, Energy and International Business Transactions* 31 <http://www.dundee.ac.uk/cepmlp/gateway/index.php?news=28140> accessed 18 August 2014.

[20] See Rudolph Dolzer, 'The Impact of International Investment Treaties on Domestic Administrative Law' (2005) 37 NYU JILP 953, 953–4; Franck (n 17) 341; Schill (n 16) 62.

to be made within an externally supervised framework of correspondingly externally derived rules and principles.[21] The existence of this external body of law governing states' relationships with foreign investors coupled with a system of dispute resolution that automatically elevates settlement of state-investor disputes to an international forum therefore constrains state power more effectively than patchy and *ad-hoc* institutional changes implemented through reforms promoted by international development agencies.

IIAs 'lock in' institutional and regulatory changes by making it difficult for states to renege on their commitments to liberalise investment regimes and to establish principles for the treatment of foreign investors that is not dependent on domestic laws or administrative decision-making. Host state regulatory prerogatives are constrained by these agreements through substantive treaty guarantees – including assurances against expropriation without compensation, the fair and equitable treatment (FET) of investors by the host state and guarantees of full protection and security – supported by the right to enforce them outside the host state's legal system through international arbitral tribunals.[22] This right of investors to pursue claims directly against host states in an international forum is a landmark in international law, constituting the broadest expansion of legal personality of private actors in the postwar period. The distinctiveness of this contemporary universe of IIAs is that 'they are designed to function without the political involvement of either host or home governments', enabling, in the majority of cases, foreign investors to file claims against host states before international arbitral tribunals without 'exhausting local remedies at host states' courts, and without authorisation from or endorsement by their own home states.'[23]

---

[21] Santiago Montt, *State Liability in Investment Treaty Arbitration: Global Constitutional and Administrative Law in the BIT Generation* (Hart Publishing 2012) 1–2 and 146–7; W Michael Reisman and Robert D Sloane, 'Indirect Expropriation and its Valuation in the BIT Generation' (2004) 75(1) BYIL 115, 116–17.

[22] Franck (n 17) 342; Montt (n 21) 127.

[23] Montt (n 21) 1–2. This can be contrasted with the so-called 'denial of justice' system under the previous era of investment disputes premised on the customary international legal principle of state responsibility for the mistreatment of aliens; see Montt (n 21) 17–19. Here, the diplomatic protection of home states could only be sought by a foreign investor in a claim against the host state 'once domestic courts [in host states] had acted on the case under dispute' and were found wanting in this regard; ibid.

The reference to an external source of law and enforcement of obligations by an international dispute settlement body conforms ostensibly with the standards of good governance and the rule of law, notably with regard to state action. It situates the exercise of governmental authority within a framework of publicly articulated rules and principles and enables the scrutiny of a state's administrative and legislative acts by an independent tribunal based on its interpretation of these rules and principles.[24] IIAs purportedly resolve what Yackee terms 'the central *problematique* of host state-foreign investor relations': that of the 'obsolescing bargain' where 'the host state will opportunistically interfere with the investment's profitability once the investment has been sunk.'[25] These agreements also overcome the so-called 'dynamic inconsistency problem' for host states, enabling states to commit to an investment project without fear that a future government will interfere with the rights guaranteed to the investor.[26]

The current international investment architecture is therefore said to promote greater investment certainty protecting foreign investors against the risk of reliance on: a) potentially mutable domestic laws of host states governing their investments; and b) potentially partial, politically motivated or incompetent local courts to adjudicate on disputes arising from such investments.[27] Additionally, the privity of an arbitration process designed for commercial disputes also generally restricts the involvement of third parties and excludes considerations of broader social and economic policy issues outside the subject matter of the dispute (a subject to which we return in Section V). In the eyes of foreign investors,

---

[24] Montt (n 21) 147; UNCTAD, 'The Role of International Investment Agreements in Attracting Foreign Direct Investment to Developing Countries' (UNCTAD Series on International Investment Policies for Development 2009) 14–15.

[25] Jason Webb Yackee, 'Bilateral Investment Treaties, Credible Commitment and the Rule of (International) Law: Do BITs Promote Foreign Direct Investment?' (2008) 42(4) *Law and Society Review* 805, 807.

[26] Tom Ginsburg, 'International Substitutes for Domestic Institutions: Bilateral Investment Treaties and Governance' (2005) 25 *International Review of Law and Economics* 107, 113.

[27] Ronald J Daniels, 'Defecting on Development: Bilateral Investment Treaties and the Subversion of the Law of Law in the Developing World' (University of Toronto, Draft dated 23 March 2004) 22–3 <www.unisi.it/lawandeconomics/stile2004/daniels.pdf> accessed 10 January 2014. There is a contrary argument of course that this regime does little to promote certainty in practice due to the broad nature of the provisions in IIAs which render them open to expansive interpretation (see discussion in Section IV.B).

this guards against political opportunism and regulatory interference with investor rights induced by claims from interest groups in host states.[28]

Accordingly, accession to IIAs is often viewed as a corollary development to 'good governance' and 'investment climate' reforms, with entry into such agreements regarded as an indicator of a host state's commitment to enabling a hospitable legal environment for foreign investment. IIA advocates argue that such a commitment by a host state encourages inward investment by signalling 'receptivity to foreign investments' or 'enhancing the state's credibility as a reputable international actor'.[29] Thus, it has been argued that IIAs often serve as substitutes for 'domestic institutional quality',[30] providing a mechanism for the protection of investor rights where such domestic guarantees are weak.[31]

B. Incentivising Domestic Institutions

The importance of IIAs as an indicator of investment governance has led to arguments that the contemporary investment regime incentivises domestic governance reforms. States with weak institutional capacity are compelled to develop 'an effective normative framework' for governance that includes, inter alia, 'impartial courts, an efficient and legally restrained bureaucracy, and the measure of transparency in decision[making] that has increasingly been recognized as a control mechanism over governments.'[32] Recent studies have indicated that IIAs can attract FDI to developing countries but only as a complement rather than a substitute to a hospitable institutional environment.[33] In other words, while international investment agreements can lend credibility to countries with a

---

[28] UNCTAD (n 24) 14–15; Wälde (n 18) 28–9.

[29] Franck (n 17) 341, drawing on Jennifer Tobin and Susan Rose-Ackerman, 'When BITs Have Some Bite: The Political-Economic Environment for Bilateral Investment Treaties' (2011) 6(1) *Review of International Organizations* 1; Andrew Guzman, 'Why LDCs Sign Treaties that Hurt Them: Explaining the Popularity of Bilateral Investment Treaties' (1998) 38(4) Va JIL 639; Kenneth J Vandevelde, 'The Economics of Bilateral Investment Treaties' (2000) 41(2) Harv ILJ 469.

[30] Eric Neumayer and Laura Spess, 'Do Bilateral Investment Treaties Increase Foreign Direct Investment to Developing Countries?' (2005) 33(10) *World Development* 1567, 1578.

[31] Ibid; Ginsburg (n 26) 14.

[32] Reisman and Sloane (n 21) 117.

[33] For example, Tobin and Rose-Ackerman's latest study on BITs and inward investment found that 'the marginal benefit of entering into a BIT is higher for a developing country with a better institutional quality ranking', less

qualitatively adequate institutional framework, 'they cannot bootstrap a high risk country' to the same level as countries with more robust institutions for investor protection.[34]

This impetus to improve domestic institutional quality is driven primarily by the financial threat of non-compliance with IIAs. Host state signatories to IIAs risk incurring significant costs if they do not reform domestic institutions to give effect to treaty standards of protection, including direct costs of litigation for treaty breaches and any ensuing compensatory damages to the foreign investor as well as indirect costs, such as the aforementioned effects of reputational loss.[35] Given the broad and open-ended nature of most IIA provisions, this commitment to governance reform is significant, involving not only the liberalisation of economic sectors under the non-discrimination obligations but also changes in domestic law, administrative and regulatory policy and practice to conform with states' obligations under the FET standard and transparency principles and compliance with standards of expropriation and compensation.

Governance reforms induced by IIAs have been posited, in some circles, as welcome incentives to shift government behaviours for the betterment of their domestic constituents, conferring upon international investment law a broader function of enabling social and political development. These changes occur on several registers. First, it has been argued that the liberalisation of a host state's investment regime can result in greater competition in economic sectors, breaking up existing monopolies and oligopolies and entrenched political interests in previously closed door economies. These structural reforms, viewed in corollary to the aforementioned 'investment climate approach' promulgated by development agencies and donors, are mapped as part of a broader virtuous circle of free markets and the rule of law. Here, an international commitment to liberalisation can be perceived as 'a domestic defense mechanism to insulate the state from local rent-seeking efforts' and spurring competition among domestic as well as foreign investors.[36]

---

of an impact 'in the riskiest environments' and 'a larger positive effect for countries with moderate levels of political risk'; see Tobin and Rose-Ackerman (n 29) 6; see also Yackee (n 25).

[34] Tobin and Rose-Ackerman (n 29) 6.

[35] See Todd Allee and Clint Peinhardt, 'Contingent Credibility: The Impact of Investment Treaty Violations on Foreign Direct Investment' (2011) 65(3) *International Organisation* 401; Tobin and Rose-Ackerman (n 29); Yackee (n 25).

[36] Ginsburg (n 26) 119; Alvarez (n 17) 378.

Second, liberalisation reforms of IIAs are buttressed by substantive and procedural investor protection provisions and their increasingly expansive interpretation by arbitral tribunals. Expressions of good governance and the rule of law have featured prominently in tribunal interpretations of substantive treaty standards, notably in considerations of the FET and transparency principles. Specifically, interpretations of the former standard, regarded as the 'alpha and the omega' of the so-called 'BIT generation',[37] have clustered around a core of 'normative principles' identified by Kingsbury and Schill forming the contours of what constitutes 'good administrative governance' in host states.[38] These include requirements of 'stability predictability and consistency' of the host state's legal framework;[39] 'protection of legitimate expectations';[40] 'administrative due process and prohibition of denial of justice'[41] and the 'requirement of transparency'.[42]

The use of the language of good governance to justify this expansive reach of international investment law into the domestic sovereign realm has been justified and indeed promoted by its proponents who argue that such 'normative seepage'[43] can influence the positive development of legal, regulatory and administrative institutions in host states. For example, it has been argued that requirements for transparency in and accountability for regulatory change and administrative decision-making may in turn combat political corruption and temper arbitrary or discretionary exercises of state power.[44] Meanwhile, it is argued that regulatory

---

[37] Montt (n 21) 294.

[38] Benedict Kingsbury and Stephan W Schill, 'Investor-State Arbitration as Governance: Fair and Equitable Treatment, Proportionality and the Emerging Global Administrative Law' IILJ Working Paper 2009/6, New York University School of Law (2009) 8–10 <http://iilj.org/publications/documents/2009-6.kingsburyschill.pdf> accessed 18 August 2014.

[39] *CMS Gas Transmission Company v The Republic of Argentina*, ICSID Case No ARB/01/8, Final Award (12 May 2005); *Metalclad Corporation v The United Mexican States*, ICSID Case No ARB(AF)/97/1, Award (30 August 2000).

[40] *Técnicas Medioambientales Tecmed SA v The United Mexican States,* ICSID Case No ARB(AF)/00/2, Award (29 May 2003); *International Thunderbird Gaming Corporation v The United Mexican States,* UNCITRAL, Arbitral Award (26 January 2006).

[41] *Metalclad v Mexico* (n 39).

[42] Ibid; *Tecmed v Mexico* (n 40); see Kingsbury and Schill (n 38) 8–15.

[43] Ibid 16.

[44] Kingsbury and Schill (n 38) 16–17; Juanita Olaya, 'Good Governance and International Investment Law: The Challenges of Lack of Transparency and Corruption' (Second Biennial Global Conference, University of Barcelona,

competition between domestic courts and international arbitral mechanisms can incentivise local courts to 'compete for the business of resolving commercial disputes and therefore improve their quality.'[45]

In other words, it has been contended that institutional reforms induced by IIAs to protect foreign investors can 'trickle down' to host state constituents generally, including domestic investors as well as other stakeholders. Competition with or mimicry of external legal or regulatory regimes can, in some instances, strengthen weak internal governance and force governments to confront weak administrative and legal institutions. It can, in some circumstances, embed a culture of transparency and accountability that may lead not only to economic growth but also broader social development and political franchise. In these contexts, the language of good governance is used here to leverage transformations in the legal, regulatory and political institutions of host state developing countries similar to the way in which the concept is expressed in development policy and practice discussed in Section II to justify the governance reforms promulgated by development agencies and donors.

IV. TAKING GOVERNANCE TO TASK

A. Enclaves and Exclusions

The progressive expansion of the scope of protection offered under BITs and other IIAs by arbitral tribunals has meant that there are few aspects of host state regulatory authority that are not covered by their treaty obligations and potentially subject to review by international arbitrators, raising significant concerns about the negative correlation between investment law and domestic governance mechanisms. The positive correlation between international investment law *and* institutional development and the rule of law in host states is tenuous despite the arguments forwarded by proponents of IIAs discussed in Section III. Instead, there is mounting evidence to suggest that the constraints levelled on states by IIAs and the elevation of investor-state disputes to an international arbitral system premised on adjudicating upon primarily commercial matters is having a negative effect on good governance and the rule of law in host states.

Society of International Economic Law, Barcelona, 8–10 July 2010) 3–5 <http://papers.ssrn.com/sol3/papers.cfm?abstract_id=1635437> accessed 18 August 2014.

[45] Ginsburg (n 26) 119.

First, there is criticism that an international regime for investment protection that relies primarily on an external authority for the source of rules and principles and on an extra-territorial means of dispute settlement does not provide sufficient motivation for endogenous local development. According to Ginsburg, this 'decision to bypass domestic courts may reduce courts' incentives to improve performance by depriving key actors from a need to invest in institutional improvement.'[46] Unlike the governance and rule of law interventions of the international development community (see Section II), states are expected to independently manage the process of regulatory and institutional compliance with IIA provisions. Without financial support or technical expertise, coupled with limited institutional and professional capacity in many developing countries, host states will struggle with improving judicial quality to the standards expected by foreign investors who, given an option, would prefer international arbitration over domestic remedies.

Second, the removal of local courts and laws from the jurisdiction of foreign investment claims results in the creation of 'legal enclaves'[47] which enable foreign investors to exit domestic jurisdictions and rely on an external legal regime for protection of their rights and adjudication of their disputes with host states.[48] This 'siphoning off' of foreign investor-host state conflict to another jurisdiction for contest can undermine the function of the local judiciary and legal system.[49] Inasmuch as commitment to IIAs and international arbitration can signal host state credibility in the treatment of foreign investors within its domestic legal and administrative environment, these same commitments can also signal the host state's own loss of confidence in the same institutions to do the same.

The practice of 'allowing foreign investors to leap-frog over domestic courts' has major ramifications on standards of good governance within host states.[50] The provision of a right to international arbitration as the first recourse under most IIAs supplant the public rationales which still underpin the time-honoured local remedies rule – still applied by most

---

46 Ibid.

47 Daniels (n 27).

48 Ibid; Ginsburg (n 26).

49 Ibid.

50 Luke Eric Peterson, 'Evaluating Canada's 2004 Model Foreign Investment Protection Agreement in Light of Civil Society Concerns' (CCIC June 2006) 1–2 <http://www.ccic.ca/_files/en/what_we_do/trade_2006–06_foreign_investment_memo_e.pdf> accessed 18 August 2014.

international and regional dispute settlement bodies, such as the European Court of Human Rights and the International Court of Justice (ICJ) – and promulgate a near universal distrust of local legal regimes, irrespective of their reliability.[51] The limitation or removal of the local remedies rule in IIAs presume that local courts are incapable of delivering justice and deny domestic institutions the opportunity to review and, if necessary, redress the substance of the claims against the host government.[52]

Third, the limited role of local courts in investment disputes, effectively rendering them little more than enforcers of external arbitral decisions, has an impact on public confidence in the domestic legal system. This is particularly striking when courts have little option but to give effect to an award which may have negative ramifications on public interests with little opportunity to review the merits of the award. Enabling foreign investors to bypass local legal systems can also prevent the endogenous evolution of law through judicial precedent and statutory interpretation. This is particularly relevant in common law systems where such judicial activism is central to the development of law and which rely on test and novel cases to further the development of specific arenas of law and policy.

Finally and crucially, the relocation of foreign investment disputes away from local courts and the subjection of these disputes to external law remove incentives for foreign investors to participate as civic actors within home states, enabling the withdrawal of their voice from domestic debates on legal and judicial reform and regulatory change. This system can create a two-tiered regime of investment governance in which foreign and domestic investors are subjected to different systems of rules and adjudication and allow a government 'to segment its reputation among domestic and foreign actors.'[53] This can lead to asymmetries in the treatment of foreign and local investors with foreign investors benefiting from a highly specialised, institutionalised and often more efficient mechanism for adjudication while consigning domestic investors to often overburdened local courts.[54]

---

[51] Gus Van Harten and Martin Loughlin, 'Investment Treaty Arbitration as a Species of Global Administrative Law' (2006) 17(1) EJIL 121, 130.

[52] Ibid; see also Alvarez (n 17) 68–69.

[53] Ginsburg (n 26) 119.

[54] In *Glamis Gold Ltd v The United States of America*, UNCITRAL, Award (8 June 2009), for example, the foreign mining company sought to challenge Californian mining regulations under the North American Free Trade Agreement's Chapter 11 provision for arbitration rather than in a Californian Court; see

B. Regulatory Chill and the Social Contract

The governance concerns stemming from reliance on external institutions for adjudication is compounded by the significant shortcomings of the arbitral system to which a rapidly rising number of investment disputes are referred.[55] These concerns, which are well-documented, fall broadly into two categories: a) criticism of the expansionist scale of tribunal decisions and their impact on host states and their local constituents; and b) critique of the procedural deficiencies of the process of international arbitration. Underlying these concerns is what Schill terms the 'public law challenge'[56] of a system that is public in character but private in form, charged with the review of inherently public and civic issues but operationally and conceptually premised on a framework that was designed for commercial disputes between private actors. The open-ended nature of substantive content of investment agreements coupled with the overarching *raison d'état* of investment treaties to minimise political and regulatory risk has meant that the arbitral system has been called upon to adjudicate matters of public concern in host states without the corresponding institutional framework or professional expertise to support it.

Acting under the auspices of BITs and other IIAs, arbitral tribunals have been called upon to evaluate claims relating to a wide range of governmental action ranging from termination of water concession contracts[57] to government failure to renew a licence for the operation of a landfill[58] and refusal of a permit to operate a hazardous waste disposal

---

Brynn Olsen, 'International Local Government Law: The Effect of NAFTA Chapter 11 on Local Land Use Planning' (2007) 4 *International Law and Management Review* 53.

[55] The number of known investor-state dispute settlement (ISDS) cases has risen exponentially since the mid-1990s. In 2012, there were at least 58 new cases filed, constituting the 'highest number of known treaty-based disputes ever filed in one year', the majority of which were filed against developing countries and economies in transition; see UNCTAD, 'Recent Developments in Investor-State Dispute Settlement (ISDS), Updated for the Multilateral Dialogue on Investment, 28–29 May 2013' IIA Issues Note No 1 (May 2013) 1 <http://unctad.org/en/PublicationsLibrary/webdiaepcb2013d3_en.pdf> accessed 18 August 2014. At the end of 2011, there were a total of 514 known treaty-based investment cases; ibid 3.

[56] Schill (n 16) 67.

[57] See *Biwater Gauff (Tanzania) Ltd v United Republic of Tanzania*, ICSID Case No ARB/05/22, Award (24 July 2008).

[58] See *Tecmed v Mexico* (n 40).

facility[59] to the institution of environmental and cultural impact assessments[60] and government bans on gasoline additives.[61] In a series of cases resulting from the Argentinean financial crisis in 2000–2001, arbitral tribunals have had to examine the legitimacy of government acts to redenominate the local currency in the midst of economic exigencies.[62]

In many of these cases, tribunals have been called upon to assess the quality of governance in host states by evaluating not only the appropriate scope of governmental action but also the efficacy of state institutions when carrying out the functions of government.[63] Frequently called upon to 'resolve wider conflicts of rights and interests between international investors, on the one hand, and individuals who benefit from domestic regulation of business on the other',[64] arbitral tribunals are regularly entertaining 'claims that would otherwise lie with the exclusive province of constitutional and supreme courts in host states.'[65] Under municipal law, this review of governmental action is normally conducted by the public judicial system, usually honouring the constitutional separation of powers that enables citizenry rights to be guaranteed by judicial review of executive or legislative action. Removing the forum for review to an external system has significant ramifications not only for the conduct of government in host state but also the relationship between state and its constituents.

A key concern arising from the deficiencies of the investment arbitral system is that the stability and predictability afforded by the legal protections under international investment law for foreign investors has translated into a corresponding instability and lack of predictability for host states and their domestic constituents. Governments may now be

---

[59] See *Metalclad v Mexico* (n 39).

[60] See *Glamis Gold v USA* (n 54).

[61] See *Methanex Corporation v United States of America*, UNCITRAL, Arbitral Award (3 August 2005).

[62] See *CMS Gas v Argentine Republic* (n 39); *Enron Corporation and Ponderosa Assets LP v Argentine Republic,* ICSID Case No ARB/01/3, Award (22 May 2007); *Sempra Energy International v The Argentine Republic,* ICSID Case No ARB/02/16, Award (28 September 2007).

[63] As Dolzer observes, '[t]he appropriate time for filing an appeal, the process of determining a relevant fact, and the judicial administration of justice in general have all been subject to review by this growing jurisprudence'; see Dolzer (n 20) 970.

[64] Gus Van Harten, 'Private Authority and Transnational Governance: The Contours of the International System of Investor Protection' (2005) 12(4) *Review of International Political Economy* 600, 615.

[65] Montt (n 21) 126.

reluctant to institute regulatory or administrative changes even where such reforms are necessary for the protection of public interest. In seeking to manage 'political risk' and 'regulatory opportunism' by host states (see Section II), international investment law conversely exerts a 'regulatory chill' on host governments through substantive treaty provisions and stabilisation clauses in investment contracts that seek to freeze regulations in host states, including changes necessitated by shifting economic and environmental circumstances.[66]

This creates what Schneiderman describes as a 'political economy of certainty' which insulates 'key aspects of economic life from the pressures of majoritarian politics.'[67] In many host states, the decision of the executive to enter into IIAs has been taken without adequate consultation with local communities and other domestic constituents, including local businesses that may be affected by the substantive terms of such treaties. Despite the wide-ranging scope of IIAs and their significant impact on the capacity of host states to act in the public interest, host states have routinely entered into these agreements without satisfactory consultation and debate.[68] In some countries where entry into an international agreement remains the prerogative of the executive, the waiver of government authority in this manner has raised significant questions over the exercise of state power.

Additionally, the shift from domestic lawmaking and adjudication mechanisms to a process that enshrines in private adjudicators 'the authority to review the legitimacy of state action and omissions according to undefined standards of review'[69] exerts a constitutional toll on the social compact between the host state and its citizens. Aside from the privileging of foreign investors discussed in Section III, the extensive constraints placed on state's regulatory prerogatives by IIAs and arbitral jurisprudence can undermine the institution of the state itself, calling into question the very function of government and government institutions.

---

[66] *Metalclad Corporation v Mexico* (n 39); *CMS Gas v Argentine Republic* (n 39); *Enron Corporation and Ponderosa Assets LP v Argentine Republic* (n 62); *Sempra Energy International v Argentine Republic* (n 62); *LG&E Energy Corp, LG&E Capital Corp and LG&E International Inc v Argentine Republic,* ICSID Case No ARB/02/1, Award (25 July 2007).

[67] David Schneiderman, *Constitutionalizing Economic Globalization: Investment Rules and Democracy's Promise* (CUP 2008) 205–7.

[68] Gus Van Harten, 'Investment Treaty Arbitration, Procedural Fairness and the Rule of Law' in Stephan W Schill (ed.), *International Investment Law and Comparative Public Law* (OUP 2010) 630.

[69] Montt (n 21) 126.

This is particularly acute in host states with fragile political coalitions, those emerging from economic crisis, natural disasters or armed conflict or indeed states transiting from authoritarian rule where consolidated state authority remains pivotal in consolidating a fragmented national polity.

C. Arbitral Assaults on Governance

The transplantation of a private framework of adjudication to issues of public policy has resulted in critical procedural anomalies which, paradoxically, sit in opposition to the standards of governance the very same arbitral tribunals seek to enforce in host states. First, the appointment and conduct of investment arbitrators challenges the core 'principles of public accountability and judicial independence that underlie public law.'[70] In particular, the *ad hoc* nature of appointments – by disputing parties or designated external authorities[71] on a case-by-case basis – mean that the '[i]nstitutional safeguards of judicial independence' that are normally present in the resolution of public law disputes, such as security of tenure, bars on external remuneration, and objective and independent assignment of cases to judges, are absent in investment arbitration.[72] This, it has been argued, predisposes arbitrators to bias by increasing their financial and professional dependence on both foreign investors as the sole prospective claimants under the asymmetrical structure of investment arbitration and on officials in the designating arbitral centres.[73]

These perceptions of bias are attenuated by criticisms that the 'club' of individuals from which arbitrators are selected form a closed circle of advocates 'who serve as counsel in some cases and as arbitrators in others, often obtaining repeated appointments, thereby raising concerns about potential conflicts of interest.'[74] Additionally, there are concerns that although they are adjudicating on cases involving public interest,

---

70 Van Harten (n 64) 615.

71 IIAs often prescribe a designating authority for appointing arbitrators, such as the ICSID or the International Chamber of Commerce (ICC) International Court of Arbitration (ICA); see Van Harten (n 68) 4, n 1.

72 Gus Van Harten, 'Contributions and Limitations of Empirical Research on Independence and Impartiality in International Investment Arbitration' (2011) 1(4) *Oñati Socio-Legal Series* 1, 3–4.

73 Ibid; Van Harten (n 68) 643–51; Gus Van Harten, *Investment Treaty Arbitration and Public Law* (OUP 2008) 167–8.

74 UNCTAD, *World Investment Report 2012: Towards a New Generation of Investment Policies* (United Nations 2012) 88; see also Van Harten (n 64)

many arbitrators lack the professional expertise in public policy and are not accountable to stakeholders other than the parties to the dispute.[75] This contrasts with the practice in domestic legal regimes and in other public international arenas, such as the ICJ and the World Trade Organisation's dispute settlement body, where adjudicators tasked with review of government conduct are drawn from a wider pool of expertise and where the terms of appointments are reflective of the public character of the cases they hear.

Concerns with the lack of transparency in the selection of arbitrators are matched by concerns over the lack of transparency in arbitral proceedings more generally. Here, the transposition of a system established for commercial disputes – with confidentiality as one of its 'distinctive features'[76] – sits uncomfortably with its new reality of hearing cases of public interest. A hallmark of this system has been its presumption of privacy that has greatly limited public access to arbitral proceedings, both in terms of documentary disclosure and third party participation in tribunal hearings. This adjudicative model premised on party autonomy, party consent and commercial confidentiality transplants uneasily to disputes involving matters of public concern which go beyond the interests of the parties to the case.[77] In recent years, there has been progress towards facilitating greater openness in arbitral proceedings but these new rules remain highly qualified and still fall short of the disclosure rules of many domestic legal regimes in cases that deal with public interest matters (see Section V.A).

The informational and representation deficits of the arbitral system are further compounded by the lack of institutional hierarchy within the arbitral regime that has resulted in conflicting decisions on cases filed in multiple fora by foreign investors and by the absence of an effective and independent appellate mechanism that can redress these inconsistencies and other procedural deficits.[78] Paradoxically, the problem of inconsistency in awards by different tribunals – illustrated by the *Lauder* and *SGS*

615–16; Andrea K Bjorklund, 'The Emerging Civilization of Investment Arbitration' (2009) 113(4) Penn State LRev 1269, 1297–8.

[75] Ibid.

[76] Bjorklund (n 74) 1287.

[77] Ibid; Franck (n 17); Susan D Franck, 'The Legitimacy Crisis in Investment Arbitration: Privatizing Public International Law Through Inconsistent Decisions' (2005) 73 Fordham LRev 1521, 1541–2; UNCTAD (n 74); Van Harten (n 64).

[78] See Franck, 'The Legitimacy Crisis in Investment Arbitration' (n 77) 1586.

arbitrations[79] – and the absence of the doctrine of precedent in arbitral practice, impact not only on the regulatory authority of host states but also on their ability to meet their obligations to foreign investors. If the purpose of IIAs is to serve as credible commitment devices to ensure regulatory certainty and manage regulatory risk, then the indeterminacy of the arbitral process risks undermining the capacity of states to formulate and implement coherent regulatory policy.

The question of damages also reflects the hybrid nature of the investment regime which transposes a private adjudicatory regime to matters of international public interest. Inconsistent awards aside, the use of damages 'as a public law remedy' contrary to the practice of most international legal regimes[80] highlights the fundamentally pecuniary nature of the investment arbitral system and contradicts arguments that such cases can work towards incentivising the improvement of domestic governance (see Section III.B). Without clear and prospective means of enforcing state obligations – such as trade sanctions available at the WTO – the investment regime relies on retrospective financial sanctions as a deterrent to supervise state compliance with their obligations at the same time as it seeks to use the same damages to compensate private actors for losses suffered as a consequence of host state treaty violations. However, the system lacks the public interest qualifications that apply to the award of damages in other international legal regimes, such as the Court of Justice of the European Union, that provide for damages to individual claimants, including thresholds of culpability and limits to the quantum of damages recoverable, despite the significant financial implications of such awards on host states, particularly developing country states.[81]

---

79 *Ronald S Lauder v The Czech Republic*, UNCITRAL, Final Award (3 September 2001); *CME Czech Republic BV v The Czech Republic*, UNCITRAL, Partial Award (13 September 2001); *SGS Société Générale de Surveillance SA v Islamic Republic of Pakistan,* ICSID Case No ARB/01/13, Decision of the Tribunal on Objections to Jurisdiction (6 August 2003) and *SGS Société Générale de Surveillance SA v Republic of the Philippines,* ICSID Case No ARB/02/6, Decision of the Tribunal on Objections to Jurisdiction (29 January 2004). The former two tribunals (*Lauder* and *CME*) reached conflicting decisions regarding 'the same facts, related parties and similar investment rights' while the latter two (*SGS* arbitrations) resulted in differing opinions regarding the similar investment rights and commercial situations for different sets of parties; see Franck (n 77) 1558–74.

80 Van Harten and Loughlin (n 51) 131.

81 Ibid 131–3; Andreas Kulick, *Global Public Interest in International Investment Law* (CUP 2012) 82–3.

V. GOVERNANCE AS RECALIBRATION

A. Rewriting Wrongs

As the language of good governance becomes increasingly expressed in the law, policy and practice of the investment regime, there are increasing expectations that these narratives may be utilised to transform the deficiencies of the regime itself. In recent years, as global criticism of and dissatisfaction with the current investment law framework have intensified, the narratives of good governance and development have re-emerged as potential scripts for countering the legitimacy and credibility crisis in international investment law. As discussed in Section II, the discourse of good governance has been appropriated by proponents of the contemporary framework of international investment law to justify its prevailing norms and structures, particularly the constraints the system imposes on the political and economic institutions in host states.

The concepts of good governance and the rule of law are now forming an important plank in efforts to recalibrate international investment law. On the one hand, notions of good governance and the rule of law provide the language through which claims of different stakeholders of the regime – host states, civil society groups and communities at the frontline of adverse foreign investment outcomes – can be articulated and through which the normative agenda of international investment may be challenged. At the same time, the discourse of good governance can also be viewed as supplying the scripts for countering the current legitimacy and credibility crisis in the investment regime through attempts to embed a broader social and public agenda into the system. In practice, both registers operate in tandem, reflecting the iterative process of sustained critique and incremental change.

As a starting point, the good governance agenda has provided a conceptual and operational framework for forwarding critique of the procedural deficiencies of the investment arbitration regime. In particular, the discourse of the rule of law has supplied a valuable tool for highlighting the paradox of a system that purports to uphold standards of good governmental conduct (at least *vis-à-vis* investors) yet fails to engender such values within its institutional structure. Civil society groups, sometimes but not always, in conjunction with host states, have successfully lobbied for greater access to the arbitral process using the language of transparency, due process and good governance.[82] Here, the rule of law has served as a valuable resource to leverage greater openness in the arbitral process, leading to incremental changes in public disclosure of and third party representation in arbitral proceedings.

UNCTAD in its revised paper on 'transparency' observes the significant changes to the way in which transparency issues have been expressed in IIAs and arbitral practice since its last iteration of the note in 2004, noting in particular 'the emergence of investor responsibilities' and 'the introduction of a transparency dimension into investor-state dispute settlement.'[83] With respect to the latter, the organisation notes that the linking of sustainable development objectives with the language of good governance has led to changes in arbitral procedure that has enabled greater public participation in disputes that have implications for development strategies in host states, including increased public disclosure of documents, public access to hearings and third party representation via the submission of amicus briefs.[84]

In this context, the parties to the North American Free Trade Agreement (NAFTA) had paved the way for greater public disclosure and access to arbitral proceedings, providing expressly that, subject to certain elementary redactions, nothing in the NAFTA precludes parties to the agreement 'from providing public access to documents submitted to, or issued by a Chapter Eleven tribunal.'[85] This reflects in part an extension of what Bjorklund identifies as the 'strong cultures of open access to government information' in North America, notably the US and Canada,[86] but also demonstrates the strength and increasing professionalization of domestic advocacy, mainly by civil society groups, on these broader investment-related issues. The NAFTA practice has been extended in the new generation of model BITs issued by Canada and the

---

[82] NGOs, such as the Canadian-based International Institute for Sustainable Development (IISD) and the Washington DC-based Centre for International Environmental Law (CIEL), have been active in monitoring IIAs and evaluating their public interest impacts as well as forwarding claims from stakeholders and civil society groups in developing countries affected by foreign investment projects.

[83] UNCTAD, *Transparency: A Sequel* (UNCTAD Series on Issues in International Investment Agreements II, United Nations 2012) xi.

[84] Ibid 36–7.

[85] NAFTA Free Trade Commission (2001), 'NAFTA: Notes of Interpretation of Certain Chapter 11 Provisions' (31 July 2001) s A(1) <http://www.sice.oas.org/tpd/nafta/Commission/CH11understanding_e.asp> accessed 18 August 2014.

[86] Mexico only recently amended its Constitution to allow for a guarantee of a right to government information; see Bjorklund (n 74) 1288.

US in 2003 and 2004 respectively, leading to a series of IIAs now containing extensive provisions on disclosure of documents and awards of arbitral tribunals, access to hearings and allowance of third party submissions in arbitration.[87]

Meanwhile, amendments to the ICSID Convention Arbitration Rules (ICSID Rules)[88] and ICSID Additional Facility Rules (ICSID Additional Rules)[89] in 2006 have enabled 'access to the legal reasoning behind awards in cases administered by ICSID' with express consent of the parties but 'stop short of requiring the disclosure of the pleadings or the memorials submitted by the parties.'[90] The recently adopted UNCITRAL Rules on Transparency (UNCITRAL Transparency Rules)[91] go further than the ICSID amendments and provide for transparency throughout the entire lifecycle of a treaty-based investor-state arbitration conducted under the UNCITRAL Arbitration Rules, including the disclosure of a wide range of documents, such as party submissions and expert reports, subject to certain exceptions.[92] Crucially, in a departure from other arbitral practice, the new rules require hearings to be open subject to limitations.[93]

The UNCITRAL Transparency Rules also allow for third party involvement in investor-state disputes, continuing a trend towards broadening access to such hearings in other arbitral regimes. NAFTA parties set the precedent for amicus curiae submissions with the landmark

---

87 See UNCTAD (n 83) 37–43; Kyla Tienhaara, 'Third Party Participation in Investment-Environment Disputes: Recent Developments' (2007) 16(2) *Review of European Community & International Environmental Law* 230, 232–3.

88 ICSID Convention Rules for Arbitration Proceedings (Arbitration Rules); see ICSID, 'ICSID Convention, Regulations and Rules' (ICSID/15) (ICSID April 2006) 99ff <https://icsid.worldbank.org/ICSID/StaticFiles/basicdoc/CRR_English-final.pdf> accessed 18 August 2014.

89 ICSID Additional Facility Rules in ibid.

90 Bjorklund (n 74) 1290; Rule 37 ICSID Rules.

91 UNCITRAL, 'Rules on Transparency in Treaty-bound Investor-State Arbitration' (2013) <http://www.uncitral.org/pdf/english/texts/arbitration/rules-on-transparency/Rules-on-Transparency-E.pdf> accessed 18 August 2014.

92 Exceptions include confidential or protected business or security information or if disclosure would jeopardise the integrity of the arbitral process; see UNCITRAL, 'Rules on Transparency' (n 91) art 7; see Lise Johnson and Nathalie Bernasconi-Osterwalder, 'New UNCITRAL Arbitration Rules on Transparency: Application, Content and Next Steps' (2013) 4(4) *Investment Treaty News* 3.

93 UNCITRAL, 'Rules on Transparency' (n 91) art 6. These limitations are similar to the exceptions to documentary disclosure (above n 92), including on grounds of confidentiality.

receipt of such briefs by the tribunal in *Methanex Corporation v US*[94] and later, in the case of *UPS v Canada*,[95] a practice effectively codified in a latter statement by the Free Trade Commission in 2003.[96] Since then, a series of arbitral tribunals have accepted amicus submissions and allowed third party participation in investor-state disputes to varying degrees,[97] highlighting in particular the public interest rationale in their reasoning for accepting these briefs.[98] In addition to the expertise and alternative perspectives that amici may contribute to the substantive claims, tribunals have grounded their decision to allow amicus briefs in the wider legitimacy import of allowing such submissions. Specifically, tribunals have stressed the significance that acceptance of third party submissions would contribute towards enhancing the public image of the arbitral process.[99]

Aside from challenging the procedural deficits of the arbitral system, critics of the investment regime have similarly harnessed the language of good governance to forward substantive arguments, usually in support of host states in defence of communities affected by investment projects and

---

[94] *Methanex Corporation v USA* (n 61).

[95] *United Parcel Service of America Inc v Government of Canada*, UNCITRAL, Award on the Merits (11 June 2007).

[96] NAFTA Free Trade Commission, 'Statement of the Free Trade Commission on Non-Disputing Party Participation' (2003) <www.state.gov/documents/organization/38791.pdf> accessed 10 January 2014; see also Tienhaara (n 87) 232.

[97] See *Methanex Corporation v USA* (n 94); *United Parcel Service of America Inc v Government of Canada* (n 94); *Glamis Gold v USA* (n 54); *Aguas del Tunari SA v Republic of Bolivia*, ICSID Case No ARB/02/3, Decision on Respondent's Objections to Jurisdiction (21 October 2005); *Suez, Sociedad General de Aguas de Barcelona SA and Vivendi Universal SA v Argentine Republic*, ICSID Case No ARB/03/19, Decision on Jurisdiction (3 August 2006); *Suez, Sociedad General de Aguas de Barcelona SA and InterAgua Servicios Integrales del Agua SA v Argentine Republic*, ICSID Case No ARB/03/17, Decision on Liability (30 July 2010); *Biwater Gauff v Tanzania* (n 57).

[98] James Harrison, 'Human Rights Arguments in *Amicus Curiae* Submissions: Promoting Social Justice?' in Pierre-Marie Dupuy, Ernst-Ulrich Petersmann and Francesco Francioni (eds), *Human Rights in International Investment Law and Arbitration* (OUP 2009) 404; Eugenia Levine, '*Amicus Curiae* in International Investment Arbitration: The Implications of an Increase in Third-Party Participation' (2011) 29(1) Berkeley JIL 200, 205–6.

[99] See *Methanex Corporation v USA* (n 94); *Suez, Sociedad General de Aguas de Barcelona SA and InterAgua Servicios Integrales del Agua SA v Argentine Republic* (n 97); see also the discussion below, Section V.B.

arbitral claims. Harrison, for example, notes the increasing frequency in which human rights arguments, framed in the context of substantive and procedural fairness and social justice, are raised by groups intervening in investment disputes.[100] While the two concepts should not be conflated, it is instructive to note Harrison's assessment of why such discourses are attractive to those who seek to challenge the premise of international investment law. According to Harrison, a rights-framework posits an alternative claim on host states' regulatory authority, creating primary legal obligations on states to intervene on behalf of their citizens where their rights – enshrined either via domestic constitutions or regional or international human rights law – are violated by third parties.[101]

Similarly, the language of good governance supplies those stakeholders whose interests stand in opposition to the foreign investor's proprietary rights protected by investment contracts and IIAs with a frame of reference under which their rights can be articulated and taken into account, both within and outside and the legal regime. Within the legal architecture of investment protection, the terminology afforded by the discourse of good governance, human rights and the rule of law 'gives legal expression' to certain values, such as social welfare and environmental protection, that would otherwise find little currency in the world of arbitration and international law-making.[102] Operationalised through amicus submissions, these discourses 'translate ... public concerns' into specialised terms of art that can be filtered and understood by arbitrators whose narrow field of expertise and limited parameters of engagement precludes them from hearing otherwise.[103]

Outside the legal framework, the good governance agenda marshals public support for challenging the overarching universe of IIAs and investment policy by providing a language through which broader citizenry action against the constraints of the investment regime may be mobilised. In this manner, the good governance agenda may have mobilised greater recognition among policymakers of the need to shift the previously narrow focus of the investment regime. UNCTAD's flagship report, the *World Investment Report*, in 2012 notes that innovations in recently concluded IIAs have included features 'to ensure that the treaty does not interfere with, but instead contributes to, countries'

---

[100] Harrison (n 98).
[101] Ibid 413.
[102] Ibid.
[103] Ibid.

sustainable development strategies', including those that 'provide treatment and protection guarantees to investors without hindering the government's power to regulate in the public interest' or those that undermine domestic laws, including environmental and labour laws.[104] Towards this end, UNCTAD itself has developed its 'Investment Policy Framework for Sustainable Development' which it is offering as a policy tool for governments developing national and international investment policies, including the reorientation of investment regimes towards more inclusive growth and sustainable development.[105]

Importantly, the language of good governance has also been utilised to recalibrate the asymmetry between investment protection and investment regulation by placing emphasis on investor responsibilities in addition to investor rights. As noted previously, investor behaviour is increasingly being featured in newer generations of IIAs and state investment policy. Two prominent regional agreements in Africa – the Investment Agreement for the Common Market for Eastern and Southern Africa (COMESA) Common Investment Area 2007 and the Protocol on Finance and Investment of the Southern African Development Community (SADC) 2006 – both contain provisions on 'investor obligation' and 'corporate responsibility' respectively, effectively placing obligations on foreign investors to comply with domestic laws, policies and administrative measures.[106] The SADC's model BIT further includes measures to combat corruption and sets standards for human rights, environment, labour and corporate governance while upholding the right of host states to regulate in the interest of development.[107]

B. Recalibration or Relegitimation

The recalibration of investment law via the transformative language of good governance must be located within the limitations of the current framework of international law and crucially the geopolitical and economic realities of interstate relations and relations between host states and foreign investors. While concepts of good governance and the rule of law can serve 'as a resource available to social movements to countervail the power of dominant social and economic forces', it can also be used as a means of 'inhibiting the possibilities for political action.'[108] The utility

---

104 UNCTAD (n 74) 89.
105 Ibid.
106 See UNCTAD (n 83) 31–2, Box 20 and 21.
107 UNCTAD (n 74) 89.
108 Schneiderman (n 67) 207.

of the good governance agenda as an instrument of public change must therefore be placed within the caveat. As previously discussed, changes in the framework of investment law and arbitration have been relatively incremental despite the extensive criticism directed at the regime and it is questionable whether the largely procedural reforms would have an impact on the substantive scope of international investment law.

While there have been reforms towards greater transparency in and access to arbitral proceedings, discussed in the previous section, these innovations are not universal and remain subject to restrictions and exceptions. For example, under the amended ICSID Rules, disclosure of awards still requires the parties' consent and there is no requirement to make public other documents, such as submissions and pleadings.[109] Similarly, the more comprehensive new UNCITRAL Transparency Rules (see above) only came into effect after 1 April 2014 and applies only to IIAs concluded after that date, allowing states parties to opt out or modify application of the rules.[110] Disputes arising from treaties concluded before the Rules' entry into force will be heard using the existing UNCITRAL Arbitration Rules. Moreover, since IIAs frequently provide for a menu of dispute settlement options, parties to an investment dispute could choose to have their disputes heard in other arbitral fora, such as the ICSID, or organisations such as the ICC's International Court of Arbitration or the Stockholm Chamber of Commerce that have maintained the *status quo* on confidentiality.

Correspondingly, provisions for third party participation in hearings remain limited largely to written submissions from the amici although tribunals can allow access to (but not participation in) the proceedings.[111] Further, the right to participate is subject to the tribunal's approval and tribunals can and have rejected amicus curiae applications. While there has been a gradual acceptance of amicus curiae submissions by tribunals from interested third parties since the *Methanex* case, the extent to which the tribunals feel they are able and willing to give weight to the considerations raised by these submissions is questionable.[112]

Additionally, formal access to arbitral proceedings does not necessarily translate into useful disclosure of information nor does it ensure effective participation by relevant stakeholders. The crux of the problem remains the diversion of disputes involving wider questions of public interest to

---

109 Bjorklund (n 74); Rule 37 ICSID Rules.

110 UNCITRAL, 'Rules on Transparency' (n 91) arts 1–3.

111 NAFTA Free Trade Commission (n 96); ICSID Rules, Rule 32(2) and 37(2); UNCITRAL, 'Rules on Transparency' (n 91) arts 4(1) and 6.

112 Harrison (n 98).

an external regime that is inaccessible to local constituents and further disenfranchises participation in public processes of decision-making and adjudication. Access to information on arbitral proceedings can be limited by virtue of the language, commonly English, used in the pleadings and decisions and unfamiliarity with the law applied in these cases.

Moreover, while this recognition constitutes a step in the right direction, there are questions as to whether submissions brought by amici groups are sufficiently representative of the public interest in the disputes brought to tribunals. Given that access to such hearings requires a heavy investment of financial resources and expertise, amici curiae submissions may continue to constitute the preserve of well-organised, often metropolitan and externally funded organisations at the expense of local, grassroots organisations that may be at the sharp end of the ultimate outcome of arbitral decisions.

At the same time, there are also significant concerns that the process of 'recapturing the public sphere' of arbitral proceedings[113] may be utilised as a mechanism of relegitimising the authority of the arbitral process rather than a genuine attempt to reform the system. As Harrison and Tienhaara's respective surveys of amicus submissions demonstrate, tribunals have typically justified their inclusion of such briefs as a means of strengthening the legitimacy of the arbitral process.[114]

The tribunal in *Suez/Interaguas v Argentina* for example noted:

> The acceptance of *amicus* submissions would have the additional desirable consequence of increasing the transparency of investor–state arbitration. Public acceptance of the legitimacy of international arbitral processes, particularly when they involve states and matters of public interest, is strengthened by increased openness and increased knowledge as to how these processes function. ... Through the participation of appropriate representatives of civil society in appropriate cases, the public will gain increased understanding of ICSID processes.[115]

---

[113] Barnali Choudhury, 'Recapturing Public Power: Is Investment Arbitration's Engagement of the Public Interest Contributing to the Democratic Deficit?' (2008) 41 Vand JTL 775.

[114] Harrison (n 98); Tienhaara (n 87).

[115] *Suez, Sociedad General de Aguas de Barcelona SA and InterAgua Servicios Integrales del Agua SA v Argentine Republic*, ICSID Case No ARB/03/17, Order in Response to a Petition for Participation as Amicus Curiae (17 March 2006) para 21.

In other words, the good governance narrative is increasingly acting as a 'prose of counter insurgency'[116] to quell the incipient crisis of faith in the investment regime, similar to the manner in which it was utilised to respond to crisis in development policymaking discussed in Section II.

VI. CONCLUSION

This chapter has sought to consider the relationship between investment law, development and good governance. Good governance is a construct that is rooted in temporal and policy space and its utilisation as a conceptual scaffold on which to evaluate the legitimacy and deficiencies within the international investment regime must be located within this broader construction of its emergence as this tool of international development policy. In the realm of investment law, the language of good governance and associated rule of law narrative have been the traditional *leitmotif* justifying the normative and institutional evolution of law and policy in this area. For the proponents of the contemporary legal universe of international investment, the framework of IIAs and investment arbitration tribunals create a regime that provides an enabling climate for foreign investment, particularly in developing countries and transition economies.

The narratives of good governance and the rule of law 'legitimise a certain view of the legal system and its relation with the economy, and to naturalise a particular kind of economic structure', the equation of law with progress and a market economy that prioritises investor rights as a *sine qua non* of economic development and a pre-requisite of social progress.[117] In this sense, 'BITs consciously seek to approximate in the developing, capital-importing state the minimal legal, administrative, and regulatory framework that fosters and sustains investment in industrialized capital-exporting states.'[118] The refashioned 'rule of international economic law' offers a multilateral protection that the good governance agenda sought to deliver locally by providing a framework through which the contemporary regulatory state can be disciplined.

The aforementioned discussion has demonstrated that, both substantively and procedurally, at national and international levels, the current

---

[116] James Thuo Gathii, 'Good Governance as a Counter Insurgency Agenda to Oppositional and Transformative Social Projects in International Law' (1999) 5 *Buffalo Human Rights Law Review* 107.

[117] Humphreys (n 3) 142.

[118] Reisman and Sloane (n 21) 115–18.

framework of investment law fails to meet the standards of good governance even as measured in their own terms. The good governance agenda must therefore be located within the conceptual premise of international investment law and mainstream development policy that problematises the role of state and upholds the primacy of market actors in delivering an enabling climate for social and economic development.

This underlying conceptual legacy can and does limit the efficacy of the good governance discourse as a tool for recalibrating the imbalances of international investment law in favour of development and public interest outcomes. At its best, incorporating these concepts loads greater complexity onto a system that is currently ill-equipped with the expertise and institutional structure to support it while doing little to engender economic development and further the interests of social and ecological justice. At its most insidious, the discourse of good governance and its associated, aforementioned language of 'counter insurgency'[119] seeks to mitigate critique of the regime while masking and further legitimising its systemic deficiencies.

---

[119] See Gathii (n 116); Sundhya Pahuja, 'Technologies of Empire: IMF Conditionality and the Reinscription of the North/South Divide' (2000) 13(4) Leiden JIL 749.

7. Aspiring for a constructive TWAIL approach towards the international investment regime

Antonius R. Hippolyte

I. INTRODUCTION

Development in its myriad forms and meanings has been an important post-colonial desire of developing countries,[1] and these countries have responded to it in different ways. Significantly, developing countries desired international law's reconstruction to take into account their socio-economic interests as newly emergent countries. Thus, in the post-colonial era, Third World Approaches to International Law (TWAIL) surfaced as an analytical tool, which sought to appraise the validity and universality of international law's relationship with developing countries.[2] TWAIL emerged as an alternative narrative, which sought to supplant what it considered the domination of international law by the West.[3] TWAIL's criticisms of international law are manifold and international

[1] In this chapter, the terms 'developing countries', 'developing world', and 'the South' are used interchangeably to denote the countries that emerged shortly after World War II, with the exception of Latin American countries that had previously attained their independence between 1810 and 1900. What these countries have in common is that their economies are relatively undeveloped compared to that of their former colonial masters. Similarly, 'industrialized countries', 'developed countries', 'the Western World', and 'the North' are used interchangeably to denote former colonial powers and modern economic powers in the international community.

[2] Opeoluwa A Badaru, 'Examining the Utility of Third World Approaches to International Law for International Human Rights Law' (2008) 10 *International Community Law Review* 379, 380.

[3] Mohsen Al Attar and Rosalie Miller, 'Towards an Emancipatory International Law: The Bolivarian Reconstruction' (2010) 31(3) *Third World Quarterly* 347.

economic law has been no exception.[4] Acutely aware of their post-colonial situation, developing countries sought to re-evaluate and suggest changes to international economic governance that would enable their national governments to reclaim control of domestic economies, thereby giving substance to their newfound independence.[5]

Today, the debate has witnessed a paradigm shift that places less emphasis on having control over one's domestic economy than the national economic control (NEC) model, which presupposes a sort of isolationist, or at least a conceptual, distinction between national and foreign economies. It refers to a country's right to exercise sovereignty over its domestic economy without subscribing to the rules of international economic governance.[6] This early 20th century NEC model influenced the failed New International Economic Order (NIEO) project. The NIEO model, however, more accurately refers to developing countries' attempts, from the 1960s through 1980s, to restructure international economic relations in order to establish an equilibrium between developing economies and industrial economies, thereby challenging the unfair international trading, investment and finance rules advanced by developed countries.[7] Contemporary analysis, instead, places greater emphasis on the constraints and conditions that determine how developing economies integrate into the global economy. The debate has changed its focus from its post-colonial preoccupation of developing countries' economic independence, towards greater critical analysis of these countries' engagement with the global economy and, in particular, the existing investment regime.

Nonetheless, some NEC and NIEO concerns still permeate international economic governance. Given their vast natural resources, concerns are manifested in the insufficient manner in which developing countries have participated in the international economic system, particularly in the international investment regime, since decolonization. Developing countries view the manner in which rules of international investment are crafted, applied and adjudicated between industrialized

---

4 Karin Mickelson, 'Rhetoric and Rage: Third World Voices in International Legal Discourse' (1998) 16(2) Wisc ILJ 353, 362.

5 Patrick M Norton, 'A Law of the Future or a Law of the Past? Modern Tribunals and the International Law of Expropriation' (1991) 85 AJIL 474, 478.

6 James T Gathii, 'Third World Approaches to International Economic Governance' in Richard Falk, Balakrishnan Rajagopal and Jacqueline Stevens (eds), *International Law and the Third World: Reshaping Justice* (Routledge 2008) 255, 256–7.

7 Ibid 256–8.

and developing countries, or between developing countries and the interest of global capital, as 'unfair'. They reject the biased manner in which choices are made between alternative ways of crafting investment rules, the meaning ascribed to a particular rule in its application by administrative agencies or at the adjudication stage by international tribunals when the interests of developing countries are at stake.[8] These suspicions have given rise to the 'regime bias critique'. Employing TWAIL's analytical sting, the regime bias model seeks to illustrate that international tribunals interpret and apply international economic law to disempower economically vulnerable countries inconsistently with its liberal promise of fairness.[9]

Regime bias in international investment law has emerged as a site of major modern concern.[10] These concerns have placed considerable pressure on bilateral investment treaties (BITs) and investor-State arbitration.[11] Arbitration which is the pre-eminent method of settling investment disputes, and without which the entire system faces collapse,[12] has found itself under intense scrutiny.[13] Developing countries find themselves uncomfortable with the investor-State arbitration processes. This is particularly significant taking into account the types of disputes that are being brought to arbitration. Whereas earlier disputes concerned breaches of contract or nationalizations, modern disputes hinge on matters relating to public policy,[14] such as environmental regulation,[15] or human rights protection.[16] There is growing concern among developing countries that

---

8 Gus Van Harten, 'TWAIL and the Dabhol Arbitration' (Osgoode Hall Law School Research Paper No 19/2011, 2011) 136 <http://digitalcommons.osgoode.yorku.ca/cgi/viewcontent.cgi?article=1057&context=clpe> accessed 10 May 2014; see also Gathii (n 6) 261.

9 Gathii (n 6) 256–7.

10 Van Harten (n 8) 136.

11 Gathii (n 6) 261.

12 Christopher F Dugan and others, *Investor–State Arbitration* (OUP 2008) 2–3.

13 Susan D Franck, 'The ICSID Effect? Considering Potential Variations in Arbitration Awards' (2011) 51 Va JIL 825, 841.

14 Nicolette Butler and Surya P Subedi, 'Kyla Tienhaara, The Expropriation of Environmental Governance: Protecting Foreign Investors at the Expense of Public Policy, Cambridge University Press, 2009' (2011) 4 *Journal of World Energy Law and Business* 201.

15 *Técnicas Medioambientales Tecmed, SA v The United Mexican States*, ICSID Case No ARB(AF)/00/2, Award (29 May 2003).

16 *Capital India Power Mauritius I and Energy Enterprises (Mauritius), Company v Maharashtra Power Development Corporation Limited, Maharashtra*

resorting to investor-State arbitration is a guise for forcing Western values upon the rest of the world.[17]

TWAIL's critique of the international investment regime has garnered a significant degree of sophistication since it emerged. However, while it may be the appropriate conceptual framework for leveling criticisms against the international investment regime, TWAIL's criticism fails to offer constructive proposals for improvement. TWAIL deconstructs, but offers little assistance in formulating suggestions for reforming the system. TWAIL criticism fails to acknowledge that developing countries are generally not participating in the international economic system to the degree that is necessary to augment their economies both at the national and international levels. This is problematic as it creates an adversarial relationship between developing countries and international law, thereby masking the potential for these countries to develop under the aegis of the current regime.

Therefore, there exists the need for a more theoretically informed analysis than the lump critique which generates the argument that international law, including international investment law, as currently angled, fails to take into account developing countries' interests. TWAIL should aspire to be more than merely a tool of system-criticism, as there exists a need for a more sophisticated approach that encourages greater beneficial engagement of developing countries with the international investment regime. It would be more beneficial for TWAIL to aspire to be a source of reform, or more appropriately, a forum for constructive engagement of these countries with the international investment regime, as this would create more meaningful participation of developing countries in the global economy. Initiatives similar to the Southern African Development Community (SADC) development-centered model BIT[18] would pave the way for greater influence of developing countries over the international investment regime, as it would take into account their vulnerable economic positions in the future development of international investment agreements. Afro-Asian countries have achieved a measured degree of success in the area of international arbitration, as illustrated by the establishment of five arbitration centers in the African-Asian region under the auspices of the African-Asian Legal Consultative Organization

---

States Electricity Board and the State of Maharashtra, ICC Case No 12913/MS, Final Award (27 April 2005).

17 Butler and Subedi (n 14) 201.

18 UNCTAD, 'SADC Moving Forward on Bilateral Investment Treaty Template' (6 August 2012) <unctad.org/en/pages/newsdetails.aspx?OriginalVersionID=210> accessed 23 June 2014.

(AALCO).[19] Greater engagement with the international investment regime will only result in greater benefits for developing countries, replacing current fears with confident participation in the system. This chapter highlights that notwithstanding TWAIL's exposure of international economic governance's discrepancies, particularly in the international investment regime, developing countries should augment their engagement with the international investment regime.

Part II introduces TWAIL, which emerged in response to developing countries' claims that international law was biased against them, thereby frustrating their development aspirations. Part III focuses on the paradigm shifts that have characterized international economic governance since decolonization. It reveals developing countries' historic preoccupation with domestic economic control as revealed by the NEC model, which later influenced the NIEO model. Today the debate is less about the NEC or NIEO models. More recent concerns engage the regime bias critique and particularly in how some areas of international economic governance have persistently evaded the influence of developing countries. Part IV focuses on the incidence of regime bias in international investment law. It considers the lack of real participation by developing countries in BIT negotiation and the manner in which these instruments are interpreted and applied to deny developing countries sufficient voice in investor-State dispute settlement fora, such as the International Centre for Settlement of Investment Disputes (ICSID). Part V advocates for TWAIL's constructive engagement with the international investment regime. It posits the benefits of developing countries working within the contours of the international investment regime, if they are to augment their participation in the global economic system in years to come.

II. THIRD WORLD APPROACHES TO INTERNATIONAL LAW

TWAIL emerged after decolonization in response to the continued dominance of international relations by former colonial powers, in particular, the manner in which developed countries continued to manipulate international law to maintain a colonial-style economic relationship with developing countries.[20] Although independent, developing countries

[19] R Rajesh Babu, 'International Commercial Arbitration and the Developing Countries' (2006) 4 *AALCO Quarterly Bulletin* 386, 398.

[20] Arghyrios A Fatouros, 'International Law and the Third World' (1964) 50 Va LRev 783, 800.

found that their economies were still subject to external economic forces.[21] While holding the best part of the world's most important resources, developing countries continued to participate only marginally in the international economic system after decolonization.[22] Although these resources were located in developing countries, they remained in the ownership of corporations which had their hubs in metropolitan countries, similar to the chartered companies of the colonial era.[23] Even where this was not the case, for example, as a result of large-scale post-colonial nationalization agendas, developing countries' continued dependence on foreign capital to explore, extract, produce and transport their many natural resources to industrialized markets inhibited their independence.

TWAIL emerged from developing countries' resistance, as an analytical tool which sought to appraise the validity and universality of international law's relationship with developing countries.[24] TWAIL is part of the long tradition of post-colonial critical internationalism that swept the globe after World War II.[25] This campaign draws heavily from earlier Latin American opposition to Western domination;[26] however, its intellectual and inspirational roots emerged with Afro-Asian anti-colonial struggles from the 1940s to the 1960s.[27] From the 1970s, sustained work started to emerge from the Centre for International Legal Studies at Jawaharlal Nehru University in India under Ram Prakash Anand's inspired guidance. These works fought for an international law that was cognizant of the aspirations of Southern peoples.[28] TWAIL questioned international law's ability to safeguard developing countries' post-colonial interests, since this same regime had subjected them to colonial

---

21 Nana Poku and Lloyd Pettiford (eds), *Redefining the Third World* (Macmillan Press 1998) XIII.

22 Kamal Hossain (ed.), *Legal Aspects of the New International Economic Order* (Pinter 1980) 2.

23 Fernand Braudel, *The Perspective of the World: Civilization and Capitalism 15th–18th Century*, vol III (Fontana Press 1985) 220–35.

24 Badaru (n 2) 380.

25 Makau Mutua, 'What is TWAIL?' (2000) 94 ASIL Proceedings 31.

26 Ibid 32.

27 Obiora C Okafor, 'Newness, Imperialism, and International Legal Reform in Our Time: A TWAIL Perspective' (2005) 43 *Osgoode Hall Law Journal* 171, 177.

28 Bhupinder S Chimni, 'The World of TWAIL: Introduction to the Special Issue' (2011) 3(1) *Trade, Law and Development* 14, 17.

domination just a few years prior.[29] Significantly, it questioned the ability of international economic governance to safeguard developing countries' interests in the global economy.

A. Methodological Pluralism and Common Concerns

Mutua defines TWAIL as a 'broad dialectic of opposition to international law' by the developing world.[30] Al Attar and Miller, define it as 'an alternative narrative to international law that has developed in opposition to the realities of domination and subordination prevalent in the international legal apparatus.'[31] To others, TWAIL sets to reclaim law, while harnessing the critical insights of new approaches to international law in constructing a more nuanced style of critique, especially in terms of the relationship between notions of law and neo-liberal policies of development. TWAIL is an alternative method of international legal theory.[32] It is certainly as much a method as feminism, critical legal studies and international relations/international law.[33] But it is not solely a 'method', if by 'method' we refer to a means of solely determining 'what the law is'.[34] It is a polemical or counter-hegemonic term designed to rupture received thinking, challenging the colonialist and Eurocentric foundations of international law.[35] It is united in its opposition to the politics of empire.[36] At the very least, TWAIL falls under the umbrellas of both 'theory' and 'methodology' for analyzing international law and its institutions,[37] and exposing international law's hegemonic tendencies in

---

[29] Antony Anghie, 'TWAIL: Past and Future' (2008) 10(4) *International Community Law Review* 479, 480.

[30] Mutua (n 25) 31.

[31] Al Attar and Miller (n 3).

[32] Obiora C Okafor, 'Critical Third World Approaches to International Law (TWAIL): Theory, Methodology, or Both?' (2008) 10 *International Community Law Review* 371, 376.

[33] Antony Anghie and Bhupinder S Chimni, 'Third World Approaches to International Law and Individual Responsibility in Internal Conflict' (2003) 2 *Chinese Journal of International Law* 77.

[34] Ibid.

[35] James T Gathii, 'Alternative and Critical: The Contribution of Research and Scholarship on Developing Countries to International Legal Theory' (2000) 41 Harv ILJ 163, 274.

[36] Chimni (n 28) 17.

[37] Okafor (n 32) 377.

relation to developing countries. TWAIL is committed to addressing the explicitly political questions of agency, resistance, and the future of international law.[38]

TWAIL therefore refers to opposition to the generally unjust character of international law, that all too often (but not always) helps subject developing countries to domination, subordination, and serious disadvantage.[39] It seeks to transform international law from a language of oppression to a language of emancipation – a body of rules and practices that reflect and embody the struggles and aspirations of developing countries and their people and that, thereby, promote truly global justice.[40] Thus, TWAIL offers histories and mentalities of self-determination and self-governance. It insists on the recognition of cultural and civilizational plurality and diversity.[41] TWAIL provides a methodological framework for unpacking the manner in which national policies of developing countries are dictated by conditionalities imposed by international institutions and in the interest of economically powerful countries.[42]

There is arguably no credible theoretical approach which unites TWAIL jurists; they merely share a sensibility and a political orientation.[43] TWAIL harnesses critical insights from a variety of disciplines, including post-colonialism, cultural studies, Marxism, critical race theory and critical legal theory.[44] Yet, TWAIL should not suffer reproach due to its internal diversity. As long as it continues to cohere around a broadly unifying intellectual idea, or set of ideas, its relatively minor, but still creative internal contestations, should not be mistaken for incoherence.[45] TWAIL jurists acknowledge that TWAIL's parameters are not well

---

38 Ruth Buchanan, 'Writing Resistance Into International Law' (2008) 10 *International Community Law Review* 445, 447.

39 Okafor (n 27) 176.

40 Anghie and Chimni (n 33) 78.

41 Upendra Baxi, 'What May the "Third World" Expect from International Law?' (2006) 27 *Third World Quarterly* 713, 714.

42 Jalia Kangave, '"Taxing" TWAIL: A Preliminary Inquiry into TWAIL's Application to the Taxation of Foreign Direct Investment' (2008) 10 *International Community Law Review* 389, 390.

43 Luis Eslava and Sundhya Pahuja, 'Between Resistance and Reform: TWAIL and the Universality of International Law' (2011) 3 *Trade, Law and Development* 104.

44 James T Gathii, 'Neoliberalism, Colonialism and International Governance: Decentering the International Law of Governmental Legitimacy' (2000) 98 Mich LRev 1996, 1997 ff.

45 Okafor (n 32) 376.

defined, but it is generally understood that TWAIL seeks to oppose international law's hegemony.[46] TWAIL is therefore defined by a commonality of concerns. These concerns center on attempts to attune the operation of international law to those sites and subjects that have traditionally been positioned as the 'others' of international law.[47] So while far from a theology, it represents a 'chorus of voices' rather than a monolithic collegium.[48] To be part of the TWAIL movement, one does not have to subscribe to a party program. It is simply a loose network of jurists whose work is animated by the concern to establish a truly universal international law that is sympathetic to developing countries' concerns.[49]

B. Substantive Themes of the TWAIL Analysis

TWAIL jurists have written extensively on international law's role in marginalizing developing countries; most of the literature centers on what may loosely be categorized as self-determination.[50] They have explored the war on terror,[51] the role of social movements, women, the environment[52] and the Third World from an indigenous perspective.[53] Additionally, TWAIL debates have focused, inter alia, on the concept of statehood, State sovereignty, economic intervention[54] and the role that international law, and international institutions in particular, play in buttressing colonialism today.[55]

Thus, a foremost purpose of TWAIL is to make international law truly universal by writing resistance into it, in an effort to make international

---

46 Okafor (n 27) 176; see also Gathii (n 35) 274; Chimni (n 28) 18.

47 Chimni (n 28) 18; see also Eslava and Pahuja (n 43) 117.

48 Okafor (n 27) 176.

49 Bhupinder S Chimni, 'Third World Approaches to International Law: A Manifesto' (2006) 8 *International Community Law Review* 3, 18; Kangave (n 42) 389.

50 Kangave (n 42) 390.

51 Obiora C Okafor, 'The Third World, International Law, and the "Post-9/11 Era": An Introduction' (2005) 43(1/2) *Osgoode Hall Law Journal* 1.

52 Sara L Seck, 'Transnational Business and Environmental Harm: A TWAIL Analysis of Home State Obligations' (2011) 3(1) *Trade, Law and Development* 164.

53 Kangave (n 42) 390 ff.

54 Gathii (n 6).

55 Kangave (n 42) 390.

law 'recognize' the plight of developing countries.[56] Without such recognition, even potentially resistant discourses, such as development, will become swallowed up in the expanding scope of international law's hegemony.[57] TWAIL helps jurists to appreciate how international law is often manipulated to promote Western neo-liberal objectives.[58] It helps jurists critique the oft-proclaimed high moral ground occupied by the West and mainstream international law, especially as it relates to socio-economic under-development of developing countries.[59] For example, developing countries have the prospect of development, but only if they 'follow' the path of and in so far as they do not interfere with the economic needs and aspirations of former colonial masters.[60]

TWAIL opposes Western hegemony, which the UN legitimizes through the cloak of universality. TWAIL reveals the flagrant disregard by the UN of developing countries' problems and how the selective use of UN organs to advance Western foreign policy stands in direct contradiction to its high sounding morals.[61] A TWAIL perspective, therefore, helps scholars to understand international law's inconsistencies, particularly in the perpetuation of injustice against developing countries.[62] TWAIL demonstrates the discrepancy between the contradictory languages that international law adopts in its different subject streams.[63] For example, while international law purports to promote State sovereignty and self-determination, it seems to pay little attention when the application of other regimes or rules of international law restrict the sovereignty of developing countries. Neither universality nor its promise of global order make international law a 'legitimate' code of global governance.[64] Thus, *prima facie*, an intellectual goal of TWAIL is to deconstruct international law in order to show its internal inconsistencies.[65]

TWAIL attacks international law's machinery that legitimizes global moral depravity. Depravity, not unlike law, is a product of society. To

---

56 Balakrishnan Rajagopal, *International Law from Below: Development Social Movements and Third World Resistance* (CUP 2003) 1–5.

57 Buchanan (n 38) 448.

58 Badaru (n 2) 383.

59 Ibid.

60 James T Gathii, 'International Law and Eurocentricity' (1998) 9 EJIL 184, 200.

61 Mutua (n 25) 37.

62 Badaru (n 2) 383.

63 Ibid.

64 Ibid.

65 Andrew F Sunter, 'TWAIL as Naturalized Epistemological Inquiry' (2007) 20 *Canadian Journal of Law and Jurisprudence* 475, 477.

counter it, TWAIL seeks to reform the social paradigm that lay at the heart of the bipolar division,[66] manifesting itself in the economic gap between developed and developing countries.[67] TWAIL is united in its rejection of what its champions regard as an unjust relationship between developing countries and international law.[68] TWAIL exposes how international law preserves a power hierarchy much like the one experienced during the colonial era.[69] TWAIL claims that classical international law was based on the supremacy of white Europeans and their 'duty' to civilize and control non-Europeans.[70] Thus, TWAIL is anti-hierarchical, and, therefore, views the current international law regime as illegitimate, given that much, if not all, of international law has been driven by complexes of superiority. Hence, since its emergence, TWAIL has sought through scholarship, policy and politics, to eradicate the conditions of underdevelopment and to embark on a mission aimed at improving the socio-economic status of developing countries.[71]

III. PARADIGM SHIFT IN THE INTERNATIONAL ECONOMIC GOVERNANCE CRITIQUE

A. Moving Away from NEC and NIEO Models

For a long time, TWAIL preoccupied itself with colonialism and the colonial origin of international law. Great emphasis was placed on colonialism and how it legitimized the suppression of the non-European world.[72] TWAIL's engagement with international economic governance became part of the dominant discourse in the developing world, following the post-colonial realization that critique of colonialism was fruitless; in fact, the new 'political kingdom' was a hollow edifice of neo-colonial control.[73] To a large extent, this was informed by earlier Latin American

---

66 Al Attar and Miller (n 3) 348.

67 Chimni (n 49) 18.

68 Ibid.

69 Madhav Khosla, 'The TWAIL Discourse: The Emergence of the New Phase' (2007) 9 *International Community Law Review* 291, 296.

70 Mutua (n 25) 36.

71 Ibid 31.

72 Khosla (n 69) 297.

73 Joseph Oloka-Onyango, 'Heretical Reflections on the Right to Self-Determination: Prospects and Problems for a Democratic Global Future in the New Millennium' (1999) 15 *American University International Law Review* 151, 172.

NEC claims,[74] which refer to the right of a country to exercise its sovereignty over its economy without subscribing to the rules of international law. After decolonization, the NEC debate continued to influence developing countries' engagement with international economic governance. This later gave way to the NIEO debate that permeated international relations from the 1960s through to the 1980s. By an NIEO, developing countries sought to restructure international economic relations by establishing an equilibrium between the primarily raw-material-producing developing economies and Western industrial economies, thereby challenging the application to them of unfair international trading, investment and finance rules.[75]

Wrought by the deepening gloom brought on by expanding mechanisms of indirect economic governance by international economic institutions and the creation of an integrated global economic governance structure that constrained and supplanted the economies of (especially poorer) countries, the G-77, a group of developing countries, rebelled against the structure of the international economic governance.[76] Like TWAIL, the G-77 emerged in the post-colonial era and can be linked back to Afro-Asian post-colonial struggles. The Group of 77 was established in 1963, with seventy-five nations, composed of African, Asian, and Latin American States. However, it was not until 1964, in Geneva, that the Group introduced the 'Joint Declaration of the Developing Countries' into the United Nations Conference on Trade and Development (UNCTAD)[77] and began to act as a unit on substantive issues. From there a new collective diplomacy had come into being along with the creation of the Group of 77.[78] Notably, these countries revolted against the continued domination of international economic relations by developed countries upon the realization that political independence had not guaranteed similar economic independence. Developing countries devoted significant attention to the international investment regime, and

---

74 Antonio Cassese, *International Law in a Divided World* (OUP 1992) 51.

75 Gathii (n 6) 256–8.

76 Buchanan (n 38) 447.

77 Joint Declaration of Seventy-Seven Countries Made at the Conclusion of the United Nations Conference on Trade and Development, Geneva, 15 June 1964 <http://www.g77.org/doc/Joint%20Declaration.html> accessed on 27 August 2014.

78 Alan G Friedman and Cynthia A Williams, 'The Group of 77 at the United Nations: An Emergent Force in the Law of the Sea' (1979) 16 San Diego LRev 555, 557–9.

the methods by which investment disputes were settled.[79] Nevertheless, with greater participation in international economic relations, developing countries moved away from the NEC and NIEO models due to their growing irrelevance in an international economic system where protectionism meant economic suicide.

Today, debates surrounding international economic governance place less emphasis on having control over one's domestic economy as set out earlier in the NEC model or overhauling international economic law as set out in the NIEO model. TWAIL now engenders a broader critical sting towards analyzing how developing countries participate in international governance. Contemporary analysis places more emphasis on the ability of developing countries to participate in the global economy.[80] TWAIL maintains as paramount its objective of improving the socio-economic situation in the South in accordance with the development aspirations of developing countries. Despite this paradigm shift, TWAIL continues to provide a forthright critique of contemporary international economic governance, using historical and cultural evidence, such as the failed NIEO project, to show that the central doctrines of international economic law are not universal, that is, representative of the values and beliefs of the entire international community.[81] Nevertheless, some NEC and NIEO concerns continue to permeate TWAIL's engagement with international economic governance. These concerns manifest themselves in the unequal participation by developing countries in the global economy and the inability of developing countries to fairly participate in international economic governance as illustrated by the 'regime bias' debate.[82] By regime bias, reference is made to the manner in which international economic law is often manipulated when investor's interests are at stake. Unfairness relates to the structural inability of developing countries to retake control of domestic economies without facing costly and biased dispute settlement processes that threaten to frustrate their development goals.[83]

---

[79] Antony Anghie, *Imperialism, Sovereignty and the Making of International Law* (2nd edn, CUP 2007) 224–5.

[80] Gathii (n 6) 261.

[81] Sunter (n 65) 476.

[82] Gathii (n 6) 261.

[83] Olivia Chung, 'The Lopsided International Investment Law Regime and Its Effect on the Future of Investor-State Arbitration' (2007) 47 Va JIL 953, 955.

B. TWAIL's Engagement with the Regime Bias Debate

Regime bias is the latest in a series of developing world critiques of international economic governance. It refers to the manner in which 'rules of international trade, commerce and investment are crafted, applied and adjudicated between developed and developing countries, or between developing countries and the interest of global capital.'[84] It also refers to an examination of the choices made between alternative ways of crafting legal rules, the meaning ascribed to a particular rule in its application by administrative agencies or at the adjudication stage by domestic judicial bodies or international tribunals.[85] To TWAIL jurists, considerations of regime bias manifests in the following considerations: first, international economic law is not a neutral and objective set of rules, but an instrument employed in a context of power relations between developed and developing countries; second, international economic law reflects an underlying racism against former colonies that remain 'others' in international relations; and third, international institutions may interpret and apply international law in ways that are biased systematically against developing countries' interests.[86]

Unlike the NEC and NIEO models,[87] proponents of the regime bias critique claim that it also exposes the political, legal and other stakes between developed and developing economies. For example, Shalakany, in examining 'bias' in investor-State arbitration, argues that bias in this context is not the discernible and determinate outcome of doctrines and institutions.[88] He tries to illustrate how three Libyan arbitrations,[89] concerning three similar expropriations in the 1970s,[90] decided by three different arbitrators, each resulted in three different awards, although all

---

[84] Van Harten (n 8) 136; see also Gathii (n 6) 261.

[85] Gathii (n 6) 261; see also Van Harten (n 8) 136.

[86] Van Harten (n 8) 1–25.

[87] Gathii (n 6) 255–60.

[88] Amr Shalakany, 'Arbitration and the Third World: A Plea for Reassessing Bias under the Spectre of Neoliberalism' (2000) 41 Harv ILJ 419, 453; see also Gathii (n 35) 270.

[89] *British Petroleum Exploration Company Ltd v The Government of the Libyan Arab Republic* (10 October 1973) (1979) 53 ILR 297; *Libyan American Oil Company (LIAMCO) v The Government of the Libyan Arab Republic* (12 April 1977) (1981) 20 ILM 1; *Texaco Overseas Petroleum Company and California Asiatic Oil Company v The Government of the Libyan Arab Republic*, Award (19 January 1977) (1979) 53 ILR 389.

[90] These expropriations resulted from Colonel Gaddafi's desire for Libyan oil, which had hitherto been controlled by foreigners, to be controlled by the Libyan Government.

three were against Libya.[91] Shalakany argues that international law's legal indeterminacy is a plausible explanatory tool to understand bias, and that exclusive reliance on legal logic to account for bias is simply inadequate.[92] Shalakany reveals that three bipolar manifestations of the public/private distinction might enrich doctrinal analysis: contract/politics, equal/unequal and property/sovereignty. Once Libya's actions were associated with politics and the coercive exercise of sovereign powers in an unequal relationship, Libya was denied access to a host of legal interpretations, which would have been more favorable to its position. Consequently, the arbitrators were able to argue that the controversy was contractual and not political, between two equal parties, and about property and not sovereignty.[93]

Thus, a regime bias analysis shows how legal interpretations of international economic law enable powerful economies to manage the tensions of engaging in international commerce to 'buy-off' losers from international trade within their economies.[94] Even where the North and South are framed as formally equal before the law, the premises of the legal form and its basic concepts, such as contract and property, inherently favor those endowed with economic power.[95] Advocates argue that regime bias also helps demonstrate the discrepancy between the contradictory languages that international law adopts in its different subject streams.[96] While international law purports to promote development, it seems to pay little attention when international dispute resolution's vices consistently violate the development aspirations of developing countries. Such technocratic turns arise from the adoption of stylized legal reasoning that has a well-articulated template of competing doctrinal definitions, sources and authorities. This stylized legal reasoning is the backdrop against which legal indeterminacy gives the individuals presiding over international disputes different technocratic solutions that appear legitimate.[97] Advocates of the regime bias critique claim that it exposes the way in which the 'ideology' or consciousness of

---

91 Shalakany (n 88).

92 Ibid 452; see also Gathii (n 35) 271.

93 Shalakany (n 88) 457–59; see also Gathii (n 35) 271

94 Gathii (n 6) 263–4.

95 John Reynolds, 'The Political Economy of States of Emergency' (2012) 14 *Oregon Review of International Law* 85, 92.

96 Badaru (n 2) 383.

97 Shalakany (n 88) 419.

decision-makers in international dispute settlement often legitimates the *status quo* by disguising the internal and external flaws of international law.[98]

Regime bias uses historical examples, such as colonialism, as a sort of benchmark by which contemporary regimes are measured. For example, it foregrounds the inability of developing countries to effectively participate in the international investment regime on the ever evolving nature of international law and its manifold contemporary devices that continue to constrict developing countries' engagement with this regime. Subscribers to the TWAIL philosophy claim that whereas classical international law respected the sovereignty and prevented international law from scrutinizing or legally assessing the character of a State's government,[99] for developing countries infringement on their sovereign capacity to determine national economic policies remains the norm. The regime bias critique helps draw attention to the manner in which colonial discourse interacts with contemporary international law by attributing the persistent economic inequality of developing countries to inferior characteristics of 'otherness' and therefore rationalizes the continuing domination of the South by the North as a product of Northern superiority.[100] Regime bias illustrates how international law commonly serves as an agent of First World interests and overwhelmingly reflects continental legal thought shaped during colonialism.[101] So structured, the regime bias critique reveals the replication of a subtler form of colonialism through international law. It reveals how developed countries simultaneously impose First World ambitions upon the rest of the world, while reproducing colonial domination and exploitation within a formalized system of hegemony.[102] Its disguised liberal framework legitimates significant conglomerations of power, preserving and extending the legal shorthand of private property rights, commandeering control over resources and labor to moneyed elites. Thus, a comparative analysis of the ways in which international law facilitated the economic exploitation of non-Europeans during colonialism and the extent to which its role is too often repeated,

---

98 Chantal Thomas, 'Critical Race Theory and Postcolonial Development Theory: Observations on Methodology' (2000) 45 Villanova LRev 1195.

99 Antony Anghie, 'Civilization and Commerce: The Concept of Governance in Historical Perspective' (2000) 45 Villanova LRev 887, 895–6.

100 Thomas (n 98) 1208.

101 Al Attar and Miller (n 3) 353.

102 Ibid.

reveals that international economic law is being interpreted and applied in ways that supplant developing countries' economic interests.[103]

Consequently, a regime bias analysis reveals that rules are capable of being construed unfavorably towards vulnerable economies. However, its value is primarily in exposing how the construal or application of specific rules entrench uneven consequences between developed and developing countries. It illustrates specifically how these rules can be applied and adjudicated in ways that are inimical to developing economies.[104] It does so by foregrounding a particular way of tracing adverse outcomes for these countries in the global economy and showing that these outcomes are not inevitable. An example that comes to mind, in this context, is the manner in which the arbitral tribunal established pursuant to the rules of the International Chamber of Commerce (ICC) in the *Dabhol Arbitration*[105] approached the dispute. This arbitration produced the only publicly available award in a series of disputes between the Indian government, on the one hand, and Bechtel, Enron and General Electric, on the other, following the termination of an agreement to construct natural gas-fired electricity plants in Maharashtra. In addition to the non-equitability of the agreement, which was far more profitable to the investors than it was to India, India cited numerous irregularities in relation to the investment, stemming from corruption and lack of transparency, human rights abuses and environmental risks, as the main reasons for terminating the agreement. Even the World Bank declined to finance the project.[106] Nonetheless, the tribunal held that India's termination was tantamount to expropriation and awarded Bechtel USD 94 million plus interest at the rate of 6 percent.[107] The point of contention in this award is the manner in which the dispute was removed from the Indian context and placed in the sphere of international arbitration, notwithstanding the absence of any reference in the agreement to international arbitration and the fact that an Indian court had ruled against any reference to international arbitration.[108]

---

[103] Baxi (n 41) 715.

[104] Gathii (n 6) 260–63.

[105] *Capital India Power* (n 16).

[106] Human Rights Watch, 'The Enron Corporation: Corporate Complicity and Human Rights Violations' <http://www.hrw.org/reports/pdfs/i/india/enron991.pdf> accessed 18 August 2014.

[107] Van Harten (n 8) 1–25.

[108] Ibid 136.

To TWAIL jurists, regime bias exposes the biased manner in which international tribunals interpret and apply rules in dispute resolution to further the phenomenon of neoliberalism, which is a common characteristic of economies of most industrialized countries and the global economy, inconsistently with its liberal promise of fairness.[109] It challenges the neo-liberal agenda of deeply integrating developing economies into the Western-dominated global economy using international dispute resolution. TWAIL claims that institutions charged with regulating the global economy, such as the WTO, NAFTA and ICSID principally reward winners in the metropolis, that is, developed countries, at the expense of losers in the periphery, that is, developing countries.[110] Moreover, globalization has significantly facilitated the proliferation of international tribunals that subordinate the roles of domestic tribunals in resolving disputes. These range from the WTO Dispute Settlement Understanding (DSU) to investor-State arbitration tribunals. However, it is not the greater internationalization that is problematic, but the biased application of rules for developing countries and their impact on these countries.[111] Nowhere is regime bias clearer than in international investment law and the manner in which developing countries have engaged with this regime.

IV. PARTICIPATION OF DEVELOPING COUNTRIES IN INTERNATIONAL INVESTMENT LAW

Emerging from colonialism, initially, Latin American countries denounced investor-State dispute resolution mechanisms that sought to pry disputes from domestic settings, as illustrated by the Calvo doctrine. This stipulated that aliens relinquished the right to request the diplomatic protection of their home State and agreed to have disputes settled by domestic tribunals.[112] It sought to limit legal and political intervention in Latin America, which often constituted the pretext or the occasion for armed expeditions, political pressure, or other forms of economic interference.[113] These experiences continued to influence the reaction of

---

109 Ibid.

110 José E Alvarez, 'Contemporary Foreign Investment Law: "An Empire of Law" or the "Law of Empire"?' (2009) 60 Alabama LRev 943, 951.

111 Chimni (n 49) 13.

112 Cassese (n 74) 50.

113 Ibid.

other developing countries towards international investment law after decolonization.[114] Thus, even though BITs and ICSID had both been in existence since the 1960s, they were not employed with any frequency until the 1990s.[115] Today, developing countries continue to view investor-State dispute settlement as unfair, undemocratic and biased against States, particularly countries with limited resources.[116]

Regime bias concerns in investor-State dispute resolution are sites of contemporary interests for developing countries.[117] This interest is manifested predominantly in the legitimacy concerns that continue to characterize the manner in which developing countries engage with the international investment regime.[118] BIT negotiation[119] and investor-State arbitration, both of which continue to elude developing countries' effective participation, are sites of concern.[120] Therefore, several developing countries have expressed skeptical views on the current state of the international investment regime.[121] Skepticism relates to the reverence of BITs and investor-State arbitration in Western circles, while highlighting how they negatively impact developing countries. Due to developing countries' desire to attract investment, North-South BIT negotiation, in particular, often seems lopsided in favor of developed countries as a consequence of the uneven participation of developing countries.[122] Unfortunately, these treaties bind them when disputes arise.

---

[114] Ibironke T Odumosu, 'The Law and Politics of Engaging Resistance in Investment Dispute Settlement' (2007) 26 Penn State ILRev 251, 256.

[115] Chung (n 83) 954.

[116] Butler and Subedi (n 14) 201.

[117] Van Harten (n 8) 136.

[118] Charles N Brower and Stephan W Schill, 'Is Arbitration a Threat or a Boom to the Legitimacy of International Investment Law?' (2009) 9 Chi JIL 471.

[119] Jeswald W Salacuse, 'Your Draft or Mine?' (2007) 5 *Negotiation Journal* 337.

[120] Odumosu (n 114) 253–4.

[121] Franck (n 13) 826–914; see *Occidental Exploration and Production Company v The Republic of Ecuador*, LCIA Case No UN 3467, Final Award (1 July 2004).

[122] Chung (n 83) 955.

A. The Lack of Real Participation of Developing Countries in International Investment Rule-Making

With the colonial mechanism no longer available, new investment rules were desirable. Developed countries desired a means to maintain the colonial-style procurement of raw materials from newly independent, resource-rich developing countries, and novel mechanisms to ensure the protection of such resource procurement. To give the façade of neutrality, these mechanisms had to be depoliticized from both the governance structures of an investor's home country and country of investment. Due to fears of bias on both sides, neither States nor investors wished for disputes to be resolved under either of their national legal systems. This saw the emergence of BITs as regulators of international investments.

In 1959, West Germany and Pakistan signed the first BIT.[123] In 2003, the world BIT count was slightly above 2000.[124] Today, there are over 3000 BITs.[125] BITs' success stem from their overt preferential treatment of investors. This is an anathema to what some recognize as the particular 'susceptibility' of investors *vis-à-vis* host governments. BITs lessen sovereign authority in matters over which national law otherwise grants complete authority.[126] States may be inhibited from taking regulatory action over investor behavior, even where public policy demands it and national law authorizes a sovereign to do so. Thus, capital exporting countries see BITs as a means of investment protection, removing governments from the difficult role of espousal and depoliticization.[127] BITs seek to promote the fidelity of contractual agreements, and limit undue hindrance of market-driven commitments of capital.[128] Therefore, BITs have become part of the normal investment landscape.[129] They

---

123 Tom Ginsburg, 'International Substitutes for Domestic Institutions: Bilateral Investment Treaties and Governance' (2005) 25 *International Review of Law and Economics* 107, 108; see also Alvarez (n 110) 960.

124 Ginsburg (n 123) 108.

125 UNCTAD, *World Investment Report 2015: Reforming International Investment Governance* (United Nations 2015) 106.

126 Ginsburg (n 123) 108.

127 Carlos G Garcia, 'All the Other Dirty Little Secrets: Investment Treaties, Latin America, and the Necessary Evil of Investor-State Arbitration' (2004) 16 Florida JIL 301, 312–14.

128 Andrew T Guzman, 'Why LDCs Sign Treaties That Hurt Them: Explaining The Popularity of Bilateral Investment Treaties' (1998) 38 Va JIL 639.

129 Ibid.

represent a crucial part of international investment regulation, spelling out the duties of host States.

Critics reveal that with all the attention attributed to them, BITs are rather obscure instruments. Precisely how and when a State's liability under its own law gives rise to a breach of BIT protection is impossible to determine and there is little jurisprudence to help draw the line.[130] TWAIL views the rapid evolution of the BIT regime as not being by chance, but part of the normative agenda of developed countries to dominate international economic governance. TWAIL sees BITs as *de facto* enforcers of an international investment regime that seeks to rein in recalcitrant investment hosts in the developing world.[131] So, despite the reverence for BITs among developed countries and the recent surge in the participation of developing countries in the process,[132] a critique of BITs casts a shadow on the entire system.[133]

TWAIL claims that due to economic vulnerability, developing countries have generally failed to participate meaningfully in the evolution of the BIT regime. Effective negotiation is supplanted by developing countries' desire to attract foreign capital.[134] Due to the economic-relief needs of developing countries, they have generally entered into agreements with developed countries that they otherwise would not have.[135] In the competition to attract investment, potential host States end up in a bidding contest for investment capital. Olivia Chung reveals that 'developing countries may feel compelled to undermine interests and concerns

---

[130] Garcia (n 127) 328.

[131] See, e.g., Agreement for the Promotion and Protection of Investment (Netherlands-Philippines) (adopted 27 February 1985, entered into force 1 October 1987) [1985] Tractatenblad (Neth) No 86, art 2 [hereinafter Netherlands-Philippines Treaty] states: 'Each Contracting Party shall encourage and create favorable conditions for investments, consistent with its national objectives, of nationals of the other Contracting Party, subject to the laws and regulations of the Party in whose territory the investment is made ...' See Jeswald W Salacuse, 'Bit by Bit: The Growth of Bilateral Investment Treaties and Their Impact on Foreign Investment in Developing Countries' (1990) 24 *The International Lawyer* 675, 666.

[132] Jennifer L Tobin and Marc L Busch, 'A Bit is Better than a Lot: Bilateral Investment Treaties and Preferential Trade Agreements' (2010) 62 *World Politics* 1.

[133] Odumosu (n 114) 254.

[134] Chung (n 83) 955.

[135] Antonius R Hippolyte, 'Calls for National Intervention in the Toxic Waste Trade with Africa: A Contemporary Issue in the Environmental Justice Debate' (2012) 58 Loyola LRev 301, 302.

in exchange for greater incentives to investors, such as tax breaks, reduced pollution controls, and relaxed employment regulations.'[136] Thus TWAIL views developing countries as being in a disadvantaged position when negotiating BITs with wealthier States whose investors can choose among numerous developing countries. Thus, lack of economic clout has resulted in BIT negotiation, where the benefits for developed countries vastly outweigh the benefit to developing countries.[137]

The *realpolitik* of relationships between countries like the United States, for example, and their BIT counterparts offer an even darker picture of the BIT negotiating process.[138] José E. Alvarez, a former member of the US State Department BIT-negotiating team, describes it in the following terms:

> For many, a BIT relationship is hardly a voluntary, 'uncoerced' transaction. They [US BIT partners] feel that they must enter into the arrangement, or that they would be foolish not to. For Latin American countries, the BIT represents a return to the earlier days of reliance on FDI – before they learned to fear becoming dependent. But the truth is to date the US model BIT has been regarded as, generally-speaking, a 'take it or leave it' proposition, with the United States calling the shots and the BIT partner as supplicant. … A BIT negotiation is not a discussion between sovereign equals. It is more like an intensive training seminar conducted by the United States, on US terms, on what it would take to comply with the US draft.[139]

Unfortunately, neither has there been concern for poorer countries affected, nor for the fact that the fundamental bases of the discipline are being distorted. It is a sad episode, which demonstrates that 'greed' and not 'need' drives the international investment regime.[140] Developed countries continue to dominate the international investment regime, while developing countries play a subordinate role. Indeed, while there is an increasing number of South-South BITs, UNCTAD data reveals that there are only a handful of Southern States with the capacity to invest any meaningful capital in other developing or industrialized countries.[141] In 2013, almost half of the FDI from developing and transition economy

---

136 Chung (n 83) 958.

137 Salacuse (n 119) 337–41.

138 Guzman (n 128); see also Garcia (n 127) 316.

139 Jose E Alvarez, 'Remarks' (1992) 86 ASIL Proceedings 550, 552–53.

140 Muthucumaraswamy Sornarajah, 'Mutations of Neo-Liberalism in International Investment Law' (2011) 3 *Trade, Law and Development* 203, 207.

141 UNCTAD, 'Trends in Outward Investments by Transnational Corporations in 2013 and Prospects for 2014–15' (29 April 2014) <http://unctad.org/en/pages/newsdetails.aspx?OriginalVersionID=729> accessed 20 June 2014.

transnational corporations (TNCs) was in equity, while developed countries held 'large amounts of cash reserves in their foreign affiliates as part of reinvested earnings. The latter were at record levels of 67 per cent of total FDI outflows from developed countries.'[142] While it is true that investment activity abroad by TNCs from developing economies grew in 2013, reaching a record level of USD 460 billion, more than two-thirds of the international community is comprised of developing countries with vast resources, yet together with those from transition economies (USD 100 billion) they account for merely 39 percent of global foreign direct investment (FDI) outflows, while TNCs from a few developed countries held USD 858 billion worth or 55 percent of global investments.[143] So debates surrounding the emergence of more South-South BITs have been belied by the fact that investment flows from the South are still insignificant compared to North-South investment flows.

In addition to BIT negotiation, TWAIL continues to look upon developing countries' minimal participation in the evolution of the rules of international investment regulation with disdain. Due to the incidence of developed countries emerging as respondents in investment disputes in the present course of international investment law,[144] these countries are once again significantly engaging in the re-development of the rules governing foreign investments. TWAIL reveals that before the 1990s, investment rules seemed settled, at least from the perspective of developed countries, until rules formerly applied almost exclusively to developing countries in dispute settlement proceedings were extended to developed countries. Suddenly, the rules appeared inadequate and biased in favor of investors, and developed countries increasingly adopted the formerly untenable arguments of developing countries.[145] Therefore, while the distinct investment protection purpose still predominates, it competes with the new agenda of some developed countries to rewrite, or at least to amend applicable rules to accommodate their interest as defendants.[146]

TWAIL jurists reveal that international investment law has evolved in a manner that methodically resists peculiar influence of developing countries. To them, there exists a significant lack of participation from developing countries in promulgating the rules of the international investment regime. The rules are now being reformulated to protect the

---

142 Ibid.
143 UNCTAD (n 141).
144 Alvarez (n 110) 943–75.
145 Odumosu (n 114) 256.
146 Sornarajah (n 140) 203.

interests of developed countries in investor-State dispute proceedings.[147] The rationales for the emerging rules are strikingly familiar as they echo earlier arguments of developing countries (which were not favorably received) on the invasive nature of some international investment rules.[148] Arguments earlier rejected, including concerns about sovereignty erosion, have gained currency in some forums.[149] According to TWAIL, these changes in the international investment regime resemble the general trend in international economic law where accepted rules mostly derive from the initiative of economically powerful States, or at least sanctioned by them.[150] For this reason, even though the system is beginning to incorporate developed countries as defendants,[151] investment arbitration, for example, has been described as a discipline that applies mostly to developing countries.[152] Unfortunately, however, developing countries have generally incorporated the construction of North-South BITs in South-South BITs, not because they accept the structure of North-South BITs, but again due to their desire to present themselves as attractive havens for investment capital to their Southern neighbors. Nonetheless, due to the manner in which BITs are currently construed, developing countries desire a BIT model that balances their national interest against investors' economic interests when disputes arise.

B. The Attitude Towards Investor-State Dispute Settlement in the Developing World: A Review of ICSID

Today, most BITs offer investors a menu of arbitration options; these can include the Stockholm Chamber of Commerce, the London Court of International Arbitration, the International Chamber of Commerce or arbitration without any supervising institution, for example pursuant to the Arbitration Rules of the United Nations Commission on International Trade Law (UNCITRAL).[153] Nonetheless, the most popular has become the World Bank's ICSID. ICSID was established during a time of intense

147 Odumosu (n 114) 255–6.

148 Anghie (n 79) 211.

149 Odumosu (n 114) 256.

150 Mickelson (n 4) 362.

151 UNCTAD, 'Latest Developments in Investor-State Dispute Settlement', IIA Monitor No 1 (April 2009) 2 <http://unctad.org/en/Docs/webdiaeia20096_en.pdf> accessed 18 August 2014.

152 Sornarajah (n 140) 203.

153 Noah Rubins and Azizjon Nazarov, 'Investment Treaties and the Russian Federation: Baiting the Bear?' (2008) 29 *Business Law International* 101.

debate about the meaning of international investment law and the scope of substantive protection for expropriation.[154] Aaron Broches shifted the discussion by focusing on the procedural mechanisms to resolve investment disputes. As General Counsel of the World Bank, Broches advocated for the creation of an impartial and stable forum, governed by a set of procedures, to settle investment disputes.[155] Thus, in 1966, the Convention on the Settlement of Investment Disputes Between States and Nationals of other States (ICSID Convention or Washington Convention)[156] established ICSID as an organ of the World Bank to help resolve investment disputes between foreigners and host countries. As of 30 May 2014, 159 countries had signed the Washington Convention and 150 had deposited their instruments of ratification.[157]

In the mainstream discourse, ICSID is considered to be today's leading institution devoted to investor-State dispute settlement. Mainstream advocates claim that this is supported by ICSID's large membership, substantial caseload and by the many references to its arbitration services in investment treaties and laws. According to them, ICSID stands to play a significant role in the field of international investment and economic development.[158] It is a key element in an international dispute settlement process that aspires to promote global sustainable development and foreign investment. Noted arbitrator Johnny Veeder, claims that 'ICSID is the best institution in its field, the best run, the best staffed, with the best rules and the best treaty.'[159] Others believe that ICSID's scrutiny flows merely from its prominence and affiliation with the World Bank.[160]

Nevertheless, to TWAIL jurists, the development of international investment law remains consumed by the agenda of developed States in a

---

154 Franck (n 13) 837.

155 Ibid.

156 Convention on the Settlement of Investment Disputes Between States and Nationals of other States (ICSID Convention) (adopted 18 March 1965, entered into force 14 October 1966) 575 UNTS 159.

157 ICSID, 'Member States' <http://icsid.worldbank.org/ICSID/FrontServlet?requestType=CasesRH&actionVal=ShowHome&pageName=MemberStates_Home> accessed 31 May 2014.

158 Charles E Aduaka, 'The Enforcement Mechanism under the International Centre for Settlement of Investment Dispute (ICSID) Arbitration Award: Issues and Challenges' (2013) 20 *Journal of Law, Policy and Globalization* 134, 134.

159 Franck (n 13) 848.

160 Ibid 841.

manner that eludes particular influence of developing countries.[161] Notwithstanding ICSID's high-sounding ideals, TWAIL views it as an institution consumed by metropolitan influence. TWAIL reminds us that ICSID is not an autonomous body, but the judicial arm of an international organization whose key stakeholders are developed countries. It is recorded that the US, which holds the largest share of the World Bank's shares, significantly influenced the bank's lending policies in the 1990s[162] and, notwithstanding the fact that different arbitrators decide these disputes, could just as easily influence ICSID's dispute settlement processes.

Moreover, the manner in which ICSID has evolved reflects the neo-liberal attitude of developed countries towards the international investment regime.[163] This can be seen in TWAIL literature surrounding ICSID's emergence.[164] For instance, ICSID was originally envisioned as an entity providing dispute resolution services for disputes arising out of agreements between investors and States that had ratified the Washington Convention. Nonetheless, in 1978, ICSID's Administrative Council created the Additional Facility (AF) Rules.[165] The AF Rules expanded dispute resolution services to provide an additional ground for securing recourse to arbitration for those cases where only one of the parties to the dispute was a convention signatory or an investor from a convention signatory, thereby expanding ICSID's jurisdiction. Although AF arbitrations are not ICSID awards for enforcement purposes, they still benefit from nearly identical arbitration rules and ICSID's administrative support and processes. TWAIL views this development as a further attempt to rein in recalcitrant developing countries, that had not ratified the Washington Convention, which was drafted in the heydays of nationalist convergence in the developing world.

ICSID was established in the euphoria of these times. Due to ICSID's establishment, investor-State dispute settlement was institutionalized for the first time as a depoliticized system.[166] According to TWAIL jurists,

---

161 Reynolds (n 95) 121.

162 Thomas Barnebeck Andersen, Henrik Hansen and Thomas Markussen, 'US Politics and World Bank IDA-lending' (2006) 42(5) *Journal of Development Studies* 772.

163 Guzman (n 128).

164 Odumosu (n 114).

165 Franck (n 13) 840.

166 Odumosu (n 114) 254.

several factors shaped the emergence and character of ICSID.[167] After World War II, investment disputes became increasingly internationalized because they were subject to international arbitration and international law emerged as the primarily applicable substantive law.[168] TWAIL views this development as a consequence of the investors' perception that the application of the host State's law and adjudication by domestic tribunals were prejudicial to their interests.[169] Thus, by placing investment disputes within the international domain, developed countries ensured that their economic interests remained within structures that were accessible to (and dominated by) them.[170] It filled the need to protect foreign investment in developing countries and the promise that investment protection would attract foreign investment to the developing world.

In spite of the suspicions surrounding international dispute settlement at the time, a considerable number of developing countries, excluding most Latin American countries, signed the ICSID Convention with hopes of reaping the institution's benefits. Although Latin American countries had achieved their independence much earlier, the disinclination towards ICSID in these countries, like most of the developing world, was the result of their opposition to the domination of international economic relations by the West.[171] Nonetheless, with the need to protect investors' interests and the desire of developing countries to increase inflows of investment capital, ICSID found its place in the multifarious world of international investment dispute settlement.[172]

Nevertheless, recent legitimacy concerns emanating from the developing world have, again, left ICSID shrouded in controversy. The disregard displayed towards developing countries in the proceedings before ICSID, is a major cause of concern. According to TWAIL, parties to arbitration proceedings are generally construed narrowly as the investor and the host State as private entities, with the arbitration itself framed as a commercial matter. Public interest considerations and the needs and desires of vulnerable economies and poverty stricken populations are incidental.[173] Additionally, investor-State arbitration as conducted by ICSID has no

---

167 Ibid.

168 Ibid.

169 Shalakany (n 88) 419–68.

170 Odumosu (n 114) 254.

171 AF Abbott, 'Latin America and International Arbitration Conventions: The Quandary of Non-Ratification' (1976) 17 Harv ILJ 131.

172 Odumosu (n 114) 255.

173 Reynolds (n 95) 121.

determinate outcome and is subject to the manner in which the rules of international economic law are interpreted by the tribunal. This, in turn, may be affected by the desire to protect private property rights which is essential to the continuation of Western economic domination, and not because these developing countries are pre-disposed to being unsuccessful. Thus, a lack of effective and consistent review or appeal mechanism is quickly emerging as the most glaring defect of ICSID arbitration.[174] The possibility for mischief and intellectual dishonesty is real. Arbitrators who wish to be review-proof may simply ignore or distort facts, and on the basis of a skewed view of reality proceed to decide the case with impeccable legal reasoning and grounding and certainly not in a manner that could ever be characterized as an excess of jurisdiction. The mere fact that arbitral rules require written, reasoned awards is of little assistance in the unclear, open world of investor protection norms, where international law allows a decision maker to draw upon (or ignore) many sources in crafting reasons.[175] With no right to challenge errors of law or unsupported findings of fact, the losing party has no real hope of overturning even egregious decisions.

Thus, the invocation of the TWAIL perspective in international dispute settlement has recognized 'regime bias' in this modus operandi of investor-State arbitration.[176] TWAIL attributes bias in the dispute settlement process to the fact that international tribunals, such as those established under ICSID, have found themselves in the habit of widely reviewing the national economic policies of developing countries. This is biased against developing countries, because the level of transparency often required from developing countries by ICSID is seldom achievable in developed countries that have more sophisticated governance structures.[177] This was seen in *Tecnicas Medioambientales (Tecmed), S.A. v. United Mexican States*.[178] The dispute arose out of Mexico's denial of an operational permit to operate a hazardous waste landfill, which was dangerously close to a populated municipality. An ICSID tribunal held that Mexico had violated the 1995 Spain-Mexico BIT by indirectly expropriating the company's interest by refusing to issue the permit, since without the permit all other real and personal property was of little value to the investor. For reasons such as the outcome in *Tecmed*, developing countries generally, and many Latin American countries in

---

174 Garcia (n 127) 340.
175 Ibid 342.
176 Van Harten (n 8) 131–63.
177 Alvarez (n 110) 965.
178 *Tecmed v Mexico* (n 15).

particular, have expressed concerns in relation to allegations of bias and vehemently dismissed the idea of investor-State arbitration as a neutral forum.[179] In 2009, in expressing his discontent with ICSID, President of Ecuador, Rafael Correa, propounded that Ecuador's withdrawal from ICSID is necessary for 'the liberation of our countries because [it] signifies colonialism, slavery with respect to transnationals, with respect to Washington, with respect to the World Bank.'[180] Moreover, the apparent emerging pattern in ICSID jurisprudence, as seen in relation to the Argentine economic emergency, suggests the possibility of investment dispute resolutions as a site of resistance for developing countries.[181] Some have even declared that investment arbitration is not 'a fair, dependent and balanced method for the resolution of investment disputes and therefore should not be relied on.'[182]

Thus, in contrast to their domestic counterparts, international arbitral tribunals, like those established under ICSID, have found themselves in the unique position of having to defend themselves on a regular basis against attacks on their legitimacy as mechanisms for resolving disputes about the scope and limits of State sovereignty.[183] A debate has erupted about whether ICSID is an appropriate and fair forum for resolving investment treaty disputes. Some developing countries have alleged that ICSID is biased and unfair, withdrawn from the ICSID Convention, and advocated creating alternative arbitral institutions.[184] Critics have attacked ICSID's institutional legitimacy and suggested that ICSID is biased; these criticisms have gone so far as to say that the system is rigged, and ICSID represents the inequities of an international institution biased against developing countries.[185] This distrust in the system is vivid as seen in the withdrawal from ICSID of certain Latin American countries since 2007.[186]

---

[179] Nigel Blackaby, 'Arbitration' (2006) *Latin Lawyer Review* 1–5.

[180] See 'ICSID in Crisis: Straight-Jacket or Investment Protection?' Bretton Woods Project (10 July 2009) <http://www.brettonwoodsproject.org/art-564878> accessed 12 September 2014.

[181] Reynolds (n 95) 120.

[182] Gus Van Harten and others, 'Public Statement on the International Investment Regime' (31 August 2010) <http://www.osgoode.yorku.ca/public-statement/documents/Public%20Statement%20%28June%202011%29.pdf> accessed 27 February 2014.

[183] Brower and Schill (n 118) 471.

[184] Franck (n 13) 825–8.

[185] Van Harten and others (n 182).

[186] Franck (n 13) 847.

To combat 'perceived' Western dominance of investor-State arbitration, a coalition of various Latin American and Caribbean countries, known as the *Bolivarian Alternative for the People of the Americas (ALBA)*, has advocated the creation of an institution that mimics the functions of ICSID, but offers a more legitimate arbitration process.[187] As has been seen so far, developing countries have a different attitude towards international law and Latin American countries in particular have historically expressed dissenting views towards international dispute resolution. Therefore, ALBA seeks to establish a judicial arm capable of resolving investor-State disputes without having to subscribe to conventional mediums of Western interpretations of international investment law.

TWAIL reveals that while it may be argued that developing countries consent to investor-State dispute settlement processes such as that of ICSID, such arguments ignore the threat or actual incidence of economic coercion of developing countries by developed countries.[188] Developing countries who refuse to participate in these processes risk experiencing the wrath of developing countries. A notable example is the US 'First Hickenlooper Amendment'.[189] The statute represents an attempt on the part of the United States to provide an enforcement mechanism, through domestic law, that could carry out the American interpretation of international law. This law requires that the President:

> [t]erminate aid to any country that has seized American-controlled property,[190] has repudiated or nullified contracts with Americans,[191] or has imposed or enforced discriminatory taxes or other exactions, or restrictive maintenance or operational conditions,[192] [and that has failed to] discharge its obligation under international law ... including speedy compensation for such property in convertible foreign exchange, equivalent to the full value thereof ...[193]

---

[187] Joel D Hirst, 'The Bolivarian Alliance of the Americas – Hugo Chavez's Bold Plan' (*International Business and Diplomatic Exchange,* December 2010) <http://ibde.org/component/content/article/111-the-bolivarian-alliance-of-the-americas-hugo-chavezs-bold-plan.html> accessed 25 April 2014.

[188] Chimni (n 49) 3.

[189] Foreign Assistance Act of 1961, Pub L No 87–195, 77 Stat 386 (1963) (codified as amended at 22 USC § 2370(e)(1)(1994)).

[190] 22 USC § 2370(e)(1)(A) (1982).

[191] 22 USC § 2370(e)(1)(B) (1982).

[192] 22 USC § 2370(e)(1)(C) (1982).

[193] 22 USC § 2370(e)(1) (1982).

Since its adoption, this statute has been invoked twice, once against Sri Lanka in 1963 and once against Ethiopia in 1979.[194]

V. THE CALL FOR A CONSTRUCTIVE TWAIL ENGAGEMENT WITH THE INTERNATIONAL INVESTMENT REGIME

Under-development is a major concern to developing countries.[195] Concerns stem mainly from the delayed growth of most of their economies and their persistent reliance on external finance mechanisms, either in international aid,[196] or FDI that have come to dominate domestic economies.[197] TWAIL attributes development delay in developing countries to their colonial history. A pre-independence analysis of developing countries reveals that they existed to supply raw materials for their colonial masters.[198] After independence, these countries were encouraged to and continued trading in raw materials, which naturally achieve a lower price than manufactured goods. Therefore, in the post-colonial era most were unable to garner the capital required to exploit and export their resources.[199] This has had dire consequences on the socio-economic development of developing countries. Today, a person born in Niger can still expect to live 29 fewer years, to have 9 fewer years of education, and to consume 53 times fewer goods than a person born in Denmark.[200] A popular refrain among economists is that for all their sweat, developing countries are not catching up with developed countries. For every step they take forward, industrialized countries take two. Even China, the

---

194 Patricia McKinstry Robin, 'The BIT Won't Bite: The American Bilateral Investment Treaty Program' (1984) 33 *American University Law Review* 931, 938–9.

195 Chung (n 83) 958.

196 Georg Sorensen, Nana Poku and Lloyd Pettiford, 'Introduction: Redefining the Third World?' in Nana Poku and Lloyd Pettiford (eds), *Redefining the Third World* (Palgrave Macmillan 1998) 1, 8–9.

197 Burns H Weston, 'The Charter of Economic Right and Duties of States and the Deprivation of Foreign-Owned Wealth' (1981) 75 AJIL 437, 461.

198 Herschel I Grossman and Murat F Iyigun, 'Population Increase and the End of Colonialism' (1997) 64 *Economica* 483, 483.

199 Winston E Langley, 'The Third World: Towards a Definition' (1981) 2 *Boston College Third World Law Journal* 1, 13.

200 Jonathan Power, 'The Third World Is Catching Up' (12 January 2011) <http://www.oldsite.transnational.org/Columns_Power/2011/2.ThirdWorld.html> accessed 18 August 2014.

world's fastest growing economy, cannot play catch-up.[201] While forecasted to overtake the US economy by the end of 2014,[202] socio-economic conditions as measured by per capita income are vastly superior in the United States when compared to those of China.[203] Moreover, although the socio-economic gap between countries like China, India and Brazil, on the one hand, and the United States and Western Europe, on the other, seems to be shrinking, it will be a long time before such conditions in China and the rest of the developing world rival that of the developed world. In the mean time, living standards remain superior in the industrialized world. Contemporary development aspirations of developing countries, therefore, manifest themselves in their unhindered ability to follow the development patterns of developed countries. Developing countries aim to achieve socio-economic conditions that rival that of developed countries. In line with these desires, the next section highlights the many benefits associated with encouraging a positive inflow of foreign investment into developing countries.

A. The Benefits of Attracting FDI to Developing Countries

Today, the ability to attract investment in developing countries, capable of assisting in building growth of infrastructural facilities to enhance their sustainable development, is critical.[204] This involves the mobilization of investment funds into the host economy. It may be in the form of transfer of ownership from domestic to foreign investors, or in the form of expansion in productive capacity and capital formation in that country.[205] An FDI inflow has the potential of greatly enhancing the country's development. Not only does it facilitate the transfer of technology, in effect bringing modern technology to developing countries, but it also

---

201 Ibid.

202 'Crowning the Dragon: China Will Become the World's Largest Economy by the End of the Year' *The Economist* (London, 30 April 2014) <http://www.economist.com/blogs/graphicdetail/2014/04/daily-chart-19> accessed 18 August 2014.

203 World Bank Data, 'GDP per Capita' <http://data.worldbank.org/indicator/NY.GDP.PCAP.CD> accessed 18 August 2014; see also Ami Sedghi, 'China v The US: How the Superpowers Compare' *The Guardian* (London, 7 June 2013) <http://www.theguardian.com/news/datablog/2013/jun/07/china-us-how-superpowers-compare-datablog#> accessed 18 August 2014.

204 Ismail Adelopo, Kamil Omoteso and Musa Obalola, 'Impact of Corporate Governance on Foreign Direct Investment in Nigeria' (2009) <http://ssrn.com/abstract=1514982> accessed 22 October 2015.

205 Ibid.

stands to enhance their socio-economic climate.[206] A steady in-flow of investment capital creates new sources of revenue, as countries are now able to implement taxation policies on equipment coming into the country. The taxation of non-native raw materials is a very important part of a country's revenue.[207] Indeed, developing countries are famous for attracting investment in relation to resource production.[208] However, even where investment agreements include concessionary tax benefits as an incentive for establishing businesses in that particular country, there are still benefits to be deduced from such establishment.[209]

Investments also come with significant skill transfers in terms of human resource development that can improve the economic performance of the host country.[210] Investments create more sources of employment. Furthermore, they have the potential of alleviating poverty through the creation of more employment and empowerment of locals through improved acquisition of skills and training. The economic growth of developing countries is heavily dependent upon development of technological and managerial skills.[211] Thus, developing countries can ensure that investment agreements cater to the employment of citizens as well as the effective training of local technical and managerial staff. Governments should ensure that development contracts reflect the limits within which investors are free to bring in foreign employees and the time schedule for replacing foreign staff with local staff.[212] Nigeria is a case in point. Under Nigerian law,[213] foreign investors are obligated to employ a certain percentage of Nigerian employees. Such policies play a significant role in raising the overall social status of the country as a result of the employment opportunities created. This culminates in developing a countries' freedom to fix the main lines of its development policy.

---

[206] Eric A Schwartz, 'The Role of International Arbitration in Economic Development' (2009) 12 *International Trade and Business Law Review* 126, 128.

[207] David Hummels, Jun Ishii, Kei-Mu Yi, 'The Nature and Growth of Vertical Specialization in World Trade' (2001) 54 *Journal of International Economics* 75, 76.

[208] Ibid.

[209] Philippines Incentives Act s 7(d).

[210] Adelopo, Omoteso and Obalola (n 204) 4.

[211] Martin Bell and Keith Pavitt, 'Technological Accumulation and Industrial Growth: Contrasts Between Developed and Developing Countries' in Daniele Archibugi and Jonathan Michie (eds), *Technology, Globalisation and Economic Performance* (CUP 1997) 83, 83–4.

[212] Kevin W Ryan, 'Investment Contracts and the Developing Countries' (1970) 9 *Australian Yearbook of International Law* 91, 98.

[213] Nigerian Contents and Development Act 2010.

Mechanisms whereby investors who enter into development agreements with developing countries are taken to have done so with knowledge of its development policy and subject to it are therefore desirable.[214] Thus, in marketing and selling commodities originating from developing countries, a foreign investor will take into consideration the development policies of that country.[215]

One cannot but acknowledge that the international investment regime has the potential to benefit all countries, and merely needs to be more sensitive to the plight of developing countries compared to the fixation on foreign capital.[216] TWAIL claims, however, that the international investment regime still remains largely insulated from the sensibilities of developing countries and does not necessarily take developing countries' welfare into account.[217] Instead, in dispute settlement, tribunals adopt a depoliticized (or apolitical) conception of international investment law,[218] thereby removing disputes from the reach of domestic tribunals. So whereas investors are not equal to States when dealing in the context of a pure public law relationship, as soon as the State crosses over into the private law domain by entering into commercial agreements with investors, theoretically investors are on the same level as States, with equal bargaining powers.[219] Moreover, while the foreign investor includes the corporation and its shareholders, the State is construed as an abstract, artificial entity, divorced from its population. To TWAIL critics, such interpretation of international investment law seeks to protect the interest of investors to the detriment of developing countries.[220] Nonetheless, such a deconstructive focus, disregards the benefits of international investment law.

---

214 S Prakash Sinha, 'Perspectives of the Newly Independent States on the Binding Quality of International Law' in Frederick E Snyder and Surakiart Sathirathai (eds), *Third World Attitudes towards International Law: An Introduction* (Martinus Nijhoff Publishers 1987) 23, 28–9.

215 Ryan (n 212) 98.

216 Karl-Heinz Böckstiegel, 'Enterprise v State: The New David and Goliath?' (2007) 23 *Arbitration International* 93–101.

217 Odumosu (n 114) 257.

218 Robin CA White, 'Expropriation of the Libyan Oil Concessions – Two Conflicting International Arbitrations' (1981) 30 ICLQ 1.

219 Engela C Schlemmer, 'A New International Law on Foreign Investment' [2005] *Journal of South African Law* 531, 535.

220 Odumosu (n 114) 257.

B. The Need for a More Constructive Approach towards the International Investment Regime

Thus, TWAIL's current engagement with the international investment regime reveals that, while TWAIL may serve as the apt critique in examining the place of developing countries in this system, any critique should serve as a means to an end, and not an end in itself. Hence, there exists the need for more pragmatic solutions than the often lump critique that generates the argument that international law as currently oriented fails to take into account the developing countries' interests. This critique fails to make proper use of any forceful methodological instruments. It fails to offer constructive proposals for improving the system. TWAIL should, therefore, aspire to be more than merely an instrument of system-criticism. It should strive for a constructive engagement of developing countries with the international investment regime and develop ideas as to what that engagement could look like in practical terms. It would be more beneficial to developing countries for TWAIL to aspire to be a source of reform or, more appropriately, a forum for the constructive engagement of developing countries with the international investment regime.

TWAIL should aim towards greater sophistication of the regime bias critique, particularly surrounding the future ability of developing countries to fairly participate in BIT negotiation and investment arbitration. Effective use of the regime bias critique in relation to the current state of international investment governance would generate a more theoretically informed analysis to demonstrate that the international investment regime, as currently constituted, is at odds with developing countries' aspirations, while at the same time offering constructive proposals for reform. One may notice the difficulties in concluding the international trade and investment agreement between Canada and the Bahamas, since the government of the Bahamas is of the opinion that the Agreement's dispute settlement mechanism is at odds with its domestic interests.[221] One way of overcoming this is for the Caribbean Community (CARICOM), as the representative of that region's interest in international relations, to establish a regional arbitration center in the Caribbean Basin in order to cater to the region's investor-State dispute settlement needs. Either way, TWAIL should foster developing countries' engagement with

---

[221] Alison Lowe, 'Canada Demands Controversial Investor Rights Clause' *The Nassau Guardian* (Nassau, 15 April 2014) <http://www.thenassauguardian.com/index.php?option=com_content&view=article&id=46666&Itemid=2> accessed 21 April 2014.

the present orientation of the international investment regime. This includes providing ways for remedying, first, their disadvantaged position in treaty negotiation due to the economic vulnerability of most of these countries, and second, the impact of this vulnerability in their ability to participate fairly in international dispute settlement.

Moreover, TWAIL should seek to eradicate the conditions of under-development in developing countries.[222] This includes the possibility of developing countries spearheading the adoption by the international community of a regime of substantive international investment law and investor-State arbitration that takes into account the economic vulnerability of developing countries in BIT negotiations and investor-State arbitration. The establishment of a draft code of procedure will prove essential in supplanting fears of Western conventional arbitration mechanisms among developing countries. Unlike the NIEO project that sought to revamp the entire regime of international economic governance, contemporary revolutionary aims would target the international investment regime specifically to make it more consistent with the development aims of developing countries. Perhaps a TWAIL-type ideology should also endeavor to extend its borders beyond legal studies and embrace disciplines such as economics and development theory, for these collectively would create the forceful methodological instrument that has so far been lacking in TWAIL analysis. Instead of the lump critique of international law, TWAIL should take the development dialogue further, given the South's economic aspirations and the premise that socio-economic progress would be wrought by a positive inflow of foreign investments. Developing countries' socio-economic goals could be achieved by a constructive body of international development law that is as far reaching as the current body of international investment law, and that is based on international law principles such as equity and natural justice. There is merit in TWAIL's argument that developing countries did not arrive on the international scene in the same manner and at the same time as industrialized countries; and for this reason it is unjust for these countries to have applied to them rules that fail to take their development interests into account. Therefore, it is necessary that these rules are not applied to them until they too have achieved some degree of industrialization.

222 Mutua (n 25) 31.

C. Constructive Approaches Towards the International Investment Regime

A development-inspired investment treaty model would also go a long way in safeguarding developing countries' development aspirations. Ideally, this would set the stage for the negotiation of more equitable treaties. A useful starting point would be UNCTAD's Investment Policy Framework for Sustainable Development (IPFSD), which aims to guide the development of international investment policy and options on international investment agreements.[223] The IPFSD seeks to integrate investment policy into overall development strategies, enhancing sustainable development as part of investment policies, balancing rights and obligations of States and investors in the context of investment protection and promotion, including corporate social responsibility, into investment policy-making and encouraging international cooperation on investment-related challenges.[224]

UNCTAD's IPFSD framework significantly influenced the recently completed Southern African Development Community (SADC) model investment treaty,[225] which is perceived to be more equitable than the conventional Northern BIT model due to its development-centered focus. SADC's BIT model has all the trappings of conventional BITs; however, it strives towards more equitable participation of developing countries in the international investment regime. It aspires to embody harmonized approaches that will assist its Member States in their individual and collective negotiations of BITs with third countries, as well as in revisiting existing treaties. The model represents a distinct effort to enhance the sustainable development dimension of future BITs, by including provisions on environmental and social impact assessments, measures against corruption, standards for human rights, environment, labor, corporate governance and the right to regulate and pursue countries' development goals.[226] It is hoped that such engagement with the international investment regime would create the welcoming environment that developing countries need to enhance participation in international investment regime.

---

[223] UNCTAD, *Investment Policy Framework for Sustainable Development* (United Nations 2012) <http://unctad.org/en/PublicationsLibrary/webdiaepcb2012d6_en.pdf> accessed 18 August 2014.

[224] Ibid.

[225] UNCTAD (n 18).

[226] Ibid.

Another notable move in that direction was the work done by the Asian-African Legal Consultative Committee (AALCC). Like TWAIL,[227] the AALCC has its origin in the historic Bandung Conference, held in Indonesia in April 1955 by several Asian countries and Egypt. While TWAIL has permeated primarily in academic circles, the AALCC is considered the tangible outcome of the Bandung Conference. Thus, in April 1958, in order to secure greater participation of African countries, the AALCC was established.[228] One of its most notable accomplishments was the establishment of several arbitration centers in the Afro-Asian region, which AALCC proposed as a follow-up to the work of UNCITRAL in the field of international commercial arbitration during its Thirteenth Annual Session held in Nigeria in 1973.[229]

AALCC proposed to conduct an independent study on some of the more important practical problems relating to international arbitration from the point of view of the African-Asian region.[230] AALCC saw it as necessary to develop the procedure of international arbitration, establish institutional support, develop necessary expertise and create an environment favorable to conduct arbitration in the African and Asian regions. As such, AALCC endorsed the recommendations of its Trade Law Sub-Committee that efforts should be made by Member States to develop institutional arbitration in the Asia-African region and that a network of Regional Arbitration Centers would be established functioning under the auspices of AALCC.[231] This, it was thought, would minimize fears of the developing countries *vis-à-vis* international arbitration and act as a viable alternative to the conventional Western arbitration institutions such as ICSID.

In pursuance of this goal, AALCC, in cooperation with its Member States, established the Kuala Lumpur Regional Arbitration Centre in 1978, the Cairo Regional Centre for International Commercial Arbitration in 1979, the Lagos Regional Centre for International Commercial Arbitration in 1980 and the Tehran Regional Arbitration Centre in 1996.[232] The name of the Committee was changed to Asian-African Legal

---

227 Mutua (n 25) 31.

228 Asian-African Legal Consultative Organization, 'About AALCO' <http://www.aalco.int/scripts/view-posting.asp?recordid=1> accessed 19 April 2014.

229 Asian-African Legal Consultative Organization, 'Report on the AALCO's Regional Arbitration Centres' <http://www.aalco.int/userfiles/File/Arbitration 2012.pdf> accessed 25 January 2014.

230 Ibid.

231 Ibid.

232 Babu (n 19) 398.

Consultative Organization (AALCO) at the Committee's 40th Session in New Delhi in 2001. In 2007, the Nairobi Regional Arbitration Centre was established under this new international organization.[233]

The establishment of these arbitration centers is welcome news in developing countries, which have historically been averse to international arbitration. This illustrates the positive engagement that developing countries require to survive in the international investment regime. Instead of resisting the international investment regime, the establishment of these arbitral centers seeks to facilitate the participation of developing countries in this system.

VI. CONCLUSION

Using TWAIL theory, jurists unveil the existence of an ideological gap that exists between the development aspirations of developing countries and the current orientation of international law, which is premised on bringing about development. The foregoing has considered the parameters of TWAIL theory, which sees international law as illegitimate and since its emergence has sought to redirect international law's focus to the plight of developing countries. Here, TWAIL focused particularly on the shift away from the NEC and NIEO approaches. NEC and NIEO matters have largely become matters of historical relevance. The regime bias critique has come to dominate TWAIL's analysis of international economic governance. Regime bias as a methodological extension of the TWAIL critique is emblematic of the entire system of international law, but is more visible in international dispute resolution. Therefore, given the importance of international investments to the development aspirations in developing countries, an area of significant concern has been investor-State arbitration. The regime bias critique illustrates the skeptical attitude of developing countries towards international investment regulation, encompassing both investment treaty negotiation and arbitration.

Nevertheless, there is a general failure by TWAIL to offer avenues for the constructive engagement of developing countries with the international investment regime. TWAIL's shortcomings have highlighted the need for a pragmatic solution, rather than mere critique of foreign investment regulation. As seen above, developing countries are starting to develop their own model BITs, as illustrated by the recent SADC initiative. Afro-Asian countries have responded through AALCO to

233 Asian-African Legal Consultative Organization (n 229).

concerns surrounding the use of conventional Western investment dispute settlement by establishing a network of regional arbitration centers. These initiatives represent a pragmatic solution for alleviating developing countries' fears of investor-State arbitration, by veering off the traditional course of TWAIL's systematic critique of international law while ensuring their continued participation in the international investment regime. Together, these initiatives pave the way for the constructive engagement of developing countries with the international investment regime and reveal in practical terms what that engagement can look like. Initiatives such as these are what developing countries require, ensuring their effective participation in international economic governance and ultimately the international economic system in years to come.

PART III

Development and self-determination

8. Sovereignty over natural resources and international investment law: The elusive search for equilibrium

Melaku Geboye Desta*

I. INTRODUCTION

The relationship between national sovereignty over natural resources and protection of foreign investment is a complex one. Natural resources,[1] such as oil and gas reserves or mineral deposits, are often in such high demand that resource companies are mostly willing to put their capital and reputation at serious risk in order to acquire a stake in their development. Likewise, as soon as the presence of a reasonable deposit of some valuable resource in the territory of a particular country becomes public, governments come under intense 'economic and political pressure' to develop it.[2] The comparative lack of complete geological information in most developing countries means that the majority of new and worthwhile resource discoveries today and in the future are likely to be in these countries, while only firms from mainly developed countries have the necessary financial, technical and managerial capability to unlock the resource and transform it into actual wealth.[3]

* This chapter was presented at the Frankfurt Investment Law Workshop (March 2013). I thank my two commentators at the workshop, Prof Nico Schrijver and Prof Isabel Feichtner, for their insightful comments and remarks. My thanks also go to Dr Abba Kolo and Prof Moshe Hirsch for their helpful comments on earlier drafts of this chapter. All errors remain solely my own.

1 Throughout this chapter, I use the term 'natural resources' to mean hydrocarbons and minerals.

2 See Paul Stevens and others, 'Conflict and Coexistence in the Extractive Industries' (Chatham House Report, 1 November 2013) x.

3 This picture is changing with the arrival of major resource companies from emerging countries, such as Brazil, China and Malaysia, but by far the dominant players in the sector still come from the OECD.

Almost inevitably, the involvement of foreign firms, especially if they are successful in their primary task of producing and exporting the resource, tends, sooner or later, to provoke nationalist sentiment and accusations about loss of host country sovereignty, or worse. As a result, the story of investment in natural resources is mostly a story of foreign private firms operating in developing countries, on terms usually negotiated on project-specific bases and kept hidden from public view; while their exploration, production and exportation activities are all too visible to the local communities in the form of adverse environmental and social externalities and, in far too many cases, a 'resource curse' situation where resource revenues are used in order to maintain unaccountable ruling elites in power, often leading to violent competition for control of resources and civil conflict.[4] From this perspective, the natural resources sectors particularly in developing countries have long been the laboratory within which the legal experiment to find the optimal point of balance between host state sovereignty, on the one hand, and attraction and protection of foreign investment, on the other, occurs. That optimal point has, however, been elusive, fluctuating with the investment cycle itself, commodity prices on world markets, and whatever is the dominant ideology of the day.

This contribution starts with a highlight of the literature on the relationship between foreign investors and host states in the extractive sectors. Focusing on Raymond Vernon's obsolescing bargains model,[5] Section II introduces this highly insightful theoretical perspective. Section III provides a brief introduction to the principle of sovereignty over natural resources and how it interacts with the evolving regime of

---

[4] For more on this see World Bank, 'The World Bank Group Program of Support for the Chad-Cameroon Petroleum Development and Pipeline Construction Program Performance Assessment Report' (Report No 503 15, 16 September 2009) <http://www-wds.worldbank.org/external/default/WDSContentServer/WDSP/IB/2009/09/29/000333037_20090929000309/Rendered/PDF/503150PPAR0P05101Official0use0only1.pdf> accessed 17 July 2014. UNCTAD also reported 'a strong link between dependence on natural resources and the risk of civil war and other conflicts and their prolongation' as well as 'detrimental impacts of natural resource dependence on governance and human rights … particularly in sub-Saharan Africa. Oil and diamonds in Angola, diamonds in Sierra Leone and Liberia, cobalt and other minerals in the Democratic Republic of the Congo and oil in Sudan have fuelled lengthy civil wars', see UNCTAD, *World Investment Report 2007: Transnational Corporations, Extractive Industries and Development* (United Nations 2008) 95.

[5] See Raymond Vernon, *Sovereignty at Bay: The Multinational Spread of US Enterprises* (Basic Books 1971).

international investment law. There is ample literature on this subject already[6] and this contribution is a narrowly focused examination of how the fast-evolving body of international investment law affects the host state's exercise of permanent sovereignty over its natural resources. To this end, I start that section with an outline of the major principles of international investment law, which I describe simply as principles of international law designed to protect foreign investment from the host state.[7] I then look at the principle of sovereignty in very broad terms, as a bundle of powers and prerogatives that are available only to a state with internal and external dimensions. Internally, sovereignty manifests itself in the inherent qualities of the state as being endowed with supreme authority to do as it pleases within its territory subject only to constraints it has wilfully undertaken, while the external dimension implies the right to be left alone (non-intervention from abroad) and the right to be recognised and treated as an equal in international affairs.[8] Section IV then considers the broad question of whether, or to what extent, international investment law hampers the exercise of sovereignty by the state over its natural resources. Section V concludes with thoughts about the current trends, threats and opportunities. Using historical and doctrinal approaches, this contribution attempts to examine the issues from the perspective of poor developing countries like those in sub-Saharan Africa.

II. THEORETICAL INSIGHTS: THE OBSOLESCING BARGAINS MODEL

Too many countries with abundant natural resources, such as potentially valuable fossil fuel and mineral deposits, suffer from extreme poverty and political instability while, at the same time, there is often an external

---

[6] See Nico Schrijver, *Sovereignty over Natural Resources: Balancing Rights and Duties* (CUP 1997), and Sundhya Pahuja, *Decolonising International Law: Development, Economic Growth and the Politics of Universality* (CUP 2011).

[7] There is a large and growing body of literature in this area. For an authoritative and critical analysis of the investment regime see M Sornarajah, *The International Law on Foreign Investment* (2nd edn, CUP 2004).

[8] See, e.g., Rafael Domingo, 'The Crisis of International Law' (2009) 42 Vand JLT 1543, 1557 (noting that sovereignty is 'a property inherent to any state, which gives it supreme power in its territory, control of its legal system, and the right to recognize external bodies or entities that establish contact with it').

world market that offers attractive prices for their resources. Although governments in these countries are desperate to develop their resources, there is little they can do by themselves. In the absence of home-grown capital, technology and know-how, attracting foreign investment becomes the only option.[9] Depending on the quality and quantity of resource endowment and the situation on the market for the relevant commodities, countries may have to compete amongst themselves in order to stand out in the eyes of foreign firms, such as by way of enacting new laws, reducing royalties and other taxes, promising exemptions from import and export duties and the like.[10]

Once companies have set their eyes on a particularly attractive-looking country, the chances of winning additional concessions are often highest at the outset. Unlike in most developed countries where the major terms of investment are provided in general legislation, investment terms in most developing countries are decided by negotiations, a game that typically brings overly keen but inexperienced host government officials face to face with a foreign investor that is likely to be a repeat player in the negotiations game, with a wealth of professional experience and expertise to draw on. The resulting investment contract is often so comprehensive, and its terms so specific, that it can effectively replace national law for most purposes of the investment.[11] In case that might not

---

[9] International financial institutions, such as the World Bank and regional development banks, could also provide financing for natural resources projects, but they often put the involvement of foreign mining or oil and gas companies as a condition for financing such projects. As Professor Wälde noted three decades ago, 'financial institutions are unwilling to contribute capital if they are not assured that an experienced mining company will be in charge of operations and will assume strict completion guarantees', Thomas W Wälde, 'Permanent Sovereignty over Natural Resources: Recent Developments in the Mineral Sector' (1983) 7(3) *Natural Resources Forum* 239, 245.

[10] In order to attract foreign investment, World Bank advice to resource-rich countries would emphasise the need to put in place a guarantee of mining rights before starting exploration, to institute a well-established mining code and a system of contractual stability, a stable fiscal regime, accelerated depreciation and amortization, opportunities for profit repatriation, and access to foreign exchange at realistic rates, see World Bank, 'Strategy for African Mining' (World Bank Technical Paper No 181, 1992) 17.

[11] The World Bank also observed that '[a]n investment agreement is often an indispensable condition for foreign investors for major projects in developing countries where the risk of unilateral changes by the government to the investment rules is considered unduly high by investors because of political circumstances, lack of track record and economic difficulties' see World Bank (n 10) 25.

be enough, and recognising that such good days never last forever, investment contracts in the extractive industries in particular often contain a clause that aims to freeze, as of the date of the contract, the legal regime governing their operations for up to several decades into the future.[12] Finally, they also typically provide for the use of international arbitration to settle any future disputes, further insulating the investment not just from the application of local law but also from the jurisdiction of local courts. While investment contracts are generally intended to protect foreign firms from non-commercial risks that are inherent in such long-term and vulnerable projects,[13] in practice they are also used to lock-in terms and conditions extracted from the host state at a time when its bargaining power is at its weakest.[14] It is also this far-reaching nature of investment contracts and the lack of balance they embody that usually raises sovereignty concerns not long after they are signed and puts their continued validity into question.

In his recent book about ExxonMobil, Steve Coll recounts the widely-reported story of the contract signed between Exxon (together with project partners Chevron and Petronas), on the one hand, and the government of Chad, on the other, for the exploration, exploitation and transportation of Chad's hydrocarbon resources.[15] Coll observes that the terms of the contract were highly favourable to Exxon, which were insulated from subsequent unilateral government action by a stringent stabilization and supremacy clause under which the terms of the contract were to prevail over any existing or future law of Chad. He then quotes a member of Chadian President Deby's cabinet at the time as saying that the president 'did not take time to go through [the contract]. ... Only later did he realize that the terms were not as favourable as he wanted.'[16]

---

[12] For a recent survey of stabilisation clauses see Andrea Shemberg, 'Stabilization Clauses and Human Rights' (Research Project Conducted for IFC and the United Nations Special Representative of the Secretary General on Business and Human Rights, 27 May 2009).

[13] The World Bank noted that average return on equity required or targeted on investment in developing countries was 25 to 30 per cent, with a payback of two to four years as opposed to 20 per cent and a payback of five to six years in industrialized countries; see World Bank (n 10) 17.

[14] Through these contracts, firms win 'special privileges or exemptions regarding taxes and foreign exchange regulations'; see ibid 30.

[15] According to Coll, 'Chad's take of less than two thirds of revenue after expenses compared to rates closer to 90 percent in Nigeria', Steve Coll, *Private Empire: ExxonMobil and American Power* (Allen Lane 2012) 160.

[16] Ibid 159–60.

Coll quotes Christopher Goldthwait, then US Ambassador to Chad, as marvelling: 'just how much control the government [of Chad] has ceded to Esso [Exxon's local subsidiary] over what happens in the south, almost a loss of sovereignty!'[17] It is here that Vernon's theory comes in as a helpful device to explain, and perhaps even predict, the behaviours and expectations of the main protagonists in the natural resources contractual relationship.

The obsolescing bargains theory predicts that once an agreement has been reached between the foreign investor and the host government, and a certain amount of foreign capital invested in projects, the bargaining power starts to shift from companies to host states. In his pioneering analysis, Raymond Vernon showed that investment contracts in the natural resources sector are 'generally assumed' to come unstuck through a process that 'leads governments repeatedly – almost predictably – to reopen the issues involved in the exploitation of raw materials.'[18] This, according to Vernon, is inter alia because the initial contractual obligations on the government side 'consist of a series of self-denying commitments,' which make them obsolete in the eyes of the government almost immediately after signature of the contract.[19] Vernon's insights are not limited to the political economy of the natural resource investment contract; he also understood the legal innovations that were taking place to deal with the perceived extra political and regulatory risks involved for multinational corporations operating in the developing world. 'If the raw material operation is located in an advanced country,' wrote Vernon, 'as a rule, the enterprises have been brought into the country under the provisions of general law, without extraordinary concessions of an extensive sort, and they are expected to continue on that basis' while in the less-developed countries, 'special provisions generally surround the foreign operations.'[20]

---

[17] Ibid 170. Coll does not say when the *Convention for Exploration, Exploitation and Transportation of Hydrocarbons* was signed but we can find an indication of the time from the fact that Goldthwait served as US Ambassador to Chad between October 1999 and January 2004.

[18] Vernon (n 5) 46. Wälde and Ndi call this the 'unavoidable, natural tendency of governments to seek adjustments to long-term investment relations in response to both political pressure and the evolution of circumstances', Thomas W Wälde and George Ndi, 'Stabilizing International Investment Commitments: International Law versus Contract Interpretation' (1996) 31 Tex ILJ 215, 220.

[19] Vernon (n 5) 47.

[20] Ibid 48.

The enduring validity of Vernon's perception on this particular issue has been confirmed and reconfirmed by subsequent research and analysis.[21] Writing in the mid-1990s, Wälde and Ndi observed that '[d]eveloped Western nations rarely contract with foreign investors under a specific, individual investment regime derogating from the generally applicable law,'[22] while Cameron wrote, in 2012, that 'stabilization clauses in state contracts remain near-standard practice around the world but are rarely ever conceded by governments in OECD countries in their attempts to attract investment in their natural resources.'[23] Finally, Vernon also showed how natural resources operators particularly in the poorest developing countries are likely to undermine the sovereignty of their hosts by dominating the national economy, and sometimes dictating national policy as governments depend on tax or other revenues from such companies for their daily operations.[24]

Vernon's powerful insights have been further refined by subsequent analyses, the work of Hogan and Sturzenegger being perhaps the most recent and comprehensive.[25] Using the notion of the 'natural resources trap' as their analytical tool, Hogan and Sturzenegger make a compelling case as follows:

---

[21] See also Amnon Lehavi and Amir N Licht, 'BITs and Pieces of Property' (2011) 36 Yale JIL (2011) 115–66 (highlighting the political economy context within which Vernon coined the theory, the empirical evidence from the 1970s that proved the predictive power of the theory, and the debt crisis of the 1980s, along with the triumph of market liberalism starting from the late 1980s, which led to a marginalisation of the theory).

[22] See Wälde and Ndi (n 18) 221.

[23] Peter D Cameron, 'Reflections on Sovereignty over Natural Resources and the Enforcement of Stabilization Clauses' in Karl P Sauvant (ed.), *Yearbook on International Investment Law & Policy 2011–2012* (OUP 2013) 313.

[24] Vernon (n 5) wrote at 52: 'As foreign raw material operations become more and more integrated in the economic life of host countries – through increasing payments to government and the increasing use of local labor, materials, and resources – the vulnerability of the economy to changes in these operations inevitably seems to increase. The psychic sense of dependence on foreign interests generated by this situation has produced occasional eruptions. … the sense of dependence that host governments experienced was at times beyond bearing.'

[25] See William Hogan and Federico Sturzenegger (eds), *The Natural Resources Trap – Private Investment Without Public Commitment* (MIT Press 2010).

> Because MNCs anticipate expropriation, they will offer a contract that compensates them for the risk. But this forces the [host country] to expropriate; if they do not firms will be rewarded with windfall gain that may be politically intolerable. It is a double trap, because lack of credibility not only creates a contract that in itself is more vulnerable, but also because it forces even those governments that would prefer to operate in a stable and law-abiding context to fall in the vicious cycle with the rest.[26]

The logical conclusion of Vernon's obsolescing bargains model or Hogan and Sturzenegger's natural resources trap model appears clear: whatever states give at the beginning of the investment relationship they will try to take back afterwards, making a dispute with the foreign investor all but inevitable. The natural assumption that investment contracts are designed to maximise the investor's share of the pie at the expense of the host state's, and the 'self-denying' nature of the initial commitments, are likely to lead the state to overreaction later. It is also worth noting that this unfortunate cycle is by no means unique to developing countries; it is only more frequent there. Dieter Helm described the UK's own processes of nationalisation and privatisation in the second half of the 20th century as a classic time-inconsistency problem in which governments have 'an incentive to promise ex ante that investors will be able to earn at least normal profits but then ex post to intervene to force down prices, claw back profits, and change outputs.'[27]

When states take action, they often justify it through one ill-defined and often least-understood notion – sovereignty. Their argument can take many different forms: the terms of the original investment contract were unduly skewed in favour of the foreign investor and therefore contrary to the host country's national interest; those terms undermine the sovereign rights of the host state over its natural resources, making the agreements null and void; the political-economy circumstances within which the contract was negotiated have undergone significant transformation, making continued validity of the contract anomalous; etc. The sad fact that poor countries that are rich in natural resources are prone to suffer from

---

[26] Ibid 3.

[27] See Dieter Helm, 'Credibility, Commitment, and Regulation: Ex Ante Price Caps and Ex Post Interventions' in Hogan and Sturzenegger (n 25) 294. In a Comment on Helm, Jeffrey Frankel defines the time-inconsistency problem to mean the situation where 'the incentive you have to promise ahead of time is different from the incentive you have after the investment has been made'; ibid 326.

resource curse[28] – also known as the 'paradox of plenty' – makes it all the more likely that their governments will also try to find a scapegoat in foreign investors. Today's international investment law regime[29] is the direct or indirect product of competing claims and counterclaims as they evolved over time. The story of this evolution can be told as a process of fine-tuning the point of equilibrium between the claim for the fullest possible measure of sovereignty in traditionally capital-importing (host) states and the desire for the fullest possible protection of foreign investment by capital-exporting (home) states.

III. SOVEREIGNTY V. INVESTMENT PROTECTION: HISTORICAL OVERVIEW

Under traditional international law, the right of diplomatic protection through the home state was essentially the only peaceful remedy available to an alien that has suffered damage at the hands of a host state.[30] Diplomatic protection itself was available only on restricted grounds, and normally only after exhaustion of local remedies.[31] How times change! Today's international investment law is probably unrecognisable to international lawyers of just a generation ago. I contend that the decolonisation of a large part of the world after the Second World War,

---

[28] Professor Paul Collier describes the resource curse phenomenon as 'the tendency for many low-income commodity exporters to experience slower economic growth than countries that are less well-endowed with resources', Paul Collier, 'Essay: Laws and Codes for the Resource Curse' (2008) 11 *Yale Human Rights and Development Law Journal* 9, 11; see also Emeka Duruigbo, 'Permanent Sovereignty and Peoples' Ownership of Natural Resources in International Law' (2006) 38 *George Washington International Law Review* 33–100 (noting at 34 that the problem in this area can better be described as a 'leadership curse' whereby 'kleptocratic rulers cause a wake of thieving frenzy, a cascade of catastrophes').

[29] For a treatment of present-day international investment law as a regime see Jeswald W Salacuse, 'The Emerging Global Regime for Investment' (2010) 51(2) Harv ILJ 427–73.

[30] Under the principle of diplomatic protection, if a foreign investor company suffers from an unlawful act, 'the general rule of international law authorizes the national State of the company alone to make a claim'; see *Barcelona Traction, Light and Power Company, Ltd (Belgium v Spain)* [1970] ICJ Rep 3, 47.

[31] See, e.g., William S Dodge, 'National Courts and International Arbitration: Exhaustion of Remedies and Res Judicata under Chapter Eleven of NAFTA' (1999/2000) 23 *Hastings International and Comparative Law Review* 357–83.

which promised the hitherto-inconceivable luxuries of sovereignty to former colonies, exposed the inadequacies of diplomatic protection to safeguard continuing foreign economic interests inside the territories of those newly-born states. Two types of interests were in need of special protection from the threats of sovereignty in these new states: access to their natural resources through foreign direct investment, and access to their markets through trade – the same twin motives that drove the colonial project in a previous era.[32]

The special protection agenda was set in the middle of the Second World War in the *Atlantic Charter*, a short but highly influential joint 'communiqué' between US President Franklin D. Roosevelt and British Prime Minister Winston Churchill on 14 August 1941.[33] By this document, the two superpowers of the day 'deem[ed] it right to make known certain common principles in the national policies of their respective countries on which they base[d] their hopes for a better future for the world.'[34] The fourth principle in a list of eight committed the two powers to 'endeavor, with due respect for their existing obligations, to further the enjoyment by all States, great or small, victor or vanquished, of *access, on equal terms, to the trade and to the raw materials of the world which are needed for their economic prosperity*.'[35] The International Trade Organisation (ITO) project that was launched right after the War was designed to give effect to this principle of the Atlantic Charter.[36]

Fifty-three countries signed the ITO Charter but only Liberia ratified it; all others were waiting for the US to move first but when, in 1950, the

---

[32] The dominant economic view of the era of economic imperialism demanded possession of African territory, which was deemed 'necessary in order to serve as a market for the products, and a source of the raw materials of the industry, of the citizens of European States.' Leonard Woolf, *Empire and Commerce in Africa: A Study in Economic Imperialism* (London 1919, republished 2012 by Forgotten Books) 324.

[33] The Atlantic Charter was just that, a communiqué; it was not even signed by the two leaders in order to avoid having to have it ratified as a treaty by the US Senate. For an insightful account of the drafting history of the Atlantic Charter see Benn Steil, *The Battle of Bretton Woods: John Maynard Keynes, Harry Dexter White, and the Making of a New World Order* (Princeton UP 2013) 118–21.

[34] See US Department of State, *The Atlantic Charter* (1941) <http://infousa.state.gov/government/overview/53.html> accessed 19 March 2013.

[35] Ibid (emphasis added). Steil (n 33) 119 describes the negotiation process on the fourth principle as 'the hornet's nest'.

[36] On the history of the ITO project see Douglas A Irwin, Petros C Mavroidis, and Alan O Sykes, *The Genesis of the GATT* (CUP 2008).

US government decided not to seek ratification from Congress, the ITO Charter was effectively dead.[37] There are several reasons for this failure, including dissatisfaction in capital-exporting nations with the excessive sovereignty-protective provisions of the Charter's investment chapter.[38] At this point, the supposedly provisional General Agreement on Tariffs and Trade (GATT) was assigned to take care of the trade concerns – which was essentially a market-opening tool for industrial goods, the type produced only in the advanced countries, but which left national governments unfettered with respect to those goods, such as agricultural products and other primary commodities, over which generally the poorest countries have a comparative advantage. No GATT-type multilateral alternative existed for the issue of access to natural resources, which took a different direction altogether. With the decolonisation movement about to enter its 'most active phase,'[39] international law needed an innovative solution for the problem.

A. Independence: The Promises and Challenges of Sovereignty

When the newly-independent countries looked inside the sovereignty box, they sensed that it was different from the one their former colonial masters had enjoyed for a long time; they realised that independence did not necessarily mean full sovereignty over their natural resources; the political independence they proudly proclaimed appeared to lack sufficient economic content. They realised that, even after independence, companies from metropolitan territories were to continue with large, generous and long-term concessions granted prior to independence; international commitments undertaken on their behalf by former colonial rulers would remain valid, potentially for ever; their inheritance was not just the great assets they had expected, but also enormous constraints and potential liabilities.[40] It was clear that recognition of the sovereignty of

---

[37] See GATT, *Analytical Index: Guide to GATT Law and Practice* (Updated 6th edn, WTO and Bernan Press 1995) 6.

[38] See Salacuse (n 29) 88.

[39] See Matthew Craven, *The Decolonization of International Law: State Succession and the Law of Treaties* (OUP 2007) 90. Ghana became the first country in sub-Saharan Africa to gain its independence in 1957.

[40] For early views of the debate whether newly independent states were to start with a clean slate or be subjected to restrictions and commitments undertaken during colonial days see Mohammed Bedjaoui, 'First Report on Succession of States in Respect of Rights and Duties Resulting from Sources other than Treaties' (ILC Document A/CN.4/204 1968), arguing at 115 that 'a concessionary contract must end with the extinction of the personality of the

these countries was, at least in economic terms, mere 'courteous pretence.'[41] Frustrated by this perceived injustice, but also encouraged by their growing numerical strength in global bodies such as the UN General Assembly, developing countries launched their quest for an unequivocal affirmation of their rights over their natural resources as early as 1952. The delegate of Burma to the UN at the time is quoted to have said: 'The principle of the sovereign rights of nations over their own resources would seem so obvious as not to require elucidation.'[42] As subsequent developments demonstrated, he was clearly right and clearly wrong at the same time.

Indeed, no one in their right mind would have questioned the sovereignty of, say, the United Kingdom over the natural resources within its territory; that was merely an aspect of British territorial sovereignty. The very concept of sovereignty would lose its core meaning if it did not imply at least this much. British sovereignty was indivisible. The only question was whether the newly-independent countries of the Third World were fit to assert that same principle on the same basis as the likes of Britain. Again, there was nothing new here; Grotius himself 'insisted that "[s]overeignty beyond Europe, unlike sovereignty within Europe, was … very much a divisible notion and was to remain so within all subsequent conceptions" of relationship with the non-Western world.'[43] It took ten years for these new states to get a declaration of their sovereignty over their natural resources, in the form of the famous UN General Assembly Resolution 1803.[44] However, far from a simple acknowledgment of their sovereignty over their natural resources, Resolution 1803 was drafted as a compromise between the state's sovereign

---

ceding State and could survive the change of sovereignty only at the express wish of the new authority.' For a modern analysis of the doctrines of clean slate v succession see Craven (n 39) 29–52.

[41] Susan Strange, *The Retreat of the State: The Diffusion of Power in the World Economy* (CUP 1996) 13.

[42] See Stephen M Schwebel, 'The Story of the UN's Declaration on Permanent Sovereignty over Natural Resources' (1963) 49 *American Bar Association Journal* 463.

[43] Anthony Pagden, 'The Empire's New Clothes: From Empire to Federation, Yesterday and Today' (2006) 12 *Common Knowledge* 41, as quoted in BS Chimni, 'Just World under Law: A View from the South' (2006/07) 22 *American University International Law Review* 199, 202.

[44] UNGA Res 1803 (XVII) on the 'Permanent Sovereignty over Natural Resources' (14 December 1962) was passed by 87 votes in favour, two against, and 12 abstentions, see Schwebel (n 42).

rights, on the one hand, and its obligations towards the foreign investor, on the other.

If we look at some of the provisions of Resolution 1803 just on the surface, the first paragraph declares:

> The right of peoples and nations to permanent sovereignty over their natural wealth and resources must be exercised in the interest of their national development and of the well-being of the people of the state concerned.

This was immediately followed, in the second and third paragraphs, by a recognition that decisions regarding the exploration of resources, and whether or not to allow foreign investment for that purpose, would be left to the free choice of the state; however the text adds in paragraph 3:

> In cases where authorization is granted, the capital imported and the earnings on that capital shall be governed by the terms thereof, by the national legislation in force, and by international law. The profits derived must be shared in the proportions freely agreed upon in each case, between the investors and the recipient state, due care being taken to ensure that there is no impairment, for any reason, of that state's sovereignty over its natural wealth and resources.

Likewise, paragraph 7 affirms that,

> Violation of the rights of peoples and nations to sovereignty over their natural wealth and resources is contrary to the spirit and principles of the Charter of the United Nations and hinders the development of international co-operation and the maintenance of peace.

Paragraph 8 reintroduces the investor's side, this time with the apparent elevation of the investment contract to a quasi-treaty:

> Foreign investment agreements freely entered into by, or between, sovereign states shall be observed in good faith; states and international organizations shall strictly and conscientiously respect the sovereignty of peoples and nations over their natural wealth and resources in accordance with the Charter and the principles set forth in the present resolution.[45]

Finally, paragraph 4, which recognises the state's right to nationalise foreign investments under certain circumstances, makes the right conditional on the payment of 'appropriate compensation, in accordance

---

45 This point in particular was later used to support the emerging concept of internationalization of state contracts; see infra Section IV.A.

with the rules in force in the state taking such measures in the exercise of its sovereignty and in accordance with international law'; and in the event of a dispute, it reaffirms the doctrine of exhaustion of local remedies, but also introduces consensual international arbitration as an option.

Needless to say, the title of Resolution 1803 – 'permanent sovereignty over natural resources' – does not adequately represent its content; in fact, it is a resolution as much about the protection of foreign investment as it is about sovereignty over natural resources. The resolution would probably have been more aptly named: 'the state's sovereignty over its natural resources and its obligations towards the foreign investor.' By keeping the investment protection aspect of Resolution 1803 out of the title, the drafters gave the false impression that this Resolution marked the beginning of the Permanent Sovereignty over Natural Resources (PSNR) principle; in fact this same resolution also represented the start of the post-War experiment to develop a new species of international law for the protection of foreign investment from the risks posed by these newly-independent states. That this happened within the natural resources sector is somewhat inevitable; virtually all foreign investment at the time was concentrated in the natural resources sector, a fact that remains largely the case in sub-Saharan Africa even today.[46] Furthermore, continuing access to natural resources was a matter of national security and strategic priority for the major powers at the time.[47] Only with these economic realities and strategic imperatives in mind can one appreciate the conjoined nature of the birth of PSNR and investment protection principles as we know them today. In no other sector do these two sets of principles clash so directly, and in no other multilateral instrument before the 1962 resolution can one find the substantive and procedural principles

---

[46] See, e.g., UNCTAD, *World Investment Report 2010: Investing in a Low-Carbon Economy* (United Nations 2010) 33, and UNCTAD, *Economic Development in Africa: Rethinking the Role of Foreign Direct Investment* (United Nations 2005) 9 and 69.

[47] Daniel Yergin, in his authoritative account of the oil industry in the 20th century, recounts the story of oil contract renegotiations that started with the fifty-fifty formula in Venezuela in 1943 and spread to Saudi Arabia and others around 1950 and the nationalization of the Anglo-Iranian oil company by the Mossadegh government in 1951, the nationalization of the Suez Canal company by the Nasser government in Egypt in 1956, etc, all of which would naturally have shaped the position of the capital exporting countries during the PSNR negotiations, see Daniel Yergin, *The Prize: The Epic Quest for Oil, Money and Power* (Pocket Books 1991) 431–98. The formation of OPEC in 1960 could only exacerbate their concerns.

of investment protection articulated in so much detail, and with so much similarity to their modern form.

Resolution 1803 was broadly considered a success, but not unanimously, nor indefinitely. On further reflection, some developing countries began to feel that Resolution 1803 may have 'harmed rather than furthered' their interests.[48] This perception, coupled with the continuing rapid increase in the ranks of new members of the UN General Assembly in the 1960s and early 1970s, led to many more resolutions reasserting sovereignty over natural resources in ever more strident language, culminating in Resolution 3201 (S-VI: 1974) on the establishment of the New International Economic Order (NIEO)[49] and Resolution 3281 (XXIX: 1974) on the Charter of Economic Rights and Duties of States.[50] The PSNR principle was recognised as one of several principles on which basis 'the new international economic order should be founded.'[51] By rejecting the earlier concept of internationalization of state contracts, this Resolution explicitly put investment and PSNR on a direct collision course, stating:

> In order to safeguard these resources, each State is entitled to exercise effective control over them and their exploitation with means suitable to its own situation, including the right to nationalization or transfer of ownership to its nationals, this right being an expression of the full permanent sovereignty of the State. No State may be subjected to economic, political or any other type of coercion to prevent the free and full exercise of this inalienable right.[52]

Mainly because of its aversion to the foreign investor's rights, the Texaco tribunal that recognised Resolution 1803 (1962) as a codification of existing international customary law specifically rejected Resolution 3201 (S-VI: 1974) on the establishment of the NIEO and Resolution 3281 (XXIX: 1974) on the Charter of Economic Rights and Duties of States.[53] Stephen Schwebel later called the 1974 Charter 'the high water

---

[48] See Antony Anghie, *Imperialism, Sovereignty and the Making of International Law* (CUP 2005) 221.

[49] See Declaration on the Establishment of a New International Economic Order, UNGA Res 3201 (S-VI) (1 May 1974) UN Doc A/RES/S-6/3201, para e.

[50] See Charter of Economic Rights and Duties of States, UNGA Res 3281 (XXIX) (12 December 1974).

[51] See Resolution 3201 (n 49) para e.

[52] Ibid.

[53] See *Texaco Overseas Petroleum Company v The Government of the Libyan Arab Republic*, Award (1978) 17 ILM 1, paras 88–91.

mark of disregard, if not denigration, of the international law relating to foreign investment.'[54] The 1974 Charter also represented the high point of the NIEO movement; sovereignty's ascendancy peaked about this time, while the investment protection agenda was only just taking off.[55]

B. Investment Protection: Deflating Sovereignty

Richard Gardner, by then already an influential figure inside the US government, wrote in *Foreign Affairs* in 1974 that 'in three decades of negotiations since [the Atlantic Charter], our focus has been almost exclusively on access to markets. In the next decades, we will need to place new emphasis on arrangements to assure reasonable access to scarce resources.'[56] This agenda was pursued systematically, consistently and, with the benefit of hindsight, successfully. While developing countries were arguing passionately over the PSNR text and its successors in New York and elsewhere, the blueprint of the future investment protection project was being developed, quietly, at the World Bank in Washington.[57] The Washington Convention of 1965, which established ICSID, is the outcome.[58] Professor Andreas Lowenfeld, who participated in the process representing the US, recalls that the World Bank prepared the Washington Convention text using only legal experts, and not national diplomats or politicians, because '[t]hey did not want this effort to

---

[54] See Stephen M Schwebel, 'Investor-State Disputes and the Development of International Law: The Influence of Bilateral Investment Treaties on Customary International Law' (2004) 98 ASIL Proceedings 28.

[55] See José E Alvarez, *The Public International Law Regime Governing International Investment* (Brill 2011) 124.

[56] Richard Gardner, 'The Hard Road to World Order' (1974) 52 *Foreign Affairs* 564.

[57] Thomas Wälde later observed that some global institutions like the World Bank 'act as successors to the former colonial administrations, with a social-engineering mandate for economic development that seems to succeed rarely if ever.' See Thomas W Wälde, 'International Standards in Transnational Investment & Commercial Disputes: The Role of International Standards, Soft Law, Guidelines, Voluntary and Self-Regulation in International Arbitration, Negotiation and other Forms of Dispute Management: Preliminary Study' (2004) 1(4) TDM 14.

[58] For a fascinating story of how the negotiations for this Convention took place see Andreas F Lowenfeld, 'The ICSID Convention: Origins and Transformation' (2009) 38(1) Georgia JICL 47–61.

replicate the experience of the United Nations.'[59] As Puig noted in his recent historical study of ICSID, 'one of the reasons ICSID was established under the auspices of the World Bank was to insulate the discussion from the UN General Assembly.'[60] Instead of calling a diplomatic conference as is usual in such matters, the Bank got the Convention approved by a resolution of its Board of Governors – a body whose decision-making procedures more accurately reflect the prevailing balance of power than the size of its membership. The resolution was passed despite 21 developing countries voting against it. According to Lowenfeld, 'this was the first time that a major resolution of the World Bank had been pressed forward with so much opposition.'[61] Just as it was born without any diplomatic fanfare, ICSID lived its early days quietly and unthreateningly; only after the arrival of bilateral investment treaties (BITs) of the highly investor-protective variety, that came particularly since the late 1980s, did it start to bite properly.[62]

The claim of sovereignty over natural resources that was asserted with so much passion and emotion has since faded, while the investment protection agenda has never been stronger. The lesson for developing countries is clear: numerical superiority alone is not enough to bring changes to international law; if there were any illusions to that effect, they are no more. They now realise that, in the words of Professor Michael Reisman, '[i]nternational law's arithmetic may be one state – one vote, but international political arithmetic … still holds that ninety-nine minus one ofttimes equals zero, and that one plus one ofttimes equals one hundred. Getting your numbers wrong in world politics is as perilous as getting your physics wrong on a superhighway.'[63]

Developing countries got their arithmetic wrong, and found themselves driving down the BIT superhighway, one at a time. Several initiatives for a multilateral investment agreement failed, leaving the bilateral route almost as the only option, and many took it – in some cases probably

---

59 See ibid 52.

60 Sergio Puig, 'Emergence & Dynamism in International Organizations: ICSID, Investor-State Arbitration & International Investment Law' (2012/13) 44 Georgetown JIL 531, 542–3.

61 See Lowenfeld (n 58) 54.

62 As Lowenfeld noted, 'only eleven disputes were brought to the Centre in its first fifteen years, and only six resulted in a final award', ibid 55. As Alvarez reminds us, although the first BITs date back to the late 1950s, they were mostly weak; it was in the 1980s that truly investor-protective BITs emerged, and the US played a leading role in their birth. See Alvarez (n 55) 126.

63 W Michael Reisman, 'The Cult of Custom in the Late 20th Century' (1987) 17 Cal Western ILJ 137.

without much serious thought.[64] Those who led the development of ICSID through the World Bank Board of Governors prepared their own model BITs to further their interests as capital exporters, took them to the capitals of Third World countries, and got them signed with little modification; they became the treaty-equivalent of the contracts of adhesion.[65] They might be typical of 'agreements between a lion and a rabbit,'[66] but they meet the formalistic requirements of consent under international law. In the circumstances, it will certainly be difficult to disagree with Jan Paulsson when he says: 'those who challenge the legitimacy of international adjudication ... criticize the principle of the supremacy of international law when their real complaint has to do with the political choices of their own government in making the bargains reflected in international treaties.'[67] The next question then is this: to what extent, if at all, has this development undermined the PSNR principle?

IV. SOVEREIGNTY OVER NATURAL RESOURCES: THE RETREATING HOST STATE

Before we attempt to answer the above question, a brief discussion of the general concept of sovereignty itself is in order. The concept of sovereignty is complex, dynamic and controversial; it is often condemned and

64 For an insightful summary of the competing explanations as to why so many developing countries advocated the NIEO principles so passionately and signed BITs that completely undermine the letter and spirit of the NIEO movement see Alvarez (n 55) 123–43.

65 Carlos Calvo's home state Argentina signed a BIT with the US 'whose text is, except for its Protocol, identical to that of the 1987 US Model BIT Text'; José E Alvarez and Kathryn Khamsi, 'The Argentine Crisis and Foreign Investors: A Glimpse into the Heart of the Investment Regime' in Karl P Sauvant (ed.), *Yearbook on International Investment Law & Policy 2008–2009* (OUP 2009) 379, 408.

66 According to Nico Schrijver, Nigeria used this expression during UN General Assembly debates on Resolution 1803, apparently referring to the phrase 'freely entered into', presumably in paragraph 8 of the Resolution, which provides: 'Foreign investment agreements freely entered into by, or between, sovereign states shall be observed in good faith'. See Schrijver (n 6) 263.

67 Jan Paulsson, 'The Power of States to Make Meaningful Promises to Foreigners' (2010) 1(2) JIDS 349.

dismissed as out of date,[68] as it is defended and upheld as our salvation from chaos.[69] Professor John Jackson wonders whether the concept of sovereignty is 'perhaps purposefully, misleading';[70] for Professor Louis Henkin, state sovereignty is 'essentially a mistake, an illegitimate offspring'[71] that we must get rid of if we can. It is notable, however, that most – though not all – of the criticisms of sovereignty mainly derive from the history of abuse of the doctrine by repressive regimes that have used it as a shield against foreign intervention while perpetuating some of the most heinous human rights violations within their territories.[72] This aspect of sovereignty is out of date and must be rejected.[73] In this chapter, sovereignty is considered as it relates to the management of national natural resources, where I believe sovereignty remains positively relevant. For my purposes, I find Richard Haass's characterisation of sovereignty a good starting point:

> First, a sovereign state is one that enjoys supreme political authority and a monopoly over the legitimate use of force within its territory. Second, it is capable of regulating movements across its borders. Third, it can make its foreign policy choices freely. Finally, it is recognized by other governments as an independent entity entitled to freedom from external intervention.[74]

---

68 No less an authority than Louis Henkin has argued that 'for legal purposes at least, we might do well to relegate the term sovereignty to the shelf of history as a relic from an earlier era.' Louis Henkin, *International Law: Politics and Values* (Kluwer 1995) quoted in John H Jackson, *Sovereignty, the WTO, and Changing Fundamentals of International Law* (CUP 2006) 69.

69 See José E Alvarez, 'The Return of the State' (2011) 20(2) Minn JIL 223, 263 (referring to Michael Walzer as saying that 'only those lucky enough to live in a functioning state can afford to suggest that [sovereignty] is "withering away"').

70 See Jackson (n 68) 69.

71 In simpler days, wrote Henkin, sovereignty 'implied several key elements. Primarily, it meant political independence. It also meant territorial integrity and virtually exclusive control and jurisdiction within that territory'; Louis Henkin, 'Lecture: That "S" Word: Sovereignty, and Globalization, and Human Rights, Et Cetera' (1999) 68(1) Fordham LRev (1999) 1, 2 (footnotes omitted).

72 Ibid 2 (footnotes omitted).

73 For an eye-opening discussion of the type of atrocities, genocide and crimes against humanity that have been committed under the watch of the UN, and the ongoing struggles to stop them see Kofi Annan with Nader Mousavizadeh, *Interventions: A Life in War and Peace* (Allen Lane 2012).

74 See Richard N Haass, *Sovereignty: Existing Rights, Evolving Responsibilities: Remarks to the School of Foreign Service and the Mortara Center for*

Sovereignty described in these forms is far from absolute. After all, mere assertion of the abstract principle of sovereignty by a resource-rich developing country cannot make a meaningful difference until that resource is properly explored and exploited, which requires capital, technology and management know-how. Sovereignty over natural resources is

> a mere abstract potentiality when the means for developing these resources are lacking. The freedom to exploit natural resources implies, therefore, at least some cooperation between developed and underdeveloped states, since it is only the former that can provide to the latter the means for developing their resources. Precisely for that reason, States all the time use their sovereignty as currency in bilateral and multilateral negotiations with one another to maximize mutual gains, and in the process to voluntarily concede pieces of their sovereign space in exchange for concessions of a similar nature from others.[75]

Or, to use Richard Haass's language, governments 'trade freedom of action for the benefits of multilateral cooperation.'[76] The question, then, is on what terms will that cooperation take place. The international investment regime represents a significant part of the answer to this question at any particular point in time.

In order to analyse the relationship between sovereignty over natural resources and investment protection law, and building on Haass's characterisation, I consider sovereignty as a bundle of powers and prerogatives, available only to a state. Translated into the natural resources sector and contextualized within the domain of international investment law, governments have supreme political authority internally to make and enforce laws for the management, development and utilization of their natural resources ('internal authority' or 'exclusive jurisdiction within their own territory'); they have supreme authority to determine whether or not foreign capital can be employed to develop those resources and, once developed, whether or not the final product stays within their borders or is exported to the world market (border control); and they have complete authority to determine their foreign policy and international relations with respect to natural resources and do so on an equal basis

---

International Studies, Georgetown University (Washington, DC, 14 January 2003) <http://2001–2009.state.gov/s/p/rem/2003/16648.htm> accessed 10 March 2013.

[75] Arghyrios A Fatouros, 'International Law and the Third World' (1964) 50 Va LRev 783, 804.

[76] Haass (n 74).

with every other state in the world and free of unwanted intervention (non-intervention).[77]

Understood in this way, the three traditional functions of the state – to make laws through its chosen legislator (also known as legislative jurisdiction), to administer those laws through its own executive (also known as executive jurisdiction), and to interpret those laws and administer justice through its courts (also known as judicial jurisdiction) – are all derived from, and manifestations of, national sovereignty. The key question, then, is whether, or to what extent, international investment law hampers the exercise of these three components of sovereignty in the natural resources sector. I suggest that modern investment law significantly erodes the state's sovereignty over its natural resources by, at the minimum: (1) limiting its legislative jurisdiction through the doctrine of internationalisation of the investment contract and stabilisation clauses; and (2) virtually eliminating its judicial jurisdiction through the almost uniform adoption of international arbitration as the means to settle investment disputes.

A. Legislative Sovereignty and Internationalisation of Contracts

Internationalisation of contracts refers to a process by which the parties to an international investment contract, that is, the foreign investor and the host state, could 'remove their agreement from the scope of the contracting State's legislative sovereignty'[78] and put it directly under international law.[79] The roots of this innovation date back to the 1930 *Lena Goldfields* award,[80] where the tribunal split the question of applicable law in two and ruled that, for all domestic matters, such as those

---

[77] This paraphrasing is based on Haass's description of the four main characteristics of sovereignty, see ibid.

[78] See Christopher Greenwood, 'State Contracts in International Law – the Libyan Oil Arbitrations' (1982) 53(1) BYIL 27, 41.

[79] For a useful summary of the extensive debate surrounding the concept of internationalization of state contracts see AFM Maniruzzaman, 'State Contracts in Contemporary International Law: Monist Versus Dualist Controversies' (2001) 12(2) EJIL 309–28.

[80] Arthur Nussbaum, 'The Arbitration between the Lena Goldfields, Ltd and the Soviet Government' (1950) 36 *Cornell Law Quarterly* 31–53. The award of the tribunal in *Lena Goldfields* was published in *The Times* of London on 3 September 1930 and reproduced in Nussbaum. For a modern and comprehensive account of this case see Van V Veeder, 'The Lena Goldfields Arbitration: The

relating to performance of the contract by both parties inside the USSR, Soviet law applied, while for all other purposes 'the *general principles of law* such as those recognized by Article 38 of the Statute of the Permanent Court of International Justice ... should be regarded as "the proper law of the contract".'[81] It was from this curious and unwarranted split[82] of the applicable law concept that one of the most successful legal innovations of international investment law originated. This is the first time Article 38 of the Statute of the PCIJ was used as a source of law governing the relations between a State on the one hand and a private investor, on the other.

Although there was little enthusiasm or recognition of the significance of this innovation when it first came about, the decolonisation process of the 1950s and 1960s, and the accompanying sovereignty risks to foreign property in the newly-independent states, gave new meaning and relevance to the doctrine of internationalisation. Already in 1957 Lord McNair, a leading authority in international law who had just retired from his position as President of the ICJ, was thus able to assert an emerging 'general consensus of opinion' that general principles of law recognised in civilised nations provided 'the system of law governing these contractual relationships.'[83] And, as noted earlier, in 1962, Resolution 1803 effectively elevated the investment contract to a quasi-treaty by prescribing the state's obligation to observe its contractual commitments in good faith.[84] Greenwood thus observed that 1962 was 'the high point of acceptance' of the theory of internationalization of state contracts, which was soon followed by 'growing opposition from the developing States' who considered it an insult to the sovereignty of a contracting State.[85]

Historical Roots of Three Ideas' (1998) 47 ICLQ 747–92.

[81] *Lena Goldfields Company Ltd v Soviet Union*, Award (2 September 1930) para 22, extracts reproduced in Nussbaum (n 80) 50 (emphasis added).

[82] Arthur Nussbaum rightly commented that 'such a splitting of applicable legal systems was not warranted; the "proper law" of the entire contract was Soviet'; ibid 36.

[83] See Arnold McNair, 'The Applicability of "General Principles of Law" to Contracts between a State and a Foreign National' (American Bar Association: Section of Mineral & Natural Resources Law Proceedings, 1957) 168–76; a slightly modified version of this article is also available in Arnold McNair, 'The General Principles of Law Recognized by Civilized Nations' (1957) 33 BYIL 1–19.

[84] For early reflections on this practice see Greenwood (n 78).

[85] Ibid 43.

Be that as it may, if an investment contract were to be removed from the legislative sovereignty of the host state, one would think that the parties must include an unambiguous choice of law clause to that effect.[86] But this has not always been the case.[87] In the *Abu Dhabi* arbitration, the closest to a choice of law clause was limited to a declaration by the parties to 'base their work in this Agreement on goodwill and sincerity of belief' and to interpret the Agreement 'in a fashion consistent with reason.'[88] The sole arbitrator started with a rhetorical question of what the proper law of the contract was and wrote: 'This is a contract made in Abu Dhabi and wholly to be performed in that country. If any municipal system of law were applicable, it would prima facie be that of Abu Dhabi.'[89] The arbitrator continued: 'But no such law can reasonably be said to exist. The Sheikh administers a purely discretionary justice with the assistance of the Koran; and it would be fanciful to suggest that in this very primitive region there is any settled body of legal principles applicable to the construction of modern commercial instruments.'[90] Thus the arbitrator conferred on himself an unlimited discretion to determine the law applicable to the construction of the contract. At first, he rejected the municipal law of England as inapplicable because, 'Clause 17 of the agreement … repels the notion that the municipal law of any country, as such, could be appropriate.'[91] Interestingly, however, the arbitrator ended up applying English law on the grounds that 'some of its rules are … so firmly grounded in reason, as to form part of this broad body of

---

[86] As Judge Higgins put it, 'the best way to avoid sole reliance on domestic law is, one has to say, by having a governing law clause that introduces international law. If, in the bargaining process, the private party has been unable to accomplish this, it seems doubtful that international arbitrators should remedy that which one of the negotiating parties was unable to achieve.' Rosalyn Higgins, *Problems and Process: International Law and How We Use It* (OUP 1994) 141.

[87] According to Maniruzzaman, the theory of internationalization suggests that, 'no matter what law the parties to [a state] contract choose as the proper law of the contract, international law superimposes their choice and applies automatically as the overriding governing rule'; see Maniruzzaman (n 79) 309.

[88] *Petroleum Development (Trucial Coast) Ltd v Ruler of Abu Dhabi*, Award (21 August 1951) (1952) 1 ICLQ 247–61.

[89] Ibid 252.

[90] Ibid 252–3.

[91] Ibid 253.

jurisprudence – this "modern law of nature,"' a body of 'principles rooted in the good sense and common practice of the generality of civilised nations.'[92]

The *Abu Dhabi* award might stand out for its bluntness today, but it was by no means unique in its dismissal of host state laws as totally inadequate. As Lalive has observed, many tribunals have ruled that 'the State party to the contract and to the litigation had no law of contracts, no commercial law capable of meeting the intricacies of modern international trade relations.'[93] Lalive then opined that this argument 'is not very convincing and should as a rule be disregarded.'[94] In this spirit, the *Aminoil* tribunal showed its sensitivity by emphasising that

> Kuwait law is a highly evolved system … established public international law is necessarily a part of the law of Kuwait. In their turn the general principles of law are part of public international law … and that this specifically applies to Kuwait oil concessions, duly results from the clauses included in these.[95]

In *Abu Dhabi*, English law was brought in as applicable law because it represented some form of 'modern law of nature'; in *Aminoil*, those same English law principles would apply because they would represent general principles of law recognised in a civilized nation, forming part of established public international law that is 'necessarily part of the law of Kuwait.' The routes could be straightforward as in Abu Dhabi, or meandering as in Aminoil, but the destination remained the same in all cases. The 'general principles of law recognised in civilised nations' that were used as the tool to make new law applying to new states are still on the ICJ Statute as a legitimate source of international law.

Professor Alvarez suggests that today's international lawyers 'no longer distinguish the rules applicable to the "civilized" versus "uncivilized" worlds in order to use the former to dispossess the latter.'[96] The evolution of the applicable law concept in international investment law and its practical application in the hands of international arbitrators might

---

[92] Ibid.

[93] See Jean-Flavien Lalive, 'Contracts between a State or a State Agency and a Foreign Company: Theory and Practice: Choice of Law in a New Arbitration Case' (1964) 13 ICLQ 987, 1009.

[94] See ibid.

[95] See Award in the Matter of an Arbitration between Kuwait and the American Independent Oil Company (Aminoil) (1982) 21 ILM 976,1000.

[96] José E Alvarez, 'Contemporary Foreign Investment Law: An "Empire of Law" or the "Law of Empire"' (2009) 60 Alabama LRev 943–75.

leave a question whether Alvarez's statement here is a result of hope rather than experience. The *Abu Dhabi* award may be dismissed as a case of the bad old days, but national law was never given the last word in investment arbitration; at the very least, it has always been subject to the international minimum standard. To the extent its substantive rules and principles are taken from the general principles of law in those 'civilized states', the international minimum standard is reminiscent of Lord Asquith's rejection of English law as inapplicable, only to bring it back in through the back door with a different name – as a 'modern law of nature.'[97] As Mohammed Bedjaoui put it, the general principles of law are 'in fact merely the transposition into international law of the principles of the Western countries' own domestic law.'[98] Article 42(1) of the ICSID Convention makes host state law and international law applicable law by default in the absence of a choice of law clause in the contract. But, in practice, and regardless of whether or not the parties have included a choice of law clause, arbitrators apply host state law subject to international law – that is, in the event of a conflict between the two, international law is given precedence over host state law.[99] As Dame Higgins noted two decades ago, 'whether there is only a domestic-law-proper law clause; or whether there is a mixed "international-law and domestic-law" clause (as in the Libyan arbitrations or in Article 42 of the [ICSID]), international arbitrators are very likely to find international law relevant.'[100] Many BITs that are pervasive today take this a significant step further – through the so-called umbrella clause, which purports to lift all and any breaches of investment contracts to the realm of international law.[101]

---

[97] But, the application of the international minimum standard to a country as a minimum threshold that it must make available to foreign investors in its territory is not the same as making international law the only applicable law. For a discussion of the distinction between these two see Maniruzzaman (n 79).

[98] Mohammed Bedjaoui, *Towards a New International Economic Order* (Holmes and Meier 1979) 101.

[99] See, e.g., Rudolf Dolzer and Christoph Schreuer, *Principles of International Investment Law* (OUP 2008) 271.

[100] Higgins (n 86) 141.

[101] The umbrella clause expressly requires the host state 'to observe any obligation it may have entered into with regard to foreign investments, that is converting (or purporting to convert) contracts subject to domestic law into international obligations'; see Lowenfeld (n 58) 58.

B. Legislative Sovereignty and Stabilisation Clauses

Stabilisation clauses are provisions in investment contracts that aim 'to freeze the law of the host state at the time of contracting or to insulate the contract against the impact of future legislative changes.'[102] Traditionally, stabilisation clauses are designed to freeze the law of the host state as of the day of the investment contract.[103] This is reflected in the definition adopted by the arbitral tribunal in *Total v. Argentina*, which understood stabilisation clauses as clauses in state contracts 'with the intended effect of freezing a specific host State's legal framework at a certain date, such that the adoption of any changes in the legal regulatory framework of the investment concerned (even by law of general application and without any discriminatory intent by the host State) would be illegal.'[104]

Generally intended as tools for the management of political risk, stabilisation clauses were first introduced to fill whatever room was left for national legislative sovereignty from the application of the doctrine of internationalisation. But, unlike the doctrine of internationalisation, which first came into existence through an arbitration award and later moved to contract drafting, stabilisation clauses were the creation of contracts from the 1950s, receiving recognition by arbitral tribunals afterwards. When they started in the 1950s and 1960s, they were introduced as part of the post-colonial regime to manage the impending 'sovereignty risk' in the newly sovereign states of the South.[105]

Starting in the 1980s, however, stabilisation clauses were more or less wilfully accepted by capital-starved developing countries that looked at

---

[102] Georges R Delaume, 'The Proper Law of State Contracts Revisited' (1997) 12(1) ICSID Rev 23. For a recent and thorough analysis of stabilisation clauses see Shemberg (n 12).

[103] However, stabilisation obligations today may come from international treaties as well as unilateral undertakings contained in municipal law. This chapter deals with traditional stabilisation clauses as contained in international investment contracts, for the simple reason that to the extent they are contained in municipal law or international treaties, stabilisation clauses impose constraints on sovereignty just like every other law does and in every country. Stabilisation clauses contained in investment contracts, on the other hand, are as a matter of empirical fact limited to developing countries. For more see ibid.

[104] *Total SA v Argentine Republic*, ICSID Case No ARB/04/1, Decision on Liability (27 December 2010) para 100.

[105] As Cameron rightly pointed out, the debate on stabilisation clauses first began when 'the post-colonial investment regime [was] in place'; Cameron (n 23) 311, 312.

them as 'an important tool of foreign investment promotion policy.'[106] Today, stabilisation clauses are a common feature of investment contracts, particularly those in the extractive industries between foreign companies and African governments,[107] though rare or non-existent in advanced countries.[108] In this sense, stabilisation clauses are a premium developing countries pay in order to attract private foreign capital and technology; indeed, considering administrative and institutional problems that are often associated with these countries, this might be termed a rule-of-law premium. As a result, a state party to an international investment contract that contains a stabilisation clause might commit breach of contract by the mere act of passing a new law, or as we have seen in recent jurisprudence and contract practice,[109] even a new interpretation of a pre-existing law.[110]

Given that the state has consented to such a clause in the first place, it is hardly surprising that today's international law affirms that this contractual breach entails state responsibility.[111] As an ICSID tribunal emphasised recently, a stability undertaking in an investment agreement is of 'undoubted importance for investors' because it 'freezes the laws, rules and regulations applicable to it, as they were in existence at the time the Agreement was concluded.'[112] The investor expectations created by such a clause are also likely to be considered 'legitimate', thereby triggering claims of breach of the fair and equitable treatment clause in a

---

[106] Wälde and Ndi (n 18) 218.

[107] See Shemberg (n 12) 17, 21–2 and 32.

[108] Ibid. In fact, many OECD countries do not just exclude stabilisation clauses; they often explicitly reserve the power to unilaterally modify contracts with private operators. For a discussion of such clauses in France, the UK and the US see Patrick M Norton, 'A Law of the Future or a Law of the Past? Modern Tribunals and the International Law of Expropriation' (1991) 85 AJIL 474, 492–3.

[109] For a useful analysis see Lorenzo Cotula, 'Pushing the Boundaries vs Striking a Balance: Some Reflections on Stabilization Issues in Light of Duke Energy International Investments v Republic of Peru' (2010) TDM 1.

[110] See *Duke Energy International Peru Investments No 1 Ltd v Republic of Peru*, ICSID Case No ARB/03/28, Award on the Merits (18 August 2008) para 227. For analysis of this case see Cotula (n 109).

[111] This might look obvious in the face of today's virtual consensus in the arbitration jurisprudence, but as recently as 1960, Mann argued otherwise, see FA Mann, 'State Contracts and State Responsibility' (1960) 54 AJIL 581 and 587–8.

[112] See *Aguaytia Energy LLC v Republic of Peru*, ICSID Case No ARB/06/13, Award (11 December 2008) para 95.

BIT.[113] In a recent award, the *Mobil v. Canada* tribunal observed that a state may be held responsible if it is established that it made 'clear and explicit representations … in order to induce the investment,' that such representations were 'reasonably relied upon by the Claimants,' and it subsequently repudiated those representations.[114] Unlike in earlier days,[115] however, the obligation of the state under a stabilisation clause is generally limited to the payment of compensation to affected foreign investors rather than repeal of legislation.[116] As a result, the limitations to legislative sovereignty resulting from modern stabilisation clauses have diminished over time. However, the mere fact that stabilisation clauses are common in international investment contracts for the exploitation of natural resources in developing countries, with consequent constraints on the powers of the state to change its laws – albeit remediable through financial compensation – provides further evidence that international investment law unduly and discriminatorily restricts the sovereign legislative space available to these states to manage their natural resources sectors.

C. Judicial Sovereignty and International Arbitration

As noted earlier, one key manifestation of sovereignty involves the inherent power of the state as the supreme authority to administer justice within its territory. Translated into the natural resources industry, this would inevitably mean the power to subject all natural and legal persons operating within its territory to the jurisdiction of its courts. In practice,

---

[113] See, e.g., *Total SA v Argentine Republic* (n 104) para 117.

[114] See *Mobil Investments Canada Inc v Canada*, ICSID Case No ARB(AF)/07/4, Award (22 May 2012) para 154.

[115] See the Texaco Award, where the arbitrator ordered specific performance as a remedy, but this aspect of the award became irrelevant as Libya and the companies reached a settlement soon after the award was issued. See Troy E Elder, 'The Case Against Arbitral Awards of Specific Performance in Transnational Commercial Disputes' (1997) 13(1) *Arbitration International* 1–32.

[116] A good example of this came from the mid-1970s when the ICSID tribunal in *Alcoa Minerals of Jamaica v Jamaica*, ruled that Jamaica was in breach of the stabilization clause contained in the long-term contract it had signed with Alcoa for bauxite mining. See *Alcoa Minerals of Jamaica, Inc v Government of Jamaica*, ICSID Case No ARB/74/2, excerpts in (1979) 4 *Yearbook Commercial Arbitration* 206. See Virtus Chitoo Igbokwe, 'Developing Countries and the Law Applicable to International Arbitration of Oil Investment Disputes – Has the Last Word Been Said?' (1997) 14(1) *Journal of International Arbitration* 120.

however, this is where the investment law experiment in the natural resources sector has succeeded in almost completely obliterating prior international law. In perhaps the most successful innovation designed to insulate Western corporations operating in the poorest developing countries from the jurisdiction of the local courts, access to international arbitration has since become an almost unconditional right for the foreign investor.[117]

The reputation of many of these countries as lacking independent and competent courts with the capacity to administer justice impartially explains, at least in part, investors' and home states' insistence on access to international arbitration as a condition for commitment to operate in those countries. Today, BITs have effectively guaranteed them this privilege. If the doctrine of internationalisation of state contracts was intended to ensure foreign investors remained subject only to the laws of their home countries (through the reference to the general principle of law recognised in civilised nations or some other less crude language), the provision of direct access to international arbitration is the modern day replacement of the consular courts that had exclusive jurisdiction during the colonial days.[118]

Traditional international law of course had an older, fairer and well-established mechanism of dealing with such issues by allowing foreign investors access to diplomatic protection, or even international arbitration if there was a specific agreement to that effect, once they have exhausted available remedies within the host state. General Assembly Resolution 1803 recognised this possibility when it provided: 'In any case where the question of compensation gives rise to a controversy, the national jurisdiction of the State taking such measures shall be exhausted.

---

[117] What is interesting is that even some of the leading authorities of the day did not see this coming. Writing in 1963, Professor Brierley described the doctrine of diplomatic protection, identified some of its defects, such as the fact that the home state of the foreign investor might not be willing to take up his case, possible delays, and the like, and noted: 'It has been suggested that a solution might be found by allowing individuals access in their own right to some form of international tribunal for the purpose.' Brierley then added: 'For the time being, however, the prospect of states accepting such a change is not very great'; James L Brierley, *The Law of Nations* (6th edn, OUP 1963) 277, quoted in Nigel Blackaby and Constantine Partasides with Alan Redfern and Martin Hunter, *Redfern and Hunter on International Arbitration* (OUP 2011) 467.

[118] For a discussion of capitulation agreements and how they were applied through consular courts see Salacuse (n 29) 82, and more generally Anghie (n 48).

However, upon agreement by sovereign States and other parties concerned, settlement of the dispute should be made through arbitration or international adjudication.'[119] As Professor Lowenfeld pointed out, the language of this provision was the result of serious negotiations and compromises.[120] If the use of the stronger language of 'shall' indicated that the doctrine of exhaustion of local remedies was left intact, subsequent developments under the auspices of the World Bank sowed the seed for its lasting reversal in the shape of the 1965 Washington Convention that established ICSID.[121] The doctrine of exhaustion of local remedies remains the default rule to this day,[122] except when it comes to the relations between foreign investors and developing countries, for which BITs mostly provide access to international arbitration without any such requirement.[123]

---

119 Resolution 1803 (n 44) para 4. The rest of this paragraph contains the following: 'Nationalization, expropriation or requisitioning shall be based on grounds or reasons of public utility, security or the national interest which are recognized as overriding purely individual or private interests, both domestic and foreign. In such cases the owner shall be paid appropriate compensation, in accordance with the rules in force in the state taking such measures in the exercise of its sovereignty and in accordance with international law.'

120 See Lowenfeld (n 58) 48–9 (pointing out that 'in comparison with the draft proposed by the Special Commission to the General Assembly, the first sentence was changed from "should" to "shall" – i.e. stronger for the host country, while the second sentence was changed from "may" to "should", – i.e. stronger for the investors').

121 For more on the history of ICSID, see Lowenfeld (n 58) 51.

122 The exhaustion of local remedies rule is 'an established procedural rule of customary international law that a State may not espouse the claim of one of its nationals against another State unless the national has exhausted local remedies'; George K Foster, 'Striking a Balance between Investor Protections and National Sovereignty: The Relevance of Local Remedies in Investment Treaty Arbitration (2011) 49(2) Colum JTL 201, 204.

123 As Professor Schreuer put it, 'international investment arbitration dispenses with the requirement to exhaust local remedies, at least in principle. Article 26 of the ICSID Convention specifically does away with this traditional requirement "unless otherwise stated"': Christoph Schreuer, 'Calvo's Grandchildren: The Return of Local Remedies in Investment Arbitration' (2005) 4(1) LPICT 1. Schreuer adds that while countries can insist on exhaustion of local remedies in their BITs, 'clauses of this kind seem to be rare and are found mostly in BITs of older vintage'; ibid 2.

V. CONCLUSION

A state's sovereignty over its natural resources is now one of the most prominent principles of international law that has already been recognised as a principle of customary international law. Indeed, when Resolution 1803 was issued by the General Assembly in 1962, it was 'generally considered at the time to be evidence of customary international law.'[124] Whatever doubt may have remained about its status has since evaporated. The ICJ has also, for the first time, ruled that the PSNR principle 'is a principle of customary international law.'[125] At the level of relevant treaties, too, this principle has been articulated in various instruments and in varying degrees of detail; the Energy Charter Treaty may be mentioned as just one example.[126] Finally, Professor Vaughan Lowe refers to the PSNR principle as one of the possible examples for *jus cogens* norms of international law on the same level as the principle for the prohibition of apartheid-type racial discrimination.[127] This, however, is only the easy part. As I noted earlier, I do not believe the sovereignty of states over their natural resources, per se, was ever seriously questioned; only the sovereignty of the newly independent states was – and by extension their sovereignty over their natural resources. The real question is one of balance between this principle and the principles of international law for the protection of foreign investment.

This balance has been shifting increasingly towards the latter especially over the last two decades. The changes brought about by BITs in these two decades are so revolutionary that, according to Judge Schwebel, they represent what until recently he would have considered the 'ideal' law of international investment: 'BITs specify – in terms more explicit, detailed, and far-reaching than was ever advanced under what

---

124 See Greenwood (n 78) 42. Former ICJ Judge Stephen M Schwebel also noted that the resolution 'is the capstone of more than ten years of consideration of the subject by the General Assembly, the Human Rights Commission, the Economic and Social Council and a special Commission on Permanent Sovereignty over Natural Resources'; see Schwebel (n 42) 463.

125 *Case Concerning Armed Activities on the Territory of the Congo (Democratic Republic of the Congo v Uganda)* [2005] ICJ Rep 168, para 244. For analysis of the significance of this ruling see Robert Dufresne, 'Reflections and Extrapolation on the ICJ's Approach to Illegal Resource Exploitation in the Armed Activities Case' (2008) 40 NYU JILP 171–217.

126 See ECT, art 18(1).

127 See Vaughan Lowe, *International Law* (OUP 2007) 59.

was customary international law in the time of Cordell Hull – what may be described as an ideal law of international investment.'[128] Many of the capital-importing developing countries that fought hard in the corridors of the United Nations until the mid-1970s have come to realise that all their fears have materialised, shattering their hopes for a more balanced future under the law. The dawn of hope and independence in the 1960s, which was further invigorated by the commodity price boom and accompanying confidence and assertiveness of the 1970s, was quickly replaced by the debt crisis and the pro-market ideological shift of the 1980s, the BITs of the 1990s, and the dreaded arbitrations of the 2000s.

However, I conclude not with despair, but with hope. There are presently some promising signs of change in the right direction, dictated mainly by such underlying economic factors as the role reversal of the traditional home states of FDI in the Global North increasingly finding themselves in the unusual position of having to answer for their own practices at the behest of investors coming from the traditional host states of the Global South. As a result, these countries are reconsidering their traditional positions, and in the process coming slightly closer to the position long advocated by the Global South. As Professor Alvarez observed in 2011, 'many recent investment protection treaties accord FDI host states greater room to maneuver, while simultaneously granting foreign investors fewer rights.'[129] Alvarez added that the US 'led the charge in favor of investor protections' in the 1980s, but 'it now appears to be leading the drive in the opposite direction.'[130] However, this opportunity cannot come to the poorest countries until and unless they consciously act to get it. As Alvarez warned, although many countries are following this US lead, '[m]any African states will likely remain parties to older much more pro-investor BITs based on models comparable to those of the US Model BIT of 1984.'[131]

So the challenge is clear; today's international investment law significantly erodes the sovereignty of the poorest countries over their natural

---

[128] See Schwebel (n 54) 28.

[129] Alvarez (n 69) 235.

[130] Ibid. Alvarez also shows that several other countries, including Canada and China, are following this US lead in terms of their model BITs, while several countries are also making revising their national investment laws in more sovereignty-enhancing ways; interestingly, Alvarez also suggests that even some arbitral tribunals are turning in this direction: 'The efforts to re-balance the rights of sovereigns vis-à-vis foreign investors [are] increasingly evident in the text of BITs, national laws, and even some arbitral awards …'; ibid 251–2.

[131] Alvarez (n 69) 260.

resources. While this is largely a product of history and present-day political economy, recent developments towards the treatification of investment law have brought the traditional capital exporting countries closer to the place long occupied by developing countries, including exposure to international arbitration. As a result, the developed countries are once again quickly rebalancing their international commitments and moving towards a more sovereignty-protective regime of foreign investment law. I believe the likes of sub-Saharan Africa must also move with the times and not get stuck with the model of the 1980s. If we manage to alert these countries to these developments, support them in their efforts, and stand for fairness, there is hope now more than ever to make some important changes for the better. This is a time of hope. Even Africa is changing. As *The Economist* put it recently: 'Never in the half-century since it won independence from the colonial powers has Africa been in such good shape.'[132] Rebalancing its investment commitments is likely to help transform today's hopes into tomorrow's realities of improved livelihood for Africa's citizens.

---

132 'The World's Fastest-Growing Continent: Aspiring Africa' *The Economist* (London, 2 March 2013).

9. International (investment) law and distribution conflicts over natural resources

Isabel Feichtner

I. DISTRIBUTION CONFLICTS OVER NATURAL RESOURCES IN INTERNATIONAL LAW

Natural resources – such as minerals or hydrocarbons – constitute the basis of our economies; they provide us with energy and the raw materials for infrastructure and industrial production. Extractive resources – which are the focus of this chapter – are exhaustible and distributed unequally over the globe. Their territoriality, scarcity and uneven geographical distribution lead to conflicts over access to natural resources. Due to the potentially large gains that can be reaped from natural resource exploitation and extensive social and environmental costs involved conflicts not only arise over access, but also with respect to the questions whether to extract or not, the modalities and the sharing of the costs and benefits of natural resource exploitation.

Many poor countries in the Global South have historically been and remain today the site of large scale projects for the extraction of raw materials frequently destined for export to countries in the Global North. Under colonialism, international law was instrumental for the metropolitan powers to secure access to natural resource wealth in the colonies and dependent territories. With decolonization and the inclusion of the former colonies into the international community as sovereign States access could no longer be safeguarded through formal domination. Yet, international law continued to play an important role with respect to the distribution of access to natural resources between States, a role that continues to change over time.

Already during World War II the United States and the United Kingdom anticipated that the distribution of natural resources would become a central concern after the war. In the Atlantic Charter of 1941 they stated:

> Fourth, they [the US and the UK] will endeavor, with due respect for their existing obligations, to further the enjoyment by all States, great or small, victor or vanquished, of access, on equal terms, to the trade and to the raw materials of the world which are needed for their economic prosperity.[1]

Accordingly natural resource wealth was to be equitably shared between States. Yet, with progressive decolonization the newly independent States started to promote their own views on just distribution which substantially differed from those of the industrialized States. For the new States, political independence promised that they would be able to reap the benefits of resource wealth for their own economic prosperity. Resource wealth, moreover, meant bargaining power in the endeavor to negotiate a New International Economic Order (NIEO). Just distribution with respect to natural resource exploitation for these countries implied the right to nationalize, state control over foreign investments, reparation and compensation for natural resource exploitation in the former colonies and dependent territories and market intervention to control commodity prices.[2] While distribution conflicts over natural resources were central to the debates on a NIEO, during the last decades the specific distribution conflicts surrounding natural resource exploitation no longer have been at the core of international law. Instead, international law has played a significant role in the privatization of natural resource exploitation relegating questions of distribution to 'the market'. Yet, international law's stance on resource distribution conflicts may once more be changing and resource conflicts may soon move center stage again, given the growing demand by emerging economies for raw materials, the discontents triggered by the social and environmental costs of extraction projects mainly in poor, but increasingly also in rich countries, as well as an enhanced global awareness of planetary limitations and the destructive consequences of our ever increasing consumption of natural resources.

In this chapter, I trace the developments in the relationship between international law and resource distribution conflicts. The focus will be on the role of international economic law, and in particular international investment law, in displacing efforts to create a legal framework for the

---

1 Declaration of Principles (signed and entered into force 14 August 1941) 204 LNTS 381, 384.

2 For a good overview see Nico Schrijver, *Sovereignty over Natural Resources. Balancing Rights and Duties* (CUP 1997) ch 3.

political resolution of distribution conflicts over natural resources with a market rationale of distribution which does not take account of the particularities of natural resource exploitation. I first argue that the New International Economic Order favored the political resolution of distribution conflicts over natural resources and envisaged international distribution conflicts to be addressed by the political organs of international institutions within legal procedures (II). Second, I show how the NIEO was surpassed by a different order that relied largely on the market as a distribution mechanism for raw materials and how international institutions and international law played a crucial role in the establishment of this order by promoting the privatization of natural resource exploitation and protecting foreign direct investment (FDI) and trade (III). With reference to the copper industry in Zambia, in the next section, I illustrate how international investment law, and more broadly international economic law, is shaping (and affecting the resolution of) not only distribution conflicts between, but also within States (IV). I conclude with a call for a renewed focus on an international law of resource conflicts allowing for their political resolution given the countermoves we can observe with respect to international investment law and the persistence of (violent) conflicts over natural resource exploitation within States (V).

II. THE NEW INTERNATIONAL ECONOMIC ORDER: POLITICAL RESOLUTION OF DISTRIBUTION CONFLICTS OVER NATURAL RESOURCES

The NIEO – which the newly independent States, organized in the G77, sought to establish after World War II – can be interpreted to exhibit a preference for the political resolution of natural resource conflicts. With the establishment of the principle of permanent sovereignty over natural resources it clearly allocated the right to dispose over natural resource wealth to the State within whose territory natural resources are located. Sovereignty over natural resources includes the right of States to exclude other States from access to their extractive resources.[3] As concerns internal decisions whether or not to exploit natural resources, how to exploit natural resources and how to share the benefits and burdens of natural resource exploitation, permanent sovereignty over natural resources may be interpreted to require such decisions to be the outcome

[3] On modifications of sovereignty over natural resources in particular by international environmental law see ibid 231 ff.

of democratic processes. The NIEO not only allocated disposal rights to resource States and their peoples, it also addressed questions of international distribution conflicts which the principle of permanent sovereignty – by its primary allocation of disposal rights over territorial resource wealth to individual States – potentially exacerbated. International Commodity Agreements were to provide legal frameworks for the political resolution of such international distribution conflicts.

A. Permanent Sovereignty over Natural Resources as a Political Concept

With decolonization the conflicting positions between industrialized countries, many dependent on imports of raw materials and oil, and newly independent resource-exporting States became apparent in debates within the United Nations on permanent sovereignty over natural resources. Under colonialism, the imperial/European international law had provided a justification (based on the colonies' inferior status attributed to them by international law) to the imperial powers and their corporations for the exploitation of natural resources in the colonies.[4] With political independence, however, the formerly dependent territories became the imperial powers' sovereign equals and concomitantly could assert a right to territorial sovereignty, including sovereignty over their natural resources. Since the early 1950s the principle of permanent sovereignty over natural resources was formulated in a number of General Assembly resolutions.[5] General Assembly Resolution 1803 of 1962 qualifies the principle as follows:

> The right of peoples and nations to permanent sovereignty over their natural wealth and resources must be exercised in the interest of their national development and of the well-being of the people of the state concerned.[6]

This formulation indicates that permanent sovereignty is to protect the collective autonomy of the resource States' population and has to be exercised through politics. This interpretation is supported by the international human rights covenants that link permanent sovereignty over

---

[4] Antony Anghie, *Imperialism, Sovereignty and the Making of International Law* (CUP 2005); Bernard VA Röling, *International Law in an Expanded World* (Djambatan 1960) 26 ff.

[5] UNGA Res 523 (VI) (1952); UNGA Res 626 (VII) (1952); UNGA Res 1803 (XVII) (1962).

[6] UNGA Res 1803 (XVII), ibid para 1.

natural resources to the right to self-determination.[7] The African Banjul Charter clarifies that this right can also be brought into position against a government and provides that '[i]n case of spoliation the dispossessed people shall have the right to the lawful recovery of its property as well as to an adequate compensation.'[8]

With the firm establishment of the right to permanent sovereignty over natural resources, initiatives were defeated that sought to introduce into international law obligations of resource States to grant access to their natural resources to third States or the obligation to engage in natural resource exploitation not only to promote the national, but the global public interest. The International Co-operative Alliance had proposed, for example, to place resources under the control of the United Nations and to negotiate an international convention that would provide for equal access and exploitation in the public interest.[9]

Today, international law scholars again attempt to derive from the international law principle of sovereignty international obligations of States towards other States in a range of fields.[10] Yet, the wording of the relevant passage of General Assembly Resolution 1803 makes quite clear that, when the resolution was adopted, permanent sovereignty over natural resources was not understood in that way. Why States that depended on resource imports still agreed to the Resolution and its attribution of exploitation rights solely to the people of the resource State becomes clearer when we look at how importing States could protect their own national interests in access to resources through another body of rules, namely those on investor protection.[11] What should be noted here is that permanent sovereignty over natural resources provides the basis to argue for the need of a political resolution of internal resources conflicts. On the liberal-democratic premise that autonomy can only be realized within political procedures framed by human and minority rights, important decisions on the exploitation of natural resources will

---

[7] Art 1(2) of the International Covenant on Civil and Political Rights and the International Covenant on Economic, Social and Cultural Rights.

[8] Art 21(2) of the African [Banjul] Charter on Human and Peoples' Rights (adopted 27 June 1981, entered into force on 21 October 1986) OAU Doc CAB/LEG/67/3 rev 5 (1982) 21 ILM 58.

[9] On this and other attempts to establish an obligation to use natural resources in the global interest see Schrijver (n 2) 37 ff.

[10] Eyal Benvenisti, 'Sovereigns as Trustees of Humanity' (2013) 107 AJIL 295.

[11] See infra Section III.A.

always need to be linked to democratic procedures if they are to be an expression of self-determination.[12]

As natural resource exploitation is frequently highly capital- and skill-intensive many resource-rich developing countries would not have been able to exploit their natural resources without the help of FDI. In order to attain greater economic independence they combined insistence on permanent sovereignty over natural resources with claims for substantial financial assistance by public lenders as well as transfer of technological know-how.[13] Support specifically for the economic exploitation of natural resources was to be provided by a Common Fund for Commodities.[14]

B. International Legal Procedures to Address International Resource Conflicts

While permanent sovereignty over natural resources laid the foundation for the argument that national decisions about natural resource exploitation must be an expression of collective autonomy and are to be the subject of (domestic) politics, the NIEO envisaged conflict-resolution procedures also at the international level. Conflicts between resource-exporting (producer) States and resource-importing (consumer) States were to be addressed within international organizations established by International Commodity Agreements. The Agreement Establishing the Common Fund for Commodities defined International Commodity Agreements as

> any intergovernmental arrangement to promote international cooperation in a commodity, the parties to which include producers and consumers covering the bulk of world trade in the commodity concerned.[15]

International Commodity Agreements were, as shows the distinction in the definition just mentioned, based on the premise that the interests of producer and consumer States were potentially in conflict.

---

[12] On the link between sovereignty, self-determination and democracy see Anne Peters, 'Humanity as the A and Ω of Sovereignty' (2009) 20 EJIL 513.

[13] See, e.g., International Development Strategy for the Second United Nations Development Decade, UNGA Res 2626 (XXV) (1970) paras 43 and 64.

[14] Christoph Ohler, 'Common Fund for Commodities (CFC)' in Rüdiger Wolfrum (ed.), *Encyclopedia of Public International Law* (OUP 2008) <www.mpepil.com> accessed 1 August 2014.

[15] Agreement Establishing the Common Fund for Commodities, TD/IPC/CF/CONF/25, art 1 para 2.

Developing countries advocated the establishment of International Commodity Agreements to achieve greater equity in international commodities trade and in particular to stabilize prices of primary commodities through market intervention in order to prevent a deterioration of the terms of trade to their detriment. In the 1960s and 70s when International Commodity Agreements were high on the agenda of the United Nations, and more specifically the United Nations Conference on Trade and Development (UNCTAD), stabilization was thought to be necessary to contain a perceived long-term trend of falling prices of commodities in relation to manufactured goods. The main instruments of market intervention to be implemented by International Commodity Agreements were buffer stocks and export quotas.[16] Yet, long term stabilization of commodity prices was not the only objective. Benefits of international cooperation with respect to commodities were also promised to consumer countries that were (and this is a significant difference to producer associations) to be equally represented in International Commodity Agreements. Objectives that would benefit consumer countries included the stabilization of short-term price volatility[17] and the equitable distribution of commodities in short supply through the co-ordination of commodity production and marketing policies.[18] Next to a number of further objectives International Commodity Agreements also sought to increase processing of raw materials in the resources States and to ensure fair labor standards in natural resource exploitation.[19]

The International Commodity Agreements that entered into force established international organizations, which – like other international organizations – had a main political organ, the council, consisting of representatives of all members,[20] and an executive committee with limited membership and to which the council could delegate certain powers. Decisions of these organs included, for example, the setting of reference prices for the respective commodity. Each of the two groups, consumer and producer countries, had an equal number of votes; within each group the votes were distributed proportionally to export and import

---

[16] BS Chimni, *International Commodity Agreements. A Legal Study* (Croom Helm 1987).

[17] Ibid 42, 43.

[18] UNCTAD Resolution, 'International Commodity Arrangements and Removal of Obstacles and Expansion of Trade' in *Proceedings of the United Nations Conference on Trade and Development: Final Act and Report* vol I (United Nations 1964) Annex A.II.1, 26; Chimni (n 16) 52, 53.

[19] Chimni (n 16) 53.

[20] Ibid 87 ff.

shares. Decisions had to be taken by double, or distributed, majorities, meaning that a majority of votes in each group was required.[21]

The following observation by Bhupinder Chimni with respect to decision-making in International Commodity Agreements renders a good picture of the approach to the resolution of natural resource conflicts envisaged by proponents of the NIEO, which I would call a political approach:

> The significance of decision making procedures to the effective operation of international organizations can hardly be overstated. Firstly, decisions are not likely to be observed if the procedures through which they are arrived at are perceived to be unsatisfactory. Secondly, their enforcement in the outside world is rendered difficult if all the major concerned interests are not represented in the decision making process.[22]

International Commodity Agreements never became the effective regulators that developing countries had intended them to be.[23] The consumer countries, and in particular the United States, were largely opposed to the market-intervention approach of International Commodity Agreements.[24] While a number of such agreements were concluded and some are still operative today (for coffee, cocoa, tropical timber, olive oil, sugar and wheat), they never covered the whole range of commodities that UNCTAD's Integrated Programme for Commodities foresaw to be subject to International Commodity Agreements.[25] The International Commodity Agreements which are still operative today no longer intervene in commodity markets, but instead engage in product marketing,

---

[21] Ibid 93, 94.

[22] Ibid 92.

[23] One of the most spectacular failures was the bankruptcy of the International Tin Council; see Matthias Hartwig, 'The International Tin Council (ITC)' in Wolfrum (n 14).

[24] On the US exit from the International Coffee Agreement see Matthew J Foli, 'International Coffee Agreements and the Elusive Goal of Price Stability' (1995) 4 *Minnesota Journal of Global Trade* 79, 94; P Brian Bartels, 'Preventing Coffee Cooperation from Grinding to a Halt: An Institutional Analysis of the International Coffee Agreements and Recommendations for Achieving Long-term Cooperation in the International Coffee Trade' (2009) 42 *Creighton Law Review* 279.

[25] Apart from agricultural commodities the following commodities were to be covered: bauxite, copper, iron ore, manganese, phosphates and tin: UNCTAD Resolution 93 (IV) s II.

collect information and provide fora for consultation on the respective commodity.[26]

III. PRIVATIZED NATURAL RESOURCE EXPLOITATION, INVESTMENT PROTECTION AND TRADE LIBERALIZATION: JUST DISTRIBUTION OF NATURAL RESOURCES THROUGH THE MARKET

For a number of reasons the resource distribution order envisaged by proponents of the NIEO never fully came into being. The reasons include the lack of agreement between developed and developing countries[27] as well as changing views within economics as to the best way to promote economic development.[28] Moreover – and most importantly with respect to this chapter's subject of distribution conflicts over natural resources – for industrialized countries whose industry depend on resource imports the privatization of natural resource exploitation, the promotion of a strong international investment law and the liberalization of trade proved more effective means to secure access to extractive resources than the establishment of political procedures for the resolution of international resource conflicts within the United Nations framework.

The avenue pursued by resource-importing countries to secure access to resources stands in stark contrast to Chimni's statement cited above. Resource-importing States have promoted their interests not through international cooperation with exporting States that openly acknowledges distribution conflicts, but instead have opted to strengthen investor protection. In this endeavor they have been substantially supported by international organisations, in particular international financial institutions. The latters' role has not been to resolve distribution conflicts with

[26] Frank Schorkopf, 'Internationale Rohstoffverwaltung zwischen Lenkung und Markt' (2008) 46 *Archiv des Völkerrechts* 245.

[27] On the antagonism between developing countries and developed countries in the United Nations in the 1980s see Jagdish N Bhagwati and John Gerald Ruggie (eds), *Power, Passions, and Purpose. Prospects for North-South Negotiations* (MIT Press 1984).

[28] For critiques of the economics underlying the NIEO see Anne Krueger, 'Trade Policy and Economic Development: How We Learn' (1997) 87 *American Economic Review* 1; Jagdish N Bhagwati (ed.), *The New International Economic Order* (MIT Press 1977).

the participation of all affected States. Instead, their secretariats' economic expertise promoted the exploitation of natural resources through private investors as the model most conducive to development. This model made the interest conflicts that were stressed in the NIEO disappear in a win-win scenario: The pursuit of private investors of their interests in profit-maximization would also satisfy the interests of resource exporting developing States in economic development. And coincidentally also the interests of the investors' home States: resource-dependent importing States.

The fact that resource importing States largely left the scene of international cooperation for the political resolution of resource conflicts does not mean that they did not consider supply security a national interest. Rather they could rely on supply being secured through private investment abroad and liberalized trade;[29] and even more so as international law came to protect, and international institutions came to promote, FDI. As resource exporting States sometimes impose restrictions on the export of raw materials (e.g. to promote the establishment of a domestic processing industry) the prohibition of such barriers to trade is a further objective pursued by importing States to secure access to natural resources.[30]

A. Promotion of Privatized Natural Resource Exploitation and Strengthening of Investor Rights

While in the 1960s all States represented in the United Nations could agree to a broadly phrased principle of permanent sovereignty over natural resources, what remained contentious was how this principle would affect existing and future rights of foreign investors. A number of foreign corporations held concessions for resource exploitation within the new States which ran for several decades. Aiming not only at political autonomy, but also greater economic independence the new States frequently nationalized their operations. They argued that sovereignty should not only entail a right to ownership, but also a right to nationalize foreign extraction companies. While consensus could also be reached on

---

[29] Stephen D Krasner, *Defending the National Interest. Raw Materials Investments and US Foreign Policy* (Princeton UP 1978).

[30] Where the establishment of a legal framework conducive to private investment and raw materials trade was not sufficient, import states continued to intervene. Yet, such intervention as, for example, the United States' support for the military coup against Salvador Allende in Chile in 1973, largely occurred outside the confines of international law.

this position, the industrialized countries did not agree to a right to nationalize without any limitations imposed by international law.[31] Most of the industrialized countries shared the view that nationalizations had to pursue a public interest and that the nationalizing State had to pay prompt, adequate and effective compensation. They also stressed that permanent sovereignty could be 'contracted away' by a State through entering into international agreements.[32]

The G77, by contrast, strove to consolidate their own version of a right to nationalize as part of a NIEO.[33] While Resolution 1803 of 1962 on Permanent Sovereignty over Natural Resources provided for compensation according to *international law and national law* in cases of expropriation,[34] the Declaration on a New International Economic Order and the Charter on the Economic Rights and Duties of States of 1974 aimed to expand the right to expropriate. These two instruments no longer demanded compensation according to international law and they also did not require expropriation to serve a public interest.[35] The industrialized powers, however, resisted this move by voting against the respective parts of the resolutions dealing with expropriations and subsequently international law scholars and arbitrators, most famously René-Jean Dupuy in his *Texaco* Award, for this reason concluded that they lacked legal effect.[36]

While the requirements for lawful expropriations under customary international law remain contested today[37] the protection of private investment has progressively been strengthened through the case law of arbitral tribunals, the conclusion of bilateral investment agreements and

---

31 M Sornarajah, *The International Law of Foreign Investment* (3rd edn, CUP 2010) 406 ff.

32 Schrijver (n 2) ch 2.

33 On NIEO as a project of redistributive justice see Mohammed Bedjaoui, *Towards a New International Economic Order* (Holmes Meier 1979).

34 UNGA Res 1803 (XVII) (1962) para 4: 'Nationalization, expropriation or requisitioning shall be based on grounds or reasons of public utility, security or the national interest which are recognized as overriding purely individual or private interests, both domestic and foreign'; on this formulation which was a compromise between developing countries and industrial nations see Stephen M Schwebel, 'The Story of the UN's Declaration on Permanent Sovereignty over Natural Resources' (1963) 49 *American Bar Association Journal* 463.

35 UNGA Res 3201 (S-VI) (1974) para 4 (e); UNGA Res 3281 (XXIX) (1974) art 2.

36 *Texaco Overseas Petroleum Company/California Asiatic Oil Company v The Government of the Libyan Arab Republic* (1978) 17 ILM 1.

37 Sornarajah (n 31) 412 ff.

inclusion of investment chapters into regional trade agreements. The principle of permanent sovereignty over natural resources as formulated by the General Assembly resolutions had left the door open for the argument that a State could voluntarily limit its own sovereignty by concluding international agreements. Building on this argument arbitral tribunals enhanced the protection of foreign investors by interpreting concession agreements concluded with foreign investors as constituting international agreements. Investment arbitrations in the 1970s concerning the expropriation of oil companies by Libya adopted such an interpretation and held that the petroleum concession contracts in question that had been concluded between Libya and Texaco, Liamco and BP respectively constituted 'economic development agreements' that were not part of national law, but of international law.[38] As a consequence of the characterization as economic development agreements which form part of the international legal order, contractual provisions on the application of international law or so-called stabilization clauses that mandate the application of domestic law as it existed at the time the contract was concluded could not be overturned by subsequent national legislation. This de-localization and internationalization of contracts increased the protection afforded to foreign investors, while limiting the authority of the host State.[39]

Today, this doctrinal construction has lost some of its relevance as many FDIs fall within the scope of bilateral investment agreements which were initially concluded mainly by capital-exporting (industrialized) States with capital-importing (developing) States to secure the protection of investors from the industrialized States from government incursions, such as nationalizations, in the developing country where the investment was taking place. While at first sight these agreements appear as one-sided (and are frequently interpreted to be) they also posit (like the arbitral awards mentioned above) that in order to benefit from international protection, FDI must be beneficial to economic development. Under such an interpretation transnational corporations are becoming agents of development.[40]

---

[38] Charles Leben, *The Advancement of International Law* (Hart Publishing 2010) ch 1; see also Melaku Desta, 'Sovereignty over Natural Resources and International Investment Law: The Elusive Search for Equilibrium', in this volume, 223.

[39] For a critical view see Antony Anghie, *Imperialism, Sovereignty and the Making of International Law* (CUP 2005) 229 ff.

[40] For a defense of such a conception of international investment protection see Stephan W Schill, 'Investitionen und Entwicklung' in Philipp Dann, Stefan

The same transnational corporations would have been more strictly controlled and limited in their power if the developing countries had had their will. The Declaration on a New International Economic Order had called for an obligation of home States to cooperate with developing countries in the effective control of transnational corporations.[41] Yet, the UN General Assembly never adopted the Code of Conduct on Transnational Corporations drafted by the Commission on Transnational Corporations.[42] An international competition law which might achieve some of the same objectives to date remains a mainly scholarly endeavor.[43]

The demands of developing countries for technical and increased financial assistance, too, have remained largely unfulfilled (the Common Fund for Commodities, for example, only entered into force 1989, nine years after the agreement on its establishment was concluded) and with them the realization of independence from private foreign capital. The official development assistance that was granted, in particular by the World Bank, was soon to be linked to conditions, so-called structural adjustment conditionality, that often made the receipt of financial assistance dependent on the privatization of resource extraction enterprises.[44]

B. Prohibition of Export Restrictions

The prohibition of export restrictions complements FDI as an instrument to secure access to natural resources. Recently, export restrictions have received renewed attention as the US, the EU and Japan have seen their industry's access to raw materials threatened by the imposition of export quotas and tariffs on certain rare earths and other raw materials by China. The EU Commission is very explicit in its communication 'Tackling the Challenges in Commodity Markets and on Raw Materials'[45] as to its

---

Kadelbach and Markus Kaltenborn (eds), *Entwicklung und Recht. Eine systematische Einführung* (Nomos 2014) 341.

[41] UNGA Res 3201 (S-VI) (1974) para 4(g).

[42] Commission on Transnational Corporations, 'Report on the Special Session (7–18 March and 9–21 May 1983)' Official Records of the Economic and Social Council, Suppl No 7 (1983) (E/1983/17/Rev.1) Annex II.A.

[43] Wolfgang Fikentscher, *Culture, Law and Economics: Three Berkeley Lectures* (Stämpfli und Carolina Academic Press 2004).

[44] See the case of Zambia, Section IV below.

[45] Communication from the Commission to the European Parliament, the Council, the European Economic and Social Committee and the Committee of the Regions, 'Tackling the Challenges in Commodity Markets and on Raw Materials' COM(2011) 25 final.

stance on export restrictions. Two main pillars of its raw materials initiative (set out in this communication) are: first, the negotiation of prohibitions of export restrictions, to be included in bilateral free trade agreements, regional free trade agreements and WTO accession protocols and, second, the enforcement of such rules through diplomatic means and dispute settlement.[46]

In the WTO disputes with China the EU has obtained important victories in using dispute settlement to secure access to Chinese raw materials, and in particular rare earths of which China is the main exporting State. In the first case concerning restrictions on exports of bauxite, coke, fluorspar, magnesium, manganese, silicon carbide, silicon metal, yellow phosphorus and zinc as well as in the second case concerning restrictions on exports of rare earths, tungsten and molybdenum the WTO Appellate Body confirmed the panels' findings that Chinese export duties and export quotas violated WTO law.[47] Export quotas are prohibited by Art. XI of the General Agreement on Tariffs and Trade (GATT) – the general prohibition on quantitative restrictions (unless an exception applies). Export duties, by contrast, are not prohibited by the GATT. A prohibition of export duties had, however, been negotiated in the course of China's accession to the WTO and included in the accession protocol which made it a binding obligation for China.[48] Similar obligations are included in a number of other accession protocols, including the WTO accession protocols of Mongolia and Tajikistan.

The EU's strategic use of international law to secure access to raw materials demonstrates its acknowledgment that international conflicts exist over access to resources. This acknowledgment is illustrated by the following comment of EU trade commissioner Karel de Gucht on the WTO panel report in the rare earths dispute: 'Today's ruling by the WTO on rare earths shows that no one country can hoard its raw materials from the global marketplace at the expense of its other WTO partners.'[49]

---

[46] For the implementation of these pillars see Results on Raw Materials, posted by the EU Commission on <http://ec.europa.eu/trade/policy/accessing-markets/goods-and-services/raw-materials/index_en.htm> accessed 11 August 2014.

[47] Appellate Body Report, 'China – Raw Materials' WT/DS395/AB/R; Appellate Body Report, 'China – Rare Earths' WT/DS432/AB/R.

[48] WTO, 'Accession of the People's Republic of China' Decision (10 November 2001) WT/L/432.

[49] Cited in Shawn Donnan and James Politi, 'WTO rules against China on "rare earths" export restrictions' *Financial Times* (London, 26 March 2014).

The way in which the EU uses international law to address these conflicts also shows, however, that it does not intend to revisit the idea inherent in the proposals of the NIEO to establish political procedures for the resolution of resource conflicts. Instead of promoting international procedures for an equitable resolution of resource conflicts it is 'committed to ensure that the international raw materials markets operate in a free and transparent way.'[50] This can be interpreted to mean that distribution conflicts are to be solved by the market or rather that distribution conflicts that would require political resolution will not arise if only the market is left to operate freely and transparently within a framework of binding international law rules.

IV. HOW INTERNATIONAL (INVESTMENT) LAW SHAPES DISTRIBUTION CONFLICTS OVER NATURAL RESOURCES: THE CASE OF ZAMBIA

The example of Zambia illustrates the shift towards privatized natural resource exploitation and how it was promoted by the international financial institutions. It also reveals that the win-win scenario which provides the legitimation for the promotion and protection of FDI in Zambia, as in many other resource-rich developing countries, has remained unfulfilled. Finally, it indicates how the privatization of natural resource exploitation has released the importing States from responsibility while at the same time serving their interest in resource security and how international law has come to restrict the policy space available to resource States to address internal distribution conflicts.

A. Privatization of Natural Resource Exploitation in Zambia

The Republic of Zambia is a resource-rich country. On its territory exist large deposits of copper, moreover there are known deposits of emerald, gold, zinc and diamonds. Many of the mineral deposits are concentrated in the Copperbelt region on the border of Zambia and The Democratic Republic of Congo. In 2011 Zambia was the world's seventh largest producer of copper, the second largest producer of cobalt (a by-product of copper production) and provided one fifth of the global supply of

---

50 <http://ec.europa.eu/trade/policy/accessing-markets/goods-and-services/raw-materials/index_en.htm> accessed 11 August 2014.

emeralds.[51] The first copper mine started business in 1928 in Zambia, which was then called Northern Rhodesia and was a British colony. Under colonial rule, copper exploitation was controlled by the Roan Selection Trust and the Anglo-American Corporation.[52]

After Zambia had gained independence from Great Britain in 1964 the Copper Mining industry was nationalized between 1968 and 1972 under President Kaunda, who pursued a politics of 'socialist humanism'. The State asserted its sovereign right to ownership of mineral deposits, became majority shareholder in all mining companies and established the State mining enterprise Zambia Consolidated Copper Mines (ZCCM).[53] At that time the copper industry was doing well; in 1969 Zambia had attained middle-income status. Zambia's economy was based almost exclusively on the copper industry and almost all foreign exchange income derived from copper exports.[54] In the following decades copper production started to decline; whilst production in 1972 had amounted to 700,000 metric tons, it decreased to 226,192 tons in 2000.[55] This decline was due in part to a lack of investments in the copper industry and partly to low productivity.[56] In addition to these factors, falling copper prices, which accompanied the oil crises, led to significantly decreased export earnings. As a consequence of the failing copper industry, income per capita between 1974 and 1994 declined by 50 percent and Zambia became the 25th poorest country in the world.[57]

In the 1980s Zambia was one of the most indebted countries in Africa having received bilateral loans as well as financial assistance from the International Monetary Fund and the World Bank. By the end of the 1980s donors increased their pressure for structural adjustments in which

---

[51] UNCTAD/ICC, *An Investment Guide to Zambia. Opportunities and Conditions* (2011).

[52] On the history of copper exploitation in Zambia see Larry J Butler, *Copper Empire: Mining and the Colonial State in Northern Rhodesia, c 1930–1964* (Palgrave Macmillan 2007).

[53] John Lungu, 'Copper Mining Agreements in Zambia. Renegotiation or Law Reform' (2008) 35 *Review of African Political Economy* (2008) 403, 404.

[54] Ibid.

[55] UNCTAD/ICC (n 51) 9.

[56] John Craig, 'Putting Privatization into Practice: The Case of Zambia Consolidated Copper Mines Limited' (2001) 39 *Journal of Modern African Studies* 389, 392.

[57] Lungu (n 53) 405.

privatization occupied a central position.[58] The fact that Zambia, in the 1990s, started to effectuate the demanded adjustments was on the one hand due to donor pressure and the desire of Zambia to profit from the World Bank's Highly Indebted Poor Countries initiative; on the other hand it is explained with the defeat of President Kaunda's United National Independence Party in the first multi-party elections held in Zambia in 1991 by the Movement for Multi-Party Democracy that was committed to economic liberalization and privatization.[59] The privatization programme subsequently implemented was praised by international institutions as one of the most successful privatizations in Africa for the swiftness of the process, its transparency and accountability.[60] According to a 2011 investment report by UNCTAD and the International Chamber of Commerce only 10–15 percent of economic activity in Zambia is controlled by the State as opposed to 80 percent prior to privatization.[61]

B. The Unfulfilled Promise of Privatized Natural Resource Exploitation: The Case of Zambia Continued

Since the economic reforms demanded by the international financial institutions and including privatization, trade liberalization and facilitation of administrative procedures, Zambia is internationally praised for its investor-friendliness.[62] The prosperity of the Zambian copper industry is generally attributed to privatization and FDI. According to the IMF the mining sector due to private investment and positive prospects for copper prices will continue to play a key role in the country's economic development.[63] In 2007 there were nine copper mines with majority

---

[58] On the International Financial Institution's concessional loans and their conditionality, see, Lishala C Situmbeko and Jack Jones Zulu, *Zambia: Condemned to Debt. How the IMF and the World Bank Have Undermined Development* (World Development Movement 2004).

[59] Craig (n 56) 391; Lungu (n 53) 405; Alastair Fraser and John Lungu, *For Whom the Windfalls? Winners & Losers in the Privatization of Zambia's Copper Mines* (CSTNZ/CCJDP 2007) 9.

[60] Oliver Campbell White and Anita Bhatia, *Privatization in Africa* (World Bank 1998) 111 ff.

[61] UNCTAD/ICC (n 51) 9.

[62] Ibid; Zambia is a party to two bilateral investment treaties with Germany and Switzerland which entered into force in 1972 and 1995 respectively <http://unctad.org/Sections/dite_pcbb/docs/bits_zambia.pdf> accessed 11 August 2014.

[63] IMF, Zambia 2012 Article IV Consultation.

ownership of seven transnational mining companies. The government in almost all mines holds a minority stake.[64] While there was a sharp drop in copper prices in 2008 and 2009, prices have since risen to record highs (mainly due to rising demand in emerging economies, mostly China).[65]

The prosperity of the copper industry stands in stark contrast to the prosperity of the rest of the country. According to UNDP's Human Development Index 2013, Zambia is one of the poorest and least-developed countries of the world, ranked 163rd (out of 187).[66] It is commonly acknowledged that government revenues from copper exploitation have been extremely limited. Even though mining revenues constitute a relatively high share in GDP, government revenues are very low compared to other mineral-producing countries. Government revenues from copper production between 2000 and 2007 have been below 0.5 percent of GDP even though the share of copper exports was above 20 percent of GDP.[67] A Swiss NGO, 'The Berne Declaration', states that only 5 percent of mining revenues flow into the national budget, compared with 70 percent of revenues from oil extraction in Norway.[68]

This situation is mainly due to the privileged position that was negotiated with the private investors during the privatization process as concerns royalty payments, taxation and regulatory conditions. Another important reason for the limited share of the government in mining profits is tax evasion. The exploitation rights and financial obligations that the government negotiated with foreign investors were established by so-called Development Agreements. The term Development Agreement already signifies the investors' privileged status as it refers to the doctrinal figure of 'Economic Development Agreement' that was developed by international arbitration tribunals in order to internationalize certain contracts between foreign investors and host States. The Development Agreements included clauses according to which their terms were

---

[64] The government stake is held through ownership of 87 percent of the shares in ZCCM's successor company: ZCCM Investment Holdings.

[65] IMF (n 63) 5.

[66] UNDP, 'Human Development Report 2013' (2013) <http://hdr.undp.org/en/2013-report> accessed 11 August 2014. The characterization as poor or least developed of course depends on the measurement criteria. While Zambia occupies one of the last ranks in the Human Development Index, the World Bank – based mainly on Gross National Income – classifies Zambia as a lower middle income country <http://data.worldbank.org/country/zambia> accessed 11 August 2014.

[67] IMF (n 63) 15.

[68] Erklärung von Bern (ed.), *Rohstoff: Das gefährlichste Geschäft der Schweiz* (Salis Verlag AG 2011) 115.

to supersede present and future national legislation, were intended to have a duration of between 10 and 20 years and were to be modifiable only by the mutual consent of the parties to the agreement. They also provided that conflicts between the parties could be referred to international arbitration.[69]

As concerns the substantive provisions on taxation the Development Agreements diverged from The Mines and Minerals Act of 1995 in favor of the foreign investors. Whereas the Act provided for mining royalties of 3 percent, most Development Agreements reduced this rate to 0.6 percent. As concerns corporate tax the agreements provided that losses could be carried forward for periods between 15 and 20 years and deducted from taxable profits. This had the effect that until 2012 practically no corporate tax had been paid by mining companies.[70] Capital investments were also 100 percent tax deductible under the agreements and companies were exempt from duties or import taxes on machinery and equipment. For the government to share into so-called windfall profits the agreements provided for government participation in profits from sales when copper prices exceeded a benchmark of USD 2700 per metric ton (which they did beginning 2004). Again, however, payments to the government on the basis of this participation clause were to be tax deductible.[71]

As copper prices rose to unprecedented heights beginning in 2004[72] and copper production, contrary to World Bank forecasts[73] significantly increased, discontent mounted within the population whose living conditions did not improve, but who by contrast suffered from precarious employment and the fact that schooling and medical services in the early 1990s had been privatized and were no longer provided for free.[74] NGOs, churches, trade unions and scholars pressured the government to increase the State's share in the exploitation profits. In 2006 the population of the Copperbelt region expressed their discontent with the government's policies as a majority voted members of the Patriotic Front into urban seats, a party that had promised to combat exploitation of the workforce

---

69 The content of the Development Agreements leaked in 2007 and a number of them were published on <www.minewatchzambia.com> which is now defunct. For detailed information on the contents see Fraser and Lungu (n 59).

70 IMF (n 63).

71 Fraser and Lungu (n 59) 15.

72 In 2011 prices reached record highs of over USD 10 000 per metric ton.

73 Erklärung von Bern (n 68) 113.

74 UNCTAD/ICC (n 52); Fraser and Lungu (n 59) 21ff; Erklärung von Bern (n 68) 106.

in mines, to increase corporate taxes and limit foreign ownership of mines.[75] When the content of the Development Agreements were leaked in 2007 this put further pressure on the government that announced renegotiation of the agreements with the mining companies. Plans for negotiations were abandoned in 2008 when the Zambian parliament replaced The Mines and Minerals Act of 1995 with a new Mines and Minerals Development Act which provided that 'the development agreements shall cease to be binding on the Republic.'[76] Under the 2008 Mines and Minerals Development Act the corporate tax for copper exporters was set at 35 percent of taxable income; losses could be carried forward for a maximum of 10 years; allowances on income tax for capital expenditures have been reduced and the royalty for minerals was set at 3 percent of market value.[77] Originally the 2008 Mines and Minerals Development Act had also provided for a windfall tax of 25 percent on profits in times of high copper prices. When during the 2009 recession revenue fell to USD 77.7 million compared with USD 128.4 million the previous year despite increases in production and exports and when, as a consequence, some international investors withdrew from the Zambian copper mining industry and others refused to pay taxes, the government dismantled the windfall tax.[78] After the 2011 elections newly elected President Sata of the Patriotic Front increased mining royalties further from 3 to 6 percent.[79] He also introduced a 10 percent export duty on unprocessed metals.[80]

While the reformed tax regime is intended to increase government revenues from resource exploitation, the realization of such increases depends on administrative implementation and the effectiveness of tax collection. To minimize their tax burden or to evade taxation companies

---

75 Fraser and Lungu (n 59) 1.

76 UNCTAD/ICC (n 51) 29; the Mines and Minerals Development Act of 2008 is available at <http://www.zambialii.org/files/zm/legislation/act/2008/7/mamda2008295.pdf> accessed 11 August 2014.

77 For an overview over the current mining tax regime see Zambia EITI, 'Understanding Mining Taxes' (Brochure 2011).

78 UNCTAD/ICC (n 51) 29.

79 Prospery Raymond, 'In Haiti, We Must Make Mining Revenue Work for Us' (*The Guardian*, 2 July 2012) <http://www.theguardian.com/global-development/poverty-matters/2012/jul/02/haiti-mining-revenue-benefit-people> accessed 11 August 2014.

80 Matthew Hill, 'Zambia's Sata Orders Export Tax on Unprocessed Metals Reinstated' (*Bloomberg News*, 28 October 2013) <http://www.bloomberg.com/news/2013-10-28/zambia-s-sata-orders-export-tax-on-unprocessed-metals-reinstated.html> accessed 11 August 2014.

on a large scale engage in legal and sometimes illegal maneuvers including the allocation of losses and profits to different parts of their organization. Maneuvers that are facilitated by high degrees of vertical integration and that are hard or impossible to track by tax administrations especially if they have limited staff, expertise and funding as is frequently the case in low-income countries. A few years ago, this issue received increased public attention, when the Swiss company Glencore International AG and Canadian First Quantum Mining Ltd, whose subsidiary Mopani Copper Mines is the largest mining corporation in Zambia, were charged with illegal tax evasion.[81]

C. The Responsibility Gap of Privatized Natural Resource Exploitation and its Impact on Internal Conflict Resolution

As was already indicated above, the promotion of FDI through international financial institutions and its protection by bilateral investment agreements is being justified in terms of the furtherance of economic development. The conceptualization of foreign investors as agents of economic development presents them as actors who not only aim to maximize their own profits, but at the same time contribute to economic growth and consequently economic development of the host State. Accordingly, the World Bank can argue that making financial assistance conditional upon the privatization of natural resource exploitation is in line with its development mandate.[82] Likewise bilateral investment treaties emphasize their positive impact on development.[83] By defining the protected investments as investments promoting economic development, investment treaties can be presented as mutually beneficial bargains even though, if a bilateral investment treaty is concluded between a developing capital-importing country and a capital-exporting country, it is mostly only the latters' investors that will enjoy the treaty's protection.

---

[81] Mining Watch Canada, 'Tax Evasion in Zambia: NGOs File Complaint Against Glencore, First Quantum for Violation of OECD Guidelines' (12 April 2011) <http://www.miningwatch.ca/news/tax-evasion-zambia-ngos-file-complaint-against-glencore-first-quantum-violation-oecd-guidelines> accessed 11 August 2014; Erklärung von Bern (n 68).

[82] Art I(1) Articles of Agreement of the International Bank for Reconstruction and Development.

[83] See, e.g., the following formulation in the preamble of the 2004 US Model BIT: 'Recognizing that agreement on the treatment to be accorded [foreign] investment will stimulate the flow of private capital and the economic development of the Parties.'

For natural resource exploitation the link between foreign investment and development can be concretized as follows: Foreign investment provides the necessary capital, technology and know-how in order to turn raw materials into tradable commodities. Trade in commodities and their processing will lead to economic growth and economic growth in turn will benefit the population through the creation of further jobs and business opportunities. The international financial institutions are not oblivious to the fact that economic growth does not automatically 'trickle' down. In order to ensure that financial assistance and investments ultimately lead to poverty reduction and the well-being of the population they, inter alia, advocate for 'good governance' in developing countries.[84]

The reliance by importing States on FDI to ensure access to raw materials has two important side-effects. First, the importing State that relies on FDI for access to natural resources no longer engages in international cooperation to specifically address distribution conflicts. As a consequence, and that is the second side-effect of the privatization of natural resource exploitation, importing States have largely eschewed responsibility in cases where resource extraction projects go hand in hand with government corruption, large-scale human rights violations or environmental degradation.[85] Even if permanent sovereignty over natural resources is interpreted to imply that natural resource exploitation has to meet certain requirements to be in accordance with international law (e.g. that government proceeds from natural resource exploitation need to benefit the population and not disappear on the bank accounts of government officials),[86] the fact that the importing State takes no part in the actual resource transactions means that under international law it is generally not responsible for any violation of a peoples' right of permanent sovereignty over natural resources. Yet, the corporation that concludes a concession contract with the government and that trades the primary commodities cannot be held responsible under international law either as it is not directly bound by the right to permanent sovereignty

---

84 On changes in World Bank policies to take account of changes in development economics see Philipp Dann, *The Law of Development Cooperation: A Comparative Analysis of the World Bank, the EU and Germany* (CUP 2013) pt I.

85 For the proposition that home states are obliged to ensure that multinational corporations do not act to the detriment of host states see Sornarajah (n 31) 157 ff.

86 For such an argument see Leif Wenar, 'Property Rights and the Resource Curse' (2008) 36 *Philosophy & Public Affairs* 2.

over natural resources (or human rights[87] or international environmental obligations). Thus, the main responsibility for any detrimental impact of natural resource exploitation within its territory falls on the resource State. This finally means that the internationalization of natural resource exploitation is only partial. Natural resource exploitation is internationalized to the extent that FDI falls under the protection of international law, the interests of the population and environment of the resource State by contrast remain largely territorialized as their effective protection remains dependent on national legislation and law-enforcement.

The policy space of the resource State to address domestic distribution conflicts is, however, severely limited by international economic law.[88] A clear example of such limitation is the prohibition of export restrictions currently promoted by the EU under its raw materials initiative.[89] Given the difficulties of governments and populations, not only of developing countries, to secure a share in the profits from natural resource exploitation by way of taxation, the imposition of export tariffs on raw materials provides an important alternative for the State to gain revenues. If, however, the imposition of export tariffs is prohibited by international law States may incur costly trade sanctions should they continue to impose them. International investment law also potentially restricts the choice of State measures to adjust the burden of costs and benefits of natural resource exploitation – be it because economic development agreements immunize investor privileges from national legislation or because State measures may become the subject of investor claims on the basis of international investment law.[90]

---

[87] For the duties of corporations that today are acknowledged to flow from international human rights see United Nations 'Guiding Principles on Business and Human Rights: Implementing the United Nations "Protect, Respect and Remedy" Framework', UN Doc A/HRC/17/31 (21 March 2011).

[88] Cf Dani Rodrik, *The Globalization Paradox: Democracy and the Future of the World Economy* (WW Norton 2011).

[89] Communication from the Commission to the European Parliament, the Council, the European Economic and Social Committee and the Committee of the Regions, 'Tackling the Challenges in Commodity Markets and on Raw Materials', COM(2011) 25 final.

[90] See, e.g., the initiation of arbitral proceedings by Lone Pine Resources Inc against the Government of Canada alleging that Canada's revocation of a fracking permit violated obligations under NAFTA's investment chapter; the notice of arbitration can be accessed under <http://www.international.gc.ca/trade-agreements-accords-commerciaux/assets/pdfs/disp-diff/lone-02.pdf> accessed 11 August 2014.

V. TOWARDS AN INTERNATIONAL CONFLICTS LAW OF NATURAL RESOURCES EXPLOITATION

In recent years distribution conflicts seem to be moving again to the center of attention of international law and politics. This development can be explained by two reasons in particular. First, resource States are increasingly dissatisfied with the current international legal framework and attempt to regain control over the exploitation of natural resources on their territory. Second, the governments of the emerging economies, in particular China, call into question the viability of continued reliance by Western industrialized countries on the market to secure their access to natural resources. In light of these developments we should refocus attention on political conflict resolution procedures.

A. The Return of Distribution Conflicts over Natural Resource Exploitation to International Law

The promise of win-win through privatized natural resource exploitation frequently has remained unfulfilled and has led to discontent resulting in what is often being termed 'resource nationalism'.[91] Many resource-rich poor States are afflicted by the so-called resource curse, implying a connection between natural resource exploitation on the one hand and economic and government failures up to violent conflict on the other.[92] Even where the situation is less dramatic, private capital-led natural resource exploitation often does not lead to a significant increase in a population's well-being. Disappointment with foreign investment and the intention to reap greater benefits from exploitation have led a number of governments, in particular in Latin America, Asia and Africa,[93] but also elsewhere, to attempt to regain control over natural resources exploitation. The measures taken by resource States range from changes in the

[91] Robert Mabro, 'Oil Nationalism, the Oil Industry and Energy Security Concerns', ARI 114/2007 (25 October 2007) <www.realinstitutoelcano.org/wps/portal/rielcano_in/Content?WCM_GLOBAL_CONTEXT=/elcano/Elcano_in/Zonas_in/ARI114-2007> accessed 11 August 2014; 'Resource Nationalism in Africa. Wish You Were Mine' *The Economist* (London, 11 February 2012).

[92] Macartan Humphreys, Jeffrey D Sachs and Joseph E Stiglitz (eds), *Escaping the Resource Curse* (Columbia UP 2007); Paul Collier, 'The Political Economy of Natural Resources' (2010) 77 *Social Research* 1105.

[93] For Africa see the Africa Mining Vision adopted by Heads of State at the 2009 summit of the African Union <http://www.africaminingvision.org/reports.html> accessed 11 August 2014.

tax system to export restrictions and outright nationalizations, such as in the cases of Yukos (by Russia)[94] and Repsol (by Argentina).[95] In Bolivia the intention to establish authority over national resource exploitation has been expressed in the Constitution of 2009, Art. 349:1 of which reads:

> The natural resources are the property and direct domain, indivisible and without limitation, of the Bolivian people, and the State is mandated with their administration in the collective interest.[96]

Sometimes the strengthening of State control is being justified with the aim to promote particular social groups. Thus, Zimbabwe's politics of indigenisation or South Africa's Black Empowerment Programme have been supported with the argument that they were improving ownership of the black population in the resource sector.[97] An increasing number of States are turning their back on international investment law and have terminated their membership in the International Centre for Settlement of Investment Disputes.[98] South Africa in 2012 and 2013 terminated its bilateral investment treaties with Germany, the Netherlands and Switzerland,[99] and Indonesia recently announced the termination of all its 67 bilateral investment treaties.[100]

---

[94] Jason M Waltrip, 'The Russian Oil and Gas Industry after Yukos. Outlook for Foreign Investment' (2008) 17 *Transnational Law & Contemporary Problems* 575.

[95] Jude Webber and Miles Johnson, 'Argentina to Renationalise Oil Group YPF' *Financial Times* (London, 17 April 2012).

[96] Constitution of Bolivia, art 349: 1: 'Los recursos naturales son de propiedad y dominio directo, indivisible e imprescriptible del pueblo boliviano, y corresponderá al Estado su administración en función del interés colectivo.' Art 348(1) clarifies that minerals and hydrocarbons are considered mineral resources.

[97] *The Economist* (n 91); on related ICSID proceedings see Damon Vis-Dunbar, 'European Miners and South Africa Suspend Proceedings' (*Investment Treaty Newsletter*, 2 April 2009) <www.iisd.org/itn/2009/04/02/european-miners-and-south-africa-suspend-proceedings/> accessed 11 August 2014.

[98] Venezuela terminated its BIT with the Netherlands in 2008; in 2009 Russia terminated the preliminary application of the Energy Charter Treaty and Bolivia, Ecuador and Venezuela terminated ICSID membership in 2007, 2009 and 2012 respectively.

[99] See <http://www.rh-arbitration.com/south-africa-terminates-bilateral-investment-treaties-with-germany-netherlands-and-switzerland/> accessed 11 August 2014.

[100] See <http://investvine.com/indonesia-to-end-60-bilateral-investment-treaties/> accessed 11 August 2014.

Greater control of the State over natural resource exploitation meets with support by economists who argue that given the frequent information asymmetries between resource States and investors as concerns the extent of resource deposits or the amount of profits generated by the extractive industry, States should not easily part with exploitation rights. In some situations it might be better for States to secure an equitable share in profits by engaging in exploitation through State enterprises or joint ventures than to rely on royalty payments or taxation for revenue generation.[101]

A parallel development to the strengthening of control over natural resource exploitation by resource States are the interventions of the BRIC countries' governments in order to secure their access to resources abroad. Figures published in the most recent Human Development Report illustrate this development. According to the report development finance extended to Zambia by these countries in the period from 2006–2009 amounted to merely 3 percent of the USD 3 billion development finance that Zambia received in this period. In November 2009, Zambia and China announced that China would extend a concessional loan of USD 1 billion to Zambia, a sum that amounted to 40 percent of Zambia's total public external debt.[102] In return for such assistance which is frequently linked to particular development projects, China is given access to natural resource exploitation in the recipient country.[103]

As a reaction to the proactive resource politics of the BRICs, governments, like that of Germany, who had long ceased to be actively involved in trade in natural resources as well as the European Union now attempt to secure access to natural resources by means of international law. While Germany is concluding so-called bilateral resource partnerships,[104] the EU concentrates on the prohibition of export restrictions.[105]

---

[101] Joseph E Stiglitz, 'What is the Role of the State?' in Humphreys, Sachs and Stiglitz (n 92) 23.

[102] UNDP (n 66) 57.

[103] Paul Collier, *The Plundered Planet: Why We Must – and How We Can – Manage Nature for Global Prosperity* (OUP 2010) 91, 92.

[104] Bundesministerium für Wirtschaft und Technologie, 'Rohstoffstrategie der Bundesregierung. Sicherung einer nachhaltigen Rohstoffversorgung Deutsch lands mit nicht-energetischen mineralischen Rohstoffen' (2010) <www.bmwi.de/Dateien/BMWi/PDF/rohstoffstrategie-der-bundesregierung,property=pdf,bereich=bmwi2012,sprache=de,rwb=true.pdf> accessed 11 August 2014. So far resource partnerships have been concluded with Mongolia, Kazakhstan and Chile.

[105] Communication from the Commission to the European Parliament, the Council, the European Economic and Social Committee and the Committee of

B. Re-Politicizing Resource Conflicts in International Law

The developments described in the previous section indicate that distribution conflicts will not go away, but likely will become more severe. Their equitable resolution will require the diverging interests that give rise to these conflicts to be openly acknowledged and represented in conflict resolution procedures. Such procedures must aim to re-politicize resource conflicts. For guidance on such a re-politicization we might revisit the principle of permanent sovereignty over natural resources and the NIEO's International Commodity Agreements.

1. Operationalizing permanent sovereignty over natural resources

Permanent sovereignty over natural resources requires natural resource exploitation to benefit the people. To ensure that it does, important decisions on natural resource exploitation should primarily be taken in democratic procedures while ensuring the rights of minorities and indigenous peoples who have a particular interest in the natural resource or territory in question. When designing such procedures, account must be taken of the political economy of natural resource exploitation that may lead to certain democratic failures, such as the inducement of particular election results by promises to distribute revenues from natural resource exploitation to the electorate.[106]

Responsibility to install such procedures mainly falls on States and sub-State political communities; there will be no blueprint for the 'right' procedure and therefore international financial institutions should refrain from advising on a silver bullet. What they can do is to assemble best practices of procedures that have worked well for countries and allowed them to turn resource wealth into prosperity. What they must do, arguably, is to refrain from linking financial assistance to specific modalities of natural resource exploitation. When it is recognized that important decisions on natural resource exploitation, such as the decision to grant exploitation licenses to private investors for a particular area and resource, are intrinsically political matters – as exercises of the right to self-determination – then the international financial institutions by their own Articles of Agreement are bound to refrain from such conditionality

the Regions, 'Tackling the Challenges in Commodity Markets and on Raw Materials', COM(2011) 25 final.

[106] Paul Collier, 'The Political Economy of Natural Resources' (2010) 77 *Social Research* 1105.

as they may not interfere with the political systems of their members.[107] If a State decides, on the basis of a democratic process, to (legally) nationalize the extractive sector then it should receive adequate technical and financial assistance so it can implement this decision and thus realize its right to permanent sovereignty over natural resources. That such assistance may pay out in terms of economic development is supported by the fact that payments of the G8 for resource imports from developing countries by far exceed official development assistance.[108]

Since it has become abundantly clear that economic globalization, commercial power and vertical integration pose obstacles to the effective regulation and taxation of corporations there is renewed support today for an obligation of home States to cooperate with host States in order to effectively control and tax transnational corporations.[109] A particular impediment to democratic decision-making on the distribution of benefits from resource extraction is the intransparency of revenue flows. The Extractive Industry Transparency Initiative (EITI) aims to increase transparency in order to allow the populations of resource States to actively take part in resource politics. Participation in this multi-stakeholder initiative is voluntary. If a State participates, however, and if it wants to reach the status of a 'compliant' EITI participant it has to legally oblige companies in the extractive sector to lay open all payments to the government.[110] This obligation becomes more effective if the home States of investors establish corresponding accounting obligations.[111]

2. International institutions and procedures to address international distribution conflicts

Due to the territoriality of natural resources located within national jurisdictions delocalization can never be complete and probably for a long time to come the democratic procedures necessary to realize the right to permanent sovereignty over natural resources will have better

---

107 Art IV, s 10 IBRD Articles of Agreement; art V, s 6 IDA Articles of Agreement; art IV, s 3 b) IMF Articles of Agreement.

108 Paul Collier, *The Bottom Billion. Why the Poorest Countries are Failing and What Can be Done About It* (OUP 2008) 39.

109 On the forms international tax cooperation could take see Reuven S Avi-Yonah, 'The OECD Harmful Tax Competition Report' Public Law and Legal Theory Working Paper Series, Paper No 115 (Ann Arbor, University of Michigan Law School, August 2008).

110 For information on the Extractive Industry Transparency Initiative see its website under <www.eiti.org> accessed 11 August 2014.

111 See US Securities Exchange Act of 1934, 17 CFR Parts 240 and 249; EU Accounting Directive 2013/34/EU.

chances to be implemented on the State or the sub-State level than transnationally. As a consequence, conflicts between States over access will persist. To 'perfect the market' for natural resources does not appear a feasible option to overcome such conflicts, given that many populations opt for stricter governmental control over natural resources exploitation. In this situation international cooperation that takes into account diverging interests of exporting and importing States will be the only feasible and legitimate way to protect importing States' interests in supply security. The International Commodity Agreements provide examples of international procedures that take account of both the sovereign equality of States and the diverging interests of resource-importing and resource-exporting States. A Commodity Organization could establish a framework for mutually beneficial cooperation that on the one hand provides assistance to exporting States to realize their permanent sovereignty over natural resources and that on the other hand promotes supply security of importing States, for example, through the conclusion of long-term trade agreements. Just like the suggestion to operationalize permanent sovereignty over natural resources this proposal for a Commodity Organization is motivated by the objective to place distribution conflicts over natural resources at the center of inclusive political debates and not leave their resolution to market forces.

10. Democracy, development and compensation under investment treaties: The case of transition from authoritarian rule

Jonathan Bonnitcha

I. INTRODUCTION

Over the past decades both scholars and practitioners have paid greater attention to the role of governance in development.[1] One issue that has proven particularly controversial is the relationship between the form of government within a state and its development. The rise of China has raised questions about whether non-democratic forms of government can be more successful in mobilising resources for economic growth. At the same time, countries with democratic forms of government continue to achieve better outcomes for a range of other dimensions of development. For example, famines are much less likely in democratic countries[2] and, in general, economic resources are shared more equally in democracies than in authoritarian regimes.[3]

There is, however, a more fundamental link between democratic governance and development. In order to identify and select their own

---

[1] See, e.g., World Bank, 'Governance & Anti Corruption' <http://web.worldbank.org/WBSITE/EXTERNAL/WBI/EXTWBIGOVANTCOR/0,,menuPK:1740542~pagePK:64168427~piPK:64168435~theSitePK:1740530,00.html> accessed 18 August 2014; Helen Clark, 'The Importance of Governance for Sustainable Development' (Singapore Lecture Series, Singapore, 13 March 2012) <www.undp.org/content/undp/en/home/presscenter/speeches/2012/03/13/the-importance-of-governance-for-sustainable-development.html> accessed 18 August 2014.

[2] Amartya Sen, *Development as Freedom* (OUP 1999) 178–82.

[3] Stephan Haggard and Robert Kaufman, *The Political Economy of Democratic Transitions* (Princeton UP 1995) 62.

development priorities, the people of a state must be able to participate in the government of their own country. This link between the possibility of political participation and development is recognised by Common Article 1(1) of the International Covenant on Civil and Political Rights and the International Covenant on Economic, Social and Cultural Rights:

> All peoples have the right of self-determination. By virtue of that right they freely determine their political status and freely pursue their economic, social and cultural development.[4]

Article 8 of the Vienna Declaration on Human Rights is more specific in linking democratic government to development:

> Democracy, development and respect for human rights and fundamental freedoms are interdependent and mutually reinforcing. Democracy is based on the freely expressed will of the people to determine their own political, economic, social and cultural systems and their full participation in all aspects of their lives.[5]

This chapter examines one aspect of the relationship between development, investment treaties and the form of government in the states that are bound by them. It focuses specifically on the investment treaty claims arising from transitions from authoritarian rule. In this chapter, I use the term 'transition' to refer to the period in which one form of government replaces another form of government.[6] This definition seeks to distinguish changes to the basic rules and practices governing the exercise of political power in a state from situations in which the government of a state changes according to established rules and practices in that state. I use the term 'authoritarian' in a broad, non-technical sense to refer to

---

[4] International Covenant on Civil and Political Rights (adopted on 16 December 1966, entered into force on 23 March 1976) 999 UNTS 171 (ICCPR) art 1(1); International Covenant on Economic, Social and Cultural Rights (adopted on 16 December 1966, entered into force on 3 January 1976) 993 UNTS 3 (ICESCR) art 1(1).

[5] 'Vienna Declaration and Programme of Action' World Conference on Human Rights (Vienna 14–25 June 1993) (12 July 1993) UN Doc A/CONF.157/23, art 8.

[6] Similarly, Teitel, who defines transition as 'a shift in political orders', see Ruti Teitel, *Transitional Justice* (OUP 2000) 5. Further, O'Donnell and Schmitter, who define transition as 'the interval between one political regime and another', see Guillermo O'Donnell and Philippe C Schmitter, *Transitions from Authoritarian Rule: Tentative Conclusions about Uncertain Democracies* (Johns Hopkins UP 1986) 7.

regimes in which political power is exercised by a small minority, normally with the backing of the military, and subject to few constraints (such as free elections and independent courts).[7] This focus on transition from authoritarian rule is not intended to deny that democratic regimes are sometimes overthrown, nor to suggest that the fall of an authoritarian regime inevitably results in the emergence of a new political order with democratic characteristics. Rather, the focus reflects the fact that transitions from authoritarian rule raise different legal and policy questions to the study of military coups in democracies.

This treatment is timely in light of the 'Arab Spring' and the transition currently under way in Myanmar (Burma). These political events have already given rise to several investment treaty claims – for example, *Veolia v. Egypt* and *Damac Properties v. Egypt*.[8] Other claims are yet to become public. Many of these claims arise from attempts by incoming governments to abrogate or modify laws and policies of the previous regime. These claims throw up a range of legal and policy issues about the extent to which investment treaties do, and should, allow the actions of a non-democratic government to constrain the policy choices of a successor regime. In other words, to adopt the terminology of the international human rights conventions, they raise questions about the appropriate legal limits on a people's ability to freely choose their own economic system.

This chapter is divided into two main parts. The first part examines the legal principles that currently govern investment treaty claims arising from transitions from authoritarian rule. This analysis suggests that changes in the form of government in a host state are largely irrelevant in investment treaty claims. Neither the fact that an investment was made during a period of authoritarian rule nor the fact that a subsequent regime was responsible for the alleged breach significantly affects the likelihood that a particular investment treaty claim will succeed. The second part identifies two major policy concerns that flow from this conclusion. The

---

7 For a more sophisticated definition see Juan Linz, 'An Authoritarian Regime: The Case of Spain' in Erik Allardt and Stein Rokkan (eds), *Mass Politics: Studies in Political Sociology* (Free Press 1970) 255.

8 Luke E Peterson, 'French company, Veolia, launches claim against Egypt over terminated waste contract and labor wage stabilization promises' (*IA Reporter*, 27 June 2012) <http://www.iareporter.com/articles/20120627_1> accessed 18 August 2014; David Elward, 'Egypt Faces Backlash from Dubai Investor' (*Global Arbitration Review*, 26 May 2011) <http://globalarbitrationreview.com/news/article/29498/egypt-faces-backlash-dubai-investor/> accessed 18 August 2014.

first concern stems from considerations of fairness: that it is unfair for an investor that has acquired an investment through a non-arms' length transaction with an authoritarian regime to demand full market value when the laws and policies governing the investment are amended. The second concern is consequentialist in character: that investment treaty claims may prevent incoming democratic regimes from pursuing their development priorities and, thereby, consolidating their position. I consider several possible changes that could be made to investment treaties to address these concerns. I argue that the most attractive solution would be to amend the principles that govern compensation under investment treaties.

This chapter develops arguments made in a companion article, published in the *Journal of World Investment and Trade*.[9] That article examined the political science literature on political transitions and identifies a number of insights that are relevant to debates about how investment treaties claims arising out of transitions should be resolved. The purpose of this chapter is to trace through the implications of the argument developed in the companion article for treaty reform.

II. THE APPLICATION OF INVESTMENT TREATIES IN CLAIMS ARISING FROM TRANSITIONS: THE LEX LATA

Investment treaties constrain governments in that they require a state to pay compensation if it implements certain legal and policy changes affecting foreign investors. This section clarifies the precise extent of that constraint by examining the implications of conventional doctrines of international investment law in claims arising from transition from authoritarian rule. The discussion is focused specifically on situations in which a successor regime seeks to change the laws or policies governing investments made under the predecessor regime. The analysis is structured around five different legal issues. I begin by considering the foundational question of whether treaties signed by a former regime remain binding on a successor regime. The basic principle of international law is that a successor regime does remain bound. I then consider whether Article 62 of the Vienna Convention on the Law of Treaties (VCLT) allows a successor regime to unilaterally terminate an

[9] Jonathan Bonnitcha, 'Investment Treaties and Transition from Authoritarian Rule' (2014) 15 JWIT 965.

investment treaty entered into by a predecessor, authoritarian regime. On the basis that Article 62 of the VCLT is unlikely to confer such a right, the subsequent sections consider key legal issues at the jurisdictional, merits and quantum phases in claims arising from transition from authoritarian rule.

A. Do Treaties Signed by a Former Government Bind a Successor Government?

Within international law, the conventional view is that a change in the form of government within a state is irrelevant to the nature and content of that state's treaty obligations. This follows from three foundational propositions of international law. The first is the proposition that the state is a unitary and continuing entity.[10] The second proposition is that 'an established government stands for, and has responsibility for, the State and its people for all or virtually all purposes.'[11] The third is that an established government within a state, has 'virtually unlimited' authority to bind the state for the future as a matter of international law.[12] The combined effect of these three propositions was stated succinctly by the Iran–United States Claims Tribunal in the public debt case:

> In spite of the change in head of State and the system of government in 1979, Iran remained the same subject of international law as before the Islamic Revolution. For when a Government is removed through a revolution, the State, as an international person, remains unchanged and the new Government generally assumes all the previous international rights and obligations of the State.[13]

Thus, the basic response of international law to transitions is to assert that an incoming regime in a state remains bound by the same international legal obligations that bound its predecessor.[14]

---

[10] James Crawford, 'Democracy and the Body of International Law' in Gregory H Fox and Brad R Roth (eds), *Democratic Governance and International Law* (CUP 2000) 97.

[11] Ibid 109.

[12] Ibid 97.

[13] *The United States of America v The Islamic Republic of Iran (Case No B36)* (1996) 32 Iran-US CTR 162, para 54.

[14] Crawford (n 10) 97; Malcolm N Shaw, *International Law* (6th edn, CUP 2008) 957.

B. Fundamental Change of Circumstances and the Continued Application of Investment Treaties

Article 62 of the VCLT allows a state to terminate or withdraw from a treaty in the event of an unforeseen, fundamental change of circumstances provided that two further conditions are met: the existence of the original circumstances must have constituted an 'essential basis of the consent of the parties to be bound by the treaty'; and 'the effect of the change [in those circumstances] is radically to transform the extent of obligations still to be performed under the treaty.'[15] If these conditions are satisfied a state may elect to terminate or withdraw from the treaty in question. Incoming governments may seek to argue that the change in the form of government within the state satisfies these criteria with respect to an investment treaty.

This argument is unlikely to succeed. In *Gabčikovo-Nagymaros*, Hungary argued that 'profound changes of a political nature' – specifically, Hungary's transition from a communist to a more democratic form of government – entitled it to terminate an earlier treaty with Slovakia relating to the construction of a dam.[16] The International Court of Justice rejected Hungary's argument, emphasising that the change in the political system in Hungary had not 'radically altered the extent of the obligations still to be performed.'[17] The fact that the subject matter of the treaty continued in existence, notwithstanding the change in the form of government, was also an influential factor in the Court's reasoning.[18] The situation under an investment treaty following a change in the form of government is similar, in the sense that the foreign investments that are the subject of the treaty's protections will continue to exist. Even if the obligations contained in an investment treaty place significant, normatively unjustifiable constraints on an incoming regime, it would be difficult to argue that the extent of those obligations are 'radically altered' by a change in the form of government.

---

15 Vienna Convention on the Law of Treaties (VCLT) (adopted 23 May 1969, entered into force 27 January 1980) 1155 UNTS 331, art 62(1).

16 *Case Concerning the Gabčikovo-Nagymaros Project (Hungary/Slovakia)* [1997] ICJ Rep 7, 64–5, para 104.

17 Ibid.

18 Ibid.

C. Corruption and Cronyism: Which Investments Are Entitled to the Protection of Investment Treaties?

Assuming that successor regimes are bound by investment treaties entered into by their predecessors, the next question is whether investments made under authoritarian regimes fall within the scope of protection of such treaties. A common feature of authoritarian regimes is that economic benefits, including investment opportunities, are distributed through networks of patronage and cronyism.[19] Determining the legal significance of these facts in particular cases raises questions of jurisdiction and admissibility.[20]

Relatively few investment treaty claims have considered situations in which the investor was alleged to have procured the investment through the payment of a bribe. The only investment treaty case in which a tribunal has made a finding that the investment in question was procured through the payment of a bribe is *Metal-Tech v. Uzbekistan*. In that case the Tribunal applied a BIT that contained a provision requiring investments to be made in accordance with domestic law.[21] Given that these acts of corruption were contrary to Uzbek law, the Tribunal ruled that it lacked jurisdiction to hear the claim.[22]

Broadly analogous issues were raised in *Inceysa v. El Salvador* and *Fraport v. The Philippines*, both of which considered the significance of fraud in the process of procuring or acquiring an investment.[23] Each dispute also involved the application of an investment treaty containing a provision that required investments to be made in accordance with domestic law.[24] In these circumstances, both tribunals held that fraud contrary to domestic law at the time the investment was made would

---

19 Haggard and Kaufman (n 3) 30; Thomas Pepinsky, *Economic Crises and the Breakdown of Authoritarian Regimes: Indonesia and Malaysia in Comparative Perspective* (CUP 2009) 266–7.

20 The implications of the distinction between issues of jurisdiction and admissibility are discussed in Jan Paulsson, 'Jurisdiction and Admissibility' in Gerald Aksen and others (eds), *Global Reflections on International Law, Commerce and Dispute Resolution: Liber Amicorum in Honour of Robert Briner* (ICC Publishing 2005) 601.

21 *Metal-Tech Ltd v Republic of Uzbekistan*, ICSID Case No ARB/10/3, Award (4 October 2013) para 164.

22 Ibid paras 372–4.

23 Andrea Menaker, 'The Determinative Impact of Fraud and Corruption on Investment Arbitrations' (2010) 25 ICSID Rev 67, 69.

24 *Inceysa Vallisoletana v Republic of El Salvador*, ICSID Case No ARB/03/26, Award (2 August 2006) para 221; *Fraport AG Frankfurt Airport Services*

preclude a tribunal from exercising jurisdiction. Moreover, tribunals have found that the illegality in the acquisition of an investment under domestic law renders a dispute inadmissible, even in the absence of a treaty provision explicitly requiring compliance with domestic law.[25] These decisions add further weight to the view that arbitral tribunals are likely to reject an investor's claim if an investment has been acquired corruptly and the corrupt act was inconsistent with domestic law (as it stood at the time of the allegedly corrupt act).

The decision in *World Duty Free v. Kenya* – a contract-based investor-state arbitration – rests on a principle that is broader still. In that case, the Tribunal held that corruption is contrary to 'international public policy'.[26] For this reason, the case is often cited as authority in investment treaty arbitrations.[27] While the Tribunal also found that corruption rendered the investment contract voidable under its proper law (thereby, removing the basis for jurisdiction),[28] it suggested that it would refuse to hear any claim based on a corruptly acquired investment, regardless of the legality of the corrupt acts under domestic law.[29]

Taken together, these cases demonstrate the prevailing view that corruptly acquired investments are not entitled to the protection of investment treaties, regardless of whether the corruption was tacitly condoned by the regime at the time the investment was made.[30] There are clear public policy justifications for this approach, at least insofar as transitions from authoritarian rule are concerned. Granting an investor compensation for interference with a corruptly acquired investment would allow the investor to profit from its wrongdoing at the expense of a more democratic incoming regime.

Worldwide v Republic of the Philippines, ICSID Case No ARB/03/25, Award (16 August 2007) para 401.

[25] *Plama Consortium Ltd v Republic of Bulgaria*, ICSID Case No ARB/03/24, Award (27 August 2008) para 135; *Phoenix Action Ltd v Czech Republic*, ICSID Case No ARB/06/5, Award (15 April 2009) para 101; Stephan W Schill, 'Illegal Investments in Investment Treaty Arbitration' (2012) 11 LPICT 281, 322–3.

[26] *World Duty Free v The Republic of Kenya*, ICSID Case No ARB/00/7, Award (4 October 2006) para 157.

[27] Schill (n 25) 317.

[28] *World Duty Free v Kenya* (n 26) para 188.

[29] Ibid para 157.

[30] Jason Yackee, 'Investment Treaties & Investor Corruption: An Emerging Defense for Host States' (2012) 52 Va JIL 723, 745.

The status of investments acquired through cronyistic relationships is less certain. Some guidance can be found in claims raising broader issues of impropriety in the acquisition of investments. *Plama v. Bulgaria* concerned a privatised oil refinery. The investor had agreed to purchase shares from the original private owner of the refinery, a transaction that required the approval of the Bulgarian Privatisation Agency under Bulgarian law. The Tribunal held that the investor had fraudulently misrepresented its technical and financial capacity in order to obtain regulatory approval. The question for the Tribunal concerned the significance of this misrepresentation for the purpose of the investor's treaty claim. The Tribunal dealt with the issue primarily through the prism of legality. It concluded that the investor's claim was not admissible because the misrepresentation had constituted a breach of applicable domestic law.[31] The Tribunal in *Phoenix Action v. Czech Republic* came to a similar conclusion.[32]

In the absence of illegality, no tribunal has refused to hear an investment treaty claim on the grounds that the investment was originally acquired from the host state through a transaction that was not arms' length. While the Tribunal in *KT Asia v. Kazakhstan* did reject jurisdiction partly on the basis that the claimant had acquired its investment from a related party through a transaction that was not arms' length,[33] this was in the context of considering whether a 'shell company' was entitled to bring a claim. This situation is different to the situation where the 'real' owner of an investment has acquired the original investment through a non-arms' length transaction. For this reason, the availability of investment treaty protection to investments acquired significantly below their market value is unlikely to depend on an examination of the propriety of the relationship between the investor and a predecessor authoritarian regime. Unless the acquisition of the investment was corrupt or tainted by illegality under domestic law at the time the investment was made, existing jurisprudence suggests that tribunals would allow a claim to proceed.

D. The Substantive Protection Provided by Investment Treaties

For investments falling within the scope of an investment treaty's protection, the next legal issue is the extent of substantive protection

---

31 *Plama* (n 25) para 139.

32 *Phoenix Action* (n 25) paras 102–3.

33 *KT Asia v Republic of Kazakhstan*, ICSID Case No ARB/09/8, Award (17 October 2013) para 182.

provided in claims arising from transition. From the outset, it is important to be clear that no investment treaty provides an exception to its substantive provisions for conduct that takes place during, or because of, a transition in the form of government within a state. As such, the question of whether conduct of a transitional or incoming regime breaches the terms of an investment treaty turns on the application of the core substantive provisions of the treaty – provision requiring fair and equitable treatment, national treatment, compensation for expropriation and the like – to the case in question.

Situations in which a state renationalises a factory or unilaterally cancels a concession contract can be addressed relatively simply. Assuming that the investment in question falls within the protection of the treaty, such actions would amount to expropriation and would, therefore, require compensation. While some arbitral awards have recognised certain circumstances in which regulatory measures will not amount to *indirect* expropriation,[34] these principles do not extend to situations in which a state *directly* expropriates an investment.

Claims arising from changes to the law governing foreign investments or situations in which a state unilaterally amends the terms of a concession contract without purporting to cancel it raise issues that are significantly more complex. Several disputes involving broadly similar fact scenarios have already come before investment treaty tribunals. Examples include: *Piero Foresti v. South Africa*, concerning the introduction of new affirmative action requirements in the mining sector in South Africa;[35] *Vattenfall v. Germany I*, concerning the imposition of new environmental conditions that made a project to construct and operate a coal power station project uneconomic;[36] and the Argentine gas cases, concerning unilateral modifications of the fiscal terms of gas distribution contracts.[37] In such cases,

[34] *Methanex Corporation v United States*, UNCITRAL, Final Award (2005) 44 ILM 1345, pt IV, ch D, para 7.

[35] *Piero Foresti, Laura de Carli and others v The Republic of South Africa*, ICSID Case No ARB(AF)/07/1, Award (4 August 2010).

[36] Luke E Peterson, 'Parties in *Vattenfall v Germany* Case Suspend Proceedings' (*IA Reporter*, 18 March 2010) <http://www.iareporter.com/articles/20100319_6> accessed 18 August 2014.

[37] *BG Group Plc v The Republic of Argentina*, UNCITRAL, Final Award (27 December 2007); *LG&E Energy Corp, LG&E Capital Corp and LG&E International Inc v The Argentine Republic*, ICSID Case No ARB/02/1, Award (25 July 2007); *CMS Gas Transmission Company v The Argentine Republic*, ICSID Case No ARB/01/08, Final Award (12 May 2005); *Sempra Energy International v The Argentine Republic*, ICSID Case No ARB/02/16, Award (28 September 2007).

the decisive issue is usually the extent of substantive protection provided by the fair and equitable treatment (FET) standard. The FET standard is the most significant substantive protection contained in investment treaties,[38] as it allows foreign investors to challenge a broad range of government conduct that affects their investments.[39] Investors have alleged breach of the FET standard in almost every investment treaty claim brought over the past decade,[40] and it is the claim with which investors have the best record of success.[41]

Arbitral tribunals have taken very different views on the extent of protection that the FET standard provides from legal and policy change.[42] On one hand, some tribunals have understood the FET standard as a guarantee against all significant changes to the laws and policies governing a foreign investment. For example, in *Occidental v. Ecuador I* the Tribunal held that 'the stability of the legal and business framework is … an essential element of fair and equitable treatment.'[43] Similarly, in *Tecmed v. Mexico* the Tribunal held that the FET standard protects an investor's 'basic expectations' at the time of making the investment.[44] The fullest statement of this view was made in *Frontier Petroleum v. Czech Republic*:

> Stability means that the investor's legitimate expectations based on this legal framework and on any undertakings and representations made explicitly or implicitly by the host state will be protected. The investor may rely on that

---

[38] Rudolf Dolzer and Christoph Schreuer, *Principles of International Investment Law* (2nd edn, OUP 2012) 130; Andrew Newcombe and Lluis Paradell, *Law and Practice of Investment Treaties* (Kluwer Law International 2009) 255.

[39] Rudolf Dolzer, 'Fair and Equitable Treatment' (2005) 39 *International Lawyer* 87, 90.

[40] Jeswald W Salacuse, *The Law of Investment Treaties* (OUP 2010) 218.

[41] Dolzer and Schreuer (n 38) 130; similarly, Lucy Reed and Daina Bray, 'Fair and Equitable Treatment: Fairly and Equitably Applied in Lieu of Unlawful Indirect Expropriation?' in Arthur W Rovine (ed.), *Contemporary Issues in International Arbitration and Mediation: The Fordham Papers 2007* (Martinus Nijhoff 2008) 15.

[42] Jonathan Bonnitcha, *Substantive Protection under Investment Treaties: A Legal and Economic Analysis* (CUP 2014) 169.

[43] *Occidental Exploration and Production Company v The Republic of Ecuador*, UNCITRAL (1976), LCIA Case No UN 3467, Final Award (1 July 2004) para 183.

[44] *Técnicas Medioambientales Tecmed SA v The United Mexican States*, ICSID Case No ARB(AF)/00/02, Award (29 May 2003) para 154.

> legal framework as well as on representations and undertakings made by the host state including those in legislation, treaties, decrees, licenses, and contracts.[45]

On this understanding, the FET standard protects foreign investors from both significant unilateral changes to the terms of contracts and significant changes to laws and policies of general application that govern the investment.

In contrast to this view, other tribunals have emphasised that there are circumstances in which a state may legitimately amend the laws and contractual terms governing an investment. Thus, the Tribunal in *EDF v. Romania* held that '[t]he idea that legitimate expectations, and therefore FET, imply the stability of the legal and business framework, may not be correct if stated in an overly-broad and unqualified formulation.'[46] Such tribunals have argued that claims that a state has failed to provide a stable legal and business environment should be assessed in light of the political and economic situation in the state in question 'including not only the facts surrounding the investment, but also the political, socioeconomic, cultural and historical conditions prevailing in the host State.'[47]

On this view, significant changes to the laws, policies and contractual terms governing an investment may well be justified in times of transition to a more democratic form of government. Tribunals taking this view have noted that laws and policies of general application are particularly susceptible to change,[48] but have been less sympathetic to the host state in cases involving the unilateral modification of contracts.[49]

The precise contours of the protection provided by the FET standard have been the subject of detailed examination elsewhere.[50] For present

---

[45] *Frontier Petroleum Services Ltd v The Czech Republic*, UNCITRAL (1976), Final Award (12 November 2010) para 285.

[46] *EDF (Services) Ltd v Romania*, ICSID Case No ARB/05/13, Award (8 October 2009) para 217.

[47] *Duke Energy Electroquil Partners & Electroquil SA v Republic of Ecuador*, ICSID Case No ARB/04/19, Award (18 August 2008) para 340; *Bayindir Insaat Turizm Ticaret Ve Sanayi AS v The Islamic Republic of Pakistan*, ICSID Case No ARB/03/29, Award (27 August 2009) paras 190–91; *National Grid plc v The Argentine Republic*, UNCITRAL, Award (3 November 2008) para 175.

[48] *Continental Casualty Company v The Argentine Republic*, ICSID Case No ARB/03/9, Award (5 September 2008) para 261.

[49] *El Paso Energy International Company v The Argentine Republic*, ICSID Case No ARB/03/15, Award (27 October 2011) paras 375–9.

[50] Bonnitcha (n 42) ch 4; Alexandra Diehl, *The Core Standard in International Investment Protection: Fair and Equitable Treatment* (Kluwer Law

purposes, it suffices to note that different tribunals have taken very different views of the extent to which the FET standard guarantees the stability of the laws and policies governing an investment. This contrasts with clearer substantive provisions that require compensation in the event of direct expropriation or nationalisation.

E. Principles Governing Compensation

Assuming that conduct affecting a foreign investment during a transition from authoritarian rule does breach an investment treaty, a final question arises as to the compensation owed. In the case of expropriation, most investment treaties provide that full market value compensation must be paid for the expropriated property.[51] The application of this principle requires a tribunal to determine what an arms' length buyer would have paid for the investment immediately prior to the expropriation.[52] The price that the investor originally paid for an investment may be relevant as *evidence* of an investment's market value immediately prior to expropriation,[53] particularly in circumstances where the investment has no record of profitable operation.[54] However, the principle of full market value compensation does not allow a tribunal to adjust compensation to reflect the circumstances in which, or the value for which, the investment was originally acquired.

In contrast to the express provisions governing compensation for expropriation, investment treaties do not normally address the question of compensation owing for non-expropriatory breaches of the treaty. In the absence of any express rule, tribunals have applied the rule of customary

---

International 2012); Roland Kläger, *'Fair and Equitable Treatment' in International Investment Law* (CUP 2011).

[51] See, e.g., 2012 US Model Bilateral Investment Treaty (2012) art 6(2)(b) <http://www.ustr.gov/sites/default/files/BIT%20text%20for%20ACIEP%20Meeting.pdf> accessed 18 August 2014; *Siemens AG v The Argentine Republic*, ICSID Case No ARB/02/8, Award (6 February 2007) para 353; *Compañiá de Aguas del Aconquija SA and Vivendi Universal SA v The Argentine Republic*, ICSID Case No ARB/97/3, Award (20 August 2007) para 8.2.10.

[52] W Michael Reisman and Robert D Sloane, 'Indirect Expropriation and its Valuation in the BIT Generation' (2003) 74 BYIL 115, 138; similarly *CMS Gas v Argentina* (n 37) para 402.

[53] See, e.g., *Wena Hotels Ltd v The Arab Republic of Egypt*, ICSID Case No ARB/98/4, Award (8 December 2000) paras 124–5.

[54] *Vivendi v Argentina* (n 51) para 8.3.3; Sergey Ripinsky and Kevin Williams, *Damages in International Investment Law* (BIICL 2008) 206–7.

international law governing state responsibility for an internationally wrongful act:

> [R]eparation must, as far as possible, wipe out all the consequences of the illegal act and re-establish the situation which would, in all probability, have existed if that act had not been committed.[55]

This principle requires a tribunal to ascertain the hypothetical position that an investor would be in 'but for' the breach, and calculate damages so as to put the claimant in that position.[56] This is a forward-looking exercise, which does not take into account the circumstances or the value for which an investment was acquired. While distinct in principle, application of the rule governing compensation for an expropriation and the rule governing reparation for other breaches of the treaty would lead to similar, even identical, results in most fact scenarios.[57] Regardless of which rule is applied, there is little room for 'balancing' of competing interests at the compensation stage.

Contrary to the conventional view, Tudor has argued that arbitral tribunals do have the ability to adjust compensation under the FET standard on the basis of discretionary factors.[58] This would allow arbitral tribunals to consider the circumstances surrounding the acquisition of the investment at the compensation stage, and revise the compensation payable downwards accordingly. Whatever the policy merits of her view, Tudor's argument finds little support in existing jurisprudence.[59] Most of the cases she cites were either cases in which the tribunal found the treaty had not been breached – *Fraport*, *GAMI*, *Olguin* and *Generation Ukraine* – or cases in which the tribunal in question ultimately applied the normal principles governing the quantification of damages – *CME*, *CMS*, *LG&E*

---

55 *Case Concerning Certain German Interests in Polish Upper Silesia (Germany v Poland)* (Claim for Indemnity) PCIJ Rep Series A No 17, 47.

56 Irmgard Marboe, *Calculation of Compensation and Damages in International Investment Law* (OUP 2009) 83.

57 *Waguih Elie George Siag and Clorinda Vecchi v The Arab Republic of Egypt*, ICSID Case No ARB/05/15, Award (11 May 2009) para 542; Borzu Sabahi, *Compensation and Restitution in Investor-State Arbitration: Principles and Practice* (OUP 2011) 102.

58 Ioana Tudor, *The Fair and Equitable Treatment Standard in the International Law of Foreign Investment* (OUP 2008) 228.

59 Martins Paparinskis, *The International Minimum Standard and Fair and Equitable Treatment* (OUP 2013) 9.

Energy and *Maffezini*.[60] In those cases where the tribunal did explicitly consider the investor's conduct – *Bogdanov* and *MTD* – that conduct was relevant only in determining the extent to which the wrongful act of the state had *caused* the investment's loss in value.[61] Similarly, in the recent case *Occidental v. Ecuador (II)*, the tribunal held that claimant's negligence was causally responsible for part of the investment's loss in value and adjusted the damages awarded accordingly.[62] Overall, the better view of current doctrine is that it requires a state to pay full compensation for any loss caused by a breach of an investment treaty.

There are, however, indirect ways that a change in the political regime in the host state may feed into the calculation of compensation, which are consistent with settled principles of investment treaty law. For one, the market value of an investment immediately prior to an expropriation will reflect general economic conditions in the state, which in turn may be affected by political turmoil. More specifically, to determine the position an investor would be in 'but for' the breach, a tribunal must draw a set of inferences about how political and economic circumstances in the state would have evolved absent the breach.[63] This includes making allowance for legitimate regulatory change.[64] The set of assumptions about the likely future evolution of the political and economic circumstances in a state will have an impact on the extent of damage ultimately assessed.[65] However, the significance of these factors should not be overstated. They do not allow a tribunal to adjust compensation in light of fairness considerations relating to the manner in which an investment was acquired.

---

[60] *CME Czech Republic BV v The Czech Republic*, UNCITRAL, Final Award (14 March 2003) para 508; *CMS Gas v Argentina* (n 37) para 419; *Emilio Agustín Maffezini v The Kingdom of Spain*, ICSID Case No ARB/97/7, Award (13 November 2000) para 95; *LG&E Energy v Argentina* (n 37) para 58.

[61] *Yuri Bogdanov v The Republic of Moldova*, SCC, Arbitral Award (22 September 2005) 11; *MTD Equity Sdn Bhd and MTD Chile SA v The Republic of Chile*, ICSID Case No ARB/01/7, Award (21 May 2004) para 242.

[62] *Occidental Petroleum Corporation and Occidental Exploration and Production Company v The Republic of Ecuador (II)*, ICSID Case No ARB/06/11, Award (5 October 2012) paras 669–80.

[63] Marboe (n 56) 238; *Chevron Corporation (USA) and Texaco Petroleum Company (USA) v The Republic of Ecuador (I)*, UNCITRAL, PCA Case No 34877, Partial Award on the Merits (30 March 2010) para 374.

[64] Thomas Wälde and Borzu Sabahi, 'Compensation, Damages and Valuation in International Investment Law' (2007) 4(6) TDM 1, 6.

[65] Ripinsky and Williams (n 54) 118.

F. Summary: The Extent of the Legal Constraint Placed on Incoming Regimes by Investment Treaties

A complex picture emerges from the foregoing legal discussion. International investment law offers relatively clear answers to questions concerning the continued application of investment treaties in times of transition and concerning the principles that govern compensation. Tribunals are highly likely to find that an investment treaty signed by an authoritarian regime continues to bind successor regimes and to conclude, if the treaty is breached, that compensation should be calculated on a full market value basis. The answers to questions concerning the scope and extent of protection provided by investment treaties are less clear. Tribunals are likely to decline to hear cases concerning corruptly acquired investments or investments acquired in breach of applicable domestic law. However, neither point is fully settled. The extent of substantive protection provided by investment treaties is even more elusive. While outright nationalisation or cancellation of investment contracts is likely to breach an investment treaty, tribunals have come to markedly different views about the extent to which investment treaties protect foreign investors from interferences falling short of outright nationalisation. Specifically, tribunals have disagreed about the circumstances in which changes to the legal and policy framework governing an investment will amount to a breach of the FET standard.

III. A CASE FOR TREATY REFORM?

The previous section of this chapter examined the legal principles that would govern investment treaty claims arising out of transitions. This section examines whether these legal principles are appropriate from a policy perspective. In particular, it seeks to determine whether investment treaties impose an unacceptable constraint on the ability of incoming democratic governments to adopt new economic and social development policies following a transition from authoritarian rule. In doing so, this chapter draws heavily on the insights of the *Journal of World Investment and Trade* companion article. That article identifies several insights from political science literature on transitions that are relevant to debates about how investment treaties claims arising out of transitions should be resolved.

The first insight is that authoritarian regimes often rely on the support of business elites for their survival.[66] This support is generally secured by granting preferential business concessions to the favoured elite. Accordingly, authoritarian regimes often leave behind a problematic economic legacy,[67] including assets and contractual rights granted to 'cronies' of the regime on highly favourable terms. Thus, one important policy question is the extent to which investment treaties constrain an incoming government from renationalising or unilaterally amending the terms of contracts awarded on a non-arms' length basis by the previous regime.

The second insight is that the process of transition is a contest for control of the state that is played out among various groups and actors. As such, the question of whether a transition is likely to result in a new, relatively stable, democratic regime depends in part on whether an incoming regime can secure a political and economic settlement supported by a broad coalition of civilian actors. This insight goes to the heart of the relationship between development, investment treaties and transition. It suggests that the viability of civilian government depends, in part, on the implementation of new laws and policies.

The third insight is that transition is a complex and uncertain process. Transitions do not necessarily end with the establishment of democratic regimes. Even relatively democratic regimes that emerge from transitions may prove disappointing in other respects.[68] As such, discussions about the application of investment treaties should not be premised on the assumption that new forms of government that emerge from political transitions are necessarily democratic. Nor should they rely on binary classifications between 'authoritarian' and 'democratic' regimes. This observation is borne out by the different trajectories of the 'Arab Spring' countries. At the time of writing, Libya appears to be sliding toward civil war. The democratically elected Morsi government in Egypt was removed by the military in July 2013.[69] The regime subsequently

---

[66] Haggard and Kaufman (n 3) 29; Hector E Schamis, 'Distributional Coalitions and the Politics of Economic Reform in Latin America' (1999) 51 *World Politics* 236, 239.

[67] O'Donnell and Schmitter (n 6) 46.

[68] Fareed Zakaria, 'The Rise of Illiberal Democracy' (1997) 76(6) *Foreign Affairs* 22, 42; Philippe C Schmitter, 'Twenty-Five Years, Fifteen Findings' (2010) 21 *Journal of Democracy* 17, 20.

[69] 'Egypt Crisis: Army Ousts President Mohammed Morsi' (*BBC News*, 4 July 2013) <www.bbc.co.uk/news/world-middle-east-23173794> accessed 18 August 2014.

installed has banned opposition political parties and increasingly resembles the Mubarak regime in power before the 'Arab Spring'. Only Tunisia appears to have emerged from its period of transition with a stable democratic government.

These insights from the political science literature suggest that concerns about the application of investment treaties in claims arising from transitions are likely to coalesce around two different types of cases. The first is the situation in which an incoming regime seeks to amend laws and policies of general application, consistently with its new development priorities. Such policies could include changes to the state's tax laws, labour laws and environmental regulations. The second is the situation in which an incoming seeks to renationalise or unilaterally amend the terms of contracts governing particular investment projects, perhaps in response to the perception that the investment was not originally acquired through a legitimate process. Both types of cases raise issues of fairness, as well as consequentialist concerns about the impact of treaty constraints on the process of economic reorganisation necessary for democratic consolidation.

A. Investment Treaty Claims Arising from Changes of Laws and Policies of General Application

The policy concerns arising out of the first type of cases – the amendment of laws and policies of general applications – relate primarily to the substantive protections of investment treaties. The review of applicable legal principles in the first part of this chapter concluded that relevant principles remain unsettled. As such, transitional and incoming governments are likely to find it difficult to make *ex ante* assessments of whether changes to laws and policies of general application that interfere with foreign investments are likely to infringe the state's investment treaties. This review also concluded that, when determining whether legal and policy changes falling short of outright expropriation breach an investment treaty, some established lines of jurisprudence would allow an arbitral tribunal to take the political and economic context of transition from authoritarian rule into account. For example, there is some authority in existing arbitral awards jurisprudence that the political and economic circumstances within a state should be taken into account when assessing claims that an investor has been deprived of 'legal stability' or that its 'legitimate expectations' have been disappointed. According to these lines of jurisprudence, an incoming regime would be relatively unconstrained in its ability to change labour laws, tax laws, environmental regulations, and the like.

On this basis, it seems that the policy concerns arising from the application of investment treaties in such cases could be addressed through interpretative strategies that operate within the constraints imposed by existing treaties. Arbitral tribunals should be sensitive to the political context in which investment treaty claims arise. They should endorse and apply the lines of FET jurisprudence that recognise governments' ability to amend laws and policies of general application, even if such changes are contrary to the interests of established investors.

B. Investment Treaty Claims Arising from Renationalisation of Assets and Unilateral Amendment of Contract Terms

The policy concerns arising from the second type of cases – those in which a successor regime seeks to renationalise or unilaterally amend the contractual terms of an investment – are more complex. These concerns are especially acute in cases involving assets originally acquired through non-arms' length transactions. The prevailing view is that assets acquired through corrupt transactions are not entitled to the protection of investment treaties. However, existing jurisprudence suggests that assets sold to foreign investors for a small fraction of their full market value are entitled to the protection of investment treaties provided that the transaction was lawful under the laws of the authoritarian regime as they stood at the time the investment was made. Any renationalisation of assets and significant unilateral amendments to concession contracts are likely to breach investment treaties' substantive protections. Full market value compensation would then be required. As such, investment treaties restrict the ability of an incoming regime to recover assets transferred to associates of the authoritarian regime, and to engage in more radical forms of redistribution.

As previously noted, there are two related policy concerns arising from the application of investment treaties in claims of this type. The first is that requiring a government to pay full market value compensation for the expropriation, or forced renegotiation of contract terms, of investments that were not originally acquired for full market value is *unfair*. The argument that it is unfair to require the payment of full market value compensation is simple. Full market value compensation grants an unearned windfall to associates of an authoritarian regime at the expense of the country's citizens.

The strongest argument for the opposite view – that fairness requires full market value compensation – seems to rest on libertarian norms. The argument would be that the acquisition was lawful at the time it occurred, and that fairness requires lawfully-acquired property rights to be respected, regardless of the competing considerations involved. This argument is tenable but, in my view, it is unpersuasive. When an authoritarian regime sells state assets on an arms' length basis – for example, if an open, competitive tender is held to award a mining concession – there may be fairness grounds to treat the transaction as a legitimate exercise of state authority, regardless of how reprehensible the regime is in other respects. On the other hand, a decision to transfer state assets into private ownership for a small fraction of their real value is clearly not a legitimate exercise of state authority. There is no benefit to the 'state' in selling assets for less than they are worth. Nor are such transactions in the interests of the people of the state. An authoritarian regime transfers state assets to cronies because it makes sense for the group of individuals that control the state to secure the allegiance of other influential individuals.

The second policy concern relates to the impact of investment treaties, and claims under them, on the ability of incoming democratic regimes to reorganise their economies. Transitional regimes that inherit power following a period of authoritarian rule are subject to a range of pressures. The foremost of these is the need to consolidate democracy, and avoid a coup that returns the country to authoritarian rule. Unlike its predecessor, the transitional government (and any successor regime) cannot rely on the military for its viability. Its success or failure rests on its ability to establish and secure broad-based *civilian* support. In order to establish their legitimacy, incoming regimes may need to revisit the terms of investments that are perceived to be unfair and to ensure that a greater share of the benefits of economic development flow to the people of the host state.

The transition currently underway in Myanmar provides several examples of this dynamic. In 2006, without any tendering process, the military government awarded the Myitsone Dam concession to a Chinese, state-owned enterprise. The financial terms of the contract have never been made public but are believed to be highly favourable to the investor, reflecting the government of Myanmar's dependence on Chinese government support through decades of international isolation and Western sanctions. The project was heavily criticised within Myanmar and became a focal point for democratic opposition to the military regime. In late September 2011, the transitional government announced the 'suspension' of the concession, signalling its willingness to negotiate with democrats and other opponents of the former regime. The ultimate fate of the project remains undecided. Another example, also involving a Chinese investment, is the Leptadaung copper mine. In response to protests against the mine, the transitional government appointed a commission to review the terms of the contract with the investor. The commission's recommendations – that the government of Myanmar take a greater stake in the project and that money be set aside for social projects for the benefit of the local population – then formed the basis for renegotiation of the terms of the contract with the investor.

Investment treaties, particularly the possibility of investment treaty claims in high profile projects, make the process of working through the economic legacy of authoritarianism more difficult. Transitional governments are generally subject to funding constraints. The option of paying compensation equal to each investment's full market value in order to cancel it, or to vary the terms of the original bargain, is not always realistic. Paying compensation equivalent to the full market value of the affected investments would place extraordinary strain on other aspects of an incoming regime's budget, undermining public support for the regime. Allowing investment projects to continue on the terms established under a previous authoritarian regime is equally politically difficult. Expectations of the incoming regime are likely to be high. The people of a state expect that a new government will seek to unwind the privileges conferred on associates of the former regime and ensure a more equitable distribution of economic benefits.

C. What Should Be Done?

Thus far, I have identified policy concerns arising from the application of investment treaties in claims arising from transitions from authoritarian rule. I argued that some of these concerns can be addressed under existing investment treaties through interpretative strategies, but that others cannot be addressed so easily. In particular, I argued that the requirement to pay full market value compensation in the event of renationalisation or unilateral amendment of contractual terms is both unfair and undesirable in the case of investments acquired from authoritarian regimes through transactions that were not originally on arms' length terms.

In this section, I consider three possible amendments that could be made to existing and future investment treaties in order to address these concerns. They are as follows:

1. Investment treaties could be drafted to exclude investments originally acquired from an authoritarian regime from the protection of the treaty.

2. Investment treaties could be drafted to allow tribunals to reduce compensation when an investment was originally acquired from an authoritarian regime.
3. Investment treaties could be drafted to allow tribunals to reduce compensation when an investment was originally acquired through a non-arms' length transaction.

The first option – entirely excluding investments acquired from authoritarian regimes from the protection of investment treaties – is the most radical. Adopting this option would ensure that any new democratic regime is not constrained by the actions of its authoritarian predecessor, at least insofar as investment treaties are concerned. It could also discourage foreign investors from dealing with noxious regimes, or at least shift the risk of such dealings onto the investor. However, this option would rely on tribunals' ability to classify regimes as either authoritarian or democratic. Even leaving aside the sensitivities of requiring arbitral tribunals to make such judgements, there are serious questions about whether such a distinction is viable conceptually. The political science literature on authoritarianism and democratisation suggests that regimes do not fall neatly into such categories. Rather, different regimes exhibit a range of different authoritarian or democratic characteristics. Moreover, the form of government in a state generally evolves over time, developing new and different characteristics. These observations suggest that any legal rules that rely on binary categorisation of different forms of government are likely to be unworkable.

The second option – allowing tribunals to adjust compensation to reflect the fact that an investment was acquired from an authoritarian regime – presents similar difficulties. This option would also require a tribunal to classify political regimes in states. While the consequences of this distinction are less severe – the second option would still allow an investor that acquired assets from an authoritarian regime to receive some compensation in the event of renationalisation – the same conceptual challenges relating to the classification of regimes remain.

In my view, the third option – allowing tribunals to reduce compensation if the investment was not originally acquired through an arms' length transaction – is more promising. The difference between this option and the first and second options is that it looks to the circumstances surrounding a particular *transaction*, rather than to the character of a *regime*. Investment treaties could be drafted in a way that allows a tribunal to take into account the process through which the investment was acquired and the amount originally paid for the investment, among other factors. (Some investment treaties already allow tribunals to take such factors into account when determining compensation for expropriation.)[70] The principle of full market value could remain the default rule in cases where impropriety is absent or unproven.

From a policy perspective, this third option has three advantages over the other alternatives considered. The first is that it addresses many of the concerns arising from the application of investment treaties in claims arising out of transition from authoritarian rule. This option would prevent associates of an authoritarian regime being awarded windfall gains through investment treaty arbitration at the expense of the people of the host state. It would also significantly reduce the risk of incoming regimes being discouraged from unwinding the economic privileges associated with authoritarian rule.

The second advantage is that this option relies on information that is likely to be before the arbitral tribunal, and which arbitral tribunals are well qualified to assess. At the quantum phase of investor-state arbitration, evidence relating to the acquisition of the investment is normally led by the claimant, regardless of the legal principles governing compensation that are applied. Moreover, arbitral tribunals are much better placed to assess whether a specific transaction was consistent with industry norms of arms' length dealing than whether a particular government should be classified as authoritarian or not.

The third advantage is that this option creates appropriate incentives for foreign investors. Allowing tribunals to adjust compensation in light of the circumstances in which an investment was acquired would not discourage investors from investing in countries under authoritarian rule *per se*. Rather, such a rule creates an incentive for investors to ensure that they can show that the acquisition of such investments is not tainted by cronyism and impropriety.

IV. CONCLUSION

One important dimension of development is the ability of the people of a state to freely choose their own development priorities. This chapter has examined some of the legal and policy issues raised by investment treaty claims arising from transitions from authoritarian rule. I argued that

---

[70] One example is the Agreement between the government of Hong Kong and the government of Australia for the Promotion and Protection of Investments (Australia-Hong Kong BIT) (adopted on 15 September 1993, entered into force on 15 October 1996) art 6(1).

investment treaties, as they are currently drafted, place significant constraints on the ability of incoming democratic governments to reorganise their economies and pursue new development priorities following a transition from authoritarian rule. In particular, investment treaties limit incoming governments' ability to reorganise their economies by unwinding privileges granted to foreign investors associated with the former regime. I argued that these policy concerns could be addressed through changes to the principles governing compensation under investment treaties. Specifically, states should consider drafting investment treaties in a way that allows compensation to be adjusted in light of the circumstances in which an investment was originally acquired.

11. Investment treaties and democratic transition: Does investment law authorize not to honor contracts concluded with undemocratic regimes?

Walid Ben Hamida

I. INTRODUCTION

In investment law, democratic transitions raise mainly two issues. The first, especially linked to violent transitions, is the request for compensation for some damages (destruction, theft, fire) due to the revolutionary events. The second is the revocation of contracts concluded by old regimes.

Damages arising from revolution are governed by a special clause provided in many investment treaties that are called 'clauses relating to the loss of investment owing to a natural phenomenon, civil disturbance, revolution or armed conflict.'[1] In Libya, the popular protests against long-term authoritarianism transformed themselves into a military conflict.[2] Many foreign investors that lost their investment have considered

[1] See, e.g., Art 7(4) of the BIT between the Belgo-Luxemburg Economic Union and Libya: '4. Investors of one Contracting Party whose investments suffer losses owing to war or other armed conflict, revolution, a state of national emergency or revolt in the territory of the other Contracting Party shall be granted by the latter Contracting Party a treatment, as regards restitution, indemnification, compensation or other settlement, at least equal to that which the latter Contracting Party grants to the investors of the most favoured nation.'

[2] See on Libya's transition Emin Poljarevic, 'Libya's Violent Revolution', COSMOS WP 2012/5 (2012) <http://cadmus.eui.eu/bitstream/handle/1814/26178/2012WP05COSMOS.pdf> accessed 1 January 2014.

possible indemnification claims for harm and loss owing to these violent events.[3]

In customary international law, it was asserted that the State is not responsible for damages that are owed to a popular revolution, natural catastrophe, war, national emergency and insurrection. Indeed, it has been observed that damage caused by such events are the result of either acts the State has found itself forced to carry out to ensure its own protection (wars and insurrection) or from events that are beyond human control (natural catastrophes). Consequently, these acts constitute an accidental event or a *force majeure* which cannot be attributed to the State.[4]

Investment treaties limit the scope of this non-liability rule. Bilateral investment treaties (BITs) contain specific provisions that address the consequences of armed conflict, state of emergency, revolution, insurrection, civil disturbance or similar events. They set out the treatment which the State must grant to an investor in the presence of one of these events.[5] Two categories of clauses must be distinguished. The first type of clause, which is found in BITs entered into by France, Canada and Switzerland, obliges the State to treat the prejudices caused by these events in accordance with the standards of national treatment (NT) and treatment of the most favored nation (MFN).[6] The second category can be found in American, British and Austrian BITs. It is comparable to the first in that it grants national treatment and MFN treatment in the event of

---

[3] I am aware of at least one BIT arbitration opposing a German/Tunisian investor to Libya related to damage owing to the popular revolution in this country.

[4] Teodoro Alvarado-Garaioca, 'La responsabilité de l'Etat dans les guerres civiles' in Institut de Sociologie de l'Université Libre de Bruxelles (ed.), *Mélanges Offerts à Léon-Eli Troclet, Droit Social et International* (ULB 1967) 43.

[5] For a more detailed discussion of these clauses see Walid Ben Hamida, *L'arbitrage transnational unilatéral. Réflexions sur une procédure réservée à l'initiative d'une personne privée contre une personne publique* (2003) paras 568 ff; see also Christoph Schreuer, 'The Protection of Investments in Armed Conflicts' (2012) 9(3) TDM <http://www.univie.ac.at/intlaw/wordpress/pdf/Armed%20Conflict.pdf> accessed 1 January 2014.

[6] See, e.g., Art VII of the BIT between Canada and Egypt: 'Compensation for Losses: Investors of one Contracting Party who suffer losses because their investments or returns on the territory of the other Contracting Party are affected by an armed conflict, a national emergency or a natural disaster on that territory, shall be accorded by such latter Contracting Party, in respect of restitution, indemnification, compensation or other settlement, treatment no less favourable than that which it accords to its own investors or to investors of any third State.'

damage that resulted from one of the events referred to above. Nevertheless, the clauses differ in that they require more than MFN and national treatment if the investment has been requisitioned or destroyed by the forces or authorities of the host State when this requisition or destruction was not required by the necessities of circumstance. Therefore, an investor who during a war, armed conflict, state of emergency, revolution, insurrection, civil disturbance or any other similar event suffers losses that result from the requisitioning or destruction of its investment by the forces or authorities not required by the necessity of the situation, shall be accorded restitution or compensation which in either cases shall be prompt, adequate and effective. In other words, according to compensation standards identical to those provided for expropriations.[7]

The second effect of political transitions is related to measures adopted by the transitional or successor regime against foreign investors that contracted with the former regime. Revolutions and regime changes are generally accompanied by retaliation against investors who dealt with the overthrown regime. Foreign investors can be considered as the allies of the illegitimate political power that was overturned by the popular movement. This retaliation can include the confiscation of assets, the prohibition to manage the investment, the appointment of new managers to run the project and the deprivation of enjoyment and administration of companies. Often, the new rulers try to revoke or to modify the contract

---

[7] See, e.g., Art 5 of the BIT between Austria and Libya: 'Compensation for Losses: (1) An investor of a Contracting Party who has suffered a loss relating to its investment in the territory of the other Contracting Party due to war or to other armed conflict, state of emergency, revolution, insurrection, civil disturbance, or any other similar event, or acts of God or force majeure, in the territory of the latter Contracting Party, shall be accorded by the latter Contracting Party, as regards restitution, indemnification, compensation or any other settlement, treatment no less favourable than that which it accords to its own investors or to investors of any third state, whichever is most favourable to the investor.

(2) An investor of a Contracting Party who in any of the events referred to in paragraph (1) suffers loss resulting from: (a) requisitioning of its investment or part thereof by the forces or authorities of the other Contracting Party, or (b) destruction of its investment or part thereof by the forces or authorities of the other Contracting Party, which was not required by the necessity of the situation, shall in any case be accorded by the latter Contracting Party restitution or compensation which in either case shall be prompt, adequate and effective and, with respect to compensation, shall be in accordance with Article 4(2) and (3) [on expropriation].'

On the difference between these two categories of clauses see Walid Ben Hamida, 'Arbitration and the New Political Context in Tunisia' (2011) 3 *International Journal of Arab Arbitration* 6–23.

concluded by former rulers on the ground that such contracts have been obtained through corruption or are incompatible with the public interest.

This scenario took place in Egypt. Since the uprising that toppled Husni Mubarak in 2011, many lawsuits before domestic tribunals have been brought by activists and lawyers who asserted that public companies were sold to foreign investors too cheaply in deals that were representative of corrupt business practices. Egyptian courts have issued at least 11 rulings ordering the state to reverse deals signed by the former president's administration.[8] Around fifteen requests for arbitration have been introduced against Egypt under investment treaties due to the revocation of contracts entered into by the overturned regime.[9]

The Libyan government is presently in the process of reviewing contracts signed with foreign companies prior to February 2011.[10] The same issue may present itself in a situation like the one which currently exists in Burma (Myanmar). Several contracts relating to natural resource exploitation have been concluded with the military government of the country.[11] A similar situation exists in Nigeria, where lucrative oil

---

[8] 'A New Investment Law Draft Prevents Third Parties from Challenging Contracts Signed between the Egyptian Government and Investors' (*Al Arabiya News*, 24 February 2014) <http://english.alarabiya.net/en/business/economy/2014/02/24/Egypt-investment-law-prohibits-third-party-challenge-to-contracts-source-says.html> accessed 1 April 2014. In February 2014, Prime Minister Hazem el-Biblawy approved new amendments of the investment law to prevent third parties from challenging contracts made between the government and investors see Egypt: PM Amends Investment Law (25 February 2014) <http://allafrica.com/stories/201402251685.html accessed 1 April 2014.

[9] Among the cases covered by the media, the following can be mentioned: *Hussain Sajwani, Damac Park Avenue for Real Estate Development SAE, and Damac Gamsha Bay for Development SAE v Egypt*, ICSID Case No ARB/11/16, *Bawabet Al Kuwait Holding Company v Egypt*, ICSID Case No ARB/11/6, *National Gas SAE v Egypt*, ICSID Case No ARB/11/7 and *Anwal v Egypt* (pending), on this case see Ahmed El Hadidi, 'Privatization and Revolution: A Critical Reading of the Omar Effendi Case' (thesis in partial fulfillment of the requirements for the LLM Degree in International and Comparative Law, American University in Cairo, School of Global Affairs and Public Policy, December 2012) <http://dar.aucegypt.edu/handle/10526/3350> accessed 1 April 2014; see also the cases quoted by Jonathan Bonnitcha, 'Democracy, Development and Compensation under Investment Treaties: The Case of Transition from Authoritarian Rule', in this volume, 285, 287.

[10] Andrew Watrous, 'Investment in Libya: Security, Contracts, and a New Constitution' (2013) 7 *World Commerce Review* 60–62.

[11] See Bonnitcha (n 9) 304–305.

concessions have been granted in areas belonging to minority tribes by a military dictatorship.[12]

In any case, if governments try to revoke old agreements, private investors can consider having recourse to the arbitration regime offered in international investment treaties and domestic investment laws to protect their rights. They can thus claim that the termination of contracts constitutes an unfair and unjust treatment, disguised expropriation, arbitrary treatment or a breach of the umbrella clause. Governments can defend themselves claiming that these contracts have been obtained in an illegal manner or by corruption, which poses the delicate problem of proving illegality and the continuity of the State. Yet, can a government invoke the illegal acts of a previous government which represents the State as a means of defense?

I will focus my remarks on a very special issue: the validity of contracts concluded by non-democratic regimes with foreign investors. Are such contracts illegal or not protected by international investment treaties? In light of the recent events in the Arab region after the 'Arab Spring',[13] this question is timely. This chapter does not intend to give a definitive answer to this difficult question but rather provides some comments in order to create a debate on this controversial issue. In Part II of this chapter, I will argue that international investment law does not prohibit the conclusion of contracts with non-democratic governments. However, even if the principle remains that contracts with despots are not *per se* illegal, I will explain in Part II that there is some evolution in the legal treatment of contracts concluded by undemocratic regimes. Some investment agreements are illustrative of a new trend that takes into account new values of morality and democracy.

---

12 See 'World: Africa Nigeria Suspends Military Regime Contracts' (*BBC News*, 31 May 1999) <http://news.bbc.co.uk/2/hi/africa/357457.stm> accessed 1 April 2014.

13 The Arab Spring is a term used to describe democratic transitions after a revolutionary wave of demonstrations and protests (both violent and non-violent), riots, and civil wars in the Arab world that began on 18 December 2010; see Steven Heydemann, 'Tracking the "Arab Spring" Syria and the Future of Authoritarianism' (2013) 24 *Journal of Democracy* 59; see also Eva Bellin, 'Reconsidering the Robustness of Authoritarianism in the Middle East: Lessons from the Arab Spring' (2012) 44 *Comparative Politics* 127–49.

II. THE PRINCIPLE: INTERNATIONAL INVESTMENT LAW IGNORES DEMOCRACY

From an economic point of view, the link between investment and democracy is controversial. Although many of the classic works in political science have argued that democracy has a positive impact on economic growth, there is no link established between democratic governance and foreign direct investment (FDI).[14] As it has been pointed out, '[f]or a commercial company trying to make investments, you need a stable environment. Dictatorships can give you that.'[15]

From a legal point of view, international investment law does not prohibit the conclusion of contracts with non-democratic governments. Contracts with despots are not *per se* illegal in international law. This assertion is based on the fact that international law does not provide for a democratic exception (A.), that the majority of international financial institutions do not take into consideration democratic principles when they conduct their activities (B.), and that the theory of odious debt that was invoked to support the illegality of contract concluded with despots is controversial (C.).

A. No Democratic Exception in Investment Law

International investment law ignores democracy. BITs and multilateral investment treaties do not make any reference to democracy. This means that contracts concluded by undemocratic regimes could be protected by bilateral and multilateral investment treaties.

Some investment tribunals have considered that '[t]he existence of a contribution to the economic development of the host State is a characteristic of the protected investment under international investment treaties.'[16]

However, the contribution of the investor to the development of the host state does not mean that for the investment to be protected it must be made in a democratic country. Contracts concluded with despotic regimes

---

[14] Nathan M Jensen, 'Democratic Governance and Multinational Corporations: Political Regimes and Inflows of Foreign Direct Investment' (2003) 57 *International Organization* 587–616.

[15] Christopher L Avery, 'Business and Human Rights in a Time of Change' in Menno T Kamminga and Saman Zia-Zarifi (eds), *Liability of Multinational Corporations under International Law* (Kluwer Law International 2000) 27.

[16] See, e.g., *Patrick Mitchell v Democratic Republic of Congo*, ICSID Case No ARB/99/7, Decision on Annulment (1 November 2006) para 33.

can contribute to the development of the state (for example through the construction of transport facilities, houses and energy infrastructure).

It is also true that according to the arbitral jurisprudence contracts infected by corruption are unenforceable. The arbitral tribunal in *World Duty Free Ltd. v. Kenya*[17] found that the claimant had bribed the President of Kenya to obtain a concession agreement and therefore held that this agreement was unenforceable. It dismissed the claimant's claims that Kenya had breached its contractual obligations. Recently, in the award in *Metal-Tech Ltd. v. Republic of Uzbekistan*, the tribunal found that it lacked jurisdiction to hear the parties' claims and counterclaims brought under the Israel-Uzbekistan BIT and Uzbek law due to corruption related to Metal-Tech's investment in Uzbekistan.[18] However, there is no logical link between the absence of democracy and corruption. Corruption is not necessarily connected to undemocratic governments. In most cases, non-democratic governments are corrupt. However, a non-democratic government is not necessarily corrupt. Similarly, a democratic government can be corrupted.

Some BITs provide for an 'in accordance with host State law' clause according to which investments that are in violation of host State law do not enjoy the protection of the BIT in question. It also appears that even without an 'in accordance with host State law' clause, some tribunals do not hesitate to refuse affording protection to investments that are contrary to host State law.[19] It is possible to argue that if host State law provides for a democratic form of government, for example in the constitution, investment contracts concluded by a non-democratic government do not enjoy the protection of the BIT. For example, the Constitution of Libya, in force under Gaddafi, established Libya as 'a democratic independent sovereign State.' This argument, however, could be challenged by the estoppel theory and the principle *nemo auditur propriam turpitudinem*

---

[17] *World Duty Free Co Ltd v Republic of Kenya*, ICSID Case No ARB/00/7, Award (4 October 2006).

[18] *Metal-Tech Ltd v Republic of Uzbekistan*, ICSID Case No ARB/10/3, Award (4 October 2013). See also *Niko Resources (Bangladesh) Ltd v People's Republic of Bangladesh, Bangladesh Petroleum Exploration & Production Company Limited ('Bapex'), Bangladesh Oil Gas and Mineral Corporation ('Petrobangla')*, ICSID Case No ARB/10/11 and ICSID Case No ARB/10/18, Decision on Jurisdiction (19 August 2013) paras 433–7. The Tribunal pointed out that '[it] accepts without further development that the prohibition of bribery forms part of international public policy'.

[19] *Plama Consortium Ltd v Republic of Bulgaria*, ICSID Case No ARB/03/24, Award (27 August 2008) paras 139–140, *Phoenix Action, Ltd v Czech Republic*, ICSID Case No ARB/06/5, Award (15 April 2009) para 106.

allegans (no one is heard when alleging one's own wrong). A host State that endorsed the investment in question, should be estopped from raising the argument of illegality because of the violation of the democratic principle. This issue also raises the problem of definition of democracy. Does democracy presuppose a multi-party system? What is the definition of democracy in countries like Libya under the Gaddafi regime or in Tunisia while Ben Ali was in power? Different forms of democracy are possible. Democracy could mean everything and, therefore, mean nothing.[20]

Finally, some new BITs make reference to corporate social responsibility standards. Canadian BITs contain a new article entitled 'Corporate Social Responsibility' that provides

> Each Party should encourage enterprises operating within its territory or subject to its jurisdiction to voluntarily incorporate internationally recognized standards of corporate social responsibility in their practices and internal policies, such as statements of principle that have been endorsed or are supported by the Parties. These principles address issues such as labour, the environment, human rights, community relations and anti-corruption.[21]

It is important to observe that the obligation to incorporate corporate social responsibility standards is directed to the contracting States and not to the foreign investor. Besides, it is only a best effort obligation. Further, no known international corporate social responsibility code prohibits investments in non-democratic countries. For example, the Organisation of Economic Cooperation and Development Guidelines for Multinational Enterprises recommend that the investor '[a]bstain[s] from any improper involvement in local political activities.'[22]

Therefore, the Guidelines prevent improper interference in the internal affairs of countries where multinational enterprises operate. But there is no prohibition of investing in a non-democratic country. In 2000, a

---

20 Susan Marks, 'International Law, Democracy and the End of History' in Gregory H Fox and Brad R Rot (eds), *Democratic Governance and International Law* (CUP 2000) 532. On this issue see Stephan W Schill, 'Illegal Investments in Investment Treaty Arbitration' (2012) 11 LPICT 281–323.

21 See, e.g., Free Trade Agreement between Canada and the Republic of Colombia (signed 21 November 2008, entered into force 15 August 2011) ch 8, art 816 <http://wits.worldbank.org/GPTAD/PDF/archive/canada-columbia.pdf> accessed 30 January 2015.

22 OECD, *Guidelines for Multinational Enterprises* (OECD 2011) <http://mneguidelines.oecd.org/2011GeneralPolicies.pdf> accessed 1 January 2014.

change to the text of the OECD Guidelines provided that 'enterprises should take fully into account established policies in the countries in which they operate, and consider the views of other stakeholders.'[23] This modification suggests that foreign investors must respect the political orientations, even if non-democratic, of the State in which they invest.[24]

B. The Practice of International Financial Institutions

A few regional financial institutions, such as the European Bank for Reconstruction and Development (EBRD), take into consideration democratic principles when they conduct their activities. The EBRD is a regional financial institution that supports projects in over 30 countries, from Eastern Europe to Central Asia and the Southern and Eastern Mediterranean.[25] The Bank promotes entrepreneurship and fosters transition towards open and democratic market economies. The Bank provides financing for industries and businesses, both new ventures and investments in existing companies. The mandate of the EBRD stipulates that it must only work in countries that are committed to democratic principles.[26] The preamble of the EBRD Agreement[27] provides that '[t]he contracting parties, committed to the fundamental principles of multiparty democracy, the rule of law, respect for human rights and market economics.'

Article 1 of the EBRD Agreement states:

> In contributing to economic progress and reconstruction, the purpose of the Bank shall be to foster the transition towards open market-oriented economies and to promote private and entrepreneurial initiative in the Central and Eastern European countries committed to and applying the principles of multiparty democracy, pluralism and market economics.

---

23 OECD, *Guidelines for Multinational Enterprises* (OECD 2000) 19.

24 John M Kline, 'Political Activities by Transnational Corporations: Bright Lines Versus Grey Boundaries' (2003) 12 *Transnational Corporations* 1–25.

25 See on the EBRD <http://www.ebrd.com/pages/about/faq.shtml> accessed 1 April 2014.

26 EBRD, 'Political Aspects of the Mandate of the European Bank for Reconstruction and Development' <http://www.ebrd.com/downloads/about/aspects.pdf> accessed 1 April 2014.

27 Agreement Establishing the European Bank for Reconstruction and Development (signed 29 May 1990, entered into force 28 March 1991, last modified September 2013) in EBRD, 'Basic Documents of the European Bank for Reconstruction and Development' (September 2013) 3 <http://www.ebrd.com/downloads/research/guides/basics.pdf> accessed 1 April 2014.

However, international financial institutions, including the International Monetary Fund (IMF) and the International Bank for Reconstruction and Development (IBRD or World Bank), do not take into consideration the existence of democratic values in the countries in which they conduct their activities. The IMF and the World Bank, when lending money, have not considered whether it was for a democratic government or a dictator. They simply lend to the government that is in political power at the time.[28] International financial institutions are required to base their decisions exclusively on economic considerations in the conduct of their operations regardless of the democratic regime of the State. The primary mission of such institutions is to help the people, regardless of the political system. The World Bank lends to some countries that do not have democratic political systems, or have poor human rights records.[29] It was asserted that good governance, in the narrower (World Bank) sense, could exist even in non-democratic regimes.[30] This approach led to the adoption of three almost identical provisions in the Articles of Agreement of the IBRD,[31] the IFC,[32] the IDA[33] and MIGA,[34] which was meant to

---

[28] Meena Krishnamurthy, 'International Financial Institutions' in Darrel Moellendorf and Heather Widdows (eds), *Acumen Handbook on Global Ethics* (Acumen 2014) 2 <http://home.cc.umanitoba.ca/~krishna1/resources/KrishnamurthyIntlFinancialInstitutions.pdf> accessed 1 January 2014.

[29] See World Bank, 'Projects & Lending' (2012) <http://web.worldbank.org/WBSITE/EXTERNAL/EXTSITETOOLS/0,,contentMDK:20264002~menuPK:534379~pagePK:98400~piPK:98424~theSitePK:95474,00.html> accessed 1 January 2014 ('Why does the Bank lend to some countries that do not have democratic political systems, or have poor human rights records? Our primary mission is to help the poorest people of the world, regardless of the political system in a country. In some cases, our involvement can encourage a government to consult more widely and recognize the problems of its citizens in ways it perhaps would not otherwise have done.').

[30] SWR de A Samarasinghe, 'Series on Democracy and Health Democracy and Democratization in Developing Countries' (American University & Institute for International Research Washington, DC and International Centre for Ethnic Studies Kandy, Sri Lanka, July 1994) 18 <http://www.hsph.harvard.edu/ihsg/publications/pdf/No-7-1.PDF> accessed 1 January 2014.

[31] IBRD Articles of Agreement (1944), art IV, s 10 and art III, s 5(b) <http://siteresources.worldbank.org/EXTABOUTUS/Resources/ibrd-articlesofagreement.pdf> accessed 1 January 2014.

[32] IFC Articles of Agreement (2012), art V <http://www.ifc.org/wps/wcm/connect/1c95b500484cb68d9f3dbf5f4fc3f18b/IFC_Articles_of_Agreement.pdf?MOD=AJPERES> accessed 1 January 2014.

[33] IDA <http://www.worldbank.org/ida/articles-agreement/IDA-articles-of-agreement.pdf> accessed 1 January 2014.

insulate these institutions from political intervention of their Member States and to prohibit them from taking democratic considerations into account in the conduct of their operations.[35] For example, Article IV, Sect. 10 titled 'Political Activity Prohibited' of the IBRD Agreement of 1944 provides that

> [t]he Bank and its officers shall not interfere in the political affairs of any member; nor shall they be influenced in their decisions by the political character of the member or members concerned. Only economic considerations shall be relevant to their decisions, and these considerations shall be weighed impartially in order to achieve the purposes stated in Article I.

Similarly, Article III, Section 5(b) of the IBRD Agreement restricts political considerations in Bank financing. It sets out that

> (b) [t]he Bank shall make arrangements to ensure that the proceeds of any loan are used only for the purposes for which the loan was granted, with due attention to considerations of economy and efficiency and without regard to political or other non-economic influences or considerations.

With respect to the identical provisions of the Articles of Agreement of the IBRD and the IFC, Shihata explains that 'this means that … the political character of the member is irrelevant for the purposes of the decisions of the institution.'[36] This shows that according to general practice, international economic law has refrained from taking into consideration regarding the democratic form of the State when they conduct their economic activities.

C. The Odious Debt Theory is Controversial

Odious debt or illegitimate debt is a debt incurred by a despotic regime for purposes that do not serve the best interests of the nation. Such debt

---

[34] Convention Establishing the Multilateral Investment Guarantee Agency (MIGA Convention) (adopted 11 October 1985, entered into force 12 April 1988, last modified 14 November 2010) art 34; MIGA Comm (1985) para 60 <http://www.miga.org/whoweare/index.cfm?stid=1788> accessed 1 January 2014.

[35] See on this issue Panayotis M Protopsalis, *Mutilateral Investment Guarantee Agency* (Kluwer Law International 2005) paras 339–41.

[36] Ibrahim FI Shihata, 'The World Bank and "Governance" Issues in its Borrowing Members' in Ibrahim F I Shihata, Franziska Tschofen and Antonio R Parra (eds), *The World Bank in a Changing World: Selected Essays* (Martinus Nijhoff 1991) 66.

should be, according to some authors, not enforceable. An analogy could be established between odious debt and contract concluded by despots. Like odious debt, contracts concluded with undemocratic regimes do not serve the interest of the nation; it is therefore possible to argue that they are not protected by international investment law.

The doctrine of odious debt was formalized in a 1927 treatise by Alexander Nahum Sack, a Russian professor of international law at the University of Petrograd. According to him,

> [w]hen a despotic regime contracts a debt, not for the needs or in the interests of the state, but rather to strengthen itself, to suppress a popular insurrection, etc, this debt is odious for the people of the entire state. This debt does not bind the nation; it is a debt of the regime, a personal debt contracted by the ruler, and consequently it falls with the demise of the regime.[37]

In the same vein, it is possible to assert that contracts concluded between foreign investors and despotic regimes do not take into consideration the needs or the interests of the people. Such contracts strengthen the despotic regime and help it to repress the population that fights against it, this contract is thus odious for the population of the State. The investor may not participate directly to repress the population. However, by paying taxes and other fees, he strengthens the despot and gives him the means necessary to retain power. Taxes and other fees paid by foreign investors give the non-democratic regime resources to finance police, dictatorship control authorities, secret services activities and to commit hostile acts against the population.

The legal status of the odious debt theory, however, is uncertain. In a number of situations, tribunals and States have rejected claims to adjust or sever debt obligations based on considerations of 'odiousness'. The international rules concerning State succession refuse to question the principle of continuity in relation to agreements for odious debts. Instead,

---

[37] 'Si un pouvoir despotique contracte une dette non pas pour les besoins et dans les intérêts de l'État, mais pour fortifier son régime despotique, pour réprimer la population qui le combat, etc, cette dette est odieuse pour la population de l'Etat entier. Cette dette n'est pas obligatoire pour la nation; c'est une dette de régime, dette personnelle du pouvoir qui l'a contractée, par conséquent elle tombe avec la chute de ce pouvoir', Alexander N Sack, *Les effets des transformations des Etats sur leurs dettes publiques et autres obligations financières: Traité juridique et financier* (Recueil Sirey 1927) 146 <http://cadtm.org/IMG/pdf/Alexander_Sack_DETTE_ODIEUSE.pdf> accessed 1 January 2014; see on this issue Sabine Michalowski, *Unconstitutional Regimes and the Validity of Sovereign Debt: A Legal Perspective* (Ashgate 2007) 41.

the continuity of debts, contracted on behalf of the State, is a well-established principle.[38]

The legal systems of many countries may well have concepts such as 'clean hands'[39] or 'cause illicite ou immorale', and the notion that contracts related to illegal purposes are invalid. Similarly, in international law, it was argued that a claimant's claims may be barred due to its illegal conduct in relation to the claims brought.[40]

However, it is difficult to authorize a State to oppose to the foreign investor a wrong (here: the conclusion of the contract) that it participated in committing. As the arbitral tribunal in *Inceysa v. El Salvador* observed: '[n]o legal system based on rational grounds allows the party that committed a chain of clearly illegal acts to benefit from them.'[41] A State that concludes a contract with a foreign investor cannot argue that such conduct is not clean. The State that seeks equitable relief must itself not be guilty of some form of misconduct or dubious practices.[42] Besides, it was observed that historical application of the clean hands doctrine has been inconsistent, and as such, inconclusive[43] and that some international tribunals are reluctant to apply the clean hands doctrine.[44] Finally, the ILC Articles on State Responsibility do not contain a provision on the clean hands doctrine.[45]

---

38 See Robert Howse, 'The Concept of Odious Debt in Public International Law', UNCTAD Discussion Paper (July 2007) <http://unctad.org/en/docs/osgdp20074_en.pdf> accessed 1 January 2014.

39 See on clean hand in domestic laws Ori J Herstein, 'A Normative Theory of the Clean Hands Defense', Cornell Law Faculty Publications Paper 210 (2011) <http://scholarship.law.cornell.edu/facpub/210> accessed 1 January 2014.

40 Rahim Moloo, 'A Comment on the Clean Hands Doctrine in International Law' (2011) 1 TDM 1.

41 *Inceysa Vallisoletana, S I v Republic of El Salvador*, ICSID Case No ARB/03/26, Award (2 August 2006) para 195.

42 *Niko Resources v Bangladesh* (n 18) paras 479–80. The Tribunal pointed out that the clean hand doctrine requires some form of reciprocity. Quoting the Individual Opinion of Hudson in the Diversion of Water from the Meuse case, the Tribunal observed that the Claimant could not blame the Defendant for an illegal act if this Claimant was making a similar act.

43 Moloo (n 40) 10.

44 Aleksandr Shapovalov, 'Should a Requirement of "Clean Hands" be a Prerequisite to the Exercise of Diplomatic Protection? Human Rights Implications of the International Law Commission's Debate' (2005) 20 *American University International Law Review* 842.

45 See James Crawford, 'Second Report on State Responsibility' (1999) 2(2) YBILC 83 (concluding, in quoting Charles Rousseau, *Droit international public*,

The application of the clean hands doctrine or odious debt or equivalent doctrines and theories may have far-reaching consequences for the population. Even if concluded with non-democratic regimes, investment contracts could contribute to the development of the country, generate revenues for the population, expand employment opportunities and improve income distribution, transfer knowledge and skills and ameliorate infrastructure and the environment of the host country. Arguing that such a contract with an undemocratic government is illegal will deprive the population of such benefits and increase its misery. For the same reasons, it is difficult to assert that a contract concluded with a despot that has positive impact on the population is in conflict with the transnational public policy.

III. THE EXCEPTION: THE EMERGING CONSIDERATION OF DEMOCRACY IN SOME INVESTMENT LAW INSTRUMENTS

Few authors have considered that an investment agreement made with an undemocratic regime that is universally condemned cannot be binding on a legitimate government which succeeds it. Sornarajah has argued that a norm of democratic governance has emerged in modern international law. He observed that the *Urenco Case*[46] provides a basis for this opinion, even if the claim was later withdrawn. He concluded that an investment agreement made with a regime that is universally condemned cannot be binding on a legitimate government which succeeds it. The foreign investor fishes in troubled waters in concluding agreements with such states.[47]

Sornarajah has not further developed arguments to support his conclusion on the non-binding character of contracts concluded by undemocratic regimes. Two new arguments could essentially be added to illustrate the existence of exceptions to the principle according to which contracts concluded by despots must be honored. First, contracts with

---

vol V: les rapports conflictuels (Siery 1983) 170), that 'it is not possible to consider the "clean hands" theory as an institution of general customary law').

[46] The case was brought before Dutch courts to test the validity of some contracts concluded by Dutch companies. The case was withdrawn after the independence of Namibia. On this case see Caleb M Pilgrim, 'Some Legal Aspects of Trade in the Natural Resources of Namibia' (1994) 61 BYIL 249.

[47] M Sornarajah, *The International Law on Foreign Investment* (3rd edn, CUP 2010) 470–71.

non-democratic regimes are immoral; and some regional investment treaties require that the investor behave in a moral manner (A.). Second, some BITs now make reference to democracy (B.). These instruments illustrate a new evolution and demonstrate an emerging trend that takes into consideration democratic values in investment law.

A. Contracts with Non-Democratic Regimes Are Immoral

The question of the protection of contracts concluded by undemocratic countries arises in the Arabic region after the Arab Spring. The two probably most important agreements, which both date back to the 1980s, have not been used very frequently in the past. The majority of investors from Arab States and Islamic States and even the legal community in these countries and elsewhere were not aware of the existence of these treaties. This may be partly due to the fact that the literature and many official documents relating to these agreements are available only in Arabic.

The first agreement is the Agreement on Promotion, Protection and Guarantee of Investments among Member States of the Organization of the Islamic Cooperation (OIC), which was approved and opened for signature on 1–5 June 1981 and entered into force five years later on 23 September 1986.[48] This agreement is the first multilateral agreement that provides foreign investors with the right to initiate arbitration against their host country, many years before the creation of the North American Free Trade Agreement or the Energy Charter Treaty. Article 17 of the Agreement offers resort to arbitration:

> 2. Arbitration. If the two parties to the dispute do not reach an agreement as a result of their resort to conciliation, or if the conciliator is unable to issue his report within the prescribed period, or if the two parties do not accept the solutions proposed therein, then each party has the right to resort to the Arbitration Tribunal for a final decision on the dispute.[49]

The Agreement was signed and/or ratified by numerous Arab countries, including Egypt, Libya, Morocco, Tunisia and Yemen.[50]

---

48 Available at <http://www.comcec.org/TR_YE/Yeni_Site_Dokumanlar/Agreements/APPGI.pdf> accessed 1 January 2014.

49 On this agreement see Walid Ben Hamida, 'A Fabulous Discovery: The Arbitration Offer under the Organization of Islamic Cooperation Agreement Related to Investment' (2013) 30 *Journal of International Arbitration* 637–6.

50 See the ratifications and the signatories of the OIC Agreement <www.oic-oci.org/english/ convenion/Accords_Eng_31_01.pdf> accessed 1 April 2014.

The other not very known agreement is the Unified Agreement for the Investment of Arab Capital in the Arab States, which was signed on 26 November 1980 and entered into force on 7 September 1981.[51] This Agreement establishes the Arab Investment Court, which is open to States and investors. In 2003, the Saudi company *Tanmiah* decided to sue the Tunisian government to settle an investment dispute under the 1980 Arab Agreement of Investment. The Court confirmed its jurisdiction and rendered its first decision on 12 October 2004.[52] Until now, the Court issued five decisions relating to disputes opposing Arab investors to Arab States.[53] Many cases are pending before it. During the 3rd Arab Economic and Social Development Summit organized in Riyadh on 21–22 January 2013, the Arab leaders decided to amend certain provisions of this agreement. The entry into force of the new agreement of 2013 requires ratification by five contracting States.[54]

With the recent developments in the Arab region and the revolutions that swept across Egypt, Tunisia, Libya and Yemen, these regional investment protection agreements are set to attract even more attention. In particular, since in many Arab countries post-revolution governments revoked investment contracts made by the former regimes, foreign investors are exploring legal options, many of these cases are related to the protection under these regional agreement of contracts that were concluded by formerly undemocratic countries.

One of the specificities of the OIC Agreement of 1981 and the Arab Agreement of 1980 is that they adopt a balanced approach that takes into consideration both the interests of the State and the investor.

In contrast with a large number of investment agreements, the Arab Investment Agreement of 1980 provides some obligations that investors must observe. First, the investor must, as far as possible, coordinate with the host State and its various institutions and authorities. Second, the Arab investor must respect the laws and regulations of the State that are

---

[51] Available at <http://unctad.org/Sections/dite/iia/docs/compendium/en/36%20volume%202.pdf> accessed 1 January 2014.

[52] Walid Ben Hamida, 'The First Arab Investment Court Decision' (2006) 7 JWIT 699–721.

[53] See Walid Ben Hamida, 'The Development of the Arab Investment Court Jurisprudence: New Decisions of the Arab Investment Court Rendered' (2014) 6 *International Journal of Arab Arbitration* 3–18.

[54] Until now the process of ratification was engaged in Morocco <http://arabic.arabianbusiness.com/politics-economics/2013/nov/29/348170/#.UsqJ-dLuIQc> accessed 1 January 2014, and in the United Arab Emirates <http://www.mubasher.info/CASE/news/> accessed 1 January 2014.

'consistent with this Agreement.' Third, in establishing, administering and developing Arab investment projects, every investor must comply with the host's State development plans and its national development programmes. The investor must also employ all means which reinforce the structure of the host State and enhance Arab economic integration. Finally, the Arab investor shall refrain from any action which might violate public order and morality or involve illegitimate gains. Indeed, according to Article 14

> 1. [i]n the various aspects of his activity, the Arab investor must, as far as possible, liaise with the State in which the investment is made and with its various institutions and authorities. He must respect its laws and regulations in a manner consistent with this Agreement and, in establishing, administering and developing Arab investment projects, must comply with the development plans and programmes drawn up by the State for the purpose of national economic development by employing all means which reinforce its structure and promote Arab economic integration. In so doing, he shall refrain from any action which might violate public order and morality or involve illegitimate gains.
> 2. The Arab investor shall bear liability for any breach of the obligations set forth in the preceding paragraph in accordance with the law in force in the State in which the investment is made or in which the breach occurs.[55]

In the same vein, according to Article 9 of the OIC agreement of 1981,

> the Investor shall be bound by the laws and regulations in force in the host state and shall refrain from all acts that may disturb public order or morals or that may be prejudicial to the public interest. He is also to refrain from exercising restrictive practices and from trying to achieve gains through unlawful means.

The reference found in the two agreements to moral behaviors by foreign investor and the respect of public interest could support the fact that contracts concluded by undemocratic governments are immoral and, therefore, are not protected by the two regional investment agreements. However, according to the investors, contracting with an undemocratic regime is not *per se* immoral. Even when concluded with despots, such

---

[55] The Amended Arab Investment Agreement of 2013 did not provide for the obligation Arab investors to refrain from any action that might violate public order and morality or involve illegitimate gains. This Amended agreement is not yet entered into force, see the critique of Hamed El-Kady, 'The Amendments to the 1980 Arab League Investment Agreement: Implications on the Right to Regulate Investment in Arab Countries' (2014) 11 TDM 3.

contracts contributed to the development of the State and improved the living conditions of the population.

(Im)morality of contracts concluded between foreign investors and States will certainly be discussed before the Arab Investment Court and the international arbitral tribunal established under the OIC agreement in the forthcoming days. Many cases submitted before the Court and these tribunals are related to the revocation of contracts concluded between investor and the former non democratic regimes.

B. Reference to Democracy in Some International Treaties

Even if investment treaties do not make reference to democracy, democratic principles could be taken into consideration in certain situations.[56] The Cotonou Partnership Agreement concluded in June 2000[57] is the most comprehensive partnership agreement between 79 developing countries from Africa, the Caribbean and the Pacific (ACP) and the European Union (EU). Article 1 of this agreement sets out the objective of the partnership. It provides that

> [t]he Community and its Member States, of the one part, and the ACP States, of the other part, hereinafter referred to as the 'Parties' hereby conclude this Agreement in order to promote and expedite the economic, cultural and social development of the ACP States, with a view to contributing to peace and security and to promoting a stable and democratic political environment.

The reference to 'democratic political environment' could be taken into consideration when interpreting provisions of BITs concluded between European countries and ACP countries. Indeed, the Cotonou Agreement contains an Article 78 entitled 'Investment protection' that provides that

---

[56] There is a reference to democracy in the preamble of the Norway Draft Model on BITs of December 2007. The preamble of this model provides: 'Reaffirming their commitment to democracy, the rule of law, human rights and fundamental freedoms in accordance with their obligations under international law, including the principles set out in the United Nations Charter and the Universal Declaration of Human Rights.' This model wasn't adopted.

[57] Partnership Agreement between the Members of the African, Caribbean and Pacific Group of States of the one part, and the European Community and its Member States, of the other part, signed in Cotonou on 23 June 2000 (Cotonou Agreement) (signed 23 June 2000, entered into force 1 April 2003) OJ L 317 (15 December 2000).

> 1. [t]he ACP States and the Community and its Member States, within the scope of their respective competencies, affirm the need to promote and protect either Party's investments on their respective territories, and in this context affirm the importance of concluding, in their mutual interest, investment promotion and protection agreements which could also provide the basis for insurance and guarantee schemes.

Therefore, it is possible to establish a link between democracy as it is referred to in the Preamble of the Cotonou Agreement and the different BITs concluded between European and ACP countries. In fact, the Cotonou Agreement establishes a general framework for a broad range of areas of cooperation, including investment. Hence, the interpretation of investment promotion and protection agreements must take into consideration the democratic environment set out in the Agreement's Article 1.

Similarly, the 2002 EU-Chile Free Trade Agreement[58] makes reference in its Preamble to the Parties' 'full commitment to the respect for democratic principles and fundamental human rights as set out in the United Nations Universal Declaration of Human Rights; – their attachment to the principles of the rule of law and of good governance.'

Article 1 of the same agreement provides that

> 1. [r]espect for democratic principles and fundamental human rights as laid down in the United Nations Universal Declaration of Human Rights and for the principle of the rule of law underpins the internal and international policies of the Parties and constitutes an essential element of this Agreement.
> 2. The promotion of sustainable economic and social development and the equitable distribution of the benefits of the Association are guiding principles for the implementation of this Agreement.

Like the Cotonou Agreement, the EU-Chile FTA makes reference to international investment treaties, even if it is formulated differently. Article 134 provides that

> 2. [w]ith the objective of progressive liberalisation of investment conditions, the Parties affirm their commitment to review the investment legal framework, the investment environment and the flow of investment between them consistent with their commitments in international investment agreements, no later than three years after the entry into force of this Agreement.

---

58 Agreement Establishing an Association between the European Community and the Republic of Chile (signed 18 November 2002, entered into force 1 March 2005) OJ L 352 (30 December 2002).

Principles of treaty interpretation, especially the principle set out in Article 31(3)(a) of the Vienna Convention on the Law of Treaties according to which the interpretation of a treaty shall take into account any subsequent agreement between the parties regarding the interpretation of the treaty or the application of its provisions, reinforces the link between large scope economic treaties and linked sectorial treaties, such as those related to investment. If provided in subsequent treaties, democratic principles could be taken into consideration when interpreting an investment treaty.

Finally, it is important to note that following the entry into force of the Treaty of Lisbon, foreign direct investment is included in the list of matters falling under the common commercial policy. Art. 205 of the Treaty on the Functioning of the European Union (TFEU) states that the common commercial policy should be guided by the general principles of the EU's external action, including the promotion of democracy, the rule of law, the furtherance of the respect of human rights and contribute to sustainable economic, social and environmental development of developing countries. Since investment is now part of the EU's common commercial policy, the EU may include in its investment treaties a reference to democratic values and impose the respect of democratic principles. The European Commission outlined its approach for the EU's future investment policy in its Communication 'Towards a comprehensive European international investment policy' in 2010.[59] While the Communication refers to many principles, it did not contain any explicit reference to democracy. According to the Commission, 'a common investment policy should also be guided by the principles and objectives of the Union's external action more generally, including the promotion of the rule of law, human rights and sustainable development (Article 205 TFEU and Article 21 TEU).'

Even if the Commission did not mention democracy, we should wait for the conclusion of the first investment agreement by the EU. Such an agreement could make reference to the promotion of democracy considered, without any doubt, as a general principle of the EU's external action.

---

[59] European Commission, 'Communication from the Commission to the Council, the European Parliament, the European Economic and Social Committee and the Committee of Regions: Towards a Comprehensive European International Investment Policy' COM(2010)343 final (Brussels, 7 July 2010) <http://trade.ec.europa.eu/doclib/docs/2011/may/tradoc_147884.pdf> accessed 1 January 2014.

IV. CONCLUSION

International investment law does not authorize investors or States not to honor a contract concluded by an undemocratic regime. This principle is confirmed by the rule of law and by practice. However, there is a new trend in some investment agreements to take into consideration new values of morality and democracy. This new trend finds some support before arbitral tribunals. Jonathan Bonnitcha has pointed out in his chapter that there are lines of jurisprudence that suggest that economy-wide legal and policy changes introduced by an incoming democratic regime would not, ordinarily, breach an investment treaty.[60] Until now, this new trend is modest and limited. But it is important and needs to be stressed. The near future will indicate if this new trend towards more values in investment law will be confirmed to reverse the principle of validity of contracts concluded by undemocratic regimes or if the principle will resist and remain. Investment law is at a crossroads, or as we say in French 'à *la croisé des chemins*'. Investment law is in a transitional situation.

60 Bonnitcha (n 9) 293–297, 302.

PART IV

Development and social inclusion

12. The international mandate for development: Building compliant investment within the state's development decision-making processes

Diane A. Desierto

... development stands for the development of human beings and not for the development of countries, the production of things, their distribution within social systems or the transformation of social structures. These may be the means towards the end but they should not be confused with the end, which is that of developing the entire human being and all human beings.[1]

Development consists of the removal of various types of unfreedoms that leave people with little choice and little opportunity of exercising their reasoned agency.[2]

I. A 'VENN DIAGRAM' OVERLAP: POSTULATING INVESTMENT AND DEVELOPMENT RULES

Is investment separable from development? Discourses about the legal regimes governing development and investment often approach both concepts either from a historiographical trajectory leading towards some convergence,[3] from descriptions of an ongoing polar divide illustrated by

[1] Jagdish Narain Saxena, 'Uprooted People and Development' in Subrata Roy Chowdhury, Erik M G Denters, Paul J I M De Waart (eds), *The Right to Development in International Law* (Martinus Nijhoff 1992) 179.

[2] Amartya Sen, *Development as Freedom* (Random House LLC 2011) xii.

[3] See Yannick Radi, 'International Investment Law and Development: A History of Two Concepts', in this volume, 69; Anna Joubin-Bret, Marie-Estelle Rey and Jörg Weber, 'International Investment Law and Development' in Marie-Claire Cordonier Segger, Markus W Gehring and Andrew Newcombe

certain investor-State arbitral awards,[4] or from the incipient efforts to rewrite international investment agreements towards a 'rebalancing'[5] interests that guarantee policy space for governments to pursue development targets through the design of legislation and administrative regulations.[6] These approaches presuppose some incompatibility, conceptual ambiguity, competing rival ideologies, or teleological disharmony when States plan and operationalize international investment transactions and projects as part of their national development goals and strategies.[7] Indeed, discursive positions on this question often oscillate within the binary of 'defenders' and 'abolitionists' of international investment law – between those who stress the essential importance of foreign investment for achieving economic growth and the State's overall development,[8] and those who argue that the international investment legal system is devoid of any possibilities for reform because of inherent defects creating

(eds), *Sustainable Development in World Investment Law* (Kluwer Law International 2011) 15.

[4] See Diane A Desierto, 'Development as an International Right: Investment in the New Trade-Based IIAs' (2011) 3(2) *Trade, Law and Development* 296; Diane A Desierto, 'Deciding IIA Applicability: The Development Argument in Investment' in Freya Baetens (ed.), *Investment Law within International Law: Integrationist Perspectives* (CUP 2013) ch 11.

[5] See Karl P Sauvant, 'Foreign Direct Investment for Development: The United Nations Code of Conduct and the Search for Balance in International Investment Rules' in Todd Weiler and Freya Baetens (eds), *New Directions in International Economic Law: In Memoriam Thomas Wälde* (Martinus Nijhoff 2011) 179.

[6] See UNCTAD, *Investment Policy Framework for Sustainable Development* (United Nations 2012) 36–64 <http://unctad.org/en/PublicationsLibrary/webdiaepcb2012d6_en.pdf> accessed 18 August 2014.

[7] See Daniel D Bradlow, 'Development Decision-Making and the Content of International Development Law' (2004) 27(2) *Boston College Law Review* 195; see Stephen Marks, 'The Human Right to Development: Between Rhetoric and Reality' (2004) 17 *Harvard Human Rights Law Journal* 137; Isabella D Bunn, 'The Right to Development: Implications for International Economic Law' (2000) 15(6) *American University International Law Review* 1425, 1442.

[8] See Liesbeth Colen, Miet Maertens and Johan Swinnen, 'Foreign Direct Investment as an Engine for Economic Growth and Human Development: A Review of the Arguments and Empirical Evidence' in Olivier De Schutter, Johan Swinnen and Jan Wouters (eds), *Foreign Direct Investment and Human Development: The Law and Economics of International Investment Agreements* (Routledge 2013) 70, 114.

prohibitive obstacles for the State against feasibly accomplishing development objectives.[9] As with any complex question traversing law and authoritative decision-making (and which requires one to engage various intellectual disciplines and analytical tools examining social phenomena[10]), however, the question of the actual nature of the relationship between the legal regimes governing investment and development will not always yield a linear answer in all cases.

Part of the quandary lies with the fluid notion of the concept of development as an international right articulated in the 1986 United Nations Declaration on the Right to Development [hereafter, 'the Declaration'].[11] Article 1(1) of the Declaration sets forth a rather tautological definition:

> 1. The right to development is an inalienable human right by virtue of which every human person and all peoples entitled to participate in, contribute to, and enjoy *economic, social, cultural, and political development,* in which all human rights and fundamental freedoms can be fully realized.[12]

The definition then goes on to specify other rights included within the right to development by implication:

> 2. The human right to development *also implies the full realization of the right of the peoples to self-determination*, which includes, subject to the relevant provisions of both International Covenants on Human Rights, the exercise of their inalienable right to full sovereignty over all their natural wealth and resources.[13]

As opposed to other identifiable rights within the major human rights treaties, the right to development under the Declaration contains an inherent overlap with all other human rights.[14] This has certainly not lent

---

9 See 'Public Statement on the International Investment Regime' (Osgoode Hall Law School of York University, Toronto, Canada, 31 August 2010) <issuu.com/embajadaecuusa/docs/public_statement__final___dec_2013_> accessed 18 August 2014.

10 W Michael Reisman, 'The View from the New Haven School of International Law' (1992) 86 ASIL Proceedings 118, 120.

11 Declaration on the Right to Development, UNGA Res 41/128 (4 December 1986) UN Doc A/RES/41/128 <http://www.un.org/documents/ga/res/41/a41r128.htm> accessed 18 August 2014.

12 Declaration (n 11) art 1, para 1 (emphasis added).

13 Ibid art 1, para 2 (emphasis added).

14 See Philip Alston, 'Making Space for New Human Rights: The Case of the Right to Development' (1988) 1 *Harvard Human Rights Yearbook* 3, 21, 32.

more clarity to the right and its implementation. The textual analysis offered by Arjun Sengupta, the UN's first independent expert on the right to development, interpreted the right to development not as an end value, but as the individual entitlement to a means or a *process* of achieving certain desired human outcomes, such process being governed by specific principles elaborated further in the subsequent sections of the Declaration:[15]

> The right to development refers to *a process of development* which leads to the realization of each human right and of all of them together and which has to be carried out in a manner known as *rights-based, in accordance with the international human rights standards, as a participatory, non-discriminatory, accountable and transparent* process with *equity in decision-making and sharing of the fruits of the process* ...[16]

The contested content of the right to development,[17] along with its debatable provenance from a UN General Assembly declaration,[18] rather than from express formulation in any of the binding major human rights treaties,[19] certainly makes it unsurprising that widespread State recognition of the right to development has proven elusive thus far.[20] As far back as the 1979 Hague Academy of International Law Colloquium on the right to development at an international level, Philip Alston already anticipated many of the pivotal criticisms against recognizing a right to development:

---

[15] Arjun Sengupta, 'Right to Development as a Human Right' (2001) 36(27) *Economic and Political Weekly* 2527, 2528–9.

[16] Arjun Sengupta, 'On The Theory and Practice of the Right to Development' (2002) 24(4) *Human Rights Quarterly* 837, 846 (emphasis added).

[17] See Anja Lindroos, *The Right to Development* (University of Helsinki 1999) 43; Qerim Qerimi, *Development in International Law: A Policy-Oriented Inquiry* (Martinus Nijhoff 2012) 26–7; Arne Vandenbogaerde, 'The Right to Development in International Human Rights Law' (2013) 31(2) *Netherlands Quarterly of Human Rights* 187.

[18] See Philip Alston, 'Conjuring Up New Human Rights: A Proposal for Quality Control' (1984) 78(3) AJIL 607, 612.

[19] See Isabella D Bunn, *The Right to Development and International Economic Law: Legal and Moral Dimensions* (Hart 2012) 31–57.

[20] Felix Kirchmeier, 'The Right to Development – Where Do We Stand? State of the Debate on the Right to Development' (Dialogue on Globalization, Friedrich-Ebert-Stiftung, Occasional Papers No 23, July 2006) 13–15 <http://www.fes-globalization.org/publicationsGeneva/FESOccPapers23.pdf> accessed 18 August 2014.

a) None of the studies undertaken to date has conclusively established the existence of a right to development …
b) The international community has not agreed in any specific legal instrument that the right exists, and it therefore does not …
c) Recognition of the right to development constitutes an admission that existing human rights guarantees are inadequate and thus challenges a consensus which took 20 years to achieve …
d) If the right to development is essentially a synthesis of existing rights it serves no new purpose …
e) The right to development will be interpreted as a collective rather than an individual right and could thus be used to justify human rights violations which occur in the course of the quest for development …
f) Millions of people will never realize their right to development and it is thus foolish to posit that it is a right at all.[21]

Notwithstanding the above criticisms, he anchored the significance of recognizing a right to development on three policy reasons. First, he saw the recognition of the right as 'the logical next step in the programme of decolonization … a major turning point in terms of the economic, social, and cultural emancipation of [decolonized] States.'[22]

Second, he argued that the right to development brings a focus to 'the interaction between both human rights and development issues … two fundamental areas of United Nations endeavor which have to date developed as parallel lines',[23] allowing for the direct translation of respect for human rights into the content of national and international development policies. Finally, he stressed that recognition of the right would 'inject a stronger ethical component into analyses of international relations'.[24]

While many of Philip Alston's anticipated institutional, ideological, and interpretive criticisms still resonate today,[25] there are likewise many others who have since concurred with him on the historic, symbolic,

---

21 Philip Alston, 'The Right to Development at the International Level' in René-Jean Dupuy (ed.), *The Right to Development at the International Level* (Sitjhoff & Noordhoff 1980) 99, 106–9.

22 Alston (n 21) 110–11.

23 Ibid 111.

24 Ibid.

25 See among others Srirang Jha, 'A Critique of the Right to Development' (2012) 1(4) *Journal of Politics & Governance* 17; Richard Warren Perry, 'Rethinking the Right to Development: After the Critique of Development, After the Critique of Rights' (1996) 18(2) *Law & Policy* 225; Bunn (n 7) 1434–6; Mesenba Assefa Tadeg, 'Reflections on the Right to Development: Challenges and Prospects' (2010) 10 *African Human Rights Law Journal* 325, 336–9.

ethical value and importance of recognizing a right to development despite ambiguities and implementation difficulties.[26] After over two decades since he first issued his Hague study, however, it is significant that Alston himself expressed some frustration over the protracted debate militating against the full implementation of the right to development:

> the subsequent quarter of a century of debates over the implications of the right to development and how it could make a meaningful practical contribution to the quest to link human rights and development has not produced a great deal. The main results seem to be innumerable speeches, major diplomatic battles over the wording of resolutions, and the creation of a UN expert working group followed by a UN governmental working group, followed by a UN independent expert, followed by a new UN working group. At the end of the day, it is clear that something, at least, is not working.[27]

This chapter does not propose to continue the conceptual debates on the definition and binding scope of the right to development in international law. Rather, I proceed from the perspective of international investment as a particular form of States' economic decision-making,[28] and the right to development as the specific responsibility of States to build in an enabling environment for international human rights protection as part of the State's economic decision-making processes.[29] I thus focus on the practical implementation of this right in States' international investment planning as part of their broader development economic decision-making

---

[26] See Bunn (n 19) 58–82; Wade Mansell and Joanne Scott, 'Why Bother About a Right to Development?' (1994) 21(2) *Journal of Law and Society* 171; Brigitte I Hamm, 'A Human Rights Approach to Development' (2001) 23(4) *Human Rights Quarterly* 1005.

[27] Philip Alston, 'Ships Passing in the Night: The Current State of the Human Rights and Development Debate through the Lens of the Millennium Development Goals' (2005) 27(3) *Human Rights Quarterly* 755, 798.

[28] See Jeswald W Salacuse, 'Making Transnational Law Work through Regime-Building: The Case of International Investment Law' in Pieter HF Bekker, Rudolf Dolzer and Michael Waibel (eds), *Making Transnational Law Work in the Global Economy: Essays in Honour of Detlev Vagts* (CUP 2010) 406, 418.

[29] See Beate Rudolf, 'The Relation of the Right to Development to Existing Substantive Treaty Regimes' in Stephen P Marks (ed.), *Implementing the Right to Development: The Role of International Law* (Friedrich-Ebert-Stiftung 2008) 107 <http://www.fes-globalization.org/geneva/documents/HumanRights/August08_Publication_RtD.pdf> accessed 18 August 2014.

strategies,[30] recognizing that both international investment law and the right to development ultimately entail *processes* of decision of the State's authoritative decision-makers.[31]

When a State determines the acceptable scope of qualitative protection afforded to foreign investments under its bilateral or multilateral investment treaties;[32] the terms of contractual or project commitments it assumes vis-à-vis multinational firms conducting investment operations in its jurisdiction;[33] as well as the prescribed breadth of the State's legislative and administrative rules governing foreign investment;[34] the State is engaged in a process of economic decision-making and governance that has long-term consequences and impacts, not just on its overall macro-economy but more to the point, upon the welfare of the State's constituents.[35] It is this process of decision-making that can be tested and assessed against the rights-based, participatory, transparent and equitable process prescribed under the right to development. Regardless of the debated genealogy and precise scope of the right to development

---

30 Joseph Martial Ribeiro, *International Development Project Appraisal, Execution Planning and Monitoring* (Presses Internationales Polytechnique 2011) 74–81.

31 See Myres S McDougal, 'Law as a Process of Decision: A Policy-Oriented Approach to Legal Study' (1956) 1 *Natural Law Forum* 53, 55–6.

32 See Kenneth J Vandevelde, 'The Political Economy of a Bilateral Investment Treaty' in Fiona Beveridge (ed.), *Globalization and International Investment* (Ashgate 2005) 47, 61, also originally published as (1998) 92 AJIL 621.

33 See Thomas L Brewer, 'Government Policies, Market Imperfections and Foreign Direct Investment' (1993) 24(1) *Journal of International Business Studies* 101; UNCTAD, *State Contracts* (UNCTAD Series on International Investment Agreements, United Nations 2004) 23–30 <http://unctad.org/en/Docs/iteiit200411_en.pdf> accessed 18 August 2014.

34 Jeswald W Salacuse, *The Three Laws of International Investment: National, Contractual, and International Frameworks for Foreign Capital* (OUP 2013) 89–136.

35 See Laixun Zhao, 'The Impact of Foreign Direct Investment on Wages and Employment' (1998) 50(2) *Oxford Economic Papers* 284; John M Rothgeb Jr, 'The Effects of Foreign Investment on Overall and Sectoral Growth in Third World States' (1984) 21(1) *Journal of Peace Research* 5; Kevin Lehnert, Mamoun Benmamoun and Hongxin Zhao, 'FDI Inflow and Human Development: Analysis of FDI's Impact on Host Countries' Social Welfare and Infrastructure' (2013) 55(3) *Thunderbird International Business Review* 285; Theodore H Moran, *Foreign Direct Investment and Development: The New Policy Agenda for Developing Countries and Economies in Transition* (Institute for International Economics 1998) 155–68.

(whether as an individual right or as a composite right spanning all economic, social and cultural rights),[36] there is little doubt that there would be some overlap in the practical consequences arising from the rules postulated by States for international investment, with those postulated for achieving the State's overall development.[37] When States decide to open new frontiers of their economies to foreign investment projects – whether through standard build-operate-transfer contracting, energy and utilities concessions, infrastructure development, portfolio financing activities, or new forms of public-private partnerships[38] – these decisions also impact on how the right to development is realized within their jurisdictions.[39] Testing the mode and manner of State decision-making in international investment transactions from the prism of the right to development would very likely yield polemical Hayekian-Keynesian[40] views on the role of the State in responding to inequality and determining

---

[36] Bunn (n 19) 112–21; Arjun Sengupta, 'Implementing the Right to Development' in Nico J Schrijver and Friedl Weiss (eds), *International Law and Sustainable Development: Principles and Practice* (Martinus Nijhoff 2004) 341, 349.

[37] See Celine Tan, 'Reviving the Emperor's Old Clothes: The Good Governance Agenda, Development and International Investment Law', in this volume, 147; Diane A Desierto, 'Calibrating Human Rights and Investment in Economic Emergencies: Prospects of Treaty and Valuation Defenses' (2012) 9 *Manchester Journal of International Economic Law* 162; also J Saul Lizondo, 'Foreign Direct Investment' in Research Department of the International Monetary Fund, *Determinants and Systemic Consequences of International Capital Flows* (IMF 1991) 68, 79–80.

[38] See Peter Carroll and Peter Steane, 'Public-Private Partnerships' in Stephen P Osborne (ed.), *Public-Private Partnerships: Theory and Practice in International Perspective* (Routledge 2002) 36; Gavin Drewry, 'Public-Private Partnerships: Rethinking the Boundary between Public and Private Law' in Osborne (ed.), ibid 57; Stephen P Osborne and Vic Murray, 'Understanding the Process of Public-Private Partnerships' in Osborne (ed.), ibid 70; Kimberly Evans, 'Foreign Portfolio and Direct Investment' (OECD Global Forum on International Investment: Attracting Foreign Direct Investment for Development, Shanghai, 5–6 December 2002) <http://www.oecd.org/investment/investmentfordevelopment/2764407.pdf> accessed 18 August 2014.

[39] See Olivier De Schutter, Johan Swinnen and Jan Wouters, 'Introduction: Foreign Direct Investment and Development' in De Schutter, Swinnen and Wouters (n 8) 1.

[40] See John Maynard Keynes, *General Theory of Employment, Interest and Money* (Atlantic 2006) 147; Friedrich A Hayek, *The Road To Serfdom* (University of Chicago Press 2009) 133; Mario Seccarecia, 'The Role of Public Investment as a Principal Macroeconomic Tool to Promote Long-Term Growth: Keynes' Legacy' (2012) 40(4) *International Journal of Political Economy* 62.

the accumulation, use, and allocation of capital within and across intra-State and inter-State channels.[41]

One could well explore options for how the right to development could inform and be interwoven into the State's processes of international investment decision-making.[42] Certainly, this decision does not only implicate the conventional sources of international investment law (e.g. international investment agreements such as bilateral or multilateral investment treaties),[43] but also the mass of operational rules covering the investment project, such as the foreign investment contract, interrelated external or international financing components to the prospective investment project, and specifically applicable administrative regulations and national legislation or statutes.[44] From my perspective, the State's international investment decision-making process does not only engage the front end of postulating rules at the time of the establishment of the investment, but also the back end of implementing the State's regulatory decisions for the duration of the investment, well as the defense and calibration of such decisions should investor-State disputes arise.

As rightly pointed out by its progenitors among United Nations experts and international legal scholars,[45] the right to development is an entitlement to a form and process of governance. Part II (Operationalizing the Right to Development as a Governance Process) discusses the right to development through the lens of principles already derived from pre-existing international human rights norms, but which are now specifically

---

41 See Thomas Piketty, *Capital in the Twenty-First Century* (Harvard UP 2014) pts III and IV.

42 See Angelica Bonfanti, 'Applying Corporate Social Responsibility to Foreign Investment: Failures and Prospects' in Tullio Treves, Francesco Seatzu and Seline Trevisanut (eds), *Foreign Investment, International Law and Common Concerns* (Routledge 2014) 230.

43 See J Anthony VanDuzer, Penelope Simons and Graham Mayeda, *Integrating Sustainable Development into International Investment Agreements: A Guide for Developing Country Negotiators* (Commonwealth Secretariat 2013).

44 See Thomas Pollan, *Legal Framework for the Admission of FDI* (Eleven International Publishing 2006) 136–234; Hilmar Raeschke-Kessler and Dorothee Gottwald, 'Corruption' in Peter Muchlinski, Federico Ortino and Christoph Schreuer (eds), *The Oxford Handbook of International Investment Law* (OUP 2008) 584, 600–601.

45 See Tamara Kunanayakam, 'The Declaration on the Right to Development in the Context of United Nations Standard-Setting' in United Nations Office of the High Commissioner for Human Rights, *Realizing the Right to Development: Essays in Commemoration of 25 Years of the United Nations Declaration on the Right to Development* (United Nations 2013) 17.

situated into States' economic decision-making and governance strategies. These principles, I contend, augur a particular form of governance to be intermediated into States' economic decision-making processes, as they would best ensure compliance with international human rights pursuant to their fundamental duties under the UN Charter.[46] Over twenty-five years since the 1986 UN Declaration on the Right to Development, the right has since evolved more identifiably into a prescription for a particular human rights-driven process or mode of economic governance by States. As indicated in a Report of the UN Secretary-General,[47] the duties that flow for States under the right to development include *duties of cooperation* to promote the realization of the right to development, applicable both to State conduct towards people living under their jurisdiction as well as to the conduct in relation with other States, as well as *duties to guarantee meaningful participation* for affected individuals and processes in the development decision-making process.[48]

Part III (Building 'HR-Compliant' Investment in State Development Decisions) proceeds to translate the international duties of cooperation and participation flowing from the right to development into various aspects of the State's investment decision-making processes. I discuss concrete aspects of foreign investment project planning and implementation where these State duties flowing from the right to development could potentially inform the process behind the State's spectrum of decisions on foreign investment – from the design of eligibilities, qualifications, and conditions for foreign investors bidding for the State's investment projects;[49] clauses on cooperation, participation, transparency and human rights-oriented due diligence for the foreign investment contract and related sovereign or international financing contracts;[50] the design of the State's investment promotion and investment monitoring institutions;[51]

---

[46] Charter of the United Nations (adopted on 26 June 1945, entered into force on 24 October 1945) 15 UNCIO 355 (UN Charter) arts 1(3) and 55(c).

[47] Report of the Secretary-General, 'The Emergence of the Right to Development' in UN 2013 Right to Development (n 45) 3, 12–13.

[48] Ibid 14.

[49] Andrew Edkins and Alan Smith, 'Designing the Project' in Terry M Williams and Knut Samset (eds), *Project Governance: Getting Investments Right* (Palgrave Macmillan 2012) 135.

[50] Lorenzo Cotula and Kyla Tienhaara, 'Reconfiguring Investment Contracts to Promote Sustainable Development' in Karl P Sauvant (ed.), *Yearbook on International Investment Law & Policy (2011–2012)* (OUP 2013) 281.

[51] See UNCTAD, 'The World of Investment Promotion at a Glance: A Survey of Investment Promotion Practices' ASIT Advisory Studies No 17,

clauses to consider in the negotiation of international investment agreements;[52] as well as the State's internal administrative processes for deciding how to manage and resolve investor-State disputes as they arise.[53] In the Conclusion, I return to Professor Alston's theory of the significance of the right to development, and show why this theory remains vital for the ongoing reform and reframing of international investment law, despite Professor Alston's own misgivings about the potentially imprecise and delegitimating co-optation of human rights in economic law regimes.[54]

II. OPERATIONALIZING THE RIGHT TO DEVELOPMENT AS A GOVERNANCE PROCESS

State duties flowing from the right to development are easily encompassed within the UN Charter Purpose of 'promoting and encouraging respect for human rights and for fundamental freedoms for all without distinction as to race, sex, language, or religion'.[55] UN Human Rights Commissioner Navi Pillay identifies six constituent elements of the right to development as defined in Article 1 of the Declaration, along with specific prescriptions contained in the Declaration for the realization of this right:

> Like all human rights, the right to development also contains a specific entitlement – in this case the *right 'to participate in, contribute to, and enjoy economic, social, cultural and political development'*. This basic entitlement,

---

UNCTAD/ITE/IPC/3 (2001) <http://unctad.org/en/Docs/poiteipcd3.en.pdf> accessed 18 August 2014; Neil Gunningham, 'Voluntary Approaches to Environmental Protection: Lessons from the Mining and Forestry Sectors' in OECD, *Foreign Direct Investment and the Environment: Lessons from the Mining Sector* (OECD 2002) 157, 176–7.

52 VanDuzer, Simons and Mayeda (n 43) 252–406; Peter Muchlinski, 'Holistic Approaches to Development in International Investment Law: The Role of International Investment Agreements' in Julio Faundez and Celine Tan (eds), *International Law, Economic Globalization and Developing Countries* (Edward Elgar 2010) 180.

53 See Roberto Echandi, 'Complementing Investor-State Dispute Resolution: A Conceptual Framework for Investor-State Conflict Management' in Roberto Echandi and Pierre Sauvé (eds), *Prospects in International Investment Law and Policy: World Trade Forum* (CUP 2013) 270.

54 Philip Alston, 'Resisting the Merger and Acquisition of Human Rights by Trade Law: A Reply to Petersmann' (2002) 13(4) EJIL 815.

55 UN Charter (n 46) art 1(3); see also ibid, art 55(c).

set out with perfect clarity in article 1 of the Declaration, includes a number of constituent elements, enumerated subsequently in the Declaration. Among them are:

- *People-centred development.* The Declaration identifies 'the human person' as the central subject, participant and beneficiary of development.
- *A human rights-based approach.* The Declaration specifically requires that development be carried out in a manner 'in which all human rights and fundamental freedoms can be fully realized'.
- *Participation.* The Declaration calls for the 'active, free and meaningful participation' of people in development.
- *Equity.* The Declaration underlines the need for 'the fair distribution of the benefits' of development.
- *Non-discrimination.* The Declaration permits 'no distinction as to race, sex, language or religion'.
- *Self-determination.* The Declaration integrates self-determination, including full sovereignty over natural resources, as a constituent element of the right to development.[56]

The UN Millennium Declaration clearly prioritizes the realization of the right to development:

> [w]e are committed to making the right to development a reality for everyone and to freeing the entire human race from want … We resolve therefore to create an environment – at the national and global levels alike – which is conducive to development and to the elimination of poverty.[57]

The implementation of the right to development from the framework of State decision-making processes and governance is likewise envisaged in numerous international instruments, UN reports, and statements issued by UN specialized agencies.[58] Significantly, a 2004 study commissioned by

---

[56] Statement by Navi Pillay, UN High Commissioner for Human Rights, 'Development Is a Human Right for All' <http://www.ohchr.org/EN/Issues/Development/Pages/IntroductionStatement.aspx> accessed 18 August 2014.

[57] United Nations Millenium Declaration, UNGA Res 55/2 (8 September 2000) paras 11–12 <http://www.un.org/millennium/declaration/ares552e.htm> accessed 18 August 2014.

[58] See among others 'Report of the Working Group on the Right to Development on its First Session', Chairman-Rapporteur Mr Mohamed Ennaceur, E/CN.4/1994/21 (13 December 1993) paras 39–49, 50–63; 'Report of the Working Group on the Right to Development on its Third Session', Chairman-Rapporteur Mr Mohamed Ennaceur, E/CN.4/1995/27 (11 November 1994) paras 14–35, 36–49; 'Report of the Intergovernmental Group of Experts on Right to Development on its Second Session', Chairman-Rapporteur Mr Antonio Garcia Revilla, E/CN.4/1998/29 (7 November 1997) paras 65–81; UN Economic and

the UN Office of the High Commissioner for Human Rights focused on '[m]ainstreaming the right to development into international trade law and policy at the World Trade Organization'.[59] The 2004 study stressed that

> the right to development entails the exploration of policies that allow the realization of human rights and economic growth to be mutually reinforcing … [it] requires that the goals and outcomes of development-related laws and policies be stipulated and assessed in terms of the enhancement of human capacities and the meeting of human needs as reflected in the range of civil and political, and economic, social and cultural rights.[60]

The 2004 report illustrated how the right to development could be mainstreamed into WTO practices through: 1) the assessment of trade rules and policies under the Trade Policy Review Mechanism (TPRM); 2) technical assistance activities especially to government decision-makers in developing countries; 3) the reform of the WTO architecture and its governance procedures; and 4) the use of the right to development in the interpretation of WTO law.[61]

There is, as yet, no distinct counter-report to the aforementioned 2004 study on mainstreaming the right to development in international investment law.[62] Isabella Bunn's 2012 book on the right to development in international law posited six principles extrapolated from the Declaration

---

Social Council, 'Question of the Realization of the Right to Development, Report of the Secretary-General Submitted in Accordance with Commission Resolution 1997/72', E/CN.4/1998/28 (16 February 1998); 'Report of the Working Group on the Right to Development on its Fourth Session', Chairman-Rapporteur Mr Mohamed Ennaceur, E/CN.4/1996/10 (25 August 1995) paras 11–13; 'Report of the Working Group on the Right to Development on its Sixth Session', Chairperson-Rapporteur Ibrahim Salama, E/CN.4/2005/25 (3 March 2005) paras 46–56.

59 UN Commission on Human Rights, Sub-Commission on the Promotion and Protection of Human Rights, 'Mainstreaming the Right to Development into International Trade Law and Policy at the World Trade Organization', E/CN.4/Sub.2/2004/17 (9 June 2004).

60 Ibid paras 14–15.

61 Ibid paras 26–49.

62 See among others Jan Wouters, Sanderijn Duquet and Nicholas Hachez, 'International Investment Law: The Perpetual Search for Consensus' in De Schutter, Swinnen and Wouters (n 8) 25; Ursula Kriebaum (ed.), *Special Issue on Aligning Human Rights and Investment Protection* (2013) 1 TDM <http://www.transnational-dispute-management.com/journal-browse-issues-toc.asp?key=46> accessed 18 August 2014; Bruno Simma and Theodore Kill, 'Harmonizing Investment Protection and International Human Rights: First Steps towards a

('respect for human rights, equality of opportunity, differential treatment of developing countries, participation, accountability and expansion of social responsibility'[63]), and applied the same to international trade, international financing, and corporate responsibility.[64] It did not, however, include any analysis situating the right to development specifically in international investment law and the typically hybrid spectrum of applicable law in investor-State transactions.[65] Likewise, the UN Office of the High Commissioner's landmark 2013 compilation of published essays on realizing the right to development[66] contained various works on mainstreaming the right to development on issues of poverty,[67] women,[68] indigenous peoples,[69] global governance,[70] the Millennium Development Goals,[71] the Paris Declaration on Aid Effectiveness,[72] the WTO and other economic partnership agreements,[73] debt relief,[74] climate change and environmental issues[75] – but it also did not contain any discussion on

---

Methodology' in Christina Binder and others (eds), *International Investment Law for the 21st Century* (OUP 2009) 678.

63 Bunn (n 19) 177.

64 Ibid 204–76.

65 See Salacuse (n 34) 33–48; Yas Banifatemi, 'The Law Applicable in Investment Treaty Arbitration' in Katia Yannaca-Small (ed.), *Arbitration under International Investment Agreements: A Guide to the Key Issues* (OUP 2010) 191.

66 UN 2013 Right to Development (n 45).

67 See Irene I Hadiprayitno, 'Poverty' in UN 2013 Right to Development (n 45) 137.

68 Fareda Banda, 'Women, Human Rights and Development' in UN 2013 Right to Development (n 45) 149.

69 Koen De Feyter, 'Indigenous Peoples' in UN 2013 Right to Development (n 45) 159.

70 Balakrishnan Rajagopal, 'Global Governance: Old and New Challenges' in UN 2013 Right to Development (n 45) 169.

71 Sakiko Fukuda-Parr, 'The Right to Development Critique of Millennium Development Goal 8' in UN 2013 Right to Development (n 45) 201.

72 Roberto Bissio, 'The Paris Declaration on Aid Effectiveness' in UN 2013 Right to Development (n 45) 233.

73 Robert Howse, 'Mainstreaming the Right to Development into the World Trade Organization' in UN 2013 Right to Development (n 45) 249; James Thuo Gathii, 'The Cotonou Agreement and Economic Partnership Agreements' in UN 2013 Right to Development (n 45) 259.

74 Boris Gamarra, Malvina Pollock, Dörte Dömeland and Carlos A Primo Braga, 'Debt Relief and Sustainability' in UN 2013 Right to Development (n 45) 275.

75 Marcos Orellana, 'Climate Change, Sustainable Development, and the Clean Development Mechanism' in UN 2013 Right to Development (n 45) 321.

how the right to development could be specifically mainstreamed into the shape and evolving content of modern international investment rules, norms, and institutions.[76] Much of the emergent work in this area focuses on the implementation of rights guaranteed under the International Covenant on Economic, Social, and Cultural Rights (ICESCR),[77] and not particularly the right to development as articulated under the UN Declaration on the Right to Development. The recent periodic review work of the Committee on Economic, Social and Cultural Rights with States Parties to the ICESCR, in particular, specifically considers the consistency of States Parties' trade and investment agreements on their ability to discharge obligations under the ICESCR.[78] In 2011, the UN Human Rights Council also adopted 'Guiding Principles on human rights impact assessments of trade and investment agreements'.[79]

In 2000, the UN Conference on Trade and Development (UNCTAD) issued its own study on how to build in flexibility for development in the terms of international investment agreements,[80] but other than a cursory reference to the Declaration on the Right to Development (which was also at the earliest stages of conceptual and interpretive development

---

76 See Committee on Economic, Social and Cultural Rights (CESCR), 'Statement of the Committee on Economic, Social and Cultural Rights to the Third Ministerial Conference of the World Trade Organization' E/C/12/1999/9 (26 November 1999) paras 2–3.

77 See Diane A Desierto, *Public Policy in International Economic Law: The ICESCR in Trade, Finance, and Investment* (OUP 2015); Hans Morten Haugen, 'Trade and Investment Agreements: What Role for Economic, Social and Cultural Rights in International Economic Law?' in Eibe Riedel, Gilles Giacca, Christophe Golay (eds), *Economic, Social and Cultural Rights in International Law: Contemporary Issues and Challenges* (OUP 2014) 227.

78 See among others CESCR, 'Consideration of Reports Submitted by States Parties under Articles 16 and 17 of the Covenant: Kenya' E/C.12/KEN/CO/1 (19 November 2008) para 11; CESCR, 'Concluding Observations of the CESCR: Canada' E/C.12/CAN/CO/4 and E/C.12/CAN/CO/5 (22 May 2006) para 68; CESCR, 'Concluding Observations of the CESCR: Dominican Republic' E/C.12/DOM/CO/3 (26 November 2010) para 8.

79 UN Human Rights Council, Report of the Special Rapporteur on the Right to Food, Olivier De Schutter, 'Guiding Principles on Human Rights Impact Assessments of Trade and Investment Agreements' A/HRC/19/59/Add.5 (19 December 2011).

80 UNCTAD, *International Investment Agreements: Flexibility for Development* (UNCTAD Series on Issues in International Investment Agreements, United Nations 2000) <http://unctad.org/en/docs/psiteiitd18.en.pdf> accessed 18 August 2014.

among practitioners and scholars),[81] the UNCTAD 2000 study did not apply specific elements of the right to development contained in the Declaration. UNCTAD premised its 2000 study from the view of development as involving

> the attainment of sufficient levels of economic growth to allow for a progressive improvement in the material standard of living of the populations of these countries … also encompass[ing] wider social objectives for which wealth creation is only a starting point.[82]

The UNCTAD 2000 study ultimately focused on prescribing various formulations of standards of protection and substantive provisions in international investment agreements (such as the scope and definition of investment, most favored nation/MFN treatment, fair and equitable treatment/FET, national treatment/NT, conditions for admission and establishment of investment)[83] that would enable host States to preserve policy or regulatory space for development objectives (and if necessary, operationally implement rules that might potentially injure foreign investments or dilute treaty-guaranteed international investor protection, but would be otherwise justified if the host State's regulatory actions were meant to serve development objectives). The as-yet untested 'special and differential treatment' (SDT) principle in trade law[84] (which permits developing countries to modify the terms of their compliance with trade law rules for developmental purposes) is one example of prescribed reform of investment treaty language.[85]

The UNCTAD's approach in its 2000 Study, however, begged the question of what were constitutive elements of the right to development

---

[81] UNCTAD (n 80) 26, box II.

[82] Ibid 11.

[83] Ibid 69–114.

[84] See Constantine Michalopoulos, 'The Role of Special and Differential Treatment for Developing Countries in GATT and the World Trade Organization' (World Bank Paper) <http://elibrary.worldbank.org/doi/pdf/10.1596/1813-9450-2388> accessed 18 August 2014. On adopting the SDT as a 'contextual' norm in international investment law, see Emily A Alexander, 'Taking Account of Reality: Adopting Contextual Standards for Developing Countries in International Investment Law' (2008) 48(4) Va JIL 815, 817–18.

[85] UNCTAD (n 80) 61–75; 2010 ASEAN Comprehensive Investment Agreement (adopted on 26 February 2009, entered into force on 29 March 2012) art 23(c); ASEAN-Korea Investment Agreement (adopted on 2 June 2009, entered into force on 1 September 2009) art 16(d); ASEAN-Australia-New Zealand Free Trade Agreement (adopted on 27 February 2009, entered into force on 10 January 2012) chapter on investment, art 15(d).

and the State duties arising from this right. The UNCTAD 2000 Study seemed to presuppose that States initiating regulatory changes to the investment protection framework generally act according to self-judged development objectives.[86] As noted in both investor-State arbitral awards and academic commentaries, however, not all regulatory actions that are sought to be justified on the host State's right to regulate are always benign – in some instances, the right to regulate could also be invoked in a 'pretextual' manner to evade State obligations to foreign investors.[87] It is in this sense that the latest conceptual, institutional, and interpretive developments on the right to development as defined in the Declaration on Development, could help inform and shape the assessment of the objective content of 'development' whenever invoked by a host State to justify regulatory changes.[88]

Possibly more updated guidance for translating the right to development into international investment law may be had from the UNCTAD Investment Policy Framework for Sustainable Development (IPFSD).[89] The IPFSD prescribes eleven Core Principles on investment for sustainable development, policy coherence, public governance and institutions, dynamic policymaking, balanced rights and obligations in investment policies, the right to regulate of States, openness to investment, investment protection and treatment, investment promotion and facilitation, corporate governance and responsibility, and international cooperation.[90] The UNCTAD IPFSD sees the 'new generation' of investment policymaking to refer to those that

> systematically integrate sustainable development and operationalize it in concrete measures and mechanisms at the national and international level, and at the level of policy-making and implementation.[91]

However, much of the focus of the UNCTAD IPFSD appears to lie primarily with the design of international investment agreements and

---

86 UNCTAD (n 80) 6.

87 See among others, *ADC Affiliate Ltd and ADC & ADMC Management Ltd v The Republic of Hungary*, ICSID Case No ARB/03/16, Award (2 October 2006) paras 423–4; Rahim Maloo and Justin Jacinto, 'Environmental and Health Regulation: Assessing Liability under Investment Treaties' (2011) 29(1) Berkeley JIL 1, 42.

88 See *Abaclat and others v The Argentine Republic,* ICSID Case No ARB/07/5, Dissenting Opinion, Georges Abi-Saab (28 October 2011) para 50.

89 IPFSD (n 6).

90 Ibid 11.

91 Ibid 6.

national investment laws of host States. In particular, the UNCTAD IPFSD does not specifically reference the UN Declaration on the Right to Development, although UNCTAD has clarified that other international instruments inform the IPFSD Core Principles, such as the Universal Declaration on Human Rights, the UN Guiding Principles on Business and Human Rights, the Convention on the Establishment of the Multilateral Investment Guarantee Agency (MIGA), the World Bank Guidelines on the Treatment of Foreign Direct Investment, the UN Global Compact, the OECD Guidelines for Multinational Enterprises and the ILO Tripartite Declaration of Principles Concerning Multinational Enterprises and Social Policy, and World Trade Organization (WTO) agreements such as the General Agreement on Trade in Services (GATS), the Agreement on Trade-Related Investment Measures (TRIMS), and the Agreement on Government Procurement.[92]

For the purpose of advancing specific proposals in Part III on ways to mainstream the right to development in international law into international investment transactions, I focus on the content of the right to development as it lays out three principles: '(a) there is an inalienable human right that is called the right to development; (b) there is a particular process of economic, social, cultural and political development, in which all human rights and fundamental freedoms can be fully realized; and (c) the right to development is a human right by virtue of which every human person and all peoples are entitled to participate in, contribute to, and enjoy that particular process of development.'[93] These principles, I submit, can well be translated into a host State's design of its international investment regulatory architecture.

As to the first principle, treating the right to development as an 'inalienable' right establishes its fundamental priority within the overall strategic objectives of the host State's international investment planning. For example, when a State opens up publicly-held enterprises, utilities, among other State assets to some degree of privatization and foreign investment, for example, it has to assess whether its objective for doing so is truly aimed at

> the constant improvement of the well-being of the entire population and of all individuals, on the basis of their active, free and meaningful participation in development and in the fair distribution of benefits resulting therefrom.[94]

---

[92] Ibid 10.

[93] Arjun K Sengupta, 'Conceptualizing the Right to Development for the Twenty-First Century' in UN 2013 Right to Development (n 45) 67, 68.

[94] Declaration on the Right to Development (n 11) Preamble.

As the historical record of failed privatization projects bear out,[95] in some instances, the failure to properly design environmental and social compliance in investors' expectation of risks and returns and the ultimate pricing mechanism for the investment project would have made it more prudent in hindsight to put off or delay project commencement until these regulatory safeguards were put in place.[96] A State that is fully cognizant of its duties under the right to development should thus already proceed from this baseline when making the initial threshold decisions on whether to invite foreign participation in any investment project; and how the State would design the investment project needs in a manner that fully maximizes welfare impacts, enables free participation especially of affected communities and vulnerable groups, and ensures that the benefits and returns that the State reaps from the investment project are indeed fairly distributed among its constituencies.[97]

With respect to the second principle of the right to development, I submit that establishing a 'particular process of economic, social, cultural and political development' within the host State's international investment planning process calls for building in an architecture for compliance with the host State's human rights obligations directly into the contractual, administrative, and regulatory infrastructure of the international investment project, which can be operationalized under current corporate social responsibility mechanisms, human rights due diligence processes, environmental and social impact assessments accompanying the contract planning, formation, and monitoring processes.[98] To this end,

---

95 See Antonio Estache and Lourdes Trujillo, 'Privatization in Latin America: The Good, the Ugly, and the Unfair' in Gerard Roland (ed.), *Privatization: Successes and Failures* (Columbia UP 2013) 136.

96 See, e.g., World Bank Program of Support for the Chad-Cameroon Petroleum Development and Pipeline Construction, Program Performance Assessment Report No 50315 (20 November 2009) <http://siteresources.worldbank.org/INTOED/Resources/ChadCamReport.pdf> accessed 18 August 2014.

97 See Statement of Chairperson Ariranga G Pillay, CESCR (30 November 2012) <http://cesr.org/downloads/CESCR_ChairLetterSPto_ICESCR_30.11.12.pdf> accessed 18 August 2014; CESCR, 'Statement on the Obligations of States Parties Regarding the Corporate Sector and Economic, Social and Cultural Rights' E/C.12/2011/1 (12 July 2011) para 5.

98 See, among others, Bruno Simma, 'Foreign Investment Arbitration: A Place for Human Rights?' (2011) 60(3) ICLQ 573; Peter Muchlinski, 'Towards a Coherent International Investment System: Key Issues in the Reform of International Investment Law' in Echandi and Sauvé (n 53) 411, 423 (on building in human rights due diligence in investment planning); World Bank, 'Human Rights

it is significant that recent developments from the United Nations on the empirical monitoring of human rights compliance could now help facilitate the design of the international human rights compliance process in the investment monitoring aspects of the project.[99] The State's international investment planning process is but one form or permutation of its overall economic programming governed by the right to development, which, concomitantly, should also be 'participatory … decisions will have to be taken with the full involvement of the beneficiaries … .'[100] Grounding the international investment planning process on the right to development manifests a 'human rights approach to development … [that] focuses on claims that individuals have on the conduct of the State and other agents to secure their capabilities and freedoms.'[101] When the right to development is at the core of the State's decision-making calculus on economic programming, the economic growth and investment yields of international investment transactions would have to be globally reassessed to factor in social protection needs and the resource demands necessary to achieve compliance with the host State's international human rights obligations.[102]

Finally, the third element of the right to development requires that State have

> a duty to formulate, according to article 2, paragraph 3 … [national development policies that] should have two characteristics: (a) they must be *participatory* ('on the basis of … active, free and meaningful participation');

Impact Assessments: A Review of the Literature, Differences with other Forms of Assessments and Relevance for Development' (February 2013) <http://siteresources.worldbank.org/PROJECTS/Resources/40940-1331068268558/HRIA_Web.pdf> accessed 18 August 2014.

[99] Report on Indicators for Promoting and Monitoring the Implementation of Human Rights, HRI/MC/2008/3 (6 June 2008) para 2 <http://www2.ohchr.org/english/issues/indicators/docs/HRI.MC.2008.3_en.pdf> accessed 18 August 2014; United Nations Office of the High Commissioner for Human Rights, *Economic, Social and Cultural Rights: Handbook for National Human Rights Institutions* (Professional Training Series No 12, United Nations 2005) <http://www.ohchr.org/Documents/Publications/training12en.pdf> accessed 18 August 2014. See also Todd Landman, 'Measuring Human Rights: Principle, Practice, and Policy' (2004) 26(4) *Human Rights Quarterly* 906.

[100] Sengupta (n 93) 69.

[101] Ibid 70.

[102] See Urban Jonsson, 'Human Rights Approach to Development Programming' (UNICEF, April 2003) <http://www.unicef.org/spanish/rightsresults/files/HRBDP_Urban_Jonsson_April_2003.pdf> accessed 18 August 2014.

> and (b) *equitable* ('the fair distribution of benefits') … if States acting on their own are unable to formulate and execute those policies … they have the right to claim cooperation and help from other States and international agencies.[103]

In the context of a State's international investment planning process, this would require ensuring the broadest possible consultation of, participation in, and revenue-sharing possibilities for all directly affected local communities, vulnerable groups, and other stakeholders in the planning, execution, and monitoring of international investment projects. Lorenzo Cotula has written extensively about ensuring the preservation of resource rights of local groups, consultation and benefit-sharing tools, and introducing social impact assessments and safeguards for natural resource investment projects in Africa.[104] The World Bank and other international agencies have likewise provided guidance on how to ensure significant and meaningful local community consultation, participation in, and 'ownership' by these communities of the implementation process in the delivery of services from States' international investment projects with foreign investor consortia, showing that the success of foreign investment in these projects depended heavily on successful engagement and partnership with local communities.[105]

As seen in the foregoing discussion, it is not altogether impossible to translate the constitutive elements of the right to development into the general features of a State's international investment planning process. In the following Part III, I explore structural considerations for ensuring the

---

[103] Sengupta (n 93) 72 (emphasis added).

[104] See Lorenzo Cotula, *Legal Empowerment for Local Resource Control: Securing Local Resource Rights within Foreign Investment Projects in Africa* (IIED 2007) <http://dlc.dlib.indiana.edu/dlc/bitstream/handle/10535/5396/08_IIED_legal_empowerment.pdf> accessed 18 August 2014.

[105] See World Bank/International Finance Corporation (IFC), *Investing in People: Sustaining Communities through Improved Business Practice* (IFC 2000) <http://www.ifc.org/wps/wcm/connect/1dc2e100488658 11b3fef36a6515bb18/CommunityGuide.pdf?MOD=AJPERES> accessed 18 August 2014; Overseas Development Institute, 'Community Content: The Interface of Community Investment Programmes with Local Content Practices in the Oil and Gas Development Sector' ODI Briefing Note No 9 <http://www.odi.org.uk/sites/odi.org.uk/files/odi-assets/publications-opinion-files/2087.pdf> accessed 18 August 2014; Food and Agriculture Organization of the United Nations (FAO), 'Trends and Impacts of Foreign Investment in Developing Country Agriculture: Evidence from Case Studies' (FAO 2012) <http://www.fao.org/fileadmin/templates/est/INTERNATIONAL-TRADE/FDIs/Trends_publication_12_November_2012.pdf> accessed 18 August 2014.

admission and implementation of human rights-compliant investment across the State's development decisions from the pre-contractual stage, the foreign investment contracting stage, the establishment of investment promotion and investment monitoring institutions, to the State's design preferences in its international investment agreement (IIA) programme as well as its internal administrative process for deciding how to manage and resolve investor-State disputes. The discussion is by no means comprehensive. Rather, it is an initial attempt to visualize a State's international investment transaction from the development process standpoint – and one that seeks to embed and institutionalize human rights compliance at the outset from project design.

III. BUILDING 'HR-COMPLIANT' INVESTMENT IN STATE DEVELOPMENT DECISIONS

States have sufficient tools at their disposal to ensure that their international investment planning process truly encapsulates the governance process required under the right to development, by building in compliance with their international human rights obligations at every phase of international investment projects.[106] In this Part III, I focus on five aspects: 1) the host State's pre-contract procedures; 2) the host State's approval of all related contract documents in the international investment projects; 3) the host State's management of investment promotion and investment monitoring institutions; 4) the host State's negotiation of terms in its international investment agreements; and 5) the host State's internal administrative process for deciding how it will prevent, manage, and resolve investor-State disputes. These aspects of international investment planning, I submit, are distinct opportunities for States to pragmatically implement the right to development, notwithstanding the usual

---

[106] See among others, Lorenzo Cotula, *Investment Contracts and Sustainable Development: How to Make Contracts for Fairer and More Sustainable Natural Resource Investments* (IIED 2010); Kate Miles, *The Origins of International Investment Law: Empire, Environment, and the Safeguarding of Capital* (CUP 2013) 348–85; Sheldon Leader, 'Risk Management, Project Finance and Rights-Based Management' in Sheldon Leader and David Ong (eds), *Global Project Finance, Human Rights and Sustainable Development* (CUP 2011) 107; Tamara Wiher Fernandez, 'Human Rights Impact Assessments and Project Finance' in Leader and Ong (eds), ibid 174; Markus W Gehring and Avidan Kent, 'Sustainable Development and IIAs: From Objective to Practice' in Armand de Mestral and Celine Levesque (eds), *Improving International Investment Agreements* (Routledge 2013) 284.

disparities in bargaining leverage between capital-importing States and foreign investors and their corresponding home States.[107] While the conventional wisdom is indeed that ‘before investments start international investors have more bargaining power than host states, whereas after investment takes place, the bargaining power shifts in favor of the other side’,[108] this does not have to mean that host States have to incentivize and attract international investment by a regulatory ‘race to the bottom’ leaving out human rights compliance from international investment projects.[109] Rather, as others have argued, failure to build in human rights compliance as part of prudential risk management in international investment transactions tends to be more costly to all participants (host States and investors) in the long run, as to make a State’s respect for human rights an incentive for attracting foreign investment.[110] It is, ultimately, up to the authoritative decision-makers of the host State to define the terms under which they are willing to exact immediate and long-term economic benefits from the infusion of capital from external sources such as foreign investors. The following discussion attempts to reorient that process of definition towards the long view espoused under the right to development.

A. Pre-Contract Procedures

Investor-host State contracts

> define the terms of an investment project, and the way risks, costs, and benefits are distributed, who has the authority to sign the contract and through what process greatly influences the extent to which people can have their voices heard.[111]

---

107 See UNCTAD, ‘Bargaining between TNCs and Host Countries’ <http://unctc.unctad.org/data/e92iia21h.pdf> accessed 18 August 2014.

108 Mustafa Erkan, *International Energy Investment Law: Stability through Contractual Clauses* (Kluwer Law International 2011) 47.

109 See Peter M Madsen, ‘Does Corporate Investment Drive a “Race to the Bottom” in Environmental Protection? A Reexamination of the Effect of Environmental Regulation in Investment’ (2009) 52(6) *Academy of Management Journal* 1297.

110 See Institute for Human Rights and Business (IHRB), *Investing the Right Way: A Guide for Investors on Business and Human Rights* (IHRB 2013) <http://www.ihrb.org/pdf/Investing-the-Rights-Way/Investing-the-Rights-Way.pdf> accessed 18 August 2014.

111 Lorenzo Cotula, ‘Rethinking Investor-State Contracts through a Sustainable Development Lens’ (*Investment Treaty News*, 7 October 2011) <http://

Even before these contracts are signed, States define project needs, investor eligibilities, as well as terms and conditions for participation in the bidding procedures. These pre-contract procedures – and how the State can intermediate human rights compliance as a requirement in these procedures – will depend on the form and mode of foreign investment chosen. Wholly-owned foreign direct investments (FDI), for example, will involve foreign investor contracts with private parties possessing the target asset or acquisition, and obtaining the necessary permissions from host State governmental agencies to operate the investment or avail of statutory or regulatory tax and non-tax incentives.[112] At this stage, the host State's governmental or regulatory agencies may already require a human rights impact assessment as part of the pre-acquisition scoping and due diligence process, which would, in turn, enable the investor to more accurately assess investment risks.[113] The host State should likewise make clear that the scope of applicability of its international human rights obligations and duties to protect, respect, and fulfill international human rights guarantees should be read as part of the regulatory framework binding upon all entities operating in its territorial jurisdiction.[114] This would ensure that the nationality of the FDI operator (whether as a branch of the foreign investor company, or as an independent subsidiary of the foreign investor parent organized under host State laws) would not be material insofar as the binding coverage of the host State's duty to comply with its international human rights obligations,

---

www.iisd.org/itn/2011/10/07/rethinking-investor-state-contracts-through-a-sustainable-development-lens/> accessed 18 August 2014.

[112] Salacuse (n 34) 204.

[113] See Liesbeth Colen, Miet Maertens and Jo Swinnen, 'Foreign Direct Investment as an Engine for Economic Growth and Human Development: A Review of the Arguments and Empirical Evidence' (Leuven Centre for Global Governance Studies Working Paper No 16, September 2008) <https://ghum.kuleuven.be/ggs/publications/working_papers/new_series/wp11-20/wp16.pdf> accessed 18 August 2014; Aaron Bernstein, 'Incorporating Labor and Human Rights Risk into Investment Decisions' (Harvard Occasional Paper Series No 2, September 2008) <http://www.law.harvard.edu/programs/lwp/pensions/publications/occpapers/occasional_paper2.pdf> accessed 18 August 2014.

[114] See August Reinisch, 'The Changing International Legal Framework for Dealing with Non-State Actors' in Philip Alston (ed.), *Non-State Actors and Human Rights* (OUP 2005) 37; Jochen von Bernstorff, 'The Global "Land-Grab", Sovereignty and Human Rights' (2013) 2(9) *ESIL Reflections* <http://www.esil-sedi.eu/sites/default/files/ESIL%20Reflections%20-%20von%20Bernstorff_0.pdf> accessed 18 August 2014.

including the host State's implementation of these international obligations by local statute, administrative action, or regulatory rules.[115]

Despite differences in the ultimate structure of the investment vehicle (e.g. whether through FDI, international joint venture agreements, project financing for international infrastructure projects under build-operate-transfer/BOT agreements, concession contracts, consortium agreements, or international loan contracts),[116] the host State can already indicate in the 'pre-negotiation' or 'pre-contract' phase that prospective investors must already include compliance with the host State's international human rights obligations as part of the investment regulatory framework. Part of the minimum qualifications that the host State could set for participating bidders or potential investment project operators would be scrutiny into the entity's design of its due diligence process, its track record for ensuring respect, protection, and fulfillment of international human rights in project operations, as well as the corporate social responsibility (CSR) capacity of the bidder or prospective investment operator. At the pre-negotiation or pre-contract phase, the host State could already signal to all potential bidders that compliance with the host State's fundamental human rights obligations is a critical baseline requirement of the investment project.

A crucial issue for the pre-contract or pre-negotiation phases of international investments is the extent of public participation and transparency permitted in the process.[117] In the first instance, the latent question underlying this issue is the manner by which the host State represents the interests of its constituents. Those advocating separate representation by other groups in the pre-contract and pre-negotiation phases do so on the belief that the public policy dimensions involved in the contract are not satisfactorily represented or considered by the host State in the development decision-making process. The clamor for transparency at this stage is certainly a justifiable one, especially for local communities that stand to be directly affected by a foreign investment

---

[115] See Special Rapporteur on the right to food Olivier De Schutter, 'Regulating Transnational Corporations: A Duty under International Human Rights Law' (March 2014) <http://www.ohchr.org/Documents/Issues/Food/EcuadorMtgBusinessAndHR.pdf> accessed 18 August 2014.

[116] Salacuse (n 34) 205–44.

[117] Cotula and Tienhaara (n 50) 286–91.

project.[118] A host State cognizant of its duties under the international right of development would be careful to ensure that the international investment planning process affords the widest possible participation at the outset of the project. Local participation and transparency need not be feared as factors that could 'scuttle' prospective investment projects for the host State, but rather, should be seen as prudent measures that better enable foreign investors to estimate and price investment risks, build more durable partnerships with the host State, foster systems of accountability for all participants to the project, deter corruption, and ensure more widespread acceptance and commitment to the success of the investment project.[119]

B. Host State Approval of Investment Contracts and Related Contracts: Registration and Performance Requirements

Various international investment treaties provide for host State registration and approvals for certain forms of investment, subject to certain conditions and/or required consultations for the registration and approval process, as well as performance requirements (such as required local content/employment and training, required submission of environmental impact assessments, among others).[120] Where their international investment treaties would not be inconsistent with the inclusion of registration and performance requirements that create a 'human rights screening'

[118] See Julie A Maupin, 'Transparency in International Investment Law: The Good, the Bad, the Murky' in Andrea Bianchi and Anne Peters (eds), *Transparency in International Law* (CUP 2013) 142, 148; Valentina Vadi, *Public Health in International Investment Law and Arbitration* (Routledge 2012) 49.

[119] See Emma Wilson and Judy Kuszewski, *Shared Value, Shared Responsibility: A New Approach to Managing Contracting Chains in the Oil and Gas Sector* (IIED 2011) 11–24; Beata S Javorcik and Mariana Spatareanu, 'To Share or Not to Share: Does Local Participation Matter for Spillovers from Foreign Direct Investment?' (Rutgers University Newark Working Paper No 2006-001, February 2006); World Bank, *Implementing the Extractive Industries Transparency Initiative: Applying Early Lessons from the Field* (World Bank 2008) 7–56.

[120] See, among others, Treaty between the United States of America and the Czech and Slovak Federal Republic Concerning the Reciprocal Encouragement and Protection of Investments (adopted on 22 October 1991, entered into force on 19 December 1992) para 10 <http://investmentpolicyhub.unctad.org/Download/TreatyFile/994> accessed 5 February 2015; UNCTAD, *Foreign Direct Investment and Performance Requirements: New Evidence from Selected Countries* (United Nations 2003) <http://unctad.org/en/docs/iteiia20037_en.pdf> accessed 18 August 2014.

process, host States can implement the right to development in their design of registration approvals and performance requirements.[121] Where host States provide for investment treaty coverage for investments 'in accordance with law',[122] in particular, host States can ensure and notify investors at the outset that its human rights obligations form part of the corpus of host State law that are of such fundamental importance that they must be included in the due diligence to be conducted by the investor and the host State.[123] While there is a line of arbitral awards that narrowly identifies host State's corporate registration requirements as the only 'law' contemplated by this clause,[124] there are also other arbitral awards that suggest that the clause applies to other sources of law that are consistent with the teleological purposes of an IIA,[125] such as anti-dummy legislation, bribery laws, contractual fraud, and central bank

---

[121] See, e.g., Global Reporting Initiative, 'Indicator Protocols Set for Human Rights' <https://www.globalreporting.org/resourcelibrary/G3.1-Human-Rights-Indicator-Protocol.pdf> accessed 18 August 2014; Nathalie Bernasconi-Osterwalder and Mahnaz Malik, 'Registration and Approval Requirements in Investment Treaties' (IISD December 2012) <http://www.iisd.org/pdf/2013/best_practices_registration_requirements.pdf> accessed 18 August 2014.

[122] *MTD Equity Sdn Bhd and MTD Chile SA v The Republic of Chile*, ICSID Case No ARB/01/7, Award (25 May 2004) paras 190, 197; Stephan W Schill, 'Illegal Investments in Investment Arbitration' (2012) 11 LPICT 281.

[123] *Fraport AG Frankfurt Airport Services Worldwide v The Republic of the Philippines*, ICSID Case No ARB/03/25, Award (16 August 2007) para 396; *SGS Société Générale de Surveillance SA v The Republic of the Philippines*, ICSID Case No ARB/02/6, Decision on Objections to Jurisdiction and Separate Declaration (29 January 2004) paras 99–112.

[124] *Veteran Petroleum Ltd v Russian Federation*, PCA Case No AA 228, Interim Award on Jurisdiction and Admissibility (30 November 2009) paras 20–21; *Yaung Chi Oo Trading Pte Ltd v Government of the Union of Myanmar*, ASEAN Case No ARB/01/1 (31 March 2003) para 62; *Waguih Elie George Siag and Clorinda Vecchi v The Arab Republic of Egypt*, ICSID Case No ARB/05/15, Decision on Jurisdiction and Partial Dissenting Opinion (11 April 2007) paras 198–201; *Middle East Cement Shipping and Handling Co SA v The Arab Republic of Egypt*, ICSID Case No ARB/99/6, Award (12 April 2002) paras 131–8.

[125] *Salini Costruttori SpA and Italstrade SpA v The Kingdom of Morocco*, ICSID Case No ARB/00/4, Decision on Jurisdiction (23 July 2001) para 46; *Mytilineos Holdings SA v Serbia and Montenegro and Serbia*, UNCITRAL, Partial Award on Jurisdiction and Dissenting Opinion (8 September 2006) para 152.

regulations.[126] The host State can likewise ensure that its definition of applicable law includes human rights compliance and due diligence processes for all related or interdependent contracts with the international investment project.[127] These requirements would not come as a surprise for many institutional investors as well as global development banking institutions who already accept socially responsible investment[128] practices under the UN Principles on Responsible Investment (UN PRI)[129] and the Equator Principles (the financial industry voluntary benchmark for determining and assessing environmental and social risks in international project financing).[130]

C. Design of Investment Promotion and Investment Monitoring Institutions

Host States can further implement the right to development in the manner by which they design investment promotion and investment monitoring institutions. Investment promotion, by definition, covers

> all activities and measures aimed at creating favourable determinants for foreign investment in the host country. These determinants include the policy framework for foreign investment, economic determinants, and business facilitation.[131]

---

[126] *Fraport AG v Philippines* (n 123) (involving local anti-dummy legislation); *World Duty Free Company Ltd v The Republic of Kenya*, ICSID Case No ARB/00/7, Award (25 September 2006); *Inceysa Vallisoletane SL v El Salvador*, ICSID Case No ARB/03/26, Award (2 August 2006); *Anderson and Others v Costa Rica*, ICSID Case No ARB (AF)/07/3, Award (10 May 2010) paras 55–9.

[127] See Nii Ashie Kotey and Poku Adusei, 'Project Finance Mechanisms, Human Rights and Sustainable Development in Ghana's Mining Sector: The Newmont and Anglogold Mining Projects' (IIED April 2009) <http://pubs.iied.org/pdfs/G02488.pdf> accessed 18 August 2014; Aldo Caliari, 'Trade, Investment, Finance and Human Rights: Assessment and Strategy Paper' (2009) 6(11) *Sur Revista Internacional de Direitos Humanos* 141 <http://www.scielo.br/scielo.php?pid=S1806-64452009000200008&script=sci_arttext&tlng=en> accessed 18 August 2014.

[128] Hung-Gay Fung, Sheryl A Law and Jot Yau, *Socially Responsible Investment in a Global Environment* (Edward Elgar 2010) 1–43.

[129] 'UN Principles of Responsible Investment' <http://www.unpri.org/about-pri/the-six-principles/> accessed 18 August 2014.

[130] See 'Equator Principles' (June 2013) <http://www.equator-principles.com/resources/equator_principles_III.pdf> accessed 18 August 2014.

[131] UNCTAD, *Investment Promotion Provisions in International Investment Agreements* (United Nations 2008) 1.

Investment promotion often includes some reference to cooperation on information-sharing as well as some administrative facility for investment promotion activities.[132]

To date, few governments have explicitly incorporated their human rights obligations under their export credit and investment promotion policies,[133] making it a continuing obligation for the State to implement its duties flowing from the right to development by revisiting the current structure and content of its investment promotion strategies and institutions.[134] The usual models of investment promotion tend to focus on single-window service delivery to more expeditiously facilitate investment operations,[135] rather than to use investment promotion also as a platform for cooperation with the foreign investor in ensuring mutual transparency and information cooperation to foster international human rights compliance in investment projects. When properly designed, investment promotion activities can help

> improve the transparency and reduce the burden of domestic regulation a host state … support the operation of home state investors in the host state by reducing the burden of regulation and making its operation more predictable … the home state's support for investment promotion may be used as a bargaining chip in exchange for the host state's agreement to protect the home state's investors through an IIA.[136]

Ensuring consistency between the host State's investment promotion activities with its international human rights obligations, at the outset, clearly conveys that the admission and establishment of investment

[132] See OECD, *Policy Framework for Investment: A Review of Good Practices* (OECD 2006) ch 2 Investment Promotion and Facilitation <http://www.oecd.org/investment/investment-policy/40287315.pdf> accessed 18 August 2014.

[133] See Peter Newell, 'Climate Change, Human Rights, and Corporate Accountability' in Stephen Humphreys (ed.), *Human Rights and Climate Change* (CUP 2010) 126, 153.

[134] Hubert Brossard, 'Importance of Organizations for Investment Promotion during an Investment Decision-Making Process: An Exploratory Study' (1998) 38(3) *Management International Review* 203; UNCTAD, 'Evaluating Investment Promotion Agencies' (2008) <http://unctad.org/en/Docs/diaepcb20082_en.pdf> accessed 18 August 2014.

[135] See Pravakar Sahoo, 'Foreign Direct Investment in India: Unfinished Agenda' in Philippa Dee (ed.), *Economic Reform Processes in South Asia: Toward Policy Efficiency* (Routledge 2012) 109, 114–15.

[136] VanDuzer, Simons and Mayeda (n 43) 496.

would be contingent upon the investor's continuous compliance with human rights standards in all phases of investment operations.

Investment monitoring institutions are not often included in international investment agreements,[137] but the host State and the foreign investor may provide for such institutions within the terms of the investment contract to facilitate easier access to the sharing of regulatory information, as well as to enable parties to ventilate concerns early on regarding potential or actual human rights violations arising from investment operations. After the investor and the host State respectively conduct corresponding human rights due diligence processes[138] at the time of the admission and establishment of the investment, the investment monitoring institution will be crucial for ensuring centralized and continued human rights impact monitoring during the life of the investment. The investment monitoring institution can also serve as a valuable resource for receiving information about the environmental and social impacts of the investment, as well as for initiating independent inquiries and consultations with local communities and other project stakeholders on the economic, environmental, and social consequences they experience from the investment project.[139]

[137] See among others, Treaty Between the United States of America and the Oriental Republic of Uruguay Concerning the Encouragement and Reciprocal Protection of Investment (United States/Uruguay BIT) (adopted 4 November 2005, entered into force 1 November 2006) S Treaty Doc No 109-9 (2006) art 30(3); Agreement between the United Mexican States and the Government of the Republic of India on the Promotion and Reciprocal Protection of Investments (India/Mexico BIT) (adopted 21 May 2007, entered into force 23 February 2008) IC-BT 742 (2007) art 29(2); Agreement between the Government of Canada and the Government of the Czech and Slovak Federal Republic for the Promotion and Protection of Investments (Canada/Czech Republic BIT) (adopted 6 May 2009, entered into force 22 January 2012) art X(6); North American Free Trade Agreement (NAFTA) (adopted 17 December 1992, entered into force 1 January 1994) IC-MT 002 (1992) ch 11: Investment, art 2001 (The Free Trade Commission); Dominican Republic-Central America-United States Free Trade Agreement (DR-CAFTA) (adopted 5 August 2004, entered into force 1 January 2009) IC-MT 012 (2004) ch 10: Investment, art 10.22(3) (Governing Law).

[138] James Harrison, 'Establishing a Meaningful Due Diligence Process for Corporations: Learning from the Experience of Human Rights Impact Assessment' (2013) 31(2) *Impact Assessment and Project Appraisal* 107 <http://www.tandfonline.com/doi/pdf/10.1080/14615517.2013.774718> accessed 18 August 2014.

[139] See Matthias Sant'ana, 'Risk Managers or Risk Promoters? The Impacts of Export Credit and Investment Insurance Agencies on Human Development and Human Rights' in De Schutter, Swinnen and Wouters (n 8) 189, 229.

Ultimately, the extent of the 'redesign' of investment promotion and investment monitoring activities of the host State will depend on the host State's commitment to embed its economic programming – as well as all international investment planning activities – within the fundamental framework of the right to development and the State's duties to respect, protect, and fulfill human rights obligations to its constituents. This kind of redesign of investment promotion and monitoring strategies and institutions purposely adopts a 'development perspective' that situates international investment within the State's development process[140] – one that 'considers the factors that determine noncompliance and how policies and interventions can change the context, alter incentives, and affect outcomes.'[141] The redesign of investment promotion and investment monitoring strategies and institutions should facilitate the sharing of information between the host State and the foreign investor to enable the accurate pricing of the risks and returns of the investment. As I have stressed in other works,[142] there is a critical need to revisit how investment risks are being estimated in each investment project, given host States' social protection obligations, particularly under the International Covenant on Economic, Social and Cultural Rights. Investment promotion agencies and monitoring institutions can act as useful information conduits on the human rights obligations of the host State and the projected environmental, economic, and social impacts of the proposed investment. By so doing, these institutions can help set a more realistic baseline of regulatory expectations,[143] as well as assist in the investor's estimation of political risks and investment returns, and ultimately, the

140 See Peter Uvin, 'From the Right to Development to the Rights-Based Approach: How "Human Rights" Entered Development' (2007) 17(4) *Development in Practice* 597.

141 Gordon Betcherman, 'Placing Core Labor Standards in the Development Context' in *Monitoring International Labor Standards: Human Capital Investment* (National Academies Press 2003) 6.

142 See Diane A Desierto, 'ICESCR Minimum Core Obligations and Recasting the Non-Expropriation Compensation Model during Financial Crises' (2012) 44(3) *George Washington International Law Review* 473; Desierto (n 37); Diane A Desierto, 'Conflict of Treaties, Interpretation, and Decision-Making on Human Rights and Investment During Economic Crises' (2013) 1 TDM.

143 See Christoph Schreuer and Ursula Kriebaum, 'At What Time Must Legitimate Expectations Exist?' 7–8 <http://www.univie.ac.at/intlaw/pdf/97_atwhattime.pdf> accessed 18 August 2014.

acceptable threshold of the investment price that would be determinative of the initial decision to invest. If an investor were to be apprised early on of the host State's fundamental human rights obligations and the expected impacts of the proposed investment project on those obligations, and the investor nevertheless proceeds with the investment decision having already assumed the risk on the basis of sufficient knowledge of these regulatory matters, then surely the investor's 'legitimate expectations' need not be drastically adverse to, or disparate from, that of the host State's core constituencies.[144]

D. Negotiating the Host State's International Investment Agreements

To implement the State's duties flowing from the right to development into the design of IIAs, much more would be required than an incremental revision of sundry IIA provisions to create 'policy space'[145] for the State to regulate for development objectives. I submit that we would have to attempt a thematic overhaul of what is conventionally understood to be 'current' IIA design (e.g. with the heavy focus on investor protection treatment standards and investor-State dispute settlement).[146] Redesigning IIAs from the standpoint of State duties under the right to development would have to consider two interrelated aspects: first, that the international right to development requires a particular form of *rights-based governance process* owed by the State towards its constituents; and second, that the international right to development also means that States purposely engage in *international cooperation* to ensure respect, protection, and fulfillment of international human rights. Thus, rather than sundry references to human rights provisions in international investment agreements (which for the present focuses on the IIA's consistency with the host State's environmental and labor obligations),[147] an IIA designed to implement the State's pre-existing duties under the right to development would have to devise an entire

---

[144] See Thomas C Berry and Joan C Junkus, 'Socially Responsible Investing: An Investor Perspective' (2013) 112(4) *Journal of Business Ethics* 707; Debora Spar, 'Foreign Investment and Human Rights' (1999) 42(1) *Challenge* 55.

[145] See Suzanne A Spears, 'The Quest for Policy Space in the New Generation of International Investment Agreements' (2010) 13(4) JIEL 1037.

[146] See Andrew Newcombe, 'Developments in IIA Treaty-Making' in de Mestral and Levesque (n 106) 15.

[147] See 2012 United States Model Bilateral Investment Treaty, arts 12, 13; 2004 Canada Model Bilateral Investment Treaty, art 11.

governance process for the international investment project that is conducive and enabling for the realization and achievement of human rights standards and obligations; accepts the broadest possible participation for all local communities and vulnerable groups that would be affected by the State's investment project decisions; provides an equitable balance of redress, recourse, and remedies for both investors injured by host State actions as well as local communities, groups, and other stakeholders who are adversely affected by investor conduct and operations; and ultimately establishes a system of investment governance that justly allocates risks between investors and States, enables information access to all interested parties, and internalizes accountability for all parties to the investment transaction or project. The home State of the investor would have its own duties of international cooperation to ensure that its investor-national does not prevent or obstruct the respect, protection, and fulfillment of international human rights obligations of the host State. While there is no such IIA in existence,[148] the 2005 IISD Model Agreement on Investment for Sustainable Development does attempt to put forward many of the foregoing concerns.[149]

E. Internal Process for Managing Investor-State Disputes

Finally, a State cognizant of its duties under the right to development should also be conscious of reflecting the same in its decisions on the management, resolution, and/or settlement of investor-State disputes.[150] There is a tremendous literature seeking reforms of the investor-State dispute settlement system (primarily in the form of investor-State arbitration),[151] and to that extent the host State must indeed decide the dispute

---

148 Marc Jacob, 'International Investment Agreements and Human Rights' (INEF Research Paper Series on Human Rights, Corporate Responsibility and Sustainable Development, March 2010) <http://www.humanrights-business.org/files/international_investment_agreements_and_human_rights.pdf> accessed 18 August 2014.

149 IISD Model International Agreement on Investment for Sustainable Development (2005) <http://www.iisd.org/pdf/2005/investment_model_int_agreement.pdf> accessed 18 August 2014.

150 Chester Brown, 'Resolving International Investment Disputes' in Natalie Klein (ed.), *Litigating International Law Disputes: Weighing the Options* (CUP 2014) 401.

151 See among others Anna Joubin-Bret and Jean E Kalicki (eds), *Reform of Investor-State Dispute Settlement: In Search of a Roadmap* (2014) 1 TDM, including among others, Christian T Campbell, 'Assessing Treaty-based Investor-State Dispute Settlement: Abandon, Retain or Reform?'; Christoph H Schreuer,

resolution system suitable for it to implement the right to development. Venezuela, Ecuador, and Bolivia, have opted to withdraw altogether from the ICSID Convention, a move that has been remarked as 'counterproductive' or disadvantageous to these states.[152] Australia opted to remove any investor-State dispute settlement mechanism in its negotiations of the Australia-US Free Trade Agreement.[153] Indonesia announced plans to terminate over sixty bilateral investment treaties in order to prevent multinational companies from suing Indonesia in investor-State arbitrations.[154] Others advocate system reform, given the overall effectiveness and salience of the investor-State dispute settlement processes.[155]

There is no settled path for any State's ultimate decision whether or not to participate in or subscribe to investor-State arbitration as the prescribed form of dispute settlement in its international investment agreements. There are, of course, other modes of dispute prevention, settlement, and resolution, each with their own idiosyncratic advantages and disadvantages.[156] Considering its duties under the right to development, however, the host State has to consider the extent to which the

---

'Do We Need Investment Arbitration?'; Rudolf Dolzer, 'Perspectives for Investment Arbitration: Consistency as a Policy Goal?'; and Antonio R Parra, 'Advancing Reform at ICSID'.

[152] See Diana Marie Wick, 'The Counter-Productivity of ICSID Denunciation and Proposals for Change' (2012) 12 *Journal of International Business and Law* 241.

[153] Kyla Tienhaara and Patricia Ranald, 'Australia's Rejection of Investor-State Dispute Settlement: Four Potential Contributing Factors' (*Investment Treaty News*, 12 July 2011) <http://www.iisd.org/itn/2011/07/12/australias-rejection-of-investor-state-dispute-settlement-four-potential-contributing-factors/> accessed 18 August 2014.

[154] Ben Bland and Shawn Donnan, 'Indonesia to Terminate More than 60 Bilateral Investment Treaties' *The Financial Times* (London, 26 March 2014) <http://www.ft.com/intl/cms/s/0/3755c1b2-b4e2-11e3-af92-00144feabdc0.html#axzz34iOmf2ul> accessed 18 August 2014.

[155] Charles N Brower and Sadie Blanchard, 'From "Dealing in Virtue" to "Profiting from Injustice": The Case Against "Re-Statification" of Investment Dispute Settlement' (2014) 55 *Harvard International Law Journal Online* 45–59 <http://www.harvardilj.org/wp-content/uploads/2014/01/Brower_Blanchard_to_Publish.
pdf> accessed 18 August 2014; Christoph H Schreuer, 'Do We Need Investment Arbitration?' <http://www.univie.ac.at/intlaw/wordpress/wp-content/uploads/2014/01/Do-we-Need.pdf> accessed 18 August 2014.

[156] See UNCTAD, *Investor-State Disputes: Prevention and Alternatives to Arbitration* (United Nations 2010) <http://unctad.org/en/docs/diaeia200911_en.pdf> accessed 18 August 2014.

investor-State dispute settlement system – in tandem with the host State's investment treaty programme – would enable the host State to maintain the international investment project as a rights-based governance process. On the one hand, the host State has to 'anticipate the practical and legal consequences of the inclusion of an arbitration clause', 'select, where appropriate, the recognized arbitration rules most suited to the agreement', and 'draft specific language governing arbitration under the agreement.'[157] If the international investment planning process is but one aspect of the State's broader development programming, then the State should also weigh the costs of opening the door to investor-State arbitration, alongside its short-term and long-term capacity to undertake an effective defense in the event it is brought to compulsory arbitration under investment treaty-based consent to arbitration.[158] Some may well argue that developing States, in particular, require international technical assistance to develop more capacity to review their international investment treaty programme, as well as for cultivating the necessary in-house expertise to ably defend the host Stage against investor claims in international investment treaty arbitration.[159]

IV. CONCLUSION: AVOIDING SILOS – INVESTMENT WITHIN THE DEVELOPMENT PROCESS

Writing in 2002, Philip Alston resisted Ernst-Ulrich Petersmann's proposal to realign international human rights law with tenets of international economic law, particularly under the aegis of the World Trade Organization:

---

[157] Joseph T McLaughlin, 'Arbitration and Developing Countries' (1979) 13(2) *The International Lawyer* 211, 215.

[158] See Kevin P Gallagher and Elen Shrestha, 'Investment Treaty Arbitration and Developing Countries: A Re-Appraisal' (GDAE Working Paper No 11-01, May 2011) <http://ase.tufts.edu/gdae/Pubs/wp/11-01TreatyArbitrationReappraisal.pdf> accessed 18 August 2014.

[159] See Eric Gottwald, 'Leveling the Playing Field: Is it Time for a Legal Assistance Center for Developing Nations in Investment Treaty Arbitration?' (2007) 22 *American University International Law Review* 237; UNCTAD, 'Development Implications of International Investment Agreements' IIA Monitor No 2 (2007) <http://bit.escwa.org.lb/CMSPages/GetFile.aspx?nodeguid=0867d2c9-1fa8-4a31-a52f-cc8540ea84ff> accessed 18 August 2014; George Kahale III, 'Is Investor-State Arbitration Broken?' (2012) 7 TDM.

> The most fundamental change is that human rights would … become detached from their foundations in human dignity and would instead be viewed primarily as instrumental means for the achievement of economic policy objectives.[160]

While these misgivings were certainly justified, they do not contradict attempts now to reframe and reform international investment law within the broader panorama of obligations and international duties of States under the right to development. Investment decision-making is but one aspect of the State's development decision-making processes, and to approach the former as a separate phenomenon from the latter is what invites a deep discord, in the first place, between guaranteeing adequate investment protection while maintaining the State's ability to realize the full spectrum of human rights. The burgeoning of human rights claims in international investment arbitrations[161] have merely begun to unravel the crux of the problem. When States do not include their international human rights obligations as part of the continuing regulatory fabric governing international investment project planning, they fail to convey the precise degree of regulatory and political risk to be anticipated from the investment, and ultimately cause the 'mis-pricing' of the investment as a whole while sparing investors from any degree of accountability for the environmental and social impacts of their operations. The State's mandate under the right to development makes this silo mentality anathema to the difficult public choices in economic programming – which require embedding international human rights at every step of development decision-making.

---

[160] Alston (n 54) 843.

[161] See Pierre-Marie Dupuy, 'Unification Rather than Fragmentation of International Law? The Case of International Investment Law and Human Rights Law' in Pierre-Marie Dupuy, Francesco Francioni and Ernst-Ulrich Petersmann (eds), *Human Rights in International Investment Law and Arbitration* (OUP 2009) 45.

13. The law of investment protection and poverty reduction

Krista Nadakavukaren Schefer*

I. INTRODUCTION

The contribution of foreign direct investment to a nation's economic growth and development has long been hypothesized, investigated, and backed up by data showing it to be true. Skeptics seemingly never tire of pointing out the ambiguity of the numbers and the questionable causation between investment flows and development indicators, but there does seem to be agreement that sustained economic development requires at least some measure of economic growth and that economic growth, in turn, will require the inflow of resources (money, goods, services, technologies, or knowledge) to an economy. Thus, while it would be rash (and certainly wrong) to assert that investment alone will lead to development, it is safe to assume that foreign investment contributes to economic growth, which itself is a requirement for development.

The contributions in this volume examine the ways in which the law of protecting foreign investors from host state actions impact on development and developing countries. This question is important because development is an explicit goal of many international investment agreements (IIAs), and both host and home state governments rely on investment to 'work' to stimulate development and improve standards of living as well as the economic capacity of the host. But development is a broad term – maybe even more appropriately called a concept – and exactly which aspects are furthered by investment and investment protection (themselves arguably two different questions) may be unclear if treating it as a whole. A narrower question, asking what is the relationship between investment law and poverty reduction, is more suited to a single chapter, and it is that which I propose to do here.

* My sincere thanks go to Julian Powell for his assistance in preparing the manuscript for publication and to Christian Arnsperger for his helpful insights.

Why poverty reduction? Partly because poverty reduction is at the top of the global political agenda. From the poignant statements by our leaders as to the need for combatting its causes and effects, to the vigorous debates as to whether foreign aid contributes or detracts from a state's ability to reduce it and the well-orchestrated photo-shoots of movie stars with its victims, poverty is something that everyone seems to recognize as needing to be attacked, even if the methods for doing so are not agreed upon. Connected closely, as much of investment law is, with institutions and states that are committed to poverty reduction, it seems natural that investment law itself would be examined from the perspective of its relationship with poverty.

Poverty reduction is also important because it is a challenge for industrialized countries as well as developing ones. Whereas the most severe physical consequences of poverty are suffered in states of the global South, poor individuals are found in every nation of the world. In the world's wealthiest country, the official estimate of the number of persons without a home on any given day is 640,000,[1] well over half of the states have more than 20 percent of their children growing up with 'food insecurity',[2] and the situation of the working poor is deteriorating. The shifting currents of investment flows, then, will not resolve the investment-poverty reduction relationship. It will remain relevant for years to come.

Finally, despite its political prominence, poverty reduction is largely ignored by international law. There is no recognized legal duty on the part of governments to reduce poverty (although there is a demand on states to alleviate the most apparent consequences of financial deprivation). Nor is there a legal duty to assist other states in their attempts to reduce poverty. Asking if, and if so how, investment law affects those attempts, cannot end with an analysis of legal conflict of laws. It requires considering how we can approach the question of whether the legal

---

[1] US Department of Housing and Urban Development, 'Opening Doors: Federal Strategic Plan to Prevent and End Homelessness 2010' <http://usich.gov/opening_doors/> accessed 5 November 2013; this number is corroborated by the National Alliance to End Homelessness (NAEH), whose 2012 report noted the 1% drop in the number of homeless between 2009 and 2011, to just over 636,000 in 2011; NAEH, 'State of Homelessness in America 2012' <http://www.endhomelessness.org/library/entry/the-state-of-homelessness-in-america-2012> accessed 5 November 2013.

[2] See Craig Gundersen and others, *Map the Meal Gap 2013* (Feeding America 2013) <http://feedingamerica.org/hunger-in-america/hunger-studies/map-the-meal-gap.aspx> accessed 5 November 2013.

system of investor protection is compatible with a further evolution of the international legal system toward a duty to reduce poverty.

In this chapter, I set out the contours of such an analysis with no illusions of providing a comprehensive examination of the problem or answering the ultimate question. While my preliminary conclusion leads to the suspicion that investment law – as a system primarily aimed at protecting existing resource distributions and status quo property rights – is incompatible with the emergence of an international right to poverty reduction to the extent that such a right would entail a duty of international assistance – this is not intended to be normative. One might decide that what needs to be changed is the idea that the law of investment protection is about development at all.

Part II sets out a short account of what poverty is and why poverty reduction is a goal of the international community. In Part III, the relationship between investment law and poverty is examined. The conclusions of Part IV suggest a way forward for scholars of investment law and poverty law.

II. POVERTY IN A NUTSHELL

A. Defining Poverty

Defining the term 'poverty' is a more challenging undertaking than one might think if one is not in the habit of doing so. Like a diamond, it has rough versions and polished ones, the latter with multiple facets. The rough version of poverty is the obvious connection of poverty with a lack of money – an individual living in poverty lives without (or with a low) income and without capital. The results of such deprivation range from the extreme (starvation, homelessness) to the moderate (the inability to purchase goods that others in the community have and value), and are assessed by poverty scholars as indicating either absolute (or extreme) poverty or 'relative' poverty.[3]

The more advanced definitions of poverty rely on the results of deprivation rather than on the depth of deprivation. The most popular of these accounts is that promoted by Amartya Sen, who recognizes the consequences of rough 'income poverty' in his analysis of human

---

[3] See Krista Nadakavukaren Schefer, 'Preface' in Krista Nadakavukaren Schefer (ed.), *Poverty and the International Economic Legal System: Duties to the World's Poor* (CUP 2013) xxv–xxvi (describing the forms of poverty).

development.[4] Sen takes into account monetary deprivation's direct effects on purchasing power, but also the social deprivations deriving from a broader notion of poverty. The idea of poverty as an 'unfreedom' extends the term 'poverty' to include low levels of education and poor health, frequently to economic exploitation, and a disproportionate exposure to violence and crime.[5] Moreover – and this is implied in Sen's choice of the label 'unfreedom' income poverty leads to a lack of voice in the political process, which, together with the other social disadvantages leads to a life of limited opportunities.

The unfreedom conception of poverty can be taken further to highlight the less tangible aspects of deprivation on the individual – anxiety and depression. The former arises from the uncertainty that accompanies lives of poverty. It is not only that impoverished individuals face fewer opportunities to pursue personally satisfying lives, they face uncertainty of opportunities. Research on the financial behavior of families living in extreme poverty point out that the 'dollar-a-day' poor are actually not receiving one dollar per day.[6] They may receive two dollars today, and no dollars for the rest of the week, with a five dollar day next month. Knowing when the dollars will come in, however, could be as important for relieving poverty's psychological burden as having more total dollars at the end of the month. The anxiety caused by uncertainty is common among those facing poverty, whether the poverty is extreme or relative.[7]

Depression and social exclusion are other effects of poverty, ones which are often seen in situations of relative poverty (where subsistence needs are fulfilled but where the inequality of resources is apparent).[8] For

---

[4] See, e.g., Amartya Sen, *Development as Freedom* (OUP 1999).

[5] Ibid 88–92.

[6] Daryl Collins and others, *Portfolios of the Poor: How the World's Poor Live on $2 a Day* (PUP 2009) 39–52 (describing income uncertainty as the second prong of the 'triple whammy' of poverty: low income, uncertainty of income, and ill-suited financial institutions).

[7] See generally Deepa Narayan and others, *Voices of the Poor: Crying Out for Change* (OUP/World Bank 2000) 21–43; see particularly 37 (explaining the psychological effects of poverty and quoting an impoverished person from Russia as saying 'Wellbeing is a life free from daily worries about lack of money').

[8] See, e.g., Christopher J Hudson, 'Socioeconomic Status and Mental Illness: Tests of Social Causation and Selection Hypotheses' (2005) 75 *American Journal of Orthopsychiatry* 3; Jane D McLeod and Michael J Shanahan, 'Trajectories of Poverty and Children's Mental Health' (1996) 37 *Journal of Health and Social Behavior* 207 (finding that poverty in childhood affects the likelihood of mental health and that the duration of experience poverty corresponds to the level of problems); see also The Lancet's 2007 and 2011 series on

the poor in industrialized countries, the problems of poverty may be different than those of the starving in sub-Saharan Africa, but nevertheless debilitating. In the case of relative poverty, the unfreedom stems from the inequality itself – the inability to access social resources pushes those with little property into positions of social inferiority, which in turn reinforces and perpetuates the socio-economic division. The social norms that emerge to shield the non-poor make reducing relative poverty potentially more difficult than reducing extreme poverty.

B. The Problematization of Poverty: Why the Call for Poverty Reduction

That extreme poverty is a 'problem' for individuals is clear. Indeed, it is built into the definition, which indicates a deprivation of resources so severe that the individual (or family) cannot meet its subsistence needs. That relative poverty is a problem for individuals is also clear, given the readily recognizable limits on opportunities to lead a life one values that accompany such a condition.

As this chapter focuses on investment law and poverty reduction, however, we must not only concern ourselves with how poverty affects the individual. We need to know why poverty is a problem for states, for it is the state-led poverty reduction program that is the potential target of investors' legal claims.

It is here that the matter gets complicated, for states' concern with *extreme* poverty can clearly be linked to the emergence of the ethic of the state as a guarantor of the general welfare of the citizen. This has grown with the solidification of human rights' emphasis on the positive duties of the state to protect basic rights. Yet, the reason behind governments' attention to *relative* poverty is less transparent.

The legal basis for such attention (which may or may not be the politically relevant one) must stem from the idea of equality. Any poverty reduction programs that extend beyond the provision of basic sustenance rely, on a theoretical level, on the role of the government in protecting the right of each person to equal opportunities of access to public goods. Thus, the analysis of investment law and poverty must address how

---

global mental health, which demonstrate the established links between poverty and mental illness in industrialized countries but only incipient research on the problems in developing countries <http://www.thelancet.com/series/global-mental-health> accessed 5 November 2013 and <http://www.thelancet.com/journals/lancet/issue/vol378no9801/PIIS0140-6736%2811%29X6043-9> accessed 5 November 2013.

investment law responds to attempts to remedy unequal distributions of resources, and not just how it helps or hinders the provision of food, water, or land.

1. Poverty reduction: The new moral minimum?

There is a clear and widely held belief in the ethical value of reducing poverty in today's world. Surprising to many of us, this was not always the case. Although the social and religious importance of the poor has been recognized for centuries, their importance was mainly a function of their effect – as poor persons – on the rest of society. Rulers and the wealthy *needed* the poor – as laborers, as subjects, or – intriguingly – as objects of mercy.[9] The role of charity and philanthropy in earlier societies, therefore, was different than today's efforts to reduce the number of people living in destitution.[10] Alms and public provision of food and shelter for the poor were to minimize suffering, maximize the forgiveness of one's sins, reduce the threat of political upheaval, or foster a particular vision of society – not to reduce the number of people in poverty. The same can be said for numerous other efforts of poverty relief which emphasized the easing of the hardships of the poor without questioning whether there should be the poor at all.

It was not until ideas of equality spread that poverty became an element of the political landscape. The identification of the poor themselves as poor-but-equal-in-inherent-rights ignited their awareness of the lack of power that accompanied their poverty, and with that self-realization came demands for change. It was the (political) demands of equality that therefore spurred the pursuit of poverty reduction. No longer was an alleviation of the worst effects of poverty – hunger and lack of shelter – the sole ethical command.

The moral minimum of the modern age is one that recognizes all humans as equal in inherent dignity. This has been transposed into law through the system of international human rights, a system that itself has fundamentally changed international law from its pre-World War II limits of state-centrality. Equality before the law and the non-discriminatory treatment as rights that an individual can demand from her own government form the basis of the international human rights system. Because living in poverty subjects persons to situations antithetical to dignity,

---

[9] Bronislaw Geremek, *Poverty: A History* (Blackwell Publishers 1997) 20 (noting the role of poverty in the doctrine of charitable giving set out in the *Life of St Eligius*).

[10] See generally ibid for a discussion of how ideas about poverty and poverty reduction were considered in the Middle Ages in Europe.

poverty must be combatted. Thus, all individuals must have access to adequate food and water, all individuals must have access to adequate shelter, and all children must have access to basic education. These minimum standards are the basis of the current international commitment to poverty reduction.

The ethic of poverty reduction has been taken up by the world's political institutions with enthusiasm: the United Nations' Millennium Development Goals set out a goal of reducing poverty by half by 2015 and the post-2015 Agenda aims even further – at eradicating extreme poverty by 2030;[11] the UN Development Program calls poverty reduction an 'overarching goal' and a 'core' of its work;[12] the EU 2020 program aims to move 20 million Europeans out of poverty by 2020;[13] USAID has set a target of eliminating extreme poverty by 2050;[14] the ASEAN Foundation spends a large portion of its funds seeking to alleviate poverty and its effects;[15] and the Organization of Islamic Conference's Fund for Poverty Reduction implements the Islamic Development Bank's 'strategic' of reducing poverty levels.[16] Numerous other political institutions – national, regional, local – have similar aims. Private institutions and individual opinion leaders, too, promote poverty reduction as an

---

11 Report of the Secretary-General of the United Nations, 'A Life of Dignity for All: Accelerating Progress Towards the Millennium Development Goals and Advancing the United Nations Development Agenda Beyond 2015', A/68/202 para 73.

12 UNDP, 'Fast Facts' (January 2013) <http://www.undp.org/content/dam/undp/library/corporate/fast-facts/english/FF-Poverty-Reduction.pdf> accessed 23 January 2014.

13 See European Commission, 'European Platform Against Poverty and Social Exclusion' <http://ec.europa.eu/social/main.jsp?catId=961> accessed 23 January 2014; see also European Commission, 'Europe 2020' <http://ec.europa.eu/europe2020/index_en.htm> accessed 26 April 2014 (official website of the Europe 2020 program, setting out priorities, targets, flagship initiatives, country-specific recommendations, and other information about the projects and progress as well as links).

14 USAID, 'Ending Extreme Poverty' <http://www.usaid.gov/endextremepoverty> accessed 23 January 2014.

15 Filemon A Uriarte, 'Poverty Alleviation: Initiatives of the ASEAN Foundation' (ASEAN Foundation 2008) 5, 16, 18 <http://www.aseanfoundation.org/documents/brochure/poverty%2010oct08.pdf> accessed 26 April 2014.

16 Islamic Development Bank, 'Policy Paper on Poverty Reduction' (April 2007) 6; see also Amadou Boubacar Cisse, 'Tackling Poverty Reduction: The Role of the Islamic Development Bank', XLV UN Chronicle 1 what is this? (March 2008) <http://unchronicle.un.org/article/tackling-poverty-reduction-role-islamic-development-bank/> accessed 23 January 2014.

ethic. The Ford Foundation, the Bill and Melinda Gates Foundation, Warren Buffett and his wealthy friends, and countless other personalities, rock stars, football players, actors and actresses – all of them see reducing poverty as a moral call. Moreover, unlike on many ethical issues, there are few voices that openly challenge this dominant perspective on the 'goodness' of reducing poverty.

There is more to the human rights dimension of poverty than that of fulfilling subsistence needs, however. Human rights' foundations in the inherent dignity of each individual means that equality is also valued. By considering this as extending to the equality of opportunities, the moral value of eliminating poverty can be recognized as including relative poverty as well as absolute poverty.

2. Poverty reduction as an economic necessity?

Parallel to the ethical turn toward recognizing poverty as incompatible with the fulfillment of human rights, economists recognize widespread poverty as a hindrance to development and have called for poverty reduction in the name of macroeconomic health.[17] The findings of researchers from across the political spectrum have confirmed the fact that nations cannot attain lasting economic growth where a majority (or even significant minority) of the population is occupied with ensuring its mere survival.[18] Deep markets will not form where would-be consumers have incomes that are small and unpredictable. Production will falter where employees are regularly absent due to diseases that may be preventable, but whose cure is too costly. Technology-driven growth will elude states where families must send children into paid work instead of schools. The effects of poverty are detrimental to economic development by limiting production and consumption, the drivers of macroeconomic growth.

3. Poverty reduction as a legal norm? Not yet

The widespread ethical and economic agreement that poverty should be reduced does not mean, however, that reducing poverty is regarded by all – or even by many – as a duty that should be enforced by law. Legal institutions have been less quick to take on the challenge of poverty

---

[17] See, e.g., Humberto Lopez and Luis Servén, 'Too Poor to Grow', Policy Research Working Paper 5012 (World Bank, August 2009) (including numerous further references to the literature).

[18] Both Milton Friedman, *Capitalism and Freedom* (Chicago UP 2002) and Amartya Sen (n 4) agree that poverty can hinder development. The difference between the two is how to address poverty.

reduction. Thus, the legal demands to help the impoverished are indirect – through redistributive tax systems that pay for income supplements, subsidized health care, or public education systems.

Moreover, the rights and duties involved in the laws relating to poverty reduction are local. The legal demands for more equitable wealth distribution remain within national boundaries, with the rights of state sovereignty ensuring on the one hand that governments with large populations of impoverished residents can deflect international attempts to improve internal financial redistribution as intervention in their domestic affairs, and on the other that wealthy states can remain impervious to efforts to establish supranational mechanisms of resource transfers. Poverty reduction, in fact, can only become a legal issue for international law if poverty were to be seen as a threat to international peace or recognized as a condition that prevents individuals from living a life of dignity.

The latter, of course, opens the door to seeing poverty reduction as a matter of human rights.[19] And indeed, as viewed currently, poverty has mainly been discussed as a matter of economic and social rights.[20] To be sure, the provisions of the International Covenant on Economic, Social, and Cultural Rights (ICESCR)[21] clearly correspond to the situation of the poor, and the duties on states to ensure a minimum core of the basic economic rights contained in Articles 23, 25, and 26 can be combined to imply a right to not live in extreme poverty.[22] The arguments as to the fundamental importance of ensuring such rights have been made *in extenso* elsewhere. Here, the critical issue is that viewing poverty reduction as an economic right can address the most immediately obvious detriments of being extremely poor (hunger, lack of shelter, lack of education), but the duties of the state to protect individuals from such

---

19 Besson warns against making all problems facing humanity an issue of human rights law; Samantha Besson, 'The Allocation of Anti-Poverty Rights Duties' in Nadakavukaren Schefer (n 3) 431.

20 This, despite the recognition of the interdependence of all human rights as set out in the Maastricht Principles on Extraterritorial Obligations of States in the area of Economic, Social and Cultural Rights (28 February 2012).

21 UNGA Res 2200A (XXI) (1966) UN Doc A/6316; 993 UNTS 3; (1967) 6 ILM 368.

22 See Shareen Hertel and Lanse Minkler, 'Introduction: Economic Rights: The Terrain' in Shareen Hertel and Lanse Minkler (eds), *Economic Rights: Conceptual, Measurement and Policy Issues* (CUP 2007) 3–6.

hardships remain basic and – despite at least a decade of scholarship – controversial.[23]

International human rights law has not fully developed a theory for protecting the rights of the relatively poor, although the growing regard to the political implications of poverty in the domestic context is a step in this direction.[24] A more effective human rights approach to poverty would require the international legal community to further examine the political and civil rights implications of resource deprivations on individuals and families. Here, the primary analytical focus must be the rule of equality of persons. It is only through this call to treat all individuals as equals before the law (except where the public interest can override the discriminatory treatment) that human rights approaches to poverty can fully begin the process of juridifying the moral duties of poverty reduction on an international scale.

Finally, the lack of consensus regarding the extraterritorial duties of states to promote and protect human rights leaves the case for international resource transfers open.[25] Despite the recognition of the dangers of global wealth inequalities to world peace and the detriments to sustainable economic growth, governments have no enforceable obligation to offer financial assistance to one another in even the most extreme situations of need. Correspondingly, no government has a right to demand assistance from another or from the international community. That poverty reduction *should* be pursued is not in dispute, but national governments cannot rely on their neighbors to help them to reach such a goal. In the end, it is the national government that must act to the full extent possible within its means to fulfill its human rights obligations. While asking other governments for help is a part of fulfilling its attempts to satisfy its duties, there is no corresponding duty on other states to respond. This becomes important to the analysis of investment law's role in poverty reduction, as I will now explain.

---

[23] See Monica Hakimi, 'Human Rights Obligations to the Poor' in Nadakavukaren Schefer (n 3) 406.

[24] Recall the discussions surrounding the actions of several States of the United States to restrict voting rights in the run-up to the 2012 elections. Framed by the courts as a matter of racial inequality, the basic issue was one of economic deprivation as a functional limit on the right of an individual to vote; see, e.g., Wendy Weiser and Diana Kasdan, 'Voting Law Changes: Election Update' (Brennan Center for Justice 2012).

[25] Hakimi notes that extraterritorial duties would only arise where the state has complete control over the territory of another state or has 'substantially' enabled a human rights violator to act without appropriate restraint; Hakimi (n 23) 401–02.

III. INVESTMENT LAW AND POVERTY REDUCTION

Turning our attention to the context of investment (that is, the activity of placing resources in a foreign state territory and managing the profit-making activity) and investment law (the rules on protection of an investment from host state actions), the role of poverty and poverty reduction becomes very diffuse because the legal relationship at the heart of rules for investment protection is confined to the contours of the investor's interests in maintaining her property rights. While it is the state's actions that are assessed, it is only in so far as those actions impact on the investor's interests that they are of legal interest.

Likewise, it is only in so far as the reasons behind the actions can justify the impacts on the investor that they are relevant at all to investment law. Even then they may not relieve the state of its duties toward the investor. Thus, poverty reduction measures, if they affect the investor's interests, become relevant to investment law as measures affecting the investment relationship, not as measures to reduce poverty. While this may seem obvious, it has implications on the suitability of the investment law system to adapt to changes in the law of poverty.

A. The Aims of Investment Law

Before beginning to consider how investment law and poverty are related, and to what extent the former can contribute to the reduction of the latter, it is helpful to recall what it is that investment law is intended to achieve. The short answer to this is that it aims to increase the amount of wealth available in the world by incentivizing property owners to put their property to productive use. The specific role of the investment protection rules (i.e., those that are found in international investment agreements), is to guarantee those property owners the continued ownership of their property and any financial profits flowing from such productive use of it. As important as the wealth-increasing goal is, it is the IIA rules that are seen as the cornerstone of the investment law system. It is the protection rules that are to act as the incentive to the increased use of foreign property owners' wealth, and therefore it is by understanding such rules that we can determine the norms underlying the system.

1. Historical development of investment protection

International investment law[26] did not originate from any development impulses, much less from considerations of poverty reduction. From its beginnings (which we can take to be the nineteenth century, even though the rules of sovereign courtesy which promised no uncompensated takings of foreign property stem from at least the Middle Ages), investment law was concerned with securing the *investor's* well-being, not the condition of the host state before or after the investment and certainly not the well-being of the host's native population.[27]

While the large foreign investments of the nineteenth century did increase the amount of wealth in the world, and undeniably contributed to the economic capacities of host territories, the great majority of investors (most of whom had never seen the tangible effects of their capital) were more interested in securing their own profits than in promoting any cosmopolitan views of global development. Unable to effectively protect their rights to their foreign property against host state governments on their own, investors turned to their home governments for diplomatic protection of their economic interests. This need for the involvement of the home state fostered the evolution of a practice of promoting public international investment rules that centered on the distinctly private interests of the investor's rights in his property and its profit-making potential. While the home state could conceivably have pursued development goals as a foreign policy while pursuing diplomatic protection (such as the creation of consumer markets or more capable allies), this was rarely the actual motivation for action. Governments meant to ensure that their investors received the economic value of the investment (the income flows it was to provide) rather than the host's interests in the property that was the primary feature of such interactions.

The legal principles arising from such practices thus evolved so as to shield those who had capital to risk from suffering avoidable financial losses that might arise due to a host government taking advantage of its sovereignty over the physical presence of the foreigner's assets within its jurisdiction. As the actions of host states in this respect were often in violation of the rule of law (being arbitrary, discriminatory, or not in the

---

26 While no multilateral investment protection treaty exists, the large number of bilateral investment treaties (BITs) and growing number of regional investment agreements with both similar terms and commitment-multilateralizing clauses within them means that one can write of 'international investment law' without risking too much inaccuracy.

27 Krista Nadakavukaren Schefer, *International Investment Law: Text, Cases and Materials* (Edward Elgar Publishing 2013) 3–5.

public's interest), the law of investment protection became a bulwark against unjust governmental interference in the investor's rights to her property. From the beginnings of the globalized economy, then, 'investment law' was the 'law of investment protection' – a transboundary protection of the right to property.

2. Investment law today

This traditional commitment to the protection of the investor's right to property continues in modern investment law. True, today it is frequently combined with a firm nod toward the host state's own interests, with IIA preambular language sometimes stressing the assumed developmental benefits of the treaty's protections and several tribunals demonstrating a readiness to grant hosts policy space to regulate investors' activities.

Modifying the law's basic premise that justice requires that the rules of investment protection presume that individuals are 'entitled' to their holdings, no matter how morally arbitrary the original distribution of holdings is, entails creative interpretation and a teleological approach to the decision-making role of arbitrators. And even then, investment law rules demonstrate a strong resistance to wealth redistributions.[28]

B. How Investment Activities Affect Poverty Levels: The Role of the State

1. What to ask

When looking to the specific poverty impacts of investment law, generalizations are only of limited value. National legislation on admitting investments as well as any contracts investors conclude with the State would need to be examined for indications of the basis on which permission is given: are there requirements ensuring that investments will create jobs for local populations? Are investments permitted in sectors that might create competition for industries of particular importance to disadvantaged groups? Is there a minimum duration for investments? Do investors proposing profitable but polluting activities have to submit to an environmental impact assessment before receiving admission?

Regulations applicable to admitted investments (again both general legislation and the investment contracts are relevant) must be scrutinized on the basis of the protection they afford to impoverished persons

---

[28] Robert Nozick is the philosopher most readily identified with the entitlement theory, claiming that the state should have no role in the redistribution of property; see Robert Nozick, *Anarchy, State, and Utopia* (Basic Books 1974).

working for the investment, living in the area of the investment, or impacted on by the investment: do minimum wage requirements apply to the foreign concern? Are environmental laws in place that will adequately ensure that resident populations will not be exposed to toxic levels of emissions from the investment? Will persons displaced from their homes be adequately provided for through resettlement and compensation?

Another angle requiring examination would be that of the enforcement procedures utilized by the host government. These would need to be tracked to determine whether investments that violate rules in place that would have helped the disadvantaged populations are pursued legally and sanctioned effectively.

2. What to answer – or think about in answering

The question of how an investment may affect poverty levels in the host territory can only be fully answered by empirical analysis, but can be thought of as follows. Investment is considered a prerequisite for long term economic growth and thus, going one step farther, for poverty reduction. The accuracy of this assumption may falter on the second step, but that is dependent upon the host state's policies regarding how the investment operates and how the profits are used. If the host state consciously shapes investment policies – from market access policymaking through the initial licensing of a project, to the regulation of the investor's operations – so as to maximize a distribution of the profits (for instance through increasing public service provision proportionately to the increase in the growth of tax base), secure the contribution of the investment to the long term growth of the local economy (by requiring technology transfers or local personnel training), and minimize negative externalities on the surrounding communities (including by adequately enforcing environmental and labor regulations), the investment is likely to contribute to poverty reduction.

Where the government ignores the interests of the poor, on the other hand, there is no security that the economic growth spurred by the investment will have any beneficial effects on the incomes (let alone on the lives) of the poor. This is because there is nothing inherent in the investment relationship to ensure that the profits of the investment are redistributed to the local population. While in most cases this would simply result in no improvements in the levels of poverty, the effects can be serious enough to result in a violation of the state's duties to protect its population's basic rights where there had not been any before (as when a foreign company's purchase of a water-supply concession fails to include maximum pricing clauses to safeguard the impoverished individuals' de facto right of access to an adequate supply of water).

C. How Investment Law Might Regard Poverty Reduction Measures

Unlike the empirical collection of information that is necessary for assessing how investment relates to poverty, those interested in the relationship could consider what sorts of policies governments might implement to reduce poverty and determine whether they would violate investment protection provisions.

Numerous investment and human rights analyses examining the legality of governmental policies result in findings similar to what one can discover when analyzing investment and poverty.[29] Such results depend on a view of poverty as identical to deprivations of economic and social human rights: that is, poverty as *extreme* poverty. The more problematic relationship is looking at investment law and its effects on poverty reduction when the efforts of governments are aimed fundamentally at eliminating inequalities: that is, poverty as *relative* poverty. Investment law, as was alluded to above, concerns itself with protecting property holders' rights to their property: rights that they hold against all others, including those who have no property. To this extent, international investment law is based on protecting existing inequalities.

There are numerous poverty reduction policies that could come within the scope of an investment dispute, because there are so many paths that could be chosen to reduce poverty. Land redistributions or monetary transfers are two examples, but so are the fixing of maximum prices for basic commodities and the offer of publicly provided goods and services.

The investment law implications of any type of property (tangible or intangible) transfer are clear – once a governmental measure is classified as an expropriation (or a measure tantamount to an expropriation), treaty provisions will require the state to compensate the investor for takings, justified or not. Investment law is particularly strict in this respect, with no recognized exceptions to the rule on compensation. The tribunal in *Santa Elena v. Costa Rica* stated this plainly in the context of environmental protection measures:

> Expropriatory environmental measures – no matter how laudable and beneficial to society as a whole – are, in this respect, similar to any other expropriatory measures that a state may take in order to implement its policies (…).[30]

---

[29] See, e.g., Marc Jacobs, 'International Investment Agreements and Human Rights', INEF Research Paper Series (2010).

[30] *Santa Elena v Costa Rica*, ICSID Case No ARB/96/1, Award (17 February 2000) para 72; see also the more recent reaffirmation of this position in *Marion*

Thus, where Tanzania reversed its privatization of the water supply, its rescission of the concession was deemed compensable.[31] The investor's inability to provide its services to the local population was not relevant to the issue of whether or not the government took property from the investor, and so had no impact on the imposition of compensation – the ultimate decision to not award damages was because of the investor's own financial insolvency.[32]

Moreover, given the ambiguity of the scope tribunals will apply in determining whether a particular regulation is a taking, governments may be hesitant to implement a poverty-relief measure that could have an impact on a foreign investor. While examples of actions not taken are difficult to find, there are some reports of such occurrences. The Canadian government, for example, reportedly backed down from promoting cigarette-labeling legislation aimed at reducing smoking in the face of threats by the tobacco industry to bring an investment claim on the basis of an alleged expropriation of trademark rights. Admittedly not a poverty-reduction measure, the cigarette labeling dispute shows the regulatory chill that can be placed on public interest legislation by the ambiguity of expropriation's scope combined with its unavoidable compensation requirement.

Finally, even where a regulation does not deprive the investor of the use or control of her property, protections against unfair or unreasonable treatment may restrict how governments respond to poverty. Argentina's measures to counter its 2007 financial crisis were the focus of numerous arbitration disputes, nearly all of which ended in decisions granting investors compensation. Tribunals found Argentina's conversion of dollar-denominated debts into pesos and the imposed rigidity of concession terms to be violations of the obligation of fair and equitable treatment.[33] Once again, the host state's appeals to the concerns for the effects of the economic situation on its impoverished residents were subordinated to the government's obligations to its investors and their income.

Unglaube v Republic of Costa Rica, ICSID Case No ARB/08/1, Award (16 May 2012) para 217.

[31] *Biwater Gauff (Tanzania) v United Republic of Tanzania*, ICSID Case No ARB/05/22, Award (24 July 2008) para 519.

[32] Ibid para 807.

[33] See, e.g., *CMS v Republic of Argentina*, ICSID Case No ARB/01/8, Award (12 May 2005); *BG Group Plc v Republic of Argentina*, UNCITRAL. Award (24 December 2007); *National Grid Plc v Republic of Argentina*, UNCITRAL, Award (3 November 2008).

A different aspect to consider is whether investment law promotes poverty reduction where governments are inactive. This is a particularly important angle where the interests of the host government are more closely aligned with those of the investor than with those of its impoverished citizens. The structure of international investment law relies on the activity of the investor to invoke its protections. While development (and implicitly poverty reduction) may be a goal of the system, its pursuit is not an obligation owed to the investor or the states parties to the IIA. Thus, the law of investment is likely to be relatively resistant to poverty reduction apathy. Investment arbitration provides no opening for the interests of the impoverished to be heard outside of the investor or the host's arguments. A host state's refusal to redistribute income from an investment will hardly be complained of by an investor, and those whom such an action should benefit (the poor themselves) will have no standing to complain. Even where tribunals allow third persons to submit views, such amicus submissions must relate to the legal issues of the dispute – not to the social circumstances in general.[34]

A more fundamental approach to the question of investment law's relationship to poverty calls for an examination of whether investment law's core function is compatible with the essence of poverty reduction. Under this approach, the specifics of the cases are less important than the general directions of legal development.

As a legal claim, a call for poverty reduction is more than the sum total of calling for adherence to the rights to basic economic subsistence. As important as fulfillment of the rights to food, shelter, and an adequate income is, it is only by recognizing each individual's right to be treated as equal to every other individual that can capture the multifaceted disadvantages of living in poverty. The demand for equality is what allows the provision of food and shelter to be demanded and not just requested,[35] and what makes these rights 'civil' and 'political' as well as 'economic'.

For the state, the obligations corresponding to food and shelter can be satisfied by providing the food or providing the shelter – but the right to equality requires more. The government must ensure that the individual is

---

[34] See, e.g., *Suez v Republic of Argentina*, ICSID Case No ARB/03/19, Order in Response to a Petition for Participation as Amicus Curiae (17 March 2006) paras 17–18 (listing, as one of the tests for permitting a submission from an amicus, that the subject matter of the submission be appropriate to the subject matter of the case).

[35] Henry Shue, *Basic Rights: Subsistence, Affluence, and US Foreign Policy* (2nd edn, Princeton UP 1996).

given as much opportunity to pursue her life's choices as any other. While it does not entail a promise of equal income, the right to equality is incompatible with barriers to access to policymaking bodies or the courts or other differential rights based on income.

Investment law is not only unconcerned about the principle of substantive equality, it cannot accommodate it in a strong form. Investment law's claimants are restricted to propertied individuals – the definition of an 'investor' as one who makes an investment itself ensures that those without capital, knowledge, or goods will have no role in its legal regime.

The substantive principles of investment law as set out in treaties – providing for compensation for expropriations, guaranteeing 'full protection and security' of investments from damage by third persons, holding governments to minimal standards of conduct in relation to the treatment of investors and investments – further the emphasis on the non-impoverished, and promote their accumulation of further wealth. Asserting that those who have property (i.e. investors) may not be divested unlawfully or unfairly of the property they have (i.e. their investment and the flows of income from the investment), reinforces any existing inequalities and disincentivizes governmental attempts to redistribute wealth.

The procedural law of investment, offering investors access to binding arbitration in cases of alleged violations of the treaty provisions, too, supports existing holdings by promising injured investors compensation for any financial losses. As arbitration procedures are closed to claims by non-investors, the interests of the poor can have no direct voice in the proceedings.[36] Neither are the broader interests of a more equal society likely to be raised, given the arbitrators' limited jurisdictional competence.

The obvious result of the procedural and substantive rules of investment is that the calls for poverty reduction are unlikely to be made in the

[36] In some cases, the public does not even know of investment disputes brought against their government. In other cases, the dispute's existence may be public knowledge but the details of the proceedings remain confidential. The debate between confidentiality and transparency in investor-State dispute settlement is a topic of growing significance and attention; see *Telefónica SA v Mexico*, ICSID Case No ARB(AF)/12/4, Procedural Order No 1 (8 July 2013), and the dissenting opinion of Arbitrator Ramirez para. 15 (disagreeing with the majority's decision to keep the proceedings confidential, since transparency is a 'fundamental value' of arbitration proceedings when states are involved).

context of a dispute.[37] If they are made, tribunals are unlikely to permit such calls to affect the investor's holdings so as to lessen the inequality between it and the impoverished nationals of the host state.

The more insidious result of the investment law regime as perceived today is that it makes poverty reduction programs less likely to be attempted in the first place. Those governments that welcome investment likely do so in the hopes of reducing poverty by attracting foreign capital. Where economic growth results, they may not see the need to engage in further programs to reduce the wealth inequalities that often accompany such growth. On the other hand, where growth is not occurring (or where extreme poverty is absent), governments may shy away from implementing plans to reduce wealth inequalities given the likelihood of objection by their investors against such programs and the difficulty in defending them before arbitration tribunals. In these situations, making a demand for equality in a human rights context may be the only type of legal action open to the poor.

What does this mean for states' poverty reduction programs? The above analysis of investment law as a legal system based on inequalities is not intended to condemn the system of property protection that it embodies as morally bankrupt or even as not valuable. First, where foreign direct investments are placed because of protections to investments provided by treaty rules, this certainly has benefits on the reduction of absolute poverty. The direct and indirect employment offered by such investments is one part of this, but the competition for foreign investment also acts as an incentive to governments to increase the education and health of their populations in order to 'win' investments. Such improvements in the human infrastructure themselves reduce the unfreedoms of poverty.

The concerns set forth above, then, are more in relation to investment law's ability to condone reductions in relative poverty, or inequalities. In this area, the entitlement-basis of investment law is at odds with reducing great divisions of holdings. Even there, however, substantial progress can be made compatible with investment protection if the political will exists to do so, because investment law remains a creation of states. Most significantly, states have not subjected their fiscal policy competences to the compensation requirements of investment protection: taxation regulations often do not fall within the scope of IIAs. Thus, as long as taxation is not used to unjustifiably or unfairly burden foreign investors

---

[37] Christopher Kee, 'International Commercial Arbitration and Poverty, not Obvious but (Maybe) Possible' in Nadakavukaren Schefer (n 3) 144–58.

(for instance, by imposing high taxes on a specific company or by unfounded prosecutions of investors on the grounds of alleged tax fraud), states are still free to use tax policies to achieve the transfer of wealth necessary to eliminate relative poverty. Such policies need, of course, to adequately weigh the effects of taxes on investors' willingness to place investments against the poverty reduction benefits they would achieve, but the investment protection rules themselves should not be blamed as the cause of a government's decision not to use taxation-based redistribution, should this be the result of the balancing of interests.

IV. CONCLUSION

Investigating the relationship between poverty and the investment law regime is a valuable corollary to examinations of investment law's impacts on development. Investment law's emphasis on property rights and fair treatment of (propertied) foreigners is not designed to alleviate poverty directly, nor is it a regime that incorporates the voices or the interests of the poor. Yet, as its evolution into a mechanism for development continues, its potential to help or hurt those living with economic deprivation becomes worthy of sustained attention.

This chapter has left the empirical effects of investment admission and regulation on the poor to be analyzed by others, attempting instead to theorize on whether investment protection as set forth in today's IIAs and interpreted by recent arbitral tribunals can be a force for reducing poverty or if it stands in the way of poverty reduction. If my characterization of the need to pursue poverty reduction as a consequence of the right to equality is correct, there is reason to doubt investment law's full compatibility with its advancement.

To equalize resource holdings, poverty reduction must not only generate increased wealth (to ensure the elimination of absolute poverty), it must ensure that those with less receive a disproportionate share of the increase (to ensure the elimination of relative poverty). Whereas investment protection law is presumed to serve the first goal, the second is hampered because the rules assume the investors' entitlement to existing holdings. The belief in this entitlement makes investment law resistant to redistribution, and this stands at odds with efforts to address inequalities that are at the heart of poverty reduction goals. Any government-led redistribution of property is likely to entail duties on the state to compensate the investor for losses.

By thus forcing states to choose between not reducing the value of investors' property or compensating them to the extent of such losses, investment protection rules ensure that poverty reduction efforts are financed nationally. Foreign property cannot be used to reduce inequalities. With no rights for host states in general international law to receive foreign assistance and no international duties on home states to give such, the dilemma of poverty reduction versus investor protection is likely to remain a silent muffler of progress for the poor.

Investment law, however, is mainly treaty-based. Its principles and procedures are open to change by states – states which are bound by the norms of human rights to ensure the equality of treatment of individuals as well as their protection from want. The rules of investment law can be changed if there is a will to witness the implementation of human equality on a global scale.

14. Mainstreaming sustainable development into international investment agreements: What role for labor provisions?

Vid Prislan and Ruben Zandvliet

I. INTRODUCTION

The relationship between international investment law and labor rights has been subject to much less scrutiny than its trade-labor counterpart, or the relationship between investment and other areas of international regulation.[1] The existence of this relationship is nonetheless a fact, as references to labor rights are increasingly added to international investment agreements (IIAs) – be it bilateral investment treaties (BITs), be it investment chapters that are now increasingly often added to free trade

---

[1] This can partly be explained by developments in treaty-making practice. While references to labor standards are still relatively scant when it comes to investment treaties, they have now become a standard feature of many bilateral or regional trade agreements. According to the ILO, labor provisions were included in about one third of all trade agreements that came into force between 2005 and 2013; ILO, *Social Dimensions of Free Trade Agreements* (ILO 2013) 1920. Arguably, the relatively scant scholarly interest may have to do with the fact that there have not (yet) been any controversial cases of investors using investor-State arbitration to challenge domestic regulatory action in the field of labor standards. Nor have there been any inter-State arbitrations on the basis of labor provisions in IIAs, although at the time of writing this contribution formal consultations were pending between the United States and Bahrain pursuant to the US-Bahrain FTA. Also, a formal request for arbitration has previously been filed under the CAFTA-DR in relation to a complaint brought by US and Guatemalan workers' organizations against Guatemala. But that arbitration was subsequently suspended as the US and Guatemala negotiated a comprehensive enforcement plan.

agreements (FTAs) or economic partnership agreements (EPAs).[2] Indeed, the inclusion of such provisions is now considered instrumental to enhancing the sustainable development dimension of international investment policies, and to strengthen the development dimension of investment treaties in particular.[3]

In an attempt to contribute to a better understanding of the investment-labor linkage,[4] the present chapter explores the different forms in which these provisions appear in IIAs, and provides an analytical framework to evaluate their intended purpose and potential effects. It does so in the following order. After discussing the role of international labor standards, as well as the role of foreign direct investment in fostering sustainable development (Part II), the chapter presents a detailed analysis of the different types of labor clauses that are presently found in IIAs (Part III). By way of conclusion, it then evaluates the evolution in treaty language in relation to labor provisions and the prospects of such language for mainstreaming sustainable development into IIAs (Part IV).

II. SUSTAINABLE DEVELOPMENT, INTERNATIONAL LABOR STANDARDS, AND INTERNATIONAL INVESTMENT AGREEMENTS

Ever since the World Commission on Environment and Development, commonly known as the Brundtland Commission, brought it on the international agenda in its 1987 report on *The Common Future*,[5] the concept of 'sustainable development' has been widely embraced as an important objective of the global community. Today, the concept has moved beyond the stage of aspirational policy documents, having gained legal relevance through its inclusion in numerous treaty instruments, including regional economic agreements and investment treaties, which

---

[2] The term IIA is used here to refer not only to instruments providing for investment protection guarantees, but also to those containing other types of investment provisions, such as those dealing with market access or investment liberalization only.

[3] See, e.g., UNCTAD, *World Investment Report 2012: Towards a New Generation of Investment Policies* (United Nations 2012) 89–90.

[4] This chapter builds on research presented in Vid Prislan and Ruben Zandvliet, 'Labor Provisions in International Investment Agreements: Prospects for Sustainable Development' in Andrea K Bjorklund (ed.), *Yearbook of International Investment Law and Policy 2012–2013* (OUP 2014) 357–414.

[5] World Commission on Environment and Development, *Our Common Future* (OUP 1987).

list sustainable development as one of the goals that other treaty objectives – such as the expansion of trade, the promotion and the protection of investments, and enhanced economic cooperation – shall strive to achieve.[6] While the Brundtland Commission defined sustainable development as 'development that meets the needs of the present without compromising the ability of future generations to meet their own needs,'[7] there has subsequently been much debate among scholars about the term's definition, parameters, and policy implications, as well as its legal status.[8] At the policy level, however, there is a wide agreement that sustainable development is composed of three interdependent and mutually reinforcing pillars: economic development, social development and environmental protection.[9] Thus, sustainable development is not only about properly managing the natural resources and protecting the environment, or changing unsustainable patterns of production and consumption, but equally about eradicating world poverty – each of these elements must be seen as an overarching objective of, and an essential requirement for, development that is sustainable.[10]

The inclusion of a social pillar in the concept of sustainable development recognizes that development cannot disregard the position of individuals, even if the country as a whole fares well. Inasmuch as poverty is not only about a lack of income, but also a deprivation of human rights, it has now become accepted that the full realization of all human rights is essential for sustainable development, since it is crucial

---

6 Virginie Barral, 'Sustainable Development in International Law: Nature and Operation of an Evolutive Legal Norm' (2012) 23(2) EJIL 377–400.

7 World Commission on Environment and Development (n 5) 43.

8 See generally Nico Schrijver, *The Evolution of Sustainable Development in International Law: Inception, Meaning and Status* (Martinus Nijhoff 2008).

9 'Johannesburg Declaration on Sustainable Development' UN World Summit on Sustainable Development (Johannesburg, South Africa, 26 August–4 September 2000) UN Doc A/CONF.199/20 (4 September 2002). This is also expressly recognized in some IIAs. The preamble of the Protocol on Investment to the Australia-New Zealand Closer Economic Relations Trade Agreement (signed 16 February 2011, entered into force 1 March 2013) <http://www.austlii.edu.au/au/other/dfat/treaties/ATS/2013/10.html> accessed 30 March 2014, e.g., recognizes that 'a protocol on investment can assist in promoting sustainable development, including social development, economic development, and environmental protection.'

10 'World Summit Outcome Document' (UN World Summit, New York, 14–16 September 2005) UN Doc A/RES/60/1 (24 October 2005) para 48.

as such to social development.[11] Fundamental workers' rights, as a subset of human rights, play an important role in this context, given that the regulation of labor is inherently economic and that their realization can therefore be instrumental to integrating the economic and social pillar of development. States now increasingly accept that social development is a matter of intra-generational equity and not something that can only be claimed after a certain level of economic development has been met, and that the respect for workers' rights is important to mainstreaming sustainability into development.[12]

In fact, the concluding documents of all major international summits on sustainable development now contain ample references to labor rights and the work of the International Labour Organization (ILO). The final resolution of the Rio+20 summit in 2012, for instance, discusses youth unemployment, the concept of 'decent work', child labor, and occupational health issues including HIV/AIDS.[13] The ILO, in turn, increasingly uses the concept of sustainable development to integrate economic and environmental concerns in its own work, and as a platform to promote integration of ILO standards into other domains of international law and policy making.[14] In 1998, the ILO adopted the Declaration on Fundamental Principles and Rights at Work, which elevated, (1) freedom of association and collective bargaining, (2) the abolition of child labor, (3) the abolition of forced labor, and (4) the elimination of occupational discrimination, to the status of 'core' labor rights, and in doing so, emphasized that 'in the context of a global strategy for economic and social development, *economic and social policies are mutually reinforcing components* in order to create broad-based *sustainable development*.'[15]

---

[11] The link between social development and human rights has been strongly made by Amartya Sen, who argued that the fulfillment of human rights is not only a means to development but constitutes development *ipso facto*; see Sonia E Roland, *Development at the World Trade Organization* (OUP 2012) 24–8.

[12] Barral (n 6) 380. The concept of 'decent work' has been developed by the ILO and refers to the availability of employment opportunities, rights at work, social protection, and social dialogue.

[13] 'The Future We Want' (27 July 2012), UN Doc A/RES/66/288 (11 September 2012) paras 23–4.

[14] See, e.g., ILO, 'Director-General's Introduction to the International Labour Conference: Decent Work for Sustainable Development', ILC 96-2007/ Report I (A) (2007) 4 <http://www.ilo.org/public/english/standards/relm/ilc/ilc96/pdf/rep-i-a.pdf> accessed 15 December 2013.

[15] ILO, 'Declaration on Fundamental Principles and Rights at Work and Its Follow-Up' (18 June 1998, revised 15 June 2010) <http://www.ilo.org/

Indeed, embedding labor rights into a holistic definition of sustainable development aligns with the 'principle of integration, [which] reflects the interdependence of social, economic, financial, environmental and human rights aspects of principles and rules of international law relating to sustainable development.'[16]

However, the relationship between the economic, social, and environmental pillar of sustainable development remains profoundly complex, which can clearly be seen in relation to the role of foreign direct investment in the implementation of sustainable development. Attracting foreign investment flows has long been recognized as 'critical to the ability of developing countries to achieve needed economic growth to improve the welfare of their populations and to meet their basic needs in a sustainable manner.'[17]

But capital liberalization and the legal framework for attracting and protecting investment flows, established primarily in the form of IIAs, may lead to conflicts between economic interests, on the one hand, and social or environmental concerns, on the other.

Presently, there are around 3000 IIAs in force that protect, and in some cases also liberalize, foreign investment flows.[18] Most of these treaties still follow the traditional model of BITs developed by European States in the 1960s, which remain premised on the assumption that the proper treatment of investors would automatically contribute to the flow of capital and technology, and thereby to the development of the host State, and are thus designed with a strong focus on investment protection. Although traditionally concluded between a developed and a developing country, these BITs do not specifically address developmental concerns,

---

declaration/thedeclaration/textdeclaration/lang–en/index.htm> accessed 11 September 2013) (emphasis added).

16 ILO, 'New Delhi Declaration of Principles of International Law Relating to Sustainable Development' (2002) 2 *International Environmental Agreements: Politics, Law and Economics* 211–16.

17 United Nations Conference on Environment & Development, 'Agenda 21: Programme of Action for Sustainable Development', UN Doc A/CONF.151/6/Rev.1 (1992) 31 ILM 874, para 2.23; see also UN, 'Monterrey Consensus of the International Conference on Financing for Development: The Final Text of Agreements and Commitments Adopted at the International Conference on Financing for Development' (Monterrey, Mexico, 18–22 March 2002) para 20 <http://www.un.org/esa/ffd/monterrey/MonterreyConsensus.pdf> accessed 11 September 2013.

18 According to UNCTAD, *World Investment Report 2013: Global Value Chains: Investment and Trade for Development* (United Nations 2013) 101, there were a total of 2857 BITs and 339 other IIAs at the end of 2012.

since their primary purpose is the promotion of economic growth of *both* contracting parties, not only the State receiving investment. Nor are they intended to actively promote a holistic concept of sustainable development, since their emphasis is on economic concerns, with non-economic objectives perhaps only tacitly expected to follow from the increase in FDI flows, as a positive spillover effect.[19]

But as States have increasingly begun to accept that observance of labor standards may function as a prerequisite for free trade and investment policies – rejecting thereby the premises of neo-liberal laissez-faire economics, which refuted any normative floor to global economic integration and considered labor standards merely as producing 'rigidities' in markets and frustrating development[20] – the issue of the investment-labor linkage has started to influence the design of IIAs. The issue of whether to include labor provisions in IIAs is essentially part of the debate on how to achieve the appropriate balance between the promotion and protection of foreign investment flows, on the one hand, and the sovereign right to regulate labor matters, on the other.

There are essentially three types of risk associated with the fostering of investment flows through the conclusion of IIAs which have an impact on the regulation of labor standards and which therefore provide the main rationale for the investment-labor linkage. One of the risks is that investment liberalization, which is now actively pursued by some IIAs that grant pre-establishment rights to foreign investors, could lead to regulatory distortions resulting from States competing with each other to attract (specific) investments by means of derogations from labor standards. Another, different kind of risk is that the imbalances of rights created by the currently-dominating model of IIAs – which confer only rights upon investors, without creating concomitant rights for host States, or subjecting investors to any specific obligations – could lead to a regulatory chill, since the predominantly protective nature of IIAs could arguably make States hesitate to adopt new labor regulations out of fear

---

[19] See Anna Joubin-Bret, Marie-Estelle Rey and Jörg Weber, 'International Investment Law and Development' in Marie-Claire Cordonier Segger, Markus Gehring and Andrew Newcombe (eds), *Sustainable Development in World Investment Law* (Kluwer 2010) 19–20; and Federico Ortino, 'The Social Dimension of International Investment Agreements: Drafting a New BIT/MIT Model?' (2005) 7 *International Law FORUM du Droit International* 243.

[20] Robert Howse and Brian Langille with Julien Burda, 'The World Trade Organization and Labour Rights: Man Bites Dog' in Virginia A Leary and Daniel Warner (eds), *Social Issues, Globalisation and International Institutions* (Martinus Nijhoff 2006) 159.

that this might violate the terms of the investment agreement. A third, related risk is that the absence of specific investors' obligations in IIAs could undermine the encouragement of investors' responsibility in the field of labor rights. As discussed in the following Part, the labor clauses that are presently found in IIAs, in one way or another, seek to respond to these risks.

III. SUBSTANTIVE LABOR OBLIGATIONS IN IIAS

Although the inclusion of separate labor provisions is a relatively new development in investment treaty practice, references to labor rights in IIAs are not of recent vintage. Since the beginning of the 1990s, preambulatory statements have begun to be added to BITs that express the belief that the development of economic and business ties can contribute to the well-being of workers and promote internationally accepted labor standards.[21] Statements of this kind were premised on the belief that increased FDI flows will, by themselves, inevitably lead to an improvement of labor standards in recipient countries. But with the growing realization that the liberalization of investment flows can have both positive and negative impacts on the position of workers of the contracting parties, there has been considerable evolution in, as well as diversification of, treaty language.

In general, one can discern three modes of regulation: (1) provisions responding to potential derogations in the level of labor rights; (2) provisions aimed at the preservation of the parties' policy space in labor matters; and (3) provisions focusing on the observance of labor standards by foreign investors.[22] Apart from that, however, the labor provisions that

---

[21] For an early reference, see the preamble of Treaty between the United States of America and the Republic of Poland concerning Business and Economic Relations (adopted 21 March 1990, entered into force 6 August 1994) <http://tcc.export.gov/trade_agreements/all_trade_agreements/exp_005367.asp> accessed 31 March 2014, recognizing 'that the development of business and economic ties can contribute to the well-being of workers in both countries and promote respect for fundamental worker rights.'

[22] This is not to say that these three categories encompass all kinds of provisions that may have a bearing on the position of workers. For example, the latter may also benefit from provisions on entry and sojourn of foreign nationals, which are occasionally included in IIAs (see, e.g., Art 2(4) of the Agreement Between the Government of the Republic of Botswana and the Government of the People's Republic of China on promotion and protection of investments (12 June 2000) <http://unctad.org/sections/dite/iia/docs/bits/china_botswana.pdf>

are presently found in IIAs exhibit a great deal of diversity. This is not only obvious when it comes to their form – which ranges from brief preambulatory statements and self-standing treaty clauses, to separate treaty chapters and side-agreements – but also with regard to the scope of commitments that they impose and the arrangements they put in place for the supervision and enforcement of those commitments.

A. Provisions Concerning Labor Rights Derogations

The large majority of labor provisions that are presently found in IIAs require that contracting parties refrain from relaxing labor rights as an incentive to attract foreign investment. In that, they respond to the danger that States would use the level of labor standards to enhance their competitiveness vis-à-vis others, which could lead to 'regulatory distortions'.[23] In view of their purpose, these types of clauses are more likely to be found in IIAs that pursue a stronger liberalization agenda, such as those concluded by the United States, Canada, and Japan, which extend the obligation of national treatment to the establishment and/or acquisition of investments (pre-establishment rights).[24] However, they increasingly feature also in BITs that are based on the traditional admission control model, such as those concluded by Austria or the Belgium-Luxembourg Economic Union (BLEU), which suggests that regulatory distortions may have become a system-wide concern.

The language in which these provisions are couched varies between IIAs. Some treaties do not go much further than merely recognizing the inappropriateness of encouraging investment through the relaxation of

accessed 31 March 2014). But strictly speaking, such provisions do not directly relate to the issue of labor rights and will therefore remain outside the scope of this chapter.

23 The term 'regulatory distortions' can be used to describe situations in which jurisdictional competition leads to a level of labor standards that would have been different from the outcome in a baseline scenario. Such distortions can occur by way of explicit derogations from current levels of labor standards, or by way of promises not to increase standards in the future. On the issue of regulatory competition, see, e.g., David Charney, 'Regulatory Competition and the Global Coordination of Labor Standards' (2000) 3(2) JIEL 283.

24 On the distinction between the 'traditional' and 'liberalizing' IIAs, see, e.g., UNCTAD, *The Role of International Investment Agreements in Attracting Foreign Direct Investment to Developing Countries* (United Nations 2009) 20.

domestic labor standards.[25] In most cases, however, the language is quite elaborate. A typical example is the labor clause in the United States-Uruguay BIT, which provides that:

> [t]he Parties recognize that it is inappropriate to encourage investment by weakening or reducing the protections afforded in domestic labor laws. Accordingly, each Party shall strive to ensure that it does not waive or otherwise derogate from, or offer to waive or otherwise derogate from, such laws in a manner that weakens or reduces adherence to the internationally recognized labor rights … as an encouragement for the establishment, acquisition, expansion, or retention of an investment in its territory … .[26]

What most labor clauses of this type have in common is that they are formulated broadly, in that they prohibit not only outright derogations, but also any offers to do so; in that they do not require a systemic pattern of behavior (with the consequence that a single derogation would be sufficient for a violation to occur); and in that they do not distinguish between the ways in which derogations take place (with the consequence that the abolition of a formal law would have the same effect as a contract in which the State promises not to enforce its labor laws within an export processing zone). Moreover, they are broader in scope than the traditional investment disciplines, in that the obligations they impose are mostly not limited to the weakening of labor standards in favor of investments by nationals of the other contracting party, but equally apply to the weakening of labor standards in favor of investments of third States. At the same time, their focus is limited to derogations that are used as a means to encourage investment, not to prohibiting derogations as such.

---

25 See, e.g., Agreement for the Promotion and Protection of Investment between the Government of the Republic of Austria and the Government of the Republic of Kosovo (22 January 2010) art 5(1) <http://www.parlament.gv.at/PAKT/VHG/XXIV/I/I_01332/imfname_224247.pdf> accessed 31 March 2014.

26 Treaty between the United States of America and the Oriental Republic of Uruguay concerning the encouragement and reciprocal protection of investment (adopted 4 November 2005, entered into force 1 November 2006) art 13(1) <http://www.ustr.gov/sites/default/files/uploads/agreements/bit/asset_upload_file748_9005.pdf> accessed 31 March 2014. Identical provisions can also be found in the US treaty with Rwanda, as well as in many treaties concluded by BLEU; see, e.g., Agreement between the Belgium-Luxembourg Economic Union and the Republic of Mauritius on the Reciprocal Promotion and Protection of Investments (30 November 2005) Art 6 <http://unctad.org/sections/dite/iia/docs/bits/BLEU-Mauritius-eng.pdf> accessed 31 March 2014.

In spite of their commonalities, however, there are also important differences within this type of clause. One of the aspects in which IIAs differ is in the nature of the commitments undertaken by the contracting parties. Some IIAs, particularly those concluded by Japan, contain only aspirational language in that they stipulate that the contracting parties 'should not' waive or otherwise derogate from their domestic labor standards.[27] A large number of IIAs, however, contain more demanding language, even though there are differences in the type of obligations imposed.

In most cases, the commitments in question are formulated as obligations of conduct, in that they require that the Contracting Parties 'shall strive to ensure' that they do not waive or otherwise derogate from their domestic labor legislation. This type of language is currently present in several BITs concluded by BLEU,[28] in some of the BITs and FTAs concluded by the United States,[29] and occasionally in FTAs concluded by other States.[30] On the other hand, there are several IIAs that go a step further and impose obligations of result, by providing either that the parties 'shall not'/'will not' derogate from their labor legislation, or that they 'shall ensure' that no derogations take place. This has become the

---

[27] See, e.g., Agreement between Japan and the Republic of Peru for the Promotion, Protection and Liberalisation of Investment (adopted 21 November 2008, entered into force 1 March 2012) art 26 <http://www.mofa.go.jp/region/latin/peru/agree0811.pdf> accessed 31 March 2014. Similar provisions can also be found in treaties that Japan concluded with Uzbekistan, Switzerland FTA, Colombia, Papua New Guinea, and Iraq.

[28] See, e.g., Agreement between the Belgium-Luxembourg Economic Union and the Government of the Republic of Guatemala on the Reciprocal Promotion and Protection of Investments (14 April 2005, not yet in force) art 14(2) <http://unctad.org/sections/dite/iia/docs/bits/BLEU-Guatemala-eng.pdf> accessed 31 March 2014, and the corresponding provisions in the BITs that BLEU concluded with Bahrain, Botswana, Congo DR, Libya, Madagascar, Mauritius, Mozambique, Peru, Qatar, and Sudan.

[29] See, e.g., US-Uruguay BIT (n 26) art 13(1); or Agreement between the United States of America and the Hashemite Kingdom of Jordan on the Establishment of a Free Trade Area (adopted 24 October 2000, entered into force 17 December 2001) art 6(2) <http://www.ustr.gov/sites/default/files/Jordan%20FTA.pdf> accessed 31 March 2014. Similar language can also be found in FTAs that the US concluded with Singapore, Chile, Australia, Bahrain, Dominican Republic/Central America, Morocco, and Oman.

[30] Agreement between Japan and the Republic of the Philippines for an Economic Partnership (adopted 9 September 2006, entered into force 11 December 2008) art 103(1) <http://www.mofa.go.jp/region/asia-paci/philippine/epa0609/main.pdf> accessed 31 March 2014.

preferred drafting method in recent US FTAs,[31] though such language can also be found in labor chapters/side agreements of FTAs concluded by Canada, Korea, the European Free Trade Association (EFTA) States, and the European Union (EU).[32] In general, however, provisions imposing more stringent commitments are still relatively limited, and still rarely found in traditional BITs.[33]

Significant differences also exist when it comes to the scope of commitments undertaken in labor clauses. First, some IIAs are more comprehensive than others with regard to the manner in which impermissible relaxations of labor standards take place. While many IIAs currently address only derogations from domestic labor legislation by way of positive action (through changes in legislation or by way of administrative measures), some IIAs demand in addition that derogations shall also not occur as a result of omissions. Thus, a number of labor chapters in US FTAs contain provisions to the effect that a party 'shall not fail to effectively enforce its labor laws … through a sustained or recurring

[31] See, e.g., United States-Peru Trade Promotion Agreement (adopted 12 April 2006, entered into force 1 February 2009) art 17.2(2) <http://www.ustr.gov/trade-agreements/free-trade-agreements/peru-tpa/final-text> accessed 31 March 2014. Same language can also be found in the US FTAs with Colombia, Panama, and Korea.

[32] See, e.g., Agreement on Labour Cooperation between Canada and the Republic of Peru (adopted 29 May 2008, entered into force 1 August 2009) art 2 <http://www.labour.gc.ca/eng/relations/international/agreements/lca_peru.shtml#cpalc>; Agreement on Labour between the EFTA States and Hong Kong, China (adopted 21 June 2011, entered into force 1 October 2012) art 2 <http://www.efta.int/~/media/Documents/legal-texts/free-trade-relations/hong-kong-china/Agreement%20on%20Labour.pdf> accessed 31 March 2014; Peru-Korea Free Trade Agreement (adopted 14 November 2010, entered into force 1 August 2011) art 18.2(2) <http://www.sice.oas.org/trade/PER_KOR_FTA/Texts_26JUL2011_e/PER_KOR_ToC_e.asp> accessed 31 March 2014; or Canada-European Union Comprehensive Economic and Trade Agreement (consolidated text, publicly available as of 26 September 2014) Chapter X+1, art 3 <http://trade.ec.europa.eu/doclib/docs/2014/september/tradoc_152806.pdf> accessed 15 August 2015.

[33] See Agreement between United Arab Emirates and the Belgium-Luxembourg Economic Union (adopted 8 March 2004, entered into force 10 November 2007) art 6.2 <http://unctad.org/sections/dite/iia/docs/bits/UAE_Belglux.pdf> accessed 31 March 2014; or Agreement for the Promotion and Reciprocal Protection of Investment between the Government of the Republic of Austria and the Government of the Republic of Kazakhstan (12 January 2010, not yet in force) art 5(1) <http://www.parlament.gv.at/PAKT/VHG/XXIV/I/I_01333/imfname_224254.pdf> accessed 31 March 2014.

course of action or inaction, in a manner affecting trade or investment between the Parties.'[34]

But similar requirements can also be found in labor chapters and side agreements of FTAs concluded by Canada, Korea, and the EFTA States.[35] This type of language considerably strengthens labor provisions, since the weakening of labor standards often occurs through a lack of enforcement instead of formal derogations. Interestingly, some US FTAs go as far as to also limit the 'enforcement' discretion of the contracting parties by additionally stipulating that a party cannot defend failure to enforce its labor laws on the basis of resource limitations or decisions to prioritize other enforcement issues.[36]

Second, IIAs sometimes differ in the type of changes that the parties are allowed to introduce to their domestic labor legislation, and in the scope of the labor legislation to which the non-derogation provisions apply. To date, there has seemingly been no IIA that would seek to prohibit derogations from any labor law, regardless of its type. Most non-derogation provisions apply only to that part of domestic labor legislation that directly relates to a set of international labor standards. However, while some IIAs prohibit any derogations from such laws,[37] others prohibit only those derogations that are actually inconsistent with ILO norms.[38] This means that the party that currently observes, in its

---

34 United States-Colombia Trade Promotion Agreement (adopted 22 November 2006, entered into force 15 May 2012) art 5(1) <http://www.ustr.gov/trade-agreements/free-trade-agreements/colombia-fta/final-text> accessed 31 March 2014. Similar provisions are present in all US FTAs.

35 See, e.g., Canada-Peru LCA (n 32) art 3; Peru-Korea FTA (n 32) art 18.2(1); or Free Trade Agreement between the EFTA States and Montenegro (14 November 2011, entered into force 1 November 2012) art 34(1) <http://www.efta.int/media/documents/legal-texts/free-trade-relations/montenegro/montenegro-main-agreement.pdf> accessed 31 March 2014.

36 See, e.g., US-Peru FTA (n 31) art 17.3(1)(b). Similar language can be found in the US FTAs with Panama, Colombia, and Korea. This differs from earlier US FTAs, which recognized that each party 'retains the right to exercise discretion with respect to investigatory, prosecutorial, regulatory, and compliance matters and to make decisions regarding the allocation of resources to enforcement with respect to other labor matters determined to have higher priorities,' see United States-Singapore Free Trade Agreement (adopted 15 January 2003, entered into force 1 January 2004) art 17(2)(1)(b) <http://www.ustr.gov/trade-agreements/free-trade-agreements/singapore-fta/final-text> accessed 31 March 2014.

37 Japan-Peru BIT (n 27) art 26.

38 See, e.g., US-Uruguay BIT (n 26) art 13(1).

domestic legislation, labor standards above those required by the ILO can thus lower its standards without violating the labor clause.

Furthermore, differences also exist with regard to the set of international labor standards that are to serve as a benchmark for permissible derogations. For this purpose, no IIA actually refers to the 'international labor code' as such, which in total comprises 189 binding ILO Conventions and 202 non-binding Recommendations, dealing with matters ranging from rights for migrant workers to workplace-related HIV/AIDS issues. Rather, the majority of IIAs refers to: (1) freedom of association and the effective recognition of the right to collective bargaining, (2) elimination of all forms of forced or compulsory labor, (3) effective abolition of child labor, and (4) acceptable conditions of work with respect to minimum wages, hours of work, and occupational safety and health. These correspond to the standards traditionally treated as 'internationally recognized labor rights' by the United States in its domestic legislation relating to the enforcement of labor rights through trade measures.[39] However, they depart from the four 'core labor rights' listed in the 1998 ILO Declaration, in that they include acceptable conditions of work, but exclude the elimination of discrimination in respect of employment and occupation which is otherwise listed in that Declaration as a core labor right. However, the discrepancy between the US 'internationally recognized labor rights' and the ILO 'core labor rights' is beginning to wither away. The principle of non-discrimination in respect of employment and occupation is increasingly added to the other 'internationally recognized labor rights' as a fifth non-derogable right. Such expanded lists can presently be found in more recent US FTAs,[40] in some Austrian BITs, and in several Labor Cooperation Agreements (LCAs) concluded by Canada as counterparts to its FTAs.[41]

Last but not least, IIAs diverge in the institutional arrangements they create for the purpose of overseeing the parties' compliance with non-derogation obligations, as well as in the procedures that they provide for their enforcement. At one end of the spectrum there are BITs that tend not to create any permanent institutions, but usually provide for

[39] These can be found in Section 301 of the US Trade Act, 19 USC Ch 12 (1974) and in the US Generalized System of Preferences.

[40] See US-Peru FTA (n 31) art 16.2(1); see also the US FTAs with Panama, Colombia, and Korea.

[41] See, e.g., Canada-Peru LCA (n 32) art 1(1). This and some other Canadian agreements even cover additional labor standards, such as the rights of migrant workers, which are not present in other IIAs.

expert or political consultations to be convened on an ad hoc basis.[42] At the other end of the spectrum, there are FTAs with labor chapters and separate labor agreements that establish permanent institutional arrangements that are often very comprehensive in nature. The most extensive arrangements can be found under the North American Agreement on Labor Cooperation (NAALC)[43] that was concluded alongside the North American Free Trade Agreement (NAFTA), and in US FTAs and Canadian LCAs that were modeled on its basis.[44] All these agreements establish supranational bodies of various designations, composed of minister-level representatives that are generally tasked with overseeing the implementation of the treaty (sometimes supported by a permanent secretariat), and national administrative offices that serve primarily as a contact point for all interested parties and that can receive and review petitions from private persons.

When it comes to mechanisms available for the enforcement of labor provisions, these usually differ from those available for the enforcement of investment protection guarantees. In the case of FTAs with investment chapters/labor side agreements, investor-State arbitration is typically available only for obligations under the investment chapter. Matters arising under the labor chapter are instead to be dealt with on the inter-State level, primarily through consultation, with inter-State arbitration sometimes available as an option.[45]

---

[42] See, e.g., BLEU-Mauritius BIT (n 26) art 6(4), which provides for the possibility of convening 'expert consultations' on any matter falling under the purpose of the labor provisions.

[43] North American Agreement on Labor Cooperation (adopted 14 September 1993, entered into force 1 January 1994) arts 8–19 <http://www.dol.gov/ilab/regs/naalc/naalc.htm> accessed 31 March 2014.

[44] See, e.g., Canada-Peru LCA (n 32) arts 7–11; or US-Singapore FTA (n 36) art 17.4.

[45] The NAALC, some earlier US FTAs, and some Canadian LCAs limit the types of matters that can be submitted to inter-State arbitration to those that relate to the failure by a party to effectively enforce its labor laws through a sustained or recurring course of action or inaction in a manner affecting trade and/or investment between the Parties, and place limits on monetary penalties for breaches of such labor provisions. In contrast, under the more recent US FTAs with Peru, Colombia, Panama, and South Korea, recourse to inter-State dispute settlement is available with regard to all obligations under the labor chapters and without any caps on potential penalties; see, e.g., US-Peru FTA (n 31) art 21.2. Similarly, the Japanese FTAs with the Philippines and Switzerland contain no carve-outs in relation to their labor clauses; see, e.g., Japan-Philippines FTA (n 30) arts 149–59. On the other hand, there are some FTAs, such as the Peru-Korea FTA (n 32) art 18.7, or the EFTA-Hong Kong Agreement on Labor

When it comes to BITs, the differences in treaty-making practice are more pronounced. In US BITs, for example, the labor clause remains outside the scope of both investor-State and inter-State arbitration, but is subject to its own consultations procedure.[46] Other BITs, particularly those concluded by BLEU or Austria, permit the labor clause to be used as a basis for claims in both investor-State and inter-State dispute settlement procedures.[47] At any rate, the practical effects of some of these limitations are not necessarily detrimental to the position of the investor. Even though they may not be able to bring direct claims in relation to the labor provisions, investors are not prevented from invoking the failure of the host State to respect internationally recognized labor rights or to effectively enforce its domestic labor legislation as part of their principal or subsidiary claims in relation to other investment protection standards available under IIAs, particularly if different labor standards are applicable to domestic as opposed to foreign investors.[48]

All in all, the inclusion of non-derogation provisions appears to be justified by both economic and legal dynamics. While studies have shown that inward-FDI generally leads to improvements in labor conditions,[49] and that (the risk of) a 'race to the bottom' is essentially non-existent, there is plenty of anecdotal evidence on situations of regulatory distortions which occurred as an incentive to attract FDI.[50] Such distortions do

---

(n 32) art 6(2), where the labor chapters/labor agreements are expressly excluded from any form of binding, third-party dispute settlement.

[46] See US-Uruguay BIT (n 26) arts 13(1), 24(1), and 37(5).

[47] See, e.g., BLEU-Mauritius BIT (n 26) art 6(4), 12–13; or Austria-Kosovo BIT (n 25) arts 13–14, 21. Occasionally, however, the option to invoke labor provisions in investor-State arbitration is excluded due to limitations in the scope of consent to arbitrate; see, e.g., Japan-Peru BIT (n 27) art 18(1).

[48] There are certainly situations where a foreign investor will have an interest in the host State's complying with its international labor legislation; see, e.g., *United Parcel Service of America Inc v Government of Canada*, UNCITRAL, Award on Jurisdiction (22 November 2002) paras 83–99; and Award on the Merits (24 May 2007) paras 186, 102–19, 173–81.

[49] Layna Mosley, *Labor Rights and Multinational Production* (CUP 2011).

[50] Recorded instances of regulatory distortion range from the 'Hobbit labor laws' in New Zealand, where film industry workers were reclassified from employees to 'independent contractors' in order to deny them union contracts, to the prohibition of trade unions in Bangladeshi export processing zones, which was demanded by Japan and South Korea on behalf of their own investors; see 'New Zealand Passes Hobbit Labour Law' (*CBC News*, 30 October 2010) <http://www.cbc.ca/news/arts/film/story/2010/10/30/hobbit-nz-labour.html> accessed 18 March 2014, and Economist Intelligence Unit, 'Bangladesh: Country Report' (April 2001) 19 cited in Theodore H Moran, *Harnessing*

not only have an impact on the position of host State workers and potentially constitute a violation of international labor and human rights agreements, but to the extent that they affect investment flows, they also lead to economic injury of third States, which in turn, may decide to respond with counterincentives. This provides sufficient policy justification for curtailing States' ability to influence FDI inflows through the deregulation of labor.

B. Preserving Policy Space

The second type of labor provisions address the problem of host States' regulatory space by stipulating, either expressly or implicitly, that the standards of treatment imposed by IIAs ought not to result in host States' being prevented from establishing their own levels of domestic labor rights. While IIAs do not expressly prohibit changes to the domestic regulatory framework, their strong focus on economic objectives and the attendant emphasis on the high level of protection to investments[51] have been said to produce stabilizing effects, with the consequence that host States may become hesitant to implement measures in pursuit of social policy objectives, which may even lead up to a regulatory chill.[52] Arguably, such 'stabilizing' or 'chilling' effects further ensue from the possibility for foreign investors to challenge undesirable regulatory measures through binding arbitration that is available under most IIAs, as investors have already demonstrated being capable of doing in relation to measures adopted for the promotion of public health or the protection of the environment.[53] In light of these precedents, trade unions have

---

Foreign Direct Investment for Development: Policies for Developed and Developing Countries (Center for Global Development 2006) 58.

[51] The reason for this is a historical one, as IIAs were specifically designed to provide investors of capital-exporting States with protection additional to that under the host State's domestic laws and under the rules of customary international law on the minimum standards of treatment of aliens, at a time when the latter have come under challenge by newly independent post-colonial States; see Kate Miles, *The Origins of International Investment Law: Empire, Environment and the Safeguarding of Capital* (CUP 2013) 88–9.

[52] The importance of these concerns has been acknowledged in UNCTAD, *Investment Policy Framework for Sustainable Development* (UNCTAD 2012) 40.

[53] For recent examples see *Philip Morris Asia Limited v Australia*, UNCITRAL, PCA Case No 2012-12 and *Philip Morris Brands Sàrl, Philip Morris Products SA and Abal Hermanos SA v Oriental Republic of Uruguay*, ICSID Case No ARB/10/7, arising out of the adoption by, respectively, Australia and Uruguay of stringent tobacco labeling legislation; or *Vattenfall v Federal*

occasionally expressed the fear that investors might bring similar claims in response to the introduction or significant increase of a minimum wage, introduction or strengthening of collective bargaining rights, constraints on the use of casual labor, or the failure to end industrial disputes or strikes.[54] Indeed, even though there have so far been no reported cases of investors bringing a claim under an IIA in relation to the imposition of higher labor standards, the potential for investors using IIAs in such manner are not remote.[55]

In response to these concerns, a great deal of IIAs now include provisions which expressly recognize the host State's right to regulate labor standards (and other matters of public policy concern), or have the effect of doing so indirectly (1). Some of these provisions, furthermore, impose additional obligations geared at the progressive improvement of labor standards (2).

1. Right to regulate

Provisions aimed at preserving the contracting parties' regulatory autonomy in labor matters are often added to treaty clauses prohibiting derogations from labor standards and are couched in the form of statements '[r]ecognizing the right of each Party to establish its own

Republic of Germany, ICSID Case No ARB/12/12, arising out of Germany's decision regarding its nuclear phase-out.

[54] See, e.g., Bill Rosenberg, 'Labour Rights and Investment Agreements' (2 March 2012) <http://union.org.nz/sites/union.org.nz/files/Labour-Rights-and-TPPA-March2012.ppt> accessed 31 March 2014.

[55] The propensity of foreign investors to use arbitration to challenge legislative measures concerning labor regulation has been attested to, among others, in the cases of *Centerra Gold Inc and Kumtor Gold Company v The Kyrgyz Republic*, UNCITRAL, PCA Case No AA278 (arising out of amendments to labor legislation regarding the payment of high altitude premiums to mining workers), *Veolia Propreté v Egypt*, ICSID Case No ARB/12/15 (partly concerning Egypt's increase of minimum wages), *Sergei Paushok, CJSC Golden East Company and CJSC Vostokneftegaz Company v The Government of Mongolia*, UNCITRAL, Award on jurisdiction and liability (18 April 2011) (partly relating to new mining legislation, which penalized the employment of foreign citizens in an effort to achieve greater participation of Mongolian workers in mining operations), and *PieroForesti, Laura de Carli & Others v Republic of South Africa*, ICSID Case No ARB(AF)/07/01, Award (4 August 2012) (partly relating to obligations concerning the hiring of 'historically disadvantaged South Africans' under South Africa's new Mining Charter). While the former two cases were based on an investment contract (and therefore may have limited precedential value from the perspective of investment treaty arbitration), the latter two cases concerned alleged breaches of IIAs.

domestic labor standards, and to adopt or modify accordingly its labor laws and regulations.'[56] Such statements can presently be found in several US FTAs, in BITs concluded by BLEU, as well as in FTAs concluded by other States.[57] Eventually, they can also be couched in the form of statements 'recogniz[ing] the right of each Contracting Party to establish … its own sustainable development policy and priorities.'[58]

More often, however, the parties' regulatory discretion in labor matters is simply recognized in preambulatory statements, either by way of clarifying that investment protection must not be implemented at the cost of labor standards, or by way of adding the improvement of such standards as self-standing treaty objectives. An example of the former can be found in the preamble of the United States-Uruguay BIT, which expresses the desire 'to achieve these [treaty] objectives in a manner consistent with the protection of health, safety, and the environment, *and the promotion of internationally recognized labor rights.*'[59] An example of the latter can be found in the Preamble of the Netherlands-Mozambique BIT, which recognizes 'that the development of economic and business ties should *promote internationally accepted labour rights*.'[60]

---

[56] US-Singapore FTA (n 36) art 17.1 (2).

[57] See, e.g., BLEU-Mauritius BIT (n 26) art 6(1); or EFTA-Hong Kong Agreement on Labor (n 32) art 3.

[58] Agreement on Encouragement and Reciprocal Protection of Investments between the Kingdom of the Netherlands and the United Arab Emirates (26 November 2013, not yet in force) art 2(2) <http://wetten.overheid.nl/BWBV0006303/geldigheidsdatum_13-03-2014#AuthentiekEN> accessed 4 April 2014.

[59] US-Uruguay BIT (n 26) Preamble (emphasis added). Similar statements also appear in the preambles of BITs recently concluded by Turkey, such as Agreement between the Government of the Republic of Turkey and the Government of the Republic of Cameroon concerning the Reciprocal Promotion and Protection of Investments (24 April 2012, not yet in force) <http://unctad.org/Sections/dite/iia/docs/bits/Turkey_Cameroon%20BIT.pdf> accessed 4 April 2014.

[60] Agreement between the Government of the Republic of Mozambique and the Government of the Kingdom of the Netherlands concerning the Encouragement and Reciprocal Protection of Investment (adopted 18 December 2001, entered into force 1 September 2004) Preamble <http://unctad.org/sections/dite/iia/docs/bits/netherlands_mozambique.pdf> accessed 4 April 2014 (emphasis added). Identical language is also present in a few other BITs concluded by the Netherlands. See also the preambles of the Agreement on the Promotion and Protection of Investments between the Government of the Republic of Finland and Bosnia and Herzegovina (adopted 1 November 2000, entered into force 8

Other preambulatory statements are bound to have similar effects, even without making reference to labor rights explicitly. The Preamble to the Canada-Jordan BIT, for example, recognizes 'that the promotion and the protection of investments ... will be conducive to the stimulation of mutually beneficial business activity, to the development of economic cooperation between [the parties] *and to the promotion of sustainable development*.'[61] The latter includes the promotion of international labor standards, given that sustainable development requires the integration of economic, environmental, and social objectives.

This type of preambulatory language has not evolved in relation to labor rights issues specifically, but has been part of a broader response to IIAs' potential restrictions on host States' regulatory autonomy in matters of general societal concern.[62] In the same category one must therefore consider also other treaty provisions that have been included in IIAs for the purpose of preventing investment protection disciplines from impinging upon the ability of host States to safeguard non-economic concerns and which may have the effect of preserving the parties' policy space in labor matters, even without necessarily making reference to labor rights as such. This is certainly true with regard to various interpretative statements, through which some States have sought to clarify the scope of the most commonly invoked standards of treatment, such as expropriation, fair and equitable treatment, and non-discrimination.

A number of US and Canadian IIAs, for example, contain annexes clarifying that non-discriminatory regulatory actions by a party that are 'designed and applied to protect legitimate public welfare objectives, such as health, safety and the environment' do not constitute indirect expropriations, except in rare circumstances when those actions are not

---

December 2001) <http://unctad.org/sections/dite/iia/docs/bits/finland_bosnia.pdf> accessed 4 April 2014 and of the Agreement Between the Government of the Slovak Republic and the Government of the Republic of Kenya for the Promotion and Reciprocal Protection of Investments (adopted 14 December 2011, not yet in force) <http://unctad.org/Sections/dite/iia/docs/bits/Slovakia_Kenya.pdf> accessed 4 April 2014.

61 Agreement between Canada and the Hashemite Kingdom of Jordan for the Promotion and Protection of Investments (adopted 28 June 2009, entered in force 14 December 2009) Preamble <http://www.treaty-accord.gc.ca/text-texte.aspx?id=105176> accessed 4 April 2014 (emphasis added).

62 On the policy response to this problem in general see Suzanne A Spears, 'The Quest for Policy Space in a New Generation of International Investment Agreements' (2010) 13(4) JIEL 1037–75.

adopted and applied in good faith.[63] Similar explanatory language can also be found in IIAs concluded by African and Asian countries, such as the Investment Agreement for the Common Market for Eastern and Southern Africa (COMESA) Common Investment Area (2007)[64] and the Association of Southeast Asian Nations (ASEAN) Comprehensive Investment Agreement (2009).[65] In principle, the language used in such explanatory statements will equally apply to regulatory actions aimed at the improvement of labor rights, given that these also represent legitimate public welfare objectives.

Another technique has been to include general exceptions clauses, which provide the contracting parties with the possibility of derogation – subject to several substantive or procedural requirements – from their investment treaty obligations in situations where compliance would prevent a party from adopting or enforcing measures necessary for the achievement of certain non-investment policy goals. Inasmuch as such clauses affect the application of investment protection standards, they operate at a different level than other policy-space provisions, which primarily affect the interpretation of those standards. This is why exception clauses are sometimes used in the alternative to, and sometimes in combination with, other provisions. Although none of the clauses that are currently found in IIAs provides specific exceptions for measures aimed at the improvement of labor rights, several other exceptions could, under certain circumstances, be construed as applying to measures related to the improvement of labor standards. This is particularly the case with exceptions applicable to measures necessary to protect public morals (for, there is nothing moral about forced labor, for example), or human life or health (as this obviously includes occupational safety and health).[66] The wording of these general exception

---

[63] See, e.g., Canada-Jordan BIT (n 61) Annex B.13(1); or US-Uruguay BIT (n 26) Annex B.

[64] Investment Agreement for the COMESA Common Investment Area (adopted 23 May 2007, not yet in force) art 20(8) <http://vi.unctad.org/files/wksp/iiawksp08/docs/wednesday/Exercise%20Materials/invagreecomesa.pdf> accessed 4 April 2014, where interpretative guidance has been added as an integral part of the provision concerned.

[65] ASEAN Comprehensive Investment Agreement (adopted 26 February 2009, entered into force 29 March 2012) Annex 2 <http://www.asean.org/images/2012/Economic/AIA/Agreement/ASEAN%20Comprehensive%20Investment%20Agreement%20(ACIA)%202012.pdf> accessed 4 April 2014.

[66] See, e.g., ibid art 17(1)(b) and (c); see also Agreement between the Government of the Republic of Korea and the Government of Japan for the Liberalization, Promotion and Protection of Investment (adopted 22 March 2002,

clauses mirrors to a large extent those found in WTO law, most notably Article XX GATT. Their practical application, however, differs significantly. The public morals and human life or health exceptions in trade law can arguably be used to prevent the importation of goods produced under immoral or unhealthy circumstances abroad.[67] This extraterritorial effect is absent in investment law, as the exception can be invoked to defend measures redressing immoral or unhealthy labor conditions within the jurisdiction of the host State itself against potential claims from foreign investors.

2. Improvement of labor standards

Apart from attempting to preserve policy space, it is not uncommon for labor provisions to contain commitments concerning the improvement of domestic labor standards, even though the IIAs' normative ambitions in this regard diverge. Some IIAs focus only on preventing derogations of labor standards as a means to encourage investment, without being concerned with the level of those standards, not even implicitly. For example, the labor clause in the United States-Uruguay BIT, while requiring that the parties do not derogate from their labor legislation, does not explicitly demand that such legislation be consistent with internationally recognized labor rights, nor impose any obligation to bring this legislation in conformity with such rights.[68] Other IIAs, in contrast, pursue a more progressive agenda. While no IIA lays down a commitment to fully harmonize the level of labor standards between the parties, some IIAs impose commitments to improve domestic labor laws in light of international minimum standards. Most paradigmatic in this regard is the 'Statement of Shared Commitment' in the United States-Singapore FTA, which provides:

> Recognizing the right of each Party to establish its own domestic labor standards, and to adopt or modify accordingly its labor laws and regulations, *each Party shall strive to ensure that its laws provide for labor standards consistent with the internationally recognized labor rights … and shall strive to improve those standards in that light.*[69]

---

entered into force 1 January 2003) art 16(1)(c) <http://unctad.org/sections/dite/iia/docs/bits/korea_japan.pdf> accessed 4 April 2014.

[67] See Robert Howse, 'The World Trade Organization and the Protection of Workers' Rights' (1999) 3 *Journal of Small & Emerging Business Law* 131–72.

[68] US-Uruguay BIT (n 26) art 13(1).

[69] US-Singapore FTA (n 36) art 17.1 (2) (emphasis added).

Similar language is present in some other FTAs concluded by the United States, as well as in many BITs concluded by BLEU. The Canada-Peru LCA, by contrast, formulates such commitments as obligations of result, requiring that each party 'shall ensure that its statutes and regulations, and practices thereunder, embody and provide protection for ... internationally recognized labour principles and rights.'[70] But then again, these internationally recognized labor rights are nothing but a bare minimum.

A different approach is notable in IIAs concluded between more developed treaty partners. Under the NAALC, 'each Party shall ensure that its labor laws and regulations provide for *high* labor standards, consistent with high quality and productivity workplaces, and shall continue to strive to improve those standards in that light.'[71] The standards referred to in the NAALC are not limited to the internationally recognized labor rights and core labor standards, but are broader, as they also encompass the right to strike, equal pay for women and men, prevention of occupational injuries and illnesses, compensation in cases of occupational injuries and illnesses, and protection of migrant workers.[72] Similarly, under the Canada-EU Comprehensive Economic and Trade Agreement (CETA), each Party 'shall ensure' that its labor law and practices, not only 'embody and provide protection' for the fundamental principles and rights at work, but also 'promote' health and safety at work, including the prevention of occupational injuries and illnesses and the provision of compensation; the establishment of acceptable minimum employment standards for wage earners, including those not covered by collective agreements; and non-discrimination in respect of working conditions, including for migrant workers.[73] Furthermore, 'each Party shall strive to continue to improve those laws and policies with the goal of providing *high* levels of labour protection.'[74]

With a view to enhancing the parties' cooperation in the adoption, maintenance, and further improvement of labor standards, NAALC – as well as many US and Canadian IIAs – also mandate the development of special collaborative mechanisms, through which the parties are expected to cooperate on establishing priorities for cooperative activities on labor matters and their subsequent development, exchanging information on

70 Canada-Peru LCA (n 32) art 1(1).
71 NAALC (n 43) art 2 (emphasis added).
72 Ibid art 1 and Annex 1.
73 CETA (n 32) Chapter X+1, art 3.
74 Ibid art 2 (emphasis added).

labor legislation and practice, and implementing the principles reflected in the ILO Declaration.[75]

3. The problem of regulatory chill

At the end of the day, the question remains whether the standards of treatment that are presently found in IIAs – in particular, the prohibition of indirect expropriations and the obligation to provide fair and equitable treatment – would actually bar the adoption and implementation of higher labor standards where clauses acknowledging the host State's right to regulate are lacking. Considering that their object and purpose is not to shield the foreign investor and its investment from any and all interferences by the host State, but only from those that are undue, IIAs ought merely to dissuade the host State from amending its laws in a capricious or opportunistic way, but do not stand in the way of bona fide law reform. It is essentially the task of arbitral tribunals to find the right balance between the host State's regulatory discretion and the investor's interest that such discretion is not abused. It cannot be denied that, in performing this task, tribunals have regularly sought to strike a balance of interests between investors' legitimate and reasonable expectations, on the one hand, and the host State's legitimate regulatory interests, on the other.[76]

However, the balancing act is to be performed by each arbitral tribunal. Considering that under the current system, States cannot decisively influence the composition of such tribunals and that there is no guarantee that these will take due account of host State's regulatory interests, nor adopt consistent decisions in interpreting the same standards, it is no surprise that some States preferred to amend the language of their IIAs,

---

[75] See, e.g., US-Singapore FTA (n 36) Annex 17A paras 1–4; NAALC (n 43) art 11; Canada-Peru LCA (n 32) art 9.

[76] Such balancing has been considered necessary to establish whether a regulatory measure of general application amounted to an indirect expropriation (see, e.g., *Técnicas Medioambientales Tecmed, SA v The United Mexican States*, ICSID Case No ARB (AF)/00/2, Award (29 May 2003) para 122; or *Methanex v United States*, UNCITRAL, Final Award (3 August 2005) pt IV, ch D 7), as well to determining a breach of the fair and equitable treatment standard (see, e.g., *Saluka Investments BV v The Czech Republic*, UNCITRAL, Partial Award (17 March 2006) paras 305–6). As part of this balancing, tribunals have also rejected the idea that the fair and equitable treatment obligation could be interpreted as implying the total chilling of the host State's legal framework (see, e.g., *Parkerings-Compagniet AS v Republic of Lithuania*, ICSID Case No ARB/05/8, Award (11 September 2007) para 332; or *EDF (Services) Limited v Romania*, ICSID Case No ARB/05/13, Award (8 October 2009) paras 217–19).

with a view to expressly recognizing policy space in non-investment matters. These amendments certainly provide an additional impetus for investment tribunals to properly take account of public policy concerns of the host State, including their interest in the adoption and further improvement of labor standards. Furthermore, the inclusion of labor provisions in IIAs reduces the potential of normative conflicts between treaty regimes, as inconsistencies between different issue areas must now be resolved at the level of the same instrument.[77] At any rate, one must not forget that, even though on a proper construction, investment protection standards ought to take into account public policy concerns, threats are cheap and investors can still make claims even when these may have little chance of success. In the end, perception matters.[78]

C. Fostering Compliance by Foreign Investors

The third, and thus far the least frequent type of labor provisions are those directed at fostering compliance with labor standards by foreign investors. These are the most recent innovation in treaty language, and form part of a broader trend towards enhancing the responsibility of all relevant stakeholders benefiting from the international investment regime.[79] Although IIAs have often been accused of 'granting rights without responsibilities,'[80] their purpose has never been to make foreign

---

[77] In more technical terms, it shifts the question of how to interpret protection standards from Article 31(3)(C) to the, arguably less problematic, arts 31(1) and 31(2) VCLT. On this see Campbell McLachlan, 'The Principle of Systemic Integration and Article 31(3)(C) of the Vienna Convention' (2005) 54 ICLQ 279, 281.

[78] See, e.g., Kyla Tienhaara, 'Regulatory Chill and the Threat of Arbitration: A View From Political Science' in Chester Brown and Kate Miles (eds), *Evolution in Investment Treaty Law and Arbitration* (CUP 2011) 606–28, who argues on these grounds that the repeated dismissals of the regulatory chill hypothesis by some practitioners and legal scholars are both premature and lacking in analytical rigor.

[79] See John Gaffney and Janani Sarvanantham, 'Achieving Sustainable Development Objectives in International Investment: Could Future IIAs Impose Sustainable Development-Related Obligations on Investors?' (Columbia FDI Perspective No 108, 13 November 2013) <http://www.vcc.columbia.edu/content/achieving-sustainable-development-objectives-international-investment-could-future-iias-impo> accessed 4 April 2014.

[80] See Jarrod Hepburn and Vuyelwa Kuuya, 'Corporate Social Responsibility and Investment Treaties' in Marie-Claire Cordonier Segger, Markus Gehring and Andrew Newcombe (eds), *Sustainable Development in World Investment Law* (Kluwer 2010) 589, 607.

investors immune from regulation. Both the home State of the investor and the host State will always remain in the position to regulate investors' conduct through their national legal systems. Thus, the issue is not about the responsibility of foreign investors as such, but whether this responsibility should be regulated more directly in IIAs rather than merely through domestic legislation as under the present system.

Insofar as investors' compliance with labor standards is concerned, the motivations for pursuing regulation through IIAs are essentially two-fold: on the one hand, the conduct of investors can eventually be made subject to compliance with some external standards, independent of those enshrined in domestic legislation; on the other hand, the inclusion of more direct obligations may prevent abuses of the system of investor-State arbitration by investments that fail to respect such standards. Both rationales are reflected in current treaty language, as a distinction can be drawn between provisions that seek to promote investor's compliance with labor standards as a matter of corporate social responsibility (CSR) (1), and provisions that impose obligations directly upon investors in relation to their adherence to domestic (labor) legislation and/or international labor standards as such (2).

1. Corporate social responsibility provisions

References to CSR appear in a variety of forms. In the case of some FTAs concluded by Canada or EFTA States, for example, they are found in preambulatory statements recognizing the importance of CSR for sustainable development and affirming the contracting parties' commitment 'to encourage' their enterprises to 'respect' or 'take into account' internationally recognized standards, principles, and best practices.[81] In some other IIAs, on the other hand, they feature in separate treaty provisions on CSR. For example, in the investment chapter of the Canada-Peru FTA (2008), as well as in investment chapters of some other Canadian FTAs, one can find clauses stipulating that:

> Each Party should encourage enterprises operating within its territory or subject to its jurisdiction to voluntarily incorporate internationally recognized standards of corporate social responsibility in their internal policies, such as statements of principle that have been endorsed or are supported by the Parties. These principles address issues such as labour, the environment,

[81] See, e.g., Preambles of EFTA-Montenegro FTA (n 35), or Canada-Peru Free Trade Agreement (adopted 29 May 2008, entered into force 1 August 2009) <http://www.international.gc.ca/trade-agreements-accords-commerciaux/agr-acc/peru-perou/peru-toc-perou-tdm.aspx> accessed 4 April 2014.

> human rights, community relations and anti-corruption. The Parties therefore remind those enterprises of the importance of incorporating such corporate social responsibility standards in their internal policies.[82]

A different example is the clause appearing in the Netherlands-United Arab Emirates BIT (2013), which provides that '[e]ach Contracting Party shall promote as far as possible and in accordance with their domestic laws the application of the OECD Guidelines for Multinational Enterprises to the extent that is not contrary to their domestic laws.'[83] The reference to the OECD Guidelines – which is probably the first such reference found in IIAs – makes the content of the aspired CSR norms more concrete than in most of the abovementioned provisions.

While currently found in only a handful of IIAs, CSR clauses are likely to appear in some important IIAs that are currently in the making, as attested to by, among other examples, the leaked investment chapter of the Trans-Pacific Partnership Agreement[84] and the Shared Principles for International Investment which will serve as a basis for the drafting of the US-EU Transatlantic Trade and Investment Partnership (TTIP) between the United States and the EU.[85] It is moreover expected that such clauses will become a standard feature of future trade and investment agreements negotiated by the EU.[86] Indeed, provisions encouraging

---

[82] Canada-Peru FTA (n 81) art 810. Similar CSR clauses can also be found in Canada-Colombia Free Trade Agreement (adopted 21 November 2008, entered into force 15 August 2011) art 816 <http://www.international.gc.ca/trade-agreements-accords-commerciaux/agr-acc/colombia-colombie/can-colombia-toc-tdm-can-colombie.aspx> accessed 4 April 2014; Canada-Panama Free Trade Agreement (adopted 14 May 2010, entered into force 1 April 2013) art 9.17 <http://www.international.gc.ca/trade-agreements-accords-commerciaux/agr-acc/panama/panama-toc-panama-tdm.aspx> accessed 4 April 2014; and Canada-Honduras Free Trade Agreement (adopted 5 November 2013, entered into force 1 October 2014) art 10.16 <http://www.international.gc.ca/trade-agreements-accords-commerciaux/agr-acc/honduras/10.aspx?lang=eng> accessed 4 April 2014.

[83] Netherlands-UAE BIT (n 58) art 2(3).

[84] Trans-Pacific Partnership Agreement (June 2012) draft art 12.15 *bis* <http://www.citizenstrade.org/ctc/wp-content/uploads/2012/06/tppinvestment.pdf> accessed 4 April 2014.

[85] Statement of the European Union and the United States on Shared Principles for International Investment (10 April 2012) 1 <http://trade.ec.europa.eu/doclib/docs/2012/april/tradoc_149331.pdf> accessed 4 April 2014.

[86] See European Parliament, Resolution of 25 November 2010 on Corporate Social Responsibility in International Trade Agreements (2009/2201(INI)) (2012/C 99 E/19), in which the proposal was made that future EU FTAs 'should

businesses to adopt practices that promote economic, social and environmental objectives have already been included in the CETA.[87]

In general, the commitments imposed by CSR provisions are still much less demanding than those under the non-derogation and policy space-type provisions, since they are usually phrased in a 'double-soft law' manner: States are required to *remind* or *encourage* investors to adopt *voluntary* standards. While such language apparently seeks to capture the benefits of the voluntary approach that has usually been pursued in relation to CSR issues,[88] it has also been suggested that the clauses would be given additional weight if IIAs would also instruct tribunals to take into account investor's compliance with the relevant standards in deciding investors' claims.[89] Even in their 'soft' form, however, CSR clauses are not necessarily redundant, as they can influence the interpretation of other investment protection standards found in IIAs. Exceptionally, however, one can also find CSR clauses that are cast in more stringent language and require from the parties specific legislative action at the domestic level. The CARIFORUM-EU Economic Partnership Agreement (2008), for example, provides that the parties

> shall cooperate and take, within their own respective territories, such measures as may be necessary, inter alia, through domestic legislation, to ensure that … Investors act in accordance with core labour standards as required by the International Labour Organization (ILO) Declaration on Fundamental Principles and Rights at Work, 1998 [and that] Investors do not manage or operate their investments in a manner that circumvents international … labour obligations arising from agreements to which the EC Party and the Signatory CARIFORUM States are parties.[90]

All in all, in terms of regulatory impact, CSR clauses constitute an important step towards ensuring greater compliance by foreign investors with labor standards, in that they are not directed solely at the State party which is the recipient of the investment and which may lack the capacity

---

incorporate a chapter on sustainable development which includes a CSR clause, based, in part, on the 2010 update of the OECD Guidelines for Multinational Enterprises.'

[87] See CETA (n 32) art XX.3.

[88] See on this Hepburn and Kuuya (n 80) 589–609.

[89] See UNCTAD, *Investment Policy Framework for Sustainable Development* (n 52) 58.

[90] Economic Partnership Agreement between the CARIFORUM States, of the one part, and the European Community and its Member States, of the other part (signed 15 October 2008, not yet in force) art 72, paras (b) and (c), OJ L 289 (30 October 2008).

and/or political will to ensure respect of labor rights, but also at the State party within whose 'territory' the enterprises operate or within whose 'jurisdiction' they fall, which equally (and perhaps primarily) means the capital-exporting State. In doing so, CSR clauses reaffirm the responsibilities that States have under international law to ensure respect of human rights by corporations even when these operate extraterritorially, an element which has been embraced as one of the central pillars of the Guidelines developed by the UN Special Representative John Ruggie in 2011.[91]

2. Provisions imposing direct obligations

In terms of structure, however, CSR provisions do not depart from the paradigmatic way in which IIAs are drafted. That is, they do not impose obligations upon investors directly, but rely for the purpose of regulation upon the contracting parties to the IIA which are expected to 'encourage' investors' compliance with CSR norms essentially by means of national legislation and administrative measures. From the perspective of contemporary international law, however, there are certainly no conceptual arguments explaining why IIAs could not impose specific obligations upon foreign investors directly: if they are capable of vesting foreign investors with direct rights, such as the right to commence arbitration against the host State, they are certainly capable of also subjecting them to specific obligations. Yet, just as attempts to impose standards of good behavior upon corporations through internationally binding legal instruments have generally failed to garner political support,[92] so have capital-exporting States generally resisted the inclusion in their IIAs of

[91] See UN Human Rights Council, 'Report of the Special Representative of the Secretary-General on the Issue of Human Rights and Transnational Corporations and Other Business Enterprises, John Ruggie: Guiding Principles on Business and Human Rights: Implementing the United Nations "Protect, Respect and Remedy" framework' UN Doc A/HRC/17/31 (21 March 2011) 9. See generally Jennifer A Zerk, *Multinationals and Corporate Social Responsibility: Limitations and Opportunities in International Law* (CUP 2006) 104–42.

[92] Reference can be made to the aborted United Nations Code of Conduct on Transnational Corporations (1983) <http://unctad.org/sections/dite/iia/docs/Compendium/en/13%20volume%201.pdf> accessed 4 April 2014 which emphasized the responsibility of investors to comply with host State regulations, respect their sovereign right to regulate and contribute to the host State's development; or the equally unsuccessful Norms on the Responsibilities of Transnational Corporations and Other Business Enterprises with Regard to Human Rights (UN Doc E/CN.4/Sub.2/2003/12/Rev.2 (13 August 2003)), which sought to impose upon companies, directly under international law, the same range of human rights

obligations relating to investor's conduct.[93] Recently however, this has begun to change, as a few IIAs have been adopted which impose specific obligations upon foreign investors directly, demanding from them, among others, compliance with domestic and/or international labor standards.

An early example is the Investment Agreement for the COMESA Common Investment Area (2007), which stipulates that 'COMESA investors and their investments shall comply with all applicable domestic measures of the Member State in which their investment is made.'[94] This provision does not yet prescribe any particular obligation of conduct in relation to labor standards; it does however impose an additional obligation under international law to comply with the domestic legislation of the host State, including, among other obligations, its labor code. A further, more comprehensive example are the Community Rules on Investment that were adopted by the Economic Community of West African States (ECOWAS) in 2008, which contain a complete chapter devoted to obligations and duties of investors and investments (Chapter III).[95] While confirming that investors

> are subject to the laws and regulations of the host State, [these Rules specifically provide that investors] shall strive, through their management policies and practices, to contribute to the development objectives of the host States and the local levels of government where the investment is located.[96]

For that purpose, the Rules require that, once established in the host State, investors

---

duties that States have accepted for themselves. On this see Peter T Muchlinski, 'International Corporate Social Responsibility and International Law' in Todd Weiler and Freya Baetens (eds), *New Directions in International Economic Law: In Memoriam Thomas Wälde* (Martinus Nijhoff 2011) 223–44.

93 The draft of the later aborted Multilateral Agreement on Investment did contain a provision that would 'associate' the OECD Guidelines on Multinational Enterprises to that agreement. But the Guidelines themselves are not legally binding; see OECD, 'The Multilateral Agreement on Investment: The MAI Negotiating Text' (22 April 1998) 95 <http://www1.oecd.org/daf/mai/pdf/ng/ng987r1e.pdf> accessed 4 April 2014.

94 Investment Agreement for the COMESA Common Investment Area (n 64) art 13.

95 See Supplementary Act A/SA.3/12/08 Adopting Community Rules on Investment and the Modalities for their Implementation with ECOWAS (19 December 2008) <http://www.privatesector.ecowas.int/en/III/Supplementary_Act_Investment.pdf> accessed 4 April 2014.

96 Art 11(1) and Article 11(3), respectively.

> *shall* uphold human rights in the workplace and the community in which they are located. Investors shall not undertake or cause to be undertaken, acts that breach such human rights. Investors shall not manage or operate the investments in a manner that circumvents human rights obligations, labour standards as well as regional environmental and social obligations, to which the host State and/or home State are Parties.[97]

Furthermore, the rule states that '[i]nvestors and investments shall act in accordance with fundamental labour standards as stipulated in the ILO Declaration on Fundamental Principles and Rights of Work, 1998.'[98]

These examples suggest that it is not inconceivable for future IIAs to impose more demanding commitments on investors, including specific obligations of conduct in relation to labor standards. Attesting to this trend are also several Model BITs that were developed in the past few years that impose extensive labor-related obligations on investors.[99] Moreover, UNCTAD identified the inclusion of obligations concerning investors' compliance with investment-related national laws as one of the four areas of evolution in IIA treaty-making practice that could serve to address sustainable development challenges.[100]

---

[97] Art 14(2) (emphasis added).

[98] Art 14(4).

[99] See, e.g., Article 14 of the IISD Model International Agreement on Investment for Sustainable Development (2005) <http://www.iisd.org/pdf/2005/investment_model_int_agreement.pdf> accessed 4 April 2014 which demands, inter alia, that investors and investments 'should uphold human rights in the workplace' and 'shall act in accordance with core labour standards as required by the ILO Declaration on Fundamental Principles and Rights of Work, 1998'; and Article 15 of the Southern African Development Community Model Bilateral Investment Treaty Template (2012) <http://www.iisd.org/itn/wp-content/uploads/2012/10/SADC-Model-BIT-Template-Final.pdf> accessed 4 April 2014 which similarly provides that investors 'have a duty to respect human rights in the workplace', 'shall act in accordance with core labour standards as required by the ILO Declaration on Fundamental Principles and Rights of Work, 1998', and 'shall not [establish,] manage or operate Investments in a manner inconsistent with international environmental, labour, and human rights obligations binding on the Host State or the Home State, whichever obligations are higher.' As these are only model instruments, it remains to be seen whether capital-exporting States will be willing to accept such commitments in their treaties.

[100] UNCTAD, *Investment Policy Framework* (n 52) 39. In addition to including general provisions demanding investors' compliance with domestic laws, UNCTAD also proposes the introduction of a two-way umbrella clause that would require not only the host country, but also the investor to observe specific obligations in relation to an investment under an investment contract concluded between the investor and the host country; ibid 54.

The imposition of more direct obligations on investors will have consequences especially for investment treaty arbitration. In the absence of such provisions, the possibility for the host State to raise the issue of the investor's compliance with domestic laws as an independent head of claim has generally been limited. Since under most IIAs the right of recourse to investor-State arbitration pertains solely to the foreign investor, the host State only has the option to raise the issue of non-compliance as a counter-claim, once the investor has already initiated arbitration proceedings. Though, the threshold for successfully invoking counter-claims has generally been difficult to meet and the inclusion of direct obligations for investors would therefore alleviate some of these problems.[101]

At the same time, one should not forget that under present IIAs, host States have already been able to raise the issue of the investor's non-compliance with domestic legislation indirectly, as an argument in defense of their liability. This has been in the form of an objection to the jurisdiction of the arbitral tribunal or the admissibility of the investor's claim, in which case the question was one of determining whether the foreign investor complied with the domestic laws of the host State when making its investment.[102] Alternatively, it has been raised as a defense on the merits, in which case allegations of illegalities in the management and operation of the investment and the conduct of the investor in general

---

[101] Inasmuch as counterclaims must fall within the scope of consent to arbitration as expressed in the IIA and must arise directly out of the subject-matter of the dispute or must have a close connection with the primary claim to which they are a response, it has been practically impossible to bring counter-claims in relation to the investor's own conduct, particularly where consent was limited to disputes concerning breaches of obligations under the IIA in question, which only imposed obligations on the host State. For an exceptional situation where counter-claims were permitted, see *Antoine Goetz & Others and SA Affinage des Metaux v Republic of Burundi*, ICSID Case No ARB/01/2, Award (21 June 2012) paras 267–87.

[102] The test whether investors complied with host States' domestic laws in the making of an investment has often been conducted by investment tribunals, which occasionally also declined jurisdiction over claims because the underlying investments were illegal; see *Inceysa Vallisoletana SL v Republic of El Salvador*, ICSID Case No ARB/03/26, Award (2 August 2006); or *Fraport AG Frankfurt Airport Services Worldwide v Philippines*, ICSID Case No ARB/03/25, Award (16 August 2007). The legality test is still in an emerging state and the scope of domestic law violations that are covered by this test often depends on specific IIA provisions; see further Stephan W Schill, 'Illegal Investments in Investment Treaty Arbitration' (2012) 11 LPICT 281–323.

were assessed against the conduct of the host State in determining the latter's breaches of investment protection standards.[103]

At the end of the day, however, it is not the purpose of investment arbitration to function as a mechanism for ensuring the investor's compliance with domestic labor laws, as this remains the task for domestic authorities of the host State. Nor is investment arbitration an appropriate mechanism for such ends. In particular, considering that its function is to settle bilateral disputes between foreign investors and host States, investment arbitration does not enable other aggrieved stakeholders, such as workers, to bring claims before an investment tribunal.[104]

IV. INNOVATION IN TREATY LANGUAGE – PROSPECTS FOR SUSTAINABLE DEVELOPMENT?

Since the early 1990s, the inclusion of labor provisions into IIAs has steadily been gaining momentum. Less than a decade ago, it was still considered a 'general rule' that investment treaties of OECD countries did not include special provisions bearing on the protection of labor rights, with the United States and BLEU being mentioned as the only two exceptions.[105] Today, such provisions are regularly found in IIAs concluded by Austria, Korea, Japan, Canada, and EFTA. Very likely, they will also be inserted in some important IIAs that are currently in the making, such as the TTIP.

Admittedly, when it comes to BITs, the occurrence of labor provisions is still somewhat exceptional. But the practice of concluding BITs as such has begun to lose momentum, as States increasingly prefer to

---

[103] On this see Peter T Muchlinski, '"Caveat Investor"? The Relevance of the Conduct of the Investor Under the Fair and Equitable Treatment Standard' (2006) 55 ICLQ 536–56; and Andrew Newcombe, 'Investor Misconduct: Jurisdiction, Admissibility or Merits?' in Brown and Miles (n 78) 187–200.

[104] The only way for interested stakeholders to raise the issue of labor standards in the context of investor-State arbitration is through their limited participation as non-disputing parties; see, e.g., *UPS v Canada,* UNCITRAL, Decision of the tribunal on petitions for intervention and participation as *amici curiae* (17 October 2001), for one of the earliest instances of an investment tribunal deciding to accept amicus curiae briefs from a trade union.

[105] OECD, 'Novel Features in Recent OECD Bilateral Investment Treaties', International Investment Perspectives 2006 (OECD 2006) 157.

regulate the promotion and protection of foreign investment in conjunction with other issues of economic cooperation, resulting in investment chapters now often being added to FTAs or economic partnership agreements. In comparison with BITs, these instruments are much more comprehensive in nature, since they frequently deal with important non-economic matters as well, such as labor and the environment. The potential for regulating the interface between investment and labor rights in a comprehensive and integrated manner has thereby increased, and with it the prospects of IIAs becoming instruments for the achievement of sustainable development.[106]

In the meantime, the language of labor clauses has also changed in accordance with the diverging rationales for the investment-labor linkage. Whereas twenty years ago improvements in host State labor conditions were seen as an automatic spillover effect of inward FDI (and such beliefs are occasionally still reflected in treaty preambles), contemporary IIAs are more conscious of the risks brought about by investment liberalization and protection for labor issues, as reflected in inclusion of labor provisions in IIAs. Non-derogation clauses are probably still dominating – and developments in treaty practice even demonstrate a trend towards broadening and strengthening the commitments undertaken in these clauses, with obligations of result gradually replacing hortatory statements. But the relaxation of labor standards is no longer the sole concern. An issue of equal importance is the preservation of States' regulatory autonomy in labor and other matters of societal concern. In addition, the fostering of investors' compliance with international labor rights has become somewhat of an emerging issue.

All in all, more attention today is devoted to achieving a better balance between investment and non-investment policy objectives, and to ensure that IIAs no longer allow the goal of economic development to be achieved at the expense of social concerns, but instead promote a more holistic concept of sustainable development. The goal remains to achieve a coherent normative framework that enables States to reap the benefits of inward FDI without compromising decent labor standards.

---

[106] Provided, of course, that the conclusion of such comprehensive treaties does not lead to a potentially dangerous multiplication of treaty layers; see on this concern UNCTAD, *World Investment Report 2013* (n 18) 105–6.

15. Investment, development and indigenous peoples

Christina Binder

I. INTRODUCTION

In the investment law and development debate, the concerns of indigenous peoples gain increasing importance. One of the reasons is their recent recognition as culturally distinct peoples, which goes along with a stronger protection of their land rights in international law. At the same time, the always denser net of bilateral investment treaties (BITs) – more than 2800 by the end of 2012[1] plays a role. These developments increase the likelihood of interactions between indigenous peoples' rights and international investment law and make the need for coordination between both systems more acute; even if, so far, indigenous rights have been dealt with only in very few investment cases.[2]

Also, conceptually, the debate on investment law, development and indigenous peoples seems of particular interest. It is more complex than the debate on investment law, development and human rights.[3] For

---

[1] UNCTAD, *World Investment Report 2013* (United Nations 2013) x <http://unctad.org/en/publicationslibrary/wir2013_en.pdf> accessed 7 February 2014.

[2] See infra Section III for details.

[3] On the investment and human rights debate, see generally Ursula Kriebaum, 'Human Rights of the Population of the Host State in International Investment Arbitration' (2009) 10 JWIT 653; Bruno Simma and Theodore Kill, 'Harmonizing Investment Protection and International Human Rights: First Steps Towards a Methodology' in Christina Binder and others (eds), *International Investment Law for the 21st Century* (OUP 2009) 678; Ursula Kriebaum, 'Foreign Investments and Human Rights: The Actors and Their Different Roles' in N Jansen Calamita, David Earnest and Markus Burgstaller (eds), *Current Issues in Investment Treaty Law*, vol IV (BIICL 2013) 45; Pierre-Marie Dupuy, 'Unification Rather than Fragmentation of International Law? The Case of International Investment Law and Human Rights Law' in Pierre-Marie Dupuy,

example, when investment and development are discussed in a human rights-related context, the debate concentrates on whether investment protection is favourable to the human rights situation of the host state's population – for example, by raising standards of living via economic development; or whether investment protection is detrimental thereto as, for instance, the protection of foreign investors might prevent the host state from exercising its police powers and adopting measures to safeguard the human rights of its population. Still, in the investment, development and human rights context, the host state's (democratically elected) government may in principle be assumed to represent the interests of its population. An additional dimension is added when indigenous peoples are concerned. Since indigenous peoples usually live as minorities in nation states,[4] they are not necessarily represented by the government of that state (i.e. the host state).

It seems thus of particular interest to examine the complex relationship between international investment law, development and indigenous peoples. In doing so, this contribution adopts an inclusive development concept with a focus on sustainability. It considers that the protection of indigenous peoples as culturally distinct peoples is a necessary part of sustainable development[5] and thus rejects the more restrictive development concept which is primarily focused on the (economic) development/ well being of the host state.[6] The underlying assumption being, that for

---

Francesco Francioni and Ernst-Ulrich Petersmann (eds), *Human Rights in International Investment Law and Arbitration* (OUP 2009) 45; Ursula Kriebaum, 'Privatizing Human Rights. The Interface Between Investment Protection and Human Rights' in August Reinisch and Ursula Kriebaum (eds), *The Law of International Relations – Liber Amicorum Hanspeter Neuhold* (Eleven International Publishing 2007) 165; Eric De Brabandere, 'Human Rights Considerations in International Investment Arbitration', Grotius Centre Working Paper 2013/001-IEL <http://papers.ssrn.com/sol3/papers.cfm?abstract_id=2230305> accessed 7 February 2014.

[4] Exceptions are Guatemala and Bolivia, where indigenous peoples are the majority population.

[5] See IFAD, 'Indigenous Peoples and Sustainable Development' Discussion Paper (2003) <http://www.ifad.org/gbdocs/gc/26/e/ip.pdf> accessed 21 March 2014; IWGIA, 'Sustainable Development and Indigenous Peoples' (2012) <http://www.iwgia.org/environment-and-development/sustainable-development> accessed 21 March 2014. On sustainable development in general see Ulrich Beyerlin, 'Sustainable Development' in Rüdiger Wolfrum (ed.), *Max Planck Encyclopedia of Public International Law* (2012), vol IX, 716 (online version at <http://opil.ouplaw.com/> accessed 21 March 2014).

[6] On the different notions of development see Alhagi Marong, 'Development, Right to, International Protection' in Wolfrum (n 5), vol III, 85. Note that

an inclusive development concept, the rights of indigenous peoples have to be respected to the maximum extent.

This contribution argues accordingly that to realize such an inclusive development, de lege lata as well as de lege ferenda options to incorporate the rights of indigenous peoples in investment treaties and proceedings have to be further explored. In order to do this, this contribution first addresses the complex relationship between indigenous peoples' rights and investment law, outlining the specific characteristics of indigenous peoples, the growing recognition of their rights in international instruments and the potential for conflicts between both systems as evidenced in relevant jurisprudence by international human rights monitoring institutions (Part II). Against that background, Part III gives an overview of investment cases where indigenous peoples' issues were at stake. Part IV discusses already existing legal techniques to deal with indigenous peoples' rights in investment proceedings. Part V examines de lege ferenda options to coordinate between the systems and to incorporate indigenous concerns. Part VI concludes.

II. INVESTMENT LAW VERSUS INDIGENOUS PEOPLES? POSSIBLE CONFLICTS

The growing need to deal with indigenous peoples and international investment law stems, on the one hand, from the specific cultural identity of indigenous peoples and the possible negative impacts of investment projects on indigenous lands (A.). At the same time, the stronger international protection of indigenous peoples' rights increases the potential for conflicts between their rights and those of foreign investors (B.). This is evidenced in recent jurisprudence of human rights monitoring institutions (C.).

A. Indigenous Peoples and Their Lands

A defining characteristic of indigenous peoples is the (at least partial) maintenance of their traditional ways of life with respect to decision

---

in such a restrictive development concept, an affirmation of indigenous peoples' rights might even be considered detrimental to the host state's development; namely when their protection seemingly contravenes the economic interests – for example, in resource exploitation by foreign investors – of the majority population.

making and institutions[7] as well as the special relationship to their lands.[8] Indigenous lands and territories generally have a spiritual and emotional value and are of vital importance for the indigenous culture.[9] In view of this importance, indigenous peoples are particularly vulnerable to encroachments on their lands (logging activities, mineral exploitation, etc.) by (foreign) investors. The problem is acerbated by the fact that indigenous territories are often resource-rich areas which are of particular interest for exploitation. Moreover, their difference from the majority population, especially their traditional ways of life,[10] make indigenous peoples particularly vulnerable to external influence and pressure. Indigenous rights that are most at risk in an investment-related context are thus land and resource rights as well as their right to cultural identity (and cultural heritage).[11] These rights have seen recently an increasing recognition and protection by international instruments.

B. International Standards on Indigenous Rights

For a long time, indigenous peoples were neglected at the international sphere. However, a growing recognition of indigenous rights has taken place in the last decades, as evidenced by the adoption of specialized

---

7 See Art 1 of the Convention (No 169) concerning Indigenous and Tribal Peoples in Independent Countries (adopted 27 June 1989, entered into force 5 September 1991) (ILO Convention No 169) which stipulates the 'maintenance of some or all of their own social, economic, cultural and political institutions' as the defining characteristic of indigenous peoples.

8 Robert A Williams, 'Encounters on the Frontiers of International Human Rights Law: Redefining the Terms of Indigenous Peoples' Survival in the World' (1990) 39 Duke LJ 660, 681.

9 See International Law Association, 'Rights of Indigenous Peoples: Conference Report' 75th ILA Conference (Sofia, Bulgaria, 26–30 August 2012) 3, which lists the special relationship with its ancestral lands in addition to self-identification as one of the two essential criteria for a community to be considered as an indigenous people <http://www.ila-hq.org/en/committees/index.cfm/cid/1024> accessed 7 February 2014.

10 See Gudmundur Alfredsson, 'Indigenous Peoples and Autonomy' in Markku Suksi (ed.), *Autonomy: Applications and Implications* (Kluwer 1998) 125.

11 See in this sense also Federico Lenzerini, 'Foreign Investment in the Energy Sector and Indigenous Peoples' Rights' in Eric De Brabandere and Tarcisio Gazzini (eds), *Foreign Investment in the Energy Sector: Balancing Private and Public Interests* (Martinus Nijhoff Publishers 2014) 192, 194.

instruments on indigenous rights.[12] The 1989 ILO Convention No 169[13] is, together with its predecessor the 1957 ILO Convention No 107,[14] the only formally binding instrument which is especially dedicated to indigenous rights. ILO Convention No 169 grants important rights. It recognizes indigenous peoples as culturally distinct peoples (e.g. in Articles 1 and 5). Most importantly, ILO Convention No 169 values the specific relationship of indigenous peoples to their lands (Article 13) and recognizes the rights of indigenous peoples to the lands and territories which they traditionally occupy (Article 14). ILO Convention No 169 also establishes their rights to surface resources on their lands (Article 15). For sub-surface resources, a right to consultation is provided for (Article 15(2)).

The 2007 UN Declaration on the Rights of Indigenous Peoples goes even further.[15] The Declaration recognizes a right to self-determination of indigenous peoples (Article 3), their distinct cultural identity (e.g. in Articles 5, 8, 9, 11, 12), the specific relationship to their territories (Article 25) and far reaching land rights (Article 26). The latter includes the right to lands, territories and resources which indigenous peoples have traditionally owned, occupied or otherwise used (Article 26). It also obliges states to cooperate and consult with indigenous peoples in good faith in order to obtain their free, prior and informed consent before adopting or implementing measures that may affect them (Article 19) especially as regards projects affecting their lands (Article 32). As a General Assembly resolution, the UN Declaration is not legally binding,

---

[12] The increasing protection of indigenous peoples in international law goes hand in hand with a growing domestic recognition of indigenous rights especially in Latin American countries; see, e.g., the constitutions of Brazil, Bolivia, Colombia, Ecuador, Nicaragua, Paraguay, and Venezuela (for further reference see International Law Association, 'The Rights of Indigenous Peoples: Conference Report' 74th ILA Conference (The Hague, Netherlands, 15–20 August 2010) 23 <http://www.ila-hq.org/en/committees/index.cfm/cid/1024> accessed 7 February 2013.

[13] ILO Convention No 169 (n 7); as of January 2014, the ILO Convention was ratified by 20 states (for the status of ratifications see <http://www.ilo.org/indigenous/Conventions/no169/lang–en/index.htm> accessed 7 February 2014).

[14] Convention (No 107) concerning the Protection and Integration of Indigenous and Other Tribal and Semi-Tribal Populations in Independent Countries, adopted 26 June 1957 by the General Conference of the International Labour Organisation (ILO), 40th session, entered into force 2 June 1959.

[15] Declaration on the Rights of Indigenous Peoples, UNGA Res 61/295 (13 September 2007).

but it has been shown that especially its land rights provisions codify customary international law.[16]

In addition, general international human rights instruments provide protection. Human rights monitoring institutions interpret their provisions so as to protect indigenous peoples' rights. For example, at the universal level, the Human Rights Committee (HRC) interpreted Article 27 of the International Covenant on Civil and Political Rights (CCPR), i.e. the right to cultural integrity, in a way so as to protect indigenous lands against outside interference.[17] Also, the Committee on Economic, Social and Cultural Rights and the Committee on the Elimination of Racial Discrimination have confirmed high standards. Both Committees maintained, for instance, elevated consultation requirements in cases of resource exploitation on indigenous territories. States are therefore required to conduct consultations with indigenous peoples with the objective to gain their prior informed consent.[18] Likewise, regional human rights monitoring institutions have protected indigenous ancestral lands.[19] Especially the Inter-American Court of Human Rights has been proactive in this regard. It found that the rights of indigenous peoples on lands traditionally occupied by them were protected by the right to property of the American Convention on Human Rights (ACHR, Article 21).[20] In addition, in view of the vital importance of lands for the indigenous culture, the Inter-American Court, in *Xákmok Kásek v*

---

[16] See ILA (n 12) 22–23.

[17] See, e.g., HRC, *Länsman et al v Finland*, Communication No 511/1992 (8 November 1994); HRC, *Apiraina Mahuika et al v New Zealand* (15 November 2000) UN Doc CCPR/C/70/D/547/1993 (the CCPR does not include a right to property).

[18] See Committee on Economic, Social and Cultural Rights, General Comment No 21, 'Right of Everyone to Take Part in Cultural Life (Art 15(1) (a) of the International Covenant on Economic, Social and Cultural Rights)', UN Doc E/C.12/GC/21 of 21 December 2009, especially paras 37 and 55; CERD Committee, Consideration of Reports submitted by States Parties under Art 9 of the Convention, Concluding Observations on Ecuador (62nd 2003), UN Doc CERD/C/62/CO/2 of 2 June 2003, para 16; see Lenzerini (n 11) for further references and discussion.

[19] For the jurisprudence of the ECtHR and the European Commission on Human Rights see Timo Koivurova, 'Jurisprudence of the European Court of Human Rights Regarding Indigenous Peoples: Retrospect and Prospects' (2011) 18 *International Journal on Minority and Group Rights* 1; see also the decision of the African Commission on Human and Peoples' Rights in the Ogoni Peoples case infra Section II.C.

[20] See infra Section II.C. for details on the jurisprudence of Inter-American Court of Human Rights.

Paraguay, held that disruption of the linkages between indigenous peoples and their traditional territories amounted to inhumane treatment.[21]

Overall, increasingly far-reaching international standards protect indigenous rights to lands and territories, with due recognition of the cultural values at stake. This entails the obvious 'danger' of conflicting obligations in human rights and investment law.

C. Investment Law versus Indigenous Peoples? Possible Conflicts

A growing number of cases before international human rights monitoring institutions involve investment projects on indigenous lands. Especially the far-reaching jurisprudence of the Inter-American Court of Human Rights evidences possible conflicts between indigenous and foreign investors' rights. Already in its 2001 landmark decision *Awas Tingni v Nicaragua* (2001), the Court found Nicaragua in violation of the indigenous Awas Tingni community's right to property (Article 21 ACHR) for having consented to timber logging activities by a South Korean corporation on lands traditionally occupied by the Awas Tingni community.[22] This jurisprudence was confirmed in subsequent cases. In *Saramaka People v Suriname* (2007), the Inter-American Court found that Suriname breached Article 21 ACHR for issuing mining concessions to foreign companies on territories traditionally occupied by the Saramaka community without the establishment of adequate safeguards to ensure that the concessions would not cause harm to the community and its territories.[23] In *Yakye Axa v Paraguay* (2005) and *Sawhoyamaxa Indigenous Community v Paraguay* (2006), the Inter-American Court of Human Rights ordered Paraguay to restore ancestral land which was in

---

[21] The Inter-American Court of Human Rights held that 'the sorrow that [the indigenous persons concerned] and the other members of the Community feel owing to the failure to restore their traditional lands, the gradual loss of their culture … give rise to sufferings that necessarily violate the mental and moral integrity of all the members of the Community', resulting in a breach of the right to human treatment defended by Art 5 of the same Convention; *Xákmok Kásek Indigenous Community v Paraguay*, Inter-American Court of Human Rights Series C No 214 (24 August 2010) para 244.

[22] *Mayagna (Sumo) Awas Tingni Community v Nicaragua*, Inter-American Court of Human Rights Series C No 79 (31 August 2001).

[23] *Saramaka People v Suriname*, Inter-American Court of Human Rights (28 November 2007) paras 174, 175, 214.

the hands of private investors to indigenous groups.[24] In *Pueblo Indígena Kichwa de Sarayaku v Ecuador* (2012), the Inter-American Court found that Ecuador violated the land rights as well as the right to cultural identity of the Sarayaku indigenous community which had not been consulted before resource exploitation projects by foreign investors were carried out in its traditional lands.[25]

Likewise, the Inter-American Commission on Human Rights issued relevant decisions. In *Mary and Carrie Dann v United States,* the Commission found that the United States had not acted in conformity with their obligations under the 1948 American Declaration of the Rights and Duties of Man when granting gold mining prospects within the traditional lands of the Western Shoshone's indigenous people which affected the Dann's use of the lands and polluted the water.[26]

Also, in Africa, the potential for conflicting state obligations is evidenced in the jurisprudence of regional human rights monitoring institutions. For instance, the African Commission on Human and Peoples' Rights found Nigeria in violation of numerous provisions of the African Charter on Human and Peoples' Rights in relation to a project of oil production on the lands of the indigenous Ogoni community which had resulted in environmental degradation and health problems of members of the Ogoni.[27]

The above-mentioned cases show possible conflicts in case of competing state obligations towards indigenous peoples and foreign investors. Often, the controversy's origin is the state's granting of an extractive

---

[24] *Indigenous Community Yakye Axa v Paraguay*, Inter-American Court of Human Rights Series C No 125 (17 June 2005) paras 148, 217, 218; *Sawhoyamaxa Indigenous Community v Paraguay*, Inter-American Court of Human Rights Series C No 146 (29 March 2006) paras 135–41 and 210–14.

[25] See especially *Pueblo Indígena Kichwa de Sarayaku v Ecuador*, Inter-American Court of Human Rights (27 June 2012) paras 177, 220. The case concerns a dispute which was also dealt with by an investment tribunal in *Burlington v Ecuador*; see *Burlington Resources Inc v Republic of Ecuador*, ICSID Case No ARB/08/5, Decision on Jurisdiction (2 June 2010) <https://icsid.worldbank.org/ICSID/FrontServlet?requestType=CasesRH&actionVal=showDoc&docId=DC1530_En&caseId=C300> accessed 7 February 2014; see infra Section III for details.

[26] Inter-American Commission on Human Rights, *Mary and Carrie Dann v United States*, Case 11.140 (27 December 2002) Report No 75/02, para 172.

[27] See *The Social and Economic Rights Action Center and the Center for Economic and Social Rights v Nigeria*, Communication No 155/96 (2001) <http://www1.umn.edu/humanrts/africa/comcases/155-96.html> accessed 7 February 2014, especially paras 55 ff; see Lenzerini (n 11) 212–13.

activity or resource exploitation project in contradiction to pre-existing rights of indigenous peoples.[28] This risk is acute since indigenous territories are partly still undefined for lack of demarcation of indigenous ancestral lands. When the state subsequently wants to correct such situation by imposing specific regulations to safeguard indigenous (land) rights without compensating the investor, an investment dispute scenario may arise and the foreign investor may resort to investment arbitration in view of the host state's interference with his or her investment. Possible investment claims at stake are unlawful expropriation (when governmental measures to protect indigenous lands reduce the economic value of an investment project to an extent that this amounts to expropriation) as well as breaches of the fair and equitable treatment (FET) standard, of non-discrimination or of full protection and security clauses.[29]

This is less an issue of incompatible obligations than one of monetary compensation of foreign investors.[30] The expropriation of foreign investors to give effect to competing territorial claims of indigenous peoples is not as such illegal. Rather, compensation has to be paid. Still, the usually high amounts of compensation may pose a problem to host states. It seems therefore of particular interest which cases have effectively been brought before investment tribunals.

III. INVESTMENT CASES INVOLVING INDIGENOUS PEOPLES

So far, indigenous issues have been at stake in only very few investment cases.[31] Merely a handful of controversies arising from investment projects on indigenous lands have reached the adjudication phase before international tribunals and even less have been declared admissible. This may be explained by the fact that some disputes are settled at the national level, others are resolved through 'extra-judiciary settlements'. In other cases, no dispute is brought before investment tribunals since domestic

---

[28] See generally Kriebaum (n 3) 657.

[29] See the respective investment cases infra Section III.

[30] As was rightly pointed out by Kriebaum (n 3) 656: 'The obligations incumbent upon the State under human rights treaties will not normally lead to a conflict in a strict sense with investment protection standards. Human rights treaties do not impose a duty on States to expropriate without compensation or to treat investors in an unfair or inequitable or discriminatory manner … .'

[31] See generally Lenzerini (n 11) 201–9.

authorities are complicit in the violations of indigenous land rights and abstain from interfering with the rights of foreign investors.

Among the cases which reached the international adjudication phase, the first and perhaps best known is *Glamis Gold v the United States* (2009).[32] *Glamis Gold* concerned US federal and Californian measures in relation to open pit mining operations which impacted on indigenous (the Quechan Indian Nation's) cultural sites. The measures – including regulations requiring the backfilling of mines – inter alia aimed at the protection of these cultural sites. Glamis submitted a claim under NAFTA in 2003, arguing that the destruction of the economic value of its investment amounted to expropriation, that the FET standard was violated and that it was discriminated against since its project was subject to more onerous regulations than those of other operators. The US government relied on federal and state laws which accorded protection to tribal sacred sites and other tribal resources. The indigenous Quechan tribe participated as amicus curiae.[33] In the award, the *Glamis Gold* tribunal did not find the United States in breach of their obligations. The required backfilling measures were not of sufficient economic impact on the investment to amount to expropriation.[34] Likewise, the FET standard was not breached since the measures were of general application.[35] The award is thus, in result, favourable to the Quechan Indian Nation's rights since the US measures which accorded protection to their sacred sites were accepted. However, the indigenous concerns played, at best, a minor role in the tribunal's reasoning.

In *Chevron Corporation and Texaco Petroleum Company v Ecuador*,[36] Chevron resorted to investment arbitration before the Permanent Court of Arbitration against the judgment of an Ecuadorian court, ordering that it

---

32 *Glamis Gold, Ltd and United States of America*, UNCITRAL, Award (8 June 2009) <http://www.state.gov/gov/documents/organization/51052.pdf> accessed 7 February 2014.

33 Non-Party Supplemental Submission by the Quechan Indian Nation, *Glamis Gold Ltd v United States* <http://www.state.gov/documents/organization/75016.pdf> accessed 7 February 2014; see infra Section IV.D. for details.

34 *Glamis Gold* (n 32) para 536.

35 Ibid paras 598–830. This was, as held by Kriebaum and Schreuer, in application of a particularly high threshold for the standard; see Christoph Schreuer and Ursula Kriebaum, 'From Individual to Community Interest in International Investment Law' in Ulrich Fastenrath and others (eds), *From Bilateralism to Community Interest. Essays in Honour of Judge Bruno Simma* (OUP 2011) 1079, 1086.

36 *Chevron Corporation and Texaco Petroleum Corporation v The Republic of Ecuador*, PCA Case No 2009-23 (pending).

had to pay USD 18.2 billion to indigenous communities as damages for dumping toxic waste in the Amazon.[37] Chevron argued, inter alia, a breach of Ecuador's obligations under the US-Ecuador BIT, including a violation of the FET standard, full protection and security as well as of non-arbitrary and non-discriminatory treatment.[38] Chevron asked the tribunal to declare that any (domestic) judgment on the issue was not final and enforceable.[39] While the Tribunal had issued several interim awards ordering Ecuador to stop enforcing the judgment,[40] the dispute was still pending at the time of writing.

In *Burlington v Ecuador*,[41] claimant, a US oil and gas company which had obtained a hydrocarbon concession in the Amazon rainforest, argued that Ecuador was responsible for not providing full protection and security to its investment against attacks from local indigenous communities opposing the project. The ICSID tribunal however dismissed the claim on procedural grounds.[42] It therefore did not deal with this issue on its merits.

---

[37] *Maria Aguinda et al v Chevron Texaco Corporation*, Proceeding No 002-2003 (Sup Ct of Justice, Nueva Loja, Ecuador). The dispute was called 'Lago Agrio Litigation' because the Ecuadorian court was situated in the town of Lago Agrio. In January 2012 the judgment was upheld by the Ecuadorian court of appeals; see 'Ecuador Court Upholds US$ 8.6 Billion Ruling Against Chevron' (*CNN*, 4 January 2012) <http://edition.cnn.com/2012/01/04/world/americas/ecuador-chevron-lawsuit/index.html> accessed 7 February 2014 with according efforts to enforce the judgment in Argentina, Brazil, Canada and the United States; see Braden Reddall, 'Tribunal Presses Ecuador to Halt Chevron Case Enforcement' (*Reuters*, 8 February 2013) <http://www.reuters.com/article/2013/02/09/chevron-ecuador-idUSL1N0B8FBB20130209> accessed 7 February 2014; see Lenzerini (n 11) 207–9 for details.

[38] *Chevron Corporation and Texaco Petroleum Corporation v the Republic of Ecuador*, UNCITRAL, PCA Case No 2009-23, Claimants' Memorial on the Merits, paras 456 ff.

[39] Ibid para 547.

[40] See, e.g., *Chevron Corporation and Texaco Petroleum Corporation v The Republic of Ecuador* (n 38) Fourth Interim Award on Interim Measures (7 February 2013) operative paras 2 ff <http://www.italaw.com/sites/default/files/case-documents/italaw1274.pdf> accessed 21 March 2014.

[41] *Burlington* (n 25) para 342.

[42] Ibid para 315. Note, however, that the tribunal decided on the merits of Burlington's expropriation claim and found Ecuador in breach of its obligations; see *Burlington Resources Inc v The Republic of Ecuador*, Decision on Liability (14 December 2012) para 546. This, however, without touching upon indigenous rights.

Gallo v. Canada[43] concerns an investment in open-pit mining and the adjacent construction of a rubbish dump site in the Canadian state of Ontario. The Ontario government had enacted legislation which prevented the investor from acquiring the lands next to its project for the construction of the rubbish dump site.[44] On this basis, the investor (Gallo) brought a claim under NAFTA for unlawful expropriation and also claimed a violation of the FET standard. In defence, Canada relied inter alia on the rights of local aboriginal peoples, especially land rights, which would have been violated had the purchase of the land by the investor been permitted.[45] The NAFTA tribunal dismissed the investor's claim for lack of jurisdiction and consequently did not discuss the merits of the case.[46]

In the above cases, the activities of foreign investors interfered or had the potential to interfere with the rights of indigenous peoples. The investors were thus potential perpetrators of human/indigenous rights violations. Investments and economic activities conflicted with the non-economic, cultural rights of indigenous peoples.[47]

---

43 *Vito G Gallo v Government of Canada*, UNCITRAL (NAFTA), Award (15 September 2011) <http://www.italaw.com/sites/default/files/case-documents/ita0351_0.pdf> accessed 7 February 2014.

44 See *Vito G Gallo v Government of Canada*, Investor's Memorial (1 March 2010) para 8 <http://www.international.gc.ca/trade-agreements-accords-commerciaux/topics-domaines/disp-diff/gallo.aspx?lang=eng> accessed 7 February 2014.

45 See *Vito G Gallo v Government of Canada*, Government of Canada Counter Memorial (29 June 2010) para 137 <http://www.international.gc.ca/trade-agreements-accords-commerciaux/topics-domaines/disp-diff/gallo.aspx?lang=eng> accessed 7 February 2014.

46 *Gallo* (n 43) para 341.

47 See also the procedural order in the Joint ICSID Cases *Bernhard von Pezold and others v Republic of Zimbabwe*, ICSID Case ARB/10/15, *Border Timbers Limited, Border Timbers International (Private) Limited, and Hangani Development Co (Private) Limited v Republic of Zimbabwe*, ICSID Case ARB/10/25, Procedural Order No 2 (26 June 2012), where the arbitral tribunal denied an amicus petition submitted jointly by four indigenous communities from Zimbabwe and a European NGO. The indigenous amicus petitioners had argued that land at stake in the investment dispute was part of their ancestral territory and that they thus had a significant interest in the outcome of the investment proceedings. For further reference and a critical view on the investment tribunal's denial to admit the amicus petition see Christian Schliemann, 'Requirements for *Amicus Curiae* Participation in International Investment Arbitration. A Deconstruction of the Procedural Wall Erected in Joint ICSID Cases ARB/10/25 and ARB/10/15' (2013) 12 LPICT 365.

Conversely, in *Grand River Enterprises Six Nations, Ltd. v United States*, the foreign investors themselves were indigenous and relied on their First Nation status to argue preferential treatment in a NAFTA arbitration.[48] Put differently, they claimed special economic privileges in reliance on their indigeneity. *Grand River* is thus one of the exceptional cases where investors refer to their status as indigenous peoples to support their claims.[49] The claimants controlled a Canadian company which engaged in the tobacco exporting business to the United States. They maintained that their investment had been harmed by a US regulation which required contributions of tobacco companies to health expenses for tobacco patients. Their arguments inter alia referred to the issue that the measures amounted to expropriation and breached also the customary international law minimum standard of fair and equitable treatment. With reference to their First Nation status, claimants stated that the US measures were inconsistent with their 'legitimate expectation … not to be subject to regulatory action'[50] because of their status as one of the First Nations in North America. The tribunal did not decide on the claim for immunity from state regulation but rather held that there could not be a reasonable expectation not to be subject to state regulation when engaging in a large scale tobacco distribution business.[51] It also found that the measure did not amount to expropriation since the claimants' business remained profitable.[52] In the end, the *Grand River* tribunal dismissed the claim. Still, the award remains interesting for its far reaching reference to indigenous rights.[53]

---

48 *Grand River Enterprises Six Nations, Ltd et al v United States*, UNCITRAL, Award (12 January 2011) <http://www.state.gov/s/l/c11935.htm> accessed 7 February 2014; see for details Christina Binder, 'Investment Law and Indigenous Peoples: The Grand River Case' (2013) 2 *Rivista dell'Arbitrato* 487.

49 Also more generally, investors rarely argue a violation of their human rights as investors; see Schreuer and Kriebaum (n 35) 1089 (for further references).

50 *Grand River* (n 48) para 128.

51 Ibid paras 141 ff.

52 Ibid paras 152–3.

53 The *Grand River* tribunal criticized, inter alia, the lacking involvement of First Nations and tribal governments in the development of the proposed amendments to the MSA (para 185) as well as the missing sensitivity of the US states vis-à-vis the Claimants'/the indigenous nations' interests (para 186). The tribunal also more generally referred to the growing protection of indigenous rights (para 186). It went so far as to affirm a customary right to consultation of indigenous rights by holding that 'it may well be … that there does exist a principle of customary international law requiring governmental authorities to

All these cases thus relate to indigenous peoples. Although reliance on indigenous rights does not play an important role for their outcome, they reflect the need to deal with indigenous peoples in investment proceedings. Grosso modo, two types of situations may be distinguished: the reliance on indigenous peoples' rights as 'shield' (see, e.g., *Glamis Gold, Burlington, Chevron*) and as 'sword' (*Grand River Enterprises*). As regards the former, host states, when taking action to protect indigenous peoples which interferes with investors' rights, are in principle able to use indigenous rights as 'shield'. Reliance on indigenous rights thus serves as defence against alleged breaches of investment agreements. Reliance on indigenous rights as 'sword', conversely, relates to claims of preferential treatment by investors. Indigenous investors then claim economic privileges for being indigenous.

Both constellations raise the question of interactions – including possible conflicts – between indigenous and investors' rights. Thus, how should interactions between both – 'indigenous rights' and 'investment law' – be dealt with?

IV. EXISTING MEANS TO DEAL WITH INDIGENOUS RIGHTS IN INVESTMENT CONTEXTS

The question of how to deal with indigenous rights in investment claims goes to the core of the fragmentation debate.[54] It reflects the need to coordinate between different (sub-)regimes of international law – here: investment law and indigenous peoples' rights – when these interact or conflict with each other. This seems of particular interest in view of the challenges posed. In fact, the specific characteristics of indigenous peoples as culturally distinct peoples who generally live as minorities in

consult indigenous peoples on governmental policies or actions significantly affecting them. One member of the Tribunal has written that there is such a customary rule' (para 210). While the Tribunal maintained that such obligation to consult with indigenous peoples was not to be equalled with an obligation to consult with individual investors (para 211), it held that consultations should have occurred with the First Nations whose members could and were being affected by the MSA and related measures (para 212). Put differently, the Tribunal 'operationalized' the obligation to consult with indigenous peoples by applying it to the case before it.

[54] See generally the report of the Study Group of the International Law Commission (finalized by M Koskenniemi), 'Fragmentation of International Law: Difficulties Arising from the Diversification and Expansion of International Law' UN Doc A/CN.4/L.682 (2006).

nation states require specific means to coordinate between the regimes. While these are partly identical to those used for coordination between investment law and human rights, at times, farther-reaching approaches are necessary.

As will be shown, there are several possibilities – de lege lata and de lege ferenda – to take indigenous rights into account in investment disputes. These include jurisdiction and applicable law (A.), treaty interpretation (B.) and the amicus curiae participation of indigenous peoples in investment proceedings (C.). Also, enhanced transparency requirements of investment proceedings (D.) and the human/indigenous rights education of arbitrators (E.) may further the indigenous cause.

Still, notwithstanding these possibilities, investment tribunals seem so far not to have made use of them: not in relation to indigenous rights, and to a very limited extent in the broader investment law and human rights only debate. One major reason for this lack of judicial treatment certainly lies in the fact that the parties rarely put forward indigenous or human rights arguments in investment proceedings.[55] For this reason, the different techniques will have to be discussed mostly in the abstract.

A. Jurisdiction and Applicable Law

A first possibility to incorporate indigenous rights into investment disputes relates to an investment tribunal's jurisdiction and the applicable law.[56] This in case of both: when reliance on indigenous rights is used as a 'shield', i.e. as defence by the host state; and also when indigenous rights are referred to as 'sword', i.e., when investors argue preferential treatment for being indigenous. Still, the following considerations refer to the reliance on indigenous rights as 'shield' given their more imminent relevance.

In fact, a first determinant for a tribunal's competence to rely on the rights of indigenous peoples is the jurisdictional clause in the investment treaty. A tribunal's jurisdiction is limited to what the parties have consented to. Thus, the broader a jurisdictional clause is framed, the more room is – in principle – left to a tribunal for the possible

---

55 See Schreuer and Kriebaum (n 35) 1096 '... arbitrators are prone to reacting to the parties submissions who will invoke community interests [including human rights] only when it serves their particular interests. It would be untypical for a tribunal to investigate and promote community interests on its own initiative.'

56 See for a general discussion on jurisdiction and applicable law Kriebaum (n 3) 660 ff.

consideration of alleged violations of indigenous rights, if and to the extent that they affect the investment.[57] Article IX of the Norway-Lithuania BIT is an example for a broad jurisdictional clause. It covers 'any dispute which may arise between an Investor of one Contracting Party and the other Contracting Party in connection with an investment … .'[58] In case of such broad jurisdictional clauses it would be – at least in principle – within the scope of jurisdiction of the investment tribunal to examine violations of indigenous peoples' rights should they arise 'in connection with an investment'.[59]

Also, the applicable law may open some room for an investment tribunal to look into alleged violations of indigenous peoples' rights which relate to the investment dispute. Typical choice of law clauses in investment treaties refer to the law of the host country and such rules of international law as are applicable.[60] Tribunals could thus – provided that the jurisdictional clause is broad enough – draw upon relevant instruments for the protection of indigenous rights as part of the applicable international law of treaties[61] or as applicable customary international law. In a similar vein, tribunals could also apply indigenous rights as part of the law of the host state. In case of conflicting obligations – for example, when indigenous land rights conflict with competing claims of the foreign investor – tribunals could draw on relevant techniques for the resolution of norm conflicts (especially the lex posterior, lex specialis principles).[62] A tribunal might even consider a hierarchy of norms in case

---

[57] Ibid 661.

[58] Art IX of the Norway-Lithuania BIT.

[59] Conversely, narrow jurisdictional clauses – restricting jurisdiction to violations of the investment treaty – will thus leave very little room to refer to indigenous rights; see, e.g., Art 9 of the Netherlands-El Salvador BIT as example for a narrow jurisdiction clause: '… disputes which arise within the scope of this agreement between one Contracting Party and an investor of the other Contracting Party concerning an investment of that investor in the territory of the other Contracting Party … .'

[60] See, e.g., Art 10(7) Netherlands-Argentina BIT; see also Art 42(1) of the ICSID Convention which states that if there is no agreed choice of law 'the Tribunal shall apply the law of the Contracting State Party to the dispute and such rules of international law as may be applicable;' see Kriebaum (n 3) 661 for further references.

[61] See, e.g., ILO Convention No 169.

[62] See Tarcisio Gazzini and Yannik Radi, 'Foreign Investment with a Human Face, with Special Reference to Indigenous Peoples' Rights' in Rainer Hofmann and Christian Tams (eds), *International Investment Law and Its Others*

of ius cogens obligations. Indigenous rights which would trump competing investor claims for being classified as ius cogens might include the right to self-determination of indigenous peoples or their right not to be subject to cultural genocide in case of consistent violations of their territories and their cultural heritage.[63] So far, however, these techniques do not seem to have ever been applied by investment tribunals.

Also 'in accordance with host state law-clauses' can be a means to give effect to indigenous rights, to the extent that these rights are part of the law of the host state. Several investment treaties include 'in accordance with host state law-clauses' in the definition of the investment.[64] Investments which are made in violation of host state laws do not enjoy protection under the BIT. Investors can thus lose their protection in cases of serious violations of indigenous rights which are at the same time a breach of the domestic law of the host state. What is more, even without 'in accordance with host state law-clauses', tribunals have examined whether investments were made in accordance with the law of the host state before granting protection.[65] As was generally affirmed by the ICSID-tribunal in *Phoenix Action v Czech Republic*[66] an obiter dictum:

> To take an extreme example, nobody would suggest that ICSID protection should be granted to investments made in violation of the most fundamental rules of protection of human rights, like investments in pursuance of torture or genocide or in support of slavery or trafficking of human organs.[67]

(Nomos 2012) 87 <http://papers.ssrn.com/sol3/papers.cfm?abstract_id=2030871> accessed 7 February 2014.

[63] See Valentina S Vadi, 'When Cultures Collide: Foreign Direct Investment, Natural Resources, and Indigenous Heritage in International Investment Law' (2011) 42 *Columbia Human Rights Law Review* 798, 857 ff.

[64] See, e.g., Art 1.1 of the Germany-Philippines BIT; Art 1.4 of the Spain-Mexico BIT; see Kriebaum (n 3) 664 for further reference.

[65] The ICSID tribunal in *Plama Consortium Limited v Bulgaria* observed that: '[u]nlike a number of Bilateral Investment Treaties, the ECT [Energy Charter Treaty] does not contain a provision requiring the conformity of the Investment with the particular law. This does not mean, however, that the protections provided for by the ECT cover all kinds of investments, including those contrary to domestic or international law'; *Plama Consortium Limited v Bulgaria*, ICSID Case No ARB/03/24, Award (27 August 2008) para 138; see Kriebaum (n 3) 665.

[66] *Phoenix Action, Ltd v Czech Republic*, ICSID Case No ARB/06/5, Award (15 April 2009).

[67] Ibid para 78.

The requirement that investments must not to be made in violation of the domestic law of the host state can thus be a means to protect indigenous rights. More problematic are situations where a state wants to subsequently – after an investment was made – amend its laws to give effect to indigenous rights. 'In accordance with host state law-clauses' usually refer to the time the investment is made.[68] They will thus not cover subsequent legislative changes enacted, by a state, for instance to bring its law into line with relevant standards on indigenous rights.[69] Such subsequent legislative changes may conflict with foreign investors' rights accordingly.

Thus, the possible reference to indigenous rights depends to a large extent on the wording/provisions of the respective investment treaty as well as, obviously, on the arguments put forward by the parties.

B. Treaty Interpretation

Treaty interpretation may also be a technique to refer to indigenous peoples' rights.[70] Especially the so-called 'principle of systemic integration' contained in Article 31(3)(c) VCLT is of relevance. It provides that in the interpretation of a treaty 'there shall be taken into account, together with the context … any relevant rules of international law applicable in

---

[68] An exception to the contrary is the China-Malta BIT which requires investments to be continuously in accordance with host state law. Art 2(2) of the China Malta BIT (2009) states: 'Investments of either contracting Party shall be made, and shall, for their whole duration, continuously be in line with the respective domestic laws.' Such wording would thus allow for an even broader consideration of indigenous rights, thus encompassing even subsequent legal changes; see generally Ursula Kriebaum, 'The States' Duty to Protect Human Rights. Investment and Human Rights', p 8, available at <https://typo3.univie.ac.at/fileadmin/user_upload/int_beziehungen/Personal/Publikationen_Kriebaum/states_duty_protect_human_rights.pdf> accessed 10 February 2015.

[69] When contracts between investor and host state include stabilization clauses, such subsequent legislative changes seem even more difficult. On stabilization clauses and human rights see IFC/UN, 'Stabilization Clauses and Human Rights' (11 March 2008) <http://www.reports-and-materials.org/Stabilization-Clauses-and-Human-Rights-11-Mar-2008.pdf> accessed 7 February 2014.

[70] As to the relevance of the principle of systemic integration see, e.g., Simma and Kill (n 3); see also the reference to Art 31(3)(c) VCLT in the ILC Fragmentation Report (n 54) para 423; Richard Gardiner, *Treaty Interpretation* (OUP 2008) 260; Campbell McLachlan, 'The Principle of Systemic Integration and Article 31(1)(c) of the Vienna Convention' (2005) 54 ICLQ 279.

the relations between the parties.' Article 31(3)(c) VCLT may thus, in principle, be an important tool to interpret an investment treaty in accordance with relevant indigenous – or human – rights. First, an investment tribunal could refer to standards on indigenous rights – insofar as they are binding between the parties – when indigenous investors claim preferential treatment for being indigenous. The tribunal could thus interpret the relevant investment treaty provisions in a way which is favourable to the claims of the indigenous investors.

Second, reference to indigenous rights may be made when a host state relies on indigenous rights as 'shield'. An investment tribunal could thus refer to relevant standards on indigenous rights – insofar as they are binding between the parties – to adopt an 'indigenous rights' friendly interpretation of the investment treaty's provisions and take a position which is favourable to the host state's defences. This especially in case of broad treaty terms, for instance when determining the meaning of the FET standard, when interpreting full protection and security clauses or in relation to direct or indirect expropriation.[71]

However, there are clear limits to the application of Article 31(3)(c) VCLT. The treaty text is the starting and – usually – end point of any interpretation: 'in claris cessat interpretatio' ('interpretation stops in the face of clarity'). It is the task of an international tribunal to interpret, not to replace a treaty provision. In the words of the arbitral tribunal in the *Laguna del Desierto* case, interpretation is 'a judicial function, whose purpose is to determine the precise meaning of a provision, but which cannot change it.'[72] What is more, so far, practice is scarce and there seems to be a certain reluctance of investment tribunals to take external norms – i.e., relevant human and indigenous rights – into account.

The reasons for this limited reference are multiple. First, the narrow object and purpose of most BITs – being focused on investment protection – may prevent due reference to relevant human and indigenous rights through interpretation.[73] Also, the private law background of many investment arbitrators may play a role in the limited reliance on human rights treaties and on instruments enshrining indigenous rights.[74] Finally,

---

[71] See Kriebaum (n 3) 668 as regards human rights.

[72] *Dispute concerning the Course of the Frontier between BP 62 and Mount Fitzroy 'Laguna del Desierto' (Argentina v Chile)*, Award (21 October 1994) (1999) 113 ILR 1, 45, para 75.

[73] See Art 31(1) VCLT's reference to object and purpose of a treaty for treaty interpretation; see also infra Section V.B.

[74] See infra Section IV.E. for details.

if alleged violations of indigenous rights are not raised in the submissions of the parties to the dispute, the investment tribunal may not even know about them.[75]

C. Amicus Curiae Participation of Indigenous Peoples in Investment Proceedings

The – so far – limited reference to indigenous rights in investment proceedings raises questions of how best to inform an investment tribunal about the indigenous concerns at stake. The participation of indigenous people through amicus curiae/non-disputing party submissions therefore seems most important. Since indigenous peoples typically are not parties to the proceedings, but 'merely' affected by investment activities, amicus curiae submissions are an important procedural means to voice their concerns.

Amicus curiae submissions should support the tribunal in achieving a more complete vision of the factual and legal background of a case.[76] They are sometimes explicitly dealt with in investment treaties. Certain BITs refer to the possibility to submit amicus curiae and generally leave it to the discretion of the arbitral tribunal to accept amicus curiae submissions.[77] Also, if nothing is explicitly mentioned in an investment treaty, it is within the discretion of ICSID tribunals whether to allow amicus curiae briefs.[78]

---

[75] Note respectively that also proportionality reasoning may be used as a conflict-solving technique and cross-regime harmonization between investment law and indigenous rights; see, for example, Stephan W Schill, 'Cross-Regime Harmonization through Proportionality Analysis: The Case of International Investment Law, the Law of State Immunity and Human Rights' (2012) 27 ICSID Rev 87 <http://icsidreview.oxfordjournals.org/content/27/1/87.short> accessed 21 March 2014, for further reference.

[76] See Kriebaum (n 3) 658, n 21 for relevant case law on amicus curiae petitions by civil rights groups and human rights NGOs.

[77] See Art 10.20 of the Australia-Chile FTA (Conduct of Arbitration): '2. The tribunal shall have the authority to accept and consider amicus curiae written submissions that may assist the tribunal in evaluating the submissions and arguments of the disputing parties from a person or entity that is not a disputing party … .'

[78] See Rule 37 of the ICSID Rules as amended 2006.

The investment cases which have touched upon indigenous issues so far have shown a certain practical relevance of amicus curiae submissions.[79] In *Glamis Gold*, the Quechan Indian Nation submitted an amicus curiae brief which supported the US government's position as regards the necessary preservation and protection of indigenous rights in ancestral lands.[80] An amicus curiae brief was likewise filed in *Chevron v Ecuador*, maintaining that the dispute was both outside the jurisdiction of an investor-state tribunal and non-justiciable.[81] Also, in the *Grand River* case, the Office of the National Chief of the Assembly of Canadian First Nations supported the indigenous investors through an amicus curiae brief.[82] In these cases, amicus curiae submissions were thus a means to transport indigenous concerns, even though they do not seem to have influenced the outcome of the cases.[83]

D. Transparency of Investment Proceedings

Enhanced requirements of transparency may also be important to further the respect for indigenous rights.[84] Transparency requirements subject

---

[79] See, however, the arbitral tribunal's denial to admit the amicus curiae petition in *von Pezold and Border Timbers Limited* (n 47). See supra n 47 for further reference.

[80] See, e.g., *Glamis Gold Ltd v United States,* Non-Party Supplemental Submission by the Quechan Indian Nation (16 October 2006) 1, which maintains: 'That the preservation and protection of indigenous rights in ancestral land is an obligation of customary international law which must be observed, by both the NAFTA Parties and any treaty interpreter, in accordance with the principle of good faith; and that an investor seeking compensation for an alleged taking of property cannot rely upon a claim to acquired rights in which no legitimate expectation to enjoy such rights existed' <http://www.state.gov/documents/organization/75016.pdf> accessed 7 February 2014.

[81] Fundación Pachamama, *The International Institute for Sustainable Development* (IISD 5 November 2010) para 1.4.

[82] Office of the National Chief of the Assembly of Canadian First Nations (19 January 2009) <http://www.state.gov/documents/organization/117812.pdf> accessed 7 February 2014.

[83] The reasons for the limited impact are various. Some cases are declared inadmissible, see *Burlington* (n 25) and *Gallo* (n 43). In *Glamis Gold* (n 32), conversely, considerations of indigenous peoples' rights do not seem to have played any role for the tribunals' deliberations. In *Grand River* (n 48), the amicus submission overwhelmingly reiterated and supported the claimants' arguments already put forward in the memorial and was thus of somehow limited relevance; see generally supra Section III.

[84] See Vadi (n 63) 878.

investment proceedings to public scrutiny by civil society, media and NGOs. They thus counter the often criticized secrecy of investment proceedings. True, far-reaching transparency requirements in investment treaties are still rare.[85] Still, there is a general trend towards more transparency. It is evidenced, most importantly, in the recent UNCITRAL Rules on Transparency in Treaty Based Investor-State Arbitration.[86] This may be beneficial to the indigenous cause because violations of indigenous peoples' rights are exposed to public scrutiny and pressure.

E. Human/Indigenous Rights Expertise of Arbitrators

Finally, the education and expertise of individual arbitrators is a relevant factor for the promotion of indigenous rights in investment proceedings. The private/commercial law bias of investment proceedings has been viewed as a possible impediment to a due appreciation of common concerns, including human rights concerns.[87] A broader public international law expertise might thus induce arbitrators to also consider the

---

85 2014 UNCITRAL Rules on Transparency in Treaty Based Investor-State Arbitration, <http://www.uncitral.org/pdf/english/texts/arbitration/rules-on-transparency/Rules-on-Transparency-E.pdf> accessed 20 March 2014. For a model example as regards transparency see Art 10.22 (Transparency of Arbitral Proceedings) of the Australia-Chile FTA: '1. Subject to paragraphs 2 and 4, the respondent shall, after receiving the following documents, make them available to the public at their cost: a. the notice of intent … . b. the notice of arbitration … . c. pleadings, memorials and briefs submitted to the tribunal by a disputing party and any written submissions … . d. Minutes or transcripts of hearings of the tribunal, where available; and e. orders, awards, and decisions of the tribunal. 2. The tribunal shall conduct hearings open to the public and shall determine, in consultation with the disputing parties, the appropriate logistical arrangements. However, any disputing party that intends to use information designated as confidential business information or information that is privileged or otherwise protected from disclosure under a Party's law in a hearing shall so advise the tribunal. The tribunal shall make appropriate arrangements to protect the information from disclosure including closing the hearing for the duration of any discussion of confidential information.' See similar provisions in the 2007 Norwegian Draft Model BIT (Art 29), the 2012 US Model BIT (Art 29) and the Canadian Model FIPA 2004 (Art 38); see generally Kriebaum (n 3) 659.

86 In this sense Kriebaum (n 3) 659.

87 See Schreuer and Kriebaum (n 35) 1096: 'A restraining factor in the consideration of community interests is the origin of investment arbitration in commercial arbitration. Not infrequently tribunals are focused on the settlement of the particular dispute without regard to the wider repercussions of their decisions … .'

relevant public interests – including human rights considerations – at stake, beyond the resolution of a particular investment dispute. In fact, specific human or indigenous rights expertise might be particularly beneficial for the arbitrators' comprehension of indigenous concerns. In *Grand River*, such expertise was ensured by one of the three arbitrators, James Anaya, the (former) Special Rapporteur on the Rights of Indigenous Peoples. His expertise becomes apparent between the lines of the award[88] and seems to have positively contributed to a harmonious reading of both systems, indigenous rights and investment law.

F. Résumé

Several possibilities exist to take indigenous rights into account in investment disputes. They range from a tribunal's jurisdiction and the applicable law to procedural means such as amicus curiae submissions by indigenous peoples and the human/indigenous rights education of arbitrators. In principle, these techniques apply to both, when indigenous rights are used as a 'shield', i.e. as defence by the host state to escape liability in investment disputes; and as a 'sword', when indigenous investors refer to relevant standards on indigenous rights to argue preferential treatment. Most importantly, these techniques should be drawn upon in a comprehensive approach so that they contribute in a mutually complementary way to give maximum respect to indigenous rights.

V. IMPROVED SOLUTIONS TO DEAL WITH INVESTMENT LAW AND INDIGENOUS RIGHTS

Most of the abovementioned solutions can be implemented on the basis of existing law/de lege lata. In addition, there are certain de lege ferenda means to even further promote indigenous rights. These relate to the relevant substantive law (such as explicit references to human/indigenous rights in investment treaties (A.) or cultural exception clauses (B.)). They also include procedural means, such as a right to intervention of indigenous peoples (C.) or mandatory ex ante human rights or cultural impact assessments (D.). Still, some of these de lege ferenda solutions

88 See, e.g., the *Grand River* Award (n 48) para 210: 'It may well be, as the Claimants urged, that there does exist a principle of customary international law requiring governmental authorities to consult indigenous peoples on governmental policies or actions significantly affecting them. One member of the Tribunal has written that there is such a customary rule.'

have to be handled with care in order not to lose sight of the primary aim of international investment arbitration, namely the timely resolution of investment disputes.

A. Reference to Human/Indigenous Rights in Investment Treaties

Explicit references to human (or indigenous) rights in investment treaties may be an additional means to strengthen indigenous rights. For example, references to human rights in the preamble of an investment treaty may induce arbitrators to interpret the treaty in accordance with relevant human rights standards.[89] The incorporation of human rights provisions is thus a potentially forceful tool. However, an investment treaty with a general reference to human (or even indigenous) rights is still missing.[90] The seemingly only document with explicit reference to human rights is the Norwegian Draft Model BIT.[91] It has, however, not been adopted.

An even more effective means to further investors' respect for human/indigenous rights could be strong 'in accordance with host state law-clauses' with explicit reference to human/indigenous rights.[92] A fortiori, these clauses could require that investments have to be made 'in accordance with host state law' not only at the time of admission but during the entire duration of the investment.[93] This would have the advantage that foreign investors, who (seriously) violate human/indigenous rights during the duration of their investment, lose the

[89] See supra Section IV.C.

[90] Certain BITs refer to labour rights or the protection of health and safety in their preamble; see, e.g., the US-Albania BIT, the US-Argentina BIT, the US-Armenia BIT, the US-Azerbaijan BIT, the US-Bolivia BIT, the US-Ecuador BIT, the US-Estonia BIT; see generally Kriebaum (n 68) 8.

[91] The Norwegian Model BIT contains a commitment to human rights as set out in the UN Charter and the Universal Declaration of Human Rights in its Preamble: 'Reaffirming their commitment to democracy, the rule of law, human rights and fundamental freedoms in accordance with their obligations under international law, including the principles set out in the United Nations Charter and the Universal Declaration of Human Rights; …' <http://www.regjeringen.no/upload/NHD/Vedlegg/hoeringer/Utkast%20til%20modellavtale2.doc)> accessed 7 February 2014; see discussion in Letter from Norwegian Centre for Human Rights to Business and Industry Department (15 April 2008) <http://www.humanrights.uio.no/nasjonalinstitusjon/overvakning/horinger/2008/investeringer.pdf> accessed 7 February 2014.

[92] See Kriebaum (n 68) 21.

[93] See Art 2(2) China-Malta BIT 2009 (n 68), which, however, does not contain an explicit reference to human rights.

protection under the investment treaty. At the same time, overly broad 'in accordance with host state law-clauses' pose the risk of abuse by host states. They thus have to be handled with care and, for instance, be restricted to compliance with domestic human rights law during the duration of the investment.

B. Cultural Exception Clauses in Investment Treaties

Other de lege ferenda possibilities to strengthen indigenous rights include cultural exception clauses in investment treaties which may be relied upon by the host state to protect sites of cultural value, including indigenous cultural heritage.[94] Such exceptions may also relate to affirmative action measures to remedy past injustices. Cultural (or similar) exception clauses in investment treaties enable host states to uphold their police powers to implement social policies – here, to protect indigenous peoples – which accordingly should not constitute violations of the respective investment treaties. They thus imply, positively, that the host state retains its full regulatory powers for a specific situation. At the same time, such carve-outs burden the investor with the economic consequences of the host state's regulatory measures. Consequently, cultural (and similar) exception clauses have to be used with caution and should only be included exceptionally and with clearly defined criteria in investment treaties.

Certain investment treaties already incorporate exceptions of this kind. Malaysia excluded measures designed to promote the economic empowerment of the Bumiputras ethnic group from the scope of its BITs.[95] South African BITs provide for carve outs for affirmative action programs to remedy past injustices.[96] A further going – de lege ferenda –

---

[94] Generally on cultural exceptions see Vadi (n 63) 868 ff.

[95] See Howard Mann, 'International Investment Agreements, Business and Human Rights: Key Issues and Opportunities' (International Institute for Sustainable Development, February 2008) <http://www.iisd.org/pdf/2008/iia_business_human_rights.pdf> accessed 7 February 2014.

[96] See, e.g., Art 3.4.c of the Agreement between the Government of the Republic of Mauritius and the Government of the Republic of South Africa for the Promotion and Reciprocal Protection of Investments (1998) <http://www.unctad.org/sections/dite/iia/docs/bits/mauritius_southafrica.pdf> accessed 7 February 2014; Art 3.3.c of the Agreement between the Czech Republic and the Republic of South Africa for the Promotion and Reciprocal Protection of Investments (1998, entry into force pending) <http://www.unctad.org/sections/dite/iia/docs/bits/czech_southafrica.pdf> accessed 7 February 2014; see Schreuer and Kriebaum (n 35) 1093 for further reference.

incorporation of similar clauses also in other investment treaties might, with the above caveat, thus be a means for states to pursue affirmative action programs in support of indigenous peoples and their traditional activities without running the danger of being accused of breaching, for example, the investment treaty's national treatment or non-discrimination provisions.

C. A Right to Intervention of Indigenous Peoples?

Procedurally, some commentators have even called for a right to intervention of indigenous peoples.[97] Such right to intervention would include indigenous peoples as parties to the proceedings, allowing them to submit briefs with no page limits, attend and participate in oral hearings and access to records.[98] This would go further than amicus curiae submissions.

There are certainly arguments in favour of a right to intervention. It reflects the distinct cultural identity of indigenous peoples whose interests, even if they are affected by the outcome of investment proceedings, are at risk of not being adequately represented by the host state of the investment.[99] It is thus in line with the idea of cultural distinctiveness and indigenous self-determination.

However, to incorporate such a far-reaching right to intervention in investment treaties seems undesirable.[100] A right to intervention considerably burdens investment proceedings, including through the necessary identification of the third parties (here: the indigenous peoples) affected by the outcome, the lengthening of proceedings and a possible re-politization of the dispute. As convincingly argued by Vadi:

> Admitting third parties, such a[s] indigenous persons, to act as parties in the proceeding would take judicialization too far, and as a matter of procedure, it would be undesirable. When states agree to a BIT, they accept investor-state arbitration as the dispute settlement mechanism to solve investment disputes with foreign nationals, not with other parties with varying interests.[101]

---

97 Patrick Wieland, 'Why the *Amicus Curia* Institution is Ill-suited to Address Indigenous Peoples' Rights before Investor-State Arbitration Tribunals: *Glamis Gold* and the Right of Intervention' (2011) 3(2) *Trade, Law and Development* 334.

98 Ibid 366. Thus, a right to intervention, in principle, extends indigenous peoples' procedural rights.

99 See ibid 361 ff for further reference.

100 See Vadi (n 63) 886.

101 Ibid.

In short, a de lege ferenda right to intervention seems too far reaching.

D. Mandatory ex ante Human Rights/Cultural Impact Assessments?

Another means appears more useful to give room to indigenous concerns, namely to require ex ante human rights or cultural impact assessments.[102] Both, human rights and cultural impact assessments, follow a similar logic. They are a technical instrument to identify the effects of a proposed activity on human rights (or cultural values) and also a means to avoid or mitigate them. To include mandatory cultural or human rights impact assessments as admission criterion for an investment in investment treaties should thus further the protection of indigenous rights. So far, investment treaties do not seem to require such impact assessments. Still, some domestic systems provide for them.[103]

De lege ferenda, it might be useful to incorporate mandatory human rights or cultural impact assessments in investment treaties especially for large scale investment projects with potentially severe effects for the affected local communities. Impact assessments might therefore be an important de lege ferenda tool to avoid or mitigate the possibly negative consequences of an investment project for indigenous peoples before they occur.

E. Résumé

A range of de lege ferenda options exist to improve the incorporation of indigenous concerns in investment proceedings. They concern the applicable substantive law – i.e., the incorporation of references to human/ indigenous rights or cultural exception clauses in investment treaties – as well as procedural means, such as a right to intervention of indigenous peoples or mandatory ex ante human rights or cultural impact assessments. Some, such as references to human and indigenous rights in

---

[102] On human rights impact assessments see, e.g., ÖFSE, 'Human Rights Impact Assessments as a New Tool for Development Policy?' (January 2013) <http://www.oefse.at/Downloads/publikationen/WP37_Human_Rights.pdf> accessed 7 February 2014; James Harrison, 'Measuring Human Rights: Reflections on the Practice of Human Rights Impact Assessment and Lessons for the Future' Legal Studies Research Paper No 2010-26 (2010) <http://papers.ssrn.com/sol3/papers.cfm?abstract_id=1706742##> accessed 7 February 2014; see Vadi (n 63) 797 for further reference on cultural impact assessments.

[103] For instance, in New Zealand cultural impact assessments are conducted with regard to activities that may affect Maori cultural values and heritage; see Vadi (n 63) 874.

investment treaties appear a reasonable and necessary means to further promote the indigenous cause. Others, conversely, such as a right to intervention of indigenous peoples, go too far and may put at risk the effectiveness of investment dispute settlement. Thus, a careful weighing of the arguments in favour and against should precede any incorporation of additional means to enhance the promotion of indigenous rights in investment proceedings.

VI. CONCLUDING APPRECIATION

The trias 'investment, development and indigenous peoples' raises difficult questions. In view of the specific characteristic of indigenous peoples as culturally distinct peoples with a specific attachment to their lands, these even transcend the complexity of the investment and human rights debate. This is so because indigenous peoples usually live as minorities in nation states and are not necessarily represented by the government of that state (i.e. the host state).

So far, indigenous concerns have found very little reflection in investment proceedings. In merely a handful of cases were indigenous peoples' rights explicitly addressed in the parties' memorials or in amicus curiae submissions. Substantive decisions of investment tribunals on indigenous rights are even more rare. Only the *Grand River* tribunal seems to have pronounced itself more extensively on indigenous rights.

At the same time, the rights of indigenous peoples, as culturally distinct peoples with a specific attachment to their lands, are increasingly recognized, at the domestic as well as at the international level. Also, the number of investment treaties (and investment disputes) is growing. This increases the likelihood of interactions – as well as of conflicts – between indigenous/human rights and investment law as two different sub-systems of international law and evidences an obvious need for coordination between these systems.

International (investment) law provides for various techniques to deal with indigenous rights in investment proceedings, to coordinate and address potential conflicts between the systems. Possibilities comprise a tribunal's jurisdiction and the applicable law, which includes international law in general and hence rules protecting indigenous peoples, methods of treaty interpretation (Article 31(3)(c) VCLT), and procedural means such as amicus curiae submissions. Still, arbitrators seem to make surprisingly little use of these techniques. Thus, more is needed de lege ferenda, such as explicit references to human (indigenous) rights in investment treaties or the incorporation of human rights or cultural exception clauses in these treaties. Overall, as shown in the *Grand River* case, the personal expertise of individual arbitrators is among the most important factors to give due recognition to indigenous concerns. In the end, to reach a truly holistic approach to investment, development and indigenous peoples, a combination of these tools should increasingly be resorted to.

Index